FROM VERSAILLES TO LOCARNO

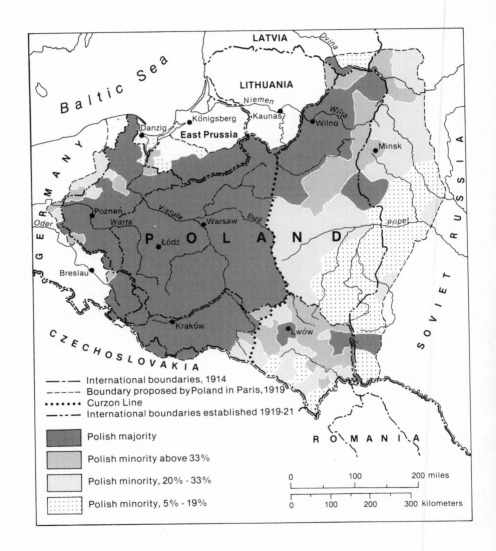

Map 1. Polish Population and Boundaries

FROM

VERSAILLES

TO

LOCARNO

KEYS TO
POLISH FOREIGN POLICY, 1919-25

Anna M. Cienciala and Titus Komarnicki

UNIVERSITY PRESS OF KANSAS

Published by the University Press of Kansas (Lawrence, Kansas 66045),
which was organized by the Kansas Board of Regents
and is operated and funded by Emporia State University, Fort Hays State
University, Kansas State University, Pittsburg State
University, the University of Kansas, and Wichita State University

Library of Congress Cataloging in Publication Data

Cienciala, Anna M.
From Versailles to Locarno.
Bibliography: p.
Includes index.
1. Poland—Foreign relations—1918-1945. I. Komarnicki,
Titus. II. Title.
DK4403.5.C54 1984   327.438   84-2302
ISBN 0-7006-0247-X

Printed in the United States of America

IN MEMORY OF
TITUS KOMARNICKI

Polish Diplomat and Historian
(1896–1967)

*Generous support for the publication of this book
is gratefully acknowledged from*

*The de Brzezie Lanckoroński Foundation,
Friburg, Switzerland*

*The Scholarly Publications Revolving Fund of the
University of Kansas, Lawrence*

*The Joseph B. Slotkowski Publication Fund of the
Kosciuszko Foundation, New York*

Contents

List of Maps

Upper Silesia,'' in Robert Machray, *The Problem of Upper Silesia* (London, 1945), map 9; (2) all other data—from "Upper Silesia: Results of the Plebiscite Shown by Districts (Kreise); Maps by the British Section, Interallied Administrative and Plebiscite Commission, Upper Silesia,'' in Sarah Wambaugh, *Plebiscites since the World War* (Washington, D.C., 1933), vol. 1, facing p. 267.

This map is based on "Polsko-Litewskie linie demarkacyjne (1919-1920)," in Piotr Łossowski, *Stosunki polsko-litewskie w latach 1919-1920* (Warsaw, 1966), end map.

This map is based on these sources: (1) Polish Majority—from "Pologne, Frontières Orientales" (see map 1); (2) Curzon Line, lines A, B—from "Galicie Orientale," printed in *Documents on British Foreign Policy,* 1st ser., vol. 3 (London, 1949), facing p. 840; (3) all other linear data—from "The Riga Settlement," in Norman Davies, *White Eagle, Red Star: The Polish-Soviet War, 1919-20* (London, 1972), endpiece.

Preface

The inspiration for this book stemmed from an unpublished manuscript by Dr. Titus Komarnicki, author of a well-known study of the rebirth of Poland, in the years 1914 to 1920,[1] and editor of three of the four volumes of the papers of Jan Szembek, Polish undersecretary of state for foreign affairs from 1932 to 1939.[2] The manuscript continued the story of Polish foreign policy to March 1923. After Dr. Komarnicki's death in 1967, his family asked me to prepare the work for publication. I accepted this task willingly, both because I owed him a debt of gratitude for advice and assistance in my doctoral research and because I believed, as he did, that an English-language study of key Polish foreign-policy problems in the early nineteen twenties would be useful to Western historians.

The increasing availability of new sources after 1967 compelled me to devote more time to the project than I had planned, while my own interests led me to change the structure of the manuscript and to extend the period covered. Thus, I have written a new Introduction and omitted seven of the original eleven chapters, while using some of the material for new ones. Also, I have added two new chapters on the period 1924/25, because the Locarno Treaties were a more important turning point for both Poland and Europe than was Allied recognition of Poland's eastern frontier in March 1923. I would like to stress that I share most of Dr. Komarnicki's views on the nature of the problems that Poland faced in her foreign policy from 1919 to 1925. I wish to express my gratitude to the Komarnicki family for their patience, and I hope that the end result will bear out the adage "Nothing good happens fast"—which applies equally to good history and good wine.

It is my hope that this book will help Western historians understand the key problems of Polish foreign policy and its objectives at this time. I trust that

xi

it will enable them to view Western and Eastern Europe as an interdependent whole.

I wish to thank all those who, either through their published work or personally, have helped me write this book. I must first acknowledge my debt to Polish historians both in Poland and abroad. I was fortunate enough to receive my training as a diplomatic historian from Professor Piotr S. Wandycz, formerly of Indiana University, now at Yale. His meticulous scholarship has always been a model for me—though, of course, I am responsible for any errors of fact and for the opinions expressed in this book. Furthermore, without his brilliant study of Soviet-Polish relations from 1917 to 1921 and his pioneering work on France's relations with Poland and Czechoslovakia from 1919 to 1925 this book would not have been possible.[3] I am greatly indebted to Professor Piotr Łossowski's excellent study of Polish-Lithuanian relations from 1918 to 1920;[4] to Dr. Zofia Zaks, for the data and insight I obtained from her dissertation and articles on East Galicia;[5] to Dr. Maria Nowak-Kiełbikowa, whose comprehensive study of Anglo-Polish relations from 1919 to 1923 I found most rewarding.[6] I also owe much to Dr. Wiesław Balcerak, whose detailed study of Polish foreign policy during the Locarno era I found most enlightening.[7]

For my understanding of French policy on Upper Silesia I am much indebted to the pioneering work of Dr. Georges Henri Soutou,[8] and my limited knowledge of the role of international finance in international relations at this time stems from the work of Dr. Denise Artaud.[9]

I wish to thank the Honorable Margaret Lambert and Dr. Eleanor Breuning for their helpful comments on British foreign policy and German-Soviet relations. I wish especially to thank Dr. Breuning for permission to use her excellent dissertation on that subject.[10] Also, I wish to thank them both for their help in providing critical books and Xerox copies. I owe a debt of gratitude to Dr. Ann Orde, whose dissertation on British foreign policy—later abridged in book form—filled many gaps in my knowledge.[11] Lady Phipps kindly allowed me to read her husband's papers, and Dr. Sybil Crowe supplied a most interesting note on Danzig in 1919 written by her father, Sir Eyre Crowe. Finally, my knowledge of the diplomacy of 1919 would have been much poorer without the experience of editing the papers of Sir James W. Headlam-Morley,[12] for which I am grateful to his daughter, Professor Agnes Headlam-Morley.

I wish to thank the staffs of the British Public Records Office; the Foreign Office and Commonwealth Library, London; the French Diplomatic Archives at the Quai d'Orsay, Paris; the German Diplomatic Archives, Bonn; the League of Nations Archives, Geneva; the Polish Institute and General Sikorski Museum, London; the Józef Piłsudski Institute of America, New

York; the Polish Modern Archives, Warsaw; and the Provincial State Archives, Gdańsk, for their unfailing patience and help.

I wish to thank Professor Wandycz, for his most helpful comments, and Virginia Seaver, managing editor of the University Press of Kansas, for her most valuable help.

My thanks go to members of the secretarial staff at the University of Kansas, without whose help this manuscript could not have been prepared for publication: Darlene Haycock, of Soviet and East European Studies; Goldie Schlink, Connie Randel, Janet Crow, and Debbie Rhoton, of the History Department; and Pam Le Row and Penny Parker of the Word Processing Center, who showed so much good will and patience with my numerous changes and corrections.

Research on the Danzig question was done with the aid of University of Kansas General Research Grants, 1965-73, a Fulbright-Hays NDEA Center Faculty Grant, 1968/69, and a sabbatical leave from the University of Kansas, 1971; some of the writing was supported by University of Kansas General Research Grants, an SSRC/ACLS grant, 1975, and grants from the Alfred Jurzykowski Foundation (distributed by the Kuściuszko Foundation), 1975 and 1982.

Dr. A. Dietrich Long, director of the University of Kansas Cartographic Service, drew the maps, the costs of which were partially covered by a small grant from the Office of the Vice-Chancellor for Research, Graduate Studies, and Public Service of the University of Kansas.

ANNA M. CIENCIALA

Lawrence, Kansas
September 1983

List of Abbreviations

AAA	Archiv des Auswärtigen Amtes (German Foreign Ministry, Bonn)
AAN	Archiwum Akt Nowych (Polish Modern Archives, Warsaw)
AARK/KP	Akten der alten Reichskanzlei, Kabinett Protokolle (Documents of the Old Imperial Chancellery, Cabinet Protocols)
ADAP	*Akten zur deutschen auswärtigen Politik* (Documents on German Foreign Policy)
AD/MAE	Archives diplomatiques, Ministère des affaires étrangères (Diplomatic Archives, French Foreign Ministry, Paris)
APEL	Archives of the Polish Embassy, London
APIP	*Archiwum polityczne Ignacego Paderewskiego* (Political Archives of Ignacy Paderewski)
ARKWR/KP	*Akten der Reichskanzlei Weimarer Republik, Kabinett Protokolle* (Documents of the Imperial Chancellery of the Weimar Republic, Cabinet Protocols)
BRN	Brockdorff-Rantzau Nachlass
CA	Conference of Ambassadors
CAB	Cabinet Minutes
CID	Committee of Imperial Defence
Cmd.	Command Papers, Great Britain
CP	Cabinet Papers
CPRAC	*Conférence de la paix: Recueil des actes de la conférence* (Peace Conference: Collected Documents)

Danzig Documents	League of Nations Council Series
DBFP	*Documents on British Foreign Policy*
DDCPLQV	*Documents diplomatiques: Conxit polono-lithuanien: Question de Vilna* (Diplomatic Documents: The Polish-Lithuanian Conflict: The Question of Vilna)
DDI	*Documenti diplomatici italiani* (Italian Diplomatic Documents)
DDRPL	*Documents diplomatiques concernant les relations polono-lithuaniennes* (Diplomatic Documents Concerning Polish-Lithuanian Relations)
DGFP	*Documents on German Foreign Policy*
DIM	*Dokumenty i materiały do historii stosunków polsko-radzieckich* (Documents and Materials for the History of Polish-Soviet Relations)
DNVP	Deutschnationale Volkspartei (German National People's Party)
DVP	Deutsche Volkspartei (German People's Party)
DVPSSSR	*Dokumenty Vneshnei Politiki SSSR* (Documents on the Foreign Policy of the USSR)
DZG. Sen.	Danzig Senate Archives, Gdańsk
FO	Foreign Office
FRUS	*Papers Relating to the Foreign Relations of the United States*
GFM	German Foreign Ministry Microfilms
Kolekcja	Dr. Henryk M. Serejski, Kolekcja opracowań i odpisów dokumentów dotyczących stosunków Polski z Łotwą, Litwą, Rosją Radziecką, Gdańskiem i Ukrainą w latach 1914–1928 (Collection of studies and copies of documents concerning Poland's relations with Latvia, Lithuania, Soviet Russia, Danzig, and the Ukraine in the years 1914–1928)
LK 1925	*Lokarno Konferenz 1925*
LLGP	Papers of David Lloyd George
LNA	League of Nations Archives
LNOJ	*League of Nations Ozcial Journal*
Locarno	Papers of British Delegation, Locarno
MP	Member of Parliament
PA	Politisches Archiv (Political Archive)
Parl. Deb. H. C.	*Parliamentary Debates, House of Commons*
PCG/G	Archives of the Polish Commisariat General, Gdańsk
PID	Political Intelligence Department, Foreign Office
PISM	Polish Institute and Sikorski Museum
PKW	Polskie kadry wojskowe (Polish Military Cadres)

POW	Polska Organizacja Wojskowa (Polish Military Organization)
PPC	*Paris Peace Conference (FRUS)*
SIPO	Sicherheitspolizei (Security Police)
SPKPP	*Sprawy polskie na konferencji pokojowej w Paryżu w 1919r* (Polish Questions at the Paris Peace Conference, 1919)
WAP/G	Wojewódzkie Archiwum, Gdańsk (Provincial Archives, Gdańsk)
WPFP	*World Peace Foundation Pamphlets*

Introduction

Within her borders as fixed in 1921, Poland's territory covered some 150,000 square miles, making her the sixth largest state in Europe as a whole and the largest in Eastern Europe. But the Poland reborn after one hundred and twenty-three years of subjection to Prussia-Germany, Austria, and Russia faced enormous problems. From an estimated ethnic Polish population of some eighteen million in 1910, she had lost two million by 1921.[1] Material losses caused by the warring armies amounted to 73 million francs, or some $18 million of 1919 value. Polish crop production was down by 50 percent, while cattle, pigs, and sheep had been reduced by 40 percent. Over half of the railway bridges and stations and some 18 percent of her buildings lay in ruins. Much of her industrial plant—located mainly in former Russian or Congress Poland—had been dismantled and removed by the Germans and the Russians. Coal and oil production was down by one-third. On top of this, the war with Soviet Russia in 1919/20 absorbed over half of the total budget. Together with Poland's debts to the Allies, this produced a budget deficit of 91 percent in 1921.[2]

The task of reconstruction was daunting enough in itself, but it had to be accompanied by the economic and legal integration of former Prussian, Russian, and Austrian Poland into one whole. Furthermore, although the award of Upper Silesia in 1921 had made Poland the fifth largest coal producer in the world, her economy was predominantly agricultural. Three-quarters of the people lived in the countryside, and the high birth rate aggravated the problem of excess rural population. Although agricultural reform began on a large scale in 1925 and reduced the percentage of land in large estates by about half by 1939, the real answer to the problem lay in industrialization. While much was accomplished in this regard over twenty

1

years, the problem could not be solved without the massive investment of foreign capital. However, such investment as came in was too limited for Polish needs. Though foreign capital was available during the 1920s, Poland and other East European states received only minimal amounts. The reasons for this state of affairs have been ably summarized by Stephen A. Schuker:

> Central and east European countries particularly faced an intractable circular difficulty in trying to attract capital. A capital influx was a prerequisite for economic recovery, which in turn would promote greater social and political stability. Paradoxically, since such stability constituted the most reliable guarantee that investment would remain safe, foreign lenders would not offer their capital until it had already been achieved.[3]

In Poland's case, her internal instability was, if anything, increased in the years 1919 through 1921 by the war with Russia. After 1921, German and Soviet claims to Poland's territories made her seem a very high financial risk to Western investors.

Poland's social structure reflected her economy. The upper middle class constituted some 1 to 2 percent of the population, and the largely Jewish lower middle class, some 11 percent. The working class was estimated at between 20 and 27 percent, and the peasant farmers at some 53 percent. In 1921 the big landowners constituted only some 0.3 percent, but held about 38 percent of the land. The intelligentsia—that is, people with high-school or university education—numbered some 5.1 percent; of these a significant number were Jews, who dominated the legal and medical professions. Contrary to widespread Western opinion, it was not the big landowners but the intelligentsia who dominated Polish politics.[4] Most, though not all, of its members were descended from the gentry class and had inherited the latter's values, manners, and interests. This—coupled no doubt with the fact that one of Poland's early foreign ministers, Eustachy Sapieha, was both a prince and a great landowner—led to the widespread misconception that Poland was ruled by aristocratic landowners.

Although Poland was not a multinational state like Czechoslovakia and Yugoslavia, the Polish state did include sizeable minorities. Ethnic Poles made up about 64 percent of the population in 1921. Next came the Ukrainians, with some 16 percent; then the Jews, with some 8 percent; the Belorussians, with some 6 percent; and the Germans, with about 3 percent (1921).[5] While some of these minorities constituted a serious domestic problem, they did not play an important role in Polish foreign policy. An exception, in the years 1919 through 1923, were the Ukrainians of former East Galicia, but the fate of this land became an international question mainly because of British insistence on East Galician territorial autonomy. While Poland's ethnic make-up was perceived in the West as a source of danger and

2

weakness, the same perception did not, curiously enough, apply to the former Russian Empire and its successor, Soviet Russia, whose population, today as in the past, was 50 percent non-Russian.

The Polish political system was not conducive to internal stability. The Constitution of 1921 was modeled on that of the Third French Republic, that is, the president was largely ornamental, and power resided in the lower house, or Sejm. At the same time, political parties proliferated, because of the system of proportional representation, also adopted from France. It is true that the Czechoslovak Republic had the same type of constitution and proportional representation, yet was able to avoid the instability so evident in Poland. The chief reason for this difference lay probably in the great moral prestige of President Thomas G. Masaryk, who faced no rival of equal political stature, while in Poland the rivalry between Józef Piłsudski (1867–1935) and Roman Dmowski (1864–1939) polarized interwar politics. Furthermore, Czechoslovakia had inherited most of the industrial wealth of the Austro-Hungarian Empire, had a high level of literacy, well-established and disciplined political parties, and a numerous and well-trained bureaucracy. Last but not least, her potential enemies, Austria and Hungary, were small and weak, whereas Poland lay between the two greatest powers of Europe—Germany and Russia.[6]

The major Polish parties were the National Democrats, led by Dmowski; the Polish Socialists, or PPS; and the Populist or Peasant Party "Piast," led by the prewar peasant leader, Wincenty Witos. There were many other smaller parties and groups; so Poland was generally governed by coalition cabinets, which collapsed whenever the participants could not resolve their differences. Since political patronage extended down to the lowest civil-service positions, the effects were, more often than not, chaotic. As for Piłsudski, he had dissociated himself from the Socialists in order to stand above parties, very much as de Gaulle did in France after World War II. Both men lacked parliamentary experience, and both shared the same sense of destiny and responsibility to God and history, rather than to parliament.[7]

It is an accepted view in the West that foreign policy stems from domestic politics. However, this is much more the case with Great Powers that also happen to be democracies than with medium or small powers or small countries, whether they be democratic or not. Their geopolitical situation is often the decisive factor in their foreign policy, severely limiting their choice of objectives and sometimes eliminating it altogether. This sometimes applies to Great Powers as well. What Henry Kissinger wrote of the Chinese in 1972— when they resumed relations with the United States out of fear of the USSR— applied even more to the Poles during the interwar period: "Their peril had established the absolute primacy of geopolitics."[8] Poland was situated between her traditional enemies, Germany and Russia, both of whom were unreconciled to their territorial losses; therefore, Poland's immediate and constant foreign-policy goal was to safeguard her independence. In her case, this was synonymous with territorial integrity, because, as the experience of the partitions had taught the Poles, their neighbors' appetites had grown with the eating and had finally led to the total disappearance of Poland from the map of Europe. For the same reason, while Polish statesmen aimed at establishing good relations with both Germany and Russia, alliance with either was out of the question. It could only be bought at the price of territorial concessions, and these could not be made without endangering the country's independence. Furthermore, the living memory of forced Germanization and Russification made such a policy unacceptable. Finally, the experience of 1920—when Poland had barely escaped renewed Russian domination and Germany had refused to allow the passage of supplies from France to Poland—gave no reason to hope that Polish relations with Germany and Russia could start, so to speak, from a clean slate.

Thus, all Polish political parties, with the exception of the small and uninfluential Communist Party, stood for the maintenance of Poland's independence, which was synonymous with her territorial integrity. Disagreements involved not the ends but the means. The National Democrats and the Populists opposed Piłsudski's federal solution in the east in favor of outright annexation. Only the Socialists supported the federal program. In fact, Polish opinion in general supported annexation, as in the case of Vilna. Majority opinion opposed territorial autonomy for the Ukrainians of East Galicia for fear of weakening the Polish state. Only the Socialist Party supported it, and it had been the only party to attempt cooperation with Ukrainian Socialists before 1914. Majority opinion supported the alliance with France, even though the Socialists often voiced bitter criticism of French economic policy toward Poland. Majority opinion was unreconciled to the loss of part of Teschen Silesia to Czechoslovakia; this made for cool relations with that country, although there were other reasons on both sides to make relations difficult. Majority opinion objected to the plebiscite in Upper Silesia and supported the Polish insurrections there, although the Polish government was unable to provide military help. Majority opinion was hostile to Lithuania, seeing her as a ready tool of Germany or Russia. Finally, majority opinion supported the alliance with Rumania—which was also threatened by Russia—and wished for close relations with Hungary. The latter was, however, impossible, due to the Hungarian-Rumanian dispute over Transylvania. In sum, Polish foreign policy and relations with neighboring states generally enjoyed the support of public opinion in what was, at that time, a democratic if chaotic political system.

One of the serious burdens of Poland's foreign policy was her negative image in Western Europe, particularly in Great Britain. Never was there a wider gap than that between the way the Poles perceived themselves and the way they were perceived by others. Firstly, educated Poles saw their values and culture as an integral part of Western civilization. Indeed, Poland had become a member of this civilization when she accepted Christianity from Rome in A.D. 966—the date that also marked the birth of the Polish state. For centuries she had thought of herself as the "bulwark of Christendom," fighting against Tartar hordes and Turks. Her parliamentary system dated back to 1492, and her political tradition, as in England, had also stressed individual freedom and rights. Poland had produced the first written, freely voted constitution in Europe on 3 May 1791 (the Swedish constitution of 21 August 1772 was "granted by King Gustav III). For centuries Poland had welcomed Jews, respecting their rights; and the death of some three hundred and fifty Jews in 1919/20 was due less to racism than to the turmoil of war.[9] Poland had a rich literature, going back to the sixteenth century; her scholars and scientists had contributed to Western science and political thought. Until the accession of Peter the Great to the Russian throne in 1682, she had also been the main conduit for Western civilization to Russia and had remained Russia's main window to Europe. But though educated Poles were aware of all this, Polish culture was mostly unknown in Britain and was little known in France, despite the fact that Paris had been the center of Polish political thought and culture between the two uprisings of 1831 and 1863.

Secondly, the Poles believed that their country lay in the heart of Europe. Geographically this was, indeed, so. The distance between Warsaw and Paris, as the crow flies, is some 900 miles, while the comparable distance between Warsaw and Moscow is about 750 miles. However, in French and British eyes, Poland was a little-known country lying on the distant peripheries of Europe. Thirdly, the Poles believed that the existence of a large and independent Poland was essential to the preservation of the European balance of power as created by the Treaty of Versailles. This required the containment of Germany by France on the west and by Poland on the east. But British statesmen could not conceive of an economically sound and peaceful Europe without the resurgence of Germany. They also believed that many German grievances against the Versailles Treaty were justified, particularly the territorial grievances against Poland. It was not long before French statesmen, particularly Aristide Briand, came to share this view. Fourthly, the Poles believed that it was not only in their vital interest, but in that of all Europe, to contain Russia. But British statesmen believed the Russia would sooner or later regain her lost territories, including eastern Poland. As for the French, they devoutly prayed for a strong Russia—which would once again become their ally against Germany—though preferably not a Bolshevik Russia. Finally, instead of the cultured, polished image that educated Poles had of themselves, their image in the West tallied pretty much with that presented in

5

the American press in 1921. Poland was pictured there as a barbaric country specializing in the murder of Jews. At best, the Poles were seen—as they were by American diplomats and government officials—as politically immature, charming, but naughty children, who did not appreciate Great Power advice and who indulged in shoddy business practices.[10] It was small comfort to think that this image stemmed largely from Western ignorance of Polish history and culture.

Damaging as this negative image was to Polish foreign policy, it served less to motivate than to justify Western, and particularly British, policy toward Poland. But in fact, this policy should be seen in the context of Britain's traditional view of her goals and her vital interests in Europe. Britain's primary aims were to safeguard her vast Empire and to secure the restoration of world trade on which her prosperity depended. Clearly, both necessitated the establishment of a lasting peace in Europe. This, in turn, was seen as impossible without the restoration of the German economy; here we should note that Germany had been Britain's number one trading partner in Europe before 1914. Furthermore, revulsion against the Versailles Treaty and distrust of France's allegedly hegemonic ambitions in Europe formed part and parcel of British sympathy with Germany's demands for the recovery of Danzig, the Corridor or part thereof, and Upper Silesia. Few Britons knew that the Polish-German frontier was—except for Upper Silesia—the same as it had been for centuries before the partitions and that the western lands of Poland—including her part of Upper Silesia—were preponderantly Polish speaking.

As for the Polish-Russian border, the British view that Poland had unjustifiably advanced east of the Curzon Line was part not only of London's concern to avert any threat to peace but also of its view of Russia as a lucrative market for British industrial goods and as a reservoir of food and raw materials for both Britain and Europe. Furthermore, Britain thought in terms of the Entente of 1907, which had helped to save France in 1914. The argument of self-determination was often used to criticize Poland's gains in the east, but few British statesmen and officials paid attention to the fact that, while the Poles were a minority in eastern Poland, the majority of the population was not Russian but Ukrainian and Belorussian. In sum, Poland was an obstacle to British policy aims with regard to both Germany and Russia. It is not surprising, therefore, that Poland was seen as a troublemaker at odds with all her neighbors. Not only had she taken too much territory in the east, against British advice, seized Vilna against British advice, and rejected British demands that she grant teritorial autonomy to East Galicia, but she was also suspected of plotting to dominate Danzig and perhaps even to seize Memel. Douglas Dakin reflects these British views in his introduction to volume 23 of the *British Documents on Foreign Policy,* 1st series, which deals with Poland and the Baltic States in the years 1921 through 1923. He writes:

> Had Polish statesmanship been a higher order, had those responsible for the conduct of Polish foreign relations enjoyed a better reputation, had moreover Poland improved her internal administration and foreign trade, it is just conceivable that she would have been regarded as a commanding power in Northern and Eastern Europe. As it was, however, neither her position as a Baltic Power nor as an Eastern Power was dominant and, important as she was, she merely shared with self-centred and unpredictable neighbours a constant fear of Russia, who, given support from Germany, might reassert herself in areas from which she had withdrawn.[11]

The problem was that whatever might deserve the accolade of high-level statesmanship or good reputation in British eyes was, more often than not, perceived by Polish statesmen and public opinion as being contrary to vital Polish interests. It also happened, as in the case of Vilna in early 1922, that Polish public opinion opposed the federal solution that was consistently advocated by the Polish government and only belatedly taken up by Britain. Nor is it correct to say that the only thing Poland shared with her neighbors was fear of Russia. In fact, this was true of Latvia and Rumania; whereas Lithuania feared Russia less than Poland, and Czechoslovakia yearned for a common frontier with Russia, seeing her as a potential ally. In any event, the charge of self-centeredness and unpredictability frequently substitutes moral criteria for lack of comprehension. It often happens that "people who live on islands, or on half-continents of their own, find difficulty in comprehending the territorial obsessions of landlocked nations."[12] In fact, loss of territory to Russia or to Germany or to both was tantamount to the loss of Polish independence; this was so because of the traditionally predatory aims of both Germany and Russia in this part of the world. Insufficient awareness of this fact helps to explain why Poland was criticized for being overly ambitious, or even "imperialistic," and why she was so often advised to be content with purely ethnic borders, though, curiously enough, some preponderantly Polish-speaking territories like the Corridor and the eastern part of Upper Silesia were also thought to belong rightly to Germany. At bottom, British statesmen believed that nature should take its course: that is, that Eastern Europe was and should be the natural sphere of Germany or Russia, though German influence was preferred after the Bolsheviks had seized power in Russia. This, of course, could not appeal to the Poles, who believed that they could only safeguard their independence against the two powers by creating and maintaining a large Poland. Some British officials who dealt with Polish affairs came to share this point of view. Thus, J. D. Gregory, head of the

Foreign Office's Northern Department in the early 1920s, wrote in his memoirs:

> Poland, as a Great Power, will be in a far better position to come to terms with her neighbours on great controversial issues than a Poland that exists merely on suffrance and dare not move a yard in any direction for fear of compromising her very existence; and, if Warsaw is one of the key positions in Europe, which it undoubtedly is, it is to be hoped that sensible people in England will give up asking that unfortunate and unwelcome question, "Is Poland going to last?"[13]

Another high official, James W. Headlam-Morley, who had helped draft the Versailles Treaty articles on Danzig and the plebiscite in Upper Silesia and who had been very critical of Polish policy in both areas, came to see the existence of Poland and Czechoslovakia as essential to Western security against Germany.[14] However, these were unusual and eccentric views at the time.

Poland's relations with her two great neighbors were generally tense in the years 1919 through 1925. The major points of tension with Germany involved the struggle for Upper Silesia, which was resolved by the League of Nations' award in October 1921 but was not accepted by Germany, and the struggle between German and Polish interests in Danzig, where, in fact, Germany had the upper hand from the outset, though this was not apparent at the time. The political aspect of the Danzig question·was that it symbolized German grievances against Poland and that these enjoyed widespread sympathy in the West. There were, of course, other sources of tension in German-Polish relations, notably the question of German settlers or colonists who had settled in Prussian Poland with the help of the Prussian Settlement Commission and the question of German "optants," who first opted for German citizenship and residence but later wished to reside in Poland.[15] But Danzig and Upper Silesia were the key sources of Polish-German tension as well as of British sympathy for Germany in these years, and therefore they merit more detailed study.

Poland's relations with Soviet Russia were generally tense up to March 1923, in large part because of the lack of Allied recognition of the Polish-Soviet border as fixed by the Treaty of Riga two years earlier. This made Soviet claims to western Belorussia and western Ukraine (East Galicia) all the more dangerous to Poland, while the Polish-Lithuanian border, and Vilna in particular, also lacked international recognition. The Vilna question was, in turn, connected with the Memel problem, and in 1922/23 the two were linked together in Western diplomacy, although the final settlement of the Memel question dragged on for some time. Lack of Western recognition for the Riga frontier served to fuel unrest in East Galicia and supported Lithuanian opposition to any federation with Poland. It also afforded indirect support to Soviet claims to these territories, claims that were couched in terms of self-determination, though few noticed that this was to be implemented only by "workers and peasants," led, of course by the Bolshevik Party of Soviet Russia.[16]

Clearly, Polish foreign policy toward Germany and Russia cannot be studied in isolation from the policies and perceptions of France and Britain. For each of these Great Powers, Polish issues were important, not in themselves, but as part of the German or Russian problem. Hence, each power's stance on any Polish issue throws light on its attitude toward either Germany or Russia at any given time. While the two powers had frequent disagreements on the policy to be followed on any Polish-German or Polish-Russian issue, they always tried to reach agreement or at least to maintain the appearance of a unity of purpose that was, in fact, lacking. The French were more dependent on the British than vice versa, particularly with regard to Germany, but the British tried to avoid irritating or antagonizing the French in order to secure their support elsewhere. Relations occasionally became very strained as, for example, during the third Polish uprising in Upper Silesia in spring and summer 1921; but eventually agreement was always reached, although the delay was frequently harmful to Polish interests.

Polish statesmen saw their main source of support in France, but realized from the beginning that she could not act effectively without the support, or at least the agreement, of Britain. For this reason, British foreign policy merits special attention. Unfortunately for the Poles, while their alliance with France strengthened them against Germany, it also increased British fears of France's alleged hegemonic ambitions in Europe and led Britain to view Poland as a French satellite. Ironically, the negotiations that led to the alliance and military convention of 1921 revealed important French reservations with regard to Poland. Also, in the negotiations for economic agreements on which the French conditioned the ratification of the alliance and convention, they drove hard bargains at Poland's expense. Still, general French support for Poland, both before and after the alliance was signed, constituted a vital element in Polish security and foreign policy. For this reason, the complex problem of the Franco-Polish alliance and Poland's role in Franco-British relations forms the first chapter of this study.

Once the Riga frontier was finally recognized in March 1923, Poland's attention shifted again from east to west—that is, to the threat from Germany. In 1924/25 this was not, as it had been earlier, the threat of armed conflict;

rather, it concerned the consequences of Western policy for Poland. The Dawes Plan, which established a new basis for German reparations in spring 1924 and was embodied in the London agreement signed in August that year, paved the way for a political accommodation between the Western Powers and Germany. Fearing isolation and German expansion at their expense, Polish statesmen strove to prevent the exclusion not only of Poland but also of Czechoslovakia from a European security pact. However, the Locarno Treaties of October 1925 effectively limited European security against Germany to France and Belgium—a security guaranteed by Britain and Italy, which was, ironically, also excluded from the guarantees. Although Locarno undoubtedly pacified Europe in the short run, it also represented a triumph of British and German policy at the expense of Poland and Czechoslovakia, while France accepted it as the best she could get. In the Foreign Office, only James W. Headlam-Morley argued that European security was indivisible and should, therefore, include both Eastern and Western Europe. But Britain's perception of her vital interests did not extend to Eastern Europe. Thus, while the French alliance system remained in being, it was severely undermined after 1925. One of the delayed consequences of Locarno was the Polish-German Declaration of Non-Aggression of 26 January 1934.[17]

The significance of Polish foreign policy stems from the fact that the key problems it faced had a broad European import, though this was rarely perceived at the time. Poland lay in the heartland of Europe between the two greatest powers on the Continent. It is not surprising, therefore, that the Poles viewed their disputes with Germany as being much more than minor territorial issues that could be solved by compromise and negotiation. They always believed that concessions to Germany would merely fuel greater demands and would ultimately lead not only to the loss of Polish independence but also to such an increase of German strength as would threaten the whole of Europe. Similarly, they viewed Russian demands on their territory as a threat not just to their own independence but to that of their neighbors as well; they believed, furthermore, that Russia's expansion here would signal her advance into Central and perhaps Western Europe. After all, in July 1920, the Soviet commander of the Western Front, Mikhail Tukhachevsky had urged his troops to march over the corpse of White Poland toward world conflagration.[18]

As we know, these Polish perceptions of Germany and Russia were not shared by the Western Powers. Ultimately, established Western sympathy for German grievances against the Versailles Treaty helped to pave the way for German expansion under Hitler, until France and Britain were finally compelled to oppose his aggression against Poland in September 1939. Nine months later, Hitler controlled most of Europe. Likewise, old Western sympathy with Russian claims to eastern Poland—as well as to the Baltic States and Bessarabia—helped to justify Anglo-American acceptance of Soviet "security" aims during World War II. This in turn led to the establishment of Soviet domination over most of Eastern Europe and half of Germany as well.

Thus, from the point of view of both 1939 and 1945, it is useful to look more closely at Polish foreign policy on the key problems it faced in the formative years 1919 through 1925. Hopefully, this will help to clarify not only Poland's regional and international significance but also the perceptions and misperceptions that she encountered in the West.

1

The Franco-Polish Alliance and Poland in Franco-British Relations, 1920–22

Although Franco-Polish friendship had deep roots in the past, it is a great exaggeration to assert, as was sometimes done after World War I, that throughout her long history, Poland had been a mere tool of French policy. For centuries, Polish interests were focused on the problems of Eastern Europe, while France did not show a serious interest in this region until the Treaty of Westphalia in 1648. It was only in the eighteenth and early nineteenth centuries that France played an active role in Polish affairs. Polish legions fought in Napoleonic armies, and Napoleon created the duchy of Warsaw (1807–12). From 1830 to the Franco-Prussian War of 1870, the Polish cause enjoyed much sympathy in France as the symbol of struggle against absolutism and national oppression. Although this sympathy waned after 1871 and almost disappeared after the Franco-Russian alliance of 1894, it was rekindled during World War I. In Poland herself, the memories of Napoleon survived until 1918, and throughout the interwar period there was a widespread popular belief that France would always stand by the reborn Polish state, if only out of concern for her own security. Time would prove this belief to be as ill founded as had been the hope for French aid during the great Polish insurrections of 1830/31 and 1863/64.

In fact, French policy toward Poland, while officially one of sincere and complete support, was essentially ambivalent. From the last years of World War I to the Locarno Treaties of 1925, it vacillated between seeing Poland as the key element in an East European barrier checking Germany and separating her from Russia, or as an obstacle to French desire for alliance with Britain and reconciliation with Germany.

The original French goal of a strong Poland was most clearly expounded in several memoranda written in 1917/18 by Pierre Jacquin de Margerie, then

13

director of the Political and Commercial Department of the Quai d'Orsay. In November 1917 he wrote that whether the Franco-Russian alliance survived or not, a strong Poland with access to the sea would constitute the best barrier between an organized and organizing Germany and a weakened, feeble, and perhaps dismembered Russia. Also, a strong Poland could deal the heaviest blow to Germany, particularly to Prussia, the heart of Germanism. Finally, Poland and Bohemia, plus an expanded Rumania, could form a broad East European rampart against German expansion in the east. In French minds, this projected barrier came to include Finland, the Baltic States, and, temporarily, Belorussia, the Ukraine, and Bessarabia. When the Paris Peace Conference opened in January 1919, a strong Poland was viewed as the key element in the projected anti-German barrier and therefore as vital to the long-term security of France. Thus, the concept of a Polish-Czechoslovak alliance also emerged at this time.

As it turned out, however, the eastern-barrier policy, in which Poland was to play a leading role, could not be implemented by France alone since she lacked the strength to do so. Dependent on British support regarding German questions, in conflict with Britain on these and Middle Eastern questions, and, above all, anxious to achieve security on her frontier with Germany, France soon came to look on Poland and other East European allies as a secondary concern and even a burden. As soon as it was clear that Britain would not guarantee France's East European allies and that she aimed at the recovery of Germany, the obvious alternative was to seek some modus vivendi with Germany herself. Hence, some French statesmen and segments of public opinion viewed Poland as a burden and an obstacle to European peace. We should also note that when Poland was struggling to survive, France was absorbed in securing her own frontier with Germany. Finally the Franco-Polish alliance of February 1921 was signed after Poland had defeated the Red Army, and even then the French made the ratification conditional on extensive Polish economic concessions.[1]

After World War I, France enjoyed enormous prestige on the European continent, where final Allied victory was ascribed mainly to French arms and leadership. This was nowhere more true than in Poland.[2] Here, the term "Entente" actually meant France, with all the other powers coming far behind, although President Wilson's support of Poland, both during the war and at the Paris Peace Conference, and American welfare work in Poland immediately after the war were greatly appreciated and gratefully remembered. But the prestige of the United States dimmed when it withdrew from the European scene. This left Great Britain as the predominant Western power in Europe. She was generally seen as favoring Germany's interests over Poland's.

14

The supportive French attitude in the settlement of Poland's western boundary at the Peace Conference seemed to justify the pro-French sentiments entertained in Poland. But this was not the case with Poland's eastern frontier. In 1919/20, White Russian—that is, anti-Bolshevik—circles exerted considerable influence in Paris, and there was a striking incompatibility between the French hankering after an alliance with a great, non-Bolshevik Russia and the aims pursued by Józef Piłsudski. This was not surprising, for many French statesmen had been deeply involved in cooperation with prerevolutionary Russia. Only the "old tiger," Georges Clemenceau, belonged to a generation to whom sympathy for Poland was a living memory. As Jacques Bainville noted, "At the time of the alliance with Russia, French diplomats took the elementary precaution never to speak about the Poles,"[3] and this held true up to the Russian Revolution of March 1917.[4] Nor was it surprising that the pro-Russian orientation survived the war and that in 1919/20 the reemergence of a "national" Russia was eagerly awaited in Paris. Bainville described this attitude as "intellectual sluggishness and lack of imagination,"[5] but it was the natural consequence of Russian aid to France in 1914 and of the hope that Russia would once again emerge as France's powerful ally in the east.

Thus, at the Paris Peace Conference and immediately thereafter, French support for Poland was limited to German-Polish problems.[6] At the same time, France—and Great Britain—supported Czechoslovak claims to the duchy of Teschen (Cieszyn, Tešín, that is, Austrian Silesia), while the United States and Italy were, for ethnic reasons, more amenable to Polish claims in this area.[7] France was also a party to many agreements that were prejudicial to Polish interests, such as reparations, which Poland was not awarded; the Minorities Treaty; the Paris Convention of November 1920, which restricted Polish rights in Danzig as compared with the Versailles Treaty; and finally, the Supreme Council's Declaration of 8 December 1919, which established a provisional line for Polish administration in the east, approximating the eastern boundary of former Russian or Congress Poland.[8]

Another factor that had an adverse influence on Franco-Polish relations in the first postwar years was the spirit of political partisanship. Certain French and Polish parties tried to use the relationship between the two countries for their own benefit. Thus, since the French Right had been mostly responsible for the Treaty of Versailles and had cooperated with the Polish Right during the war (the Polish National Committee in Paris), the French governments of the immediate postwar years also favored the Polish Right, notably the National Democrats. The latter, in turn, claimed to be the sole promoters of Franco-Polish friendship and cooperation. This state of affairs resulted in mutual accusations and suspicions that were harmful to both countries.

The Polish Left—that is, the Socialists—objected to French interference in domestic issues and criticized the role played by French capitalists in Poland. But the French Socialists, who agreed with this view, were also hostile to the new Polish state. French papers, such as *L'Ere nouvelle* and *L'Oeuvre,* abandoned their previous support of the Polish cause and charged the Poles with narrow nationalism and with dreams of territorial expansion. This was partly due to Socialist opposition to the French Right but mainly to the revival of internationalism among the Socialists of France. They soon reestablished relations with the German Socialists and German trade unions, which adamantly rejected the Versailles settlement. These contacts reinforced traditional Socialist opposition to capitalism and imperialism, which had been muted by the war. Thus, like the British Labour Party, the great majority of French Socialists viewed the Treaty of Versailles as the work of greedy capitalists and imperialists. Out of a total of 1,420 members of the National Council of the French Socialist Party, only 54 supported the treaty.[9] Out of 53 votes cast in the Chamber of Deputies against the ratification of the treaty, 49 were Socialist. Like the Communist paper *L'Humanité,* they took the line also followed by left-wing opinion in Britain—namely, that "the Polish frontier arrangements violated the rights of peoples, and were a dangerous source of future difficulties."[10] Polish Socialists also voted in the Polish Diet against the ratification of the treaty—but for opposite reasons. They objected to the restrictions imposed on Polish sovereignty (the Minorities Treaty) as well as to the plebiscite in Upper Silesia, which, they believed, should have been awarded to Poland on ethnic grounds.

The French Socialists were not alone in their hostile attitude toward Poland. Influential Catholic circles in France were also critical of the new Polish state. Side by side with pro-Polish articles there were severe criticisms of Poland in such papers as *La Croix, La Revue catholique des idées et des faits,* and *Les Amitiées catholiques à l'étranger.* The most persistent motive for this anti-Polish attitude was the illusion that after the expected collapse of the Bolshevik Revolution, the moment would come for the reunion of the Catholic and Orthodox churches—that is, the "conversion" of Russia. Russian hostility toward Poland was seen as the major obstacle to this aim.

Franco-Polish diplomatic relations had an inauspicious beginning. While Great Britain sent a distinguished diplomat as her envoy to Poland in the person of Sir Horace Rumbold, France was represented in Warsaw by Eugene Pralon, who was a second-string diplomat and a former French consul in Antwerp. The reason for this appointment was that France at this time preferred to deal with the Polish delegation to the Peace Conference. This, in turn, consisted mainly of members of the former Polish National Committee, who, as right-wingers (National Democrats), enjoyed much more confidence in Paris than the former Socialist Piłsudski and his government in Poland. The choice of Pralon was less than fortunate. He did nothing to make himself popular and even had strained relations with the French Military Mission, which he accused of being too pro-Polish. He made many psychological blunders, for he did not know how to deal with a proud and sensitive people. In effect, he behaved more like a proconsul than a diplomat.[11] He incurred severe Polish criticism for his defense of French businessmen, who wanted quick profits and demanded exorbitant privileges.[12] Some other Frenchmen who visited Poland at this time also behaved in an overbearing manner. The French senator Léon Mougeot came to Warsaw on behalf of a group of French capitalists who were interested in the Polish petroleum industry. He spoke to the undersecretary of state in the Ministry of Industry and Trade, Dr. Henryk Strasburger, in such a manner that he felt obliged to show Mougeot the door.[13]

Poland desperately needed economic and financial aid. It soon became clear, however, that French assistance was not available.[14] This explains the moves made by the Polish government to obtain British and American financial support, as well as its attempts to establish economic relations with Germany. Before 1921 the only economic agreement signed by France and Poland was the Klotz-Olszowski convention of 20 January 1920, whereby France promised to lend Poland 500 million, or even a billion, German marks to buy out German business interests in Poland. A special Franco-Polish company was to be set up to take over these interests. A French commissioner, Maxime Vicaire, with a high salary of 5,000 francs per month, was charged with the execution of the convention. However, it remained a dead letter, apart from the salary paid regularly to Vicaire by the Polish government.[15] We should also note that, jointly with the Versailles Treaty, a special treaty was signed between Poland and the Allied Powers, which imposed some unilateral trade obligations on Poland. Article 14 of this treaty stated that pending the establishment of import tariffs by Poland, the latter would accord the same most-favored-nation treatment to the Allied Powers as had been enjoyed by the Partitioning Powers under the old German, Austro-Hungarian, and Russian tariffs of 1 July 1914. No wonder that many foreign merchants, particularly the French, tried to sell Parisian luxury articles in Poland. Even Frenchmen complained of the behavior of certain French businessmen.[16] A Polish economist, Ferdynand Zweig, wrote of France's policy toward East-Central Europe at this time: "*France* was interested in East-Central Europe only from the point of view of her vain search for security, and was neither able nor ready to offer much in the economic field."[17]

In contrast with economic relations, the cooperation between the first head of the French Military Mission, Gen. Paul Henrys, and the Polish authorities was excellent. General Henrys was very popular with the Polish army and enjoyed the trust and confidence of Piłsudski, who often called Henrys his best friend. In a letter of September 1919, written to Henrys in connection with the final settlement on General Haller's army—which had come to Poland from France fully equipped by the French—Piłsudski wrote:

> I cannot pass over in silence the great services rendered by you, General, to the Polish cause and, in particular, to the Polish Army since your arrival here. Your understanding helped to solve the difficulties in which my country was involved at the time when it resumed its historic mission. In expressing my deep gratitude to you, I am sure that I express the feelings of the whole Polish Army.[18]

It is, of course, true that during the initial period, France gave Poland substantial support in arms and equipment for the Polish army. The value of the material supplied and of services rendered was assessed at about $160 million.[19] But the French later presented a bill for this aid, which was paid in part by Polish concessions to French capital in Upper Silesia. From the Polish point of view, these arms served to support not only Poland but also the European settlement established by the Versailles Treaty, of which Poland was the eastern pillar. Therefore, the Poles felt that they should not be required to pay. After all, without a Polish victory over the Red Army, the whole European structure, as created in Paris, might well have collapsed in the summer of 1920. As Lenin said in the autumn of that year: "By destroying the Polish army, we are destroying the Versailles Treaty on which the whole system of international relations is based."[20]

Although Polish leaders duly appreciated French political support as well as assistance in military supplies and the organization of their army, they realized that they could not rely on France regarding issues in which she was neither able nor willing to cooperate. Therefore, Polish statesmen attempted to interest Britain in Poland's political and economic aims and thus to balance French with the British influence in Poland. Piłsudski held many conversations on this subject with Sir Horace Rumbold in 1919/20 and made some concrete proposals, but without result.[21]

Premier Ignacy Paderewski and the Polish envoy in London, Prince Eustachy Sapieha, also made approaches to Britain at this time. Paderewski had returned to Poland on board a British destroyer in December 1918, together with Col. H. H. Wade, who became head of the British Military Mission in Poland. Paderewski was the only Polish statesman whom Lloyd George seemed to like. He tried to use this advantage by appealing to the prime minister, through Sapieha, to dispatch Allied troops to occupy the plebiscite region of Upper Silesia in September 1919. A mixed force was finally sent later, in which the French predominated, though this was due less to Paderewski's appeal than to an Anglo-French agreement. However, Paderewski's appeal was significant for its recognition of Lloyd George's dominant influence in the Entente.[22] Likewise, lower officials and diplomats made a play for British interest. Thus Sir Horace Rumbold reported to Earl Curzon, in November 1919, the opinion of Kajetan Dzierżykraj-Morawski, head of the German section in the Ministry of Foreign Affairs, that "Great Britain could, if she liked, do more to help Poland than any other power, and for that reason the Poles were willing to accord her a predominant influence."[23] But neither the British government nor private business showed much interest in this suggestion or in the idea of Anglo-Polish cooperation in the reconstruction of Russia.[24]

Let us now turn to the origins of the Franco-Polish alliance. After the Polish-Soviet war, France, who had given Poland both moral and material support, enjoyed great prestige and a predominant influence there. In France, however, the situation was different. Some influential French circles were reluctant to undertake formal commitments to Poland, except on certain strategic and economic conditions. Marshal Ferdinand Foch and Gen. Maxime Weygand, for example, recognized the need of giving substantial aid to the Polish army but wished to delay formal commitments. Foch's view that France should not go too fast stemmed from his preference for an East European bloc including Poland, rather than a Franco-Polish alliance;[25] also, French economic interests were clamoring for far-reaching concessions. Poland, of course, wanted a formal treaty with France, both for security and for the economic and military aid that she so desperately needed. It was estimated that the modernization of the Polish army alone would require at least one billion francs.[26] Poland also needed credits to stabilize her currency and build up her industry. Thus, it was clear that Poland needed France far more than France needed her. In Poland, this alliance was strongly supported by both the Right and the Left, although the Socialists and Piłsudski's close collaborators stressed that it should not mean the subordination of Polish interests and policy to France.[27] In sum, Poland's bargaining position was very weak, and this would be decisive in the negotiations and the resulting treaties.

Despite initial objections to the Little Entente—initiated by the Czechoslovak-Yugoslav alliance against Hungary signed on 14 August 1920—France accepted it and wished Poland to join it. However, Foreign Minister Sapieha made it clear that bad Polish-Czechoslovak relations and Poland's traditional friendship for Hungary made this solution impossible, at least for the time being. Therefore, in November, Sapieha's talks with Pralon's successor, Hector de Panafieu, led to the idea of a direct Franco-Polish rapprochement that would be independent of the Little Entente. Also, at the end of November, the Polish General Staff handed a draft military convention to Gen. Henri Albert Niessel, the new head of the French Military Mission in Poland. The draft, as drawn up by Gen. T. Rozwadowski, chief of the Polish General Staff, included the sending of French units to Poland in case of war with Germany and/or Russia, while Polish units would also be sent to France. We should note that at this time Finance Minister Władysław Grabski was in Paris trying to negotiate a French loan for Poland, so that French economic interests were directly involved. Indeed, Niessel mentioned the need for both Polish economic concessions and French influence on the Polish army, when he spoke to the Polish war minister at the end of December.[28] It was no secret that Grabski was pressed to make far-reaching economic concessions. Sir Horace Rumbold feared that if Poland pledged her state monopolies, railways, and state property to France in return for a loan, "her position will be far more favourable in the future in Poland than that of Great Britain." He also warned that recent sales of British oil interests to French financial groups made some people believe that Britain was divesting herself of all her interests in Galician oil. Others hinted that Poland had already come under the "financial protection of France," a fact resented by those who wished to see the development of Anglo-Polish financial and trade relations.[29] Like many similar warnings, this one, too, failed to arouse any anxiety in London.

Despite Poland's readiness to grant extensive economic concessions to France, the results of Grabski's mission were disappointing. He could not accept the far-reaching demands of French shareholders, who wished to control most of the oil production in East Galicia on their own privileged terms. What is more, the negotiations provoked an outburst in the Polish Socialist and radical press, which accused the government of selling out the country's resources to French capitalists at the expense of the Polish working class.[30] Also, the Socialist deputy premier, Ignacy Daszyński, resigned on 4 January 1921. His resignation was mainly due to Socialist unwillingness to continue cooperation with the "reactionary" parties in the cabinet of "National Union," which had been formed under the Peasant Party leader Wincenty Witos during the critical period of the Polish-Soviet war. However, since Daszyński sharply opposed economic dependence on France, the resignation could also be interpreted as a demonstration against a Franco-Polish alliance treaty on terms unfavorable to Poland. Daszyński's resignation increased political instability, since two representatives of the Right had already resigned from the cabinet in November 1920. Also, at about this time, Warsaw approached Berlin, with the aim of easing tensions and simultaneously getting a "card up the sleeve" versus France. This was resented in

Paris. Finally, the French realized that the conclusion of an alliance was bound to strengthen Piłsudski's position in Poland at the expense of their National Democratic friends.[31]

While the coalition government of July 1920 was rapidly disintegrating in Poland, France was also passing through one of her periodical ministerial crises. Georges Leygues's cabinet was replaced with one headed by Aristide Briand, when the latter became prime minister for the fifth time on 16 January 1921. The French crisis and Piłsudski's illness in mid January delayed his departure for Paris. The French invitation to Piłsudski had been sent by the Leygues cabinet on 28 December 1920, and we should note that it did not mention an alliance or military convention but merely a political and economic agreement:

> The president of the French Republic and the government would be glad if the chief of state, Marshal Piłsudski, would kindly come to Paris. In the view of the French government, such a visit would be in the interest of both countries. It would allow an exchange of views on some important problems and, through direct conversations, would facilitate the conclusion of a political and economic agreement between Poland and France.[32]

Despite this cautious wording, the Polish Foreign Ministry instructed its missions on 2 January 1921 that the invitation foreshadowed an alliance. The ministry ignored a report by the Polish legation in Paris that in the opinion of Philippe Berthelot, the secretary general of the Quai d'Orsay, Piłsudski's visit would allow for an exchange of views on international problems, especially on Soviet Russia, and would also facilitate the conclusion of political and economic agreements. It is curious that Baron Prosper de Barante, the French chargé d'affaires in Warsaw, merely delivered to the Polish Foreign Ministry the telegram containing the invitation.[33] Piłsudski and the ministry chose to interpret it as an invitation to negotiate an alliance.

In Paris there was a clear division of opinion in political and military circles. While President Alexandre Millerand and two ministers, Louis Barthou (war) and Paul Doumer (finance), as well as the chief of the General Staff, Gen. Edmond Buat, favored the alliance, reservations were expressed by the premier and foreign minister, Aristide Briand, and by his chief adviser, Philippe Berthelot. Thus, Briand instructed Panafieu to maintain a reserved attitude in Warsaw, for he feared Poland might jeopardize her future relations with Russia and thus risk more trouble.[34] Likewise, Berthelot later advised Sapieha that Poland should not take too much "Russian land." Apart from these reservations, the Quai d'Orsay was fully aware that French businessmen and financiers insisted that Poland make economic concessions as the condition for an alliance. Finally, Marshal Foch, chief of the French General Staff, had his own reservations. His instructions to Niessel have already been noted. On 4 and 14 January 1921, Foch sent notes to Briand, in which he opined that a military convention with Poland would be premature. He observed that Poland's position had not yet been sufficiently consolidated, her frontiers were unsettled, and her army had not yet been properly organized.[35]

Despite this opposition, Millerand was bent on concluding an alliance with Poland. He took credit for having sent Weygand to Warsaw in 1920, and he saw the Polish victory as his own. He managed to obtain enough support to make his view prevail. This was already clear in the first declaration that Briand made as president of the Council of Ministers (prime minister) to the Chamber of Deputies, which foreshadowed a rapprochement with Poland. Briand not only took a strong anti-German line, declaring that there was no peace between France and Germany and that the latter should be disarmed; he also warned Moscow that in the event of a Soviet attack on France's allies, France would be forced to intervene.[36] However, the well-informed Warsaw correspondent of the *Times* (London) was quick to note that a French invitation to Piłsudski would probably not have been issued if General Wrangel had not been defeated.[37]

As far as Piłsudski was concerned, he intended to have a frank discussion of bilateral relations. He wanted to establish them on a firm basis, not of dependence, but of cooperation. His short visit to Paris was meant to accomplish this, leaving the military, financial, and economic conventions to be worked out by the competent ministers after his departure. According to one of his close associates, Piłsudski said:

> I am glad that our relations with France will be, as one should hope, clearly defined in all fields. The situation that has existed so far was—to put it mildly—rather "uncomfortable," and sometimes offensive to both sides. There have been too many "buts." At the same time, neither those who came here, nor the way in which they have behaved towards Poland, suited me. Very often, therefore, these gentlemen heard words from me that were sometimes disagreeable, and sometimes not even very diplomatic.[38]

However, while Poland was most anxious to conclude an alliance with France, she was equally anxious not to alienate Great Britain. Although Piłsudski claimed he did not want to visit Britain, he would certainly have welcomed an invitation to London as well. As the Italian envoy to Poland, Francesco Tommasini, recalled in his memoirs, one of Piłsudski's friends suggested that Tommasini induce his government to obtain an invitation for Piłsudski to visit both London and Rome. Tommasini refused, saying that Piłsudski had been invited to Paris without prior consultation with the British and Italian governments.[39] Still the suggestion was made by the British chargé d'affaires in Warsaw, Sir Percy Loraine, who wrote to Curzon on 3 January 1921:

I think it possible that a feeler may be thrown out to see whether His Majesty's Government [might] contemplate asking Marshal Pilsudski to London on a brief courtesy visit. . . . Our unpopularity here is of course considerable already. . . .

Nevertheless the Poles and in my opinion, even Marshal Pilsudski himself at the bottom, set greater store on our good opinion and on good relations with us than with anyone else.

But resentment against the Polish seizure of Vilna in October 1920 was still great in London, and Curzon answered:

I do not think that there is the least chance of H.M.G. [His Majesty's Government] inviting Marshal Pilsudski to London. Indeed we are arranging the next meeting of the Supreme Council at Paris for Jan. 19—expressly so as to miss meeting the Marshal who is to leave Paris on the preceding day.[40]

This date was set according to Piłsudski's original schedule. Though he came later, he still missed the conference, which was rescheduled again for 24–29 January 1921.

British coolness was deeply felt in Poland. It was hoped that a visit to London by Foreign Minister Sapieha would improve the situation. After Piłsudski's return, the Warsaw correspondent of the *Times* (London) reported Polish disappointment:

Gratifying as the outcome of the Paris visit was to the Poles, the Franco-Polish *entente* would have been valued ever so much more had it been endorsed by Great Britain. Unfortunately, the fact that an invitation to Marshal Pilsudski to London was not forthcoming indicated clearly enough that Great Britain, or at least Mr. Lloyd George, did not look with favour upon Poland or Marshal Pilsudski, and since Marshal Pilsudski, however numerous his political opponents, stands for Poland to-day as much as Mr. Lloyd George stands for Great Britain, Poland has felt the smart.[41]

In the meanwhile, Piłsudski, who had left for Paris on 1 February, arrived there on the third and stayed in France for only three days. He was accompanied by Foreign Minister Sapieha and War Minister Gen. Kazimierz Sosnkowski. On his way to France, Piłsudski granted an interview to the correspondent of *Le Matin,* in which he recalled the old traditions of Franco-Polish friendship and stated that the two nations were bound by ties of love and interest. He was, he declared, bringing ''the whole love of Poland for France.''[42] His reception by the French government and people was equally warm. He was welcomed with great cordiality, even though President Millerand did not meet him at the station, as was customary for heads of state. This omission was apparently due to rigid French protocol, for though Piłsudski's title was ''Chief of State,'' he was not a monarch or a president. It may be that Berthelot and a few officials who did not particularly welcome the visit had something to do with this. Whatever the cause, Piłsudski did not take it amiss. He stressed the Franco-Polish comradeship in arms; he decorated Marshal Foch with the highest Polish military decoration, the Virtuti Militari, and bestowed the same on Marshal Philippe Pétain. He also wrote a cordial letter to Marshal Joseph Joffre, in which he said: "Love for France has been consecrated in Polish hearts by tradition."[43]

Since neither side had detailed drafts ready for discussion, the decision to begin negotiations for an alliance and a military convention was made during Piłsudski's visit to Paris. No French projects for an alliance or a military convention have so far come to light. On the contrary, we have Foch's communications to Briand of 4 and 14 January 1921, in which Foch opined that a military convention would be premature. He seemed preoccupied with the danger of a Bolshevik attack from the Ukraine across the Carpathians into Eastern Europe. In a letter to Briand dated 3 February, the day of Piłsudski's arrival in Paris, Foch referred to such a danger. To counter it, he suggested a Polish-Rumanian convention to coordinate action on the upper Dniester River, while Czechoslovakia assumed the task of providing military aid. He concluded that it was desirable for Poland, Rumania, and Czechoslovakia to sign a military convention, and he expressly drew attention to the need for it in view of the forthcoming conversations between the French government and Marshal Piłsudski.[44]

If Foch's aim was to suggest an alternative to a Franco-Polish military convention, Millerand rejected it. It is possible that the exclusion of French military leaders from the political talks after the official luncheon on 5 February was intentional; at least Weygand believed this to be so. He states in his memoirs that Millerand had a talk with Foch before lunch and asked him to prepare a communique stating that there was complete unity of views between the two governments. But when Weygand called on the president shortly thereafter with the draft, Millerand said that "it was no longer to the point." After the political talks, Foch was informed that the two governments had decided to conclude an alliance.[45] We do not know exactly what was discussed at lunch and at the postluncheon talk between Millerand, Briand, Barthou, and Berthelot, on the one hand, and Piłsudski, Sapieha, and General Sosnkowski on the other. No French or Polish records of this conversation have so far come to light. But we do know they agreed that the two governments would conclude three treaties—political, economic, and military—and that the preliminary political agreement was to be so formulated as to facilitate its publication and avoid anxiety on the part of French and British opinion. Sapieha and Sosnkowski were to return to Paris to negotiate the treaties after making a visit with Piłsudski to Verdun. While arduous negotiations were still to follow, we can surmise that Barthou's and Millerand's view of Poland as a factor in maintaining the Versailles system and as a pillar of French policy in Eastern Europe prevailed over the reservations of Foch, Briand, and Berthelot.

Piłsudski's own impressions of his Paris visit, as recorded later by a close associate, throw some light on his opinion of the French statesmen. According to this source, Piłsudski said:

> I found Millerand was the easiest to get on with. He understands the Polish situation best, is well acquainted with Polish problems and understands nearly all our sore spots. He is a man free of truisms and does not pretend that he is going to make the whole of mankind happy by some blueprint for rules of action that hold good only for France. As far as France is concerned, he stands for a sound nationalism and is aware of the dangers that might arise in the future. From this point of view he appreciates Poland's role as an ally. He fully realizes the role of the army and shares my preoccupation in this respect. He is aware of the German danger menacing us and, consequently, also France. He also understands our position with regard to Russia. I was able to talk at length with him on this subject and to tell him about our troubles during our war with the Bolsheviks. To sum up, he is our friend and one who does not indulge in empty words.

Piłsudski did not have the same regard for Briand, whom he distrusted:

> My old acquaintance Briand, as Polish communiques like to call him, is, as a matter of fact, quite a fleeting acquaintance, and that amounts to very little. One listens to him as one listens to music, and at least in the opinion of our legation, I do not like music.[46]

Of Barthou, he said: "That old cynic Barthou had tears in his eyes."[47]

The French government was chary of revealing the agreement reached in principle with Poland. Briand did not want to run unnecessary risks in further negotiations with Great Britain on such problems as German reparations and disarmament and, most of all, on the Franco-British alliance which was the main goal of his policy. Therefore, he presented the agreement as one that would not involve any special engagements besides those stipulated already in the Covenant of the League of Nations. In this he succeeded. The British ambassador in Paris, Lord Hardinge of Penshurst, wrote in his memoirs that "opinion in London was reassured by Briand's statement to me that the only decisions taken were the measures to be adopted in the event of a Bolshevik attack, and the possibility of a commercial agreement discussed."[48] The Franco-Polish declaration was, indeed, couched in the most innocuous terms. As communicated by Briand to the ambassadors of Great Britain, Italy, and Japan on 6 February and subsequently published, it read:

> The two Governments of France and Poland, being equally anxious to safeguard their security and the peace of Europe, have recognized once more

the community of interests which unite the two countries in friendship. They have agreed to confirm their decision to coordinate their efforts and with this object in mind, to maintain close contact for the defense of their higher interests.[49]

The negotiations for the political agreement and military convention, which began in Paris after Piłsudski's departure, were conducted on the Polish side by Sapieha and Sosnkowski, respectively foreign minister and war minister, and on the French side by Philippe Berthelot and Jules Laroche, respectively the secretary general and the associate director of the Political and Commercial Affairs Department at the Quai d'Orsay. Millerand and Briand also took part in the talks. Berthelot and Foch continued to fight a rear-guard action. Foch reiterated his objections to the military convention in a memorandum to Briand of 11 February, in which he argued that France should not undertake precise obligations to Poland, since the latter did not yet have internationally recognized frontiers. (This was a reference to the negotiations proceeding with the Russians at Riga and to the forthcoming Upper Silesian plebiscite.) Marshal Foch wished to limit military arrangements to cooperation between the two General Staffs.[50] This was, in fact, the model established in Czechoslovakia, where Gen. Eugene Mittelhauser was both head of the French Military Mission and chief of the Czechoslovak General Staff.

Berthelot, for his part, insisted on Polish moderation toward Russia and on the need for a speedy and close rapprochement with Czechoslovakia. In a long conversation with Sapieha on 10 February, his line on Russia was very similar to that of Lloyd George and the Foreign Office. Poland should be "moderate" in fixing her eastern frontier so as not to revive Allied suspicions of her "imperialism" and to avoid alienating the Russians, both in Russia and abroad. If Poland failed to accept her "legitimate ethnographic frontiers," she would, in the future, be crushed between Russia and Germany. Russia, said Berthelot, was bound to revive as a Great Power, either as a federal or as a centralized state. As for Czechoslovakia, the secretary general said that Foreign Minister Beneš was ready to adopt a more definite attitude toward the Bolsheviks and to contribute to the military defense of Ruthenia (Eastern Galicia). To this end, said Berthelot, a close Polish-Rumanian entente was necessary. Clearly, he agreed with Foch, and gave a copy of the record of this conversation to the Czechoslovak minister in Paris, Štefan Osuský.[51] He also asked Osuský to call Beneš to Paris for talks with Sapieha. However, although the Czechoslovak foreign minister arrived immediately on 11 February, Sapieha nevertheless departed for London.[52]

On 10 February, Berthelot and Sapieha also discussed the Polish drafts for the political and military agreements. The political agreement was drafted and put into legal form by Maurycy Zamoyski, the Polish minister in Paris, and by the first secretary of the Polish legation, Tadeusz Romer.[53] It consisted of a preamble and four articles dealing with mutual consultation on foreign-policy matters, mutual aid in the execution of treaties, the development of economic cooperation, mutual defense of territorial integrity, and the conclusion of a defensive military convention.[54]

General Sosnkowski drew up a draft of the military convention and gave it to General Weygand on 8 February. In his original draft, consisting of seventeen articles and additional clauses, Sosnkowski sought to gain maximum security for Poland. The most important desiderata concerned French aid in case of a Russian attack on Poland, aid in case of German aggression that would come not only from German territory but also from German territory separated from Germany (Danzig and East Prussia), and French naval aid in the Baltic. In case of German mobilization, France was to concentrate her forces on the German frontier, but Poland's measures would depend on the situation on her eastern frontier. In case of war with Russia, France was to declare war on the latter. If attacked by both Germany and Russia, Poland was to concentrate most of her forces on the eastern frontier and put only a covering force in the west. In case of a Polish-Russian war, France was not only to secure communication lines with Poland but also to send naval units to defend the Polish coast and Poland's access to Danzig, as well as to prevent the transport of German troops by sea from Germany to East Prussia. French naval units were also to blockade Russian or German ports and to control the straits of the Kattegat. While Poland obligated herself to create an army of thirty infantry divisions and nine cavalry brigades, as well as artillery and other units, each country was to send military units to the other; these were to be put under the military leadership of the host country. Poland was to introduce two years of compulsory military service, and France was to extend the necessary loans and credits to allow for the appropriate reorganization and rearmament of the Polish army. However, the final draft, which Sosnkowski drew up in Paris and which Sapieha handed in on 10 February, was somewhat modified. It was modeled on the Franco-Russian Military Convention of 1892, but with the addition of the main Polish requirements listed in the original draft.[55]

Both Polish drafts were significantly altered by the French negotiators. Berthelot handed Sapieha the French counterproposal for the political agreement on 13 February. Here, the Polish phrase "mutual execution of treaties" was replaced by the phrase "of treaties jointly signed," a formulation that clearly showed—as Berthelot explained in any case—that the French government did not wish to give an a priori recognition of the forthcoming Polish-Soviet Treaty of Riga. The phrase "mutual aid," in article 3, was replaced by "mutual understanding"; this was explained by fear of parliamentary opposition in France and by the fact that the obligation of mutual aid was already in the military convention. For this reason, too, article 3 of the political agreement omitted the statement that a military convention would be signed. Finally, in article 4, Berthelot replaced the Polish phrase about consultation on foreign problems with one specifying consultation on policy problems in Central and Eastern Europe.[56] This was later changed to the terms used in article 1 of the treaty, but article 4 provided for consultation before new agreements were concluded that were of interest to French policy in Central and Eastern Europe.

The political agreement was signed on 19 February 1921. Article 1 provided for consultation on foreign-policy problems of interest to both states, insofar as they concerned the settlement of international questions, were in the spirit of the treaties, and were in conformity with the League of Nations Covenant. Article 2 provided for agreement on action, for mutual support of European economic recovery, and for the establishment of international peace and order in Europe. The two parties were also to develop their mutual economic relations; special agreements and a commercial convention were to be signed to this effect. Article 3 dealt with the concerting of defense measures in case one of the parties was the object of unprovoked aggression and with concerting the defense of their legitimate interests. Article 4 stipulated that the two governments would consult one another before concluding new agreements of interest to their policy in Central and Eastern Europe. Finally, article 5—which was not published at the time—provided that the agreement would enter into force upon the signing of the commercial agreements then being negotiated.[57]

The secret military convention was signed on 21 February 1921. It was much longer and more specific than the political agreement. Here too, the Poles had to make many concessions in comparison with the desiderata contained in the Sosnkowski drafts. The influence of Foch and Berthelot was clearly visible.

Article 1 was generally satisfactory from the Polish point of view, for it envisaged French aid in case of unprovoked German aggression from any territory dependent on Germany. This could be interpreted to mean Upper Silesia but not Danzig, as the Poles had wished. Moreover, it spoke of "aid" instead of "entering into war," as the Polish draft had stipulated. Article 2, which dealt with French aid in case of a Russian attack on Poland, simply pledged that France would keep Germany in check and would "aid" Poland in defending herself against the Soviet army. In Article 3, French aid in case of either German or Soviet attack was limited to sending war material, railway equipment, and technical personnel. It expressly excluded French combat troops. France undertook, within the limits of her means, to secure communication lines with Poland, including sea communications; but there was no mention of French naval units being sent into the Baltic, as the Poles had proposed. Article 4 was the most extensive. It obliged Poland to institute compulsory two-year military service and to maintain an army of thirty divisions. Further, Poland was to model her army organization on the French army and to standardize her equipment with that of France. France, for her part, was to grant Poland military credits for the years 1921 and 1922, the sum of which was to be fixed in an annex to the convention. Article 5 obliged Poland to develop a war industry according to a special plan and with French aid. Article 6 stipulated that the two General Staffs were to be in constant consultation on preparing the necessary means to carry out the convention and were to maintain their lines of communication. Article 7 specified that the officers of the French Military Mission in Poland were to be kept fully informed of current developments by the Polish military authorities; a liaison office was to be attached to the office of the Polish military attaché in Paris; and selected Polish officers were to attend courses in military instruction in France. Article 8 was added after the convention had been signed. It stipulated that the convention would not enter into force until the signing of the commercial agreements, which were then being negotiated. The annex dealt with the French loan for the Polish army.[58]

Some historians have claimed that economic motives—that is, the desire of French businessmen and financiers to obtain lucrative concessions in East Galician oil and Upper Silesian coal—finally overcame the doubts of the French Foreign Office and of the highest military authorities as to the wisdom of concluding an alliance and military convention with Poland.[59] However, we know that these agreements also had some powerful supporters. Although no detailed information about them is available, they allegedly included Gen. Edmond Buat, chief of the General Staff; War Minister Louis Barthou; Finance Minister Paul Doumer; and President Alexandre Millerand. An anonymous representative of the French high command was cited as saying that the Polish alliance was the consequence of the "bad treaty fabricated for us by the Anglo-Americans" and that it served the needs of French policy.[60]

While it is difficult to evaluate the relative weight of economic and political considerations in French thinking, it is possible to identify a direct connection between the military credits foreseen in the convention and the commercial agreements on which the French conditioned the ratification of the political and military treaties. On 7 March 1921, Peretti de la Rocca cabled Berthelot, who was in London with Briand, that the Polish minister was ready to sign not only the commercial agreement on the basis of the drafts proposed but also the bilateral agreement on "property, rights and interests," on condition that the political and military agreements would come into force immediately without waiting for the signing of the oil treaty. Berthelot's reply is significant. He telegraphed on 8 March that the political and military agreements could not enter into force until after the signing of the commercial agreements, particularly the oil agreement. He then stated:

> Briand charges me to say that he had formally stipulated this reservation, written in his hand at the bottom of the political and military agreements, and with the consent of Prince Sapieha and Count Zamoyski. . . . It is evident that any preliminary signing would prevent the signing of the oil treaty, which is of first class importance to France.[61]

Oil was also connected with the annex to the military convention specifying that France would advance Poland a loan for her military needs.[62] Sosnkowski reported a French proposal that this loan be repaid in kind, by way of an oil agreement or with Polish material guarantees.[63] A French Foreign Office note, commenting on the annex to the convention, clarifies the connection between the military loan and the oil agreement. The note states that the financial stipulations of the annex would be implemented according to a plan of reimbursement to be agreed upon by the two governments. It could be based on the export of natural or manufactured Polish products, on the exploitation of state forests, on the "partial alienation of the state refinery at Drohobycz," or on other rights that the Polish state might concede. The Polish government was to propose a reimbursement plan as soon as possible. Negotiations for the "partial recovery" of the Drohobycz refinery were to be speeded up so that they could be concluded by 1 July 1921.[64]

It is also worth noting that in one of the three conversations that took place between Berthelot and Sapieha on 10 February, the secretary general gave the Polish foreign minister a note on the demands of French oil companies with investments in East Galicia, as well as the draft of an agreement that would shield them from "arbitrary action" by the Polish authorities and from the competition of Polish state-owned oil production.[65] Sosnkowski thought the French demands were too onerous for Poland and might prove impossible to fulfill.[66] Indeed, in May 1922, the rapporteur of the Sejm Commission on Foreign Affairs, Stanisław Grabski, stated that the commercial agreements—signed on 6 February—gave France much more than the latter gave to Poland and that the oil convention was totally to France's advantage. Nevertheless, he recommended that the treaties be accepted since Poland had already been compensated by the de facto alliance of February 1921.[67]

A brief glance at the economic and commercial agreements will show that French capitalists did, indeed, obtain great advantages. While this reflected the obvious fact that Poland was the weaker party, it also demonstrated French economic aggressiveness. In the commercial treaty, France obtained the most-favored-nation (MFN) status for most of her exports to Poland. The latter was thus obliged to import such French products as wines, liqueurs, jewelry, perfumes, cosmetics—luxuries that Poland did not need and could ill afford. She also had to import French textiles, although the Polish textile industry was already well developed and had lost its prewar Russian market (mainly in the Ukraine and Belorussia). All these goods enjoyed a reduced customs duty of 50 percent. Although Polish exports to France did not enjoy MFN status, they obtained minimum tariffs or reductions varying between 25 and 75 percent. This did not, however, help Poland, since most of her exports were agricultural, and France was self-sufficient in this respect.

A second commercial convention, the so-called bilateral convention, dealt with business firms. It stipulated that the business concerns of either state could establish their branches on the territory of the other.[68] In practice, this meant the establishment of French firms in Poland.

The third economic convention, the oil convention, gave freedom of production and export to French companies after the needs of the Polish market had been met. They were also granted the right to export foreign currency, as well as exemption from capital levies and obligatory government loans. In this industry, French capital did not supplant German and Austrian funds; rather, it associated itself with them and so protected them from expropriation or compulsory purchase. Thus, the German firms working in Galicia, grouped in the Deutsche Erdöl A. G. (called D.E.A. for short), and the Austrian ones, grouped in the Österreichische Boden Credit Anstalt, sold a part of their shares to the French. In this way a new company was formed, the International Petroleum Union, which brought together the D.E.A. and the French Société des pétroles de Dabrowa. The German *Handbuch für die internationale petroleum Industrie* for 1921 noted that Franco-German cooperation here was particularly cordial.[69] Other Austrian capital merged with the French in August 1920 to constitute the Société réunie des pétroles Fanto. It was closely connected with the Banque de Paris et des Pays Bas, on the one hand, and with the American Standard Oil Company on the other. British capital, which had invested in Galician oil before the war, withdrew for lack of government and private support. Thus the Premier Oil and Pipeline Co. Ltd. sold its shares to what became a Franco-German-Austrian society.

Other important Franco-Polish economic negotiations concerned Upper Silesia; these are described elsewhere. In any case, they were so dilatory that no decisive steps were taken until after the League of Nations' verdict of 12 October 1921, which divided Upper Silesia between Poland and Germany. Finally, the first payment on the French military loan to Poland was delayed until 1924. Two of the reasons for this delay were given in a French Foreign Office note of 18 July 1922. It reported that the Ministry of Finances was absolutely opposed to the loan because of the expense of producing war material for Poland and because of the lack of guarantees for reimbursement.[70]

While the French alliance gave Poland a large measure of security, this was soon proved to be incomplete without British support. French statesmen always believed they could not commit their country to war with Germany without Britain's agreement and backing. While it was clear that Britain would aid France if Germany were to attack her, British support for France's East European friends and allies was unattainable until the spring of 1939. This was due to radically different French and British perceptions of European security. Generally speaking, France expected an independent Poland—ideally allied with Czechoslovakia and Rumania—to contain Germany in the east, while France and Britain contained her in the west. Also, an independent Poland would prevent alliance or close cooperation between Germany and Soviet Russia. The French wished to preclude German-Soviet cooperation at all costs and to keep Germany as weak as possible in order to ensure France's own security and European peace. British statesmen held very different views. They assumed from the outset that Germany would recover and should then take her rightful place in the "Concert of Europe." They believed that a large Poland was bound to bring Russia and Germany together, for it was too weak to keep them apart. Also, since the Germans' strongest resentment against the Versailles Treaty focused on the lands they had lost to Poland, the British feared a German-Polish war that would draw France into conflict with Germany and thus force Britain to support France in a war over a region where Britain believed she had no "vital" interests. Therefore, some French statesmen, who saw Poland as a stumbling block in relations with Britain, wished to trade the Franco-Polish alliance for an alliance with Britain, or at least a British guarantee of the Franco-German frontier. Indeed, in 1919, a joint Anglo-American guarantee was the paramount objective of French policy. The French only renounced a separate Rhineland state allied with France, Belgium, and Luxembourg in exchange for Anglo-American guarantees of aid against Germany. These treaties, which France signed simultaneously with both Britain and the United States on the same day as the Treaty of Versailles, promised aid to France and Belgium in case of unprovoked German aggression. The United States' secretary of state, Robert Lansing, immediately saw the implications. In a note of 29 March 1919, he wrote:

> It seemed to me that here was utter blindness as to the consequences of such action. There appears to have been no thought given as to the way other nations, like Poland, Bohemia, and the southern Slavs would view the formation of an alliance to protect France and Belgium alone. Manifestly, it would increase rather than decrease their danger from Germany since she would have to look eastward and southward for expansion. Of course, they would not accept as sufficient the guaranty of the Covenant when France and Belgium refused to do so.[71]

Although these treaties fell through when the United States Senate failed to ratify the Versailles Treaty, French acceptance in 1919 of a guarantee only for Franco-German and Belgian-German borders foreshadowed a purely Western security pact as the alternative to France's East European alliances. As we shall see, it was to be partially implemented in the Locarno Treaties of 16 October 1925.

There were, of course, other areas besides Germany where Franco-British interests clashed—for example, in the Middle East. However, in Europe the major issue was Allied policy toward Germany. Here, apart from reparations, the key question was the problem of French security, which, in turn, involved Poland. But it was clear from the outset that Britain would not undertake any commitments to France's allies in Eastern Europe—that is, Poland and, later, Czechoslovakia. Even before Franco-British discussions on a guarantee pact began in November 1921, Lloyd George defined his attitude in a conversation with Lord D'Abernon, the British ambassador to Germany, on 21 June 1921. As D'Abernon wrote, Lloyd George

> appeared inclined to agree with the view that England should guarantee to protect France in the event of unprovoked attack by the Germans. He said, however, if we guarantee their security we must make it quite clear to them that there is to be no military hegemony of Europe and no operation of military adventure. We should have to put it very clearly that, if we guarantee them from attack, they must not provoke attack by an aggressive attitude, and that they must restrain the Poles. It was a choice, in a way, between an English policy and a Polish policy.[72]

However, the question was really not one of restraining the Poles but one of possible British involvement in a war provoked by German aggression against Poland. If the Poles rejected the territorial demands of a resurgent Germany and if the latter then attacked Poland, France would inevitably be drawn in. If Germany then attacked France, Britain would be obliged to come to France's defense. This would also be the case if a German attack on France should result from a Polish-Soviet war in which Germany supported Russia against Poland and France either attacked Germany or was attacked by her. The secretary of the cabinet, Sir Maurice P. A. Hankey, had these dangers in mind when he penned a memorandum for Lloyd George in June 1921, opposing an Anglo-French alliance. France, he wrote, needed a large and "aggressive" Poland, at least until a Franco-Russian alliance was again possible. Thus, an alliance with France would continually face Britain with the dilemma of either supporting a policy that ran the risk of war or of being accused of breaking the alliance. Hankey also argued that once Germany had recovered, Britain could not fulfill her military obligations to France without introducing conscription—and this would be extremely "distasteful" to British opinion.[73]

The root of British opposition to an alliance with France lay in the conviction that Britain had no national interest to intervene in Central and Eastern Europe—nor even on the Rhine for that matter—and that such intervention would not be supported by British opinion. Philip Kerr, later Lord Lothian, who was Lloyd George's private secretary in 1919, expressed these thoughts in the broad context of imperial concerns. Writing to Lloyd George in September 1920, Kerr stated that Britain could not play an active part in Europe while simultaneously shouldering the burdens of Ireland and of empire. In any case, British opinion would reject any intervention in Europe unless the security of the British Isles were threatened. Thus, it would certainly reject intervention over such issues as Upper Silesia, an Austro-German union, the "Danzig Corridor," or even the maintenance of troops in Germany for fifteen years. France, wrote Kerr, must realize that she must choose between maintaining the Versailles treaty by herself and resigning from 50 percent of it in order to secure the support of British public opinion for the rest.[74]

Given these assumptions on the British side, it is no wonder that French efforts to obtain an alliance were doomed to failure.[75] On 21 December 1921, Briand outlined to Lloyd George his concept of a broad alliance between France and Britain, "in which the two Powers would guarantee each other's interests in all parts of the world, act closely together in all things and go to each other's assistance whenever these things were threatened." Lloyd George refused on the grounds that British opinion was not interested in Eastern Europe and was not disposed to involve itself on behalf of "unstable and excitable" populations. Briand said that he understood this reluctance but that the French people desired a firm understanding with Britain which would reduce their military burden. He thought of some arrangement such as the Quadruple Pacific Treaty, just concluded in Washington. France and Britain would be the nucleus around which other nations could gather. This would be a "general organisation to keep peace in Europe." If France and Britain were to guarantee the peace, then the Germans would probably give up their militarist designs against Poland and Russia. But Lloyd George was unmoved. It was finally agreed that Briand would send Lloyd George a memorandum on the proposed treaty and that they would meet again to discuss the matter at Cannes a day or two before the meeting of the Supreme Council there.[76]

Briand's proposal came at a bad time. Franco-British relations had barely recovered from the strain over Upper Silesia, while disputes continued over many other regions. At the end of December 1921, Foreign Secretary Earl Curzon doubted that France would give up her "anti-British" policy in

Silesia, Bavaria, Hungary, Morocco, Egypt, Syria, and Mesopotamia in return for an alliance. He saw even greater difficulties in the French attempt to "revive the old policy of State alliances, dominating and controlling the future of Europe, at a time when such arrangements were believed to have been superseded by the newer conceptions embodied in the League of Nations." But, above all, Curzon objected to the danger of France's dragging Britain into war over an area where Britain's vital interests were not involved. Still, he seemed inclined to consider Briand's suggestion of a consultation pact, provided that it was tied to the League of Nations and that Anglo-French disputes in the Near East were satisfactorily settled. If the pact were connected with the league, it would not only strengthen that organization but would also avoid any British commitments in Eastern Europe—for example, to Poland.[77]

On 4 January 1922, at Cannes, Briand and Lloyd George continued their discussion of a Franco-British alliance, but with no results. Lloyd George proposed a treaty closely resembling the abortive treaty of 1919. It would contain a British *guarantee* to assist France if the latter's soil were invaded by Germany, but there was to be no formal alliance and most certainly no guarantees of aid to East European states. Briand suggested that a Franco-British *alliance* would keep the peace. Any trouble that might occur would first be dealt with at conferences in which France and Britain would act together. He also intimated that a British guarantee to France might in itself have the effect of keeping the peace. But Lloyd George countered by enumerating certain preconditions for such a guarantee: the peaceful settlement of the Greco-Turkish war; an agreement on Tangier; an agreement on French submarine construction; and cooperation in the economic and financial reconstruction of Europe. Here, Lloyd George envisaged a conference of European states which would include Russia.[78] This proposal was to develop into the Genoa Conference.

On the following day, 5 January 1922, Briand gave Lloyd George a brief outline of his ideas on the broader guarantee treaty. He thought it might include an undertaking by Russia not to attack Poland, the Baltic States, Finland, and Czechoslovakia, as well as a similar undertaking by Germany. A general European entente could be concluded on these lines, and like the Pacific Pact, it would not entail any military obligations. When Lloyd George asked how this would differ from the League of Nations Covenant, Briand answered that he thought "the latter was not sufficiently binding in form."[79] Over the next three years, this was to be the main theme in French efforts to obtain British support for a European security treaty.

On 8 January, Briand handed Lloyd George a proposal regarding the guarantee treaty. Here Briand not only sought British guarantees of France's eastern frontier—which included a guarantee of the demilitarized zone in the Rhineland—but also tried to obtain a British commitment to defend the status quo on the eastern frontiers of Germany.[80] However, Lloyd George reiterated his former objections. He also said he could not recommend a *military* alliance with France to English public opinion, so he could go no further than sign a declaration to the effect that Britain would go to France's aid in case of a German invasion. He stated that Britain could not undertake any commitments involving her in a guarantee of the general peace of Europe. To this, Briand said he envisaged two steps: first an "Entente entre deux," and then an "accord général."[81]

It is quite clear that Lloyd George refused to think of any general agreement except in the vaguest of terms, while an alliance with France was out of the question.[82] On 10 January the British cabinet rejected Briand's proposal for a broader European pact. As the cabinet saw it, Britain's agreement would tie her to France's plans for "continental hegemony."[83]

Nevertheless, Briand accepted Lloyd George's proposal for an economic conference of all European states, including Russia—despite her unpaid and unrecognized debts to France—no doubt so as to keep the door open for some Anglo-French treaty. Given the attitude of Lloyd George, the cabinet, the Foreign Office, and the majority of British opinion, it is hard to see how Briand could have had any hope of success. In any case, his conciliatory attitude toward the British prime minister and his agreement to an economic conference aroused fears in Paris that vital French interests might suffer. When the French press published a photograph of Briand "taking a lesson" in golf from Lloyd George at Cannes, there was an uproar. Millerand and Poincaré demanded that Briand renounce any engagements he had made and return immediately to Paris. Briand returned and made a speech in the Chamber of Deputies, giving a detailed account of his negotiations at Cannes; but he did not ask for a vote. He simply resigned on 12 January.[84]

Raymond Poincaré now set about forming a new government. The tough lawyer from Lorraine—and former president of France—was the antithesis of the flexible, charming Briand; but the goal of French policy remained the same. On 14 January, Poincaré met Lloyd George at the British embassy in Paris and told the British prime minister that the latter's draft treaty was inadequate. There must be a reciprocal pact and a military convention. However, Poincaré agreed that, for the time being, lack of agreement on outstanding problems made a pact untimely.[85] The meaning of this was explained to the Polish legation in Paris. The Polish chargé d'affaires reported that, firstly, the French adamantly opposed any linkage between the alliance and the settlement of Franco-British disputes; these included the Near East, policy toward Germany, naval disarmament, Tangier, and islands in the Pacific. Therefore, the French wanted a reciprocal treaty, not a one-sided British guarantee conditional on eventual French concessions in other matters. Secondly, the French wanted a guarantee that would function automatically—that is, one that would not require an interpretation of the pact on each separate occasion. The chargé also cited a well-informed source, which reported Poincaré as having declared that European reconstruction should not be based on Germany but on the young states born of the war and Allied efforts. They should be the pillars of the new European edifice. In fact, one of Poincaré's first acts after becoming prime minister (15 January 1922) was to sign the Franco-Polish commercial agreements. These had been ready since June 1921, but Briand had laid them aside, fearing they would compromise his attempts to obtain an alliance with Britain. Poincaré signed the agreements on 6 February 1922, thus bringing into force the alliance and military convention signed a year earlier.[86]

It was now Poincaré's turn to try his hand at the British alliance. He proposed not only a British guarantee for the demilitarization of the Rhineland but also Anglo-French collaboration on all matters endangering peace—that is, the order established by the peace treaties. This, of course, included the Polish-German frontier. Also, there was to be an Anglo-French military convention for a period of thirty years.[87] Though Poincaré was willing to give up the military convention for an exchange of letters, British reaction was as negative as before.[88] French attempts to reopen the talks in May failed, and the matter was dropped in July.[89] Franco-British tension grew as France moved toward her fateful decision to occupy the Ruhr.

Although the British cabinet objected to guaranteeing both the demilitarized status of the Rhineland and the status quo in Eastern Europe, they found the latter to be the more objectionable of the two. In a memorandum dated 17 January 1922, on the Guarantee Treaties of 1814/15 and 1919, James W. Headlam-Morley wrote that Britain could probably guarantee France against aggression through the Rhineland or Belgium; "but probably the real danger in the future may lie rather on the eastern frontiers of Germany—Danzig, Poland, Czecho-Slovakia—for it is in these districts that the settlement of Paris would be, when the time came, most easily overthrown." He noted that Britain could not extend military aid to those areas, and for that reason it was impossible to satisfy the demands of France in the way that the Prussians and Austrians had been satisfied in 1814/15.[90]

Headlam-Morley was careful to state that this was only one reason for opposing French demands. He knew very well that a French-occupied or a demilitarized Rhineland was necessary to French security. At the same time, the most effective help that France could give to her East European allies, if they were attacked by Germany, was to threaten to march through the demilitarized Rhineland into the Ruhr—for demilitarization of the Rhineland would, of course, lapse as far as France was concerned should Germany attack Poland and/or Czechoslovakia. None of these French advantages was welcome to Britain, but the French alliance with Poland was the chief objection.

The British ambassador, Lord Hardinge, reported on a conversation with Poincaré: "I warned him that under any circumstances it would be useless to expect that England would intervene in the event of an attack on Poland, a statement that disconcerted him greatly."[91]

The problem was, of course, much broader. It involved Britain's attitude toward the Versailles Treaty, which was, in turn, linked to the perception of her vital interests. Arnold Toynbee gave an accurate, if partial, summary of the issues dividing the two countries, when he wrote:

> The solid fact, from the point of view of Mr. Lloyd George or Lord Curzon, was that the British Parliament and public were so little troubled by a sense of insecurity from the direction of Continental Europe, now that the German fleet had disappeared, that they would not be induced to guarantee anything on the Continent beyond the eastern frontiers of Belgium and France. On the other hand, the French people realized, from a political experience as old as that of the English, though of a different kind, that the Continent was an indivisible unit of international relations from the political and military point of view.[92]

But as we know, the cabinet thought differently. In the Foreign Office, only one high official expressed a similar view at the time. Undersecretary of State for Foreign Affairs Sir William Tyrrell agreed with his superior, Sir Eyre Crowe, that an Anglo-French alliance was desirable; but he went further. He suggested that the security of Poland and other East European states should also be assured by declarations given by the French and British governments that they would put all their resources at the disposal of the League of Nations to enforce its decisions. But Tyrrell was not taken seriously. It was rumored that his Polish sympathies were linked to his Roman Catholicism.[93]

Thus, the years 1921 and 1922 saw the failure of French efforts to link an alliance with Britain with a general European security treaty. This failure implied that sooner or later, France would have to choose between a British guarantee of aid against Germany, on the one hand, or her East European alliances, on the other, as the mainstay of her security.

It is not surprising that the failure of Franco-British negotiations encouraged those Frenchmen who had, for different motives, opposed the idea of France as "the policeman of Europe." Some of these critics favored a rapprochement with Germany for political or economic reasons, or both. Among them was Philippe Berthelot, the powerful secretary general of the French Foreign Office and a close collaborator of Briand's. Berthelot's major objective was to come to terms with Germany. He was skeptical of the

Versailles Treaty and believed that, of all the European states, Germany was the one with which France could reach the best understanding, because German civilization came closest to the level attained by France.[94] Briand's and Berthelot's desire for a political and economic rapprochement with Germany resulted in many projects for Franco-German industrial cooperation.[95] Berthelot also disliked the Poles. At a critical point in the Polish-Soviet war, he told some British and American journalists: "I agree with Proudhon that after the executioners, there is nothing more repugnant than the victim."[96] Nor was he free of certain prejudices. Thus, he favored the positivist Czechs as being more reliable than the Catholic Poles.[97] But above all, like many British statesmen, he viewed the Poles as an obstacle to good relations with Germany and Russia. Poincaré forced Berthelot to resign in 1922 because of a financial scandal, but the latter returned to the Quai d'Orsay when his patron, Briand, again became prime minister and foreign minister in 1925.

While the thought of a rapprochement with Germany did not gain much currency in France before 1925, two other trends were very much alive in 1921. One was the view that the Franco-Polish alliance was a poor substitute for the old alliance with Russia. This view vegetated for a while until it bloomed again in 1932. The other line of thought—often expressed by officials, military men, and the press—was to reduce French obligations by bringing about an alliance between Poland and Czechoslovakia. However, such an alignment was impossible in Polish eyes unless the Czechs made at least a symbolic territorial concession to Poland in return for keeping the predominantly Polish-speaking areas of the duchy of Teschen. This the Czechs were unwilling to do. Moreover, they publicly disapproved of Poland's frontiers with both Germany and Russia. They did not wish to be involved in these disputes. They did not think they had any quarrel with Germany, and they viewed Russia as a potential ally. Therefore, they saw the main danger to their security in Hungarian revisionism and, of course, in the restoration of the Habsburgs to the Austrian or/and Hungarian thrones. Finally, they believed that Czechoslovakia, not Poland, should be recognized as the dominant power in East-Central Europe.

Thus, from its inception, the Franco-Polish alliance suffered from a contradiction between theory and practice. In theory, French statesmen maintained that the alliance was necessary in order to preserve a favorable balance of power in Europe. In practice, however, they desired an alliance with Britain which, on British terms, would exclude any guarantee of the French alliance with Poland. French statesmen also dreamed of a rapprochement with Germany or Russia, or with both, which would, of course, involve

French acquiescence to at least some claims on Poland. Finally, French statesmen desired to shed the burden of defending their East European allies, and they hoped to achieve this by establishing a Polish-Czechoslovak alliance which was eminently desirable in theory but extremely difficult in practice. As far as Polish statesmen were concerned, they saw the French alliance as Poland's main security against Germany, but they were equally determined not to follow in France's wake if they perceived this to be contrary to Poland's vital interests. Some, particularly Piłsudski, also realized that French help was more than doubtful without British support and approval, which they hoped to secure at some future date. They based their hopes on the assumption that Britain would finally realize that Germany's expansion at Poland's expense would strengthen Germany enough to become a threat to the whole of Europe, including France and the British Isles.

2

The Struggle for Upper Silesia: The Background and Developments from 1919 to the Plebiscite of 20 March 1921

The fate of Upper Silesia was a major issue in European politics during the years 1919 to 1921.[1] The award of this region to Poland would give her a desperately needed industrial base and thus the means to withstand German economic domination; by the same token, an award to Germany would not only restore her entire prewar industrial potential—already the greatest in Europe in 1914—but would also lead to her economic domination of Central and Eastern Europe, including Poland. The ethnic structure of the region divided it into two parts: the predominantly German-speaking area west of the Oder River, and the predominantly Polish-speaking area along the river itself and east of it. In the latter part, however, the industrial region had a mixed population. The townspeople were mostly German, while the labor force was Polish. Poles worked in the mines, steel mills, and foundries, and they lived either on the outskirts of the towns or in the surrounding countryside. Of course, the industrial region, with its coal and zinc mines, its iron foundries and steel mills, was the prize. Its heart, the so-called Industrial Triangle, was bounded by Beuthen (Bytom), Gleiwitz (Gliwice), and Kattowitz (Katowice). On the spot the struggle was waged between Poles and Germans; while in the diplomatic arena it was waged by their respective supporters, France and Britain. In order to understand the significance and complexity of this problem, we should first consider the ethnic and socioeconomic structure of Upper Silesia and then the region's economic importance to Germany and Poland respectively.

Both the Germans and the Poles claimed Upper Silesia on ethnic grounds. An objective picture of the ethnic structure can be found in the *Handbook on Upper Silesia* prepared for the Peace Conference under the direction of the Historical Section of the British Foreign Office. Basing their observations on the German census of 1910, the authors wrote:

> If the Oder is taken as the racial boundary, the eastern part of the Regierungsbezirk forms a solid block of Polish territory. Outside the four towns of the industrial districts the percentage of Poles in the population is as high as in any other large district, Russian Poland included. Among the German inhabitants of the four towns, moreover, are military and other officials of all grades, who are not indigenous, and should not be counted in an estimate of the permanent population.[2]

The predominantly Polish character of Upper Silesia was also recognized in the Report of the Supreme War Council, Military Representatives, dated 10 July 1919, on the composition and size of the army of occupation in the plebiscite area of Upper Silesia, which stated: "The population of the plebiscite area is estimated at about 1,632,000 inhabitants (of which 570,000 are Germans and 1,062,000 Poles)."[3] These figures roughly correspond with prewar assessments made by German authors, particularly by Paul Weber in his study on the Poles in Upper Silesia (1914), according to which there were, in round figures, about 638,000 Germans and 1,121,000 Poles in the region. Another author, Johannes Ziekursch, roughly approximated "Polish Silesia" with Upper Silesia.[4] The maps enclosed in Joseph Partsch's book on Silesia (1896, 1911) show the gradual Germanization of Lower Silesia after 1790 and the immigration of a German, mostly urban population into Upper Silesia, where, however, Poles continued to be in the majority.[5] British experts who were involved in the Upper Silesian problem in the period 1919–21 recognized this fact. Thus, Hamish J. Paton stated, in a paper read at the Institute of International Affairs in December 1921, that "the German minority consisted of either Germanized Poles (as indeed is the case in Middle Silesia also) or of Germans who entered the country for purposes of trade and industry, some of them at least in comparatively recent times."[6]

Poles and Germans disputed the relative economic importance of Upper Silesian industry to each country. One of the arguments constantly used by the Germans, when the future of Upper Silesia hung in the balance, was that the industrial region was absolutely indispensable to Germany and that, if deprived of it, she would be unable to pay reparations. As we shall see, this argument later played an important role in inter-Allied disputes over the interpretation of the plebiscite results.

Unquestionably, the industrial district was an important economic asset for Germany. However, its importance to the Reich progressively diminished in the years 1870 to 1914, with the development of mining and heavy industry in the Ruhr. In 1910, total German coal production amounted to 152,828,000 tons, of which Upper Silesia accounted for 34,461,000 tons. Upper Silesian

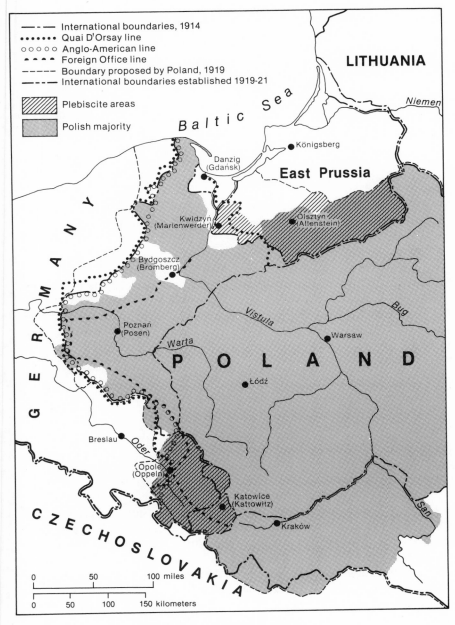

Legend

—·— International boundaries, 1914
•••••• Quai D'Orsay line
ooooo Anglo-American line
▲▲▲▲ Foreign Office line
———— Boundary proposed by Poland, 1919
—··— International boundaries established 1919-21

▨ Plebiscite areas

▨ Polish majority

LITHUANIA

Niemen

Baltic Sea

Königsberg

Danzig
(Gdańsk)

East Prussia

Kwidzyn
(Marienwerder)

Olsztyn
(Allenstein)

Bydgoszcz
(Bromberg)

G E R M A N Y

Vistula

Bug

Poznań
(Posen)

Warta

Warsaw

P O L A N D

Łódź

Breslau

Oder

Opole
(Oppeln)

Katowice
(Kattowitz)

Kraków

San

C Z E C H O S L O V A K I A

```
0        50        100 miles
|————————|————————|
0    50   100    150 kilometers
```

Map 2. The German-Polish Frontier

coal could be relatively easily replaced by increasing the production in the Ruhr. Furthermore, even before 1914, the position of the Upper Silesian coal-mining industry was precarious because of tariffs imposed on coal exported to Polish territories, which formed the natural market for this industry. Valuable information on export trends for Upper Silesian coal and coke can be found in the Foreign Office *Handbook on Upper Silesia,* cited above. This data was in turn based on an article by a German statistician, Paul Helmuth von Kulmitz, who showed that nearly half the coal produced was consumed by local industry and nonindustrial consumers, while 51.92 percent was exported. Only 28.05 percent of the total coal output was sold in the German Empire, a great part of it in Prussian Poland. The rest was exported to Russian Poland, Austrian Poland (Galicia), and other parts of the Austro-Hungarian Empire. As for coke, out of 343,657 metric tons, only 92,344 tons went to Germany—including Prussian Poland—while Russian Poland took 121,717 tons, Austrian Poland and Bukovina took 54,354 tons, and the rest was used in Upper Silesia.

The reason for the large exports to Polish territories lay in their proximity to the Upper Silesian industrial district and, obversely, in its unfavorable geographic position with regard to major German industrial centers. The authors of the *Handbook on Upper Silesia* opined that whether the district were given to Poland or were to remain in Germany, Polish territories would probably absorb most of its production. They noted that

> the development of the waterways of western Prussia has long given the coal of the Ruhr basin an advantage over that of Silesia in certain parts of Germany, which used to rely mainly upon the latter. For instance, in 1800, 72 percent of the coal consumed in Berlin was supplied in Upper Silesia, whereas in 1901 only 54 percent came from that source.[7]

Just as Upper Silesian coal and coke played a diminishing role in the German economy before 1914, so did the regional production of pig iron. In 1871 the Upper Silesian share of German pig-iron production was 14.8 percent; by 1901 it had sunk to 5.1 percent.[8]

While the share of Upper Silesian coal, coke, and pig-iron production in the German economy had shrunk between 1870 and 1914, the role of that production in the German armaments industry was still a major one. The Mines and Foundries Association of Upper Silesia was quite right in claiming that the German armaments industry could not have met the demands of the war had it not been for the production of Upper Silesia.[9] However, apart from the armaments industry, the prospects for the future were not bright. Indeed, in 1917, Upper Silesian industrialists desired the annexation of adjoining Polish territories where their industries found their major markets.[10] Professor W. J. Rose observed: "If Upper Silesia needed Poland as a market, then the

Upper Silesians who wanted their land to belong to Poland were not flying in the face of nature!''[11]

While bearing these facts in mind, it is obvious that the loss of Upper Silesian industry was bound to reduce Germany's industrial potential. In the period immediately preceding the war, Upper Silesia accounted for about 23 percent of Germany's coal production, 57 percent of her lead ore, and 72 percent of her zinc. But as later developments were to show, the loss of these resources did not prevent Germany from again becoming the greatest industrial power in Europe. Conversely, the same resources were indispensable for Poland's economic development; without them, she would have had to depend on Germany to such an extent as to make her political independence illusory.[12]

Most British statesmen and experts did not share this view, however. Thus, John Maynard Keynes wrote: ''The allies should declare that in their judgment 'economic conditions' require the inclusion of the coal districts in Germany unless the wishes of the inhabitants are decidedly to the contrary.''[13] He assumed that Germany would be ruined if the industrial district went to Poland. Many years later, Étienne Mantoux contested this view.[14] However, Keynes's opinions prevailed during the interwar period. Few people realized that while Germany could do without Upper Silesian industry, it was crucial for Poland's very existence. In fact, the part that was awarded to Poland in October 1921 produced 75 percent of her coal, 100 percent of her coke and briquettes, 66 percent of her iron, 87 percent of her zinc, and 100 percent of her lead.

The ultimate proof that Germany could dispense at least with Upper Silesian coal was provided during Polish-German negotiations for a commercial treaty in 1924/25, which were eventually broken off and led to a tariff war. The Geneva Convention (May 1922), whereby, among other things, Germany was obliged to purchase a monthly duty-free contingent of 500,000 tons of coal from Upper Silesia, was due to expire on 15 June 1925. In the course of the negotiations, which Germany tried to use for political ends, she declared that she no longer needed so much coal and would accept no more than 100,000 tons per month.[15] The news came as a shock to world opinion. Many newspapers, the *New York Times* included, observed that this meant Germany could live without Upper Silesian coal.[16] In the *Survey of International Affairs* for 1925 Arnold J. Toynbee commented: ''The situation was curious, for these provisions had been drafted largely in Germany's interest to compensate for her losses under the partition of Upper Silesia.''[17]

There is no need to give a detailed description of the political background for the Supreme Council's decision in 1919 that a plebiscite be held in Upper

Silesia. It has been recounted elsewhere.[18] Suffice it to say that the Germans had protested violently against the award of Upper Silesia to Poland in the Draft Treaty. It was Lloyd George who managed, by dint of threats and persuasion, to obtain Wilson's and Clemenceau's reluctant assent to a plebiscite, and the motive was political—to obtain Germany's signature of the Versailles Treaty.[19] This was not all, however. It is clear that the British prime minister had already made up his mind to resist such a weakening of Germany as would, in his view, lead to French "hegemony" in Europe.

Thus, it is not surprising that in his famous Fontainebleau Memorandum of 25 March 1919, Lloyd George harshly criticized French and Polish claims against Germany. He not only doubted Polish capacity for stable self-government, but, what is more important, he said he feared that Germany might throw in her lot with Bolshevism rather than sign the harsh treaty being prepared for her.[20] In Upper Silesia, he saw a plebiscite as only the second-best solution. He later told Lord D'Abernon: "We should have been favourable to giving it to Germany, but we compromised on a plebiscite." This was generally seen as an unspoken bargain: in return for the plebiscite, Germany would sign the peace treaty; and in return for the German signature, Britain would do her best to see to it that Upper Silesia would stay with Germany.[21]

The plebiscite was to be held no less than eighteen and no more than twenty-four months after the arrival of the Allied troops of occupation. This led to unrest and turmoil in Upper Silesia, exacerbated Polish-German and Anglo-French relations, and generally contributed to instability in Europe. As Paul Mantoux put it: "All these bodies that have to organize plebiscites appear to my mind like the time-bombs that the Germans used to leave in the territories from which they were obliged to withdraw."[22]

The decision to hold a plebiscite was the source of both hope and anxiety for the German government, which hoped for victory but feared defeat. In fact, fearing a Polish majority vote in Upper Silesia and the Polish Corridor, the German cabinet had decided in April 1919 not to ask for plebiscites in those areas.[23] Indeed, at the news that the draft treaty had awarded Upper Silesia to Poland, most German leaders there wanted to throw away their rifles.[24] Prussian authorities also feared that the undecided voters, who held the key, would side with the Poles in the event of a Polish occupation.[25] Thus, in the Polish uprising of August 1919, the Germans were reported as having behaved "shamelessly" because they expected a Polish victory,[26] while during the uprising of August 1920, there were fears that the show of Polish strength might swing the German vote in Poland's favor.[27] Thus, contrary to official confidence that Upper Silesia would vote for Germany, there was secret pessimism about the outcome.

Immediately after the signing of the Versailles Treaty, both sides set to work to influence the voters. The Germans had the advantage of almost absolute control in the area during fourteen of the twenty-eight months that elapsed between the signing of the armistice in November 1918 and the plebiscite on 20 March 1921. It was only after the second Polish uprising of August 1920 that the German police force was replaced by a plebiscite police force made up of both Poles and Germans. Even so, apart from some high officials who had to leave after the arrival of the Plebiscite Commission in February 1920, all administrative posts down to the lowest ranks, such as postmen and forest rangers, remained in German hands. The same applied to teachers and to technical and clerical staff in industry, mines, and agriculture. The higher Catholic clergy were German too, though most of the parish priests were Polish. Thus, the Germans enjoyed an enormous advantage over the Poles—who had struggled for their rights over the last sixty years.[28]

The development of Polish national consciousness in Upper Silesia began in the late 1840s under Bishop Bernard Joseph Bogedein, school commissioner for Oppeln (Opole) from 1848 to 1857 and later bishop of Breslau (Wrocław). Bogedein believed that children should start their education in their native tongue.[29] But later, Bismarck's Kulturkampf again banished Polish from the schools. Furthermore, no Pole could become a state or communal employee, and Polish political leaders were subject to harassment, as witness Wojciech Korfanty, elected deputy to the Reichstag in 1903. Most Poles were workers and peasants. More often than not they combined the farming of small plots of land with work in the mines and factories. Outside the industrial region, most of the province was agricultural and provided a living example of the old feudal system. Fifty-two percent of the land was in the hands of a few German magnates: the duke of Ujest, the duke of Ratibor, Prince Stollberg-Wernigerode, Prince Hohenlohe-Ingelfingen, Prince Donnersmarck, and the prince of Pless (Pszczyna). Any measures to break up these estates would have weakened their grip over Polish Silesian peasants. Furthermore, the great landowners were closely associated with German industrialists. No wonder that after the division of Upper Silesia in October 1921, the German government supported the policy of leaving great German estates intact.[30]

Besides controlling the administration, the church, and the economy, the Germans also had military forces in Upper Silesia. These were not only regular troops but also Free Corps formations. Immediately after the German collapse in November 1918, considerable regular forces were concentrated in Upper Silesia. Gen. Karl Hoefer, commander of the 117th Division, was directed to take up a position in the industrial district in November 1918. In December it was recognized as a *Grenzschutz,* or border defense unit. However, as Hoefer states in his book, the morale of his troops was very low, and it was the Free Corps which came to the rescue of the German cause.[31] The first Free Corps, under von Aulock, appeared as early as the spring of 1919. Von Oertzen, in his history of the Free Corps, states that they were used in suppressing strikes in Hindenburg (Zabrze) and, at the end of April 1919, in Gleiwitz (Gliwice). At the same time, Hasse's Free Corps appeared in the Polish areas of Pless (Pszczyna) and Rybnik. In June came the formations of the Tullmann, Eulenburg, and the Hessisch-Thüringen-Waldecksche Corps. They were followed by von Loewenfeld's Marine Free Corps and later by the most notorious of them all, the Baltic Free Corps, under Erhard. Thus, the Free Corps formations played a prominent role in the suppression of social and national unrest in Upper Silesia, and this meant mainly the Polish workers and peasants.[32]

Later, the typical Free Corpsman joined the Nazi Party. According to Robert G. L. Waite, he "was the restless Freebooter who had learned war and did not want to learn anything else."[33] This description agrees with Hoefer's statement that they preferred playing at soldiers to doing any productive work.[34] They terrorized the population by, among other things, exercising the *Feme,* or "People's justice," and murdering all those whom they classified as traitors. It was the Free Corps *Feme* which accomplished the assassination of Matthias Erzberger, on 26 August 1921, and of Walther Rathenau, on 24 June 1923. The people of Upper Silesia suffered grievously from the *Feme.* Waite writes:

> [The Feme] was a predominant feature of Freebooter activity in Upper Silesia. During the period of the Silesian plebiscite, Heinz Oskar Hauenstein gathered former *Freikorpskämpfer* about him and organized them into small shock troop formations, one of whose main functions was to "influence" German voters. Years later in a public trial Hauenstein guessed that his "Special Police" had killed "about 200 people" in Upper Silesia alone.[35]

But, at the time, the outside world knew very little about the activities of the Free Corps in Upper Silesia. Before the Versailles Treaty came into force in January 1920, the territory was under German administration, and the Allied Powers had no juridical title to intervene. It was only after the first Polish uprising in August 1919 that an Allied commission ascertained the facts about some of the atrocities. Rumors about these atrocities had been ascribed to Polish exaggeration, but some of the information was supplied by the Freebooters themselves. In February 1921 the *Times* (London) reviewed a publication of this sort, under the title "Freebooters in Arms":

> It was in Upper Silesia, during the Polish peasant rising of August, 1919, that the Ehrhardt force had the first opportunity of displaying something more than class hatred. The quelling of the insurgent "Water Pollaks," as the Silesian Poles are contemptuously termed, was a Nationalist and

48

> irredentist campaign. . . . The *Regiments-Adjutant* is in his element describing
> the intimidating of the villagers, the bombing of miners in their mineshafts,
> the bullying of "suspects."[36]

Apart from the Free Corps, the Upper Silesian Germans, with the aid of subsidies from large industrial concerns, set up their own citizens' militia. One of its organizers was Gerhard Williger, chairman of the Silesian Mining and Foundry Association.[37]

While the German government claimed that the Free Corps units were outside its control, local German authorities took strong action on Berlin's orders to keep Upper Silesia with Germany. On 31 December 1918 the president of the Regierungsbezirk Oppeln (Opole) decreed that any activity aiming at the secession of Upper Silesia from the Reich was high treason and subject to trial by military courts. On 10 January 1919, martial law was proclaimed in the industrial district and was later extended to the agricultural districts of Pless and Rybnik. All executive power was assumed by local military commanders, house searches and arrests could be carried out at any time, no public meetings were allowed, and military courts were established.[38] The German government also looked after the labor organizations. At the end of 1918 a Social-Democrat and former sergeant, Otto Hörsing, came to Kattowitz and became chairman of the Central Committee of Workers and Soldiers. Later, he was appointed state commissioner for Silesia and West Poznania, and then Reich and state commissioner, with his seat in Oppeln (Opole).[39]

But despite German control and repressive measures, strikes and unrest continued to spread. Since most of the industrial workers and peasants were Polish Silesians, the movement inevitably had the dual aspect of a socioeconomic and a national revolt. The Polish Military Organization (POW), was established here in early 1919. It grew spontaneously but received only minimum support from the Polish government, which did not want the complication of an armed uprising in Upper Silesia. On the one hand, the government realized that such an uprising would be doomed without direct assistance. On the other hand, Warsaw could not give this assistance, since Polish troops were fighting the Ukrainians in East Galicia and the Bolsheviks in the Vilna region. Moreover, expecting the Peace Conference to render a favorable decision on Upper Silesia, the Polish government did not wish to put obstacles in the conference's path. Therefore, Warsaw issued frequent warnings against any precipitate move. Wojciech Korfanty, the leader of the Polish national movement in the region, agreed. At a meeting with government officials in Poznań on 27 April 1919, he stated that an uprising would place Polish diplomacy in a hopeless position.[40] Therefore, the Polish government pressed for an Allied commission to be sent in to pacify the population.

As tension increased during the summer, the Polish government made frequent appeals to the Supreme Council to send a commission, but these were ignored. On 18 July, Paderewski asked United States Secretary of State Robert Lansing to send U.S. troops to Upper Silesia. This might, thought Paderewski, calm the population and avert an uprising.[41] On 5 August 1919 the liaison officer with the POW in Upper Silesia reported to the Polish General Staff the fear that the Polish population, exasperated by German outrages, would rise up in arms at any moment. The report warned that if the Germans did not proclaim an amnesty and if an Entente commission failed to arrive within two weeks, a spontaneous popular uprising was inevitable.[42]

It is beyond the scope of this study to deal at length with the first Polish uprising, but we should note that it was preceded by strikes and massacres of miners and workers. The uprising started on the night of 17/18 August 1919 and lasted six days. Contrary to some German assertions, particularly by Hörsing, it was not a Communist or Spartacist rising;[43] rather, it had a distinctly Polish national character. General Hoefer himself noted that since the uprising had first broken out in the predominantly Polish agricultural districts of Pless and Rybnik, it could not have been provoked by Spartacists.[44] Also, the relatively short duration of the uprising was due to the lack of Polish intervention—a fact recognized by Reich Chancellor Gustav Bauer. General Hoefer commented that irregular Polish units had no chance against the well-equipped German troops. In fact, the Germans had a total of seventy thousand men in regular and Free Corps units; the Poles had some twenty-five thousand men, and they were poorly armed.[45]

Although the uprising was a military failure, it did succeed in drawing the attention of Allied statesmen to this remote corner of Europe. It became clear that the Polish workers could bring all the mines and factories to a standstill if they so wished, and this aspect attracted the most attention in Paris and London. At a meeting of the Supreme Council on 18 August 1919, Balfour stressed the repercussions that the Upper Silesian unrest might have on coal production. He expressed no interest in the human misery involved, although Gen. Paul Henrys in Warsaw and Gen. Charles Dupont in Berlin had both sent telegrams stressing this factor. They blamed the German authorities and demanded intervention by the Entente Powers.[46] Col. G. Goodyear of the United States Army, who was then in Moravska Ostrava, sent a similar message to Herbert Hoover.[47] However, the French government, which opposed intervention, took the line that the information from Polish sources was exaggerated.[48] On 20 August, French Foreign Minister Stephen Pichon actually claimed that an Allied intervention would meet Polish wishes and that Polish workmen had brought about the strikes in order to provoke it.[49] It is most likely the French feared that an Allied intervention would mean the breakdown of the armistice with Germany.[50] Whatever the case may be, the Polish government implicitly directed its appeal to London.[51] The British chargé d'affaires in Warsaw, Sir Percy Wyndham, reported that the Polish government had succeeded, albeit with much difficulty, in controlling the army and preventing it from going to the aid of its countrymen.[52] When the question of the Entente Powers' assuming control over the plebiscite area came up, it was Balfour who urged on the Polish government that order must be maintained in the mines and that the Polish population in Silesia must be patient.[53] However, the Allied demand that Germany agree to a prompt Allied occupation of the region was refused. Finally, on 23 August, it was decided that when the treaty came into force, France should send the main contingent of troops to Upper Silesia, with smaller units being supplied by Britain and Italy. At the same time, it was decided that a Military Commission of Inquiry would be sent. This time, Berlin agreed.

The Military Commission of Inquiry consisted of Gen. Ian Malcolm and Lieutenant Colonel Tidbury of Great Britain; Col. G. Goodyear, coal representative on the Supreme Economic Council for the United States; General Dupont of France; and Gen. Roberto Bencivenga and Colonel Vaccari of Italy. The German government gave its agreement despite opposition from General Hoefer and Commissioner Hörsing.[54] German Foreign Minister Hermann Müller declared in a cabinet meeting that Germany must agree in order to combat the new wave of atrocity stories, particularly in Great Britain.[55] The commission's report stated: "There is no doubt that the repression was carried out by the Germans with great brutality, and that the troops are intensely unpopular with the Polish speaking population; far more so than either the mine managers or the civil officials, with the possible exception of Herr Hörsing." On the POW we read: "It is freely acknowledged that the Polish Military Organization—generally alluded to as the P.O.W.—is very complete and comprises nearly all the males of military age of the Polish speaking community." The commission's judgment on conflicting German and Polish views was:

> Feeling now runs so high that a balanced neutral opinion is almost unobtainable. Roughly speaking, German witnesses contend that the recent troubles are due to the labour unrest and Spartacism, which are affecting equally many other parts of the world; while the Poles contend that they are purely nationalist in origin, and are provoked by Prussian brutality. . . . The truth is that the causes are historical, religious, political, industrial and economic.[56]

51

In its Note to the German Government, the commission asked for an immediate general amnesty, except for criminal offenses, and that all arbitrary executions be stopped. Also, it asked that the persecution of women and children and the forcing of confessions by the use of threats—all facts that had been ascertained by trustworthy witnesses—should cease at once.[57] Thanks to the commission, Poland and Germany signed an agreement on 1 October 1919, providing for a general amnesty and the mutual release of political prisoners. This brought temporary calm to the plebiscite area. Thus, it may be said that though the first Polish uprising was crushed, it succeeded in ending German rule by force in Upper Silesia. Nevertheless, the demarcation line between the Poles and the Germans left the industrial region on the German side. This was due to Marshal Foch's decision that the line should run along the actual war front; it was a French concession to Britain.[58]

Shortly after these events, Hörsing committed a great mistake, which ended his career in Upper Silesia. He persuaded the German government to allow the holding of communal elections, although these were opposed by the Allied Powers. The elections were held on 9 November 1919, and they turned out to be a victory for the Poles. Out of 11,255 councillors elected, 6,822 were Poles and 4,373 were Germans. Hörsing, accused by his compatriots of having gravely jeopardized the German cause in Upper Silesia, was forced to resign.[59]

The Versailles Treaty was ratified on 10 January 1920, and the Interallied Plebiscite Commission arrived in Upper Silesia on 11 February 1920. It consisted of Gen. Henri Le Rond, president, for France; Col. H. F. P. Percival for Britain; and Gen. Armando de Marinis for Italy. The Allied troops consisted of ten French and two Italian battalions. The British were unable to furnish their contingent for the time being because of troubles in Ireland.

It was obvious from the start that the Allied troops, which numbered only twelve thousand, were not strong enough to impose their control. Although German regular troops and Free Corps formations were obliged to evacuate Upper Silesia after the Versailles Treaty had come into force, many Free Corpsmen returned as individuals and were very active in the towns.[60] They enjoyed the support of the special German *Sicherheitspolizei* (SIPO), or security police, which was organized on the model of a German infantry brigade. The Polish Military Organization also resumed its activity, although it was greatly handicapped by the German police and administrators who continued their work under Allied supervision.

After a few months of relative calm the situation again became very tense in July and August 1920, when the Red Army was advancing on Warsaw. There was general fear among the Poles that the Germans were planning to occupy Upper Silesia. In fact, the German War Ministry issued orders in July to the Seventh Army Corps to prepare for an occupation. Also, in August the German government approached the Plebiscite Commission, offering to supply it with troops to assure the neutrality of the region during the Polish-Soviet war.[61]

The outbreak of the second Polish uprising was preceded by violent anti-Polish and anti-French demonstrations in towns with German majorities, notably in Beuthen (Bytom) and Kattowitz (Katowice), from 17 to 19 August 1920. Both von Oertzen and Hoefer admit that these demonstrations degenerated into riots and attacks on Allied troops. They admit that these outbreaks were to demonstrate support for the province's neutrality in the Soviet-Polish war, but both deny that the outbreaks were organized.[62] However, Allied and Polish observers on the spot thought they portended large-scale action. The Italian foreign minister, Count Carlo Sforza, who received reports from the Italian officers with the Plebiscite Commission, wrote that in case of a Polish defeat at Warsaw, an organized German revolt was ready to break out in Upper Silesia. He also noted that in mid August, the Austrian and German press announced the capture of Warsaw by the Bolsheviks. This news led to instant and simultaneous German attacks on the Poles as well as on Allied troops.[63]

The second Polish uprising, which broke out on the night of 19/20 August 1920, was sparked by attacks on Poles in Kattowitz and other towns. The uprising was accompanied by a general strike, which spread to all mines, reducing coal production by 80 percent. The Poles saw the uprising as a measure of self-defense. It was not supposed to result in the "liberation" of Upper Silesia but was intended to counteract the German display of force and lead to the disbanding of the much-hated German security police. This aim was achieved on the fifth day of the uprising, when the Allied Commission dissolved the SIPO and set up a new plebiscite police force, which was composed half of Poles and half of Germans. Employment was guaranteed to all, as well as freedom from discrimination on religious or political grounds.[64] As Sarah Wambaugh wrote: "With the reorganization of the police, the grip of the German official machine in Upper Silesia was loosened and the situation reversed."[65] The insurgents, though they were not defeated—thanks partly to the passive support of the French troops—nevertheless feared the possible entry of German troops with official Allied permission. Korfanty, therefore, appealed to his followers to stop the fighting, since its official objective—the dissolution of the SIPO—had been achieved.

While the success of the uprising has sometimes been ascribed to organization, this is only part of the truth; it was equally due to mass support. The most important result was to demonstrate the strength of the Polish national movement, particularly since the Polish government gave no official aid, and only very limited supplies of arms and ammunition came in from

Poland. At this time, all available troops and supplies were engaged in Piłsudski's drive against the Red Army. German officials feared that Germany's chances of winning the plebiscite had greatly diminished. They thought the German Silesians, impressed with the show of Polish strength, would vote for Poland. Therefore, they advised that the plebiscite not be held before the beginning of 1921. The German cabinet approved these and other suggestions which included the proclamation that if Germany won the plebiscite, Upper Silesia would receive autonomy. This was a move to counter the Polish government's declaration to the same effect.[66]

Both sides continued their preparations for the plebiscite. As mentioned earlier, Germany had the advantage of staffing the administration and the higher clergy. Also, Germans owned the industrial plants, the mines, and most of the agricultural land. The Poles had the advantage of being in the majority. However, this did not mean that all Polish Silesians had developed a Polish national consciousness; thus, many were more sensitive to material than to national issues. While many Polish Silesians blamed their German employers for postwar unemployment and inflation, and while they resented German rule more bitterly than before, there were also those who feared that a union with Poland would deprive them of their jobs, their pensions, and other hard-earned benefits. Consequently, there was a sizeable "floating population," which was particularly responsive to material inducements.[67] In this "dance around the golden calf," the German side could count on all-out support from vested interests. In fact, the whole Upper Silesian industry and all the big landowners—with the single exception of Count Oppersdorf—generously helped to finance German propaganda.[68] Nor was the latter restricted to print. A special department for economic assistance to the poorest social strata was set up in Kattowitz and named Abteilung H.[69] The more prosperous strata were not forgotten either. When a land tax was introduced in Prussia, the cabinet decided not to extend it to Upper Silesia since this could prejudice the plebiscite results.[70] Poland was at a great disadvantage in this bidding, because she could only make promises for the future.

While stepping up their propaganda activities, both sides also prepared for every contingency, including an armed clash. On the Polish side, there was the underground Polish Military Organization; its headquarters were just across the border in Sosnowiec. Its young leaders inside Upper Silesia, particularly Michał Grażyński—later the governor of the Polish part of the province—tried to get the upper hand over the moderate Korfanty, who preferred diplomacy to military action.[71] The Polish government, fearing that an armed clash could provoke the entry of regular German troops and complicate its diplomatic situation, supported Korfanty. The Germans were also actively building up their underground organization. Unlike the POW, which consisted almost exclusively of Polish natives of the region, the

Germans accepted large numbers of volunteers from all parts of Germany and even from outside it. Hoefer, Oertzen, and Laubert describe how men, arms and munitions were smuggled into the area, mostly by night, often after clashes between German and French border detachments.[72] All these activities were directed by the German government. A special body called the Zentrale was established in Breslau under Prussian State Commissioner for Public Order and Security Dr. Karl Spiecker. Spiecker was a prominent member of the Catholic Center Party, a member of the Reichstag, a newspaper editor, and an intimate friend of Dr. Karl J. Wirth, the future chancellor of the Reich. The Zentrale took over the political, financial, and military direction of German activities in Upper Silesia. This meant, primarily, the *Oberschlesischer Selbstschutz,* or Upper Silesian Self-Defense. The Zentrale was in close touch with the military authorities, that is, General von Lequis, who was also in Breslau and who carried out the orders of the War Ministry in Berlin.[73] Another organization controlled by the Zentrale was the so-called *Spezialpolizei,* or special police. It was composed exclusively of Free Corpsmen, and its commander was Heinz Hauenstein of the Free Corps Loewenfeldt. This was an overtly terrorist organization which, as noted above, specialized in dispensing the *Feme,* or people's justice, even though, as Oertzen states, its members cared neither for the name nor for formal proceedings.[74] Oertzen admits that the terrorist activities of these Special Police were carried out with the approval of Prussian Minister of the Interior Carl Severing and of Dr. Spiecker. In fact, terrorist activities were planned and prepared by the German Intelligence Office, and all the necessary details were supplied by the German military authorities.[75] The Special Police were almost exclusively composed of Reich and Baltic Germans; the latter, having lost everything, were ready and eager to risk their lives.[76] Also, there were many criminals in the Special Police, since the authorities could not be too particular in recruiting its members.[77] The Poles, for their part, had special fighting units *(Bojówka).* These were small, consisted of local Polish Silesians, and acted independently of the Polish government. In organization and purpose they were modeled on the fighting units of the Polish Socialist Party's Military Fraction, led by Piłsudski before 1914. These units were made up of workers with some military training and were used generally for limited-purpose raids.

As the date of the plebiscite approached, two thousand British troops arrived in January 1921. One month before the vote, on 21 February, the Supreme Council decided that both the residents and the nonresidents—the ''outvoters''—should vote at the same time in the communes in which they had been born. Originally, giving the vote to ''outvoters,'' or persons who had been born in but were not residents of Upper Silesia, had been a French suggestion designed to help the Poles, for many Polish Silesians worked in the

Ruhr or in Poland.[78] However, it soon became clear that the Germans would bring in as many of their outvoters as possible. Therefore, the Poles first tried to have them disbarred from voting and, when this failed, to have the outvoters cast their ballots separately from the residents, thus ensuring a Polish majority. In this, Warsaw almost succeeded, for in November 1920 the Allies had agreed that all outvoters should cast their ballots in the Allied-occupied zone of the Rhineland, for example, in Cologne. If the Poles and Germans refused, it was agreed to adopt the French proposal that the outvoters cast their votes in Upper Silesia, but a few days after the residents had voted.[79] Both sides refused the Rhineland proposal; the Germans for fear of not being able to control the votes of the large Polish immigrant population in the Ruhr, and the Poles for fear that the Germans would do just that. Therefore, the Allies made a decision on 21 February 1921—two days after the signing of the Franco-Polish alliance, and the day on which the Military Convention was signed—that boded ill for the Poles. Ostensibly, the decision that all outvoters would vote on the same day in Upper Silesia was to prevent disorder; in reality it marked a French concession to the British. The Germans forbade any meetings of Polish outvoters living in the Ruhr and threatened them with unemployment if they left to vote for Upper Silesia. However, the Germans were also estimated to have lost some votes, since about one hundred fifty thousand of their outvoters refused to go to Upper Silesia because of the German propaganda on "Polish terror" there.[80] Finally, two days before the vote,

> the [German] outvoters were allowed to enter the area. Spurred on by propaganda, wonderfully organized throughout Germany, more than 150,000 outvoters came from all parts of the Reich and from abroad. Infirm and aged, crippled and ill, even women approaching confinement, made the journey to preserve Upper Silesia for the Fatherland. Many had not been there for decades. Free railroad tickets and free board in the area for ten days were provided by the German *Schutzbund* [protective association], which also provided for children who must be left behind and in other ways made it easy to take the journey. Some 280 trains brought them from all parts of Germany in a triumphal progress, bands playing and flags waving at every station on the journey. Their coming greatly aided the German morale as well as numbers.[81]

The long-awaited plebiscite took place on Sunday 20 March 1921, without any disturbance. The results were questionable, for they did not correspond with the real ethnic structure of the region. A total of 706,820 votes were cast for Germany and 479,418 for Poland. Out of 1,474 communes, 682 yielded Polish majorities; and 792, German ones. However, if we deduct some 180,000 outvoters for Germany and 10,000 for Poland, the respective figures are 524,532 for Germany (including some 300,000 Polish-speaking Silesians), and 469,294 for Poland. Thus, the resident German majority vote came to about 55,238.[82] Also, although the Poles had originally asked for the exclusion of the purely German districts of Neustadt and Leobschutz, west of the Oder,[83] the Allies had decided that the vote should include the whole province. This increased the German vote.

While the plebiscite results were a disappointment for Poland, their breakdown into resident and nonresident votes at least disproved the German claim that Upper Silesia was a purely German province. Indeed, while the German press celebrated victory, the Berlin stock exchange registered the fall of Upper Silesian shares and the rise of Polish notes.[84] It was clear that the plebiscite results were far from conclusive.

3

The Struggle for Upper Silesia: Interpreting the Plebiscite, 20 March to 10 October 1921

The next stage of the struggle for Upper Silesia revolved around the interpretation of the plebiscite results. Germany claimed that she had won the vote, that Upper Silesia was economically indivisible, and that division was allegedly contrary to the Versailles Treaty. While the first two claims could be argued, the third was clearly incorrect. The last sentence of paragraph 4 and paragraph 5 of the annex to article 88 of the treaty read:

> The result of the vote will be determined by communes according to the majority of votes in each commune.
> On the conclusion of the voting, the number of votes cast in each commune will be communicated by the Commission to the Principal and Associated Powers, with a full report as to the taking of the vote and a recommendation as to the line which ought to be adopted as the frontier of Germany in Upper Silesia. In this recommendation regard will be paid to the wishes of the inhabitants as shown by the vote, and to the geographical and economic conditions of the locality.

It is clear from this text that the German claim to the whole of Upper Silesia on the basis of a German majority vote did not accord with the Versailles Treaty. Nevertheless, in early April, the German government claimed the whole region and stated it did so "in the firm conviction that Upper Silesia can no more exist without Germany than Germany, bereft of Upper Silesia, would be in a position to re-establish herself economically, or recover her productive capacity. Any other solution would be contrary to the Treaty of Versailles."[1]

Thus, the German government linked its reparations' burden with Upper Silesia and claimed that any serious proposals on reparations must be based on the assumption that the region would remain with Germany.[2] Although France was even more interested than Britain in obtaining a satisfactory reparations settlement—after all, her own industrial region had been devastated during the war—it was Lloyd George who constantly argued that Germany could not pay reparations unless she had Upper Silesia. Like the Germans, he made the final reparations figure dependent on Upper Silesia's ultimate fate.[3] We should also bear in mind that in his view, the maintenance of the European balance of power depended—as one Foreign Office official put it later—on not abandoning Germany to "the mercy of a Franco-Polish alliance."[4] For this reason, he tried to keep both Danzig and Upper Silesia out of Polish hands.[5]

Poland, for her part, claimed the so-called Korfanty Line as her frontier. This line included a strip along the west bank of the Oder and all of the area east of the Oder, with the exception of the district of Kreuzburg and parts of Oppeln and Rosenberg (Susz).[6] Within this area, 673 communes had voted for Poland and 230 for Germany; the number of votes cast for Poland was 435,260 and for Germany, 409,618 (including outvoters). This area included the industrial triangle in which three out of the four large towns (Tarnowitz/ Tarnowskie Góry excepted) had a large German majority. However, as a *Times* correspondent observed, the townspeople consisted of German shop-keepers and clerical employees, while the Polish workers lived in villages or small tenement settlements around the towns.[7] Thus, even in the preponderantly German towns, the labor force was predominantly Polish.

It was in France's interest that Germany lose the industrial triangle; therefore France supported the Poles. The so-called Le Rond Line, advocated by Gen. Henri Le Rond, president of the Plebiscite Commission, was not as favorable to Poland as the Korfanty Line but included the industrial triangle where 51.40 percent of the votes had been cast for Poland.[8] French public opinion rooted for Poland, and all French political parties exerted pressure on the government to remain faithful to the text of the treaty. On 24 March 1921 the Commission on Foreign Affairs in the Chamber of Deputies voted a resolution in this sense. On 6 April, after a passionate debate in the chamber, Briand assured the deputies that the final decision on Upper Silesia would not depend on the question of reparations.[9] Nonetheless, the Polish minister in Paris warned his government that a decision would have to be reached soon, since the Quai d'Orsay feared that after May the danger of a linkage between Upper Silesia and reparations would be very great.[10]

The British position was based on both political and economic considerations. While a considerable Polish majority would no doubt have forced Lloyd George to acquiesce in a surrender of the industrial region to Poland, the apparent German preponderance played into his hands. As he told the British ambassador in Berlin, Lord D'Abernon: "My inclination is that the country

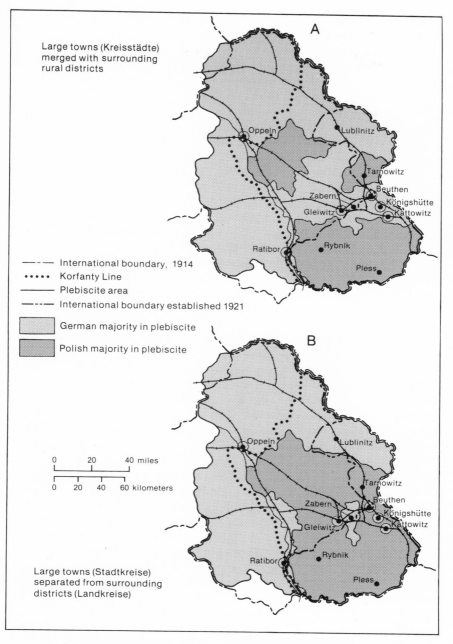

Large towns (Kreisstädte)
merged with surrounding
rural districts

A

Oppeln

Lublinitz

Tarnowitz

Zabern

Beuthen

Gleiwitz

Königshütte

Kattowitz

Ratibor

Rybnik

Piess

International boundary, 1914
Korfanty Line
Plebiscite area
International boundary established 1921

German majority in plebiscite

Polish majority in plebiscite

B

Oppeln

Lublinitz

Tarnowitz

Zabern

Beuthen

Gleiwitz

Königshütte

Kattowitz

Ratibor

Rybnik

Piess

0   20   40 miles

0   20   40   60 kilometers

Large towns (Stadtkreise)
separated from surrounding
districts (Landkreise)

Map 3. Results of the Upper Silesian Plebiscite, March 1921

61

should be kept together, and I will not agree to partition unless I am obliged to. We are all interested in German prosperity. After all, if we wish Germany to pay we have to leave them something to earn money with.''[11]

This was also the overall view of the British press, which was impressed by the German vote and stressed the economic aspect of the problem. Thus, the *Economist* of 26 March stated that ''an overwhelming majority'' of the voters had expressed the wish to remain with Germany and ''as things are, the German industralists breathe again, and so may their Allied creditors.'' Thus, when the plebiscite results were known, the British cabinet decided that the whole of Upper Silesia should go to Germany. On 22 March, Curzon instructed General Percival as follows: ''For your confidential guidance I think it well to tell you that, in view of [the] overwhelming German majority in [the] plebiscite area, the only really efficacious solution appears to us to be the recognition of German claims to the whole.'' The British representative at the Conference of Ambassadors was instructed that in the cabinet's opinion, ''the existence of isolated areas of a Polish or German majority does not justify the breaking up of the unity of Upper Silesia and attempts to do so shall be resisted.''[12]

Not only Germany's ability to pay, however, was at stake. Britain feared that if the industrial region were assigned to Poland, France would then gain control of its coal, zinc, and steel industry. These fears were fed by the signing of the Franco-Polish alliance in February 1921 and by rumors of French attempts to seize a controlling interest in the mines and steel mills. The British had frightening visions of French economic hegemony in Europe. A typical example of this is to be found in a speech by Lieutenant Commander Kenworthy, a Liberal M.P., who also served as a go-between in unofficial British contacts with Germany. On 5 May 1921, Kenworthy declared in the House of Commons that ''if the sanction is applied [to Germany, A. C.], if the French get into the Ruhr, and if the Poles get the upper silesian coal mines, France will have something like an economic hegemony of Europe through their control of coal and iron, and we are going to feel the draught very quickly.''[13] On 13 May, Kenworthy predicted the ruin of Germany if the Poles obtained Upper Silesia. On this occasion he warned that this would also mean the bankruptcy of both Britain and France,[14] though he failed to explain how a bankrupt France could exercise economic hegemony in Europe.

Franco-British differences were clearly evident immediately after the plebiscite. The first clash occurred at the meeting of the Plebiscite Commission, which was required to recommend a line for dividing the province. The British commissioner, Percival, succeeded in obtaining the support of his Italian colleague, Marinis—whom some Italians accused of pro-German tendencies[15]—and together they proposed a line in accordance with British views and wishes. However, since it was well known that France would oppose the allocation of the whole area to Germany, the Percival–Marinis Line, while assigning the industrial region to Germany, left small parts of Gleiwitz, Zabrze, Kattowitz, Beuthen, and a strip along the eastern edges of Tarnowitz, Lublinitz (Lubliniec), and Rosenberg to Poland. The agricultural areas of Pless and Rybnik were also to go to Poland.[16]

Before the plebiscite, Italian support of French, and therefore Polish, claims was available at a price. On 20 February 1921 the Italian foreign minister, Count Carlo Sforza, instructed the Italian ambassador in Paris, Lelio Bonin-Longare—whom President Millerand had approached on the subject—that Italy, in exchange for her support of the French solution for Upper Silesia, would demand the following: certain changes in the Treaty of Sèvres with Turkey; an exchange of notes on Cyprus; resignation from French claims to the Austro-Hungarian navy; and suspension of the dispute about Italian immigration to France. Millerand probably thought this price too high. In any case, Sforza refused to take up the Polish government's proposals, made at the end of February, for Polish-Italian cooperation in exploiting the mineral resources of Upper Silesia.[17]

The third Polish uprising was sparked by news of the Percival–Marinis proposal. Korfanty learned of it on 30 April from the Polish consul in Oppeln, Daniel Keszycki, who had heard it from French sources. Korfanty then decided to call for an uprising. However, he intended for it to demonstrate the Polish character of Upper Silesia, not to effect a permanent seizure of territory. Gen. Jules Gratier, who acted as president of the Plebiscite Commission during Le Rond's absence in Paris, raised no objections. Thus, on 1 May, Korfanty's German-language paper, the *Oberschlesische Grenzzeitung,* published a special issue, which informed its readers of the Anglo-Italian proposal and also of an alleged decision by German industrialists to destroy the industrial plants if Upper Silesia were awarded to Poland. By this time, many mines and foundries were already on strike; on 2 May they were joined by the remaining plants and mines. Thus it happened that on the night of 2/3 May the third Polish uprising broke out in Upper Silesia.[18] The forty thousand Poles who fought in it were for the most part mine and foundry workers who preferred to risk their lives rather than remain under German rule.[19] The German underground organization was smashed during the first stage of the insurrection and had to be reconstituted under cover of the Selbstschutz, which, as noted above, was a force made up of paramilitary units subordinated to General Hoefer.[20] The Polish forces had to rely on themselves, for they received negligible military supplies from Poland.

In fact, the Polish government had opposed plans for the insurrection. When the insurrection broke out, Warsaw tried to limit it in scope and time and to use it as a short but powerful demonstration against the proposed Percival–Marinis Line. This attitude was shared by Korfanty, but he was opposed by the young officers in the Polish Military Organization. They managed to seize the leadership and to direct the uprising onto more ambitious paths; they hoped it would lead to an occupation of Upper Silesia by the insurgents up to the Korfanty Line and thus force Allied recognition of Polish claims. Nevertheless, since in the west, Korfanty was blamed for the uprising, the Polish government dismissed him from the post of Polish commissioner in Upper Silesia. At the same time, the Polish army group under Gen. Stanisław Szeptycki, with headquarters in Kraków, received strict orders not to move and therefore never went into action.[21]

The reasons for this policy are not difficult to find. The Polish government was very much afraid of German military intervention; it also realized that its French supporters would be in a very difficult position versus the British if the uprising continued to spread. Polish Foreign Minister Sapieha had traveled to Paris at the end of April and then to London, where he arrived just before the uprising. On 2 May the undersecretary of state for foreign affairs, Erazm Piltz, telegraphed the Polish legation in London that the government was perplexed by the news of the general strike and feared it could lead to an uprising. Therefore, Premier Wincenty Witos asked Sapieha to obtain a prompt decision on Upper Silesia from the Allied Powers.[22] Two days later the Polish government resolved to issue a communique appealing to the Poles in Upper Silesia to keep calm and to end the insurrection.[23] Sapieha was informed on the same day that the Polish Council of Ministers insisted on a prompt Allied decision to prevent the insurrection from spreading.[24] On this day, too, the Polish government sent a note to the Allied Powers disclaiming any responsibility for the uprising. In another note of 7 May the government recalled the sacrifices and efforts made by the Polish workers of Upper Silesia to receive just treatment, and enumerated the measures it had taken to check the insurrection.[25] Sapieha himself gave an interview to the *Times* (London), in which he stated:

> The Polish Government was well aware that a deplorable impression would be caused by the disturbances and had done everything it could to stop them. . . . He had no doubt that M. Korfanty, the Plebiscite Commissioner, who has now been relieved of his office by the Polish Government, and who appeared to have joined the movement with a view to maintaining his influence over his countrymen, would also display a soothing spirit and try to bring back the workmen and miners to their senses. . . . The Poles considered that . . . they were entitled to the eastern part of Upper Silesia, with the mining district. . . . To leave Upper Silesia to Germany meant ruining the result of the Great War and sanctioning the "Mittel-Europa Politik" by placing all Central and Eastern Europe economically in absolute dependence on Germany.[26]

Sapieha urged his government to terminate the uprising. In a telegram dated 4 May he warned that the uprising might have a very negative effect on the Polish cause. He claimed to have assurances from Count Sforza that the latter would support Briand over Poland in the Supreme Council but that severe casualties among the Italian troops had severely jeopardized Polish interests. Briand told Sapieha that no final decision had been reached so far and that a favorable decision could only be obtained by restoring calm.[27]

Sapieha's recommendations accorded with the views of the Polish cabinet. Korfanty also agreed to work to end the uprising. On 5 May he appealed to the workers to return to work on 9 May, and they heeded him. On 10 May the insurgents signed a preliminary agreement with members of the Allied Plebiscite Commission, establishing a demarcation line for territories still remaining under their control. The Poles agreed to give up a few strategic points to the commission and, in return, demanded a line defining their sphere of operations. The signatories for the Allied Commission were: Col. L. Adam for the French, Lt. Col. Ettore Periggi for the Italians, and Captain Gastol for the British. The signatories on the Polish side were: Hauke (Karol Grzesik), Głowski, Solski, and Ludyga-Laskowski. Also present were Korfanty and the French general, Sauvage de Brantés. This was only a preliminary agreement, which had to be ratified by the whole Allied Plebiscite Commission. However, when the Germans protested and when the negative attitude of Percival and Marinis received support from London and Rome, Le Rond backed down and denied that the agreement existed.[28] In the meanwhile, Korfanty's appeal had dampened the fighting on the Polish side. This allowed the Selbstschutz to take up positions, while the Poles were content to hold the Korfanty Line, which approximated the territory they claimed. But the Conference of Ambassadors, sitting in London to discuss German reparations, issued statements on 7, 9, and 10 May, condemning the insurrection, giving assurances that no final decision had been made on the division of Upper Silesia, and blaming the Poles for the outbreak.[29] Meanwhile, Lloyd George was preparing a diplomatic offensive which was to provoke a grave crisis in Franco-British relations.

We should note that on 18 April 1921 the Reparations Commission had finally fixed Germany's total indebtedness at 132 billion gold marks (about $33 billion in 1921 dollars). It also demanded that the whole of the Reichsbank's metallic reserves be transferred to the bank's branches in the occupied areas. At the session of the Conference of Ambassadors that met in London between 29 April and 5 May, Briand demanded the immediate occupation of the Ruhr as a means of extracting German consent. However, it was eventually decided that an ultimatum would be sent requiring the German government to accept the schedule of payments established by the Reparations Commission and to fulfill the requests on disarmament contained in the Allied note of 29 January 1921. If Germany refused to comply with these demands, the Allies would occupy the Ruhr.

The acceptance of this ultimatum by the new German government of Dr. Wirth on 11 May 1921 was closely connected with the question of Upper Silesia. A few days before the new government was constituted, the German cabinet agreed that the rejection of the ultimatum might mean the loss of Upper Silesia, while acceptance was expected to strengthen British and Italian influence, which might then turn the scales in favor of Germany.[30]

The circumstances under which German acceptance of the ultimatum was negotiated show that the British used all their influence in Berlin to this end, and they may have implied a promise to support the German cause. In fact, on July 8, Chancellor Wirth told General Hoefer that he had received assurances on this point.[31] These might have come through British contacts with Gustav Stresemann. Since the British government hoped that Stresemann would accept the chancellorship in mid May and carry out a policy of fulfillment—that is, of paying reparations—he was asked to state the conditions on which he would, as chancellor, accept the ultimatum on reparations. But Stresemann first demanded some explanation of the future intentions of the British and Italian governments in regard to Upper Silesia.[32] He therefore addressed a questionnaire on this subject to the British and Italian governments. He told the British chargé d'affaires in Berlin, Lord Kilmarnock, on 9 May, that if Germany were to retain the industrial district of Upper Silesia, he thought she might, with a great effort, fulfill the conditions imposed by the Allied ultimatum. Thus, if Stresemann were assured that the British and Italian governments would stand by the proposals of their representatives on the Plebiscite Commission, he would be ready to assume responsibility for carrying out Germany's obligations. However, before deciding whether he could form a new government and accept Allied conditions, he wished to have some private assurance that the British government would not allow any other solution in Upper Silesia than that based on the report of the British representative on the commission.[33] The British ambassador in Berlin, Lord D'Abernon, realized that a formal pledge to this effect was impossible; he therefore advised his government to declare that it would adhere to a strict and impartial execution of the Versailles Treaty with respect to the industrial area.[34]

The British government could not afford to make any other statement. The Conference of Ambassadors, which was then considering the separate reports of the members of the Plebiscite Commission, failed to reach any agreement. Jules Cambon, the president of the Conference of Ambassadors, insisted that no partial decision should be made that would prejudice the French plan that, in return for the coal mines, Poland should assume part of Germany's obligations.[35] Therefore, the British declaration requested by

D'Abernon for the German government stated that the British government could not give any assurances without prior consultation with its allies; "but in our discussions with our Allies [the] German Government may rely upon our desire to pay due regard to the important German interests involved and to press for equitable settlement." D'Abernon found this communication "so unexpectedly favourable" that he was sure that if it had arrived before the creation of Wirth's cabinet (10 May), Stresemann would have accepted the chancellorship.[36] However, when the British note was disclosed at the end of July in the *New York Herald* and then the *Times* (London), Lloyd George denied that any such communication had been made.[37] The Italian government made no reply to Stresemann's questionnaire. Although the Italian ambassador in Berlin, Alfredo Frassati, supported the German cause, Count Sforza showed signs of hesitation. Thus, despite Marinis's support for the British aim of awarding the industrial area to Germany, official Italian consent seemed doubtful.

Although the uprising was petering out by mid May, Polish strength in Upper Silesia and passive French support for the Polish cause again sparked British attacks on Poland. On 13 May, Kenworthy gave the cue to Lloyd George in Parliament. He proposed that for economic reasons the whole of Upper Silesia should stay with Germany. He also suggested that the Germans be given a mandate "to clear out the Poles, if the Poles do not listen to reason."[38] In fact, the idea of warning the Poles that the Allies might not be able to restrain Germany had been mooted in a dispatch by Curzon to the British ambassador in Paris, Hardinge, on 10 May.[39] Lloyd George had apparently decided to make Parliament a sounding board for this move. He did so despite Percival's report of 11 May that Korfanty had agreed to stop the Polish advance, to make no new attacks, and to help resume work in the industrial plants and on the railways. In return, Korfanty asked that the insurgents be allowed to administer the area more or less approximating the Korfanty Line.[40] The British rejected this offer, seeing its acceptance as a "capitulation" to the insurgents.[41] Hence Lloyd George's threats.

On 13 May the prime minister prefaced his proposal by an attack on the Poles, including the charge that they had worn German uniforms and had shot at Allied troops who were fighting for the freedom of Poland during the war. Speaking about Upper Silesia he said: "Either the Allies ought to insist upon the Treaty being respected, or they ought to allow the Germans to do it. Not merely to disarm Germany, but to say that such troops as she has got are not to be permitted to take part in restoring order in what, until the decision comes, is their own province—that is not fair."[42]

French reaction was violent. Briand was in danger of falling and reportedly gave assurances that if regular German troops were sent to Upper Silesia, the French would automatically occupy the Ruhr without consulting the other Allies.[43] In public, he declared at a press conference on 15 May that "a stern and categorical warning was delivered to Germany . . . the invasion of Upper Silesia by German troops would create a situation of such terrible gravity that he declined even to contemplate it." He also backtracked from the French proposal that if the industrial district were to be given to Poland, the latter would assume part of Germany's reparations. He now insisted that the final decision should be based on equal justice for Poles and Germans. At the same time, in an *aide-mémoire* of 14 May, he rejected charges of French partiality to Poland and warned Lloyd George that direct German action would cause direct Polish involvement and put the results of the war in question. He doubted whether France or any other power could witness such events passively.[44] The situation was, indeed, tense, and not only in Paris and London. As a result of Lloyd George's speech, General Hoefer was appointed commander of the Selbstschutz. The Germans concentrated some thirty-five thousand troops in their part of Upper Silesia, and the Poles readied about the same number on their side of the border in Poland.[45]

Thus, Lloyd George's speech caused an acute crisis not only in Franco-British relations but also in Upper Silesia. Curzon warned that if French troops entered the Ruhr, the British government would view this as being inconsistent with the "spirit of the entente" and as "endangering the alliance."[46] London appealed to Rome for support over Upper Silesia, but the Italian government replied only that it would support the British in exercising pressure on the French over the Ruhr.[47] In the meanwhile, Colonel Percival's proposal that the Germans flocking into Upper Silesia be incorporated into the police force was strongly opposed by General Le Rond.[48] On 17 May, Lloyd George still hewed to his line. As he put it: "The children of the Treaty cannot be allowed to break crockery in Europe with impunity. Somebody must place a restraining hand on them, otherwise there will be continual trouble."[49] There were, however, some Englishmen who doubted whether the restraining hand should be German. Gen. Sir Henry Wilson told Austen Chamberlain, after Lloyd George's speech of 13 May, that "the Boches should be invited to carry out and execute the Treaty of Versailles," instead of being let loose on the Poles in Upper Silesia.[50]

It was rather unfortunate that Lloyd George's speech of 13 May came just at the moment when the uprising was petering out and when the Polish government was doing all it could to restrain the insurgents. On 14 May the Polish government replied to a note from the Conference of Ambassadors of 10 May, stressing the spontaneous character of the insurrection and enumerating all the measures taken to lessen the tension, such as the dismissal of Korfanty, the closing of the Polish-Silesian frontier, the prohibition of recruitment in Polish territory, and appeals to the nation to keep calm.[51] But the Poles had to refute the allegations made by Lloyd George, and Korfanty was the first to reply. In an open letter of 16 May to the British prime minister, Korfanty denied that the Polish population of Upper Silesia consisted of recent immigrants. Even the Germans had not made such a patently erroneous claim. As to the charges concerning Polish service in the German army during the war, Korfanty noted that fifteen thousand Silesian deserters or prisoners of war had joined Haller's army in France. It was cruel irony, he said, to imply that Polish Upper Silesians should have revolted against Germany during the war, when the largest armies in the world had needed four years to crush German military might. He also reminded Lloyd George that the first uprising had taken place before Germany had disarmed. Korfanty recalled that in his own speeches in the German Reichstag during the war, he had attacked Prussian militarism and had advocated Polish independence even at the risk of his life. Finally, he stressed the genuinely native character of the uprising, which would not have lasted one day if the Polish Silesians had not supported it with conviction and enthusiasm.[52] Nevertheless, on the following day, the Plebiscite Commission refused to entertain the Polish National Committee's proposal that the zone evacuated by the insurgents should be occupied by Allied troops.[53]

On 17 May the British minister in Warsaw, Sir William Max Muller, reported that the Polish prime minister would make a speech in the Sejm. The government had approved a declaration condemning the insurrection but could not publish it after Lloyd George's speech. Still, it would welcome a hint, through Muller, about a line that would be acceptable to London.[54] It seems unlikely that any answer was sent to this inquiry. On 18 May the Polish prime minister, Wincenty Witos, replied to Lloyd George. He protested the latter's unfair and unchivalrous comments about the Poles during the war. He asked for a strict interpretation of the Versailles Treaty and complained that Lloyd George's speech had only aggravated the situation. Witos recalled Polish measures to check the insurrection, and he stressed the open display of German military activity in the territory. He noted that enlistment of German soldiers for Upper Silesia was proceeding openly and that German newspapers had reported the arrival of large transports of regular troops in the area. Strangely enough, said Witos, Lloyd George seemed to be ignorant of all this and claimed that the Germans had been disarmed. Where, asked Witos, was objectivity and justice?[55]

German armed intervention in Upper Silesia was, indeed, extensive. Moreover, both General de Marinis, the Italian member of the Plebiscite Commission, and other Italian officers favored the Germans. Thanks to the connivance of the local Italian commander, Major Invrea, the first nucleus of the German Selbstschutz was organized on 3 May around Ratibor—that is, west of the Oder, where the Germans were in the majority. It was at this time that Italian troops suffered some casualties in a clash with Polish insurgents,[56] and this caused tension in Italo-Polish relations. It should be noted that some members of the notorious Oberland Free Corps took part in these operations. There were also some armed units in the northernmost tip of the province, around Kreuzburg. However, these units, consisting partly of local Germans and partly of members of the Free Corps who belonged to the Spezialpolizei, were inadequate to stem the Polish tide, aided as it was by passive French support. In fact, the whole German resistance movement would have petered out had it not been for the effective and massive support of the German government. Lloyd George's speech of 13 May gave the impetus to German counteraction. The former air-force camp at Brieg became a camp for volunteers who came from all parts of the Reich. Men came from Berlin, Bavaria, the Tyrol, and elsewhere.[57] Heydebreck's "Wehrwolves," the Rossbach storm units, and Rheinhardt's Free Corps left their work as "agricultural laborers" and set up headquarters in Upper Silesia during the first week of May. Former Baltic Free Corpsmen were already there working as "miners"; students and other volunteers arrived by the hundreds.[58] General Hoefer himself admitted that the Selbstschutz was like a small army.[59] Thus it is not true that "the complete success of the Poles was prevented, however, first, by the German inhabitants, who organized themselves for resistance under General Hoefer."[60] Only part of the Selbstschutz was made up of native Silesians, and General Hoefer's appointment was approved by Berlin.

However, we should note that the German government was seriously embarrassed by the great numbers of Free Corpsmen in the Silesian Selbstschutz. The government was well aware of their antirepublican, anti-Semitic, and generally reactionary character. Whether he knew this or not, Gen. Hans von Seeckt, chief of the Army Command, objected most strongly at cabinet meetings to the building up of volunteer corps, and he demanded that the existing Selbstschutz be supported instead.[61] General Hoefer was received on 18 May by War Minister Gessler, and Chancellor Wirth. He was ordered to restrain the Free Corps and to prevent independent actions similar to those that had taken place earlier in the Baltic region.[62] Gessler states that it was decided to organize the Selbstschutz within the framework of the Reichswehr and to supply it with artillery and munitions ordered in Soviet Russia, even if this meant spending the last gold reserves in the treasury.[63] A central fund already existed in Breslau from which the Selbstschutz was being paid.[64] Some information on the German government's direct involvement in these matters came out later in the nineteen-twenties. Thus, in December 1925, Chancellor Wirth stated in reply to the Socialist leader Phillip Scheidemann that the German government and the president of the republic, Friedrich Ebert, had organized the Selbstschutz in Upper Silesia. Similar disclosures were made about the army by Ernst Buchdrucker in his book on

Seeckt. The latter's biographer, Friedrich von Rabenau, claimed that the general, while denying any connections with the Free Corps in Upper Silesia, had secretly supplied them with arms and ammunition and had even sent military advisers in civilian clothes to their units.[65]

Warnings against the Free Corps stemmed from the fact that they violently opposed the German Republic and discredited the Selbstschutz; moreover, Western correspondents' reports on their activities shocked public opinion. Hoefer himself wrote that Free Corpsmen committed anti-Semitic excesses and even threatened to exterminate all Jews. There were many criminals among the Free Corpsmen.[66] Responsible German papers claimed that the Free Corps in Upper Silesia had "all the evil qualities of the Baltic bands. The swastika badge, the emblem of Anti-Semitism, has already made its appearance, and these corps are said to have the same tendency as that professed by their forerunners under Erhardt and Luttwitz at the time of the Kapp Putsch—namely, the ultimate overthrow of the German Republic.''[67]

In any event, the German battle against the Poles was officially waged by the Selbstschutz. This so-called self-defense organization was remarkably similar to regular army units and was heavily armed. Sixteen armored trains and a considerable amount of heavy artillery appeared at the front. Hoefer claimed that it would have been easy for the Poles, if they had had some help from Poland, to have overrun the thin German lines before they were ready.[68] However, the Polish government refused assistance and closed the frontier between Poland and Upper Silesia. Also, Korfanty had regained control over the Polish Military Organization and kept it in check. General Hoefer himself was reluctant to attack the Poles, but the commander of the Southern Group, Lt. Gen. Bernhard von Huelsen, disobeyed orders. He was egged on by the Free Corps leaders and also, allegedly, by an English officer attached to the headquarters of the Selbstschutz, a certain Major Keatinge, who was allegedly pro-German.[69] The Southern Group launched an operation against the Poles at the Annaberg (St. Anne's Mountain) on 21 May and made some gains, although both sides suffered heavy losses. Obstinate Polish resistance and German setbacks at Ratibor and Rosenberg convinced Hoefer that further operations did not have much hope of success.[70] The Free Corps, meanwhile, laid plans for the conquest of the whole of Upper Silesia. However, they were shocked on 24 May by the chancellor's decree, which forbade the formation of Free Corps and similar bodies, provided severe punishments against anyone contravening the decree, and put measures into effect to prevent Free Corpsmen from crossing the border into the plebiscite area.[71] This decree was clearly connected with the simultaneous announcement that four British battalions were to return to Upper Silesia from the Rhineland, where they had been transferred because of strikes.

On 29 May, General Hoefer ordered all his troops to remain behind the line they then occupied. However, his orders were again disobeyed, and heavy fighting continued until 6 June, when an offensive move by the Selbstschutz toward Gleiwitz was stopped by Allied troops, who interposed themselves between Germans and Poles. The latter, as mentioned above, did not have any support from Poland. This fact was confirmed by an investigation conducted by Lieutenant Commander Rawlings, R.N., who was attached to the British Military Mission in Warsaw. The results of his inquiry were communicated to German Foreign Minister Dr. Friedrich Rosen by Lord D'Abernon on 1 July 1921.[72] The Polish government had also refused Korfanty's request of 28 May for 40 million German marks and provisions. Instead, the Polish cabinet decided to provide money to liquidate the uprising.[73] Korfanty had threatened to print his own currency, but the end of the fighting aborted this plan.[74] Thus, while the German government had taken the Selbstschutz in hand and had supplied it with arms and money, the Polish government had refused to give any significant help to the insurgents. This policy was carried out despite strong pressure from Polish public opinion, which demanded that help be given to the insurgents.[75] The foreign minister, Prince Sapieha, was forced to resign. Although this was mainly the result of right-wing attacks on his policy to federate Poland and Lithuania, he found no support on the Left because of his alleged weakness in regard to Upper Silesia. In the following months it became clear that the Upper Silesian question was above all a major problem in Franco-British relations.

At the end of May the French had offered the British an olive branch. Briand delayed his full and official answer to Lloyd George's speeches of 13 and 17 May until 24 May. In the meanwhile, *aide-mémoires* crossed and recrossed the channel, and the newspapers of both countries were full of mutual recriminations. On 24 May, Briand spoke in the Chamber of Deputies. He informed his audience of the German government's decision to prohibit enlistment for the Selbstschutz on German soil. He pleaded for Allied unity and called German reactions to Lloyd George's speech a "misinterpretation." He defended the French point of view on Upper Silesia, stating: "At no time had it been in the thought of France to give Poland German territories. . . . The fact that Polish votes were to be found in rich industrial territories was no argument why these territories should be refused to Poland. In the mining districts Poland had a majority both of votes and of communes." He had no difficulty in pointing out the injustice of the British proposal for the partition of Upper Silesia: "The frontier line proposed by the British representatives would have given Poland only 194,176 electors out of 479,000 who voted for her. Thus only 40 per cent. of the Polish voters would have become Polish, while 60 per cent. would have been handed back to German domination.''[76]

Despite this criticism of the British proposal, Briand's speech had a bad press in Poland. Fears continued, even in July, that he would try to compromise with Britain at Poland's expense. Indeed, the German government was suspiciously accommodating on reparations. On 17 May it paid 150 million gold marks into the reparations account for France, and on 1 June, Chancellor Wirth declared that his government intended to loyally execute the Versailles Treaty clauses on reparations and disarmament—provided, however, that Upper Silesia remained with Germany.[77]

Although the British government and public opinion welcomed Briand's speech, French and British points of view remained literally "Poles apart," and French opinion feared that France might be outvoted in the Supreme Council. Lloyd George had, in fact, threatened, on 18 May, that the Upper Silesian question might be decided in the council by a majority vote.[78] The British government could win this vote, provided it had Italian support. The Italians, however, demurred. More than that, on 31 May, the *Corriere della sera* published a compromise proposal by Count Sforza that envisaged a partition of the plebiscite area. Sforza suggested that territory where 45 percent of the population had voted for Poland should go to her. The fate of Upper Silesia, he claimed, should be decided in accordance with the principles of the Versailles Treaty and the results of the plebiscite. Poland and Germany should each obtain territory approximating the percentage of votes received. These proposals had already been communicated to the British government on 24 May, so that Sforza was publicly challenging Lloyd George, and this made a British victory in the Supreme Council more than doubtful.[79]

Still, the French were not sure of winning their case. At the beginning of June, they opposed an early meeting of the Supreme Council. They demanded that the Poles and the Germans first disarm so that peace and order could be restored. They also asked that a commission of experts be set up to collect all the data necessary for the Supreme Council to reach a final decision. The British, for their part, desired an early meeting for the council and would not budge from the Percival–Marinis proposal to allocate the whole industrial district to Germany. Now the Italians again sided with London. As a temporary solution, Percival and Marinis jointly proposed that Upper Silesia be divided into three parts: Rybnik and Pless were to be occupied by the Poles; the western and northern parts of the plebiscite area were to be occupied by German troops; and the industrial district was to be occupied by Allied troops. This was, however, totally unacceptable to France, Poland, and Germany. Nonetheless, Briand's conciliatory stance and delaying tactics did lessen the tension between Paris and London. Furthermore, Colonel Percival suffered a nervous breakdown and resigned. He was replaced by Gen. Sir

Harold Stuart, who had been a member of the Inter-Allied Rhineland Commission. This change, in turn, improved relations between the British and French members of the Plebiscite Commission, for Percival and Le Rond had hardly been on speaking terms. Finally, the arrival of six British battalions (two additional battalions were dispatched on 26 May), numbering some three thousand men who were very heavily armed, helped to calm the local population, even though some Germans deluded themselves that the British would fight side by side with them against the French.[80] This assumption can only be explained by the fact that some British members of the commission rather openly sympathized with the German cause. According to German sources, some British officers and officials told the Germans that any transfer of part of Upper Silesia to the Poles would only be temporary. This opinion was shared by some members of the Foreign Office.[81]

In any event, the continuing discord between France and Britain stimulated German resistance to giving up any ground in Upper Silesia. While the Poles indicated readiness to evacuate the territory under their occupation provided the Germans did the same, the Selbstschutz continued its operations, with Gleiwitz—now occupied by the Poles—as the objective. The Plebiscite Commission therefore sent an ultimatum to General Hoefer, demanding that he withdraw to a specified line, and warned that in the event of refusal, French troops would evacuate the towns in the industrial area and leave them to the Poles. The German ambassador in London, Dr. Friedrich Sthamer, delivered a note on 6 June, protesting the ultimatum. The note stressed the German population's hope that British troops would liberate it from "the Polish terror." If this hope were disappointed, the German government feared that an "outbreak of despair with far-reaching consequences is inevitable." The *Times* (London) called the note "impudent."[82] A joint Franco-British *démarche* in Berlin forced the German government to order General Hoefer to stop all military operations, withdraw from the localities his forces had occupied, and in general comply with the wishes of the Plebiscite Commission. At a meeting on 7 June the German cabinet agreed that Hoefer should avoid anything that might complicate the situation. The fate of Upper Silesia, they concluded, would be decided, not on the spot, but by an inter-Allied conference.[83] Still, when the Silesian Poles agreed to evacuate Gleiwitz by 14 June, provided the Germans evacuated Annaberg, General Hoefer refused. The German cabinet decided on 15 June to tell the British and French envoys that Allied insistence on compliance with the ultimatum to General Hoefer might jeopardize the whole policy of "fulfillment" being carried out by the Wirth government. At the same time, Seeckt advised the government to deny that it had any responsibility for Hoefer's actions.[84] Thus, only when the French, British, and Italian representatives in Berlin jointly demanded on 15 June that General Hoefer obey their orders was he commanded to do so by the German government. His continued resistance had been facilitated by dissension within the Plebiscite Commission between the British General Heneker, who had demanded that the industrial towns be occupied by British troops, and Generals Le Rond and Gratier, who opposed him. This, of course, made it easier for Berlin to tolerate General Hoefer's "disobedience." War Minister General Gessler gave the real reason for this toleration. At a cabinet meeting on 21 June he proposed that the government agree to the withdrawal of troops—but on condition that the Allied troops be ready to break Polish resistance with force. He also said that if the Selbstschutz were disbanded, the men would throw their arms away and go home. Then, if the Poles did not observe the agreement, it would be technically impossible for the Germans to occupy the territory. However, some cabinet members feared prolonging the conflict. Thus, Eugen Schiffer of the Democratic Party stressed that a decision on Upper Silesia must be made soon; otherwise, Germany would lose it. He also said that even the Germans of Rybnik might welcome Polish protection against the "tyranny" of the German bands in that region.[85]

The agreement on the dissolution of forces and the evacuation of occupied territories was signed by the Poles on 24 June and by General Hoefer on the following day. By 5 July all combatants had officially left the plebiscite area. However, this did not mean that the Selbstschutz had been disbanded. According to German sources, it was partly grouped outside the area, on German soil, and partly continued its clandestine terrorist activities in Upper Silesia. The German government continued to supply the necessary funds in the belief that the dissolution of the force would encourage another Polish uprising.[86] In August, Stresemann informed a German senator that the payment of these troops—which had been temporarily suspended—had been resumed and that there was no reason to fear the dissolution of the force.[87] Thus, the "dissolution" existed mainly on paper,[88] and the Selbstschutz continued in existence until the spring of 1922. Lloyd George was certainly in error when he stated, in the House of Commons on 11 July, that both the Polish and German forces had been dissolved and reportedly had evacuated the plebiscite area.[89]

In the meanwhile, the British government continued its efforts to secure Italian support for awarding the industrial triangle and the surrounding countryside to Germany. However, on 19 June, Count Bonin-Longare suggested that the experts proposed by the French should join the Plebiscite Commission to help the latter draw up the frontier in Upper Silesia.[90] This was an omen. A few days later, on 25 June, Sforza publicly suggested that Upper Silesia be divided into three parts: the clearly Polish region, the clearly German region, and a "grey zone." This was the industrial triangle, and he proposed that this, in turn, be divided up.[91] This was a blow to the British.

We may conjecture that Sforza was continuing his game of raising the price of Italian support for either France or Britain. The Italian ambassador in Berlin, Frassati, discounted rumors that Sforza was being influenced by his beautiful Polish mistress. D'Abernon reported that a certain W (Wirth?) saw the Italians' cooperation with France as stemming from their opposition to Greek claims to Turkey, which were supported by Britain.[92] Whatever the case might be, there was deadlock; Briand and Curzon could only agree on procedures. Therefore, the Plebiscite Commission was asked to submit a unanimous report on the frontier to be drawn between Germany and Poland in Upper Silesia. If unanimity was impossible, a commission of experts, uncommitted to either side, was to review the plebiscite results and prepare the ground for a decision by the Supreme Council.[93]

However, a new crisis erupted in Anglo-French relations in the second half of July, allegedly over the continued presence of the Selbstschutz in Upper Silesia. Reacting to a British proposal of 15 July that a meeting of the Supreme Council be held on the twenty-fourth—a meeting that the French wished to avoid since they were still afraid of being outvoted—the French government sent a note to Berlin on 16 July. The note stressed that the Selbstschutz had undergone only a mock demobilization; therefore, the French government demanded the disbanding of that force as well as German assent to transit rights for Allied troops. However, this note was sent without consulting the British. Knowing this, the German foreign minister, Dr. Friedrich Rosen, asked if the request had been made in the name of the three occupying powers. He also insisted that German behavior in Upper Silesia was exemplary.[94]

The French action led to renewed tension between Paris and London. There were not only French threats to send a division to Upper Silesia but also hints from London that unless France consulted her ally, there would be a disaster.[95] The situation was further inflamed by two disclosures in the German press. The first referred to the British government's reply to Stresemann's questionnaire of May 1921; the second concerned the plan for a conference between British and German politicians to discuss all outstanding issues between the two countries.[96] The crisis died down because Briand probably never intended to do more than tweak the lion's tail in order to pressure the British and gain applause in the French press. There had been a few French casualties during house searches in Upper Silesia (which the British opposed, alleging that the French searched only German houses), and some caches of German arms had been found. However, it was a far cry from these incidents to demanding the transit of Allied troops to Upper Silesia. Obviously, Briand's main concern had been to postpone the meeting of the Supreme Council—and probably to work on the Italians. On 29 July he explained the whole matter as a misunderstanding and agreed to a meeting of the Supreme Council on 4 August, while also pledging that no French troops would leave for Upper Silesia before that time.[97] Cool heads also prevailed in London. Sir Eyre Crowe discouraged pushing for a British diplomatic victory at the expense of the alliance. Also he believed that Germany should not get all of Upper Silesia.[98] The upshot was a joint *démarche* by the French, British, and Italian ambassadors in Berlin on 3 August. The German government was asked to make the necessary arrangements for the possible transit of Allied troops to Upper Silesia.[99] On the following day, Foreign Minister Rosen agreed to the request, but at the same time, Chancellor Wirth declared in a speech at Bremen that the whole of Upper Silesia must be returned to Germany.

In the meanwhile, the Commission of Experts, which met on 25 July, could not reach an agreement. While its members agreed on rejecting the allocation of the territory *en bloc* and on not considering the vote in absolute numbers, they disagreed completely on the tracing of the frontier. The legal adviser to the Foreign Office, Sir Cecil Hurst, insisted on the indivisibility of the industrial region and argued that since the towns in that region had a German majority, it should go to Germany. This was, of course, a repetition of the arguments and proposals put forward after the plebiscite by Percival and Marinis. The French experts objected to the British exclusion of Rybnik and Pless from the industrial region, because the inclusion of these two areas would give an overall majority to the Poles.[100]

The discussions that took place in the Supreme Council between 8 and 12 August showed that Franco-British differences were unbridgeable.[101] At one point, Harold Nicolson, a member of the British delegation, told Jules Laroche, "An abyss separates us"; to which Laroche aptly replied, "Yes, but this abyss is full of Poles."[102] Indeed, the British proposals assigned almost the whole industrial region to Germany, leaving only the fringes to Poland. The British would not budge on the indivisibility of the industrial region. Laroche reminded them that in a similar case, they had not hesitated to give the whole of Transylvania to Rumania, although there was a sizeable Hungarian minority in the province. Lloyd George, in turn, accused the French of wanting to steal from the rich Germans to give to the poor Poles, and he indulged in philippics against the latter, calling them disturbers of the European peace and charging that they were incapable of using the industrial wealth they wanted. He also claimed that the population of Upper Silesia numbered 5.2 million people, of whom only 1.2 million were Poles. In fact, the whole of Upper Silesia was not at stake, only the plebiscite area. The *Times* (London), which still opposed the prime minister in most policy matters, implied that he had failed to display detachment and impartiality.[103] The Supreme Council was deadlocked. After haggling over mines, mills, Poles, and Germans, Lloyd George and Curzon were reduced to arguing that the nonindustrial part of Upper Silesia, which they proposed to give to Poland, actually had greater "potential" coal resources than the industrial area, to be ceded to Germany, which, they claimed, would be "worked out" in fifty years(!).[104] On 12 August the French cabinet again rejected the British proposals, claiming that these would allow Germany to retain her industrial arsenal for war and that Poland's small share would not be economically viable. Meanwhile, however, the crisis in Ireland made it imperative for Lloyd George to leave Paris. The British prime minister then proposed to Briand that the problems be submitted to the League of Nations. The French premier agreed.[105] Lloyd George was elated. He told his secretary, Thomas Jones, that it was his own idea to submit the issue to the League of Nations; he implied that he had triumphed by getting Briand to agree.[106] A year later, however, when the league's decision to partition Upper Silesia was criticized in the British cabinet, its secretary, Sir Maurice Hankey, prepared a statement that the idea of passing the problem to the league had come from Briand and the British Foreign Office experts.[107] But it seems that the Italians had suggested the idea to Lloyd George on 11 August and that he was under the impression that he had secured their support with the promise of a bribe. He had expressed "sympathy" with Sidney Sonnino's desire for an "Italian colony" in Turkey. He said he saw an Italian population in sparsely inhabited Anatolia as a "great asset" for Italy. He did not stop there but also urged Italy to reach an "understanding" with the Greeks over Albania—though not by written agreements that could be rejected by the League of Nations. This was a reference to the Tittoni–Venizelos agreement promising Greek support for Italian claims to Albania. It had been, however, abrogated by Sforza. Lloyd George now offered his support for a similar deal, implying that it would be his payment for Italian support of British proposals over Upper Silesia. As he said: "A gentleman . . . would pay a betting debt. . . . The attitude of a Power towards a debt of honour might be compared to this." He then urged the Italians to reach an understanding with the Greeks without waiting for another Greek victory over the Turks. It was at the end of this interesting soliloquy that the marquis della Torretta mentioned the possibility of submitting the decision on Upper Silesia to the arbitration of the League of Nations, or to "someone else." Lloyd George seized on this suggestion and made it his own.[108] He must have assumed that the British solution would, with Italian support, be adopted by the League of Nations, and therefore he proposed it the next day to Briand, who prevailed on the French cabinet to accept it. French opinion was divided on whether this was a victory or a defeat for France.[109]

Lloyd George exuded optimism in his statement to the House of Commons on 16 August. He repeated all his arguments in favor of attributing Upper Silesia to Germany, and he accused the Poles of exercising "a system of brigandage in Central Europe.'' He believed that an ''impartial'' decision of the League Council would settle the matter. As he put it:

> There will be the evidence, there will be the documents, there will be all the considerations relevant to the trial of the case, judgment will be given by the arbitrator or by the jurists in the ordinary way, and all parties will accept it. . . . The whole question goes there, and not a part of it. I mean that they are not bound in the least by any proposals or counter-proposals made either by the French, by the Italians, or by ourselves with a view to effecting an arrangement.[110]

British opinion welcomed this announcement with relief. German reaction was generally positive, although Lord D'Abernon commented on ''the invincible tendency in the German character to complain.''[111] The *Economist* reported the German prediction ''that the French contention will be badly outvoted in the Council of the League of Nations.''[112] It is clear that Lloyd George shared this assumption.

But the League Council, given its first chance to settle a major dispute that had deadlocked the two Great Powers, and assured by them of a completely free hand, made its own arrangements.[113] To begin with, at its fourth meeting of 9 September, the council decided to entrust the preliminary investigation to four members: the representatives of Belgium (Paul Hymans), Brazil (Gastaô da Cunha), Spain (J. M. Quiñones de León), and China (Wellington Koo). This deprived Lloyd George of what would have been an easy victory if the committee had been made up of the representatives of France, Britain, Italy, and Japan. Secondly, it was agreed not to make any comparisons with previously suggested solutions and not to consult any authorities that had definitely supported one or another of the earlier proposals. This disposed of the British, French, and Italian heads of the Plebiscite Commission, among whom the French would have been outvoted two to one. Thirdly, agreement was reached on the legal interpretation of articles 88 and 90 of the Versailles Treaty—that is, that the frontier should be fixed according to the wishes of the population and that geographical and economic factors should be secondary. This disposed of German economic claims and of the British proposal that the whole industrial region go to Germany. It was agreed that if the industrial region were to be considered indivisible, and therefore subject to allocation to either Poland or Germany, the wishes of the population would have to be disregarded. Therefore, the aim was, first, to find an equitable line of division according to the wishes of the population—as expressed in the plebiscite—and, second, to avoid dislocating the economic life of the region and to provide for a gradual adaptation to new conditions.[114]

The League Council appointed two experts, Professor Herald of Switzerland and Francis Hodač, a Czech industralist, to study the question and propose a boundary line.[115] The Germans were upset because they suspected the Czechoslovak government of supporting Polish claims, and indeed, Beneš did so although he did not influence the final decision.[116] The most important fact was that both the experts and the members of the committee believed that the wishes of the population—as expressed in the plebiscite in votes by commune—should prevail. Therefore, the boundary they drew up gave Poland a little over 40 percent of the population and two-thirds of the industrial triangle. But a special convention was to be negotiated by Poland and Germany to preserve the economic unity of the area.[117] This was later embodied in the Geneva, or Upper Silesian, Convention of 22 May 1922.

The league's decision came as a great shock both to Germany and to Lloyd George and his advisers. They had clearly expected a decision similar to the one reached in June on the Åland Islands. Here the League Council had decided to give Finland sovereignty over the islands, while leaving the preponderantly Swedish population a very large degree of autonomy. The islands were also demilitarized.[118] Lloyd George had expected the league either to employ arbitration by some power or to appoint a body of legal experts, such as the one that had successfully solved the dispute over the Åland Islands.[119] Therefore, he expected the industrial triangle to be allocated to Germany but with some sort of guarantees for the Poles.[120]

The Germans also supported a solution on the Åland Islands model. They even stated how they expected it to work out. On 19 August the former German foreign minister, Dr. Simons, suggested that Upper Silesia be made an administrative unit under German sovereignty, while Poland be given "a sort of economic mortgage" on the production of the province until she was able to develop her own "much greater possibilities" (?). He also suggested that minorities (from the German point of view this meant the Poles) be granted the clearest and surest guarantees possible for their national life, as had been done in the case of the Åland Islands.[121] Thus, there was a meeting of minds between Lloyd George and Simons. It was perhaps on the assumption that the league would adopt this kind of solution that on 8 September, Stresemann ordered the immediate delivery of some German industrial shares which had been promised to Germany's "English friends."[122]

But the Åland Islands solution did not stand a chance. On 29 September, Balfour reported from Geneva that the league's experts envisaged ethnographic factors to be of prime importance and economic ones to be secondary. Thus, by 29 September, it was clear that a division of the industrial triangle was likely,[123] but the decision came as a shock to both London and Berlin. On 13 October, when the outcome was known, D'Abernon sent an excerpt of his diary to Lloyd George. He noted that according to "a quite reliable source," the most influential man on the league committee was a Belgian (Hymans), who carried out French instructions. The French had kept all Czech experts under close surveillance, and the report had been drawn up by a French professor who had close ties with Czechoslovakia (Jean Monnet). Moreover, the German government claimed that the committee had chosen its witnesses from elements "notoriously in alliance with French interests." D'Abernon thought this last point untrue. A few more details filled in the picture. Thus, Balfour had allegedly been "seduced" by the French philosopher Henri Bergson, who was brought to Geneva—instead of the traditional cocotte of French spy dramas—to delight the intellectual British diplomat. Still, D'Abernon concluded that although the English had lost face, Germany had obtained a very favorable solution as compared with the Le Rond Line or with the loss of the whole of Upper Silesia as envisaged in the draft Versailles Treaty. In comparison with those alternatives, Germany's gains—due to Lloyd George's efforts—were enormous.[124]

The report from a "reliable source" was, of course, an imaginative fabrication. Balfour did not need Bergson's company to decide in favor of a partition of Upper Silesia, nor were the German allegations of biased witnesses correct. The German witnesses called were Williger, Geisenheimer, and Tomalla, respectively president, secretary, and syndic of the Oberschlesischer Berg und Huttenmännischer Verein. Franz Karger, secretary of Deutsche Freie Gewerkschaften, was called in as a representative of the workers. On the Polish side, the committee interviewed an engineer, Stanisław Grabianowski, and the vice-president of the Polish Miners' Union, Alojzy Kot.[125] Sir Maurice Hankey, however, believed the report. He commented: "Prime Minister. This makes my blood boil. It tends to confirm your and my opinion as to what happened in Geneva. M. P. A. Hankey, 21. ×. 21."[126] On the same day, Hankey sent a private letter to Secretary General of the League of Nations Sir Eric Drummond. In a note to Lloyd George, Hankey wrote that he had waited a few days "to allow my wrath to cool before I could write civilly," but the letter was neither cool nor civil. Of the league's decision Hankey wrote: "In official circles here, this is almost universally unpopular. Rightly or wrongly everyone felt that our case was so overwhelming that if it were put before a thoroughly impartial tribunal, the decision would have been completely in our favour." The British, according to Hankey, had advocated a decision by the league because they expected an impartial tribunal to make a decision on the model of the Åland Islands. He was bitterly disappointed when the case was referred to members of the council, who had not been previously concerned with the case, and had warned the Foreign Office that this was a "big risk." As for the representatives of the powers who had been chosen to sit on the council, he called the

Belgian "notoriously Francophile" and noted that of the remaining three, "two were Dagoes and one a Chink." Since both "Dagoes" were ambassadors in Paris, they did not want to lose their posts. On the final decision, Hankey wrote: "One cannot but feel the gravest anxiety that, in the long run, it will prove unworkable and that it will sow the seeds of future war. . . . I simply cannot conceive our referring any question of a vital character to ourselves with the risk of its reference to a Tribunal composed as were the Upper Silesian arbitrators."[127]

Sir Eric Drummond shed some light on his own attitude and Balfour's in two personal letters to Hankey. In the first, dated 24 October and sent in answer to a personal message transmitted through Philip Noél-Baker, Drummond wrote that when he had originally discussed the matter with Hankey in London, Drummond had favored the appointment of a commission on the same lines as for the Åland Islands. However, the opposition of council members to this proposal was too strong. He also remembered that Balfour "did not altogether favor it."[128] In replying to Hankey's letter of 21 October, Drummond refuted the latter's accusations. He stated that Paul Hymans and Quiñones de León, the most important of the four council members involved, were both "scrupulously fair." The French government had never tried to influence them, but the German government had intervened in Madrid, asking that Quiñones de León be instructed to take a pro-German line. Drummond also enclosed a statement of 10 October by Hymans regarding the opinion of the Committee of Four on the plebiscite and its interpretation.[129] As for Balfour, he stated that he had received no instructions from the British cabinet and that he had worked closely and amicably with the French representative, Léon Bourgeois.[130] We may assume that, given a free hand, Balfour had acted out of conviction that the wishes of the population came first. There is no need to doubt Drummond's statement to Sir John Simon in December 1933, that "the Upper Silesian boundary was determined after a most careful examination of a very complicated ethnological and economic situation. Lord Balfour and M. Léon Bourgeois were ultimately the principal negotiators, and the former regarded the settlement as completely fair."[131] This was also the opinion of Lord Robert Cecil. He was not favorably disposed toward the Poles, but as the most prominent British advocate of the league, he upheld the verdict and seemed to be convinced that it was just. Of course, he also believed that it could be modified after fifteen years—the life span of the convention to be signed by Poland and Germany.[132]

When the League of Nations awarded most of the industrial triangle to Poland, there were rumors not only that this had been done under French pressure but also that French economic interests in the region may have played a decisive role. In fact, neither league nor French documents bear out this charge. On the contrary, French sources indicate that French interests were not firmly established in the region before October 1921. While the French government aimed at awarding the industrial triangle to Poland, with controlling French interests, and negotiated with the Poles to this end, French business concerns showed little interest in this direction. On the contrary, some French officials and businessmen negotiated with German industrialists for control of Upper Silesian industry with a minimal German share. Thus, while the French political line was clear, economic policy was at best ambivalent. The Poles, of course, always assumed that they would obtain the industrial triangle, but they also knew that they could not exploit it without French financial aid. The French government wished Poland to have the industrial triangle, so as to weaken Germany, and was willing to make arrangements. Therefore, several conventions were signed to this effect both before and after the signing of the Franco-Polish alliance in February 1921.

Let us first look at the convention concerning state property—that is, the former Prussian fiscal mines of the region. After long negotiations that began in January 1920, the convention was signed in Paris on 1 March 1921, three weeks before the plebiscite. It was signed by the Polish plenipotentiary for economic negotiations, Professor Artur Benis, and Emmanuel M. J. de Peretti de la Rocca, deputy director of the Political and Commercial Section of the Quai d'Orsay. It was agreed that the former fiscal mines of Prussia were to be leased for a period of thirty-six years by a Franco-Polish company, the Société fermière des mines fiscales de l'Etat polonais en Haute Silésie, known as Skarboferme. This became the largest mining concern in Upper Silesia, accounting for 10 percent of the total coal production. The initial capital consisted of 300 million German marks (part of which came from the marks purchased at 1.25 francs each by the French government in Alsace-Lorraine). Half of the shares were assigned to Poland and credited to her by the French treasury. Any depreciation of the German mark was to be taken into account in the repayment of the Polish debt by adjusting it to the average rate of exchange as of the preceding month. Thus, Poland bore the brunt of German inflation. This convention was later complemented by an additional agreement signed on 16 November 1921—that is, after the league's decision. These agreements advanced the necessary capital to Poland but deprived her of all revenues from the former fiscal mines for thirty-six years—that is, until 1957. Thus, the revenues and profits of Skarboferme were used for the repayment of French loans to Poland; they were then transmitted in dollars to the United States in partial payment of French war debts.[133] We should note, however, that the value of the initial capital fell drastically as the result of German inflation and that, in any case, the Skarboferme accounted for only 10 percent of the total coal production of Upper Silesia.

It was the private German concerns that produced most of the coal and steel of Upper Silesia. The story of French tergiversations, vacillations, and negotiations with both Poles and Germans is, indeed, a fascinating one and has been well told by a French scholar, Georges Soutou, who was the first to study the relevant French documents when they became available in 1971/72.[134] The Polish and German efforts had been described earlier by Polish historians, especially Franciszek Ryszka, in studies based on the archives of the German firms that fell into Polish hands.[135] Since the Poles were prohibited from liquidating German concerns without paying compensation for them and since the Poles lacked the necessary capital to work those concerns, they naturally turned to France. The French treasury could advance the capital, for, as mentioned above, it had acquired billions of German marks in Alsace-Lorraine. Thus, mutual interest led to the signing of the Klotz-Olszowski convention of 17 January 1920, whereby France was to lend Poland up to a billion German marks. Poland was to buy out certain German enterprises and then retrocede them to Franco-Polish companies, in which 51 percent of the shares would be reserved for French financial or industrial groups and 49 percent for Polish groups.

However, before this agreement was complemented by other Franco-Polish agreements, two groups of French capitalists engaged—with the approval of the Quai d'Orsay—in negotiations with German industralists in Upper Silesia and Berlin. Thus, immediately after the Spa Conference of July 1920, certain French financial, oil, and metallurgical concerns set up the Société d'études des affaires silésiennes. This society was headed by Ernest Mercier of the Mines de Béthune and included the Comité des houillères de France (Henri de Peyerimhoff), the Comité des forges, the Banque de Paris et des Pays Bas, and the Union parisienne. The president of the Plebiscite Commission, Gen. Henri Le Rond, had the support of the Quai d'Orsay and the French treasury in trying to secure a foothold for this group in Upper Silesian industry before the plebiscite. He began negotiations with German industrialists on the spot. Jacques Seydoux, deputy director of the Commercial Department of the Quai d'Orsay, approved. He noted that if Upper Silesia remained with Germany as a result of the plebiscite, then the Franco-Polish Convention of 17 January 1920 would fall through.[136] Thus, the Le Rond negotiations were to hedge France's bets: whatever the outcome of the Polish-Soviet war or of the plebiscite, she would control the industry of Upper Silesia.

Parallel to Le Rond's efforts, another venture was launched by the French ambassador in Berlin, Charles Laurent, who also happened to be a prominent financier and chairman of the state electric power monopoly, the

Société centrale pour l'industrie electrique. Laurent reported that he had established contact with a Dr. Kleefeld, who represented the Hohenlohe family and their extensive Upper Silesian concerns. Laurent suggested that one French intermediary be appointed for all interested French groups, and he proposed Col. Ernest Weyl, who, in fact, represented Schneider-Creuzot, the major French steel concern that had not joined Le Rond's Société. Schneider-Creuzot was very active in Central and Eastern Europe. It had acquired sizeable packets of shares in the Teschen area, among others, through its Union européenne industrielle et financière. Sabatier, of the Quai d'Orsay's Commercial Department, considered Schneider-Creuzot to be an economic tsar, aiming at a complete takeover of German interests in Upper Silesia. Nevertheless, he approved Laurent's proposal and hoped for a compromise agreement between Laurent's group and Le Rond's. This came to pass in November 1920, with the approval of the Quai d'Orsay. The author of an unsigned note of 1 February 1921—two days before Piłsudski's arrival in Paris—justified the arrangement. He commented that the Poles and the French could not, in any case, provide sufficient cadres to replace the Germans, and the British would oppose such a radical solution. Furthermore, the Weyl project would give parity to the French in the supervisory councils of the German firms involved and 50 percent of the seats in the future governing council—all this for the price of letting the German industrialists keep 10 percent of the shares with an option for an additional 25 percent. Finally, the Weyl formula would be valid if Poland should lose the plebiscite. The Commercial Department, which was responsible for this note, advised that the Poles simply be presented with a *fait accompli*. [137]

All of these plans might have achieved their aim—that is, Franco-German control of most of Upper Silesian industry—if it had not been for the opposition of the German Foreign Ministry. The German government delayed negotiations by insisting that the French group guarantee the retention of Upper Silesia by Germany, which, of course, it could not do. The plebiscite of 20 March 1921 gave an overall majority to Germany, but as we know, the Polish character of the communes in the industrial triangle was the main French argument for awarding it to Poland. This policy, together with an official Polish guarantee not to liquidate German property and the signing of the political and military conventions, led to the Franco-Polish Convention of 22 March 1921, signed by Benis and Briand, granting concessions and privileges to French capital in *private* German concerns.

According to this convention, a group of French industrialists was to hold shares in the mines and foundries up to the value of 400 million marks. Within six months, it was to give up one-fourth of these shares to persons nominated by the Polish government. The French government committed itself to advance a loan of up to 100 million marks (on the basis of the convention of 17

January 1921) to the Polish group, which was to have proportional representation in the administrative bodies. In return, the Polish government guaranteed to repay the loan with 5 percent profit, up to the level of the dividends falling to the Polish group in the preceding fiscal year and not excluding other means of paying off the debt. Furthermore, the Polish government undertook to treat enterprises with French capital on an equal footing with purely Polish ones. It gave up its rights of liquidation as per article 297 of the Versailles Treaty; assured the enterprises export and transport alleviations; and freed them not only from regulations limiting foreign-currency transactions but also from capital taxes and compulsory loans.[138]

Meanwhile, Schneider-Creuzot had lost interest in Upper Silesia, except for the Hohenlohe enterprises. Therefore, on 14 November 1922 a supplementary agreement established a Franco-Polish holding company to administer future participation in the shares. Also, the French loan was augmented to 390 million marks, which were immediately transferred to Poland. This was possible because the Comité des houillères and the Comité des forges group had voluntarily renounced their indemnification for war damages to the tune of 300 million marks. But this holding arrangement finally came to naught because of differences between the French government and the two major spokesmen for the industrialists, Mercier and Peyerimhoff. The latter would not agree to the government's demand that the industrialists submit the names of the French administrators for its approval.[139] Thus, the Franco-Polish holding company was abandoned in 1923, leaving the original convention of 22 March 1921 to be worked out without that body. In any case, by 1923 the German inflation had almost wiped out the French government's capital in German marks, while French financiers and industrialists had neither the interest nor the capital to invest in Polish Upper Silesia.

French capital was also represented in a large zinc-mining concern at Lipiny, the Société des zincs de Silésie. Most of its shares belonged to a Franco-Belgian group, and the rest to German bankers. The banks involved were the Banque de l'union parisienne, its filial branch, Neuflize & Cie, and the Banque de la Société générale de Belgique. In 1924, the remaining shares were bought by the Berlin bank of Delbrück, Schinkler & Co. This company engaged in extensive smuggling of foreign currency, and the Polish government's measures against its directors led to many interventions by the French ambassador in Warsaw. There was also a banking venture. On 23 March 1921 the French and the Polish governments signed an agreement to set up the Banque de Silésie, which was to buy out former German enterprises. However, the French banks were chary of this venture, fearing further devaluation of the German mark. It was finally under strong pressure from the French government that the banks agreed to advance the capital, and on 15 December 1921, Briand and Benis signed a convention setting up the

Franco-Polish Bank of Upper Silesia. The basic capital shares were to amount to 200 million marks, advanced half and half by the French and the Poles. The French side was to advance the Polish shares.[140] However, the bank was always undercapitalized and thus failed to fulfill the aim for which it was founded.

Another Franco-Polish company in Upper Silesia was the Fondérie fiscale polonaise de Strzybnica, Société fermière de Tarnowitz (Tarnoferm), set up in 1922 to rent the former Prussian fiscal lead and silver mines in Strzybnica, near Tarnowskie Góry (Tarnowitz). Here the capital of 50 million German marks was advanced by the Société des minérais et minéraux. However, the mines made no profit and were taken over by the Polish government in 1923. The last enterprise that remains to be listed is the Hohenlohe-Werke, which, with its headquarters in Wełnowiec near Katowice, had been the largest coal-zinc business in Germany aside from the Bergwerkgesellschaft Georg von Giesche's Erbe. Schneider-Creuzot, perhaps because it did not have the capital to dominate this enterprise, acquired only a minority of the shares in it.[141] It should be noted that in 1924 the Polish government discovered many illegal practices in the Holenlohe works when Professor Artur Benis and Wojciech Korfanty were on the board of governors. These practices included false income returns and the sale of a part of the enterprise located in German Upper Silesia to its branch, Oehringen-Bergbau. However, the Polish government had to draw back from imposing a fine of 18 million marks on the works for unpaid taxes in 1922/23, because of the pressure exerted by the French government in the name of the French groups involved. In return, the French shareholders agreed to transfer to the Polish treasury the nominal half of their shares in the Hohenlohe-Werke, a transfer that should have been made in 1922 according to the terms of the Franco-Polish convention of 22 March 1921.

The mortgaging of Polish Upper Silesia to France was sharply criticized in Poland at the time and later. However, there was no alternative. The Poles had no capital of their own, while British concerns showed little interest until early in 1922. At that time, however, these British concerns received no encouragement from the Foreign Office. Ultimately, they took over control of the important Donnersmarck mines and the Laurahütte. Some industry was also taken over by Standard Oil.[142] The French did not put all their eggs in the Polish basket but hedged their bets by negotiating with German industrialists. However, for most of the time, the French supported the Polish cause, which was, after all, in their national interest.

When the league's decision on Upper Silesia became known on 12 October, the German cabinet was shocked, and at least one member claimed that Germany had been cheated.[143] Stresemann's efforts were to no avail. He appealed to Lord D'Abernon on 11 October, claiming that the Geneva verdict would disrupt international economics and violate the principle of self-determination. Stresemann therefore proposed that a new plebiscite be held.[144] This time, however, the British government recognized that nothing could be done. On 12 October, Curzon told the Polish minister in London, Władysław Wróblewski, that Britain would comply with the recommendations of the League Council without any reservations. Finally, Briand overcame the objections of the Quai d'Orsay, which feared that Germany would not be sufficiently weakened.[145]

The German government at first hesitated about whether to resign, but it did so on 23 October, three days after the Supreme Council had officially communicated its decision to accept the league's solution. The new government was again headed by Wirth. In the meanwhile, the Supreme Council decided on 15 October to refer the award to the Conference of Ambassadors, which was to settle questions of detail. The conference adopted a series of resolutions on 20 October, which, while confirming the frontier as proposed by the league, added more provisions to ensure the economic unity of Upper Silesia after the partition. Accordingly, the convention foreseen by the League Council was to be concluded between Polish and German representatives under the presidency of a person appointed by the league; this chairman was to cast the tie-breaking vote in case the two sides failed to agree.

The discussions in the Conference of Ambassadors were marked by a difference of opinion between France and Britain on whether the recommendations relating to the provisional economic regime had a binding character or were to be left to the sovereign decisions of Poland and Germany. Cambon pointed out that Polish-German negotiations might last several months, while according to paragraph 6 of annex 1 to article 88 of the Versailles Treaty, the German and Polish authorities were to take over the administration of the territories assigned to them within one month of the notification of the final frontier by the Allied and Associated Powers. The difficulty was resolved by having the decision of the powers "communicated" to the Polish and German governments, while the official "notification" was postponed until the convention had been concluded.[146] The "communication" to the two governments was made on 27 October. The German government entered a legal reservation *(Rechtsverwahrung)*, which was enclosed with a note delivered by the German ambassador in Paris on the same day. When the question of the attitude to be taken by German political parties was discussed, Stresemann asked whether the appointment of a German delegate to conduct negotiations with Poland was compatible with the reservation. He proposed that the appointment of the delegate could only take place if the Entente Powers recognized that it did not imply Germany's recognition of the league's decision.[147] Thus, the German note delivered in Paris asserted that the decision had violated the provisions of the Versailles Treaty, but the German government would appoint a delegate for negotiations with Poland. However, France and Britain rejected this point of view. On 27 October, Briand replied in the name of the Principal Allied Powers that they could not accept the German assertion that the league's decision, taken in accordance with article 88 of the Versailles Treaty, constituted a violation of the treaty; therefore, the German reservation was rejected as being unfounded.[148] Henceforth, the reservation existed only in German policy.

The Upper Silesian, or Geneva, Convention of May 1922, which created a special regime for the region for a period of fifteen years, was in many ways a model convention. It has been studied by Polish and German authors,[149] but the most valuable summary of its achievements is provided by George Kaeckenbeeck, who was president of the Upper Silesian Tribunal of Arbitration.[150] However, for all practical purposes, the convention ceased to exist in 1925, when the German government refused to renew the coal agreement under which it was to import 500,000 tons per year duty free. As has so often been the case in Central and Eastern Europe, politics had primacy over economics.

While half a million Poles were left under German domination, the league's decision was clearly in Poland's favor. Therefore, the Polish foreign minister, Konstanty Skirmunt, advised all Polish diplomats to abstain from voicing criticism.[151] We should note that Polish Upper Silesia enjoyed a semiautonomous status. It had its own parliament, with legislative competence except in military and foreign affairs, and its own law courts and tariffs. The executive established by this parliament consisted of a council of five, headed by the *voivode,* or governor of the province. According to the Polish census of 1931, out of a total population of 1,295,000, there were 1,195,000 Poles (92.3 percent) and 90,600 Germans.[152]

The German government was, of course, unreconciled to the loss of Upper Silesia, and it did everything to make public opinion believe that Germany had been wronged and that international law had been violated. On 26 October 1921, Chancellor Wirth declared in the Reichstag that the decision was illegal.[153] The president of Prussia, Adam Stegerwald, declared in the Prussian Diet that the bonds between Germany and the Germans of Upper Silesia were unbreakable.[154]

Thus, Germany pursued a revisionist policy accompanied by a propaganda campaign for the return not only of Danzig and the Corridor but also of Upper Silesia. A few examples will suffice here. Dr. Wirth, whom D'Abernon called "the embodiment of the better elements in modern German democracy,"[155] told Brockdorff-Rantzau in 1922 that in a little while, Germany would win back Upper Silesia by war; in any case, his policy aim was to "finish" Poland.[156] On 28 March 1926, Carl Severing, a Socialist who was Prussian minister of the interior, declared that the erroneous decision would be "corrected" with time in Germany's favor. On 17 September 1928, Reich President Marshal Paul von Hindenburg declared that 60 percent of the people had voted for Germany, and they were angry.[157]

A special organization subsidized by the German government, the Vereinigte Verbände Heimattreuer Oberschlesier (United Associations of Upper Silesians True to the Fatherland), served as the center for home propaganda. Another organization, whose aim was to influence Western, particularly British, opinion in Germany's favor, was the Wirtschafts-politische Gesellschaft (Economic-Political Society). Led by its able secretary, Margarete Gärtner, it worked to convince Western journalists, politicians, and historians that the Polish-German frontier would have to be changed so as to preserve lasting peace in Europe.[158] This propaganda was also conducted by means of German minority complaints to the League of Nations. While there were only two such complaints before Germany entered the league in 1926, the next three years saw the number rise to thirty-two.[159] German propaganda was largely successful in Britain because it strengthened the already widespread opinion in governmental circles and the press that Germany had been unjustly treated and that peace depended on the fulfillment of her "justified grievances" in Danzig, the Polish Corridor, and Upper Silesia.[160] The acceptance of this so-called ethnic argument, or "self-determination" for the Germans, prepared the way for later Western acquiescence to the abolition of the Demilitarized Zone in the Rhineland, to the Anschluss with Austria, and to German annexation of the Sudetenland.

4

The Free City of Danzig:
An Unworkable Compromise, 1919–25

The small, sleepy Baltic port city of Danzig—or Gdańsk, as it is called in Polish—could hardly have expected to become the storm center of international relations. Yet, the combination of its geographical location, the defeat of Germany, and the rebirth of Poland made this inevitable.

The old city had lived through periods of prosperity and decline. Originally an old Slavic fishing and trading settlement, it had belonged to Poland from 966 to 1308, when it was seized by the Teutonic Knights. With the development of trade between Eastern and Western Europe, Danzig joined the Hanseatic League and soon thereafter came into conflict with its Teutonic masters. Along with other East Prussian towns, it rebelled against their rule in the fifteenth century and acquired the status of a free city under the Polish crown. Then followed a period of great prosperity, when Danzig enjoyed the monopoly of Polish foreign trade and developed into a center of learning and the arts. It was sometimes called the Amsterdam of the East, and indeed, its wealthy, enlightened patrician families were the equals of the Dutch in their high standard of living and their beautiful houses, libraries, and works of art. However, the seventeenth-century wars, which ruined Poland, impoverished the city too; and a recovery did not begin until the second half of the eighteenth century. This was, in turn, cut short by Frederick the Great, who not only seized Polish Pomerania but also Danzig's port (Neufahrwasser) and imposed heavy taxes on goods entering Danzig (1772). After a long siege the city fell to Prussian armies in 1793, although it revolted unsuccessfully in 1797. For a few years, between 1807 and 1815, it was again a free city but was dependent on France, serving as a base for Napoleon's armies in the east. After the Congress of Vienna it reverted once more to Prussia (1815), this time for a period of one hundred and five years, until January 1920.

During this period, Danzig sank into a long sleep. The east-west trade routes established on Polish territories by the partitioning powers relegated the city to an economic backwater. After the unification of Germany in 1870/71, it played no part in the great industrial development of that power. Although the port experienced some growth during this period, its trade turnover in 1913 was only 2 million tons, and it ranked fifth among German ports. The major industry was shipbuilding, mostly for the German Imperial Navy, followed by small establishments for the manufacture of armaments, chemicals, sugar, beer, spirits, candy, and tobacco products.

During this period the native population of Danzig was outnumbered by temporary and permanent settlers from Germany. In 1891 the city became the headquarters of the Seventeenth Army Corps; it was also the administrative center for the province of West Prussia and boasted a polytechnic, founded in 1904. Thus, German soldiers, civil servants, and pensioners supplied the main purchasing power in the city. During the First World War there was a massive influx of laborers from other German states to work in the shipyards. The population of the city itself was predominantly German-speaking; but in the countryside, people spoke German, Polish, and Kashubian (a Slavic dialect). It is impossible to establish exact percentages for ethnic affiliations; in any case, most Poles and Kashubians also spoke German. In 1923, official Danzig statistics for the territory of the free city gave a figure of only 3.3 percent Poles out of a total population of 335,221,[1] but Polish estimates varied between 9 and 10 percent.[2] Polish experts also estimated that at the end of World War I, about 30 percent of the total population consisted of Germanized Kashubians, of whom about 12 percent were conscious of being Poles.[3]

The future of Danzig was linked with the Polish Question as it emerged during the First World War. Until the first Russian Revolution of March 1917, the Western Powers saw Poland as an internal matter for their ally the Russian Empire. Thus, in 1914 a British historian and consultant to the Foreign Office, Professor Bernard Pares, believed that the outcome of Polish and Russian claims to Danzig, Posen, and Upper Silesia would depend on the success of Russian arms.[4] However, by 1916 the Central Powers had defeated Russia, and in November of that year they promised to establish a Polish state in order to secure Polish manpower to fight on their side.[5] This prospect aroused both Allied fears and interest in the Poles.

As far as the British cabinet was concerned, the preferred solution was for Poland to become an autonomous state within the Russian Empire. Arthur J. Balfour, for example, then First Lord of the Admiralty, believed in October 1916 that a common Russo-German border would allow Russia to check

German expansion westwards, while Germany could check Russian expansion in the Middle and Far East.[6] The French government kept silent out of deference for its ally Russia, although vague hopes were sometimes expressed that an independent Poland would emerge from the war.[7] It was President Woodrow Wilson, speaking for a still-neutral United States, who said in his address to Congress on 17 January 1917 he assumed that statesmen everywhere were agreed that there should be a "united, independent and autonomous Poland."[8] The mention of autonomy seemed to imply Russian sovereignty. Also, the United States ambassador in Berlin, James W. Gerard, assured the German government that these words did not imply any loss of German territory. Gerard stated that the president envisaged only a free port for Poland in Danzig, with a guaranteed Polish use of German railways and canals for access to the sea.[9]

Gerard's statement summed up the view of both the British and United States governments, until the latter diverged from it toward the end of 1918. In the meanwhile, Roman Dmowski, the head of the Polish National Committee—an organization representing Poles who supported the Allies in the West—openly laid claim to Danzig and Polish Pomerania, as well as Posen and Upper Silesia, in a memorandum apparently handed to Foreign Secretary Arthur J. Balfour on 25 March 1917.[10] If, indeed, Balfour received it on that day, he probably knew its contents earlier, for at the first meeting of the Imperial War Cabinet on 22 March, ten days after the fall of tsardom in Russia, he opposed ceding Danzig to Poland on the grounds that it was a German city. He also opposed Polish acquisition of Polish Pomerania, or the Polish Corridor, although its population was preponderantly Polish. His argument was that this would hurt German emotions and interests.[11] Here he had in mind the territorial separation of East Prussia from the rest of Germany, which would be the consequence of granting the Polish claims. British opposition to granting the Corridor to Poland persisted until March 1919. In fact, the Foreign Office guidelines for the Polish-German frontier in this sector, drawn up at the end of 1918, proposed that Danzig stay with Germany and that the latter keep most of Polish Pomerania in order to ensure territorial unity with East Prussia. Poland was to be granted a small enclave on the coast from Puck (Putzig) up to and including Danzig's port (Neufahrwasser), but this would be separated from the rest of Poland by a broad belt of German territory.[12] As Lord Robert Cecil, then permanent parliamentary undersecretary of state put it, the separation of East Prussia from Germany by a Polish Corridor would be a serious "political mistake."[13] In their concluding recommendation the experts in the Foreign Office stated that awarding German Danzig and a Corridor to the sea to Poland would make Germany's position "intolerable" when she recovered. Thus, although the Corridor was acknowledged to be preponderantly Polish, it was to stay with Germany.

Poland's access to Danzig was to be assured by guarantees for her free use of the Vistula and of the German railways.[14]

However, by the end of 1918, London's views were at variance with those of Washington and Paris. Thus, Walter Lippmann wrote to Col. Edward House in October that if Poland's access to the sea were to be secured by internationalizing the Vistula and giving her the use of German canals to Hamburg and Bremen, she would be subjected to Germany, and this would create great friction.[15] The French government, as far back as November 1917, had envisaged a strong Poland, with free access to the sea, to serve as an effective buffer between Germany and Russia.[16] A year later, in December 1918, officials in the French Foreign Ministry drew up a memorandum entitled "Une méthode d'action en Pologne," wherein it was stated that Germany would not be truly beaten until she had lost her Polish provinces. Moreover, a strong Poland, allied with Bohemia and Romania, would keep Germany in check until Russia had recovered. Therefore, Danzig should go to Poland, though with safeguards for its German population. However, if United States and British opposition should prove too strong to overcome, France could agree that Danzig become a free city attached to Germany, provided that Poland owned the port facilities.[17]

Finally, we should bear in mind that the German attitude on Poland's access to the sea was public knowledge. Chancellor Max von Baden made it clear that Germany would not oppose an independent Poland, provided her access to the sea was assured through Germany's Baltic ports, railways, and canals, as well as the Vistula.[18] At the end of 1918 a German emissary to Warsaw, Count Harry Kessler, tried but failed to reach an agreement on this basis with the Polish government.[19]

At the opening of the Paris Peace Conference, the Poles received strong support for their claim to Danzig and Polish Pomerania from the United States delegation. The latter's memorandum, dated 21 January 1919 and entitled "Outline of a Tentative Report and Recommendations," argued that if Polish claims were granted, 1.6 million Germans would be cut off from Germany, but if German claims were upheld, 20 million Poles would have only a precarious access to the sea and to the port of Danzig.[20] The United States view came to dominate the thinking of Allied experts during the first phase of the conference—that is, until mid March 1919. This was not only because it coincided with French views but also because the British delegation had no specific instructions; the Foreign Office recommendations of 1918 had no mandatory character.[21] Furthermore, Lloyd George was away in London, coping with economic problems and with Ireland, while Woodrow Wilson was in the United States. Thus, the British experts in the Commission on Polish Affairs, which was set up in early February, were left to make up their own minds and swung to support Polish claims. In early February, Sir Esme

Howard, of the British delegation, and Professor Robert H. Lord, of the United States delegation, came to an informal agreement along the lines of the United States recommendations—namely, that Danzig and a strip of territory along the west bank of the Vistula should go to Poland. British experts on Poland were persuaded to accept this solution by the memoranda of two knowledgeable Admiralty officials, Hamish J. Paton and Francis B. Bourdillon, who ably pleaded the justice of the Polish case.[22] Lewis B. Namier, who opposed it, was left fuming in London.[23] Their recommendations were criticized by such senior British officials as Sir Eyre Crowe, the assistant secretary of state, and Lord Hardinge, "the organizing Ambassador." Nevertheless, by early March, these officials, as well as Foreign Secretary Balfour, had concluded that Danzig would have to go to Poland.[24]

There were already indications, however, that the British government would oppose such a solution. Thus, Lloyd George warned the House of Commons on 12 February against creating "an Alsace-Lorraine type of situation" on the Polish-German frontier.[25] Colonel House was right when he reported to Wilson, eleven days later, that while French and British experts agreed that Danzig should go to Poland, the British government was opposed.[26] It is worth noting that two days after Lloyd George made his speech, the German foreign minister, Count Ulrich von Brockdorff-Rantzau, told the National Assembly that Poland's access to the sea should be secured in ways that would not affect German sovereignty.[27] Nevertheless, the report of the Commisssion on Polish Affairs, which was completed on 11 March, recommended that Danzig and the Warsaw-Mława-Danzig railway, with the territory along it, as well as "the so-called Polish Corridor," be given to Poland.[28]

These recommendations were to be reversed by Lloyd George. When he returned to Paris on 7 March, he was faced not only with an overwhelming inclination to grant Polish claims but also with French demands for the establishment of the Rhineland as a separate state. At the same time, a bitter Franco-British dispute had developed over French claims to Syria. By 12 March, Lloyd George stated that if these demands were not dropped, war between the Allies was inevitable.[29] Thus, France and Britain were headed for a showdown in which Polish claims constituted only one of the issues. As soon as the American president returned to Paris on 14 March, the British prime minister moved swiftly to secure the former's support against French proposals for the Rhineland. Lloyd George reached agreement with Wilson that French security be assured by an Anglo-American guarantee.[30] Thus forearmed, he was able to oppose both French and Polish claims on the grounds of self-determination and the danger of a Bolshevik revolution in Germany.

On 19 March, Lloyd George launched his attack on the report of the Commission on Polish Affairs. He claimed that the award of "two million Germans" to Poland would spell trouble for the latter. Furthermore, Germany might refuse to sign such a treaty, in which case there might be another Communist uprising (one had just broken out in Bavaria). He claimed that Danzig alone had a German population of 412,000 (his source for that figure is not known), and he protested against giving the German population along the Warsaw-Mława-Danzig railway to Poland. He suggested that since Germany was to be assured free communication through the Polish Corridor, then Poland should be assured the same along this particular railway. As for Danzig, he proposed that Poland be given free use of the port. Finally, although he knew this to be untrue, he claimed that the British members of the Commission on Polish Affairs had signed its report reluctantly.[31]

It was, however, a British expert, Lt. Col. Frederick M. Kisch—a member of the military section of the British delegation, an assistant to Sir William Tyrrell, and a member of the subcommittee on the Polish-German frontier—who took up the prime minister's challenge. Kisch proposed that the commission stand by its recommendation, and he actively helped to prepare a rebuttal to Lloyd George.[32] Worse still, the Paris press published the commission's report, together with a map. The prime minister protested violently against this "leak" and threatened to leave the conference unless measures were taken to secure secrecy. The result was the transformation of the Council of Ten into the Council of Four, at which only the heads of state of Britain, France, Italy, and the United States were present with their secretaries (Italy left the Council in April over the question of Fiume). The first problem to be tackled by this new body was Danzig.[33]

Lloyd George now retired with a few advisers to think out British policy aims; the result was the famous Fontainebleau Memorandum of 25 March 1919.[34] It was on this basis that he mounted a vigorous attack on French and Polish claims, using the arguments of self-determination and the danger of a Bolshevik revolution in Germany.[35] As far as Poland was concerned, Lloyd George hoped to cut her off entirely from the sea, but this proved to be impossible.[36] He did succeed, however, in securing Wilson's support for a compromise solution by which Danzig was to become a free city—a solution originally proposed by James W. Headlam-Morley, a Foreign Office expert on German affairs. Headlam-Morley and Dr. Sidney E. Mezes, a brother-in-law and a close adviser of President Wilson's, worked out a proposal that the free city be put under the protection of the League of Nations, and this suggestion won over the president, whose main goal was the establishment of the league.[37] Agreement in principle was reached on this proposal on the afternoon of 1 April.[38] Clemenceau grudgingly gave way, probably because

Lloyd George threatened to reverse his stand on German disarmament, reparations, and the Anglo-American guarantee to France.[39] Also, Clemenceau had strained his relations with Wilson, who was threatening to leave the Peace Conference. It is possible, too, that Clemenceau's resignation over Danzig had something to do with the Anglo-French agreement to oppose Wilson's proposal that an investigative commission be sent to Syria.[40]

Whatever the reason, Clemenceau bowed to the free-city solution. It is worth noting that Headlam-Morley and Mezes agreed that Danzig should be transferred first to the Allied and Associated Powers. Headlam-Morley believed that this would allow for consultation with the Danzigers,[41] but the main advantage was to avoid further Franco-British disputes. As it was, the Versailles Treaty articles on Danzig were drafted by British experts. The most important were: 104, which dealt with Polish rights; 107, on the division of former German state property between Danzig and Poland; 108, on Danzig's share of German reparations; and 103, on the constitution and the high commissioner of the League of Nations.[42] However, the final interpretation of these articles was left specifically to the Allied and Associated Powers, who were to negotiate the final agreement between Poland and Danzig.

Lloyd George's motives in opposing the award of Danzig to Poland have been variously interpreted as: (1) fear that the Germans would refuse to sign the treaty and that this would provoke a Bolshevik revolution in Germany; (2) support of self-determination; (3) desire to gain a firm footing in Danzig for British trade. None of these interpretations, however, is backed by conclusive evidence. Thus, at about the time when he claimed to fear that a German refusal to sign the treaty would provoke a Bolshevik revolution in Germany, British diplomats and emissaries were actively encouraging German resistance to French and Polish demands and were declaring their good will toward Germany.[43] As for self-determination, Lloyd George used it selectively. Thus, he protested against the inclusion of 2 million Germans in Poland, but he did not protest against the award of 3 million Sudeten Germans to Czechoslovakia. Also, he supported Greek claims in Turkey that went far beyond ethnically Greek territories. Finally, there is no evidence that he was interested in Danzig as a base for British trade with Poland and the rest of East-Central Europe. It is true that private British capital became involved later, in 1920, in the Danzig shipbuilding and railway industries,[44] but it was Germany which showed the greatest financial and economic interest in Danzig, and this for purely political reasons. The Polish government tried but failed to interest Britain in developing mutual trade. Thus, Lloyd George's motives must be sought elsewhere.

They can most probably be found in the desire to reach a provisional solution that would leave the door open for future revisions of the treaty to Germany's advantage. This was also the method used regarding the Rhineland and the Saar. In Danzig's case, this policy aimed to preserve its German character, thus safeguarding the chances of its returning to the Reich on the basis of "self-determination." We can find a confirmation of this line of thought in Lloyd George's speech in the House of Commons on 27 July 1936. He then declared that his aim in 1919 was to prevent a union of Danzig with the Polish Corridor, because the latter had a Polish majority and because such a solution would have led to the Polonization of the city.[45] Underlying this conciliation of Germany was the fear that a Polish-German war over Danzig would involve France and therefore Britain; this would be undesirable both because Britain wished to balance France and Germany and because Eastern Europe was not viewed as a sphere of vital British interests. During the next few years, Britain was to follow a policy of defending Danzig against Polonization. This was also the policy of Danzig's German administration, directed from Berlin.

It had been agreed in Paris that on the ratification of the Versailles Treaty, Danzig and the plebiscite areas in East Prussia would be handed over to the Allied Powers. The same was to apply to Prussian Poland (Posen), but a Polish uprising in late 1918 and early 1919 placed the territory under Polish administration. Meanwhile, a German administration remained in Danzig, East Prussia, and Upper Silesia.

The mayor of Danzig, Dr. Heinrich Sahm, wasted no time in contacting British officials and informing them of his view that the literal application of articles 104, 107, and 108 of the Versailles Treaty would mean the Polonization of the city.[46] Simultaneously, he persuaded the German government to give financial aid to Danzig's key industries so as to retain the German workers there and thus prevent the enterprises from falling into Polish hands.[47] Sahm, who was to prove a doughty fighter in preserving the *Deutschtum* of Danzig, deserves a few words of introduction. He was a German civil servant who had worked in the German administration of occupied Poland during the war. In November 1918 he had been appointed mayor of Danzig. In 1920 he became the president of the Danzig Senate, a post that he held until 1930; he then became the mayor of Berlin and ended his career as German minister to Norway. Physically a giant of a man, he was a tenacious opponent of Poland. He showed great perspicacity in 1919, in proposing that Danzig stay with Germany but accept far-reaching "state servitudes" to Poland. These would include a free port under Polish administration, Polish customs regulations, Polish administration of the Vistula between Warsaw and Danzig, and Polish tariffs on the connecting German railway lines. However, this plan was bitterly opposed by Königsberg, which saw it as a selfish gambit by Danzig to monopolize Polish trade; and it was rejected by the German government.[48]

Sahm's appeal to British officials probably strengthened the British government's desire to keep Danzig out of Polish hands; it may also have suggested the legal means of achieving this aim. Whatever the case may be, in the fall of 1919 the British were able to persuade the French to divide the burden of occupation in the plebiscite territories so that British troops were preponderant in East Prussia and Danzig, while the French had preponderance in Upper Silesia.[49] In mid August, agreement was also reached that the Allied administrator in Danzig would be British,[50] while a Frenchman was to occupy the same post in Memel. It was probably at about this time or a little earlier that Lloyd George and Clemenceau reached a secret agreement that as long as an Englishman was the league's high commissioner in Danzig, so long a Frenchman would be president of the Governing Commission in the Saar. The French would also get the presidency of the Frontier Delimitation Commission in Poland.[51] Thus, Clemenceau resigned from any effective French presence in Danzig.

Unaware of this fact, the Polish government for some time suffered from the delusion that the Versailles Treaty's articles on Danzig could, in fact, be interpreted as meaning Polish administration of the port and, in general, preponderant Polish influence in the city. The first Polish draft for the convention with the free city claimed Polish administration of the port and the port railways, Polish customs officials, complete equality for Polish nationals and Danzig citizens, and last but not least, a military and naval base in the city. The draft made no mention of a high commissioner, but it did propose the use of generally accepted methods of arbitration. This proposal was heavily criticized by officials of the Foreign Office as well as the League of Nations.[52] The Polish delegation to the Conference of Ambassadors in Paris withdrew the draft but resubmitted it in January 1920 with only slight modifications.

Meanwhile, in late November 1919, the Poles received an indication of negative British reactions to their draft from Sir Reginald Tower, who had been appointed the Allied administrator for Danzig. Tower, who had previously been the British consul in Buenos Aires, knew German, for he had served in the British consulate in Munich before the war. The briefing he received on the Polish draft of the convention only confirmed the views that he had formulated after a brief visit to Berlin, Danzig, and Warsaw. He had then concluded that the Poles were only waiting to "stampede" Danzig. He also believed that they would be no match for the Germans in local negotiations.[53] In any event, it was decided that only preparatory talks would take place in Danzig, while the negotiations would be conducted in Paris. A young British diplomat, Edward Hallett Carr, who was to be intimately concerned with these negotiations, was pleased; he hoped that Polish ministers would be excluded from the negotiations in Paris.[54] Under these circumstances, Tower told Polish delegates in Paris at the end of November that, in his opinion, Poland had no right to administer the port but only the right to enjoy its "free use and service." In his report to the Foreign Office, he stated that those who believed that the Versailles Treaty gave Poland the right to administer the port were fools.[55] This British interpretation of article 104 was soon confirmed from another quarter. Gen. Sir Richard Haking, the commander of the British battalion in Danzig, had no sooner arrived there on 4 February 1920 then he cabled Tower, who was still in Paris, that the Polish-Danzig convention should be delayed until Danzig's demands had been examined. Like Sahm, he claimed that if article 104 were interpreted literally, Danzig would not be a "Free State." He also criticized the Poles for lacking experienced administrators to take over the port.[56] Tower, of course, held the same views. It was no coincidence that on the same day he voiced serious objections to Polish delegates in Paris on the Polish draft convention that had been submitted in January.[57]

Given his previous opinions, it is not surprising that after arriving in Danzig, Tower sent long and detailed reports to the Conference of Ambassadors in Paris, stressing Polish obstruction and ineptitude and blaming the Poles for the existing tension in Danzig. These reports served to build a foundation for Britain's aim of securing her interpretation of the two most important articles on Danzig in the Versailles Treaty—namely, 104 and 107. In his reports, Tower took no account of the fact that Poland herself was suffering from food shortages and chaotic administration or that the Polish military administration in the Corridor (Polish Pomerania) was no more heavy-handed than most military administrations tend to be. He did not seem to notice either that while the Poles vividly remembered Germany's policy of forced assimilation in Prussian Poland and her oppressive occupation of Russian Poland during the war,[58] the hostile attitude of the Germans in the Corridor did nothing to make things easier. Oblivious to all these factors, Tower used every incident to point out Polish shortcomings. But this was only a variation on the theme voiced by Sahm, which harmonized with Tower's views and those of Haking. This theme was that article 104 could not be interpreted as giving Poland control over the port of Danzig. Tower's arguments were directed at the representatives of the Allied Powers at the Conference of Ambassadors in Paris, since they were to negotiate the final treaty between Danzig and Poland. Here, Britain had to have arguments to gain at least Italian support in order to overcome French support of Warsaw. Thus, it is not surprising that only two weeks after his arrival in Danzig, Tower informed the Conference of Ambassadors that the Poles were "misreading" the meaning of article 104 of the treaty by claiming the right to administer the port, and he criticized "the rough and ready division of water for Poland and land for Danzig." As he wrote to E. H. Carr, he and his staff believed that such "high-handed measures" could not be carried out without doing "serious injustice to the German element" in Danzig.[59] Thus, he clearly supported President Sahm, with whom he had established a close and friendly relationship. Like Sahm, Tower believed that if paragraphs 2, 3, and 4 of article 104 were to be applied literally, Poland would, in fact, control the port and therefore the city.

Tower's opening gambit was followed by pleas to delay negotiations for the Polish-Danzig convention. These pleas were simultaneously bolstered by complaints against the Poles for continually provoking border incidents. At the same time, Tower supported Danzig's pleas for extending its borders to include the town of Tczew (Dirschau), with its important railway bridge. He also opposed Polish attempts to lease key real estate in the port of Danzig.[60] By mid March, Tower was proposing that until the convention had been signed, one of the Allied Powers should take over the administration of the port.[61] Haking, for his part, relayed alarmist reports of a possible Polish takeover of Danzig and even suggested that it might be best to withdraw Allied troops from the city. However, cooler heads prevailed; the Foreign Office, at least, believed Polish denials of military concentrations. Indeed, Poland was unlikely to attack Allied troops, not least because British naval units stood in the Bay of Danzig.[62]

Tower went to Paris at the end of April and pleaded for the modification of article 104, which, in his view (and Sahm's), implied Polish administration of the port. He met with strong resistance from the French, who were supported by the Italians.[63] However, on 7 May, Lord Derby, the British ambassador to the Conference of Ambassadors, formally proposed that the port administration be entrusted to a Mixed Harbor Board, which, he argued, worked so well in his hometown of Liverpool. The French were able to dilute this proposal to a "recommendation," but they agreed that Poland should not have a military or naval base in Danzig.[64] (We might note that on this very day, Polish troops entered Kiev, having launched this offensive against the Bolsheviks to the accompaniment of British and, to a lesser extent, French disapproval.) The conference's decision that Poland was to have no military or naval base in Danzig was a heavy blow for her. As Haking noted, no administration was effective without physical or at least moral force to back it.[65] Also, the Polish General Staff considered the defense of the Corridor impossible unless Poland had a military base in Danzig.

Heinrich Sahm was very pleased with the results of Tower's trip to Paris. He claimed in his memoirs that he had built on Lord Derby's proposal by suggesting that the Mixed Harbor Board also control the port railways.[66] It is not surprising that Polish-Danzig talks held at the end of May, under the auspices of Tower and E. H. Carr, yielded no results. The stalemate was broken, however, by the disastrous Polish retreat before the oncoming Red

Army. This gave Lloyd George leverage for furthering British aims in Danzig.

By July 1920 the Polish armies were in full retreat, hotly pursued by the Red Army. The Polish government appealed to France and Britain for help. Prime Minister Władysław Grabski was dispatched to Spa, where Lloyd George and President Alexandre Millerand were conferring on German reparations. Grabski's reception there and the terms offered to Poland have been described elsewhere.[67] Here we will concentrate on Danzig. After Grabski had accepted the conditions for Allied aid, which included an Allied decision on Danzig, Lord Curzon raised the issue on 11 July. Significantly, he stated that the "difficulty" with articles 104 and 107 of the Versailles Treaty was that if carried out, all the trade and the development of the waterways would be in Polish hands, while the land property would belong to the population of Danzig. He then claimed that Poland and Danzig had "agreed" to the establishment of a "joint authority" under a chairman appointed by the League of Nations, which would administer the port and all local transit services (i.e., the Mixed Harbor Board). Polish tariffs would apply, but the customs revenue would be divided between Poland and Danzig. Tower was instructed to start negotiations along these lines.[68] All that the French were willing or able to obtain for the Poles was a legal loophole: British assent to the word *puisse* (may) to qualify the proposal that both Danzig and Poland accept the Harbor Board.[69]

The heads of state also decided to send an Allied mission to Poland to report on the situation. However, while the French hoped for a Polish victory under Gen. Maxime Weygand (who was to replace Piłsudski as commander in chief), the British aimed to pressure the Poles into signing an armistice with the Soviets.[70] As it happened, neither of these aims was fulfilled. Piłsudski could not be replaced, and the Soviet armistice terms were rejected, with French support, although the British government had advised that they be accepted. Piłsudski then defeated the Soviet armies.[71]

Meanwhile, however, at the height of the Polish crisis, Sir Reginald Tower, on orders from London, halted the unloading of ships with supplies for Poland on the pretext that this would unleash a dockers' strike. In London, Lloyd George assured the Soviet emissaries, with whom he was negotiating a trade treaty, that no arms would reach Poland through Danzig if Poland signed an armistice with Soviet Russia.[72] Tower did not protest when the Danzig Senate proclaimed the city's neutrality on 20 August.[73] It was at this time that a shipment of horses was unloaded in the little fishing port of Gdynia in the Polish Corridor, about eighteen kilometers west of Danzig. This was an omen of things to come.

On 20 August, when Piłsudski's victory was no longer in doubt, a Franco-British clash over Danzig seemed imminent. A French cruiser, the

Gueydon, arrived with orders from Marshal Foch to effect the unloading of supplies. Foch even authorized the transfer of French troops from Memel for this purpose if necessary.[74] Lloyd George—who was then conferring with the Italian prime minister, Giovanni Giolitti, in Lucerne, Switzerland—was forced to change his stand, since the British press was indignant at his support of Soviet terms for Poland. He now declared that the Soviet government had not revealed all of its demands to him. He blamed the Danzig "local Council" for stopping the unloading of supplies for Poland, and he called for aid to Poland.[75] Tower was ordered to permit the unloading, which was resumed on 26 August. By then Poland had been saved, but the Poles could not forget Danzig's attitude during the war or the blockage of supplies there. They began to think of developing their own port in Gdynia.[76]

Although the Allies did not send help after the Russians had entered ethnic Poland—as they had promised to do at Spa—the Poles could do nothing to reverse their acceptance of future Allied decisions on Danzig. The French, for their part, decided that they could do no more than fight a diplomatic rear-guard action on Poland's behalf. This was further complicated by Franco-British disputes over the activities of Gen. Henri Le Rond, head of the Inter-Allied Plebiscite Commission in Upper Silesia, whom the British accused of having supported Polish insurrectionists in the area. When the Polish and Danzig delegations in Paris presented totally contradictory drafts for the convention, Lord Derby obtained French agreement to the proposal that the Conference of Ambassadors appoint a mixed commission to work out a draft of its own. Also, British insistence on the establishment of a Mixed Harbor Board won the day, in return for allowing General Le Rond to continue at his post in Upper Silesia, though with reduced powers.[77] Sahm had been informed ahead of time of the possibility of such a "deal" by Tower's colleague, Captain Charley.[78] Sahm, who was in Paris as the head of the Danzig delegation, also kept in close touch with E. H. Carr, the British representative on the mixed commission that was assigned the task of drafting the convention.

The heart of this draft was the Harbor Board. It was to have the right of administering the port and the port railways and of taking over whatever former German state property it needed (this involved article 107). The French obtained some minor concessions for Poland, such as the Harbor Board's obligation to "consult" her on the administration of the Vistula, her right to "object" to the board's control of the port railways, and her right to "supervise" Danzig customs officials. These slight gains were small consolation to the Poles for losing control of the port, for the prohibition of a Polish military and naval base, and for the increased powers of the high commissioner. The Danzig delegation, highly pleased with the convention, signed it on 9 November 1920. Ignacy Paderewski, now the head of the Polish delegation, was allowed some delay but finally signed on 18 November, on the promise that the league would grant Poland a "defense mandate" for Danzig.[79]

However, this mandate, when finally worked out by French and British diplomats, turned out to be worthless. As presented to the League Council on 22 June 1921 by Count Kikujiro Ishii, the rapporteur on Danzig affairs, it stipulated that the high commissioner must request the League Council to allow Polish military intervention either for the defense of Danzig or in order to restore order in the city. But the high commissioner could—and this was a concession to France—"anticipate" league instructions by asking the Polish government to intervene in an "emergency situation." Finally, as a concession to Poland, the high commissioner was to "examine" the means of providing a *port d'attache* for Polish warships in Danzig.[80] This was not to be a naval base, but a place where Polish warships could dock for refueling, supplies, and repairs.

The Polish-Danzig Convention, or, as it was more frequently referred to, the Paris Convention, was indeed "a German-Danziger Convention," as Col. A. B. Barber, head of the American Technical Mission in Poland, called it.[81] Lt. Comdr. Eric L. Wharton, R.N., head of the British Naval Mission in Poland, held similar views. He believed that if Danzig was supposed to secure Poland's access to the sea, then the Poles should be given more control of the port than the Danzigers. He also agreed with Polish military experts that the only way in which Poland could prepare against a German attack on the Corridor was to take peacetime defensive measures in Danzig. As for Polish rights in Danzig, he noted: "A convention backed by nothing but illusory guarantees of defense could lead nowhere." He reported that the Poles were saying they would let Danzig go its own way and develop Gdynia.[82] Sahm, for his part, extended his thanks to Tower for helping the Danzig cause. He wrote that while Danzig had not won, it had not been vanquished either. He likewise acknowledged General Haking's support in various disputes with Poland, including the Defense Mandate.[83] Thus, the foundations for protecting the city's *Deutschtum* had been well and truly laid.

By the summer of 1921, Danzig was under a thinly disguised German domination. German government subsidies, funneled through the German consulate general, paid for pensions and unemployment benefits. German banks controlled the assets of Danzig banks, while the great German industrialist Hugo Stinnes had already bought most of the Danzig ships in 1920.[84] The administration was, of course, German. German civil servants automatically acquired Danzig citizenship; their service in the free city was counted as service in Germany, and they could transfer automatically to the

Reich. Bernardo Attolico, who served as the high commissioner ad interim in December 1920 before Haking took up his post, reported: "Danzig is a frank and avowed German and anti-Polish community."[85] The situation was no different a year later. The deputy secretary general of the League of Nations, Joseph Avenol, reported in March 1922 that the whole constitutional and administrative organization of Danzig was based on the German model. The administrative structure was, he observed, more suitable to an empire than to a territory with a population of 360,000.[86] Danzig also had a paramilitary police force; even Haking noted the fact that it was led by former Prussian officers in close touch with Berlin. The police possessed not only rifles but also machine guns.[87] The Danzig Constitution, while guaranteed by the league, was modeled on Weimar's; and Danzig political parties, except for the small Polish Party, were branches of German parties. The same was true of the trade unions. The Danzig administration, led by the redoubtable Sahm, recognized the supremacy of politics over economics. The Danzig Senate assured Berlin that it was conducting, not Danzig economic politics, but German politics, and considered it a patriotic duty to suffer the sacrifices that this entailed.[88]

A key element in keeping Danzig German was its industry. Danzig managed to keep the most important industrial enterprises out of Polish hands; it succeeded in doing so with the help of British and French industrialists. The enterprises involved were the former Imperial Navy Yard, known as the Danziger Werft, and the railway workshops at Troyl. In 1919, Sahm had already managed to obtain German subsidies to employ the workers and to modernize the plant equipment, as well as to have both enterprises transferred to Danzig trusteeship. He succeeded in interesting the members of the Allied Commission for the Division of Former German State Property in Danzig, set up in February 1921, in a scheme of vesting the property rights in the city on condition that it would then lease them to an international company. At first the director of the navy yard, Dr. Ludwig Noë, tried to have the property taken over by an English firm, Craven's Ltd., but France foiled this plan. After long negotiations, it was finally agreed that the enterprises would be jointly vested in Danzig and Poland, who would then lease them for fifty years to the International Shipbuilding and Engineering Company Ltd. of Danzig. The shares were divided as follows: French and British representatives held 30 percent each, while Danzig and Poland held 20 percent each. Poland was, moreover, obliged to sign a contract guaranteeing orders to the railway yards for ten years. Thus, Poland lost out once more, for she had aimed either at full ownership of this valuable property or at least 50 percent control over it.[89]

Despite the setbacks of the Paris Convention and the decision on the naval shipyard and the railway workshops, Poland at first followed a policy of conciliation toward Danzig. This was most clearly visible in the Warsaw Convention, signed by Danzig and Poland on 18 October 1921. The convention established a customs union between Poland and Danzig as envisaged in the Versailles Treaty, thus abolishing import and export duties on the traffic of goods between the free city and Poland. Warsaw made many concessions to secure the city's good will. Thus, Danzig was allowed to import raw materials and half-finished goods from Germany and to export finished goods abroad. Poland also gave up the weapon of economic pressure by agreeing to supply the city with food and fuel on the same terms as her own population. She agreed to divide the customs revenues on the basis of the very favorable ratio of six Danzigers to one Pole, thus recognizing the higher standard of living in the city. However, Sahm jealously guarded the Senate's prerogative of granting Danzig citizenship and of expelling undesirable persons, as well as granting permission to buy real estate and to employ Poles. He even refused to recognize that expulsion was subject to arbitration by the high commissioner. Also, while Poles living in Danzig were guaranteed the right to establish their own schools, this was in every case subject to senatorial agreement.[90]

But the Warsaw Convention did not have the effects desired by Poland. Constant disputes raged between the two parties. In most cases the high commissioners supported Danzig, which, more often than not, also took the initiative of bringing the disputes before the League of Nations Council. The result was that over the period 1921 to 1934, seventy such disputes went to Geneva, of which forty-nine were initiated by Danzig, fifteen by the Polish government, and six by both sides.[91] These disputes included Polish demands for a 50-50 ratio in Polish and Danzig personnel to be employed by the Harbor Board; the Polish demand that the harbor police be under the authority of the board and not of Danzig; the problem of the Polish railway administration; the site of the Polish *port d'attache;* the Munitions Depot, as well as the guard there; the Polish Post Office; Polish conduct of Danzig's foreign relations; double taxation; the status of personnel in the office of the Polish commissioner general; and whether Danzig was a sovereign state or not. It would take too long to describe each dispute, so three examples must suffice. Danzig did not hand over a building for the use of the Polish Post Office until January 1925; the problems of the *port d'attache* and of the Munition Depot and its guard, though formally settled in 1925, dragged on until 1932.

Frustrated by Danzig's obstructive policy, Polish public opinion forced the government to attempt to abrogate the Paris Convention and to obtain league recognition of the Versailles Treaty as the basis for Polish rights in

Danzig. This attempt was made in July 1923, but it failed because of British opposition and lack of French support. The British government opposed the Polish request despite the fact that both Sir Eric Drummond, the secretary general of the League of Nations, and Sir William Max Muller, the British minister in Warsaw, shared the Polish view that the Paris Convention had not secured the advantages promised to Poland by article 104 of the Versailles Treaty and that changes should therefore be made. It is also worth noting that the British consul in Danzig, Basil Fry, drew certain conclusions from the experience of the free city when suggesting a statute for Memel, which he proposed should also become a free city. In December 1922 he advised against setting up a mixed harbor board in Memel, saying it "would be not only a grave and needless expense but actually prejudicial to the interest of the port." (The Poles, of course, wished to abolish the Mixed Harbor Board in Danzig.) Furthermore, he advised against a treaty that would permit the free interchange of officials with any foreign country.[92] (Danzig had such a treaty with Germany.) It is difficult to avoid the impression that the different British attitudes toward Danzig and Memel stemmed from the fact that Britain wished Memel to be free of German influence, while it assumed that Danzig would and should return to Germany at some future time.

In July 1923, British opposition was decisive. It was based on the assumptions that Poland wished to Polonize Danzig and that she should not be allowed to do so. The French failed to support the Poles, because they wished to maintain their 1919 agreement with Britain on Danzig and the Saar.[93] But the series of Polish-Danzig agreements concluded between August and December 1923 clearly demonstrates how obstructive, in fact, Danzig policy had been. Thus, Danzig agreed that the harbor police be put under the authority of the Harbor Board and that the latter should aim to employ Polish and Danzig employees on a 50-50 ratio. The board's right to apply for foreign loans was to be subject to negotiation and not be an automatic right, as ruled by the high commissioner; Poland then resumed her subventions to the board, which had been suspended since 1921. Danzig accepted Polish customs regulations as binding and agreed that differences of opinion should not delay their application. The Senate agreed to inform the Polish commissioner general of its decisions on Polish applications for the acquisition of Danzig property. Polish citizens could no longer be arrested for nonpayment of taxes, except by decision of a court of law. The high commissioner was to examine cases regarding the equal rights of Polish nationals before the Senate issued any regulations. Other agreements concerned the Polish conduct of the city's foreign relations, the diplomatic status of Polish government property and personnel, and the taxes imposed thereon. However, Danzig reserved the right to reopen the disputes by qualifying all these agreements as "provisional."[94]

The most important agreement concerned the establishment of a separate Danzig currency, and this was the clue to Sahm's concessions, provisional though they were. The city used German currency and was therefore hard hit by the galloping inflation that followed the Franco-Belgian occupation of the Ruhr in January 1923. As Sahm confessed in his memoirs, in signing the whole series of agreements and particularly the one on Danzig currency, he was motivated by the fear that if the German situation took a turn for the worse, Poland could exert economic pressure on the city, particularly by curtailing orders for the railway workshops of the Danzig Engineering and Shipbuilding Company. Therefore, much to his regret, he had to make some concessions to Poland.[95] The new currency, the gulden, valued at one-twenty-fifth of the English pound sterling, was established with the aid of a sizeable loan from British banks.[96] But as Dr. Ludwig Noë, now the director of the International Engineering and Shipbuilding Company, foresaw, the gulden was pegged too high and therefore raised costs in the port of Danzig, thus hurting it in competition with other Baltic ports.[97] An aspect unwelcome to Danzig was partial Polish control of the assets of the new Bank of Danzig, for Poland provided 28 percent of its funding capital.[98] Nonetheless, this gain was small compensation for Poland's failure to establish her own currency in Danzig. The net result of the agreements signed in the last quarter of 1923 was to strengthen the free city, not Poland.

Developments in the international situation during 1924/25 led to a more favorable attitude toward Poland on the part of Britain and, therefore, the League of Nations. The successful negotiations for the Dawes Plan in April 1924—which scaled down German reparations and set up a new schedule of payments—presaged a reconciliation between Germany, on the one hand, and France on the other, a reconciliation that was the aim of both French and British policy. The effect of this in Danzig was a change of attitude by the high commissioner. Sir Mervyn Sorley MacDonnell, who had succeeded Haking in February 1923, was as firm a supporter of the Danzig Senate as his predecessor had been. In April 1924, however, he urged Vice-President Dr. Ernst Ziehm to avoid an anti-Polish policy.[99] In the summer he urged Sahm to avoid holding congresses of German associations in Danzig for the next four or five years. He said that, for once, Danzig should reckon with Polish susceptibilities. Furthermore, he asked the president to keep disputes with Poland off the agenda of the League Council. Sahm refused to consider these requests.[100] The objective of all this advice was to achieve relatively good relations between the free city and Poland before Germany entered the League of Nations, and thus to avert Polish-German confrontations in Geneva. However, Danzig was also to be secured against any Polish encroachments. Thus, in November 1924, MacDonnell more than balanced his counsels of moderation to the Senate by declaring that Danzig was a sovereign state in the international sense of the word. Of course, Berlin supported Danzig's claim to sovereignty as a legal basis for "defending" the free city against Poland.[101]

In 1925 the prospect of Franco-German reconciliation advanced further with Gustav Stresemann's proposal for a Rhine pact—that is, an agreement guaranteeing French and Belgian frontiers with Germany. This proposal, made by the German foreign minister at the end of January to Britain and in early February to France, opened the way to negotiations that finally resulted in the Locarno Treaties of 16 October 1925. The aim of obtaining German entry into the league led the British government to press for the settlement of outstanding Polish-Danzig disputes. Furthermore, in preparation for abandoning its protectorate over the city through British high commissioners, the British government sought a new procedure that would keep these disputes off the agenda of council sessions. At the same time, the view of the British foreign secretary, Sir Austen Chamberlain, as of the majority of Foreign Office experts, was that German entry into the league would open up prospects of that body's negotiating a revision of the Polish-German frontier in the Corridor and in Upper Silesia.[102] It should be noted, however, that while Austen Chamberlain hewed to the traditional British policy of noninvolvement in Eastern Europe and rejected suggestions that times had changed so that Britain could no longer display lack of political interest there, he also opposed an immediate revision of the Polish-German frontier.[103] In 1926 he voiced strong criticism of the German policy on Danzig and of German opposition to the Polish frontier as established by the Versailles Treaty.[104] As late as May 1929 he still hoped that at some future time, revision would come by mutual Polish-German agreement.[105]

Despite its drawbacks, the year 1925 brought some Polish successes. MacDonnell reported at the March session of the league that new machinery for resolving Polish-Danzig disputes should be developed; otherwise, once Germany took her seat at the League Council, Polish-Danzig disputes would become Polish-German disputes. He suggested that the council's rapporteur on Danzig affairs could serve as arbitrator or that a committee of three be set up to deal with Polish-Danzig disputes. Finally, it was decided that MacDonnell's tenure would be extended for only one more year; the same applied to Victor Rault, the French president of the Saar Governing Commission.[106]

This state of affairs brought Poland some immediate gains. Thus, contrary to MacDonnell, who supported Danzig, J. M. Quiñones de León, the rapporteur on Danzig affairs, suggested that the dispute over the Polish mailboxes (January 1925) be submitted to the Permanent Tribunal of International Justice at The Hague, together with the recommendation that

Poland had the right to more than one building for her postal services.[107] He also overruled MacDonnell's pronouncement on Danzig's sovereignty, declaring that the status of the free city had been defined by the Versailles Treaty. Also, once again, it was decided to put the harbor police under the control of the Harbor Board.[108] In May, The Hague tribunal ruled in Poland's favor on the mailboxes—that is, that Poland had the right to set them up and to collect mail outside the premises of her one existing post-office building.[109] A commission of three was then set up to delimit the port area where the Polish postal service could operate. The commission's report favored the Polish view that the port included not only waterways but also land, and it drew a "green line," which included essential parts of the business district in the port area. Sahm's accusation that the commission was biased was rejected, as was his request that the dispute be submitted once more to The Hague.[110] Finally, the delimitation of the area for the Polish munitions depot at Westerplatte—which was designated for this purpose by the League Council in March 1924—was carried out.[111] Despite Sahm's protests, the area was handed over to Poland on 31 October 1925. In December the League Council agreed to the Polish demand that a military unit of sixty-eight enlisted men and twenty officers be assigned to guard the munitions depot. Again, this was done over Sahm's vehement protests. In December 1925 the League Council agreed, in a secret session, that MacDonnell's term should end in February 1926 and that he would be succeeded by a Dutchman, Dr. Joost van Hamel. This decision was immediately made public.[112] It was greeted with great hostility by the German and Danzig press, which claimed that Hamel had displayed an anti-German stance during the war. His term of office was made very difficult by constant attacks, not only on his policy but also on his personal reputation. It is not surprising that he ended his service as a confirmed critic of Danzig and of German policy.[113]

The year 1925 ended with Polish gains in Danzig, but also with a very difficult economic situation for Poland. The existing inflation was accelerated by the outbreak of the Polish-German tariff war in June. The apparently imminent bankruptcy of Poland seemed to bear out calculations that such a breakdown would give Germany the best chance of putting forward her demands for Danzig and the Corridor.[114] Danzig, although it also suffered from Poland's ills, looked forward hopefully to her complete collapse. Sahm believed that this would lead either to a Polish-German economic union or the return of the free city to Germany as the condition for an international loan for Poland, which was to be raised with German participation.[115] Meanwhile, in the international context, the Polish-Danzig problem was now seen as a European problem. The British ambassador in Berlin, Lord D'Abernon, noted in early January 1926 that since Locarno had reduced the danger on the Franco-German frontier, Danzig had become the "danger spot of Europe.''[116] This was, of course, the view assiduously propagated by German diplomats and statesmen. It obfuscated the real issue, which was pointed out in August 1926 by A. W. G. Randall of the Foreign Office, when he wrote:

> Danzig was less a factor in Polish-German differences than a touchstone of Polish-German relations. When Polish-German relations improve, Danzig-Polish relations will improve, and, alternatively—though perhaps to a lesser degree—when Danzig-Polish relations improve . . . , the development of Polish-German relations may be expected to start from a more favourable point of departure.[117]

Randall's opinion was, in fact, shared by Marshal Piłsudski, who always maintained that Danzig was the touchstone of Polish-German relations.[118] The history of the next fourteen years, until September 1939, was to bear out the analysis made separately by a Foreign Office official and by the greatest statesman of modern Poland.

5

The Polish-Lithuanian Dispute
over Vilna, 1918–22

The dispute between Poland and Lithuania over the city and region of Vilna,* which originated in the last years of World War I, was to poison Polish-Lithuanian relations until March 1938. As in the case of Danzig, the dispute involved far more than the fate of a city and its inhabitants.[1] In 1919 the Western Powers viewed it as part of the unresolved Russian question. As long as the White Russian forces seemed to have a chance of winning the civil war, France and Britain assumed that the Baltic provinces would return to a non-Bolshevik Russia. They also opposed the establishment of German influence in the region, fearing that this would lead to dominant German influence in Russia. From the end of 1919 onward, when the Bolsheviks were clearly winning the civil war, the British government aimed to secure good trade relations with Russia by supporting a solution of the Vilna question that would be acceptable to the Soviets. However, French support of General Wrangel required effective Polish military action against the Red Army and therefore assured selective French support for Polish aims. After Piłsudski's victory in the Polish-Soviet war in August–September 1920 and after Wrangel's debacle in the Crimea shortly thereafter, Britain generally supported Lithuania against Poland. This was because the Soviets had recognized Vilna as the capital of Lithuania in their treaty with the latter in July 1920, and so it was assumed that Britain's support for this solution would strengthen her bid for the Russian market. Also the Vilna question provided Lloyd George with a means of putting pressure on Poland with regard to East

---

* The Russian name of Vilna is used here because of its general acceptance in Western literature. The Polish name is Wilno; the Lithuanian, Vilnius.

Galicia and Memel. The French generally supported Poland—that is, Piłsudski's aim of establishing a federation with Lithuania. This was due to the French belief that Lithuania herself would be too weak to withstand German pressure. However, by May 1922, and particularly after Lloyd George's resignation as prime minister in October, the British also came to favor federation.

It is therefore in the context of the Russian question that we should see the opposing objectives of the Polish and Lithuanian leaders regarding Vilna and Polish-Lithuanian relations. On the Polish side, Józef Piłsudski, chief of state and commander in chief of the army, aimed at establishing a Polish-Lithuanian federation—including Belorussia—in order to prevent German or Russian domination of the region, to weaken Russia, and to secure one of the two "gates" against the invasion of Poland from the East. The Vilna region constituted this gate in the northeast, while East Galicia was the gate in the southeast. Between them lay the Polesie Marshes, which were impassable to armies. Secondly, the Vilna region was preponderantly Polish-speaking, and Vilna itself, though half-Polish and half-Jewish, was a historic center of Polish culture. Thirdly, the region was indispensable to Poland as a direct land connection with Latvia. Finally, Piłsudski planned to link the Polish-Lithuanian federation with a Polish-Ukrainian bloc based on an alliance between Poland and an independent Ukraine. However, majority Polish opinion opposed federation and had little or no interest in an independent Ukraine; on the contrary, it demanded the annexation of the Vilna region, western Belorussia, and East Galicia to Poland.

Federation with Poland was also violently opposed by Lithuanian public opinion. The Lithuanians aimed at the establishment of the largest possible state. They hated the Poles and played Germany off against Soviet Russia so as to prevent the establishment of any federal bonds with Poland. From the long-term point of view, a Polish-Lithuanian federation might well have been the best solution for both countries; but this idea had more enemies than friends.

The Polish-Lithuanian Commonwealth, which existed from 1569 to 1795, constituted a historical precedent for union between a reborn Poland and Lithuania. However, Lithuanian nationalism was more anti-Polish than anti-Russian. Lithuanian nationalists resented Russian domination, but in forging a modern national identity, they perceived their most dangerous enemy to be Poland. Therefore, they saw any form of union as a renewal of Polish domination. We should bear in mind that the Lithuanian and Belorussian gentry had become Polonized by the end of the seventeenth century and that until the 1880s Lithuanian had remained a predominantly

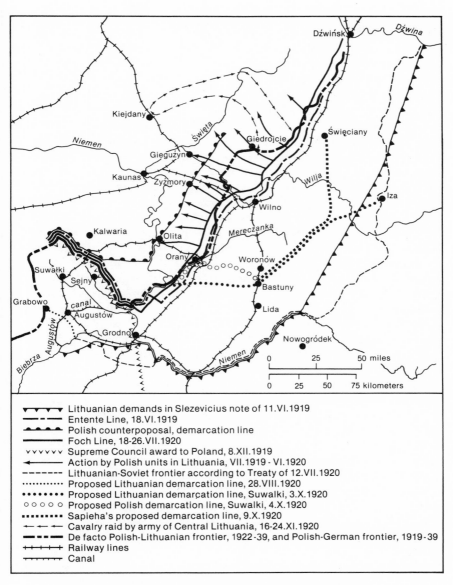

Lithuanian demands in Slezevicius note of 11.VI.1919
Entente Line, 18.VI.1919
Polish counterpoposal, demarcation line
Foch Line, 18-26.VII.1920
Supreme Council award to Poland, 8.XII.1919
Action by Polish units in Lithuania, VII.1919 - VI.1920
Lithuanian-Soviet frontier according to Treaty of 12.VII.1920
Proposed Lithuanian demarcation line, 28.VIII.1920
Proposed Lithuanian demarcation line, Suwalki, 3.X.1920
Proposed Polish demarcation line, Suwalki, 4.X.1920
Sapieha's proposed demarcation line, 9.X.1920
Cavalry raid by army of Central Lithuania, 16-24.XI.1920
De facto Polish-Lithuanian frontier, 1922-39, and Polish-German frontier, 1919-39
Railway lines
Canal

Map 4.   Polish-Lithuanian Demarcation Lines, 1919/20

115

peasant language. Since Polish nobles owned most of the land and since Poles filled most church offices, the fight for spreading the Lithuanian language in the latter part of the nineteenth century was both a cultural and a class struggle.

The cradle of modern Lithuanian nationalism was in the Trans-Niemen region. Here, prosperous Lithuanian peasant-farmers provided their sons with the means to obtain higher education, and the latter became the first leaders of the modern Lithuanian national movement.[2] They sought inspiration, not in the Polish-Lithuanian Commonwealth, but in the old Grand Duchy of Lithuania before its union with Poland. For them, Vilna symbolized the greatness of old Lithuania, which had briefly encompassed most of Belorussia, Volhynia, Podolia, and part of the Ukraine. Since the population of certain parts of the old duchy had become Polonized—which was particularly the case in the Vilna and Suwałki regions—or spoke Belorussian, the Lithuanians claimed that the land was Lithuanian "by blood" and should, therefore, be part of the Lithuanian state.[3]

This objective conflicted with the general Polish view that not only predominantly Polish-speaking territories but also those in which the Poles constituted a significant majority should belong to Poland. This program was formulated by Roman Dmowski, who called the Lithuanians a "tribe."[4] He opposed federalism on the grounds that Poland would weaken herself by absorbing areas that lacked at least a significant Polish minority. He believed that, given time and state support, such a minority would Polonize the "nationally immature" majority in any given region. Dmowski's views were shared by the vast majority of Polish opinion, which was, moreover, as much enamored of the old commonwealth as the Lithuanians were of old Lithuania.

A small part of the Polish elite, however, held that the non-Polish populations of the borderlands should enjoy home rule in a voluntary federation with Poland. These "federalists" included not only Piłsudski and his close supporters but also the Socialist Party and the left wing of the Peasant Party. This new federal concept was both revolutionary and democratic. It stemmed from the 1863 manifesto of the Polish "Reds," or radicals, who then led the revolt against Russia and offered the peoples of the old borderlands a choice between union or federation with Poland. The insurrection failed, but the idea was developed further by Polish Socialists in the period 1880 to 1900. They then combined the idea of federation with the right of national self-determination. Interestingly enough, this new concept was first applied to Poland and Lithuania, In 1891, Stanisław Mendelson rejected both the old "historic" Poland and "ethnographic" Poland. He spoke of a "revolutionary Poland," which would establish its own frontiers after crushing Russia, and of "a close revolutionary connection" between Poland and Lithuania, since Lithuania would be too weak to stand on her own.[5]

In 1892 the program of the Polish Socialist Party, which was founded that year, affirmed complete equality of rights for those nationalities that would enter the future Polish republic on the basis of "voluntary federation."[6] The Polish Socialists aimed to weaken Russia by tearing the old borderlands out of her grasp. Józef Piłsudski, who joined the party at its founding, made this his leading aim. Two years later he stressed that the Poles, Lithuanians, Latvians, and Ruthenes (Ukrainians) had a different history and different traditions from the Russians. He observed that they hated Russian national and religious oppression and had already developed a revolutionary working class, and concluded that "all these conditions allow us to assume that it is just from this area that the force will emerge that will grind the power of tsardom into dust."[7]

In 1904 he tried to secure Japanese support for a Polish uprising, in which the Poles would lead the process of breaking Russia up into her component parts and helping these parts to become self-governing units.[8] Dmowski tried to persuade the Japanese not to do so; but as it happened, though Japan defeated Russia, tsardom survived the war. From 1905 to 1917 the paths of the two Polish leaders diverged even more; Dmowski tried to obtain legal concessions from the Russian government, while Piłsudski prepared officer cadres as the core of a future Polish army to serve the independent Poland that he expected to emerge from a war between the Central Powers, on the one hand, and the Entente Powers on the other. He planned to create a Polish army that would fight for a time on the side of Austria and Germany against Russia. He foresaw that they would defeat Russia, but then would be defeated themselves by France, Britain, and probably also the United States. Under these circumstances, an independent Poland would arise.[9]

In June 1917 the thirteenth congress of the Polish Socialist Party approved a federal program. In the meanwhile, the March revolution had overthrown tsardom in Russia. The Bolsheviks seized power in November and came out with their own federal program of self-determination for the peoples of Russia, but one based on self-determination by workers and peasants—led, of course, by the Bolsheviks. In February 1918, Leon Wasilewski, the Polish Socialist expert on nationality problems, expounded the party's aims with regard to the borderlands, especially Lithuania. He wrote that in view of the ethnic complexity of the borderlands, new frontiers would have to be established by mutual agreement and in such a way as to exclude all foreign intervention and outside influence. Since the Polish state should not include too many foreign elements, it must establish political or economic relations with friendly neighbors on the basis of common interests. However, in establishing frontiers with unfriendly or hostile states, strategic considerations would be decisive. Regarding Lithuania, he wrote that if she agreed to enter a union with Poland, then some Polish-populated areas could be included in the Lithuanian state. However, if Lithuania refused, Poland would demand the Vilna region and other ethnically mixed territories in the east.[10] Wasilewski's article proved to be the blueprint for Piłsudski's policy toward Lithuania from 1918 to 1922.

But Polish majority views of Lithuania at the end of the war were strongly colored by the fact that she was dependent on Germany. The first Lithuanian government—the Taryba, or State Council—came into existence with German support in September 1917. While this was also true of the German-created Regency Council in Warsaw, most Poles expected the latter to be a temporary institution. A strong Poland would, they believed, throw off German control. Piłsudski became a national hero in summer 1917, when he refused to support the Germans and when Poland was reborn in November 1918. The Lithuanians, however, could not throw off the German yoke. After Germany's defeat, German troops stayed in Lithuania. Thus, it was easy to label the Taryba a tool of German imperialism, a charge made by Dmowski in 1919/20.

Meanwhile, Lithuanian émigré politicians in the West drew up plans for a future independent Lithuania. Thus, Juozas Gabrys—who had contacts not only with the French and American but also with German intelligence services[11]—convened the National Lithuanian Conference in Switzerland in 1917. He published a map of the new Lithuania, with the borders of the former grand duchy as it existed in 1569. This meant a territory of about 380,000 square kilometers and a population of some 16 to 17 million. Of this, only about 2.5 million people were, in fact, Lithuanian-speaking; the rest were Poles, Belorussians, Latvians, Germans, Jews, and a very small percentage of Russians. This problem was, however, brushed aside by the claim that nationality was based, not on national consciousness, culture, or language, but on "blood," meaning ancient ethnic origin. Thus, Mykolas Biržiška, a prominent Lithuanian writer and publisher, claimed that ethnic Lithuania was not limited to Lithuanian-speaking areas but also included those where Lithuanian had once prevailed.[12] In fact, even in 1569, only part of this area had been predominantly Lithuanian.[13] While there were large discrepancies between the Russian census of 1897, the German one of 1916, and the Polish one of 1921—each of which covered somewhat different areas—Polish preponderance in southern Suwałki Province and in the Vilna region was indisputable[14]

In 1917 the Poles living in these two areas established an organization called the United Polish Parties in Lithuania, which aimed at federation with Poland. In German-occupied Warsaw, where the Polish Regency Council existed under German control, the Lithuanian Commission was headed by Prince Eustachy Sapieha, who later became foreign minister of Poland. An agreement was even concluded in Berlin in June 1918 between a member of the Regency Council, Adam Ronikier, and a member of the Taryba, Augustinas Voldemaras. Ronikier recognized the existence of Lithuania and agreed with Voldemaras that the future boundaries of their respective countries would be drawn up on the basis of "ethnic, historical, and economic principles."[15] However, not only were these principles mutually contradictory, but also both sides differed radically in interpreting them. As it happened, Voldemaras formed his first cabinet in Vilna on 11 November 1918, when Polish independence was proclaimed in Warsaw. Here, Józef Piłsudski, a native of the Vilna region, became head of the reborn Polish state.

Polish and Lithuanian views seemed to be irreconcilable from the start. The Lithuanians aimed to establish a large Lithuanian state with Vilna as its capital, while most Poles envisaged a large Polish state with either an autonomous Lithuanian province or an ethnic Lithuania in some union with Poland. Piłsudski proposed union to a Lithuanian delegation in Warsaw in December 1918.[16] Shortly thereafter, a new factor complicated the dispute. On 2 January 1919 the Germans evacuated Vilna, and the Lithuanian government left with them. Polish forces took over the city but evacuated it three days later in the face of advancing units of the Red Army. On 5 January 1919 the Lithuanian Soviet Socialist Republic was proclaimed in Vilna. The Vilna Council of Workers' Deputies was headed by a Communist, Vincas Mickevičius-Kapsukas. The Poles had offered Voldemaras help in regaining Vilna, but he insisted that they first recognize a large, independent Lithuania with Vilna as its capital.[17] Voldemaras's successor, Mykolas Sleževičius, took the same line.

While Soviet Russia aimed to dominate the borderlands by means of Communist governments, Germany kept a wary eye on Lithuania, lest the latter come under Polish domination. A Foreign Ministry memorandum of February 1919 advised that Germany support all anti-Polish tendencies in Lithuania and help to establish a Lithuanian state. In May the author of another memorandum saw an independent Lithuania as a possible counterweight to Poland and as a land bridge between Germany and Russia. Since Poland was bound to become France's satellite in Eastern Europe, a Polish-Lithuanian union would be dangerous to Germany.[18] Meanwhile, a German plenipotentiary remained in Vilna, and German troops stayed in the country. This was sanctioned by the Allies, who, by the armistice of 11 November 1918, had allowed German troops to remain in former Western Russia so as to block Bolshevik expansion westward.[19] These regular troops were later replaced by various "Free Corps" units, which were to cause the Allies many headaches.

It was under these circumstances that Polish and Lithuanian claims clashed at the Paris Peace conference in 1919. Roman Dmowski, chairman of the Polish National Committee, had already presented his views and suggestions to President Woodrow Wilson in November 1918 in his memorandum "The Territory of Poland." Dmowski admitted that the Lithuanian national movement had made great strides in the past forty years, but he noted that the Lithuanians did not exceed some two million people. Arguing that no small state could survive German or Russian pressure, he proposed that ethnically Lithuanian territory should have home rule in a union with Poland. He strongly opposed Piłsudski's proposals for a federation with the peoples of the borderlands, declaring that this would only weaken Poland.[20] Dmowski maintained these views at the Peace Conference. Moreover, in his first major speech there on 29 January 1919, he tried to discredit the Lithuanian national movement by claiming that it was largely the result of "German intrigue."[21] Piłsudski's envoys, who soon joined the Polish delegation, tried to gain their colleagues' support for a federal policy, but failed. In early March the delegation rejected this alternative.[22]

Voldemaras officially stated Lithuanian demands in a note to Clemenceau of 24 March, in which he claimed the former Russian provinces of Vilna, Kaunas, and Suwałki, as well as the Lithuanian-speaking parts of former Courland (southern Latvia) and of East Prussia. He said that the Lithuanian nation rejected any union with Poland because the latter had "exploited" Lithuania since the Union of Lublin of 1569 and had "dragged her [Lithuania] down" with herself in the anarchy that led to the partitions. Finally, he said that Lithuania feared a revival of Poland's aggressive tendencies.[23]

France and Britain did not have a joint policy; instead, each pursued her own. Thus, in January 1919 the French—who hoped for a speedy settlement of Polish-Lithuanian relations so that the Poles could concentrate their forces against the Germans—believed that if Lithuania obtained Memel and the lower Niemen valley, together with some form of autonomy, she would perhaps accept a rapprochement with Poland.[24] The British had different views. In a memorandum on the former Russian Empire, dated 20 January 1919, British experts proposed that the Polish-Russian frontier run from East Prussia to a line west of Suwałki, then north to the river Niemen, then to Grodno and to the Bug River, then south along the old eastern frontier of Congress Poland down to East Galicia, where the population was to vote on its future status. Vilna was excluded from Polish territory, as was Lvov.* The

---

* The Russian name, Lvov, is used in this chapter because it was in general use at this time; the Polish name is Lwów, and the Ukrainian is L'viv; the German name was Lemberg; and the French was Léopol.

populations of these two regions could vote for Poland; if they did not, they were to be assured a cultural autonomy.[25] In its Preliminary Suggestions of 21 January 1919, the United States Inquiry Commission stated that a Polish-Lithuanian union would be acceptable, but on condition that Lithuanian demands for the provinces of Vilna, Grodno, and Minsk be met. The authors thought that if the union depended on these concessions, Poland would make them. Otherwise, Poland and Lithuania should be independent states within their ethnic boundaries.[26] But the British had more respect for Russian territory than the Americans. The Foreign Office experts advised that the Poles should not be allowed to enter the provinces of Vilna, Grodno, Minsk, Vitebsk, and Volhynia, except in agreement with the Russian Central Committee in Paris.[27] This body, known more generally as the Russian Conference, was an advisory group made up of former Russian diplomats and officials who represented the White Russian government. It was regularly consulted by Allied statesmen.[28]

British regard for Russian claims was bolstered by the key Foreign Office expert on Poland, Lewis B. Namier, who passionately opposed Dmowski's plans for a great Poland. Namier's expertise was greatest on East Galicia, where he had been born and raised; but his opposition to Polish claims in Lithuania was just as strong. He cited doubts that there was a Polish enclave around Vilna—or anywhere else in Lithuania.[29] He viewed Polish claims, both here and in East Galicia, as the expression of alleged Polish imperialism and the alleged interests of Polish landowners.[30] Furthermore, in March 1919 he warned that the extension of Polish frontiers in the east would drive the Russians and Lithuanians into the arms of Germany. What is more important, the French foreign minister, Stephen Pichon, now reached the same conclusion.[31]

At this time, Lithuania was in chaos. Soviets (Councils of Workers) had sprung up all over the country, and as mentioned above, on 5 January 1919 Vilna was taken by the Red Army. The government of Mickievičius-Kapsukas then became the government of the Soviet Lithuanian-Belorussian, or Litbel, Republic. Also in January 1919, the first units of the German Free Corps arrived in Lithuania, and their numbers continued to grow. Soon thereafter, Allied missions arrived in Kaunas, the seat of the Lithuanian government. A United States relief mission arrived on 15 March, and a French military mission, headed by Col. Constantin Reboul, arrived on 19 March. A British military mission, headed by Col. R. B. Ward, arrived in June.

On 19 April, Polish troops entered Vilna, after defeating the weak Red Army units which had tried to hold it. Piłsudski visited the city and on 22 April delivered "An Address to the Inhabitants of the Former Grand Duchy of Lithuania." He promised the population of the Vilna region that it would decide its own fate through duly elected representatives. A provisional civilian administration was created to restore order and supervise the elections. As Piłsudski admitted later, opposition to his federal policy in the Polish Sejm made him decide to march on Vilna during the Easter recess.[32]

Piłsudski's plans for Lithuania have been the subject of much controversy. On the one hand, he has been accused of aiming at outright Polish domination over Lithuania under the cloak of federalism.[33] On the other hand, he has been credited with a genuine desire to grant self-government to Lithuania in a federation with Poland.[34] All available evidence indicates that Piłsudski opposed the incorporation of non-Polish territories in the new Poland, with the exception of parts of East Galicia and Volhynia, which he believed were necessary in order to provide a defensible Polish frontier with Soviet Russia. He consistently strove for federation with Lithuania and local autonomy for Belorussia. Naturally, this went hand in hand with his primary aim of preventing German or Russian domination over Lithuania. Also, he believed that a federal solution was more acceptable to France and Britain than incorporation, and he was particularly anxious to win British recognition of Poland as a partner in the Baltic region.[35] It is true, as Piłsudski wrote to his friend Wasilewski, that he did not want to talk of federation ''without a revolver in my pocket,''[36] but this need not necessarily be interpreted as cynicism.[37] Though often described as a romantic in his overall aims, he was always a pragmatist in the implementation of policy; he knew that mere talk without a military presence would accomplish nothing. Finally, we know that he was willing to leave the Vilna region to Lithuania, provided the latter entered into a federal union with Poland.

The problem was that this was unacceptable both to Lithuanian and to Polish opinion. In Warsaw, the reaction to Piłsudski's Vilna address was violent. The National Democratic deputies in the Sejm asked whether the proclamation was legal—that is, whether it had been countersigned by a cabinet minister. On 29 April the Sejm voted that Poland should annex the northeastern territories.[38] The British and French governments expressed dismay and issued warnings. On 22 April, Balfour voiced his objections to Paderewski against a Polish occupation of Vilna; and four days later the permanent undersecretary of state for foreign affairs, Lord Hardinge, warned August Zaleski that Poland should not advance on Grodno.[39] On the same day, France subscribed to the Supreme Council warning to both Poland and Lithuania that they avoid serious complications which might lead to war. They were advised, instead, to unite in the face of the Bolshevik threat. The Supreme Council also warned that it would not recognize any frontiers established by military force, since such action contravened its right of arbitration.[40] The warning was addressed to both Poland and Lithuania; nevertheless, in view of the latter's weakness, Poland was, in fact, the main addressee. Paderewski also warned the Polish government against a policy of incorporation.[41] When he returned to Poland in mid May, he personally warned the Sejm that annexationist plans would get no support from the Western Powers and would only strengthen the position of the old Russian regime (the Russian Conference in Paris and the White leaders in Russia). As a result of these warnings, the Sejm voted for self-determination.[42] In the meanwhile, on 28 April, Polish troops occupied Grodno.

The Polish occupation of Vilna and Grodno was part of the Polish-Soviet war, but it was also designed to prevent the Lithuanians from entering these territories. Voldemaras sent a strong note to Clemenceau on 28 April, protesting against the Polish military entry into Vilna and other Lithuanian towns. Voldemaras claimed that the Lithuanian General Staff had planned to send in their own troops. Appealing to the thirteenth of Wilson's Fourteen Points—which called for an ethnic Poland—Voldemaras called the entry of Polish troops an invasion and claimed that the Lithuanians had more reason to fear the Poles than the Bolsheviks.[43]

The Lithuanian protest fitted in with French and British policy during the spring and summer of 1919. At the end of May the French and British proposed to Admiral Kolchak—whom they recognized as the Supreme Ruler of All Russia—that for the time being he agree to recognize Estonia, Latvia, and Lithuania as autonomous units. Also, he was to recognize the establishment of de facto relations between the Entente Powers and the native governments, pending the final border settlement which was to be made in consultation with the League of Nations.[44] To this, Kolchak reluctantly agreed, though he reserved for the future Russian Constituent Assembly the right to make final decisions about the borders. Meanwhile, the Commission on Baltic Affairs was set up at the Paris Peace Conference, an action that was violently criticized by the Russian Conference in Paris. The Russian Conference declared that the Commission on Baltic Affairs had no right to violate the integrity of Russian lands'' or to prejudice the decisions of the future Russian Constituent Assembly.[45] The French government explained that the commission was designed to help the existing Baltic governments in their struggle against the Bolsheviks and that it would certainly not prejudice the possibility of a future democratic Russian federation. They also claimed that the commission was needed in order to curb German influence in the region.[46] The Americans disagreed: Foreign Secretary Robert Lansing and the United States member of the commission, Samuel E. Morrison, preferred to have the Germans stay, as long as the Lithuanians could not occupy their ethnic territories.[47] But it is clear that for France and Britain the future of the Baltic provinces, or states, was closely tied to the fortunes of the Russian civil war, in which the White forces then seemed to have the upper hand. This reinforced the existing British view that the Allies had no legal grounds for disposing of old Russian territory without Russia's consent. As the British put it in early July, no final decision on the status of Lithuania could be made before the Entente Powers had reached an agreement with Russia. For the same reason, in the summer of 1919, the French also excluded any federation between Lithuania and Poland. Voldemaras, for his part, appealed to the Russian Conference to prevent the Commission on Polish Affairs from settling the Polish-Russian frontier without consulting the Russian Conference. More important was the fact that at this time the British and French governments were thinking about attaching Lithuania—with guarantees for her autonomy—to a future non-Bolshevik Russia;[48] therefore both governments opposed a Polish-Lithuanian federation.

In this context, Lithuanian moves for a rapprochement with Poland were designed both to avert further Polish military advances and to gain favor with the Allies. The Lithuanian emissary who visited Warsaw in April and May 1919, Jurgis Šaulys (a former Lithuanian minister in Berlin), refused Paderewski's proposals for a Polish-Lithuanian federation that would have a common foreign policy, military convention, treasury, railway, and postal system—even though Paderewski told Šaulys that in such a federation, Poland would not seek to put Vilna under direct Polish rule. A Polish mission was then sent to Kaunas, but it failed to make any headway. A Polish note of 24 June demanded that the withdrawal of German troops from Lithuania precede any bilateral negotiations. Also, the population in territories occupied by Polish troops was to decide its own fate.[49] The Lithuanian government refused. As Biržiška put it, the idea of a Polish-Lithuanian union came out of Polish archives and memories of the past. It was hateful to the young Lithuanian society.[50]

The Polish government now turned to a modified federal program. A draft instruction to the heads of Polish diplomatic missions, dated 7 July 1919, stated that if it should prove possible to unite the territories of the Grand Duchy of Lithuania, or most of them, with Poland, then this solution would be desirable. However, ethnically Polish territories, or those that were Polish in civilization, should be incorporated into Poland. This was to be done with the agreement of the local population, which seemed certain. Nonetheless, a plebiscite was to be avoided.[51] The Polish government wished to reconcile the federal project with Polish opinion's demand that some historically Polish regions be united with Poland; but the government also wished to avoid a precedent for holding a plebiscite in East Galicia.

At this time, Piłsudski began to explore another road to his objective. This was a settlement with a liberal Russian government, if such were to come into existence. He thought of establishing a neutral zone on each side of the proposed future Polish-Russian frontier. Vasily A. Maklakov—a prominent Russian liberal, a founder of the Russian Cadet Party in 1905, and ambassador of the Provisional Russian government in Paris in 1917—had proposed in May 1919 that the populations of some borderland territories be allowed to express the wish to be separated from Russia and thus avoid provoking Russian hatred for Poland. Piłsudski told Aleksander Skrzyński, in early July, that he would welcome such an arrangement. However, Maklakov did not have Denikin's support; so no talks took place.[52]

In the meanwhile, French and British experts on the subcommittee of the Commission for Polish Affairs in Paris were trying to resolve the problem of the Polish-Lithuanian frontier. On 8 April, Sir Esme Howard had proposed two variants, the second of which left Vilna conditionally in Polish hands. Howard's departure from previous Foreign Office proposals was due to his recent visit in Poland. He had been most favorably impressed by the spirit of the Polish leaders and people, and therefore he had incurred the bitter criticism of Lewis B. Namier.[53] But Howard was not alone in his sympathy for Poland. A line proposed by the French member of the subcommittee, Joseph Noulens, the former French ambassdor to Russia, also left Vilna on the Polish side of the frontier.[54] However, in May, reports of Kolchak's successes encouraged Russian circles in Paris to restate their claim that Lithuania and Belorussia were "purely Russian" territories.[55]

Aside from the fluctuating fortunes of the Whites and the Reds in the Russian civil-war, the experts' work in Paris was also influenced by the Allied wish to prevent fighting between Poles and Lithuanians. On the French side, Marshal Foch desired a speedy withdrawal of German troops, fearing that their presence would establish German influence in Lithuania and thus create a link between Germany and Soviet Russia. On this point, however, he was opposed by the United States secretary of state, Lansing, who preferred to have the Germans stay so as to prevent a Polish occupation.[56] Finally, the Lithuanian government appealed to the Entente Powers to establish a demarcation line between Polish and Lithuanian troops in the Suwałki region. The Commission on Baltic Affairs complied on 18 June 1919. It attributed almost the whole of Suwałki Province—except for Augustów—to Lithuania but left Vilna and Grodno in Polish hands.[57] Neither side was satisfied.

The first clashes between Polish and Lithuanian troops occurred in the northern part of the demarcation line in the Suwałki region, which the Poles crossed on 7 July. The Poles then asked Marshal Foch to modify the line so as to leave the three southern counties of Suwałki on their side, as well as more territory west of the line running from Grodno to Vilna and the river Dvina. They justified this on the grounds of military security.[58] These suggestions harmonized with Foch's objective of supporting the Poles against the Bolsheviks and thus obviating the need for German troops. Therefore, on 17 July he proposed a new demarcation line, henceforth known as the Foch Line. While this proposal was not completely satisfactory from the Polish point of view, it did put more territory on the Polish side. In particular, southern Suwałki was to be in Polish hands.[59] As noted above, this area was unquestionably Polish-speaking.[60] However, Col. R. B. Ward, the head of the British Military Mission in Kaunas, assured the Lithuanian government that the British would not allow Polish troops to advance deeper into Lithuania.[61]

Piłsudski tried to obtain Britain's support, or at least her agreement, to a further Polish advance eastward. His conversation of 16 July with the British minister in Warsaw, Sir Percy Wyndham, is a good example of Piłsudski's efforts to establish Anglo-Polish cooperation in the Baltic region and to obtain British support for his advance in the east. He told Wyndham that the Baltic Sea should be kept free of either German or Russian domination. Poland would never be a maritime state, but she did need a free Baltic for her trade and for communication with Great Britain. He also stressed the Bolshevik danger. It had to be ended, otherwise Poland could neither stop her advance nor demobilize.[62] Namier's comments were negative, as usual. Referring to Piłsudski's proposal for plebiscites in areas east of former Congress Poland, he warned against Allied agreement to what he called quasi plebiscites, to be held under Polish occupation, and against British support of a "farcical" land reform in Belorussia. He also proposed that the administration of Polish-occupied districts include representatives of the Russian Conference in Paris, proportionate in number to the percentage of the Russian population in 1914.[63] Namier could not have been unaware that even according to the Russian census of 1897 the former Russian provinces of Lithuania and Belorussia were inhabited by some five and one-half million Belorussians and six other nationalities and only half a million Russians,[64] but he believed that the Belorussians were so deficient in national consciousness that they did not count as a separate nationality.

Meanwhile, Piłsudski renewed his efforts to reach agreement with the Lithuanians. As the Polish army advanced on Minsk, the administrative center of Belorussia, he dispatched a Polish mission to Kaunas on 3 August 1919. The Polish emissaries were Leon Wasilewski, Piłsudski's closest collaborator in Lithuanian affairs, and Maj. Tadeusz Kasprzycki of the Polish army. They proposed that there be simultaneous elections in territories occupied by Polish and Lithuanian authorities. The elected representatives were then to constitute a parliament in Vilna, which would decide on the juridical-political status of Lithuania and her relationship with Poland.[65] This was, of course, the implementation of Piłsudski's address to the population of the former Grand Duchy of Lithuania on 22 April. The Lithuanians remained adamant. Prime Minister Sleževičius rejected the idea of plebiscites, claiming that all the Polish-occupied territories, except Augustów, were ethnically Lithuanian. He also stated dramatically: "If Vilna is not recognized as a Lithuanian city, that is death for Lithuania."[66] This, of course, left the same impasse as before. Wasilewski tried to obtain British support for Polish aims by offering the same economic concessions to Britain in Lithuania as those proposed by the Lithuanian government. He made this offer to Captain Brodie (Brodsky) of the British Military Mission in Riga, who attended the talks in Kaunas as an observer under instructions to work for a common Polish-Lithuanian front against the Bolsheviks.[67] Brodie could do nothing, of course, except pass on Wasilewski's proposal to his superiors.[68] There was no reply.

The failure of the Wasilewski-Kasprzycki mission led Piłsudski to make a most unfortunate decision—namely, to mount a coup in Kaunas so as to replace the existing Lithuanian government with one that would be more friendly to Poland. It seems that he reached this decision on the basis of reports from the Polish Military Organization (POW) in Kaunas, which affirmed that some prominent Lithuanians were ready to enter such a government. This expectation was not completely groundless. A Lithuanian uprising, with the aim of overthrowing the Sleževičius government, was expected at the end of August. The government was bankrupt and could not prevent the occupation of part of the country by the White Russian army of General Bermondt-Avalov. Therefore, some prominent Lithuanians were ready to form a government that would be friendly to Poland. The leading figures were Stasys Narutavičius (a relative of Piłsudski's and a half brother of the future first president of Poland, Gabriel Narutowicz, who was assassinated in December 1922) and Gen. Silvestras Žukauskas. The latter told Maj. T. Kasprzycki, on 3 August 1919, that he considered himself a Pole and that he only headed the Lithuanian army in order to reach an agreement with Poland.[69] It is doubtful, however, whether these two men could have led the country into a federation. In any case, Kaunas was forewarned by the POW seizure of Sejny on 26 August. Lithuanian troops regained Sejny but were then ousted by the Poles, who moved up to the Foch Line. Kaunas was also alerted by the cutting of telegraph wires around the city. Thus, the coup that took place at the end of August misfired. Piłsudski was branded as an aggressor, a charge that he consistently denied. However, the attempted coup confirmed the worst fears of the Lithuanian government and public opinion. Furthermore, Britain stepped up her support of Lithuania by granting the latter de facto recognition on 25 September. The British also sent twenty-one officers, led by Maj. Gen. F. Crozier, as instructors for the Lithuanian army, as well as arms and ammunition.[70] Colonel Ward supported Voldemaras's demand for a mixed commission, including representatives of the Entente Powers, to hear and arbitrate the complaints of both sides.[71] Finally, the British extended a loan to the Lithuanian government to help it overcome its financial crisis.[72]

British aid to Lithuania at this time must be seen in the context of Denikin's seemingly successful drive on Moscow. As the White Russian representative in London, E. Sablin, reported on 18 September, British military experts saw the de facto recognition of the Baltic governments as a temporary expedient, pending the reunification of these countries with Russia.[73] However, by November, Denikin's drive had turned into a retreat. Since Kolchak had been defeated in May and since General Yudenich's drive from Estonia on Petrograd had petered out in October, the British government concluded that there was little hope of a White victory in the civil war. Intervention was also most unpopular with British workers. The British now began to transfer their hopes for lucrative trade with Russia from a White to a Red government. At the end of December 1919 the Foreign Office advised the government to begin negotiations with the Bolsheviks so as to avoid political defeat and to establish trade relations.[74] H. P. B. Maxse suggested that trade with Russia would not only force the Bolsheviks to retreat from socialism but would also strengthen the British economy, threatened as it was by over-production and unemployment. Finally, he asserted that trade with Bolshevik Russia would weaken Bolshevik propaganda that was being directed at the British working class.[75] This line of thought greatly appealed to Prime Minister David Lloyd George, who adopted it as his own. For the next two years, therefore, British policy toward the Baltic States aimed to establish trade relations with Bolshevik Russia, for which the Baltic States offered important port and rail facilities. For this reason, Britain wished to avoid the establishment of German or Polish influence in the area. Finally, anxious to begin trading with the Russians, Britain wished to eliminate the danger of war between them and the Baltic governments, as well as with Poland. This policy favored Lithuania. Thus, in pursuit of peace and trade, Britain opposed any further Polish advances to the north and northeast.

France, who also had a vital interest in preventing German domination of the Baltic States, differed from Britain on other issues, including, above all, the role of Poland in this area. Thus, in October 1919, *Le Temps* hailed Poland as "the principal champion of the Allies on the shores of the Baltic."[76] This did not, however, reflect active Franco-British rivalry. The British navy dominated the Baltic Sea, and France did not have the industrial capacity to compete with Britain on the Russian market. Apart from that, nothing was further from French thoughts in 1919–21 than trade with a Bolshevik Russia which had repudiated tsarist debts to France—debts owed largely to individual French holders of Russian bonds. Thus, French policy in this region was motivated primarily by the aim of creating between Germany and Russia a strong *cordon sanitaire,* whose most vital component would clearly be Poland.[77] Still, as long as there was a spark of hope for a White victory in the Russian civil war, France opposed further Polish advances into Belorussia and the Ukraine. As early as September 1919, France threw out hints that the Poles should not act on their own initiative in the Baltic region.[78] Another element in this policy was the fear of complicating Franco-British relations. Therefore, France subscribed to the temporary eastern line of Polish administration, as announced by the Supreme Council on 8 December 1919. This ran along the Foch Line from the frontier of East Prussia to Grodno, then south to Brest-Litovsk and along the former frontier of Congress Poland to the eastern border of Galicia. Although the Supreme Council stated that the line did not prejudice the establishment of the future Polish-Russian frontier, it clearly left open the fate of the territories east of this line.[79] Also, despite Denikin's defeat in November, the Entente Powers asked Piłsudski to accept Denikin's demand that the Poles organize the administration on territories east of the Bug River in his name and that they fly the flag of imperial Russia. Piłsudski, of course, refused.[80]

Piłsudski now resolved to push for a Polish-Lithuanian federation by isolating Lithuania from the other two Baltic states. He believed that this would finally force Lithuania to accept some form of union with Poland.[81] His first move was to establish relations with Latvia by granting her de facto recognition in October 1919 and by proposing joint Polish-Latvian military action against the Bolsheviks on the river Dvina.[82] This led to an agreement not to admit Lithuanian troops onto the right bank of the river. The Latvians agreed with alacrity, since the Lithuanians had laid claims to this area.[83] Another move toward isolating Lithuania was Polish participation in conferences held by representatives of the Baltic States. Here the Poles opposed the recognition of Lithuanian territorial claims. There was a Polish observer at the first Baltic Conference held in Tartu, Estonia, in November 1919. The Soviet emissary, Maxim Litvinov, offered peace and compensation for damages done by the Red Army in the Baltic States, but this offer came to naught for lack of support from the Entente.[84] However, when a new government came to power in Estonia, it signed a preliminary peace agreement with Soviet Russia on 31 December 1919.[85] By this time, the defeat of the White Russians was conclusive, and the British now decided to support peace between the Soviets and the Baltic States.[86]

Poland also wished for peace, but at the same time she strove to counteract Soviet and German influence in the area. She therefore aimed at the creation of a Baltic bloc under her own leadership. Britain also seemed to envisage a Baltic bloc—but one that would exclude Poland.[87] Aiming at trade with Russia, Britain wished to exclude France and Poland, a desire that was shared by Moscow. It is in this context that we should view not only British warnings to the Poles against further advances in Lithuania but also British financial aid to the latter. In January 1920, Lloyd George told Polish Foreign Minister Stanisław Patek in London that he hoped the Polish-Lithuanian conflict would be resolved peacefully; he also stressed the need for Western trade with Russia.[88] On 2 March, Gen. Henry Carton de Wiart, head of the British Military Mission in Poland, asked Piłsudski to give up further action in Lithuania.[89] Since the fighting continued, on 31 March the Conference of Ambassadors accepted the resolution of the British representative, Lord Derby, warning against any further advance of Polish troops into Lithuania. On 1 April the conference agreed to inform the Polish government that Lithuania would not tolerate violations of the demarcation line.[90] Meanwhile, British financial aid to Lithuania included not only help in establishing a Lithuanian bank but also loans from British concerns to the Lithuanian government in return for the right to exploit Lithuanian forests.[91] It was not surprising that Polish efforts to isolate Lithuania at the Helsinki Conference of January 1920 failed. In March the Latvians refused to sign a military convention with Poland against Lithuania, though they did agree to military cooperation against the Bolsheviks.[92]

Lithuania now looked to Soviet Russia for help. On 31 March 1920, Voldemaras sent a note to the commissar of foreign affairs, Georgii Chicherin, demanding Soviet recognition of an independent Lithuania, which would include the provinces of Vilna, Grodno, Kaunas, and Suwałki.[93] Chicherin agreed to accept "ethnic principles" as the basis for a Soviet-Lithuanian frontier, but he proposed that a conference be held to settle the details. Soviet-Lithuanian talks began in Moscow on 7 May 1920,[94] the day on which Polish troops entered Kiev together with their Ukrainian allies.

Polish-Lithuanian relations deteriorated further when Lithuania tried to take advantage of the Polish-Soviet war in order to advance her claims. Thus, at the end of May, she refused to declare her neutrality despite considerable pressure from France.[95] On 4 July, when the Poles were in full retreat and their situation looked desperate, Foreign Minister Sapieha telegraphed Lithuanian Foreign Minister Juozas Purickis, granting Polish de facto recognition of the Lithuanian government and proposing the establishment of diplomatic relations, as well as negotiations on the status of national minorities.[96] But now the Lithuanians were riding high. They had British support for their claim to Vilna, and they were on the point of signing a treaty with Soviet Russia in which the latter recognized their claims. As we know, W. Grabski had to accept Lloyd George's demand, at Spa on 9 July, that Poland give up all her claims to territories north of Grodno and agree to accept the terms of a treaty to be signed between Soviet Russia and Lithuania. At this time, British Foreign Secretary Curzon proposed that Vilna be given to Lithuania so as to prevent a Soviet occupation. However, it was finally decided that Vilna's fate was to be settled by the Supreme Council.[97] Grabski had no choice but to accept this, as well as to leave the ultimate decision on Danzig, Upper Silesia, and East Galicia to the Allied Powers. This was the condition for the Allied aid now promised to Poland if Soviet troops should enter ethnically Polish territory.

The Spa agreement was to play a major role in later British policy toward Poland. Equally important was the Soviet-Lithuanian Peace Treaty, signed on 12 July, which henceforth provided the legal basis for Lithuanian claims. Signed at a time when Poland seemed to be on the point of collapsing under the Soviet onslaught, the treaty recognized most of the province of Vilna and part of the province of Grodno as Lithuanian. The price tag was Lithuanian agreement—in a secret protocol—to allow the passage of Soviet troops through the Vilna region and their temporary stay in Lithuania. Interestingly enough, the Soviet note of recognition stated that though the number of Lithuanians in Vilna was insignificant, the Soviet government recognized that city's great importance as the cultural and political center of Lithuania, as well as the fact that it was the most important railway junction and the main trade center of the state. However, the Soviets did not recognize Suwałki as part of Lithuania.[98] It is likely that with an embryonic Polish Communist government behind their lines, the Soviets did not wish to make it more unpopular by granting the Polish-speaking part of Suwałki to Lithuania. The careful wording on Vilna might also have been designed to leave a loophole for later negotiation. Whatever the case may be, when Lithuanian troops arrived in Vilna, they found the Red Army already there; and this was greatly resented in Kaunas. A Lithuanian-Soviet agreement was signed on 6 August, whereby the Red Army was to evacuate territories recognized as Lithuanian by the Moscow treaty. Vilna was to be evacuated by 1 September.[99]

In mid August, Piłsudski launched his great offensive from the river Wieprz and drove the Red Army out of Poland. The Soviet defeat allowed the Lithuanians to enter Vilna on 26 August. Before Piłsudski launched his offensive, the Polish delegate at a Baltic conference in Riga stated his country's desire to establish friendly relations with Lithuania. The Lithuanian delegate replied that his country would sign a defensive treaty with Poland only if the latter first signed a peace treaty with Soviet Russia.[100] Nevertheless, when the tide of war turned against the Soviets, the Poles did not resort to force but again sent a delegation to Kaunas. It was instructed to propose federation and, if this was rejected, a military convention against the Bolsheviks.[101] The Lithuanians refused on 26 August. Although the Red Army had been driven back from Warsaw, the Lithuanians thought that it might still recover and crush the Poles. They stated that Lithuania would establish diplomatic relations with Poland only if the latter would recognize Lithuanian possession of Vilna. The Poles then asked for temporary possession of the Vilna-Lida railway in order to secure their left flank. This request was also refused. Two days later, Polish troops entered the Suwałki region. On 31 August the Lithuanians broke off the negotiations in Kaunas, and Col.

Konstantinas Žukas, who conducted the negotiations on the Lithuanian side, declared that if forced to choose between Poland and Soviet Russia, Lithuania would choose the latter.[102]

Although these talks failed, it is worth noting the suggestions made to Polish authorities by a member of the Polish delegation, Capt. Adam Romer, since his proposals foreshadowed solutions that would be put forward in later negotiations and in the League of Nations. He proposed that territories with Polish and Belorussian populations be granted autonomy and their own parliament at Vilna. Another parliament was to be elected in the province of Kaunas (which had a large Polish minority). The two parliaments would then establish a common government for Lithuania. Romer believed that the Polish element in this government would be so strong that federation with Poland would naturally ensue. He also thought that the Lithuanian Peasant and Socialist parties would support this solution.[103]

Meanwhile, Polish troops advanced without Lithuanian assent. This was, of course, a continuation of the Polish drive against the Red Army, which culminated in the Battle of the Niemen in late September. However, in late August the Lithuanians reinforced their position in Suwałki Province and took Augustów on 28 August. On the same day, Lithuania declared her neutrality and proposed a demarcation line between Polish and Lithuanian troops in the southern part of Suwałki Province, leaving it in Lithuanian hands.[104] The Poles replied on 31 August by demanding that the Lithuanians withdraw beyond the Foch Line, which, in this particular case, also coincided with the Supreme Council Line of 8 December 1919. Finally, the Poles also proposed to hold direct negotiations on disputed questions.[105] Without waiting for a reply, however, Polish units called on the Lithuanians to move back beyond the Foch Line and, when they did not, entered Suwałki, which was then abandoned by the Lithuanians.

Britain tried to restrain the Poles. Curzon asked the British minister in Warsaw, Sir Horace Rumbold, to warn the Polish government against attacking the Lithuanians and trying to recover Vilna.[106] The Lithuanians were counting on a Soviet counterattack against the Poles;[107] so they launched an offensive in the Suwałki region on 5 September. This in turn led the Polish government to make a move with very serious long-term consequences. Fearing that Polish troops in the Suwałki area might not be able to hold their ground, the Council of Ministers decided to appeal to the League of Nations. This was calculated merely to win time until 15 September, when the Polish military could send more troops to Suwałki from other sectors of the front. As Wojciech Trąmpczyński, the Speaker of the Sejm, put it: "We can't take the offensive for ten days, so we will make a virtue of necessity, and our note [to the league] has this objective in mind."[108] Poland asked for the league's aid in persuading the Lithuanians to change their course of action "within a few days.''[109] Although the Polish note stated that Poland only wished the league to exert pressure on the Lithuanian government—not to intervene or mediate between the two parties—the result was to place the whole issue before the league.

The appeal to the league opened a hornets' nest for Warsaw. It gave the British, in particular, a moral basis for opposing Polish aims, in addition to the legal basis that they already possessed in article 87 of the Versailles Treaty (whereby the Allied Powers had the right to settle Poland's eastern frontier) and in the Spa agreement signed by W. Grabski. However, British concern was less moral and legal than pragmatic. After Piłsudski's victory over the Red Army, British support for Lithuania stemmed from the fear that a Polish seizure of Vilna might provoke another Soviet attack on Poland, thus disrupting trade and perhaps again threatening Germany. Therefore, the Polish drive on Vilna was called ''folly.''[110] The British supported the awarding of Vilna to Lithuania, because this had been sanctioned by the Moscow Treaty of 12 July. Therefore, Curzon instructed Rumbold to say that the British government expected Poland to leave the Lithuanian question alone until after the conclusion of a peace with Russia. Then, if no agreement could be reached between Poland and Lithuania, the matter was to be referred to the Allied Powers in accordance with the Spa agreement.[111] The Poles replied that they considered the latter to have lapsed, since the Allies had not fulfilled their pledge of aiding Poland once the Soviets had crossed into ethnically Polish territory.[112] The Poles also knew that basically, France favored their claim to Vilna, even though for the sake of good relations with Britain, France had officially warned them not to seize the city.[113]

In the meanwhile, the Polish advance continued. The High Command aimed to reach the line of the German trenches established in 1915–17. These stretched from Galicia, in the south, to a point northeast of Vilna: they included Volhynia and part of Belorussia.[114] This was a line the Poles could easily hold, but in the northeast they would have to pass through some Lithuanian-held territory in order to reach it. They therefore tried to obtain British agreement by claiming that there was military cooperation between Lithuanian and Soviet troops, that there were Soviet concentrations on Lithuanian territory in this area, and that Soviet troops were moving through it to Russia.[115] The British answer was to propose a Polish-Lithuanian conference in London.[116] The Poles countered by asking what the British attitude was toward de jure recognition of the Baltic States. Curzon frankly told Rumbold that the British government was not interested, since it did not believe in the permanence of the Baltic States and since it feared, in case they were recognized, that this might involve members of the League of Nations in a future war with Russia.[117] Here, again, the British demonstrated that they viewed the Baltic States primarily in the context of relations with Russia,

White or Red. In May the French government gave de facto recognition to Latvia and Lithuania; it also opposed recognition de jure,[118] presumably because, unlike the British government, it still hoped for a White victory in Russia.

In mid September it suited both the Poles and the Lithuanians to hold talks on drawing up a demarcation line. The Poles wished to gain time, since they were still battling the Red Army in the Niemen region; the Lithuanians were anxious to use Allied support to their own advantage. The delegates who met in the town of Kalwaria, in Suwałki Province, between 16 and 18 September, put forward virtually irreconcilable demands. The Poles wanted the Lithuanians to withdraw behind the Foch Line, which also coincided with the Supreme Council Line of 8 December 1919. The Lithuanians replied that the Poles themselves had violated the Foch Line and that the Lithuanian government had not been officially informed of the line of December 1919. Finally, the Lithuanian representatives agreed to withdraw temporarily behind the line without, however, recognizing it as binding and provided that the Poles withdrew an equal distance on their side. The Poles refused and broke off negotiations. Neither side was acting in good faith. The Lithuanians hoped for Allied support and for another Soviet offensive against the Poles, while the latter played for time, hoping that the league would put pressure on Lithuania.[119] The Lithuanians were also receiving hearty encouragement from the head of the British Military Mission in Kaunas, Colonel Ward. Sir Horace Rumbold complained, just before the negotiations began, that Ward was more Lithuanian than the Lithuanians; so the latter thought that all their actions had British approval.[120]

After the British government had dropped its proposal for a Polish-Lithuanian conference in London, the dispute over the demarcation line was taken up at the League of Nations Council between 16 and 18 September—that is, at the same time as the Kalwaria negotiations. The British attitude was strikingly pro-Lithuanian. H. A. L. Fisher supported Voldemaras's demand that Lithuania be neutral within the boundaries recognized by the Moscow Treaty of 12 July. However, the "rapporteur," the Belgian Paul Hymans, had tacit French support in proposing that the Lithuanians recognize the Supreme Council Line of 1919 as a temporary demarcation line and that they withdraw their troops beyond it. This coincided, as we have seen, with the Polish proposal at Kalwaria. But Hymans also proposed that the Poles respect Lithuanian neutrality east of this line and that observers appointed by the League of Nations be sent to keep the peace.[121] This proposal was probably the most the French could do for the Poles, and it was certainly more favorable to the latter than the British-supported demands made by Voldemaras, who at first resisted the Hymans proposal but finally accepted it. The Polish delegate, Paderewski, who was not informed of his government's strategy, considered the agreement a great success. He even stated that he no longer considered Voldemaras as his enemy and then shook hands with him. Paderewski cabled Warsaw that the decision had gone in Poland's favor.[122] However, the Polish government rejected the proposal, because recognition of Lithuanian neutrality at this time ran counter to Polish military plans. Also, on 25 September the Soviet government declared that it would recognize Lithuanian neutrality only if the Poles did so.[123] But the Battle of the Niemen was still undecided, so the Poles interpreted Lithuanian neutrality as being favorable to the Soviets. There was no guarantee that the Red Army would withdraw from Lithuania if the Poles recognized her neutrality.

In any case, Piłsudski was determined to drive the Red Army out of Lithuania and Belorussia as well as take Vilna before the Lithuanians could do so. At this point the Red Army still held Lida and Grodno, the key stations on the two railway lines to Vilna. After the Polish offensive moved forward on 23 September, Rumbold reported to Curzon that in order to take these cities as well as Minsk, the Poles would have to attack in a northwesterly direction, and therefore would have to pass through some Lithuanian territory.[124]

This was the Polish argument, but it found no support in London. The Polish offensive, and particularly the bloody Polish-Lithuanian battle at Sejny on 22 September, was severely condemned by both Britain and France.[125] The head of the French delegation to the league, Léon Bourgeois, protested to the Polish government on 25 September. Paderewski replied three days later, explaining that the Polish maneuver had been necessitated by war. To his own great relief, he could add that the Polish and Lithuanian governments had agreed to hold a conference at Suwałki beginning on 29 September.[126]

The conference did, in fact, avert serious British pressure. On 5 October, after the Poles had taken Orany—which lies midway between Grodno and Vilna—Curzon expressed great concern to Derby that the Poles had advanced beyond the "ethnic line." Curzon thought that there was no alternative but to say that if the Poles continued their campaign against Lithuania and took Vilna, the British government would withdraw its minister from Warsaw and replace him with a chargé d'affaires. He added that this action would naturally be more effective if the French government were to cooperate.[127] Two days later, Derby cabled Curzon the text of a proposed French note to Warsaw, advising that it was "loyal and wise" to assure Lithuania the possession of Vilna as her capital, whatever the sentiments of the Polish people and Piłsudski might be.[128] However, since the Polish foreign minister, Sapieha, informed Sir Percy Loraine on the same day that a Polish-Lithuanian armistice had been signed at Suwałki,[129] Curzon agreed that there was no immediate danger to Vilna and therefore no need for strong action.[130] A further reason was French reluctance to cooperate with Britain. Despite their official stance, the French did not oppose a Polish march on Vilna; they merely suggested to Poland that she justify the march on Vilna as part of her military action against the Bolsheviks, which would not prejudice the final status of this territory.[131]

Piłsudski now decided to seize Vilna in such a way that the Polish government could disclaim all responsibility and so deflect Allied fury. His decision can be dated fairly accurately to the last days of September, just at the time the Suwałki conference was in session. Since the conference included not only Polish and Lithuanian representatives but also officers of the Control Commission appointed by the league (they joined the deliberations on 4 October), any breakdown in talks would be fully reported. Piłsudski knew that the French, while supporting his aims, did not want his actions to worsen their relations with the British. What is more, Paderewski warned that a seizure of Vilna would leave Poland at the mercy of the British and the Germans in Danzig and would lead to the loss of Upper Silesia.[132] In fact, just at this time, the British and the French were at loggerheads over General Le Rond's policy of supporting the Poles in Upper Silesia and over the question of the Mixed Harbor Board in Danzig.[133] For all these reasons, Piłsudski had to choose a mode of action that would incur the least damage to Polish interests.

The method he chose was action by "rebellious" Polish troops, who would be disowned by the Polish government. It would be justified on the grounds that they were natives of the Vilna region and had been promised that they could return home at the end of the war. The instrument for this action was the Lithuanian-Belorussian Division led by Gen. Lucjan Żeligowski, a native of the Vilna region. We should note that Piłsudski had rejected the alternative suggestion to drive both the Lithuanians and the Bolsheviks into the Baltic Sea.[134] Instead, he told General Żeligowski on 30 September that the only solution was for someone to take "full responsibility" for organizing an "uprising" in Vilna with the help of the local population. He told Żeligowski that if the latter would accept this task, the Polish Parliament, all of Poland, and even he himself (Piłsudski) might have to disown Żeligowski. Therefore, Piłsudski could not "order" Żeligowski to accept. Nevertheless, Żeligowski did accept.[135]

In the meanwhile, the Suwałki Conference had convened on 20 September. Not only did the officers of the Control Commission arrive, led by Col. Auguste Pierre Chardigny, a Frenchman, but on 7 October an agreement was signed which was to enter into force three days later. The armistice line now established left eastern Lithuania, including Vilna, on the Lithuanian side.[136] If Piłsudski accepted the line, he would have to halt the Polish offensive against the Bolsheviks in the northeast and give up his Vilna plan.

But, of course, Piłsudski had already made up his mind. With his closest collaborators, Piłsudski drew up detailed plans on 2 October at Lida, a town just south of Bastuny on the northern railway line to Vilna. Before the Suwałki

Conference ended, Żeligowski had taken Vilna with the Lithuanian-Belorussian division and with the support of the local population. The division at his disposal numbered only about fourteen thousand men, but it was covered by an additional eighty thousand Polish troops. The Vilna region was not to be incorporated into Poland; instead a local civilian administration was to be set up, and the region was to receive the name of Central Lithuania. It was clear that this state could become a part of Lithuania proper only if the Lithuanian government agreed to a union or federation with Poland.[137]

On 7 October, Żeligowski told his officers that he had broken off all contacts with the Polish High Command and that he would march on Vilna.[138] The few officers who protested were detached and sent to other units. On 8 October, Żeligowski issued the order to march.[139] Curiously enough, on the previous day he had allowed the visit of two members of the League Control Commission: the British Major Pargiter and a French officer. As Colonel Ward reported to Curzon on 8 October, the Poles had told the Allied officers that they were going to march on Vilna. Ward thought that the move would be made independently of the Polish High Command, repudiating its authority, but that it would probably have the secret support of Warsaw. However, Ward's telegram did not reach the Foreign Office until 20 October,[140] presumably because his message, which was telegraphed from Vilna, was intercepted and delayed by the Poles.

When Żeligowski set off at 6 A.M. on 8 October, he had to cover a distance of fifty miles from his headquarters at Woronów, just south of the Mereczanka River. The situation was tricky, because the Lithuanian plenipotentiary in Vilna, Ignas Jonynas, had transferred his powers to the representatives of the Entente. Therefore, command of the city was taken over by the head of the French Military Mission to Lithuania, Col. Constantin Reboul, who declared a state of siege. He sent his aide-de-camp to Żeligowski, proposing that Vilna be declared a free city; but the general refused. He and his troops entered the city at about 2 P.M. on 9 October. They were supported by the Polish population, especially the railwaymen.[141]

Żeligowski now had to face Colonels Reboul, Ward, and Chardigny, the indignant representatives of the Allied Powers and the league. When they asked why he had seized the city, since Poland had signed the Suwałki agreement, he said that he wished to give the population the opportunity to decide its own fate. He then demanded that the Entente representatives and the Lithuanian troops leave Vilna by noon the next day.[142] To Chardigny's pointed questions as to where Żeligowski had obtained arms and soldiers and what he envisaged as the frontiers of the state of Central Lithuania, Żeligowski merely said that he had acted independently. The three Allied colonels left for Kaunas, whence they proceeded to Warsaw.[143]

Żeligowski set about organizing the new state of Central Lithuania. He sent a telegram to this effect to Warsaw, and he also informed the Lithuanian government, to which he proposed a plebiscite. He sent the same information to the Entente Powers and to the League of Nations.[144] On 12 October he took the title of chief of state and established the Provisional Governing Commission, which was led by a local Polish politician, Witold Abramowicz. Żeligowski then proceeded to organize the army, and he established the emblem of the new state: the eagle and the horse—the coat of arms of the former Polish-Lithuanian Commonwealth.[145] This, if anything, made Piłsudski's intention clear: the seizure of Vilna was to force the Lithuanians to accede either to a union or to a federation with Poland. The plebiscite offer to Kaunas was a threat that, otherwise, Vilna would become part of Poland.

The Żeligowski coup infuriated the British, even though the Polish government gave assurances that the coup had taken place against its will.[146] Curzon wired Derby in Paris on 11 October that the action belied the categorical assurances of Polish Foreign Minister Sapieha and was therefore "a gross breach of faith"; it showed complete "disregard" for Allied advice. It was all the more intolerable since the issue had been submitted by Poland to the League of Nations. Curzon now repeated his previous suggestion that the French and British governments withdraw their ministers from Warsaw.[147] However, Curzon's anger was due to reasons other than morality and prestige. J. D. Gregory, head of the Northern Department in the Foreign Office, told Jan Ciechanowski, the Polish chargé d'affaires in London, that the Poles were risking another partition of their country. If they rejected Allied advice and then faced disaster—by which he meant a new Soviet attack—then Britain would not be able to help. He therefore urged that Vilna be evacuated and that Żeligowski be court-martialed. But the British did not know that the Polish and Soviet delegations, which were then negotiating a preliminary peace at Riga, had agreed that Polish-Lithuanian disputes on territories west of the proposed Polish-Soviet frontier line should be negotiated directly by the two states concerned.[148]

In any case, Curzon could not do much without French cooperation, which was not forthcoming. Indeed, privately the French were not at all displeased with Żeligowski's action. The military approved it for strategic reasons, since, in their eyes, it was a move both against the Bolsheviks and against German influence in Lithuania. Thus, their advice to the Poles was to "prove" that the Polish government had had nothing to do with Żeligowski.[149] When Warsaw followed this line, even Philippe Berthelot, secretary general at the Quai d'Orsay, supported the Polish stand. Also, the French minister in Warsaw, Hector de Panafieu, expressed the view that Poland was not bound by the Spa agreements.[150] In considering French motives, we should bear in mind that in early August the French government had acted independently of Britain in recognizing the White Russian government of General Wrangel. The French clearly hoped that the Poles would inflict such a crushing defeat on the Red Army that Wrangel could recover and then counterattack from the Crimea. Finally, it was difficult for the Western Powers to proceed drastically against the Polish government because Foreign Minister Sapieha was threatening to resign.

In the face of all these problems, Curzon had to accept milder diplomatic action. He noted on 11 October: "We are merely beating the air and attempting to hide our impotence. Events will show."[151] On the following day he wired Derby that in view of Sapieha's threat to resign, the British government should refrain from taking drastic action and should merely accept a public disavowal of Żeligowski by the Polish government.[152] Thus, the Franco-British note, delivered in Warsaw on 12 October, protested against Żeligowski's *fait accompli,* warned against a policy of adventures, asked for moderation toward the "Russian People," and demanded that Poland honor the Spa agreements. Finally, it expressed the hope that the Polish government would avoid moves that could result in a threat to Poland.[153] This, of course, referred to a possible Soviet attack.

The Polish government replied that the Spa agreements had lost their validity, since the British government had not fulfilled its obligation to help Poland once the Red Army had entered ethnically Polish territory. Also, the Poles reminded the British of the latter's support of Bolshevik peace terms in early August, whose acceptance would have been synonymous with the loss of Polish independence. Finally, the Polish government asked the French and British governments not to raise new obstacles to the reconstruction of Poland immediately after the signing of a preliminary peace treaty with Soviet Russia.[154] In fact, this treaty was signed at Riga on 12 October. When Allied protests continued, Piłsudski told Loraine, on 14 October, that he might resign as chief of state and betake himself to his homeland near Vilna as a private citizen. He could not, he told the British minister, go back on his promise to Polish soldiers, who were natives of the region, that they could return home after the war. On this occasion, Piłsudski restated his views on Vilna. He told Loraine that he saw only two possible solutions. One was a Lithuanian state, with Vilna as its capital. This state would include the Lida and Grodno districts as well as the part of White Ruthenia (Belorussia) that had been assigned to Poland by the preliminary Treaty of Riga. This Lithuanian state would be united by the closest ties to Poland. The other solution was the union of Vilna with Poland.[155] Piłsudski's alternatives failed to evoke an immediate reaction from Curzon, but the threat of resignation did. It confirmed Curzon's view that the French and British should demand only an official Polish disavowal of the Żeligowski coup.[156] Therefore, the Franco-British note that was delivered in Warsaw on 17 October merely demanded a categorical disavowal of General Żeligowski, reserving Allied action until the situation in Vilna had been clarified.[157]

Public opinion in Poland was jubilant at the news of Żeligowski's action, and it confidently expected that Vilna would be incorporated into Poland. The National Democrats strongly criticized the establishment of the Central Lithuanian State, which they rightly saw as a move toward a Polish-Lithuanian federation. Thus, on 10 October the Sejm passed a resolution to incorporate Vilna into the Polish state.[158] Only the Polish Communists condemned the Żeligowski coup and warned, like Curzon, that it carried the risk of reviving the Polish-Soviet war.[159] The Polish government had to try to avert a break with the Western Powers and at the same time to mollify Polish opinion. Therefore, Prime Minister Witos told the Sejm on 14 October that the Polish government could not accept Żeligowski's "insubordination" and would investigate it. However, Witos also said that he understood the bitterness of soldiers who had been denied the right to return to their native land. Furthermore, he said that contacts would be established with the Provisional Governing Commission, asking if it intended to allow the population to decide its own fate. Finally, he warned that the occupation of Vilna by any foreign forces would be regarded by Poland as a move against self-determination.[160] On the following day, when Colonel Chardigny demanded that Poland impose a blockade on Żeligowski, this demand was rejected.[161]

The British now seemed to take a more favorable view of a Polish-Lithuanian union or federation. As usual, pragmatic considerations were uppermost. To begin with, there was no concrete evidence that the Red Army was capable of launching another offensive, but there was some fear that Germany might succeed in establishing her dominant influence in the Baltic region. J. D. Gregory noted on 17 October that Lithuania showed no signs of desiring to federate with the other Baltic States, and she was too weak to play a significant role in the region by herself. He therefore advocated a federation between Poland and Lithuania.[162] Sapieha passed on this information to Paderewski in Geneva on 18 October.[163] Loraine, writing to Gregory on 21 October, noted that although a Greater Lithuania, federated with Poland, could not absolutely prevent Germany from penetrating Russia, it could at least help to restrain German attempts in that direction.[164] Curzon may have been influenced by these arguments. On 27 October, when the question was being discussed in the League Council in Brussels, he wired the British minister there, Sir George Graham, that he preferred Lithuania, with Vilna as its capital, to be closely tied to Poland rather than be reabsorbed by Russia. He thought that a plebiscite would be a makeshift solution, and he hoped that the League Council could persuade the Poles and Lithuanians to settle the problem on a federal basis.[165] However, the French government now seemed to support—or at least it did not oppose—a plebiscite in the Vilna region, and it did not press for federation. This may have been a ploy to appease its chief delegate, Léon Bourgeois, and league supporters in France who had been outraged by Polish disregard of the league's authority.[166] Whatever the case may be, the League Council recommended that a plebiscite be held.

But the Polish government was determined to prevent a plebiscite, not because it feared to lose in Vilna, but because a plebiscite there would be a dangerous precedent for settling the Polish claim to East Galicia.[167] Therefore, while accepting the plebiscite proposal, the Polish note of 7 November was clearly designed to be unacceptable to Lithuania. The plebiscite was to be held under league supervision in regions occupied by Polish troops—that is, in Lida, Grodno, and Oszmiany. In return, Lithuania was to agree to a plebiscite in those parts of Kaunas Province that had a large Polish minority and in some other Polish-speaking regions occupied by Polish troops. The procedure was to be rapid, with open voting under the supervision of commissions that would include Polish, Lithuanian, and league officials. The Polish government could not undertake to demobilize the Żeligowski troops in the Vilna region, but it proposed that they be transformed into a local militia. Finally, the territory ceded to Poland by the preliminary Treaty of Riga could not be submitted to a plebiscite beyond the boundary set by the Treaty of Moscow.[168] Thus, the Polish government excluded plebiscites in Belorussia, Volhynia, and East Galicia.

The Lithuanian reply to the proposal of the League Council was just as uncompromising. The Lithuanians accepted the plebiscite "in principle" but refused to agree to its being held north of the demarcation line set in Suwałki on 7 October. This meant that there would be no plebiscite in the Vilna region.[169] On 23 November, Voldemaras claimed that the Lithuanian character of Vilna and the surrounding region was indisputable, for "a nation is composed more of the dead than the living." The evidence of four centuries of history should, he claimed, outweigh the revindications of a small group of Poles.[170]

The British now believed that Vilna could be the capital of Lithuania, but only within the framework of a federation with Poland.[171] Unfortunately, by now the federal concept had lost whatever limited support it had once enjoyed in Poland. Not only did the majority of Polish opinion favor the incorporation of Vilna into Poland, but so did the Provisional Governing Commission in Central Lithuania. Aside from this, Piłsudski had to oppose suggestions from the Provisional (Polish) Political Committee in Kaunas that he settle the Lithuanian-Polish problem by marching on Kaunas.[172] The Lithuanian government, for its part, opposed any kind of union or federation with

Poland. In the meanwhile, clashes had taken place between Polish and Lithuanian troops. An armistice was signed on 29 November 1920, but the league's Control Commission did not support the Lithuanian demand for the evacuation of Żeligowski's troops from Central Lithuania.[173]

The end of fighting meant that the dispute could now be dealt with by negotiation, mostly in the League of Nations. By the end of 1920, Polish prospects seemed favorable, for the Soviets were weak and the British were growing weary of Lithuania's uncompromising position. As Loraine noted, the Lithuanians' idea of negotiations was that the main points at issue should first be conceded to them. Still, even the French government's support for a federal solution was conditional on Lithuanian possession of the Vilna region. Annexation of this region by Poland was seen as dangerous, since this might lead Lithuania to opt for either Bolshevism or German domination. The French sugared the pill for the Poles by hinting that a Polish-Lithuanian federation leaving Vilna to Lithuania would, in fact, facilitate Polish domination of the latter.[174] But in Warsaw the opposition to federation was adamant. The Sejm voted in November for the annexation of the Vilna region,[175] and direct Polish-Lithuanian negotiations that had been proceeding in Warsaw were broken off on 29 December. Therefore, Hymans informed the League Council on 1 March 1921 that the plan for a plebiscite had failed. The British then suggested, and the League Council agreed, that both parties should enter into direct talks once again.[176] The Poles were considerably strengthened by the signing of the alliance with France on 19 February and of the Treaty of Riga on 18 March 1921, but they still had to keep a wary eye on Upper Silesia.

This was the setting for Foreign Minister Sapieha's new federal project, which he proposed in the latter part of March to the French, British, and Italian ministers in Warsaw. As reported on 23 March 1921 by Sir William Max Muller, the new British minister to Poland, Sapieha proposed that: (a) the federation would be based on complete equality; (b) Vilna was to go to Lithuania, on condition that the latter be transformed into a state of two cantons—Kaunas and Vilna, with Vilna as the common capital and seat of their common government and parliament; and (c) a treaty would be concluded between this Lithuanian state and Poland, providing for a common foreign policy and a joint General Staff, though the armies would remain separate. Sapieha told Muller that he did not wish to propose this plan in the name of the Polish government but that he would appreciate the views of the British government.[177]

Foreign Office reaction was positive. Sir Eyre Crowe believed the Polish terms to be so generous that the Lithuanians would be foolish to reject them. Curzon thought that the proposal was worthy of consideration, though he could not see why a "spurious parentage" should be assumed by the league or anyone else.[178] He did not understand that Sapieha was seeking British support as a lever against majority Polish opinion, which desired annexation. On 7 April, Gregory put another federation proposal to Tomas Narusevičius, the Lithuanian chargé d'affaires in London; it included provisions for cultural autonomy in the Vilna region and for Lithuania's support of the Great Powers' stance toward the Riga Treaty. In return, the Great Powers would grant de jure recognition to Lithuania and would assign Memel to her.[179] This was a bribe for Lithuania to agree to a modified federation with Poland and to secure Lithuanian support for whatever policy the Powers should decide to adopt toward the Polish-Soviet frontier. The Lithuanians demurred.

In April the Polish proposal was modified in line with suggestions made by the three Allied ministers in Warsaw. Both states were to be fully sovereign but were to share certain institutions in common. Thus, the chief of state was to be elected by the joint delegations or by representatives of the Polish and Lithuanian parliaments. There were to be joint Ministries of Foreign and Economic Affairs, of Defense, and a joint General Staff. Lithuania was to have its own legislature and administration.[180] This scheme, sometimes known as "The Three Ambassadors' Project," was reflected later in the First Hymans Plan. Sapieha accepted the modified project, but it met with strong criticism in Poland, especially from the National Democrats. In mid April the Sejm voted that the population of the Vilna region should decide its own fate.

Sapieha still hoped to work something out that would lead to a federation. He drew up a package plan, including a Polish-led Baltic federation, which, together with the Polish-Rumanian alliance, would create a united bloc between Germany and Soviet Russia. The Polish General Staff informed its French counterpart that the only obstacle to this plan was a chauvinistic Lithuania, which, if left under German domination, would provide Germany with a bridge to Russia.[181] The French government responded favorably. In a note of 26 April to London, the French only proposed to replace the word "federation" with "union." Also, the French reserved their de jure recognition of Lithuania and the possible award to the latter of Memel until a Polish-Lithuanian agreement had been reached on the lines proposed above.[182] However, the prospects of British support were dashed by the third Polish uprising in Upper Silesia. When Sapieha visited London and asked Crowe for British support on 2 May, he met with a cool reception. Indeed, at this time, Gregory tried to work out a separate project with Narusevičius. The result was a Foreign Office memorandum which guided British policy at the forthcoming session of the League Council.

The Foreign Office memorandum of 7 May stated that the British government was not bound either by the confidential Lithuanian proposals made to Hymans or by the Three Ambassadors' Project. Since no federal solution was acceptable to the Lithuanians, whereas the Poles wanted Vilna and the rest of Lithuania (which they did not, A. C.), the British government believed that the League Council should first state that Vilna belonged by right to Lithuania and that Lithuania should include both Vilna and Memel. Only after the de jure recognition of such a Lithuanian state could there be any discussion of a Polish-Lithuanian federation.[183] This, of course, strengthened Lithuania; it also reflected Britain's condemnation of the third Polish uprising in Upper Silesia.

It was not surprising that Polish-Lithuanian talks in Brussels failed to produce agreement. In late May, Hymans put forward what came to be known as the First Hyman's Plan. He collaborated closely with French diplomats in working this out, and apparently Colonel Chardigny also played an important role in its formulation.[184] It bore a striking resemblance to the Three Ambassadors' Project. Lithuania was to become a state made up of two autonomous cantons, Kaunas and Vilna, on the Swiss model. Vilna would be the capital. All ethnic groups would receive guarantees of religious and linguistic freedom; Polish and Lithuanian would both be recognized as official languages. Poland and Lithuania would recognize each other's independence and sovereignty but would also acknowledge their common interests by concluding a series of special conventions. These would include a military agreement and an economic convention. Lithuania would also assure Poland of commercial transit and free use of Lithuanian ports. There was to be a joint council for foreign affairs. Any dispute on the interpretation of these agreements would be submitted to an arbitrator named by the League of Nations. This plan was approved by Briand and Berthelot.[185]

The Lithuanian Delegation, headed by Ernestas Galvanauskas (who replaced Voldemaras), voiced strong objections. Galvanauskas not only rejected the idea of "particularist sentiments" in any part of Lithuania—meaning Vilna—but he also objected to the proposed joint institutions and to league arbitration. Finally, he said that the proposal seemed to violate Lithuanian sovereignty.[186] The Polish delegate, Prof. Szymon Askenazy, accepted the plan for the time being; but seven days later, he declared that the Polish government would accept it only on condition that representatives of the Vilna population be admitted to the talks.[187] The Lithuanian counterproposals of 30 May insisted on the independence and sovereignty of Lithuania, as well as on her possession of Vilna. Minority rights would be recognized, but Lithuania would not undertake any military cooperation with Poland until the Polish-Soviet frontier had secured international recognition—that is, by the Western Powers.

The Lithuanian stance was strengthened by British support. The Poles rejected these proposals and stated that they would never recognize Lithuanian sovereignty over Vilna. Still, at the end of June the Polish government was ready to accept the Hymans Plan, and though the Lithuanians insisted that Żeligowski first evacuate Vilna, the League Council approved the plan as it stood on 28 June.[188] Only the British delegate supported the Lithuanian demand that Żeligowski withdraw.

Though the Lithuanians rejected the plan officially on 22 July, they did not wish to bear the stigma of refusing all further negotiations in the League of Nations. The Poles, for their part, strengthened their hand on 29 July by concluding an agreement on cooperation in international affairs with Finland, Latvia, and Estonia (the Helsinki Protocol).[189] When Hymans invited both sides to continue talks at Geneva on 25 August, they accepted.[190] Each hoped for an outcome favorable to its claims.

Hymans at first conducted separate conversations with each delegation. Then, on 3 September, he submitted his Second Plan, asking that it be accepted as a package by 12 September. The Second Hymans Plan attempted to placate the Lithuanians. Thus, the Vilna canton was to have its own local government and was to elect representatives to its legislature in exact proportion to its ethnic groups, on the Swiss model. However, the joint institutions that would bind Poland and Lithuania were to be the same as in the First Plan. The annexed protocol specified that all nonnative troops occupying Vilna, as well as nonnative administrations, should leave the region as soon as possible. After the elections, the Lithuanian government was to transfer its seat to Vilna. Until then, there was to be a police force adequate to keep order and to secure the eastern frontier. Lithuanian and Polish troops should, after agreement had been reached, reinforce the police in equal numbers. A three-member commission designated by the League Council was to trace the frontier between Polish and Lithuanian territories and between the Vilna canton and the rest of Lithuania. Negotiations were then to take place on the military and economic conventions. A representative of the league was to interpret the agreement and supervise its execution.[191]

The Second Hymans Plan proved unacceptable to both Poland and Lithuania. It was supported by the British government and was surreptitiously opposed by the French. The Lithuanian government played for time and British support by accepting the plan "in principle," but it added reservations that, in fact, restated the Lithuanian point of view. Thus, the Lithuanians proposed a frontier with Poland that would give them all the territory awarded by the Moscow Treaty of 12 July. Furthermore, they proposed that the Vilna region be an autonomous unit in the Lithuanian state, with its own Diet, thus rejecting the idea of the two delegations and the joint parliament.[192]

Hymans found the Lithuanian reply unacceptable, while Askenazy regarded the Lithuanian proposal for an autonomous Vilna region in Lithuania as being contrary to federation.[193] The British and French heads of delegations, Balfour and Bourgeois, accepted the Second Hymans Plan; the

League Council endorsed it; and the League Assembly approved it on 24 September 1921.[194] At this time, Lithuania was also admitted to the League of Nations, although it had not yet been recognized de jure by members of the league. Despite Bourgeois's acceptance of the Second Hymans Plan, the French government opposed it, fearing that an autonomous Vilna region would facilitate German-Soviet contacts. Therefore, the French told the Poles that they would prefer some internationally acceptable form of incorporating the region in Poland. For this reason the French asked for the speedy removal of General Żeligowski and his troops.[195]

The French government's point of view was clearly set out to the Poles while the Second Hymans Plan was still under discussion in the League Council. Jules Laroche, deputy director of political and commercial affairs at the Quai d'Orsay, laid it out on 21 September to Józef Wielowieyski, counsellor of the Polish legation in Paris, and to the first secretary, Juliusz Łukasiewicz. Laroche made five proposals: (1) Żeligowski should leave Vilna as soon as possible. (2) Within two months an autonomous administration should be set up to organize elections to the Vilna legislature. This body, however, was to represent not only the Vilna region but also parts of the neighboring Polish districts, extending to the frontier set by the Moscow Treaty of 12 July 1920. In this way, Laroche claimed, the elections and the autonomy of the Vilna region would carry more weight with Western opinion. (3) It would be desirable to grant an amnesty to all imprisoned Lithuanians and to establish an independent Lithuanian school system in the Vilna region. (4) The Poles should accept Colonel Chardigny's suggestions that the league's Control Commission establish the frontier in Suwałki Province. This would largely follow the Curzon Line (identical here with the Foch Line), and thus leave two-thirds of the province in Polish hands. (5) All international commissions in the Vilna region should be removed as quickly as possible.[196] Laroche's proposals indicated two things: first, that the French government clearly believed that Poland was more capable than Lithuania of preventing German-Soviet cooperation and, second, that the French were anxious to make the Polish incorporation of Vilna as palatable as possible to Great Britain.

Given secret French encouragement, the Poles rejected the Second Hymans Plan. The Polish Council of Ministers did so on 30 September at Sapieha's invitation, though for the sake of appearances it agreed to additional study of the Polish-Lithuanian dispute by the League of Nations Council.[197] Piłsudski then ordered an extension of the plebiscite area to include the two districts Lida and Braslav. He also set the date of the elections for 8 January 1922. On 17 November the Polish Sejm voted for the election of a representative assembly in Vilna, which was then to determine the political and legal status of the region.[198] On 30 November, General Żeligowski resigned his position as chief of state in Central Lithuania and turned over power to a civilian administration headed by Aleksander Meysztowicz, a Polish landowner and businessman.

So far, Polish moves had followed French suggestions. But Paris was worried, and with cause, that incorporation might be effected too swiftly, thus provoking British objections and further complications. So, Paris advised against the annexation of the Vilna region too soon after the elections.[199] Like Piłsudski, the French government saw the elections as a step toward Polish-Lithuanian federation. This would be impossible if the Polish Sejm voted for incorporation, and France would then also find it impossible to defend Poland's right to Vilna.[200] Unfortunately, the bulk of Polish opinion did not favor what it viewed as a half-way solution, not least because Lithuania again appealed for Soviet support.

The Lithuanian government, in fact, requested a declaration from Moscow that the latter would view a Polish-Lithuania union as a hostile act. Chicherin obliged on 15 September. This was in keeping with the Soviet aim of preventing Polish or Western domination of Lithuania.[201] At the same time the Lithuanian government could not accept the Second Hymans Plan or negotiations with Poland because of public opposition. When Foreign Minister Juozas Puryckis sent a personal representative to Warsaw with counterproposals—which would have been rejected anyway—an attempt was made on his life. Therefore, on 3 December the Lithuanian cabinet finally decided to reject the plan and so informed the League Council on 24 December. Still, it tried to show its good will toward the league by supporting the council's resolution to guarantee the autonomy of the Vilna region, even though this had no chance of being accepted by Lithuanian opinion. As the German minister in Kaunas put it, the government had capitulated to the will of the people. Henceforth, Lithuanian supporters of the Second Hymans Plan were known as "Hymansininkas," or Hymansmen, and this became one of the most pejorative epithets in the Lithuanian political vocabulary.[202]

The Polish government also found it impossible to defy its public opinion. Therefore, it could not follow French advice to delay the incorporation. Foreign Minister Skirmunt certainly tried. He had called Zamoyski home from Paris so that the latter could personally present the French point of view, in order to convince the Political Committee of the Council of Ministers, the Sejm Foreign Affairs Commission, and the Polish politicians from the Vilna region to work for time. The British government also issued a warning. On 31 December, Max Muller said that the British government knew that the Vilna Sejm would vote for incorporation into Poland. He drew the Polish government's attention to the serious consequences of such a step: it would make a Polish-Lithuanian federation impossible later, and it would do harm to Polish relations with other Baltic States. Moreover, since the dispute was still before the League Council, such action on Poland's part would be all the more regrettable.[203] The Polish government answered that incorporation would, indeed, make the prospects for federation worse, but, it hoped, not impossible.[204]

The elections to the Vilna Sejm took place as scheduled on 8 January 1922; and as expected, they returned an incorporationist majority.[205] While Colonel Chardigny criticized the lack of voter identification at the ballot boxes and noted that the Lithuanians, Jews, and a large number of Belorussians had abstained,[206] the majority of the population was Polish and wanted to be incorporated into Poland. On 12 January the League Council resolved that its efforts at mediation had ended in failure, but warned that it would not recognize a one-sided settlement. France signed this resolution along with Great Britain. The Lithuanian delegate, Naruševičius, protested and proposed that the dispute be referred to the International Tribunal of Justice. He also requested that the League Council ask the Allied and Associated Powers to fix the eastern frontier of Poland, as they were empowered to do by article 87 of the Versailles Treaty. He stated that this act would also settle the Polish-Lithuanian dispute.[207] His appeals were seconded by the British, who warned the Poles against annexation. On 19 January, Max Muller transmitted a note to this effect to the Polish minister for foreign affairs,[208] and at the end of January, Curzon warned Sapieha, now Polish minister in London, that annexation would be the final blow to Poland's international status.[209]

Despite these warnings, the Vilna Sejm voted on 20 February for union with Poland. The Ponikowski cabinet resigned over the issue on 3 March. Four days later the government presented the act of union to the Sejm, which ratified it on the fourteenth and voted separately for the union of Vilna with Poland on the twenty-fourth. Skirmunt had warned the Council of Ministers against annexation, but his appeals could not prevail against the will of the Vilna Sejm, the Polish Sejm, and the majority of Polish opinion. Therefore, the British request that the Polish government assure a broad autonomy to the Vilna region was impossible to implement. Later, in 1922/23, British diplomacy linked Vilna with Memel, but by that time there was no talk of federation. On 14 March 1923 the Powers recognized Polish sovereignty over Vilna and gave conditional recognition to Lithuanian sovereignty over Memel.[210] While the Poles rejoiced, the Lithuanians swore not to let the world forget their claim to Vilna. The Lithuanian Constitution named it as the capital of the country, and a state of "cold war" continued to exist between the two neighbors for fifteen years. There were no diplomatic relations, no direct communications, not even a direct postal service; letters from one country to the other had to pass through a third state. Lithuanian diplomats raised the Vilna question on every possible occasion, and the Lithuanian government rejected all Polish attempts to establish normal relations until

March 1938, when they came into being as the result of a Polish ul-timatum.[211] The Poles, for their part, were unable to realize their aim of a Baltic federation. By March 1938 it was too late to make up for lost time.

A Polish-Lithuanian federation would undoubtedly have benefited both countries. It might also have made a Baltic bloc or federation a possibility. Unfortunately, neither Polish nor Lithuanian opinion was ready to accept it at the time. Western, especially French, support might have swung the scales in 1919/20, at least in Poland, for the chief opponents of federation were the National Democrats, who were self-proclaimed friends of France. However, at that time, France and Britain still counted on the victory of the Whites in the Russian civil war and therefore on the rebirth of a strong Russia, whose claims to the Baltic States they both recognized. But though France came over to the view that federation was desirable after Piłsudski's victory over the Red Army in August 1920 and though she supported Żeligowski's seizure of Vilna in October, Britain only came to accept the federal solution after much vacillation, and it then backed away, thus strengthening Lithuanian opposi-tion. Any version of the Hymans Plan, if implemented, would have estab-lished a loose Polish-Lithuanian federation while safeguarding Lithuanian sovereignty. But neither France nor Britain was willing to exert the necessary pressure on Poland and Lithuania in order to overcome the opposition of their public opinion. Perhaps this would have been possible if Paris and London had been able to set aside other disagreements, but this was not to be. Though no one saw it in such a light at the time, this was, in fact, the first failure of the League of Nations, whose efficacy depended then, as later, on the Western Powers.

6

East Galicia and the Question of Poland's Eastern Frontier, November 1918 to December 1921

In the two years that followed the signing of the Treaty of Riga, the major goal of Polish diplomacy was to secure Western recognition of Poland's eastern frontier as established by that treaty. This issue dominated Poland's relations both with the Western Powers and with her East European neighbors: Soviet Russia, the Baltic States, Rumania, and Czechoslovakia. The need to secure this frontier led to Poland's only East European alliance, the defensive alliance with Rumania against the Soviet Union, signed on 3 March 1921.[1]

The official obstacle to Western recognition of Poland's eastern frontier was the undefined status of East Galicia.* The basic reason was, however, Prime Minister Lloyd George's policy of using the issue of East Galicia both as a bargaining chip with Soviet Russia and as a means of putting pressure on Poland. East Galician oil also played a role in Allied policy. The internal aspect of the problem was the Polish struggle with the Ukrainians of East Galicia, who wanted independence, either alone or united with Great Ukraine. The undecided status of East Galicia fueled both the ferment of the Ukrainian population and repressions by the Polish authorities. These, in turn, enraged liberal opinion in Britain and strengthened the image of Poland as an "imperialist" and oppressive state. At the same time, majority Polish opinion viewed the inclusion of East Galicia in Poland as both a strategic necessity and a historic right. The East Galician capital of Lvov was an old center of Polish culture which had a predominantly Polish population. The

* The name East Galicia is used here because it was common usage at the time. Ukrainians referred to it as Halychyna, or Zahid'na Ukraina (West Ukraine), and the Polish name was Małopolska Wschodnia (East Little Poland).

bitter Polish-Ukrainian struggle over the city in 1918/19 made it even more difficult for Polish opinion to support significant concessions to the Ukrainians. Finally, Poles accounted for some 35 percent of the population east of the San River, and they were adamantly opposed to an autonomous East Galicia with a Ukrainian administration, as demanded by Britain.

The problem of East Galicia was similar in most respects to that of Vilna, since it involved an ethnically mixed territory in which the Poles formed the upper class and also part of the peasant population. Like the Vilna region, East Galicia had belonged to Poland before the partitions, but unlike Vilna, it had never been part of the Russian Empire. In both areas the non-Polish political leaders opposed Polish rule. As in Vilna, so in Lvov, the majority of the population was Polish-speaking; and there was also a high percentage of Jews. Both cities had been the capitals of non-Polish states in the early Middle Ages. As with the Lithuanians, so with the Ukrainians, the national division ran along class and language lines, with an additional religious split in East Galicia between Catholics, Uniates, and Orthodox. The Poles were preponderantly Catholic, while the majority of Ukrainians belonged to the Uniate Church and a minority belonged to the Orthodox Church.[2] There was also a large Jewish population, mostly in the towns. In both Lithuania and East Galicia, Polish culture was dominant and was seen as the major enemy by Lithuanians and Ukrainians.

The land of East Galicia (Polish—Halich; Ukrainian—Halych) had been ruled by Roman Mstyslavych and his son Daniel from the early thirteenth to the mid-fourteenth century. Then it came first under Hungarian and later under Polish rule, which spread with time to include most of the Ukraine. However, the Khmel'nyts'kyi revolt against Poland in the mid-seventeenth century led the Cossack leaders to sign a treaty of union with Russia in 1655.[3] Three years later, they signed the Union of Hadziacz with Poland, but it was repudiated by the Cossack masses. In 1667, the left bank, or East Ukraine, went to Russia, while the right bank, or West Ukraine, stayed with Poland. In 1793, Russia seized the lands west of Kiev and Volhynia. Chełm was annexed in the Third Partition and again in 1815.

Meanwhile, East Galicia came under Austrian rule in 1772. In 1848 the Austrian governor of Galicia, Count Stadion, established the Holovna Ruska Rada, or Chief Ruthene Council, which formulated the first Ukrainian territorial program. It demanded the establishment of a Ruthene crownland in the Austrian Empire, consisting of East Galicia and Sub-Carpathian Ruthenia. In 1867, Emperor Francis Joseph granted de facto autonomy to Galicia. Since the Poles formed the educated class, they now played the dominant role in the schools and in the administration. In the last years of the nineteenth century, the Ukrainian national movement was led by the great historian Mykhailo Hrushevs'kyi, who founded the Ukrainian National

Democratic Party.[4] Its goal was also a Ukrainian crownland within the Austrian Empire—this time consisting of East Galicia and Bukovina. In 1910 the Revolutionary (Socialist) Party demanded an independent Ukrainian state.

World War I exacerbated the existing Polish-Ukrainian antagonisms. The maximum goal of the Ukrainian political leaders was a great Ukraine—including both left- and right-bank Ukraine—with the support of the Central Powers; their minimum goal was a separate Ukrainian crownland within the Austrian Empire. This was the aim of the East Galician Social Democratic, Radical, and National Democratic parties, which established the Holovna Ukrainska Rada, or Chief Ukrainian Council, in August 1914. Of course, this aim collided head on with the political goal of most Polish parties in Galicia, which wanted the establishment of a Polish crownland of Galicia as the nucleus of a future Polish state. The Rada established its own military organization, the Sich, which took its name from the seventeenth-century Cossack organization but was modeled, in fact, on the Polish riflemen's organization established by Piłsudski. The most prominent Ukrainian politicians who worked for the crownland program were Kost Levytsky and Mykhailo Vassylko. However, while the Austrian government could not afford to alienate the Poles, it failed to reach agreement with its German ally on the shape of the future Polish state. In early 1918 the Austrian government favored the Ukrainians and lost the Poles, as we shall see below.

In March 1917 the first Russian Revolution led to the establishment of the Rada, or Ukrainian Central Council, in Kiev. It was chaired by Professor Hrushevs'kyi, who had returned there in 1905. The Rada desired a federal relationship with Russia, but was rebuffed by the Russian Provisional Government. The Rada therefore issued a declaration of Ukrainian autonomy on 23 June 1917. The Bolshevik Revolution of 7 November immediately affected the Ukraine. On 20 November the Rada proclaimed the Ukrainian People's Republic, as part of a Russian federation. The Bolsheviks, however, set up their own Ukrainian government in Kharkov and declared the Kiev Rada dissolved. Under these circumstances, the Rada decided to send a delegation to Brest-Litovsk to participate in the peace negotiations between the Bolsheviks and the Central Powers.[5]

On 9 February 1918, A. Sevriuk, head of the Kiev Rada's delegation, signed a separate peace treaty with the Central Powers. Furthermore, in the Treaty of Brest-Litovsk, these powers awarded the provinces of Chełm and Podlasie to the Ukrainians, despite the preponderantly Polish population in Chełm. This, of course, infuriated the Poles. Also, the Ukrainians of East Galicia signed a secret protocol to the treaty, whereby the Austrian government was to establish a Ukrainian crownland made up of East Galicia and Bukovina.[6] In late April 1918, however, the Germans abolished the Ukrainian Rada in Kiev and installed hetman Pavlo Skoropads'kyi as head of a puppet Ukrainian state. He demanded that the Ukraine include the Kuban, Bessarabia, southern Belorussia, the Crimea, the Don region, Podlasie, and Chełm.[7]

In November 1918 the former Kiev Rada created a Directorate, with V. Vynnychenko as Chairman and Simon Petlyura, F. Shvets, P. Andriyevs'kyi, and A. Makarenko as members. They led a national uprising against Skoropads'kyi and took Kiev on 14 December. The Directorate issued a radically socialist and nationalist proclamation and turned to the Entente Powers for help. Although the French showed some interest, this was limited to establishing cooperation between the Directorate's army and that of General Denikin, commander of the White armies in Odessa.[8] The Bolsheviks took Kiev on 4 February 1919, and the Directorate fled west to Vinnitsa, then to Kamenets and Rovno. At this time, Petlyura began to think of seeking help from Piłsudski.

Meanwhile, in September 1918, when the defeat of the Central Powers seemed imminent, the Ukrainians of East Galicia began to make preparations for a takeover. The Poles were caught by surprise. The POW, or Polish Military Organization, had only about thirty or forty members in Lvov, most of whom were arrested by the Austrian authorities in September 1918. The Polish legionaries under Col. Władysław Sikorski numbered about two hundred in October, while the PKW, or Polish military cadres, stood at about one hundred.[9]

On 19 October a Ukrainian conference met in Lvov and rejected union with East Ukraine. It appointed a new council, headed by Kost Levytsky. When the Austrian government would not sanction a Ukrainian takeover, the council decided on 30 October to proceed on its own. Thus, on 1 November 1918 the Ukrainians, who had gathered many of their units from the Austrian Army in the vicinity of Lvov, took over the city. They proclaimed the establishment of the West Ukrainian Republic, and a Ukrainian flag was hoisted over the town hall. But the Polish population put up a strong resistance and, after a few days, regained some key buildings. Sich riflemen arrived from Bukovina, and a detachment came from East Ukraine, but Polish troops were sent in from Kraków. They forced the Ukrainians to evacuate the city on 21 November, though it was under siege throughout the winter of 1918/19.

The Ukrainian attempt to seize Lvov, and the Polish counterattack that followed, precipitated the initial Western involvement in the problem of East Galicia. As in Vilna, so in East Galicia, the attitude of the Western Powers was governed at first by their support of the White leaders in the Russian civil war. The British attitude was officially based on the principle of self-determination, which coincided conveniently with the traditional British view of Poland as Congress, or Russian, Poland (1815–30). Moreover, in 1916, Balfour had noted that from a "selfish" point of view, Britain wished to see a small Poland, which would not be an obstacle to alliance between the Western Powers and Russia.[10] In October 1918, in what was probably his first serious consideration of East Galicia, Balfour saw it as an example of the difficulty of excluding non-Polish areas from Poland. He noted that there had been six hundred years of Polish rule in East Galicia and parts of Lithuania. However, this fact, plus the existence of a wealthy and educated Polish upper class, should not, he thought, modify the British stand at the forthcoming Peace Conference. He thought that the division of Galicia would "pain" Polish nationalists. At the same time, he noted that it would be even more difficult to include genuinely Polish areas in western Poland because of German opposition.[11]

The White Russian leaders, who were then supported by France and Britain, not only claimed East Galicia but also refused to consider the possibility of a federal Russian state. Their motto—One Great, Indivisible Russia—found support in the West. Even Lewis B. Namier, the Political Intelligence Department's expert on Eastern Europe, wrote in 1917 that "the Little Russians [Ukrainians] in the South and the White Russians [Belorussians] in the North are essentially part of the Russian nation."[12] A year later he argued that any extension of Poland's frontiers beyond ethnic lines was "fanciful" and bound in the long run to benefit the Germans. In his view, only the recovery of a Great Russia could "free" Poland from the Central Powers. If the Poles expanded in the east, they would have to use military force against the Lithuanians, the Ukrainians, and the Belorussians and would, therefore, never be free of German tutelage.[13] In August 1918 he believed that Germany could bid for Poland at the expense of the Lithuanians, Belorussians, and Ukrainians and that Berlin could rely on the Polish "nobility" and its "imperialist" interests in the east.[14] In November he claimed that the Ukrainians were determined not to submit to Polish rule and that they wanted to be under Kiev. Putting East Galicia under Polish rule would be an "outrage" and a great danger for peace. He therefore proposed that the Polish minority in East Galicia be granted autonomy.[15] Finally, a Foreign Office memorandum in December, which probably came from his pen, argued that if the Peace Conference were to give the Poles large areas of Russian or German land, this would lead to a new partition of Poland.[16] The Germans reached their own conclusion. They feared a great Poland as a barrier to German-Russian cooperation and saw her as the ally and pawn of France in Eastern Europe; therefore, they were determined to do everything possible to prevent the creation of a large Polish state.[17]

As a member of the PID (Political Intelligence Department), Namier did not, of course, formulate British policy; but he did provide it with useful arguments based both on self-determination and on alleged *Realpolitik*.[18] In fact, as was the case regarding the Baltic States, British policy aimed to leave open the door for East Galicia's union with Russia. Therefore, Namier's advice that the Poles should be ordered to reach an agreement with the Ukrainians accorded with British Policy.[19] Thus, the British note of 8 November 1918 threatened great displeasure if the Poles were to undertake military operations in East Galicia in an attempt to forestall the decisions of the Peace Conference.[20] At the same time, R. A. Leeper of the Foreign Office pointed out that Britain could only replace Germany on the Russian market if she maintained friendly relations with (White) Russia[21]—which claimed East Galicia. The Americans also were inclined to exclude this region from Poland.[22] Only the French government supported Polish claims, because its overall aim was to build a "screen" between Bolshevik Russia and the Czechs and Hungarians and, above all, between Bolshevik Russia and Germany.[23] However, even the French assumed that East Galicia would be an autonomous province within Poland.[24] As for the Poles, at the end of 1918, Roman Dmowski and the National Democrats demanded the whole of East Galicia, while Piłsudski and his supporters were content with a "minimum" line, which included Lvov and the oil fields of Drohobycz and Boryslav.[25] When the Peace Conference opened, Dmowski demanded the whole area for Poland.

At this time the British delegation's memorandum on the former Russian Empire, dated 20 January 1919, proposed that all non-Polish territories in the east be excluded from the Polish state. As for East Galicia, it was to be allowed to opt for independence or for union with the Ukraine—or even with Czechoslovakia.[26] On the same day, Namier supported the third option; he noted that the Czechs wanted a common frontier with Russia and could also "organize" that vast country. He cited Thomas G. Masaryk, the president of Czechoslovakia, on the desirability of a "federation" between East Galicia and Czechoslovakia. Namier added that the Czechs feared complete "encirclement" by the Magyars and Poles since the latter could then "dictate" terms to the Czechs on Austrian Silesia (Teschen).[27] Somehow, the wishes of the East Galician Poles, who formed about 35 percent of the population, were lost sight of in these schemes.

In any case, British and American views on East Galicia were governed primarily by the desire to keep the good will of the White Russians. The British also succeeded in holding up Haller's army in France until mid April, when it was sent to Poland on the express condition that it not be used to fight the Ukrainians in East Galicia.[28] Also, the Allies sent commissions of inquiry to the area, which were supposed to stop the fighting. The first of these, headed by Gen. Marie-Joseph Barthélemy, left for Poland in January 1919. At this time, only the French supported Polish claims, although they envisaged East Galician autonomy within Poland.[29] The French were also very interested in East Galicia's oil industry.

Oil was an important ingredient in the East Galician question. Oil production in 1913 was 2,053,150 tons. Though it had declined to a mere 900,000 tons in 1916, it still had considerable potential. In 1913, French, British, and Belgian capital represented over half of the total investments, the rest being German and Austro-Hungarian, with a small Polish involvement. At the end of the war, British capital was estimated to be 10,125,000 frs.; French, 44,800,000 frs.; and Belgian, 20,000,000 frs. Polish capital was estimated to be 10 percent of the total.[30]

Western interests were represented by the Eastern Continental Petroleum and Mining Syndicate Ltd., established in London in August 1914, and by the International Committee for the Protection of British, French, Belgian, and Other Allied Interests, established in London in October of that year. The British Premier Oil and Pipeline Co. Ltd. had a member on that committee. While French capitalists proceeded to buy out Austrian and German oil shares, the British followed another tack. Two British members of Barthélemy's mission, a Major Fordham and a man named MacIntosh, who was connected with Premier Oil, proposed in February 1919 that Polish and Ukrainian troops withdraw from the oil fields, which would then constitute a neutral zone with Polish police and administration. The oil fields, refineries, and reserves would be put under an Entente commission to be chaired by MacIntosh. Control and distribution of production was to be carried out with the participation of Polish and Ukrainian delegates.[31]

The Poles saw this project as threatening foreign annexation of East Galician oil resources;[32] so they proposed a Polish-Ukrainian agreement instead. In the meanwhile, the Ukrainians, who controlled the oil fields, had signed an agreement with the Karolyi government of Hungary to get arms in return for oil. The agreement was later ratified by Béla Kun, who set up a Communist government in Hungary in March 1919. The Ukrainians also signed an agreement with the Czechoslovak government, exchanging oil for coal.[33]

In early March 1919 the International Committee began to press its claims. Its representative, L. Litwiński, arrived in Warsaw on the eleventh and saw Piłsudski four days later. Litwiński demanded that the member companies of the International Committee be allowed to take possession of the oil wells and refineries that belonged to them. Piłsudski demanded that the committee first press the British Foreign Office to aid Poland with military equipment. One result of this was a letter from Charles Perkins, chairman of Premier Oil, to Balfour, asking for British aid to Poland.[34] However, neither this nor other interventions by Perkins had any effect. The reason may lie in the Franco-British oil agreement that will be described below.

Sir John Cadman, director of H.M. Petroleum Executive and oil adviser to the British government, negotiated an oil agreement with Senator Henri Bérenger, the French commissioner general of Petroleum Products. A draft of the agreement was submitted to the Foreign Office on 13 March 1919. On the British side it was signed by Walter Long, First Lord of the Admiralty; Bérenger signed for France. The Long-Bérenger agreement divided the oil rights in the Middle East and in Eastern Europe between the French and the British governments. In Eastern Europe they agreed on an equal division of the rights that might be obtained by either side in Rumania, Russia, and Galicia. The agreement was approved on 8 May and confirmed by Britain eight days later.[35] Although Lloyd George noted in July that he knew nothing about it,[36] he accepted it later, for Cadman and Bérenger concluded a new agreement along the same lines. Curzon and Berthelot accepted it as the basis for an oil agreement signed on 23 December 1919.[37]

In the meanwhile, Polish-Ukrainian negotiations failed because the demands of the two parties were mutually contradictory. Each side claimed the oil fields and Lvov. The British and Italians supported the Ukrainians so as to leave the door open for a union of East Galicia with Russia, while Barthélemy's proposal that the oil region be made a neutral zone on the Polish side was refused both by the Poles and by the Ukrainians.[38] At this point it is worth noting that the British General Staff took a different view from that of the Foreign Office. The General Staff favored the fusion of East Galicia with Poland and the establishment of a Polish-Rumanian frontier. Alternatively, the General Staff suggested an autonomous East Galician state, rather than having it included in the Ukraine, warning that this would give Russia access in the future to the Carpathians.[39] The General Staff was traditionally anti-Russian; therefore it feared that Russia would expand into the Eastern Balkans and dominate the Straits—the old fear of which had led the British to support the Ottoman Empire in the nineteenth century.

The Ukrainians of East Galicia now played their anti-Bolshevik card. We should note that the West Ukrainian Republic had signed an act of union with the East Ukrainian government (Directorate) in January 1919. Gen. Omelyan Pavlenko, commander of the East Galician troops, told members of the Allied subcommittee that was negotiating an armistice with the Poles that he was awaiting instructions from his government in Stanisławów (Ukrainian, Stanyslaviv) and the results of conversations with Allied representatives in Odessa on action to be taken against the Bolsheviks there.[40] Despite French denials, conversations with Petlyura's representatives there did take place. Saint Aulaire reported from Bucharest that the Ukrainian Directorate had offered to retake Odessa from the Bolsheviks, but only after an armistice had been signed in East Galicia. Then they could transfer sixty thousand men from East Galicia to Odessa.[41]

Though nothing came of this in the end, it was a factor in Pavlenko's decision to suspend the armistice and to attack the Poles in early March. This, in turn, led Jules Cambon, president of the Peace Conference, to tell the Supreme Council on 12 March that the Polish situation in Lvov was critical. If Lvov fell, he claimed there would be danger of "German intrigues" against the Polish state. On this ground, he argued that Haller's army be immediately dispatched to Poland.[42] Two days later the Franco-British commission led by General Barthélemy and the British representative, Colonel Smyth, produced a report favorable to the Poles. It warned that if East Galicia went to the Ukrainians, Russia would expand westward at Poland's expense, and there would be a new partition of Poland. The commission claimed that the Ukrainians were incapable of establishing a state because they constituted an ignorant mass with but a few educated men and were allegedly committed to implementing a Communist program (!). Therefore the commission proposed that Polish-Ukrainian hostilities be ended by force and that East Galicia be united with Poland, though with guarantees for the different nationalities and, if need be, a "reasonable" autonomy under Polish tutelage.[43]

The commission's report was obviously written under the impact of the Ukrainian attack on the Poles. While the Ukrainian intelligentsia in East Galicia was very small[44] and while the Ukrainian peasants obviously wished to divide the Polish estates among themselves, the last thing they wanted was Communism. Led by a patriotic Uniate clergy, they wanted their own government and radical land reform. In any case, the French Ministry of Foreign Affairs reacted negatively to the report. It advised the minister of war to be prudent. France should not take sides in the Polish-Ukrainian question, which was to be decided by the Peace Conference. Also, since French troops were menaced by the Bolsheviks in Kherson and Odessa, attention should be directed there. French policy, stated the author of the memorandum (probably Berthelot) had been to use Ukrainian troops against the Bolsheviks, not to attack the Ukrainians to Poland's advantage.[45]

This advice reflected the French desire to avoid antagonizing the White Russians and the British. The latter's attitude was clear. On 19 March, at a meeting of the Council of Ten, Lloyd George—who for once had an ethnic map at his disposal—pointed out that Lemberg (Lvov) was a Polish island in a Ukrainian sea. He called the Polish claims "exorbitant" and said that he believed them to be intimately related to Galician oil.[46] However, the Russian factor was paramount. On 4 April the French agreed with the British that the Ukraine could not be independent of Russia and also that the Denikin government was the only one worth supporting in South Russia.[47] Naturally, the (White) Russian Political Conference in Paris agreed. Its memorandum of

9 April to J. Cambon claimed that the new Russia must establish her relations with Poland on "a solid and just basis." The authors recalled that the Provisional Government had recognized an "ethnic" Poland on 30 March 1917, but they also stated that Poland must have Danzig.[48] Thus, the White Russians favored the ethnic principle for Poland in the east but not necessarily in the west. Not surprisingly, the Commission on Polish Affairs reported on 21 April that a definitive settlement of Poland's eastern frontier would have to await the establishment of a Russian government with which the Western Powers could deal on this question.[49]

By now the hope for the emergence of a non-Bolshevik Russia, perhaps under Denikin or Kolchak, dominated the French attitude toward East Galicia. Jules Laroche, assistant director of the Department for Political and Commercial Affairs at the Quai d'Orsay, wrote that France should work for western Polish frontiers that would conform to Polish national "aspirations" and that she should use them as a lever to make the Poles accept eastern frontiers based on the idea of "nationality." This, he noted, was contrary to the "imperialist" ambitions of many Poles. He thought that Polish claims to Lithuanian, Belorussian, and Ukrainian lands paralleled German claims to Polish lands—that is, they were based on arguments of superior wealth and culture and the possession of an administrative class. He believed that the rejection of Polish claims in the east would only affect the great landowners, who were a feeble minority in Polish society. A radical land reform would, he thought, create a strong Polish peasant class, which would in turn lead to a strong middle class. This would bring about a stable Polish state, like those of the Czechs and Serbs (!). This was all the more desirable, he wrote, since great Polish landowners had connections with German nobles and thus represented an uncertain element for France. They might work for a pro-German policy or for an equilibrium between France and Germany, thus making Poland into a new kind of Italy (!). It was therefore in France's interest to weaken the Polish landowners.[50] It is interesting that while Namier had originally attributed Poland's eastern claims to her landowners, by the spring of 1919 he had concluded that the Polish Socialists and Piłsudski were no more reasonable than the National Democrats.[51] Namier still failed to notice that Warsaw's claims to East Galicia were supported by the vast majority of Poles.

At the end of April the Commission on Polish Affairs proposed three possible solutions to the new Commission on East Galicia, headed by Gen. Louis Botha of South Africa. The three possibilities were: an independent East Galicia; an autonomous East Galicia under league control; a partition between Poland and the (Russian) Ukraine.[52] Interestingly enough, the semiofficial *Gazeta Polska* of 27 April proposed that the territory east of Lvov should go to the Ukrainians.[53] This was, of course, Piłsudski's point of view, but it went counter to a resolution voted by the Sejm on 4 April that East

Galicia should belong to Poland.[54] Now Western pressure mounted on the Polish government to stop the fighting. At the same time, Witold Jodko-Narkiewicz, director of the Political Department in the Ministry of Foreign Affairs, wrote to Paderewski from Warsaw that Sazonov's private secretary, Kvashin, claimed that Sazonov had obtained specific promises from Pichon and from the British on the future Polish-Russian frontier.[55] The Ukrainians were not idle either. At the end of April, Lord Acton, the British minister in Berne, reported proposals made by Nicholas Vasylko, an emissary of the West Ukrainian government. Vasylko said his government insisted on the line of the San but was willing to give the Poles oil concessions for fifteen years. He warned that if the Allies rejected Ukrainian claims, the Ukrainians would massacre the Poles.[56]

The Poles now accused the Ukrainians of having an agreement with the Bolsheviks to let the Red Army go through East Galicia to Hungary; the Poles also claimed that the Ukrainians had been completely "Bolshevized."[57] These Polish charges fitted in with the dominant Allied aim of fostering the emergence of a non-Bolshevik Russia. On 5 May, at a meeting of the subcomission on Poland's eastern frontiers, Colonel Kisch proposed that there be a high commissioner for East Galicia. The intent was clear, for he referred to former Russian claims, to their war sacrifices, and to the similarity between the Ukrainians of East Galicia and their eastern neighbors. General Le Rond pointed out, however, that Russia had no legal claim to East Galicia and that, if she acquired it, she would stand on the Carpathians.[58]

British opposition to Polish claims and to military operations in East Galicia stiffened perceptively when a White victory in Russia seemed almost certain. In May, Kolchak reached the Upper Volga basin, Denikin began a rapid advance from the Lower Volga toward Moscow, and Yudenich stood outside Petrograd.[59] Some British and Commonwealth officials may have believed that the problem was quite simply Polish "imperialism,"[60] but for others this argument was just a pretext to support Russian claims, especially since on 10 May the Russian Political Conference had claimed that "self-determination" for East Galicia, Bukovina, and some Hungarian counties was an "absolute necessity." The conference also demanded a common Russian-Czechoslovakian frontier, justifying this by Russia's need for Czechoslovak industrial goods.[61] On the same day, Namier advised that until Russia had recovered and a final settlement had been made, East Galicia should be put under a high commissioner appointed by the League of Nations. He noted that most of the British delegation supported this idea.[62]

Although on 13 May the Polish Sejm voted for regional autonomy in East Galicia, this did not satisfy the Allies. The British and the Americans pressed the Polish government either to accept an armistice or to risk the loss of Allied support for the restoration of the lands of Prussian Poland.[63] At the same time, the French and Italians secretly advised the Poles to proceed by *faits accomplis.* On 14 May, however, the Foreign Ministers' Conference in Paris decided that the peace treaty with Austria should include special clauses whereby Austria would resign her sovereign rights over East Galicia and transfer them to the Allied and Associated Powers. Also, economic sanctions could be used against any state that was waging war against its neighbors contrary to the will of the Powers.[64] Indeed, at the sessions of the Supreme Council on 17, 19, and 21 May, Lloyd George and Wilson proposed that very stiff sanctions be imposed against the Poles if they continued their offensive in East Galicia, launched on 14 May.[65]

Piłsudski tried to mollify the British. On 19 May he told Sir Percy Wyndham, the British minister in Warsaw, that Poland would be content with Lvov and the oil region—which had just been captured by the Poles— and leave their other claims in the area to be decided by the Peace Conference.[66] At this point, too, S. Petlyura saw Polish aid as his only hope for survival. On 27 May his envoy, Boris Kurdynovsky, signed an unofficial agreement with Paderewski in Warsaw. There was to be a joint Polish-Ukrainian struggle against the Bolsheviks under Polish command, and the Directorate renounced claims to East Galicia and Volhynia up to the river Styr. In return, Poland would support the establishment of an independent Ukraine. The rights of Poles in the Ukraine and of Ukrainians in Poland were to be guaranteed.[67] Although the agreement was rejected by the Directorate, under pressure from East Galician leaders, it foreshadowed both the final split between East and West Ukrainians and the Piłsudski-Petlyura treaties of April 1920.

Meanwhile, in Paris, both Lloyd George and Wilson were very angry with the Poles for continuing their advance in East Galicia. On 26 May the two heads of state obtained French agreement to a threat of cutting off supplies if the Poles did not accept the advice of the Peace Conference.[68] On the same day, a telegram was dispatched to the "Ruler of all Russia," Admiral Kolchak, which stipulated conditions of Allied aid to him. Although East Galicia was not mentioned, the document twice stated that disputed boundaries should be settled through the arbitration of the League of Nations.[69] This proposal tied in with the British delegation's proposal to put East Galicia under a high commissioner appointed by the league. As noted above, this was to leave open the possibility of a union with Russia.

Piłsudski countered the Allied threat to cut off supplies by explaining his advance on military grounds. He said that it was a reply to Ukrainian attacks and that he wished to effect a juncture with Rumanian forces. He argued that this was necessary since, if Germany were to cut off Poland from the west, the Poles would be able to receive Allied support only through Rumania.[70] Disclosing his real reasons in a letter to Paderewski, Piłsudski wrote that since the settlement of Poland's western frontiers depended for "nine tenths" on the Allies, he had to delay any risk of conflict with them until these frontiers were settled. After that, however, "Poland will become a first class force in Eastern Europe," and the Entente would have to recognize her as such. Piłsudski also informed Paderewski of his instructions to Sapieha, the Polish minister in London. Sapieha was to oppose the concept of a Great Russia, stretching to the Bug River. Instead, he was to gain support for Piłsudski's concept of forming a federal union between Poland and all territories lying between her and Russia proper. He was also to stimulate British interest in the Polish economy.[71]

In Paris, Paderewski confronted Lloyd George on 5 June and rebutted the latter's charges of Polish "imperialism."[72] However, this was not the real issue; the dominant factor was Allied support of Kolchak. On 11 June, Kolchak replied to the Allied message of 27 May by reserving the right to make final boundary decisions to the future Russian Constituent Assembly. He also confirmed the Provisional Government's recognition of an "ethnic Poland" of March 1917.[73] French military intelligence reported that Czechs were supporting a Moscow-oriented Ukrainian group led by Volodymyr Synhalevych, who was backed by the White Russians.[74] Meanwhile, British and United States officers in East Galicia reported that Ukrainian peasants welcomed Polish troops as guarantors of peace and order. This was clearly an impression that had been obtained through Polish sources. What is more important, these officers reported that unless Polish troops were permitted to move up to the Zbrucz River, nothing could prevent the Bolsheviks from crossing it.[75] Indeed, the commander of the West Ukrainian army, who was hard pressed by the Bolsheviks in his rear, signed an armistice with the Poles in Lvov on 16 June 1919. The Bolshevik advance was to prove the key to Allied approval of Polish military operations. Before we discuss this, however, we must turn again to the oil question.

As noted earlier, the Long-Bérenger oil agreement was confirmed by the British government on 16 May. The International Committee also pressed the Poles to allow it to buy out German and Austrian oil shares. At the end of May, Perkins of Premier Oil demanded that the Polish government allow interested British firms to take over their own property. However, the Polish government managed to stave off these demands.[76]

It is not surprising, in view of the Bolshevik threat and of Western oil interests, that the Commission on Polish Affairs recommended on 17 June that East Galicia be attached to Poland, though it also suggested that Lvov might be made a free city. The commission now argued for frontier line B, leaving Lvov and the oil fields to Poland, instead of line A, which would exclude them from the Polish state.[77] On the next day, 18 June, East Galicia was discussed by representatives of Britain, the United States, France, Italy, and Japan. Balfour stood by the former British proposals that the league appoint a high commissioner for East Galicia and that a plebiscite be held in the future. He argued that this would keep open the Ruthene option to join either Poland or Russia, or to enter into a federation with one of them. He also suggested that a study be made of a possible union with Czechoslovakia. In the meanwhile, Polish troops should be allowed to advance to the Zbrucz River, but this would not prejudge the future status of East Galicia. However, Balfour found himself isolated. The French and Italian representatives favored an autonomous East Galicia in Poland, but they opposed a future plebiscite and were joined in this by the United States representative.[78] Finally, on 25 June, the Allies agreed that Polish troops should be allowed to advance to the Zbrucz River. The Polish government was authorized to set up a civil administration in East Galicia, but it was also required to safeguard the rights of the Ukrainians and to allow them to exercise self-determination at a time to be fixed by the Allies. This allusion to a plebiscite was inserted in order to satisfy the British government, even though the Commission on Polish Affairs had advised against it.[79] This was the first legal restriction to be put on Poland with regard to East Galicia. The second came three days later with the signing of the Versailles Treaty. Article 87 stated that the frontiers of Poland that were not defined in the treaty would be decided by the Allied and Associated Powers. The third was to follow in the Treaty of St. Germain in September, in which, according to article 91, Austria ceded her sovereignty over East Galicia to the Allied and Associate Powers.

At this time, the British government and private concerns increased their interest in East Galician oil. The journal *Oil Finance* reported on 12 July that the British government had sent F. W. Robertson Butler, secretary of H.M. Petroleum Executive, and R. R. Thompson, a representative of Anglo-Persian Oil, to examine the situation in East Galicia. At the same time, the Polish Ministry of Foreign Affairs and the Ministry of Industry managed to stave off the takeover by the British Premier Oil Company of the largest oil wells and refineries, which were located in Tustanowice. Instead, the Polish government established a temporary Polish administration, though this included persons nominated by Premier Oil.[80] Polish control of all of East Galicia strengthened the government's hand with Western oil interests. In August the International Committee failed to obtain Polish assent to its takeover of German and Austrian oil property in East Galicia, even with compensation to the Polish government. Paderewski told the committee's representatives that Polish economic policy would depend on what decisions were made in Paris regarding the future of East Galicia. Premier Oil also failed in its bid to unite all former enemy refineries into one company, with great privileges for the British. Still, hopes of lucrative concessions made Perkins write Balfour on 22 August that Premier Oil could not support either a provisional decision on East Galicia or any limitations on Polish sovereignty over the province. Balfour replied that the British government could not accept or recommend the subordination of the rights and liberties of any country to the real or supposed interests of Western investors.[81] He may have been sincere in this view, but he also knew that the Treaty of Versailles, according to article 87, left the settlement of Poland's eastern frontiers in Allied hands. Also, by this time, French investors were well on the way to acquiring a dominant interest in the East Galician oil fields, thus reducing British chances.

Piłsudski had to keep the Versailles Treaty in mind when he considered Petlyura's proposal of 9 August for close cooperation. In return, the Ukrainian leader was ready to renounce claims to East Galicia. Since Piłsudski could not risk alienating the Western Powers by making an open agreement with Petlyura, the Polish foreign minister informed them that the proposed renunciation of East Galicia was unilateral and that its purpose was to coordinate the anti-Bolshevik campaign in South Russia.[82] On 30 August, Petlyura took Kiev but was ousted the next day by Denikin. The East Galician Ukrainian troops then agreed to cooperate with Denikin, in protest against Petlyura's renunciation of East Galicia. On 1 September, Petlyura signed an armistice with Poland.

Early September witnessed Denikin's greatest advance toward Moscow. The Poles feared that his victory would reduce Poland to a revived Grand Duchy of Warsaw.[83] Indeed, Denikin's press secretary, Shulgin, published a book in Rostov-on-Don entitled *Great Russia,* in which Poland was to have the eastern boundaries of 1815.[84] Polish talks with Denikin were therefore inconclusive and were undertaken only to satisfy the Entente Powers.[85] In the meanwhile, Polish representatives in Paris protested against any provisional status for East Galicia,[86] while the West Ukrainian leaders claimed that the Poles were systematically liquidating Ukrainian language and thought in the province. Some of these protests were sent from Czechoslovakia, where members of the West Ukrainian government and some troops had found refuge and support.[87] Finally, the treaty of Saint-Germain with Austria was signed on 10 September. As noted above, according to article 91, Austria renounced all rights and titles to her former territories lying beyond her new frontiers, whose fate had not yet been decided by the Allied and Associated Powers, and transferred her sovereignty to the latter. Also, in article 67 she agreed to accept such frontiers with Bulgaria, Greece, Hungary, Poland, Czechoslovakia, Rumania, and the Serbo-Croat-Slovene state as would be decided by the Allied and Associated Powers. Nine days after the signing of the Treaty of Saint-Germain, Sir Eyre Crowe, representing Balfour, told a meeting of the heads of delegations that the statute for East Galicia should leave the way open for union with Russia. As he put it, ''No obstacle should be placed in the way of an ultimate union of Eastern Galicia with Russia, and it therefore should not be made impossible for this province to separate itself from Poland.''[88]

Although Paderewski was allowed to defend Polish claims before the heads of delegations,[89] he warned Piłsudski that the Allies were counting on Denikin's success and that Poland could not afford the slightest clash, let alone conflict, with him.[90] General Rozwadowski, the Polish military representative in Paris, confirmed that this was also the French view.[91] Under these circumstances, it was not surprising that in its report of 25 September, the Commission on Polish Affairs recommended a provisional Polish eastern boundary similar to that of Congress Poland. The commission also stated that the final determination of Poland's eastern boundary would require the cooperation of a future Russian government.[92] The French had to go along, although they generally favored the Polish cause. Thus, Jules Cambon assured Paderewski privately that in his opinion, East Galicia would ultimately belong to Poland. But Cambon urged the Polish government to show generosity in granting autonomous institutions and to agree that the League of Nations Council act as arbitrator between the Polish and the East Galician diets on the application of disputed laws.[93]

It is no surprise that British insistence on a future plebiscite coincided with the demands of White Russian diplomats in Paris.[94] Lloyd George found another ally for his policy in the government of Canada, which was under pressure from numerous Ukrainians who had settled mostly in the western provinces of Saskatchewan, Alberta, and Manitoba. Lloyd George allegedly assured Sir Samuel Hughes, a Canadian M.P., that the Ukrainians of East Galicia would in all probability be allocated to the Ukraine instead of to Poland.[95] Indeed, Lloyd George was adamant that ''under no circumstances should East Galicia be annexed to Poland.'' In October he favored a Polish mandate for ten years, after which there was to be a plebiscite;[96] on 11 November, however, the British agreed to a twenty-five year Polish mandate for East Galicia.[97] Despite Denikin's defeat, all that the French proposed to the other heads of delegations on 2 December was that they recognize Polish sovereignty over *West* Galicia. At the same time, the Allies agreed on a provisional line for Polish administration north of East Galicia.[98] The proposal caused an outcry in Poland, and Foreign Minister Patek warned that the government would fall if it accepted the mandate.[99]

As the Bolsheviks mopped up the remnants of Denikin's defeated army and took Kiev, the hopes for a great non-Bolshevik Russia faded, and Poland's stock began to rise. In December, Clemenceau managed to persuade Lloyd George to retreat from the twenty-five year clause on the Polish mandate for East Galicia. However, the British prime minister insisted that this clause merely be ''suspended'' and reserved for later consideration.[100] By now, Lloyd George wished to end Allied intervention in Russia. The Foreign Office hewed to R. A. Leeper's earlier views that Great Britain should seek to establish herself as Russia's chief trading partner,[101] but this time Bolshevik Russia's. Lloyd George and Celemenceau agreed to end the intervention, and withdrawals of British troops began in December. We may assume that Lloyd George kept East Galicia up his sleeve as a card for dealing with the Bolsheviks.

As the year 1919 drew to a close, Piłsudski told Halford R. Mackinder and General Keyes, British emissaries on their way to Denikin, that the Polish army could march on Moscow in the spring, "but from a political point of view he asked himself what he should do when he got there." Referring to the territories occupied by Polish troops, Piłsudski emphatically disclaimed any imperialistic aims. He declared that he would allow plebiscites in the east as far back as the Conference Line, including Brest-Litovsk.[102] At the same time, he hinted that he would pursue his plans for an independent Ukraine and a Polish-Lithuanian-Belorussian federation.

Piłsudski gave more hints of this aim to the British and French ministers in Warsaw in early January 1920. By this time, the Soviet peace proposals to Poland were known, and the departing French minister in Warsaw, Eugène Pralon, expressed strong disapproval of Piłsudski's aims. Pralon reported on 12 January that the Polish chief of state hoped that the defeats of Kolchak and Denikin would make the French give up their policy of restoring the Russian monarchy and would induce them to support a Great Poland instead. Pralon thought the Polish aim was only a cleverly disguised plan to annex the borderlands. He believed France should oppose this, for Russian hatred of Poland might threaten the Versailles Treaty itself.[103] Thus, Pralon agreed with the Namier-Berthelot-Laroche school of thought that a large Poland at Russia's expense would lead to Russo-German cooperation. Two weeks later, Pralon reported that Piłsudski was thinking of establishing an independent Ukraine with a democratic government but one that would be "docile to his suggestions." He commented that Piłsudski had conceived this plan a long time ago.[104]

Sir Horace Rumbold, the new British minister in Warsaw, seemed to be more sympathetic to Piłsudski's aims. He reported Piłsudski's statement that there were two alternatives—either "a larger Poland" in alliance with all Russian border states, including Finland, which could then fight Bolshevik Russia; or "a lesser Poland," which would settle with the anti-Bolshevik Russians. Piłsudski's idea, wrote Rumbold, was "a kind of League of Nations in the Near East of Europe for combatting the Bolsheviks." However, two left-wing anti-Soviet Russian leaders, Boris Savinkov and Nikolai V. Chaikovskii, with whom Piłsudski discussed this idea, preferred a federation to an alliance system. Piłsudski, for his part, held that Finland and Poland could not be in a federation, since they were independent states. He thought the White Russians would at best agree to autonomy for the border states[105]—presumably within a Russian federation.

Piłsudski's plans might have had some chance of success if the French government had given up its dream of a non-Bolshevik Russia allied to France. However, this was not the case. Therefore, the French government opposed the preliminary peace proposals that Poland made to the Soviet government on 11 February—namely, that Russia give up claims to the territories lying within the Polish frontiers of 1772 and that all disputes be settled by free expression of the will of the population.[106] On 4 March, President Millerand instructed the new French minister in Warsaw, Hector de Panafieu, that it was not in Polish interests to flaunt "exaggerated" territorial claims. This was, he wrote, contrary to the principles of the Peace Treaties; also, Poland could not afford to be on bad terms with both Germany and Russia. He noted that Poland would need some time to recover her "moral unity" and that France was destined by history to be her "disinterested and friendly adviser." Therefore, Millerand instructed Panafieu to advise the Poles to avoid *maladresses* (tactless blunders) which would only make France's task more difficult. Panafieu was also to remind Warsaw that only General Le Rond was in a position to allow the Polish population of Upper Silesia to express its free opinion.[107] This attempt to pressure the Poles into giving up their demands for plebiscites in Polish-Russian borderlands smacked of blackmail. At the same time, the French supported British opposition at the Conference of Ambassadors to any plebiscites in eastern territories under Polish occupation. They still hoped that General Wrangel, whom they supported, would defeat the Bolsheviks. The British, who aimed at good trade relations with the Bolsheviks, also wished to avoid any plebiscites in what had formerly been western Russia. Therefore, the British cited Polish acceptance of future Allied decisions on the eastern frontiers in accordance with article 87 of the Versailles Treaty.[108] Rumbold made a statement along these lines to Foreign Minister Patek on 14 March.[109]

At this time, some British officials favored the idea of making the League of Nations the trustee for the eastern territories claimed by Poland. Thus, Palairet thought that the league might undertake the administration of disputed territories and hold them in trust for Russia.[110] Namier returned to the charge, claiming that Poland's eastern policy was dictated by the great landowners and that, anyway, she had been trying to break up Russia for centuries. He insisted that the Little Russians (Ukrainians) and the Belorussians were branches of the Russian nation. Finally, he argued that the results of a plebiscite would be invalidated if Poland became Bolshevik or if Russia became capitalist(!).[111] Rumbold made his own suggestions. He thought that in the eastern territories, Britain could support a mixed administration, made up of Polish and local officials, under the supervision of the League of Nations. These territories could "be held in trust" for a reconstituted Russia or, if the Allies favored autonomous states, in trust for those states.[112] J. D. Gregory, head of the Northern Department, favored Poland. Sir Eric Drummond, secretary general of the League of Nations, noted on 27 April that Gregory favored Polish sovereignty over East Galicia and Belorussia if their autonomy was guaranteed. Drummond himself thought that Poland might be given a mandate but with a very strict "organic law," providing for a large measure of autonomy. If the Powers so wished, there could be a resident commissioner to supervise Polish execution of the stipulations of the mandate.[113] As we shall see, some of these suggestions would crop up later.

Amid rumors of an impending Bolshevik offensive against Poland, Panafieu reported in mid April on Polish negotiations with Petlyura. The French minister thought that Piłsudski's aim of an alliance with a free and independent Ukraine masked a desire to find in the rich provinces of South Russia and on the Black Sea those advantages that the Poles had vainly sought on the Baltic.[114] This was only partly true, for Piłsudski's primary goal was to weaken Russia. In any event, the Polish-Ukrainian alliance was signed on 21 April, and the military convention, two days later.[115] Interestingly enough, on the same day, 23 April, East Galician and Bukovinian Communists held their first conference in Kiev and passed a resolution for the union of Galicia with the Soviet Ukraine.[116] Both sides were gearing up for war.

As we know, on 24 April the Polish armies and Petlyura's troops launched an offensive against the Ukraine. Two days later, Piłsudski issued a proclamation to the Ukrainian people. He stated that the Polish army was coming to clear the land of "foreign rulers" and that it would remain only until a legitimate Ukrainian government had established control. Petlyura issued his own proclamation on 27 April, stating that Poland was helping the Ukrainians against "a common foe" and that the blood of the two nations would cement their mutual friendship.[117]

As the Poles and the Ukrainians advanced on Kiev, French opinion was divided. On the one hand, Étienne Mantoux, head of the league's Information Department, noted on 1 May that he was "very frightened" by Polish ambitions in the East. He thought it most dangerous for Poland to claim her frontiers of 1772, even with autonomy for non-Polish populations. In his view, a Poland enlarged through the annexation of East Galicia and Belorussia would head straight for a fourth partition; in any case, the league could not accept Polish *faits accomplis*.[118] On the other hand, General Rozwadowski reported that Marshal Foch approved the Polish advance. Foch tempered this by the advice that the Poles should treat the border populations well, especially the Ukrainians, and develop their territories economically by supporting foreign capital investment. In this way, said Foch, "Poland could strengthen her rule there for a long time to our own advantage and that of the whole of Europe.''[119]

The East Galician Ukrainians were not idle, however. They tried to interest the French government in the establishment of an "ethnic" Poland and of a "neutral" East Galician state, which would serve as a "transit territory" between Poland and Russia. They proposed that this state include Chełm Province, West Volhynia, and central Grodno Province, giving it an area of 150,000 square kilometers and a population of about ten million.[120] This population was only half Ukrainian, with the rest being made up of Poles and Belorussians. However, the victorious Polish advance spurred French declarations of support for Polish claims to East Galicia.[121] The French were also gathering up the oil, and the British Foreign Office had no objections to the sale of shares of Premier Oil to French companies.[122] No wonder the Polish Foreign Ministry instructed its missions abroad to interpret article 87 of the Versailles Treaty as meaning that there would be an Allied decision on the frontiers, not of Poland, but of the plebiscite territories.[123] A few days later, the Finnish government recognized the Petlyura government as the de facto government of the Ukraine.[124] The reports from British military observers in Kiev were positive. Lieutenant Commander Rawlings was impressed by the "excellent behavior" of the Polish troops. His colleague, Major Grant, agreed. Both, however, had doubts as to the strength of Ukrainian national feeling.[125]

As we know, the Polish victory soon turned into a rout when the Red Army struck from the Ukraine and Belorussia. At Brussels on 4 July, Lloyd George insisted that Allied aid could only be given to Poland if she agreed to request it, asked for peace, agreed to come to terms with all border nations, and adopted a conciliatory attitude toward Danzig.[126] Three days later, Philip Kerr told Patek that Poland should be a national state within "ethnographic" boundaries.[127] On 8 July, Lloyd George and Foch agreed that the Lithuanians, the Ruthenes, and the Latvians should be included in Polish-Soviet peace negotiations.[128] On the same day the Revolutionary Committee of East Galicia and Bukovina, meeting in Kiev, issued an appeal to the workers and peasants of East Galicia to join the Red Army.[129] The final draft of conditions that Poland would have to accept in order to obtain Allied aid was worked out at Spa on 10 July; it included the agreement to negotiations on East Galicia under the auspices of the Peace Conference.[130]

Grabski agreed that Polish and Soviet troops should stand on the front line as of the day the armistice was signed. This was still favorable to the Poles in East Galicia, since Polish troops stood on the Zbrucz River. The insertion by the Foreign Office of an armistice line identical with line A in the report of the Commission on Polish Affairs of 17 June 1919 might have been a clerical error.[131] However, the Foreign Office was well aware of the fact that both the

Bolsheviks and the White Russians had claimed the province.[132] Only Rumania insisted that it be awarded to Poland.[133]

At a time when Poland seemed to be at the nadir of her fortunes, Edouard Beneš managed to obtain French and British assent for the definitive award of Teschen Silesia to Czechoslovakia. The story of this thorny problem has been well told elsewhere.[134] It has been known for some time that a "deal" was struck at Spa between Beneš, Laroche, and Crowe. Its exact terms are to be found in a holograph letter that Beneš wrote to Laroche, dated Spa, 11 July 1920. In it he promised that once back in Prague, he would arrange matters so that all hostilities with the Poles would cease immediately. He would speak publicly to inaugurate the new policy.[135] Beneš made the same commitments to the Polish delegates at Spa.[136] In return for these promises, his secret agreement with Laroche and Crowe stipulated that the Conference of Ambassadors—to which the Poles had unwittingly agreed to submit the Teschen dispute—would simply award the territory to Czechoslovakia.[137]

Nevertheless, the Czechoslovak blockage of war supplies to Poland continued, and on 10 August the Czechoslovak government declared its neutrality. On that same day, two significant and related events took place. Lord Curzon telegraphed the Soviet peace terms—as formulated by Kamenev in London—to Poland, advising that if they were made in good faith, Warsaw should accept them.[138] At the same time, two treaties were signed at Sèvres. The first was the Treaty of Sèvres between the Allied Powers and Turkey, in which, as one American historian has put it, Britain obtained "an imperialistic settlement following the best traditions of nineteenth century imperialism."[139] The other was the "Treaty between the British Empire and Principal Allied and Associated Powers and Poland, Rumania, the Serbo-Croat-Slovene State and the Czecho-slovak State relative to certain frontiers of those States." In this treaty, which Poland did not sign or ratify, Polish sovereignty was recognized over *Western* Galicia along line A, as in the report of the Commission on Polish Affairs of 17 June 1919.[140] Thus, Lvov and the oil fields were left outside Polish territory. East Galicia was mentioned as a separate entity, but its status was not defined. Thus, British support of the Soviet terms to Poland, the Czechoslovak declaration of neutrality, and the treaty signed at Sèvres—all indicated that both the Western Powers and Czechoslovakia aimed to leave East Galicia outside the boundaries of Poland.

The treatment of Poland at Spa and the consequent decision by the Conference of Ambassadors to award the disputed part of Teschen to Czechoslovakia created an open sore between the two countries which festered for years to come.[141] But Teschen was not the only issue dividing the two countries. The problem of East Galicia played a key role in Polish-Czechoslovak relations in the years 1919 through 1922 and contributed greatly to mutual suspicion and resentment. Aside from economic aspects, East Galicia was an illustration of the fundamentally different Polish and Czechoslovak attitudes toward Russia. Czechoslovak statesmen wanted a common frontier with Russia. In accordance with majority Czech opinion, they regarded Russia as a "big brother" and potential ally against Germany, both for their country and for other East-European states. They did not believe that any combination of these states could prevent renewed German expansion into Eastern Europe without Russian aid.[142] The Poles saw Russia as a threat both to their own independence and to that of other East-European states. The first clash between these two points of view took place over East Galicia.

As early as February 1919, Beneš thought that Poland should not be given any Ukrainian or Belorussian territories but that she should be restricted to ethnic boundaries in the east. Like Namier, with whom he was on friendly terms, Beneš warned that a Poland burdened with Ukrainian and Belorussian minorities would quarrel with Russia and thus "do the work of the Germans."[143] Such a view might sound strange coming from a statesman whose own population included one German for every two Czechs and Slovaks. However, Germany was not, at the time, claiming the Sudetenland; that was to come later. Ironically, Beneš and Masaryk justified the inclusion of the Sudetenland in Czechoslovakia on the same grounds as those on which the Poles claimed East Galicia—that is, historical, economic, and strategic ones. But the Poles, at least, could claim that some 35 percent of the population was Polish-speaking, while the Sudetenland was 90 percent German-speaking.

From the economic point of view, the Czechoslovak government hoped to play an important role in the vast Russian market, especially in the Ukraine, with its Black Sea ports. Indeed, trade agreements were signed at the end of 1918 with both the Ukrainian People's Republic of Kiev and the West Ukrainian Republic (East Galicia). A third agreement was signed with Petlyura in March 1919.[144] Besides the desire for a common frontier with Russia and economic interests, a third element in Czechoslovakia's opposition to Poland's eastern policy was her ambition to play the dominant role in Eastern Europe.[145]

After the Polish armies had advanced to the Zbrucz River with Allied consent in late June 1919, part of the West Ukrainian army crossed over to Czechoslovakia.[146] It was later joined by other units as well as by some troops that had formerly been held prisoner in Italy and, in late 1920, by some of Petlyura's troops, who, along with Ukrainian politicians, found refuge in Czechoslovakia. A Polish report of 4 January 1920 indicated the presence of some Ukrainian formations in the region of Mukačevo, Užhorod, and Horohiv.[147] Soon thereafter the West Ukrainian Republic opened a consulate in Prague.[148] At the end of July 1920 a Polish press report claimed that

President Masaryk had assured Dr. Evhen Petrushevych, president of the West Ukrainian government-in-exile, that Czechoslovakia was his ally in the struggle for East Galicia.[149] Petrushevych reportedly had assured Masaryk that East Galicia was Czechoslovakia's "window" to the whole of Eastern Europe and Asia as well.[150] The Polish press reported in early September that Petrushevych had asked the British government to establish a Czechoslovak protectorate over East Galicia.[151] As noted above, Balfour had suggested on 18 June 1919 that a study be made of a possible union between East Galicia and Czechoslovakia.[152]

The Polish victory over the Red Army in August–September 1920 seemed to eliminate the possibility of Soviet annexation, but the status of East Galicia remained formally unresolved even after the signing of the Treaty of Riga on 18 March 1921. Although in this treaty the Soviet government formally gave up its claims to East Galicia and other territories west of the new frontier, neither the Soviet Russian nor the Soviet Ukrainian government ever gave up the claim that East Galicia should be united with the Soviet Ukraine. But it was British insistence on autonomy for East Galicia that made this the key issue in Poland's relations with the Western Powers, the Soviet Union, Czechoslovakia, and the Baltic States until mid March 1923.

There is no need here to enter into a detailed account of the Polish-Soviet negotiations that led to the signing of the Treaty of Riga on 18 March 1921.[153] We will, therefore, limit ourselves to the question of East Galicia. At first, the Soviet delegates, while agreeing to a Polish frontier east of the Curzon Line, demanded that Poland recognize the independence of the Ukraine, Belorussia, and East Galicia. They also demanded a plebiscite there.[154] However, Lenin then instructed Adolf Joffe, head of the Soviet delegation, to secure peace within ten days. If necessary, Joffe was to accept the old frontier between Russia and East Galicia (the Austro-Russian frontier of 1914).[155] Although article 2 of the preliminary Soviet treaty demanded a plebiscite in East Galicia,[156] this was probably just a bargaining point. Interestingly enough, representatives of the Petrushevych government at Riga made the same demand.[157]

Petrushevych failed in his efforts to put the West Ukrainian case personally to the British Foreign Office,[158] but the French government was still reluctant to condone Polish-Soviet negotiations because of its support of General Wrangel. Thus, Askenazy reported from Paris on 10 October that Petit, secretary to President Millerand, agreed with the White Russians that article 87 of the Versailles Treaty really meant that the Allies should obtain the agreement of "real Russia" to any Polish-Russian settlement.[159] Finally, the destruction of Wrangel's army at Perekop in early November and the

French desire to acquire control of East Galician oil swung France more toward Poland.[160]

Meanwhile, the Petrushevych government was active in Western Europe. On 24 October it sent its first memorandum to the League of Nations, protesting against Polish policy in East Galicia. The Poles suspected Beneš of supporting this action, since the Czechoslovak press stridently opposed the union of East Galicia with Poland.[161] From now on, the league became the recipient of memoranda from the West Ukrainian government-in-exile. On 28 November it sent a long memorandum to the league, requesting self-determination and therefore independence for East Galicia. The Polish government rebutted Ukrainian charges of oppression and claimed that the issue did not lie within the competence of the league but within that of the Supreme Council.[162] The Czechoslovak stance was ambivalent. On the one hand, Masaryk told the Polish minister in Prague that the Czechoslovak government did not support the Ukrainians of East Galicia.[163] On the other hand, the British minister in Prague, Sir George Clerk, doubted the veracity of Masaryk's pledge. He reported that Beneš opposed the awarding of East Galicia to Poland, because he disagreed with the concept of building a "barrier" against Russia stretching from the Baltic to the Black Sea. Beneš thought it was in the interest of Western Europe to keep open the road from Czechoslovakia to Russia, and therefore he wanted an autonomous East Galicia, which, like the Baltic States, he expected eventually to enter into a federal union with a "reorganized" Russia. Gregory's comment on this report reflected his own views and those of Crowe but not those of the majority of the Foreign Office. He noted: "It is this very contribution to Pan-Slavism which we want to avoid. It is in fact the main political reason for assigning East Galicia to Poland."[164] The British military and Marshal Foch both agreed. They did not want to see the Russians standing on the Carpathians; indeed, Foch wanted the conclusion of a Polish-Rumanian-Czechoslovak military convention to prevent a Russian incursion into Central Europe.[165] However, the French Foreign Office, while basically supporting Polish sovereignty, also pressed Poland to accept a twenty-five-year mandate—despite the fact that this had been suspended, with Lloyd George's consent, in December 1919.[166] Still, Sapieha managed to obtain a French promise that the Conference of Ambassadors would send the matter to the Supreme Council, which would shelve it until better times.[167] Berthelot's pressure on Sapieha for the long-term mandate was strange, since the British Foreign Office seemed content to let the issue be. Gregory only asked Sapieha how East Galicia could be left out of a definition of Poland's eastern borders.[168]

The Treaty of Riga did not end Polish-Soviet friction. Like many European statesmen, Piłsudski did not believe that the Soviet regime would last. In 1921 there was a famine in the Ukraine, which led to some peasant resistance to the Red Army.[169] There is evidence that Polish military intelligence surreptitiously supported White Russian and Petlyurist forays into the Soviet Ukraine until late fall 1921. In May, Boris Savinkov prepared a plan for an uprising in the Ukraine. In June he established the Union for the Defense of Fatherland and Freedom in Warsaw; it envisaged the separation of the Ukraine from Russia.[170] But the Soviets were active too. Pamphlets and leaflets were smuggled into eastern Poland, calling on the population to support the union of the borderlands with Soviet Russia. Also, the Provisional Polish Revolutionary Committee of 1920 continued to exist in Soviet Russia.[171] There was also the activity of the so-called Zakordot, the foreign-aid office of the Communist Party of East Galicia, which seems to have been established in Prague sometime in 1920/21.[172] On 25 August 1921, Foreign Minister Skirmunt protested against the Soviet Ukrainian government's participation in activities aiming at the overthrow of the legal Polish government and the social structure of Poland.[173] Christian Rakovsky, the Ukrainian foreign minister, answered on 28 September, declaring that Zakordot was a Ukrainian, not a Russian, organization and that it was being liquidated.[174]

However, since both the Polish and the Soviet governments wished to avoid a break in relations, a protocol was signed in Warsaw on 7 October 1921 by the Soviet minister, Lev Karakhan, and the Polish deputy foreign minister, Jan Dąbski. According to articles 2 and 3, fourteen Russian and Ukrainian leaders who had been granted asylum in Poland were to leave that country by 20 October. Also the Polish government undertook to break off relations with "counter-revolutionary organizations," as per article 5 of the Treaty of Riga, and to move the work battalions, made up of interned troops (Ukrainians and Russians), away from the eastern frontier. In return, the Soviet government agreed to pay the first part of the promised compensation for Polish railway equipment that had been taken to Russia during the world war and to return Polish property and cultural objects.[175] The protocol smoothed Polish-Soviet relations, but Dąbski was forced to resign because of parliamentary criticism that he had violated the right of asylum.[176]

Piłsudski and his close collaborators, particularly the Military Intelligence Department, continued to support the policy of "Promethianism," that is, the goal of breaking up Soviet Russia into independent national states.[177] However, this goal enjoyed very little support and really had the character of propaganda to prepare for a future dismemberment of Russia into national states.[178] On the Soviet side, the Comintern and its member parties preached the principle of "self-determination," which was designed to prepare the disintegration of "hostile" states in Eastern Europe. This created difficulties for the Communist parties, since, except for Hungary and Bulgaria, each state contained sizeable national minorities. The Polish

Communist party was in a particularly difficult position, since it not only supported self-determination in eastern Poland—that is, the union of the borderlands with Russia—but also in western Poland—that is, the return of most of the formerly German-held territories to Germany. However, in 1923 the party was forced to recognize Polish claims to Upper Silesia.[179] As far as East Galicia was concerned, the Communists there became a branch of the Polish Communist Party.

In the meanwhile, Poland tried to improve her relations with Czechoslovakia. This meant finding a solution, or at least a compromise, for Polish-Czechoslovak territorial disputes and for the recognition of Poland's eastern frontier, especially Polish sovereignty over East Galicia. Negotiations between Foreign Minister Edouard Beneš and the Polish minister in Prague, Erazm Piltz, took place between July and October 1921. The result was a commercial and political agreement known as the Beneš-Skirmunt Pact, signed on 6 November 1921. It included mutual territorial guarantees, agreement on implementing treaties signed in common, and benevolent neutrality in wartime, including transit of war material. Czechoslovakia expressed her disinterest in East Galicia and promised to dissolve those Ukrainian organizations that worked against Poland. It was also agreed that a mixed delegation would study controversial questions in the disputed areas of Teschen, Spiš, and Orava, while the fate of Javorina and Orava was to be settled within six months. In the *secret* protocol, Czechoslovakia promised to support Poland "within the limits of her possibilities" on the issue of East Galicia and not to harm the Polish-Soviet settlement signed at Riga. Poland, in return, promised not to recognize any Habsburg attempts to regain Austria and/or Hungary.[180]

Unfortunately, the Beneš-Skirmunt Pact was not ratified. This was largely due to Czechoslovak unwillingness to cede to Poland the small Polish-speaking area of Javorina, a symbolic cession that the Polish government needed in order to have the pact ratified by the Sejm. Also, Prague continued to oppose the awarding of East Galicia to Poland and to support various West Ukrainian organizations and institutions located in Czechoslovakia.[181] Ukrainian soldiers and officers who found refuge in Czechoslovakia received the same pay as Czechs.[182] Ukrainian students also received help.[183]

Ukrainian students went to Czechoslovakia because they found it difficult to study in East Galicia. West Ukrainian émigrés constantly accused the Polish government of suppressing Ukrainian culture and education. This was true with regard to restricting Ukrainian student enrollments, but we must remember that the Poles and Ukrainians had fought bitterly in 1918/19, that the area was in constant turmoil until the spring of 1923, and that Ukrainian students were, for the most part, ardent nationalists. Indeed, many were veterans of the West Ukrainian army. Finally, due to the unrest in East Galicia, this area was under martial law at certain periods from 1919 to 1923.

176

Ukrainian students not only organized their own underground education but also led the local opposition and committed acts of political terrorism. Thus, in protest against the Polish government's announcement on 30 September 1921 that a population census would be held in Poland, including East Galicia, a Ukrainian student, Stefan Fedak, tried to assassinate Piłsudski on 25 September during the latter's visit to Lvov.[184] West Ukrainian political leaders called for a boycott of the census.[185]

Aside from the opposition of right-wing Ukrainian nationalists, the Polish authorities also had to deal with local Communists. However, the latter were weakened by internal splits and arrests made by Polish police at the St. George (Sv. Iura) Monastery in Lvov on 30 October 1921. Ironically, at the trial, which lasted from 11 November 1922 to 11 January 1923, the public prosecutor was unable to prove charges of treason. Therefore, Polish "bourgeois" justice merely succeeded in providing a public forum both for Communism and for Ukrainian national demands.[186]

Let us now turn to the development of Western policies and views regarding the eastern frontiers of Poland, and especially East Galicia, in the period between the signing of the Treaty of Riga and the end of 1921. The general line followed by France and Britain was to suspend a final decision while waiting for the Polish government to implement some type of autonomy in East Galicia which would satisfy Britain. The British government had to take into account not only its leading role in insisting on extensive East Galician autonomy in 1919 but also the support that this demand had generated in Parliament and in the liberal and left-wing press. The French government, for its part, was dependent on Britain in the question of reparations. Also it wanted Poland to grant extensive commercial privileges, especially in East Galician oil. Furthermore, the dispute over the interpretation of the Upper Silesian plebiscite was unresolved until the decision made by the League of Nations on 12 October 1921.[187] Meanwhile, in order to lessen the tension in Franco-British relations, the French government pressed the Poles to grant extensive autonomy to East Galicia. This was, of course, impossible, since the bulk of Polish opinion, as well as the Poles in East Galicia, opposed such a solution.

While insisting on autonomy, many French and British officials saw no alternative to the incorporation of East Galicia into Poland. When, at the end of March 1921, J. W. Headlam-Morley proposed that the East Galician and Upper Silesian questions be treated jointly, he was rebuffed by the permanent undersecretary of state, Sir Eyre Crowe. Headlam-Morley pointed out that the German claim to Upper Silesia was based on historic grounds and on the fact that the upper class was German. The Poles opposed this on the grounds

177

that the peasants and workers were Polish; but in East Galicia the Poles applied the same criteria as the Germans did in Upper Silesia. He therefore suggested that the Poles and the Ukrainians be allowed to argue their claims "in the glare of full publicity" before the Assembly of the League of Nations. However, Crowe commented that while Upper Silesia could be awarded either to Germany or to Poland, the only alternative to the incorporation of East Galicia into Poland was its incorporation into Russia. "This," he wrote, "is not a solution that we politically desire, as it would bring Russia right down to the Carpathians, which has never been the case before." Also, all reports indicated that the Ruthenes of East Galicia were content with the situation(!) and that it would therefore be best to avoid fresh agitation. He concluded: "We should deal with the Upper Silesian problem on its merits alone, and not complicate the situation by dragging in Eastern Galicia." Curzon initialed this without comment, thus indicating his agreement.[188]

But Headlam-Morley did not give up. In a historical memorandum on East Galicia dated 19 April, he argued again that the solution of the East Galician problem be linked with that of Upper Silesia. He also supported the British demand for a statute guaranteeing East Galician autonomy, under a Polish mandate, for twenty-five years. Crookshank agreed and suggested that the matter be raised in the Supreme Council. However, Gregory and Curzon dissented. They noted that further friction with France over Upper Silesia should be avoided.[189] The West Ukrainian politician Stefan Tomashívsky had suggested the same linkage to Philip Kerr, and the latter mentioned it in a letter to Robert Vansittart on 18 April. However, Curzon commented: "That is not practical politics."[190] Despite further urging by Crookshank in early June, the Foreign Office's motto was "Quieta non movere."[191]

Some French officials feared that the British government could make use of the same arguments against the Poles in East Galicia as the French were using in their favor in Upper Silesia. For this reason, in early June, Panafieu urged that Poland be advised to remedy the situation by satisfying legitimate Ukrainian claims. He suggested a comprehensive administrative autonomy and the end of repressions; but he clearly had received no instructions, since he asked for them to be sent.[192] Reversing Headlam-Morley's argument, Panafieu noted in August that Lloyd George, who strongly defended German rights to Upper Silesia on historic and social grounds, should, by the same token, recognize Polish rights to East Galicia.[193] But by this time the French government was pressing Warsaw to grant comprehensive autonomy.

On 3 August the French premier and foreign minister, Aristide Briand, wrote to Panafieu that Polish policy in East Galicia could provoke a popular revolt and that it only fed Bolshevik agitation. Therefore, Briand claimed that Polish policy supported the efforts of those Ukrainian émigrés and Bolsheviks who wished to suspend the "statute" and settle the issue contrary to Polish interests.[194] What he had in mind, of course, was the use that the British government might make of this situation.

However, the British government showed no desire to take up the issue. Meanwhile, the British minister in Warsaw, Sir William Max Muller, prodded the Polish government on his own initiative. On 9 June 1921 he asked a Polish minister—in connection with the latter's earlier suggestion of making oil concessions to Britain—whether such an agreement would take into account Allied sovereignty over East Galicia.[195] On 15 July, Muller reported having told Foreign Minister Konstanty Skirmunt that from a legal point of view, Poland's position in East Galicia "was merely that of a temporary caretaker." Muller added that while the Polish occupation of East Galicia was likely to be confirmed, the Allied Powers would require satisfaction that the rights of the Ruthenians were properly safeguarded. He hoped the Polish government would lose no time in submitting a scheme for autonomy to the Supreme Council for its approval.[196] Muller's initiative on this occasion may have been sparked by Lord Cecil's parliamentary question on 6 July regarding the legal status of East Galicia. Lloyd George then answered that it had not yet been fixed; he also claimed that the Polish government had made no effort to assure the self-determination of the Ruthene population according to the Supreme Council's resolution of 25 June 1919, and he charged that Poland was "colonizing" the territory.[197]

In the autumn the Polish government proceeded with the administrative incorporation of East Galicia. On 1 September the office of governor was abolished, and the land was divided into three voivodships (provinces): Lwów (Lvov, Lviv), Tarnopol (Tarnopil), and Stanisławów (Stanislaviv). This provoked Ukrainian protests at home and abroad. On 16 September the Canadian delegate to the League of Nations, the Rt. Hon. Charles J. Doherty, proposed a recommendation on the desirability of an early settlement of the status of East Galicia. This came as a great surprise to the British government. Balfour, the head of the British Delegation, asked for papers and information on East Galicia. Curzon was angry at the lack of consultation by the Canadians; he called the resolution an "impropriety" and deplored it as an effort "to force the hands of HMG."[198] The League Council adopted Doherty's resolution on 2 October and then transmitted it to the Supreme Council.[199]

Doherty's resolution spurred Max Muller to take further action in Warsaw. Muller asked again what title the Polish government had to the East Galician "crownlands." But he also complained to Curzon that he had urged more than once the necessity of having the British government expedite the East Galician question and had received no response.[200] It was the French government that now urged Warsaw to implement autonomy in East Galicia by law.[201] The political situation in Poland was, however, most unpropitious for such a move, especially after Fedak's attempt to assassinate Piłsudski. Also, Max Muller reported in early November that no Polish government would last a day if it accepted any statute for East Galicia that did not establish full Polish sovereignty over the province.[202] Given the opposition to extensive autonomy on the part of the Sejm and Polish opinion, the Polish Foreign Ministry began to work on a project that would apply the provisions of the Minorities Treaty to the Ukrainian population in the three eastern voivodships. Such a project was sent to Zamoyski in Paris on 1 December, but two weeks later he reported that it was not timely.[203] Also, August Zaleski had told Max Muller a month earlier that, in view of the attitude of the Polish population in East Galicia, he was thinking in terms of establishing Polish and Ruthene district councils in areas with large Ruthene populations. In his report, Max Muller agreed with Headlam-Morley's view of 19 April that Petrushevych and his government were able to maintain their position chiefly due to the support of the British government. Muller thought it best to have the Ruthene population "settle down" under Polish rule.[204]

By late 1921 the British government hoped that the Poles would establish an autonomous regime acceptable to London, without being asked to do so. Writing to Gregory on 15 November, Max Muller referred to the former's dispatch of 11 November, in which it was hoped that the Polish government would, of its own volition, grant a large measure of autonomy to East Galicia and thus enable the Powers to transfer to Poland their titles under article 91 of the Treaty of Saint-Germain. Max Muller commented that while the secretary of state might have cherished this hope, Muller's own archives showed that this had never been placed on record. Muller reminded Gregory that he (Muller) had first raised the question on 15 July and had referred to it several times since, but had received no indication of the views of the British government. Muller wished that the latter or the Supreme Council would tell the Poles clearly what it would do in response to various Polish moves and would not "gamble" on what the Poles might do. He thought the British government could not expect the Poles to act on their own according to British wishes, since they were not really displeased with "the present indeterminate state of affairs."[205]

The reasons for British passivity most probably lay in Anglo-French relations. As William Tyrrell noted on 6 December, there were "difficulties" with the draft proposals for the statute, and he thought it best to drop the matter. Crowe assented and observed that there was a danger of "annoying" the French and the Poles. Curzon agreed.[206] Clearly, at this time the French and Italians were not ready to support a British initiative on formulating a statute that would be unacceptable to the Poles.[207] In his December talks with Lloyd George in London, Briand apparently suggested a twenty-five year Polish administration in East Galicia, to be followed by a plebiscite, but Lloyd

George allegedly rejected this idea.[208] Since the Poles had earlier rejected a similar proposal, Briand's suggestion—if made—must be seen in the context of his goal to bring about a Franco-British alliance. As we know, Anglo-French relations were strained. Not only did Lloyd George reject Briand's proposals for a British guarantee of the Franco-Polish alliance, but there were also Franco-British disputes in the Middle East, and France had rejected Anglo-American proposals for the limitation of cruisers and submarines at the Washington Naval Disarmament Conference (12 November 1921 to 22 February 1922). The French also had serious reservations about British support for Greece in the war with Turkey. Last but not least, the French were lukewarm toward the idea of calling an international conference to discuss the reconstruction of Russia. The Genoa Conference was to draw together the many disparate threads of European politics and briefly to raise the issue of Poland's eastern frontiers—and of East Galicia in particular.

7

East Galicia and Poland's Eastern Frontier: The Genoa Conference January–June 1922

The idea of launching a great economic reconstruction of Europe, and particularly of opening up Russia for Western trade and investment, had a mixed parentage. On 28 October 1921 the Soviet foreign commissar, Georgii V. Chicherin, had proposed a conference to settle outstanding tsarist debts to the Western Powers in return for their recognition of the Soviet government.[1] The Soviets needed Western economic aid for the reconstruction that had begun in Russia in March of that year under the New Economic Policy. Western reaction was cool except in Britain, where Lloyd George had been trying to establish viable trade relations with Moscow since 1920. Now, as before, he saw trade with Russia as a way to solve Britain's economic woes, especially unemployment, which reached two million in 1921. European reconstruction was also proposed by the German foreign minister, Walther Rathenau, who suggested an international consortium for this purpose in November 1921. He saw German trade with Russia as a source for payments of German reparations. The French and British were interested in this possibility, especially since their hopes of having the United States cancel war debts had been dashed.[2] Therefore, British experts studied the possibility of establishing a syndicate for trade with Russia, in which Germany would participate so that she could pay reparations with part of her expected profits.[3] French experts also favored French participation out of fear that otherwise, Britain and Germany would go ahead on their own.[4] The French difficulty was, however, that some six million Frenchmen held Imperial Russian bonds,[5] and the government was committed not to establish relations with the Soviets unless they first agreed to honor the imperial obligations. Still, as early as August 1921, the French Foreign Office linked German ability to pay reparations with a collective Western reconstruction of Russia.[6]

On 6 January 1922, Lloyd George and Briand agreed on the terms under which Soviet Russia should be invited to a conference at Genoa. There was to be mutual recognition of different political systems and of public debts, abstention from the use of propaganda, and an undertaking by all nations to refrain from aggression against their neighbors. The Allied Powers declared they were ready to accord official recognition to Soviet Russia, but only if she accepted all their stipulations.[7] As we know, Briand was forced to resign,[8] and the new government of Poincaré was very lukewarm toward the conference.

The Polish government viewed the approaching conference with a mixture of hope and fear. Foreign Minister Konstanty Skirmunt hoped that the Allies would recognize Poland's eastern frontier, but he feared that the British might suggest that Poland pay a share of the Russian imperial debt. He was reassured by the British Foreign Office on that point, however.[9] Polish hopes for recognition of the frontier were raised by the signing of the Franco-Polish commercial conventions on 6 February 1922, which opened the way for the ratification of the alliance and the military convention of 1921.[10]

Fear that the Allies might conclude agreements with Russia at Poland's expense impelled Skirmunt to seek collective action by the East European states at Genoa. Poland participated in two conferences of the Little Entente States and organized a conference of Baltic States. Skirmunt also tried to establish cooperation with Soviet Russia. For once, Soviet and Polish interests seemed to mesh, for there was an obvious connection between the Allies' de jure recognition of Russia and Polish desire for their recognition of the Polish-Soviet frontier. Skirmunt also hoped to mediate between the Western Allies and Russia.[11] He found no takers, but Beneš managed to play the role of mediator between Poincaré and Lloyd George.

The Soviets, meanwhile, were courting both Berlin and Paris. In fact, the German-Soviet treaty that was signed later at Rapallo was fully worked out beforehand in Berlin.[12] As for Paris, Lord D'Abernon reported: "There is no doubt a good deal going on between Paris and Moscow. Poincaré knew about the pourparlers two months ago and will probably continue them. The Poles are getting alarmed, as they fully realize that their somewhat expensive charms would wane rapidly in French eyes when contrasted with those of a Moscow heiress."[13] Poincaré acknowledged that he had had contacts with Chicherin, and the French press wrote of negotiations.[14] However, nothing came of this; it was probably a Soviet bluff to put pressure on Germany.

The Poles now tried to build up a diplomatic front with other East-European states. Aleksander Skrzyński, the Polish envoy in Bucharest, represented Poland at a conference of Little Entente States there from 2 to 24 February. Polish, Czechoslovak, Rumanian, and Yugoslav representatives agreed to uphold the principle of the inviolability of treaties and the equality of participating nations at Genoa. They also agreed to oppose the settlement of

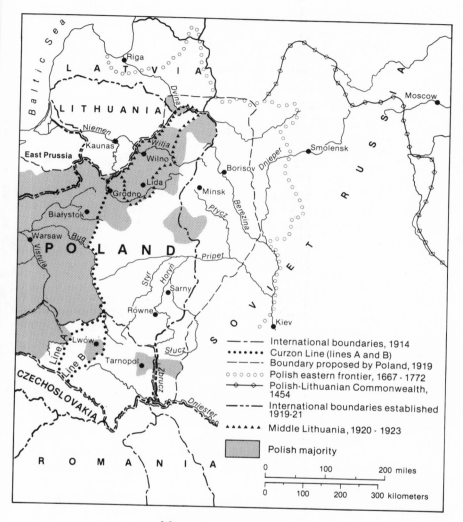

Map 5. Eastern Poland

matters of general interest by the Great Powers alone. Skrzyński stressed Poland's special position due to the Treaty of Riga, the Franco-Polish alliance, and Poland's goal of establishing cooperation with the Baltic States.[15] The experts of the three Little Entente States and Poland then met at Belgrade from 9 to 12 March in order to determine a common stand at Genoa. They agreed that "the treaties in force must not be infringed." On 15 March a communiqué was issued in Prague, stating that Czechoslovakia, Poland, Rumania, and Yugoslavia had agreed on the following: (a) to adopt a common economic line, as laid down at the Belgrade conference of experts; (b) that measures to facilitate trade and transport be compatible with the independence of the Allied states; (c) that each state should take part in the discussion of questions in which its interests were involved; and (d) to adopt a common line against revision of the existing Russian treaties.[16] This last was a veiled reference to the so-called Boulogne Declaration made by Lloyd George and Poincaré on 25 February, in which they stated their opposition to any encroachments on the rights of the League of Nations or the "treaties signed in France since the Peace."[17] This was read to imply that France and Britain might not oppose the revision of treaties that the Soviets had signed with Poland and the Baltic States.

The next Polish step was the meeting of the foreign ministers of Poland, Latvia, Estonia, and Finland in Warsaw from 13 to 17 March. The Polish goal was basically in harmony with Soviet interests, and Lev M. Karakhan, the Soviet minister in Warsaw, had been so informed on 18 February.[18] However, though Skirmunt had invited the Soviet government to send a representative to the conference, it had declined.[19] Polish objectives at the conference, as outlined by Stanisław Zalewski of the Foreign Ministry, showed that Polish and Soviet interests meshed. Zalewski's project of 7 March proposed the following: (a) the conference participants should ask Russia for assurances that she would not question her existing treaties with them and would oppose any such move by third parties; (b) the participants would oppose the establishment of one great economic consortium as well as the division of Russia into spheres of economic influence and would oppose all projects clearly aiming at the destruction of Soviet sovereignty; and (c) the participants would assure the Soviet government that their agreements on common action was not hostile to it, but that this attitude depended on Soviet implementation of existing treaties.[20]

However, Zalewski's project was abandoned. Instead, the conference dealt with mutual relations between the participating states, with recognition of their treaties with Russia, and with peaceful methods of solving disputes. The states also agreed to maintain benevolent neutrality toward any member who might become the victim of unprovoked aggression. Finally, there was agreement on a common line of action at Genoa.[21] Why were Zalewski's proposals abandoned? The reason lay in French pressure. As the British minister in Riga reported a few days later, the Lettish (Latvian) foreign minister told him that the French government had asked the conference to discuss Russian debts and international spheres of economic influence in Russia. These topics were "introduced apologetically by the Polish Minister of Foreign Affairs." Still, while the four ministers agreed in principle to the exploitation of Russia by an international syndicate, they rejected the proposal to divide her into four zones of economic influence (Petrograd for industry, Vologda for timber, the Caucasus for oil, and the Don Basin for coal). The ministers also agreed that their treaties with Russia absolved them from any responsibility for imperial Russian debts. Indeed, the Latvian foreign minister warned France that if such a claim should appear on the agenda in Genoa, it would be opposed by a bloc of Little Entente and Baltic States.[22]

The Soviet response to the Warsaw Conference was a peremptory invitation on 21 March for its members to attend a conference in Moscow on the following day.[23] This might well have been sparked by rumors of a forthcoming Finno-Polish alliance, which Finland was actually ready to sign.[24] In any event, the ministers could not go to Moscow on one day's notice, so it was agreed that their representatives would meet with the Soviet delegates to Genoa—Chicherin, Joffe, Litvinov, and Yurienev—in Riga, where they would stop on their way west.

The meeting of the Polish, Estonian, and Latvian representatives with the Soviet delegates took place in Riga on 29–30 March. The Finns only sent an observer. The result of the meeting was the so-called Riga Protocol. The two sides agreed that the inviolability of their treaties with Russia was to be the basis for a common understanding. Both declared their peaceful intentions, proposed the general disarmament of all states, and agreed to protect their frontiers only with regular troops or border guards. They also proposed to establish special zones along the frontiers, where only a minimun number of troops would be stationed. They condemned the armed bands that were ranging along the frontiers and recognized them as a threat to peace. Furthermore, both sides agreed that de jure recognition of the Soviet government by the Western states would be "desirable and useful." Both sides also agreed on the usefulness of agreements regarding trade and transport.[25]

The French press reacted to the Riga Protocol with an outburst of indignation. An editorial of 5 April in the French-controlled *Journal de Pologne* (Warsaw) asked how it was possible to reconcile Skirmunt's declarations on standing by France at Genoa with the declarations made at Riga, particularly on the official recognition of Soviet Russia. Correspondence from Paris, published in the paper on the following day, reported that Poincaré had told

Skirmunt—who was then in Paris—that the protocol had come as a surprise and had made a very bad impression.[26] The Polish government also faced sharp criticism in the Sejm, notably from the National Democrats, and Skirmunt was forced to disavow the Polish representative, Witold Jodko-Narkiewicz, for overstepping his powers in signing the protocol.[27] Thus, Skirmunt had to navigate between the Scylla of losing French support for the recognition of Poland's eastern frontier and the Charybdis of losing a line of action that Moscow had seemingly agreed to take at Genoa.

It was not an auspicious moment for trying to secure French and British promises to recognize the Polish-Soviet frontier at the forthcoming conference. However, Skirmunt forged ahead. He told Poincaré in Paris on 2 April that Jodko-Narkiewicz had gone to Riga only as an "observer" and that he had exceeded his powers by signing the protocol. But when Skirmunt asked Poincaré whether the Allied Powers would implement their right to define Poland's eastern frontier, the French premier only promised to give the matter his "most benevolent consideration."[28]

Skirmunt's paramount objective was to secure French support for official Allied recognition of the Polish-Soviet frontier. He informed Poincaré that Poland would request it, and Wielowieyski, counsellor at the Polish legation in Paris, gave Laroche the draft of a letter that Zamoyski had been instructed to address to Poincaré. However, Zamoyski said that if French reservations were such as to make the Polish government's position difficult in Warsaw, then the letter would not be sent. Laroche advised Poincaré that the French government could reply in a manner that would satisfy Polish expectations without formally prejudicing the collective Allied action foreseen in article 87 of the Versailles Treaty. The French government could recognize the Polish-Soviet frontier as traced by the Treaty of Riga, though he thought an exception should be made for the Polish-Lithuanian sector, which still had to be defined. He noted that the Polish government wished that sector to correspond with the demarcation line proposed by the League Council on 13 January 1922.[29]

However, a more elaborate note, dated 4 April 1922, was less promising for the Poles. Its author—probably Berthelot—wrote that France had never opposed the attribution of East Galicia to Poland, provided the area was granted an autonomy that would be safeguarded by serious guarantees. The Anglo-Saxon Powers, especially England, were the ones who wanted a provisional regime there under a twenty-five-year mandate for Poland, with a plebiscite at the end of this period. The French government considered these points only to be concessions to England, and the Polish government knew this. The French reply to the Polish request could mention the Treaty of Riga, but this might be inadvisable on the eve of the Genoa Conference. Therefore, the French government could reserve agreement with the other Allies, and so avert the charge of prejudicing the final decision which should be made in common. However, the French government should indicate that it would be disposed to examine the Polish eastern frontier while keeping the actual situation in mind.[30] It was this cautious policy that Poincaré finally adopted.

In the meanwhile, Skirmunt went on to London, where he held conversations with officials at the Foreign Office and was invited by the king and queen to have lunch at Windsor Castle. He also spoke with Lloyd George on 4 April. Although there is no written British record of this conversation, several sources confirm its general tenor. According to a report sent by the Polish legation in London, Lloyd George agreed that if Poland's eastern frontiers were discussed at Genoa, this would only indicate Allied recognition of the Polish-Soviet frontier as laid down in the Treaty of Riga.[31] The draft conclusions of a meeting of the British cabinet's Finance Committee of 5 April quoted Skirmunt as saying that the Poles considered the recognition of the Polish-Soviet frontier as fixed at Riga to be ''most desirable.'' Lloyd George's reply is not given, but M. P. A. Hankey, secretary of the cabinet, noted: ''He [Hanky] understood that the difficulty was connected with the future of Eastern Galicia.''[32] Zamoyski communicated a third version of the conversation to Peretti de la Rocca at the French Foreign Office on 10 April; this version was based on the account that Skirmunt had given Zamoyski at Brussels. According to Skirmunt, Lloyd George had agreed with him ''in principle'' on the need to recognize the Polish-Soviet frontier and also that the question of Russia's frontiers with her Western neighbors should be regulated at Genoa by a special treaty. Allegedly, Lloyd George added that Poland was in the same situation as Rumania. Skirmunt replied that this was not so, for Rumania did not have a treaty with Soviet Russia. The prime minister then agreed with Skirmunt that since the Polish-Soviet frontier had been fixed at Riga, the Allies should simply recognize it. Lloyd George allegedly had said that if the question had been definitely settled by Poland and Russia, then it was settled and would not be discussed at Genoa.[33] The fourth and final version of the conversation is to be found in Skirmunt's memoirs. Although he wrote them many years later during the Second World War and without the benefit of documents, they supply much interesting information. Skirmunt wrote that he told Lloyd George that the time had come for the official recognition of Poland's eastern frontier. However, according to article 87 of the Versailles Treaty, this should be done by the Powers at the Conference of Ambassadors and not by the Genoa Conference. Lloyd George seemed to agree and asked Skirmunt to see him at Genoa.[34] Of all these accounts, the most precise seems to be the version that Skirmunt gave to Zamoyski.

The Foreign Office took a favorable view of Polish demands. An unsigned memorandum of 6 April 1922, probably written by Gregory or at least approved by him, stated that Britain should ''welcome'' the settlement of some "interminable disputes," such as Vilna and East Galicia. The author of this memorandum saw no alternative to attaching East Galicia to Poland, though with local autonomy. As to Vilna, he thought that Britain should state her disinterest and leave its settlement to Poland and Lithuania.[35]

Having secured a favorable reception in London, Skirmunt now approached the French. The Polish note of 6 April, delivered by Zamoyski on 11 April, cited article 87 of the Versailles Treaty and asked for a "prompt solution."[36] Three days later, Skirmunt communicated an official note to all the Allied Powers. He stressed that the recognition of Poland's eastern frontier was essential for a lasting peace and for the economic reconstruction of Europe.[37]

The Poles did not have to wait long for the issue to surface at Genoa. The conference opened on 9 April, and after a few days it was clear that the Allied and Soviet positions were irreconcilable. The Allies demanded that the Soviets recognize imperial Russian debts and that they agree to far-reaching Western control of Soviet resources in return for economic aid. The Soviet delegation countered by claiming extensive compensation for damage done by the Allies in Russia during the civil war. On 15 April, Lloyd George tried to entice the Soviets by proposing that they discuss other questions—for example, Lithuania.[38] The next day, however, the conference faced a *fait accompli:* the German-Soviet Treaty of Rapallo.[39] But Lloyd George did not want to abandon the conference on which he had staked so much. He feared returning empty-handed to London after claiming that European, and particularly British, economic problems would be solved by an agreement on the reconstruction of Russia. The Allies drafted a sharp note to the German delegation, and Skirmunt supported Lloyd George's stand that attempts to obtain an agreement with Russia must continue. Poland, said Skirmunt, would be the first to suffer the consequences of a Russo-German alliance.[40] On the afternoon of the same day, 18 April, Lloyd George said that the Powers should do their best "to seduce Russia from the arms of Germany," for if Russian reconstruction were left completely in German hands, then it would proceed only according to German interests. Skirmunt suggested, however, that the Allies should say precisely what help they would give Soviet Russia if she were to accept their conditions.[41] This suggestion was brushed aside.

On the following day, 19 April, Poincaré finally replied to Zamoyski's note asking for prompt Allied recognition of Poland's eastern frontier. By this time there was little chance of Allied de jure recognition of Russia, and thus of the recognition of the Polish-Soviet frontier. It is not surprising, therefore, that Poincaré merely stated that the French government alone could not deal with East Galicia, but only together with the other Allies in accordance with article 87 of the Versailles Treaty. However, he assured Zamoyski that France would, as always, be inspired by sentiments of profound friendship for Poland.[42]

On 22 April the Polish Sejm rejected the Socialist resolution for the territorial autonomy for East Galicia.[43] At the same time, French and British delegates at Genoa still hoped that Poland's eastern frontier and the status of East Galicia could be settled at the conference. On 24/25 April, Hankey, Hurst, Seydoux, and Henri Fromageot agreed that the questions to be settled in connection with item 2 of the Cannes agreement—namely, peace and trade—would include the following: (1) the proposed pact of nonaggression and (2) the arrangements for the Final Act of the Conference. They then agreed that certain questions would require settlement before the Pact of Non-Aggression could be concluded: (a) the Eastern frontiers of Poland; (b) East Galicia; (c) Bessarabia and the issue of Rumanian gold in Russia.[44] Thus, they were preparing the ground for salvaging something from the conference.

At this point, Beneš suggested to Lloyd George that he oppose the recognition of the Polish-Soviet frontier. Beneš did this in violation of the agreement reached with his Polish, Rumanian, and Yugoslav colleagues to pursue a common line at the conference.[45] In his conversation with Lloyd George on 26 April, Beneš linked the proposed nonaggression pact with a British guarantee to France and with the Polish-Soviet frontier. He noted that the pact involved recognition of this frontier as laid down in the Treaty of Riga and said that his government had not recognized this treaty. He asked what would be done about Vilna and East Galicia. Lloyd George answered that there might be a clause on Vilna stating that Poland would recognize a decision by the League of Nations. As for East Galicia, he did not wish to see a separate state, so it could be said that it would belong to Poland but would have complete autonomy. When Beneš asked if Lloyd George was ready to accept the Polish boundaries as laid down by the Treaty of Riga, Lloyd George answered that if Russia had accepted them, it was not up to him to object. Beneš was not pleased. According to British notes of the conversation, he concluded by telling Lloyd George that "if, within a certain number of years, as he [Beneš] thought would occur, Russia were to attack Poland, his country would have to say that morally it was opposed to the eastern boundary drawn in the Treaty of Riga."[46]

Beneš's proposal seemed to be an attempt to lure Lloyd George into granting a British guarantee of support to France, complemented by an agreement with the Little Entente but excluding Poland. There is no evidence that Poincaré was ready to sanction this sort of arrangement, so Beneš was probably acting on his own. It is most likely that the Czechoslovak foreign minister raised the issue of Poland's eastern frontier in the context of his ongoing negotiations for trade treaties with Soviet Russia and the Soviet Ukraine. The Czechoslovak press insisted that Czechoslovakia depended on the Russian market and that on this point her interests did not coincide with those of France.[47] Beneš may have been thinking of a deal whereby Britain would give a guarantee of support to France in return for the latter's abandonment of her support for Poland over Vilna and East Galicia. Another complementary deal Beneš might have envisaged was British insistence on a type of autonomy for East Galicia that would have allowed for Soviet-Czechoslovak trade through its territory.

But Lloyd George would not be seduced into a British guarantee to France. Despite his previous declarations, neither he nor the Foreign Office nor British opinion as a whole would accept such a commitment.[48] However, Beneš may have inspired Lloyd George to raise the issue of East European frontiers. On that same evening, 26 April, the prime minister gave a speech at a dinner for the Anglo-American journalists attending the conference. He pointed to the danger of a conflagration in Eastern Europe. As he put it, "From the Baltic down to the Black Sea there is hardly a line there which is not contested, and every one of those lines involves in itself the possibility of a terrible conflict in Europe." He also spoke of "this racial lava surging right through the centre of Europe." Finally, he declared that Germany and Russia could not be kept down permanently by any combination of Powers.[49] All of these statements looked very much like signals to the Germans and Soviets that Britain was at odds with France. Most probably, Lloyd George hoped to entice the Soviets into further negotiations, or at least to secure a nonaggression pact covering Eastern Europe.[50]

Whatever the case may be, Lloyd George told the Belgian foreign minister, Henri Jaspar, and the Italian minister, Carlo Schanzer, that Beneš and Skirmunt "were very frightened" of a Russo-German bloc and that the Russians were trying to get out of the Treaty of Riga, "which was a thoroughly bad treaty."[51] Two days later, Lloyd George raised the question of the western frontiers of Russia. While agreeing with the Rumanians on their claim to Bessarabia—which Britain had recognized in 1921—he said that before there could be anything in the nature of a nonagression pact, the frontiers would have to be defined, and the Russian position on these issues would have to be known. He reiterated his view that there was a "sharp distinction" between the frontiers of Bessarabia and those of other countries. Thus, the Lithuanian frontier was still unsettled, and the East Galician question was still open, for the latter's status did not correspond with the position outlined in the treaty of Saint-Germain. He noted that the Allies had sovereignty over East Galicia and that the frontiers of this "country" had not yet been defined. This was not the case, he said, with Bessarabia, since a treaty had been signed.[52]

A few days later, on 2 May, Lloyd George took up the nonaggression pact with Barthou. He now said it was needed in order to avoid (Soviet) military operations against Poland, Czechoslovakia, or Rumania.[53] He claimed to be "absolutely certain that sooner or later the Russians, acting in collusion with the Lithuanians, would clear the Poles out of Lithuania." In such an event, the Allies could not send troops, and he reminded Barthou of Foch's opposition at Spa to sending French troops to Poland. Lloyd George also said he thought the Russians might not stop in Poland, since they might find food there(!).[54] While he was willing to leave the settlement of the Polish-Lithuanian border to the League of Nations, East Galicia was a different matter. He did not wish it to be a separate state, therefore he believed it should accept Polish sovereignty, but only with "complete domestic independence"—such as had been granted by Britain to Ireland.[55]

Barthou was uncertain as to Lloyd George's intentions; he therefore sent one of his collaborators to see Gregory. The latter thought that Lloyd George wished to recognize Polish sovereignty over East Galicia but with autonomy similiar to that stipulated for "the Ruthenes of Slovakia." Although there was a Ukrainian minority in Slovakia, Gregory may have meant the Ukrainians of Subcarpathian Ruthenia; in any case, the conversation dealt more with the need for a simultaneous settlement of Vilna and Memel than with East Galicia.[56]

The Rapallo Treaty introduced more tension into Polish-Soviet relations, and this lent some credence to Lloyd George's alarms over Eastern Europe. At the end of April, Chicherin had publicly attacked Skirmunt for having signed the Allied letter to the German Delegation condemning the Rapallo Treaty. Chicherin accused Skirmunt of having committed a serious violation of the Treaty of Riga, claiming that, by giving de jure recognition to Soviet Russia, Poland had automatically recognized Soviet Russia's right to conclude international agreements. He also accused Poland of having backed out of the Riga Protocol, which assured Polish support for Soviet efforts to obtain de jure recognition from the Allies.[57]

Skirmunt gave a sharp reply to these charges. He stated that the Soviet government had no right to intervene in Poland's relations with other states; he denied that Poland had violated sovereign Russian rights; and he claimed that she could not have violated the Riga Protocol, since it had not imposed any commitments on its signatories.[58] On 3 May the Polish press published Chicherin's letter to Schanzer, in which Chicherin claimed that some territories in Eastern Europe were still under "military occupation," citing Vilna and East Galicia.[59] He seemed to be playing Lloyd George's game.

While Skirmunt took a tough stance in public, he tried to clarify the issue and to smooth Polish-Soviet relations in a private meeting with Chicherin. The conversation took place between 2 May—when the Allied memorandum proposing financial and trade agreements was sent to the Soviet delegation—and 5 May, when Skirmunt saw Lloyd George. As Skirmunt told Lloyd

George that day, he had assured Chicherin that the Polish attitude was not hostile to Russia, but added that the Soviet government was not carrying out the agreements of the Riga Treaty. Chicherin replied that "all this was due to the fact that the Poles were too friendly with France, and were associated too closely with the group hostile to Russia."[60] In recounting this conversation to Lloyd George, Skirmunt stressed the fact that Chicherin had not touched on Polish frontiers; and when Skirmunt had alluded to Vilna, Chicherin did not take it up. Skirmunt therefore concluded that frontiers were not the issue. But Lloyd George observed that, on the contrary, this silence confirmed his impression "that if there were difficulties with Russia as the result of the present conference, the Russians would at once raise these questions."[61]

After recounting his conversation with Chicherin, Skirmunt told Lloyd George that he thought the Allied memorandum of 2 May did not go far enough on the reconstruction of Russia. He believed that the Russians wanted more credits; instead, they were offered an export credit plan which merely financed Western merchants and others who would do business in Russia. He believed that the Russians should be given at least the impression that a large loan might be considered. He also suggested that an Allied mission be sent to Russia to study the situation, similar to the one sent to Poland in the spring of 1919.

Lloyd George brushed these suggestions aside. Instead, he indulged in threats that Britain would disengage herself from Europe—which, he claimed, she did not need—and let Europe "stew in her own juice." Skirmunt answered that both he and Chicherin believed that the conference should not be broken off. Chicherin had told Skirmunt that he viewed the memorandum of 2 May, not as an ultimatum, but as a basis for discussion. While Lloyd George agreed that the conference should not be broken off, he also said that Britain would not send a "commission" to Russia. He added flippantly that if the Poles, French, and Belgians did so, they would find only typhus, and many would fail to return. Skirmunt calmly replied that there was also typhus in Poland and that his idea of a commission had nothing to do with France and Belgium.[62]

Lloyd George then raised the issues of Vilna and East Galicia, but in a way suggesting that he had given up any plans to discuss them. He said he wished it had been possible to settle these issues before the end of the conference. If there had been a reasonable chance of a European settlement, he said, these questions might have been discussed, but if the conference were to break down, this would hardly be worthwhile. Lloyd George clearly wished to sound out Skirmunt, and the latter obliged. Skirmunt referred to his conversation with Lloyd George in London (4 April) and noted that the decision on Poland's eastern frontier was reserved for the Allied and Associated Powers by article 87 of the Versailles Treaty. Skirmunt said that these questions were not the concern of the Genoa Conference but that "if a pact of non-aggression was to be reached the frontiers ought to be settled; if not at Genoa, at any rate soon. If Mr. Lloyd George would like to postpone the matter until things took a better turn at Genoa he [Skirmunt] would have no objection, but they ought to be settled in connection with the pact of non-aggression." Skirmunt cited one reason for a prompt settlement—namely, the fact that Polish elections were due toward the end of the year. Lloyd George complimented Skirmunt by saying that Skirmunt was the first Polish foreign minister he had talked to without feeling that Poland was irreconcilably opposed to Great Britain. Skirmunt then asked for another opportunity to see the prime minister before leaving Genoa, and requested that he make no decision before hearing his views. This clearly referred to Poland's eastern frontier. Lloyd George agreed to both requests. However, he also said that the existence of the Soviet Ukraine gave Russia the opportunity of intervening in East Galicia and that Lithuania would probably appeal to Russia over Vilna.[63]

On 11 May the Soviet delegation rejected the Allied proposals of 2 May. Lloyd George either expected this or had been forewarned. In any case, he startled the representatives of the inviting Powers on the morning of 10 May, by insisting that the conference discuss East Galicia. He claimed that the situation existing there could give Russia every excuse for interfering in Polish affairs, and he said that he would submit the question to the conference at its next plenary meeting. However, Schanzer proposed that the matter be referred to the Supreme Council—thus indicating that Italy would not support Britain—and Barthou, predictably, opposed the whole idea. It was perhaps because France and Italy took such a stand that Lloyd George explained that he had merely wished to have a discussion of article 2 of the agenda, which pertained to peace. Barthou then suggested that the matter be discussed in the subcommission. Lloyd George countered by stating that the conference should discuss not only East Galicia but also Lithuania and Bessarabia. However, he finally accepted Barthou's suggestion that these questions be raised in the subcommission. He threatened that if this were not done, he would raise them in plenary session "in full view of the world." As for the question of Lithuania, he admitted that this might be referred to some other body for settlement but insisted that the conference must review it.[64]

Skirmunt protested to Lloyd George, and the Polish delegation threatened to leave the conference.[65] However, on 12 May, Poland and Italy signed a trade agreement; they were also actively negotiating for an oil agreement. These developments apparently shifted Italy toward Poland, and this, together with French opposition, may have forced Lloyd George to retreat. On the morning of 13 May he merely referred to the necessity of a truce "on the basis of existing *de facto* frontiers." In this truce, Russia and her neighbors would extend mutual assurances of nonaggression.[66] Skirmunt, who had been present at this meeting, said nothing; but he restated the Polish position on the eastern frontier at another meeting in the afternoon. He said that Poland's legal position had been fixed in a treaty with Russia and that only the Western Powers considered the Polish frontier unsettled. He also said that Poland had no reason to fear Russian aggression but would be interested, from the point of view of general pacification, in the insertion of a provisional clause of nonaggression in the agreement about to be concluded with Russia.[67]

Skirmunt had a clash with Lloyd George two days later. In a discussion of the proposed nonaggression pact, Skirmunt suggested an amendment granting provisional recognition of the status quo. Lloyd George charged Skirmunt with trying to preempt a decision on the part of the League of Nations, by which he meant the Vilna question. Skirmunt denied having any such intention and repeated that the Polish-Soviet frontier was not in dispute.[68] The Polish delegation also issued a statement to the press, denying that there were important Russian reinforcements on the Polish border or that there was a partial mobilization in Poland; finally, it claimed that the Genoa Conference was not empowered to deal with Poland's eastern border.[69] Lloyd George gave up. He agreed with Barthou and Schanzer that since the drawing up of a final Allied treaty with Russia had been postponed until an investigation by a committee of experts could be made, that would also be the time to settle frontier problems in Eastern Europe.[70] As for Chicherin, he made a clear distinction between respect for and recognition of the status quo in Eastern Europe, saying: "Respect for the *status quo* between the Ukraine and Roumania, for example, did not in any way imply, for Russia, recognition of the present territorial *status quo* of Roumania, and particularly recognition of the present occupation of Bessarabia by Roumania."[71] Thus, he intimated that Moscow did not consider as binding the Allied recognition of Rumania's frontiers in 1921.

Finally, after a belated Lithuanian effort to obtain a guarantee against Polish attack—and so to raise the Vilna question—the issue of Poland's eastern frontiers was dropped.[72] Whatever Lloyd George had hoped to gain from his efforts remained his own secret. As Eyre Crowe noted in regard to a parliamentary question on the settlement of the statute and borders for East Galicia, it was difficult for the Foreign Office specialists to advise an answer, since they did not know or understand what precisely had been done about this problem at Genoa.[73] Gregory, who had been at the conference, commented later that Lloyd George's idea had been to confirm Polish sovereignty over East Galicia but also to insist on a degree of autonomy similar to that of the Irish Free State. However, Gregory also noted that the Poles would never have agreed; so it was just as well that the matter had been dropped.[74] Indeed, when former Premier Ignacy Daszyński, a prominent leader of the Polish

Socialist Party, proposed a motion in the Sejm on 30 May that East Galicia be granted a provincial diet and administration, he was soundly defeated—just as the previous Socialist motion had been defeated on 22 April.[75]

Skirmunt returned to Poland feeling that he had done everything possible to safeguard Polish interests. Piłsudski disagreed. As Skirmunt wrote in his memoirs, the marshal sharply criticized his (Skirmunt's) activity at Genoa. Piłsudski insisted that Poland was gravely threatened—by which he meant the Rapallo Treaty—and claimed that a strong government was needed in order to handle the forthcoming general elections. Therefore, the Ponikowski cabinet resigned on 2 June, and Skirmunt lost his post as foreign minister.[76] The French minister in Warsaw reported that Piłsudski had rebuked Skirmunt for not sticking with France and Belgium[77] Indeed, Zamoyski had told Peretti de la Rocca on 15 May that Skirmunt had allowed Lloyd George to "outflank him" by raising the question of Vilna and East Galicia. According to Zamoyski, Skirmunt had then decided "to go completely with the French Delegation." Peretti de la Rocca said he hoped this would always be the case.[78]

The Genoa Conference was not a defeat for Poland, but neither was it a victory. Lloyd George had failed to settle the issues of Vilna and East Galicia, contrary to Polish interests. However, Allied recognition of the Polish-Soviet frontier remained in limbo, and Beneš's policy had severely undermined Polish efforts to construct a united front of East-European states. Worst of all, the Rapallo Treaty raised the specter of a new partition of Poland.

8

East Galicia, Vilna, Memel, and the Recognition of Poland's Eastern Frontier, June 1922 to March 1923

After the Genoa Conference, the Polish government faced the formidable task of working out a statute for East Galicia that would satisfy both the British government and the Sejm. As the Polish legation in London reported on 8 July, the Powers—especially Britain—would choose their tactics according to the type of autonomy granted and how it was to be implemented.[1] While the leading British supporters of East Galician autonomy, Col. Josiah Wedgewood and Lord Cecil, asked questions in Parliament, the British and French representatives in Warsaw exerted unofficial pressure on the Polish government. On 12 July, R. H. Hoare, the British chargé d'affaires, told Kajetan Dzierżykraj-Morawski that the failure to work out a scheme of autonomy confronted the Poles with a "hopeless dilemma": if they included East Galicia in the national elections, they would be accused of usurpation; if they did not, they would be accused of disenfranchising a large part of their population. Morawski agreed, but he also said that the government had hoped to reach agreement with a sufficiently large and influential section of the Ruthene (Ukrainian) population to establish a generally acceptable form of autonomy. He claimed that these negotiations had gone well until Ukrainian hopes of independence had been raised at Genoa. In his report, Hoare observed that the British legation in Warsaw was in a difficult position on East Galicia, since it had no idea as to the intentions of its government. Max Muller's pleas for directives had been fruitless, so the legation had stopped urging the Poles to get on with plans for autonomy. Hoare thought there was not much the British government could do, except to be a little disagreeable, adding that "if the Poles offered to clear out of E(astern) Galicia tomorrow we should be in a pretty quandary!"[2]

Official British policy on East Galicia at this time was passive. Balfour simply told the Polish minister in London, Wróblewski, that if Poland presented an autonomy project, the British government would not delay discussion on it.[3] Emrys Evans, a temporary clerk in the Northern Department of the Foreign Office, had more specific ideas. In his memorandum of 28 July on the status of East Galicia, he proposed that the Polish government find a solution similar to that of Ulster, which had its own parliament but also sent deputies to Westminster. He suggested that French help be enlisted for the proposal that the Powers "mediate" between the Poles and the Ruthenes. Gregory, however, thought that Britain should not take the initiative in a matter in which she had no direct interest, and others agreed.[4] In the meanwhile, the Polish Sejm passed a resolution on 22 July calling on the government to propose a law on the self-government of voivodships (provinces) with mixed populations.[5] This resolution indicated the type of autonomy that was acceptable to the Sejm. A few days later, on 3 August, the Sejm voted to end the state of emergency that had existed off and on in East Galicia since the Austro-Hungarian government had proclaimed it on 25 June 1914.[6]

The Polish government set to work on 7 August. On that day the head of the Polish delegation to the League of Nations, the historian Szymon Askenazy, met with the Political Committee of the Council of Ministers and outlined to them the status of the East Galician problem abroad, especially in the league. The committee then resolved: (1) to prepare the text of the statute that the foreign minister would take to Paris to present to the Conference of Ambassadors; (2) to prepare the ground, before his departure, through talks with Allied envoys in Warsaw; (3) to prepare maximum concessions to the Allied Powers, especially in oil and coal, so as to ensure that they would definitively award East Galicia to Poland; (4) that the Polish government would take full responsibility for negotiating the agreement on East Galicia with the Conference of Ambassadors and would not consult the Sejm or the Covenant of Seniors (party leaders) before presenting the project for approval to the Sejm; (5) to work out the project and consult the Conference of Ambassadors by 18 August—the day on which the decree proclaiming national elections was to be published.[7] Two days later the presidium of the Council of Ministers established a commission of inquiry, which was to examine the project of the statute that had been proposed by the Entente Powers in 1919 and to see whether it could be modified in such a way as to safeguard Polish interests and secure approval by the Sejm.[8]

We should recall that, despite some disagreements, the Supreme Council had approved a statute for East Galicia in November 1919; this envisaged not only a separate, autonomous territory, with its own provincial diet and administration, but also the possibility of a plebiscite.[9] At this time, the British had insisted that the statute leave the door open for the union of East Galicia with Russia; hence these provisions. It is not surprising that the Polish project, as worked out in August 1922, departed from the key points of 1919. In any case, this kind of autonomy had failed to work in Czechoslovakia (for the Ukrainians of Sub-Carpathian Ruthenia),[10] but what was most important, massive opposition in Poland meant that even if it wanted to, the government could not secure regional autonomy for East Galicia. Therefore, the government proposed autonomy for the three Eastern voivodships of Lwów,* Tarnopol, and Stanisławów, each of which was to have its own voivode (governor) and diet. Thus, there was to be no Galician Diet with wide legislative powers, as in the Allied Supreme Council proposal project. Further, the diet of each voivodship was to be divided into Polish and Ruthene curiae; each diet was to be separately elected, meet separately, and vote separate taxes and budgets. They had to agree on mutual affairs but, again, were to vote separately.[11] The authors of the proposal clearly sought to prevent Ukrainian majority rule over the Polish minority. Therefore, they took as their model the Moravian Compromise between the Czechs and Germans of Moravia in 1905, whereby the Czech majority had accepted equality with the German minority.[12] Foreign Minister Gabriel Narutowicz presented the proposal to the Allied envoys in Warsaw.[13]

Sir William Max Muller reported his reactions on 16 August. Narutowicz had told Muller that the recognition of Polish sovereignty over East Galicia was urgent, since elections would soon be held nationwide. Max Muller vented his pent-up frustrations on the luckless Narutowicz. Rather tactlessly, Muller told him that the "pointless" dismissal of Skirmunt, who had won confidence abroad, would reduce the chances of obtaining British consent. Referring to the change of government in June, Muller castigated Poland as "a state which had once again given proof of political immaturity and inability to subordinate party to country." Narutowicz calmly replied that Polish policy had not changed but that the government had to be stronger in order to deal with the Sejm. Muller then conceded that cooperation was possible, but he said that he had no idea what the British reaction would be and that he himself was not favorably impressed by the proposal. In his report to London, Muller enclosed comments by the British consul general, Frank Savery, who analyzed the draft Polish statute and noted that the long uncertainty over the future of East Galicia had fomented turmoil. In explaining Polish objectives, Savery cited the opinion of a prominent East Galician Jew, Dr. Henryk Lowenherz, that territorial autonomy would

*Since most official documents at this time used the Polish name Lwów, it is so used in this chapter.

inevitably prepare the ground for the union of East Galicia with Russia. Savery believed that this was the main reason for the Polish government's proposal to divide the region into three separate administrative units. Finally he noted that Britain, no less than Poland, had no wish to see Russia on the Carpathians.[14]

Despite these explanations, the Foreign Office's reaction to the Polish proposal was negative. On 23 August, Emrys Evans noted that the Polish scheme was so complicated that it would be almost impossible to make it work. Also, the division of East Galicia into three provinces with local diets indicated that the scheme was "not serious," and he could not see how the British government could agree unless the proposal was amended to set up a "federal" government for the three provinces. Another official in the Northern Department, Esmond Ovey, thought that the Polish proposal did not represent "real autonomy," but he advised a wait-and-see attitude. R. C. Lindsay thought that Britain should withhold her blessings, but should also refrain from uttering curses. Finally, Curzon wrote that he thought the scheme was "a very bad one." After the prominent role that Britain had played in the question of Galician autonomy, he did not think she "ought to fall down at the first blast of the Polish trumpet."[15] Jan Ciechanowski reported on 26 August that the British government had no intention of approving any statute that did not give territorial autonomy to East Galicia. But he also noted that the Foreign Office had not made any counterproposal; therefore, he thought that Britain's protest against elections in East Galicia would only be formal and that London would not oppose them.[16]

The French reaction was more positive. Wielowieyski communicated the Polish proposal and accompanying justification to Peretti de la Rocca on 22 August,[17] who said that it would be "premature" to raise the question, since a unanimous decision by the Great Powers was impossible for the time being.[18] Still, in answer to British queries, the Quai d'Orsay stated on 6 September that the French government had examined the proposal and that "it did not seem to it that any objections could be formulated against its adoption." R. A. Leeper commented on 9 September: "The French have no conscience in this matter." He thought that the British government should inform the Poles of its opinion, but he did not want "to stir up the Ruthenes." R. C. Lindsay commented two days later that the Polish minister had advanced two arguments to him: (1) that the Polish scheme was taken from the Moravian Compromise of 1906 (1905), which had worked in a satisfactory fashion, and (2) that if only one Power refrained from accepting the proposal, the "Ruthene malcontents" would not recognize any scheme for autonomy, no matter how liberal. Lindsay asked whether the secretary of state would be helped if it could be shown that the Moravian Compromise had worked satisfactorily, but he noted that the text could not be found in the Foreign Office Library. Curzon wrote: "I doubt this is worthwhile."[19]

The foreign secretary was obviously unwilling to act. When Lindsay asked on 17 September whether the British government could declare that it was *not* in favor of a "Ruthene State," Curzon commented that he did not think the British government could make such a declaration alone.[20] One element in Britain's reluctance to tackle the issue at this time was the Greco-Turkish war in which Britain was supporting Greece, while France and Soviet Russia were supporting Turkey. This was probably the reason for the invitation extended by the chief of the British General Staff, Lord Frederick R. Cavan, to the chief of the Polish General Staff, Gen. Władysław Sikorski, who visited Britain in early September. Cavan and the head of the Political Intelligence Department, Barnet Stuart, assured Sikorski that they regretted their government's attitude toward Poland and foresaw an improvement in mutual relations in the near future. However, Sikorski made no commitments and even refused to see Lloyd George. Likewise, Stanisław Łoś, director of the Eastern Department in the Polish Foreign Ministry, would not commit himself when Frank Savery demanded in early October that Poland agree to have Rumanian military units sent to the Bosporus and the Dardanelles to bolster the British units there.[21] In fact, Poland and Rumania agreed on East Galicia, and the Poles promised to recommend to the French government that Rumania be elected to the League Council.[22] Foreign Minister Take Ionescu told Lloyd George that if East Galicia were torn away from Poland, Rumania would have to occupy the region in her own interests.[23] Nor could the British count on the Italians. The Italian government, tempted with Polish oil concessions, stated that it would not create difficulties over Allied recognition of Polish sovereignty over East Galicia.[24]

In mid September, Ukrainian protests against the forthcoming elections in East Galicia flowed into the League of Nations. On 12 September, Balfour, head of the British delegation, asked Curzon whether the latter was thinking about issuing a joint warning to the Poles that elections in East Galicia would be illegal.[25] Five days later, William Steven Fielding of the Canadian delegation moved that the League Assembly renew the (Doherty) resolution of 27 September 1921 that the League Council draw the attention of the Allied Powers to the desirability of determining the status of East Galicia at an early date.[26] On 20 September, Curzon informed Balfour of the different opinions held on the Polish proposal by the British, the French, and the Italian governments. Curzon said that he was unwilling to do anything to increase or maintain the agitation in East Galicia, while there was no point in Britain's protesting the elections alone.[27] This was also Lloyd George's view. Parliament then recessed; so the supporters of East Galician autonomy could not be heard. Finally, the head of the Polish delegation to the league, Askenazy, helped to defuse the tension by stating that the Polish government had accepted the Doherty resolution of 27 September 1921 and was working on a statute that would grant extensive autonomy in East Galicia, including language and religious rights.[28]

However, the Polish government found it impossible to secure parliamentary support even for the proposal that was so distasteful to the British. When Premier Julian Nowak sent the bill to the Sejm on 13 September, the National Democrat Stanisław Głąbiński proposed an amendment that would deprive the already diluted autonomy of any distinctive character. He proposed that the autonomous structure suggested for the three Eastern voivodships be extended to *all* the voivodships of Poland. He also proposed that limitations be placed on the competence of the diets. The Sejm approved this amendment on 26 September and stipulated that the law should be implemented within two years. The government was, however, called upon to establish a Ukrainian university.[29] This proposal was designed to conciliate the British.

The French minister in Warsaw, Panafieu, shed some light on the Polish government's difficulties and tactics in obtaining approval of this project. He reported on 2 October that Premier Nowak's bill was a compromise between the right-wing parties, who opposed a special regime for East Galicia, and the Socialists, who wanted complete territorial autonomy for that province. Nowak allegedly counted on the moderates and the Populist (peasant) Party to make up the majority. But many deputies were in a hurry to return to their electoral districts, and they therefore voted for Głąbiński's amendment almost without discussion. At the session of 26 September, at which the law was passed, only about thirty Socialists, fifteen to twenty Populists, and about one hundred deputies from the Center and the Right were present. Most of the Center deputies were absent, and this forced Nowak to accept all the amendments demanded by the National Democrats. Panafieu concluded that the law was only a timid attempt to show good will toward Allied wishes.[30]

The British Foreign Office showed little if any comprehension of the difficulties being faced by the Polish government on East Galician autonomy. It might seem surprising that men who were so proud of "the mother of parliaments" should fail to understand the significance of Polish parliamentary opposition. However, British officials thought in terms of their own government's commitment to East Galician autonomy, and particularly of the support that it enjoyed in their parliament. Therefore, Curzon sent a telegram to Max Muller on 26 September, instructing him to tell the Polish government that London would not approve the proposal as described in Muller's dispatch of 17 September, nor would it discuss suitable amendments. He said that the final British decision would depend on the nature of the proposed autonomy, both on paper and in practice.[31] This postponed British consent to some nebulous future. Muller transmitted the news to the Poles in an *aide-mémoire* on 4 October,[32] but he warned his superiors that no Polish government could be induced to go much further toward autonomy unless it was forced to do so.[33] However, Curzon's opinion remained unchanged, all the more so perhaps because the Italian government now said that it viewed the Polish law as "unsatisfactory."[34]

In the meanwhile, the situation in East Galicia was rapidly approaching a state of civil war. Knowing that the Polish government wished to demonstrate popular support for Polish sovereignty, Ukrainian political leaders, both in East Galicia and abroad, called for a boycott of the elections scheduled for November. The boycott was implemented with the aid of two terrorist organizations: the Vola (the will) and the Ukrainian Home Student Council. The latter had organized the assassination attempt on Piłsudski in September 1921, but it had not become active again until the fall of 1922. At this time, Evhen Konovalec, a former colonel of the Sich, arrived in Lwów; he assumed command of Vola and of all terrorist-diversionary activities in East Galicia.[35] Rumors circulated that Soviet troops would come in, or that the Ukrainian brigade would cross over from Czechoslovakia. There was also much talk of an uprising. However, the key weapon that was used against Ukrainians who supported the Polish authorities, and especially those who participated in organizing the elections, was terror. They received threatening letters, were attacked, and sometimes were murdered. The victims included such prominent figures as Sydor Tverdokhlib, editor of the *Ridnyi Krai;* Vassyl Pihulak; and Ivan Bakhmaschuk. There were also cases of arson and bombings, an attempt to blow up a railway bridge, and an attack on the train in which the governor was traveling.[36]

Terrorist activites peaked in September, when 116 incidents were reported, most of them involving arson.[37] Some were carried out by partisan units.[38] The Polish population was panic-stricken, and the National Democratic press demanded that the government declare a state of emergency. In Lwów, National Democratic students retaliated by beating up Ukrainians and by placing a bomb in the Prosvita building, as well as by causing explosions in the building of the Schevchenko Scientific Society and in a Ukrainian student residence.[39]

In this situation, the Polish government sent special troops to East Galicia and gave their commanders extensive judiciary powers. Their military courts could condemn and execute anyone who could be proved to have committed murder, robbery, arson, and so forth. At the same time, Polish authorities imprisoned as many Ukrainian political activists as possible, including newspaper editors. Finally, when all these measures failed, the Council of Ministers appointed Gen. Stanisław Haller as commander in chief of all military forces in the Lwów-Przemyśl (Peremyshl) military district, and gave him the power to issue directives to the civil authorities. The main reason for giving him such great powers was the government's desire to avoid armed conflict. It also feared that the Ukrainians might obtain Soviet aid.[40] Haller proved equal to his task, for the incidence of terrorism was reduced by more than half during October.

As a result of the boycott, which was carried out by all parties except the Communists, Ukrainian participation in the elections was very low. While the overall voter participation in Poland was 68 percent, it was 32 percent in Stanisławów and 32 percent in Tarnopol but 52 percent in Lwów, which, of course, had the largest Polish population.[41] The *Manchester Guardian* and the *Daily Herald* (London) called the elections "an act of lawlessness."[42] This was legally correct, since the Allied and Associated Powers still had sovereignty over East Galicia. However, they did not protest the elections and thus implicitly recognized the Polish government's right to hold them.

The national elections of 5 November 1922 gave the rightist parties 29 percent; the Center, 24 percent; the Left, 25 percent; and the "Minorities Bloc," 22 percent of the vote. In the last group, the Jews had the largest number of deputies, 34; the mostly Petlyurist Ukrainians of Volhynia had 20; the "Compromise" Ukrainians of East Galicia, who were called *khliboroby* (breadmakers), had 5; the Germans had 17; and the Belorussians had 11. When the Sejm proceeded to elect the president of Poland, the rightist candidate, Maurycy Zamoyski, obtained 222 votes in the first round; but this was not enough. In the fifth round, Piłsudski's candiate, Gabriel Narutowicz, won with 289 votes, thanks to the support of the Minorities Bloc and the Populist Party. The National Democrats, furious at Zamoyski's defeat, launched a virulent press campaign against Narutowicz, charging that he had been elected with non-Polish votes. Right-wing demonstrations took place on the day of his inauguration, when students and toughs tried to stop Jewish and Socialist deputies from reaching the Sejm building and thus to prevent a quorum for the swearing-in ceremony. They failed, but large-scale fighting was only narrowly averted. On 16 December, Narutowicz was assassinated by the right-wing fanatic, the art historian Eligiusz Niewiadomski. He was tried and sentenced to death, but some National Democratic papers made him out to be a national martyr.[43] Piłsudski, who had been Niewiadomski's primary target, was shocked and embittered. In 1923, when Piłsudski resigned from all his posts in protest against the policy of the new right-wing coalition, he extended his bitter condemnation of the National Democrats to the parliamentary system as it then existed in Poland. This paved the way for his decision to seize power in May 1926.

At the turn of 1922/23, three developments helped Poland to attain the goal of her diplomatic efforts: namely, Allied recognition of her eastern frontier and, with it, her sovereignty over East Galicia. First, Lloyd George's obstinacy in supporting the Greeks against the Turks, even at the risk of an Anglo-Turkish war, led to the breakup of his Liberal-Conservative coalition. It collapsed on 19 October 1922, and he was forced to resign. Bonar Law formed a new cabinet, and the Conservatives won the elections in November. With Lloyd George gone, Poland's chances improved. Second, on 11 January 1923, French and Belgian troops marched into the Ruhr, claiming that the Germans were not paying reparations. This created a serious crisis in Anglo-French relations. Third, and most important for Poland, on the previous day, 10 January, Lithuanian "volunteers" invaded the Memel (Polish—Kłajpeda; Lithuanian—Klajpeda) region, which had been under Allied (French) administration since January 1920. This activated the Memel question, which was, in turn, closely linked to the recognition of Poland's eastern frontier.

We should note that the Franco-Belgian invasion of the Ruhr created an atmosphere of great tension in Polish-Soviet and in Polish-German relations. On 11 January, Nikolai I. Bukharin, then chairman of the Comintern, wrote an open letter to the French Communist Boris Souvarine, stating that if there were a revolution in Germany and if Poland were then to attack Germany, Russia would probably be obliged to move against Poland. In this case, Bukharin declared, the workers of the whole world should support the German revolution and the war carried on by Soviet Russia against Poland.[44] On the same day, State Secretary Baron Ago von Maltzan spoke to the Polish chargé in Berlin, Jerzy Madeyski, about rumored Polish designs on East Prussia and Upper Silesia and warned him that any such move would have unforeseen consequences.[45] Prime Minister Sikorski refuted the rumors on 16 January,[46] but five days later an article in *Izvestia* stated that if Poincaré extended French control from the Rhine to the Vistula, this would threaten Soviet vital interests; therefore, Poland's "aggressive plans" were a direct menace to Soviet security. The same issue of *Izvestia* contained an article by Vladimir A. Antonov-Ovseenko entitled "Plans of the Polish Imperialists," in which he accused Poland of harboring designs on East Prussia.[47] Two days later, Maltzan hinted to Madeyski that Russia would intervene in case of a German-Polish conflict.[48] Since Poland had no intention of attacking either Germany or Russia, Soviet accusations were designed to check any possible Polish cooperation with France, should a revolution break out in Germany. (As we know, the Comintern planned a Communist uprising in that country, but the Communists only succeeded in seizing brief control over Saxony and Thuringia in the late spring of 1923.) These accusations were also linked with the Memel question, to which we shall now turn.

Memel had been founded by the Knights of the Sword in 1252 and had passed to the Teutonic Knights in 1328. Later it became a part of Prussia and then of the German Empire, in which it remained until 1919. The Prussian census of 1910 showed that the port city had a German majority of 92 percent and a Lithuanian minority of 8 percent out of a total population of 21,419. However, the Lithuanians constituted a majority of 66 percent in the countryside. In the Memel region as a whole, the Germans numbered 71,191, or 50.7 percent; the Lithuanians, 67,345, or 47.9 percent; and the bilinguals, who were mostly Lithuanians, 1,970, or 1.4 percent.[49]

Memel had been even more of a sleepy, provincial port than Danzig. Its main export had been lumber—for which Britain was the most important customer—and then flax. The port's development had been stifled by Prussian favoritism toward Koenigsberg, on the one hand, and Russian favoritism toward Riga, Windau, and Reval on the other. Russian development of these ports and their communications had, in effect, robbed Memel of trade with its natural "hinterland," Belorussia and the Ukraine.

Article 99 of the Versailles Treaty forced Germany to give up her rights and titles to Memel and to transfer them to the Allied and Associated Powers. German protests that the right of self-determination was thus violated, since the majority of the population was German, were rejected by the Allies. It is worth noting that on 5 June 1919, Paderewski stressed the economic significance of Memel for Poland and stated that the region was Lithuanian in character despite considerable Germanization.[50] Warsaw supported the award of Memel to Lithuania, provided the latter would enter into some form of union with Poland. The port was the natural outlet for the lumber, flax, and other agricultural products of Polish territories east of the Bug River. However, if there were to be no Polish-Lithuanian union, Warsaw favored a free city or a free state, in which Poland would have extensive rights and privileges.

France also had an interest in Memel. Part of the Anglo-French agreement that a British administrator would be sent to Danzig was that the French would have one in Memel. On 15 January 1920 a French battalion arrived in the city, followed a month later by an Alpine sharpshooter unit led by Gen. Dominique Odry. He was the Allied administrator and, later, high commissioner. He established a "directorate" to administer the city's postal, railway, and customs affairs. The majority of its members were German, as was the Civil Service. On 20 June 1920, Gabriel Pétisné was appointed as civil commissioner; he was to succeed Odry as high commissioner in 1922.

Pétisné followed a policy of encouraging local autonomy. He established good relations with the German merchant community, and he pushed French economic penetration by purchasing valuable real estate and negotiating concessions to French interests. He also tried to obtain French concessions for Polish lumber and flax, which could come down to Memel on the Niemen River. In early 1921 he hinted to the Polish delegate in Memel, Czesław Andrycz, that France's attitude toward the Lithuanian question (that is, Vilna and federation) would depend on Poland's agreeing to such concessions. However, Foreign Minister Sapieha was very cautious, and no deal was made.[51] At this time, the Poles were correct in assuming that the French "maximum program" was to make Memel a free city or a free state, under the league's protection, but with dominant French influence.[52]

The Lithuanians, of course, always claimed Memel. By October 1922 there were demonstrations for union with Lithuania, and on 11 November the Lithuanian Parliament resolved that Memel must be united with Lithuania. However, the French plan of making Memel a free city or a free state coincided with the wishes of the city's preponderantly German community. The Association for the Establishment of a Memel Free State was formed at the end of 1921. Its referendum garnered 54,329 out of a total of 71,856 votes cast in the territory. Even the German Fatherland Association supported the free-state solution.[53] Poland also favored this project, and she developed contacts with German business circles in Memel. A merchant delegation visited Warsaw in late June 1921, and a delegation of the Directorate signed a provisional one-year trade-and-transport agreement in Warsaw on 6 April 1922. The British government, however, made the reservation that the agreement could not constitute a precedent for other similar agreements.[54] Poland opposed the Memel provisions in the two Hymans plans, of May and September 1921, for a Polish-Lithuanian union in which Memel was to go to Lithuania but Poland was to have free use of the port and free transit down the river Niemen to Memel.[55] The Poles wanted the union to be signed and sealed before Memel was awarded to Lithuania.

In November 1922 the Conference of Ambassadors began to work on the Memel statute. The Polish government's program, drawn up for its delegation a month earlier, stipulated Polish interests and the right to at least a consultative voice in working out the statute. Poland wanted a "free zone" in the port and an agreement on the administration of the Niemen River by the participating states.[56] In the administration of the port, she wished to apply the bitter lessons learned in Danzig, but this time to her own benefit. Thus, the port administration was to be in the hands of a harbor board, consisting of representatives of Memel, Poland, and Lithuania, with a chairman appointed by the League of Nations. This board would also administer the city's railway system and the lower Niemen River. In Memel, Polish citizens were to enjoy the same economic rights as the natives, while the latter would enjoy equal rights in Poland. This again followed the Danzig model. Finally, the Polish government foresaw the possibility of making Memel a "free territory" under the league's protection—again on the Danzig model—but for a period of ten years. After this, a plebiscite could be held, and new decisions would be possible.[57] This would leave the door open for the awarding of the city to

Lithuania, if there were a Polish-Lithuanian union, or for a continuation of the free-territory status if a union proved impossible.

When the Conference of Ambassadors discussed the Memel question in November 1922, the Polish project seemed to have a good chance of success. Not only did it coincide with French objectives, but Joseph Krause, president of the Memel Chamber of Commerce, also came out in favor of a free state. The city's trade-union representatives demanded a referendum for either a free state or union with Germany. Even German sources confirmed that the majority of Memel Germans wanted ''independence'' under the protection of a Great Power—which could only be France. The Lithuanian delegates, of course, demanded union with Lithuania. Thus, the conference of Ambassadors leaned toward the free-state concept.[58]

No wonder the Lithuanian government decided to seize the Memel region by force, especially since it was encouraged to do so by both Germany and Russia. The German government preferred the union of Memel with Lithuania to the establishment of a free state under French protection, which would be favorable to Poland,[59] and Gen. Hans von Seeckt encouraged the Lithuanian government to seize the city.[60] The Soviet government also favored such a move. Juliusz Łukasiewicz believed there had been a meeting between Premier Galvanauskas, the German minister to Lithuania, Franz Olshausen, and Chicherin on 28 November 1922, at which they discussed the plan and the military operations as well as diplomatic action.[61] Indeed, Galvanauskas confirmed this in his memoirs. He wrote that he met Chicherin at the Kaunas railway station, when the Soviet foreign commissar was on his way to the Lausanne Conference. Chicherin had no objections to the plan.[62] The Soviet minister also warned the British, French, and Italian governments in December that Memel was so important to the Soviet Russian and Belorussian republics that the latter would not consider a settlement made without their participation as binding.[63]

Thus, by the end of 1922 the Lithuanian government was assured of both German and Soviet support if it should seize Memel. The date was set for 10 January—one day before the Franco-Belgian occupation of the Ruhr was due to take place. On the evening of 3 January 1923 the French Council of Ministers had set the date of 11 January; and, as we know, on 9 January the Reparations Commission declared Germany in default on her coal deliveries. The Lithuanians may have gotten wind of this and chosen their timing accordingly. Whatever the case may be, the Lithuanian coup came as no surprise to the French. On 7 January 1923 the deputy Polish delegate in Memel, Wołowski, was informed of the impending Lithuanian attack by none other than Commissioner Pétisné himself.[64] Two days later the Polish minister in Riga, Jodko-Narkiewicz, telegraphed Warsaw that according to the French legation, the Lithuanian attack would take place the next day.

French intelligence even knew the number of troops involved.[65] On the same day the French informed the British that they were thinking about sending a cruiser to Memel and asked if the British would send one too.[66]

The Lithuanians decided to follow Żeligowski's precedent, but with a variation. Instead of a "mutiny" by regular troops, they chose a "partisan" uprising by regular troops in civilian clothes; these troops infiltrated the territory on 10 January. Commissioner Pétisné issued a formal protest and declared that he would resist. One hundred and fifty French soldiers and two hundred Memel policemen manned trenches around the city. British, French, and Italian representatives protested to Galvanauskas, but he disclaimed any responsibility.[67] Fighting broke out on 12 January, but Pétisné's forces were hopelessly outnumbered. The French and British now made a show of force. The British cruiser *Caledon* and the French torpedo boats *Senégal* and *Algérien* were sent in, while the cruiser *Voltaire* was ordered to make its way thence.[68] On 13 January the Conference of Ambassadors demanded that the Lithuanian government withdraw its regular troops from Memel and asked the Legal Commission to draw up a report.[69] At the same time, Colonel Trousson of the French Military Mission in Poland was ordered to Memel. However, two days later, when Trousson left Danzig aboard a Polish gunboat,[70] an armistice was signed in Memel.[71] On the following day, Lithuanian units began to evacuate the city in a move designed to mollify the Allied Powers. On 17 January the Conference of Ambassadors decided to send a Commission of Inquiry to Memel, made up of Georges Clinchant, head of the Asian Department of the Quai d'Orsay, who was appointed chairman of the commission; Consul Fry; and Consul Bertanzi from Danzig.[72] (Bertanzi was soon replaced by Pompeo Aloisi, former Italian consul in Copenhagen.) On 20 January the captain of HMS *Caledon* received a delegation of Lithuanian "partisans" on board his cruiser and advised them to evacuate the city. He said that this would have a positive effect upon the forthcoming decision on Memel by the Conference of Ambassadors.[73] However, the next day the newly elected president of the Memel Region, Erdman Simonaitis, telegraphed President Poincaré that peace reigned in Memel. He blamed the French troops and Pétisné, in particular, for violating the armistice. He said that the population would fight for its freedom, and he demanded the withdrawal of French troops.[74] The Conference of Ambassadors instructed Pétisné to observe the armistice and to await the arrival of the Allied commission.[75] Jules Laroche, chairman of the conference's Memel Committee, now abandoned his former support of autonomy for the city and instead proposed that sovereignty be granted immediately to Lithuania. The British feared this would lead to Warsaw's demand for recognition of its sovereignty over Vilna, which they opposed because their aim was the simultaneous settlement of the Vilna and Memel issues.[76] But Curzon believed that nothing could reinstate the Lithuanians in Vilna; so he was inclined to accept what he called "the double outrage."[77]

On 29 January the Commission of Inquiry appealed to the Lithuanian "partisans" to leave the city and declared that the Conference of Ambassadors desired a solution that would be acceptable to the population. Two days later the commission issued an ultimatum, but this, too, had no effect. The French government then decided to withdraw Pétisné, replacing him with his financial adviser, Malin. All these gestures clearly indicated that the Powers were seeking a face-saving way out of the situation. Indeed, the Conference of Ambassadors only wished to preserve some appearance of legality before handing the city over to the Lithuanians.[78] On 4 February the members of the commission were ordered to leave within a week, together with Pétisné; they finally left on 19 February. The Lithuanians took over the administration at the end of the month.

The Conference of Ambassadors tried to cover up its discomfiture by resolving that Memel would go to Lithuania, provided the latter agreed to grant the city an autonomous administration and a representative regime. Furthermore, the Lithuanian government was to organize free land and river transit to benefit both Polish and Lithuanian interests, for which Memel was the natural outlet. Once the Lithuanian government had accepted these terms, a Memel statute would be drawn up by the conference in Paris with the participation of representatives from Lithuania and Memel, and an appropriate convention would be drawn up for Lithuania to sign.[79]

In the meanwhile, Mussolini proposed on 30 January that the Memel problem and the recognition of Poland's eastern frontier be placed before the Conference of Ambassadors.[80] This move was not unconnected with the Polish-Italian oil agreement, due to be signed the next day. The British also softened their position. On 31 January, Sir William Max Muller informed Foreign Minister Skrzyński of British satisfaction that Poland "had remained quiet on the Memel question" (probably a reference to rumors that the Poles intended to seize Danzig). He said that this had made an excellent impression in Britain, and he implied that his government was ready to recognize Poland's eastern frontier.[81]

The Polish government now launched a diplomatic campaign to secure this recognition. On 6 February, Skrzyński delivered an exposé in the Sejm, warning the Great Powers against indecision in regard to unsettled international conflicts.[82] On 8 February, Zamoyski paid a visit to Peretti de la Rocca at the Quai d'Orsay, during which he expressed Polish hopes for the swift liquidation of all unsettled questions of interest to Poland. Zamoyski claimed that this state of affairs allowed Germany to foment trouble over the statute for Memel, over Polish transit on the Niemen River, the Polish-Lithuanian frontier, and the recognition of the Polish-Soviet frontier. Peretti de la Rocca answered that the French government would examine all these questions but that perhaps the right moment had not yet come. In any case, he thought that all the issues should not be examined at once. Zamoyski replied by quoting Mussolini that the question of recognition was urgent. Zamoyski also delivered a letter for Poincaré, which accused the German government of trying to persuade the Lithuanians to attack Vilna and reported German troop concentrations in East Prussia. He therefore suggested that the Conference of Ambassadors recognize the Polish-Soviet frontier as laid down in the Treaty of Riga. He observed that for Poland to be a pillar of the European order, she must have Allied support.[83]

The Italian ambassador in Warsaw, Tommasini, officially informed the Polish government on 9 February that his government was ready to help with the recognition of Poland's eastern frontier. He also mentioned this unofficially in private conversations with Polish journalists.[84] However, the French were still reluctant to tackle the issue. A French Foreign Office note, dated 10 February, stated that the time was right, but the difficulty lay in satisfying Poland while granting the Ruthenes national freedoms that would be compatible with the unity of the Polish state.[85] This referred, of course, to British opposition to the type of autonomy that had been voted by the Polish Sejm in September 1922. Thus, in answering Zamoyski's letter on 12 February, Poincaré stated the need for a convention on Memel and promised to obtain a swift decision from the Conference of Ambassadors concerning the Polish-Lithuanian frontier. With regard to other parts of the frontier, however, he said that France must act together with her allies. Nevertheless, if Poland so desired, France would take the initiative in asking the conference to consider the question as soon as possible.[86]

In transmitting the text of this letter to Panafieu in Warsaw, Poincaré added some secret information. Referring to the statement made by the Italian minister in Warsaw that the Italian ambassador in Paris had proposed that the conference regulate Poland's eastern frontier, Poincaré claimed this was "false on all points." He stated that the Italian ambassador had only asked Jules Cambon whether it was opportune to raise the question of East Galicia. Poincaré had been told that the French government believed that the Polish government did *not* wish to raise the question *(sic)*. In any case, continued Poincaré, Zamoyski had not raised it. If the Polish government *did* wish to raise it, however, the French government was willing to do so, provided the British made no difficulties. He added that all the questions could not be settled at once and that Vilna could not be attributed to Poland without a convention being signed on Memel. In fact, Zamoyski had mentioned the Memel problem first, but he had included East Galicia by asking for the recognition of the Polish-Soviet frontier. However, the French government seemed determined to settle the Memel question first. On 12

February the conference learned that Poincaré insisted on fully safeguarding Polish interests in Memel.[87]

The Polish government now increased its pressure on Paris. On 12 February the Sejm passed a resolution demanding that the Allies recognize Poland's eastern frontier, and Foreign Minister Skrzyński told Max Muller that he would request recognition from the Conference of Ambassadors.[88] Premier Władysław Sikorski wrote a letter to Poincaré on 12 February, which Zamoyski delivered at the Quai d'Orsay four days later. Sikorski stated that a decisive intervention by the Great Powers would avert the need for the Polish government to settle its disputes with Kaunas "directly." (This was a reference both to Vilna and to a small sector of the frontier, decided by the League of Nations on 3 February, but not accepted by Lithuania.) He claimed that Memel was the pretext for a German campaign of calumnies against Poland. (This was a reference to German accusations that Poland was planning to invade East Prussia or Upper Silesia—accusations originally made by Moscow.) He mentioned the Sejm resolution demanding Allied recognition and announced a forthcoming Polish *démarche* to the Conference of Ambassadors. According to the terms of this *démarche,* the conference was to recognize the frontiers of Poland, on the one hand, and those of Russia and the Ukraine on the other, "such as had been traced by the Treaty of Riga of 18 March 1921." Sikorski added that the results of Polish conversations in Rome and London were favorable and that he hoped France would support Poland.[89] On 15 February the Polish delegation to the Peace Conference addressed a request to Poincaré, as president of the Conference of Ambassadors, for the settlement of the eastern frontier of Poland as defined by the Treaty of Riga; the delegation also asked that such recognition be considered as fulfilling article 87 of the Versailles Treaty.[90]

On 16 February the Conference of Ambassadors passed a resolution on Memel, which was to be awarded to Lithuania, but on certain conditions: the city was to have autonomy; there would be guarantees for free trade and free transit to Memel, including safeguards for Polish interests; Lithuania was to pay the costs of Allied administration and occupation from 1920 to 1923, as well as a share of German reparations; Lithuania was to accept the Memel statute and sign a convention to this effect. On the same day, the conference considered a Polish note stating that the Polish government could not accept any compromise on Memel, unless it received simultaneous guarantees on the use of Memel harbor and navigation on the Niemen River; also, the Polish government insisted that the Polish-Lithuanian frontier be defined and settled in Poland's favor. However, the conference decided that it was inadvisable to make a final decision on Vilna, on the grounds that this might precipitate a Polish-Lithuanian war.[91]

On the following day, August Zaleski, the Polish minister in Rome, wrote to the Italian deputy foreign minister, Ernesto Vassallo, setting out the Polish point of view on Memel. Zaleski stated that if the Conference of Ambassadors leaned toward awarding it to Lithuania, Poland would demand safeguards for her economic interests, including a Polish free zone in the port. He also stated that if Lithuania recognized Polish possession of Vilna and if Lithuania reduced her army to a level that would guarantee her peaceful intentions, she could expect Poland to reduce some of her demands in Memel. These matters could be discussed in bilateral negotiations and could be guaranteed in a peace treaty.[92]

Meanwhile, the Lithuanians gained no credit with the Allied Powers by their actions. After the Commission of Inquiry had left Memel on 19 February, regular Lithuanian troops entered the city and ordered the Polish delegate and his staff to leave immediately. To distract attention from Memel, the Lithuanian government protested to the League of Nations against alleged Polish aggression. This led to a minor scandal. General Carton de Wiart and Major Grant, of the British Military Mission in Poland, accompanied by two Polish officers, left Vilna by car for Orany on 20 February to investigate the alleged Polish aggression. The whole party disappeared. It later turned out that they had been arrested by Lithuanian border guards and had been detained. Both Gregory and Curzon made comments about Lithuanian stupidity.[93]

On 21 February, Poincaré informed Panafieu that he had just received Sikorski's letter of the twelfth; he also instructed him to thank Sikorski and to say that he (Poincaré) would send a reply by the next bag. Panafieu was also to say that the French delegation to the Conference of Ambassadors would propose that morning that the representatives immediately ask their governments to authorize the conference to regulate the unsettled frontiers of Poland. Poincaré added that the French government would do everything it could to find a solution in conformity with Polish wishes.[94] Indeed, the French delegation presented such a resolution at the conference that very morning; simultaneously, the delegation proposed that the Polish-Lithuanian frontier be settled so as to give Vilna to Poland. The conference also discussed the Soviet note to the Polish and Lithuanian governments, which vaguely threatened intervention if the Polish-Lithuanian frontier were to be settled without Soviet participation. This note was clearly welcomed by the Lithuanian premier, Galvanauskas, who told the British minister in Kovno on 25 February, that Russian interests would be prejudiced by any international agreement on the Niemen and on Memel.[95] However, the French delegation proposed that the transfer of sovereignty over Memel to Lithuania be conditional on Lithuanian acceptance of the conference's decision of 16 February.[96]

The French government's willingness to raise both the Vilna and the Memel issues, and its favorable reaction to Polish demands, stemmed not only from the Lithuanian coup in Memel but also from the knowledge that Italy supported Poland. But Mussolini, who had suggested on 30 January that Poland's eastern frontier be finally recognized, now introduced a complication. On 22 February the Italian foreign minister instructed the Italian ambassador in Paris that their government favored the French proposal; but he also stated that he thought the settlement of the Polish-Lithuanian frontier should be left to the League of Nations, which had already been concerned with it and whose decision the two parties were more likely to accept. The Polish government disagreed. Skrzyński visited the Italian minister in Warsaw, Tommasini, and asked him to see to it that the Polish-Lithuanian dispute not be left up to the league. He said that if the decision on Vilna should go in Lithuania's favor, the Polish government could not resist public pressure for military action. Tommasini telegraphed this message to Rome. On the same day, Zaleski told the Italian Foreign Ministry that Italy was the only obstacle to the solution of the Polish-Lithuanian frontier that would be satisfactory to Poland. Mussolini backed down.[97]

The British now raised difficulties over East Galicia. On 22 February, Curzon saw Skirmunt, the Polish minister in London. The British foreign secretary made it clear that his government would not desist from its stand on autonomy for East Galicia. He also said that the Polish-Lithuanian dispute should be settled peacefully. Skirmunt assured Curzon that the recognition of the Riga frontier would not prejudice British views and reservations regarding East Galicia.[98] Two days later the Quai d'Orsay sent instructions to its ambassadors and ministers in London, Rome, and Warsaw, recapitulating French proposals and asking for replies from the governments to which these diplomats were accredited. The date proposed for discussing the issue was 28 February.[99]

The Polish government continued to put pressure on Paris. On 25 February, Juliusz Łukasiewicz—formerly first secretary and counsellor at the Polish legation in Paris, now head of the Eastern Department in Warsaw—came to see Laroche. Łukasiewicz criticized Allied "patience" with Lithuania. Presumably he referred to the fact that the Conference of Ambassadors was still waiting for the Lithuanian reply to its Memel resolution of 16 February. Łukasiewicz asked that Lithuania not be informed that the conference would determine Poland's eastern frontier, and he suggested different formulas for Vilna and the rest of the frontier.[100] But the French government foresaw problems. An unsigned note for Poincaré of 23 February observed that France should avoid "recognizing" the Treaty of Riga. In any case, the Polish government was reported to be asking the Allies to "recognize" the frontiers as laid down by the Treaty of Riga but to "settle" the frontier between Poland and Lithuania. The first point was intended to avoid any official French recognition of the Soviet government, and the second, to settle the Polish-Lithuanian dispute over Vilna and a small section of the border.[101]

At this point the British announced their attitude on the issue of recognition. On 26 February, Curzon telegraphed the British ambassador in Paris, Lord Crewe, that he was not averse to settling the Polish-Lithuanian frontier in such a way as to include Vilna in Poland. Curzon also believed that the frontier should be defined at a point between Suwałki and Vilna, where the demarcation line was unclear. Furthermore, the British government was disposed to comply with French and Italian wishes to recognize the Polish-Russian frontier as laid down by the Treaty of Riga, but subject to two reservations. On East Galicia, Curzon suggested a stipulation that the Polish government furnish satisfactory evidence of its intentions to grant the region a special measure of autonomy if it were placed under Polish sovereignty. He also wanted a formula to avert British responsibility for the Polish-Russian frontier in case of Russian attack, as per article 10 of the League Covenant (which obligated league members to go to the aid of a member who was the victim of aggression). As Eyre Crowe explained to the French ambassador in London, Saint Aulaire, both reservations were meant to satisfy certain elements of British parliamentary opinion, especially the supporters of Lloyd George.[102] The British ambassador transmitted his government's views to the conference on 28 February.[103]

Crewe objected to Curzon's instructions. He reported that both the French and the Italian governments had already notified Warsaw that they considered the autonomy granted by Poland to East Galicia as sufficient and satisfactory. If Crewe were to demand special assurances from the Polish government, he would be in a minority of one. As to reservations on article 10 of the League Covenant, he thought that it would be difficult to make a case, since none had been made regarding the Russian-Rumanian frontier (in Bessarabia) in the treaty signed on 28 October 1920.[104] Curzon tried to find a way out. He replied that the British government could not follow the French and the Italian governments in formally recognizing the Polish scheme for East Galician autonomy. He therefore suggested that the Allies simply state that their recognition of Polish sovereignty over East Galicia was being given in consideration of Poland's undertaking that East Galicia would enjoy a suitable measure of autonomy.[105]

It was clear that the British government was ready to accept a face-saving formula so that it could join France and Italy in recognizing the Polish-Soviet frontier and, in particular, Polish sovereignty over East Galicia. As Curzon explained it to Lord Robert Cecil—the most vociferous supporter of the Ukrainian cause in Parliament—the British government desired a solution in

East Galicia because "nationalist passions" there were a threat to peace. Cecil's proposal that the matter be submitted to the league would not expedite it, since in that forum, Britain would also have to face opposition from France, Poland, and Italy. Finally, in view of Italian support for Poland, the British government saw no alternative but to award East Galicia to Poland.[106] The Powers now wanted to be rid of the burden; presumably for the same reason the Conference of Ambassadors ignored a request from the Committee of Jewish Delegations in Paris that a special Jewish council be set up in East Galicia to look after the considerable Jewish population there.[107]

In early March, however, when recognition of Poland's eastern frontier seemed imminent, the British attempted to delay the decision. This was connected with the Memel problem. As Crewe reported to Curzon on 7 March, the counsellor of the Polish legation in Paris, Wielowieyski, had called on his counterpart at the British embassy, Eric Phipps. Wielowieyski suggested that the surest way to avert Polish-Lithuanian hostilities would be to settle all of the Polish eastern frontier as soon as possible. But Crewe was still inclined to believe that Memel should be settled first. If the Lithuanians were ready to negotiate on it, he wrote, then Allied recognition of Polish sovereignty over Vilna and East Galicia would alienate them and thus lessen the chance of solving the Memel problem.[108] Crewe's advice tied in with the British policy, established in July 1922, of solving the two issues at the same time. In fact, Orme Sargent, first secretary at the British embassy in Paris and a member of the British delegation to the Conference of Ambassadors, had sent a letter to Jules Laroche on 2 March, asking the conference to delay its recognition of Poland's eastern frontier pending Lithuanian agreement to the Memel conditions of 16 February. Otherwise, wrote Sargent, the Lithuanians would "argue" if the Poles were given Vilna. Laroche, who was chairman of the Committee on Memel, objected to the delay, but Sargent said that he was merely repeating the views of the British ambassador.[109] Sargent restated these arguments in a conversation with Laroche on 3 March.[110]

Three days later, Jan Ciechanowski asked Gregory for an explanation of Sargent's action. Gregory took cover in explaining that Ambassador Crewe had "misunderstood" his (Gregory's) instructions. He repeated this to Ciechanowski later and showed him the text of an additional telegram, which had been sent to Paris, stating that recognition of Poland's eastern frontier would not be conditional on any previous settlement of the Memel question. He also said that he expected the conference to make its decision on 15 March.[111] This was not surprising, since the Lithuanian government had been given the deadline of 10 March for its answer.

Although on 10 March the Lithuanian government indicated its general assent to the conference's conditions of 16 February, this was not considered satisfactory. It was presumably for this reason that the French and British wished to gain more time. They agreed to ask the Polish government to sign the Treaty of Sèvres of 10 August 1920, regarding frontiers in Eastern Europe, and they objected to the fact that there was as yet no fixed frontier between Poland and Latvia.[112] Thus it was that on 10 March, Laroche suddenly proposed to Juliusz Łukasiewicz that Poland sign the Treaty of Sèvres, or at least that she ratify the Treaty of Saint-Germain.[113] Zamoyski replied two days later that as soon as the Powers had transferred sovereignty over East Galicia to Poland, the Polish government would do what was necessary in order to ratify the Treaty of Saint-Germain.[114]

Meanwhile, also on 10 March, the Political Committee of the Polish Council of Ministers drew up instructions for Foreign Minister Skrzyński, who was supposed to press the Polish case in Paris. Besides reaffirming that the Powers must recognize Polish sovereignty over East Galicia before Warsaw would implement its plans for the region, the committee also demanded recognition of Polish sovereignty over Spiš and Orava, territories that Poland claimed from Czechoslovakia. Further, Poland insisted on keeping Vilna and asked for a correction in the demarcation line proposed by the league in the Orany-Vilna sector on 3 February 1923.[115] Two days later, Premier Sikorski stated these demands in his speech to the Sejm.[116] We should note that in demanding recognition of Polish sovereignty over Spiš and Orava, the Polish government hoped to put pressure on the Czechoslovak government to agree to cede at least Javorina to Poland—which was in turn necessary in order for the Sejm to ratify the Polish-Czechoslovak agreements signed in 1922. However, the French government decided not to raise the issue, since any decision was bound to dissatisfy either Poland or Czechoslovakia.[117]

The French government did not welcome Skrzyński's visit. Laroche noted caustically on 13 March that the Polish foreign minister seemed to think that he and his cabinet were responsible for reestablishing good relations between the two allies. Further, wrote Laroche, it was important to impress on Skrzyński that the French government had never ceased to defend Polish interests. Therefore, Laroche wrote, Polish interventions for the recognition of the eastern frontier had merely succeeded in "breaking down an open door."[118]

Two other interventions took place on 13 March. A certain Miss Jane Anderson, representing Bainbridge Colby, former secretary of state under President Wilson, asked to be heard on the attribution of East Galicia to Poland.[119] As it turned out, Colby was involved in an attempt by the Petrushevych government's representatives in Canada and the United States to float 6 percent bonds secured by East Galician oil.[120] The other intervention came in the form of notes from the Soviet Russian and the Soviet

Ukrainian governments, protesting the settlement of East Galicia's fate without their participation.[121]

Finally, also on 13 March, Foreign Minister Galvanauskas accepted the conference's conditions on Memel. He stated that the Lithuanian government, in its note of 10 March, "in no way meant to reserve its adhesion to the principles of February 16." The conference found this satisfactory,[122] and the last obstacle to granting Polish wishes was removed. On 14 March the Conference of Ambassadors finally recognized the Polish-Lithuanian and the Polish-Soviet frontiers. However, the British reservation with regard to article 10 of the League Covenant could not be fully met. As Eric Phipps reported, all that the members could recommend to relieve their governments of the responsibility of guaranteeing the Polish-Soviet frontier, as per article 10, was the insertion of the words "sous leur responsabilité" (on their responsibility), in the paragraph referring to the frontier agreed upon by Poland and Russia in the Treaty of Riga.[123] This signified, of course, that the Western Powers did not bear any responsibility for this frontier.

As for East Galicia, Poincaré, informed Panafieu that the formula used was the one proposed by the Polish government.[124] The decision stated that concerning the eastern part of Galicia, Poland recognized that ethnographic conditions necessitated an autonomous regime. Further, in the treaty of 28 June 1919 (the Minorities Treaty), Poland had accepted special guarantees for racial, linguistic, or religious minorities.[125] As far as the Polish-Russian frontier was concerned, the conference accepted "the line traced and marked in agreement between the two states and on their responsibility, on 23 November 1922." The conference also delimited the Polish-Lithuanian frontier, leaving any rectifications to the two states concerned. Finally, the conference recognized, and Poland accepted, all sovereign rights over the territories between the Polish-Lithuanian and the Polish-Russian frontiers, on the one hand, and the remaining Polish frontiers on the other, while reserving the dispositions of the Treaty of Saint-Germain concerning the charges and obligations incumbent on states taking over the territory of the former Austro-Hungarian Empire.[126] The conference's decision was signed by Eric Phipps for Britain, Romano Avezzano for Italy, Raymond Poincaré for France, M. Matsuda for Japan, and Maurycy Zamoyski for Poland.

Sikorski thanked Poincaré for France's aid in obtaining this decision.[127] However, when Skrzyński and Wielowieyski talked to Laroche on 17 March, they expressed anxiety on the formulation that had been used regarding the Polish-Russian frontier. Skrzyński feared that the phrase "on their responsibility" could mean that a new Russian government, succeeding the Bolsheviks, would not be bound to recognize the frontier. Wielowieyski said he had explained to Skrzyński that the phrase meant that the Powers did not wish to be bound by a guarantee of the frontier as per article 10 of the League

Covenant. Skrzyński, however, wished to have this confirmed so that he could reply to questions in the Sejm. Laroche claimed that there was a more precise reason for the formula. The frontier, he said, had been slightly modified since the Treaty of Riga, but the Polish government had not furnished the procès-verbal of these modifications to the Powers. So, at Poland's request, members of the conference had limited themselves to the recognition of a *fait accompli,* and they could take no responsibility for it.[128] This was, of course, a piece of juridical sophistry. Internal correspondence indicates that the key factor was French resentment at Poland's signing the Treaty of Riga, despite French opposition to recognizing the Soviet government. Also, French statesmen wished to keep open the door to a future revision of the Polish-Russian frontier to the advantage of a non-Bolshevik Russia. Since neither fact could be admitted publicly, the French took refuge in a formula that also had the virtue of releasing the Powers from the obligation of coming to Poland's aid if she were attacked by Russia—an obligation that France had undertaken in the Military Convention of 1921. Finally, the letter that Skrzyński had requested was sent on 30 March. It stated that the Polish government had asked the Powers not to determine but to "recognize" Poland's eastern frontier. Therefore, the Conference of Ambassadors could not assume responsibility for it toward the League of Nations.[129] As for Memel, although the Lithuanians had accepted the conference conditions on 13 March 1923, the appropriate convention was not signed until 17 May 1924 and was not ratified until 25 August 1925.

The recognition of Poland's sovereignty over East Galicia had an immediate impact both on the West Ukrainian government-in-exile and in the land itself. Petrushevych and his ministers had expected the Powers to support complete independence for East Galicia, or at least to impose territorial autonomy. On 5 March, Petrushevych had demanded that East Galicia be established as an independent state under the protection of the Powers or of the League of Nations.[130] On 14 March he arrived in Paris with Levytsky, and they were joined by the Uniate metropolitan of Lwów, Andrei Sheptyts'kyi. They appealed the conference's decision, but Poincaré told Sheptyts'kyi that the decision was final.[131] There were combined Czechoslovak and Ukrainian demonstrations in Prague, and the Czech press condemned the decision.[132] However, Petrushevych and his policy were discredited. At the end of April he established a liquidation commission to wind up his government.[133]

In East Galicia the Ukrainian leaders protested the decision but were forced to reassess their policy. Since independence was now out of the question, the Trudovik (labor) party adopted a program of territorial autonomy for all Ukrainian lands that were inside the Polish state.[134] This was, of course, a rejection of the voivodship (provincial) autonomy voted by the Polish Sejm, but it was a retreat from the demand for independence. The Ukrainian Social Democratic Party declared that it would never accept the conference's decision but failed to secure the backing of the masses.[135] Most people decided to make the best of a bad situation. As for the exiles, some, such as Hrushevs'kyi, decided to settle in the Soviet Ukraine; some stayed abroad; and some returned to East Galicia. The Ukrainian Military Organization and its political party, the UNDO, made their headquarters in Berlin. Many exiles settled in Czechoslovakia.[136] The Petlyurist Ukrainian government in exile continued to exist in Warsaw.

As far as the Russians were concerned, both Monarchists and Communists protested the conference's decision. Former Premier A. F. Trepov protested to Poincaré in the second half of March.[137] On 17 March, *Izvestia* printed an article by Iurii Steklov, in which he protested that the decision was directed against Russia. The Soviet envoy to Warsaw, Leonid L. Obolensky, told the Jewish newspaper *Hajnt* that Russia could not remain indifferent to the disturbance of "the political balance" on her western frontiers.[138] On 12 April, at the second session of the Central Committee of the Ukrainian Communist Party, Christian Rakovsky rejected the conference's decision as being "an act of violence." He declared that the Soviet Ukraine would never recognize the union of East Galicia with Poland.[139]

Like many peace settlements, the one concerning East Galicia satisfied one party and embittered the other. While the Poles were relieved, the Ukrainians resented not having either their own government or, at least, home rule. However, it is difficult to see any realistic alternative to the solution that was finally reached. The vast majority of Polish opinion opposed independence or autonomy for East Galicia for fear that this would lead to its union with Soviet Ukraine and thus threaten Polish security. Finally, the Polish minority in East Galicia, which amounted to some 35 percent, was violently opposed to East Galician autonomy, since it would have meant a Ukrainian instead of a Polish administration.

For Britain—or, rather, for Lloyd George—insistence on East Galician autonomy had been a carrot for Soviet Russia and a stick for the Poles. It is clear, of course, that the Ukrainians would not have welcomed Polish sovereignty had it been granted by the Allies in 1919, but it is also clear that the unresolved status of the region kept up the hopes of the Petrushevych government and its supporters and therefore the turmoil that almost erupted into civil war in September 1922. It seems fair to assume that an earlier recognition of Polish sovereignty—which the Powers could not, in fact, ultimately deny—would have spared much suffering on both sides.

9

Toward Locarno: Poland the Western Powers, and Germany January 1924 to September 1925

The road to Locarno began with France's failure to squeeze reparations from Germany by occupying the Ruhr. The subsequent galloping German inflation threatened to kill the goose that could lay the golden egg; so, both Western and German statesmen agreed that a different solution must be found. Gustav Stresemann, who became chancellor of Germany in August 1923 and was foreign minister until his death in October 1929, chose a policy of "fulfillment," or coming to terms with France and Britain, both in order to restore the German economy and to gain Western support for his objective of revising the Polish-German frontier. American bankers insisted on a strictly financial approach to reparations, and President Poincaré agreed to a meeting of experts in Paris. The Dawes Committee reported in April that German finances must be reorganized with the help of foreign loans.[1] On 24 August the Dawes Plan was ratified in the London Agreement. Arnold Toynbee emphasized the breakthrough in relations between Germany and her former enemies when he wrote: "It would be hardly an exaggeration to say that these were the first conversations between representatives of Germany and the Allies which had taken place in a normal atmosphere since the outbreak of the War of 1914."[2]

In the meanwhile, the French elections of 11 May 1924 led to the victory of Édouard Herriot's Cartel des Gauches over Poincaré's Cartel Bleu. The French Socialists who now came to power had advocated the scaling down of reparations and were critical of the Versailles Treaty. Thus, there was a meeting of the minds with the British Labour Party. Furthermore, both Ramsay MacDonald and Édouard Herriot declared that they would strengthen the League of Nations, base their policy on the League Convenant, and work for Germany's entry into the league.[3]

The London Conference, which resulted in the adoption of the Dawes Plan in August 1924, was Stresemann's first victory in foreign affairs. As he later told a German audience, Germany was like a man up to his neck in debt; all his creditors were interested in his health so that he could at least pay them the interest.[4] The Dawes Plan drew up a schedule for reparations payments on a reduced scale until the first normal year, which, ironically, was to be 1929/30. At the rate of payments established, it would have taken Germany forty years to pay 100 billion gold marks, while the initial figure set by the Allies in March 1921 was 132 billion gold marks. Having obtained this schedule, Stresemann planned to reduce reparations further in the future.

The new policy toward Germany reflected established British views and, therefore, British preponderance in the Entente. This did not augur well for Poland. All hues of political opinion in Britain supported the revision of the Polish-German frontier, and the Labour Party had specifically included that issue in its election platform of 1922. Philip Snowden, the chancellor of the Exchequer, publicly advocated revision of the treaty early in February 1924, specifically with regard to reparations.[5] The secretary for home affairs, Arthur Henderson, urged the revision of the Versailles Treaty in a speech on 23 February at the Burnley election. However, MacDonald had no intention of damaging the new rapprochement with France and therefore decided to play down the issue. He gave the same explanation to the Polish minister, Konstanty Skirmunt, as he gave to the House of Commons. MacDonald said he had known nothing of Henderson's plans for the speech, which had been made on the latter's initiative. Furthermore, while revision of the treaty was in the Labour Party's program, it was not in the government's.[6] The party paper, the *Daily Herald*, immediately commented that there was no need of cabinet authorization for a policy that was approved throughout the land.[7] The Liberal *Manchester Guardian*, however, took a different line. It warned that to upset the whole fabric of the treaty would throw Europe into turmoil and would accomplish nothing,[8] but this did not imply support for the treaty. In early March the *Guardian* stated that Britain could give no unilateral guarantee to France, nor could she guarantee the status quo of Poland or Czechoslovakia.[9] Despite MacDonald's public stance, the Labour Party's attitude toward Poland was not encouraging. In January, W. N. Ewer, the editor of the *Daily Herald*, told Jan Ciechanowski, counsellor at the Polish legation, that while the trade-union group favored the preservation of the Entente, the intellectuals were pro-German. Also, most Labourites disliked Poland, whose "imperialist" image of 1920 was still very much alive.[10]

France also worried her ally Poland. Herriot made no secret of his desire to normalize relations with Russia, a fact that raised fears of a Franco-Russian alliance in Polish minds. What was more important, there were growing indications that France aimed at concluding an alliance with Britain to safeguard her frontier with Germany, while leaving Poland and Czechoslovakia to shift for themselves. In February 1924, immediately after the conclusion of the Franco-Czechoslovak alliance, Marshal Foch had sent a memorandum to Polish and Czechoslovak authorities suggesting a military convention between the two countries.[11] This proposal met with far-reaching reservations in Warsaw and Prague. Still, the policy of the French General Staff was much more favorable to Poland than the policy of the Cartel des Gauches. The Quai d'Orsay, for its part, viewed the Little Entente, reinforced by Poland and under French leadership, as an organ of the first importance for safeguarding peace. This was, in fact, the strategic-political testament of the Bloc National (or Cartel Bleu);[12] but the Cartel des Gauches soon moved in another direction. In September, Panafieu informed the Polish Foreign Ministry that France would conclude a guarantee pact with Britain and Belgium. Poland was therefore advised to conclude an alliance with Czechoslovakia; later, both groups would reach an understanding. Maciej Rataj, the Speaker of the Sejm, thought that this would be fatal, since it would mean the abrogation of the Franco-Polish alliance.[13] When Foreign Minister Skrzyński asked Prime Minister Herriot about Panafieu's *démarche*, Herriot claimed that a long-lost paper had been sent to Warsaw simply by way of information.[14] He did not convince anybody with this story.

Polish suspicions were fed by French behavior in the months that followed. On 2 October the League of Nations accepted the text of the Geneva Protocol. Unlike the draft Treaty of Mutual Assistance of September 1923, the protocol seemed to have a good chance of being accepted.[15] It included provisions for security, general disarmament, and Germany's entry into the league. France—its main proponent—and nine other countries, including Poland and Czechoslovakia, signed it immediately. The Polish government now faced the task of adapting the Franco-Polish alliance to the protocol and of preventing the devaluation of the alliance by a Franco-British-Belgian security pact. There were also fears of a Franco-Soviet alliance. In fact, the French minister in Moscow, Jean Herbette, had proposed a close Franco-Soviet understanding in August.[16] Under these circumstances, General Sikorski's visit to France in October–November 1924—which was undertaken at the invitation of the French war minister, Gen. Charles Nollet—took on a political as well as a military significance.

Sikorski's visit—which seems to have taken place against the wishes of Foreign Minister Skrzyński[17]—made French hesitations clear to the naked eye. Sikorski had two main objectives: to reach an agreement on the consequences of the Geneva Protocol for both states, and to give the Franco-Polish Military Convention of 1921 the form of a document that would be binding not only on the French military but also on the government. The French, however, side-stepped the first issue, proposing that it be left for further discussion. With regard to the second, they agreed only that the convention of 1921 should remain in force. Finally, they even hesitated to give formal recognition of Poland's frontiers in the protocol. After much difficulty, General Sikorski obtained the following statement:

> The Polish war minister presents considerations relating to Polish frontiers. The French war minister and the minister of the marine take note of these and refer, in this respect, to the engagements resulting from different decisions of the Conference of Ambassadors and the treaties signed by France concerning Polish frontiers.[18]

Sikorski told Rataj that Herriot had at first refused to sign the protocol but had agreed to do so at the last moment; so the passage on Polish frontiers was inserted in a different hand.[19] It was probably no coincidence that France officially recognized the Soviet Union on 24 October 1924, but the problem went deeper. On 30 October, Jules Laroche, political director at the Quai d'Orsay, rejected the proposal of Marshal Foch and General Debeney that France should in fact maintain the Franco-Polish Military Convention of 1921 while registering an anodyne text with the League of Nations. Laroche objected to the words in the Foch-Debeney text—that both sides "engage to act in common in case of aggression"—as being too extreme, although no such objections had been raised in 1921. The French General Staff was right in seeing this as a sign that the Quai d'Orsay—and of course Herriot—wished to loosen the alliance.[20] Nevertheless, the General Staff did succeed in pressuring the government into making a speedy advance, in August 1924, of the 400 million francs, promised in 1921, to rearm Polish military forces. Also, French supplies were promised in case of war, and France promised to support the expansion of the Polish navy.[21]

Meanwhile, a trend toward rapprochement appeared in Polish-Czechoslovak relations. This became evident at the time of the signing of the Geneva Protocol, of which Beneš was one of the principal authors. Beneš then agreed with Skrzyński to work for better relations and to surmount existing difficulties. Pro-Polish demonstrations took place in Czechoslovakia when the remains of the great Polish writer Henryk Sienkiewicz were transported through that country to Poland in the autumn of 1924. At about this time, Beneš told the Polish Socialist leader Mieczysław Niedziałkowski that "on his word of honor" he wanted an agreement with Poland and that he considered this possible. Beneš gave assurances that he no longer wanted a Czechoslovak-Russian frontier; he also said that in case of a Polish-Soviet war, Czechoslovakia would be neutral; but if Germany moved against Poland, this would be a *casus belli*. He thought the Bolsheviks would collapse. He promised to support Poland against German revisionist demands for the Corridor and Upper Silesia, even declaring that if Germany were to recover them,

Czechoslovakia's turn would be next. Rataj was skeptical.[22] His doubts were to be confirmed a few months later.

Another disappointment awaited Poland with regard to Polish-Soviet relations. Skrzyński wished to see an improvement so as to strengthen Poland vis-à-vis both France and Germany. On 22 August, immediately on taking up his post as foreign minister, he sent a note to Georgii Chicherin, the Soviet commissar for foreign affairs, proposing a conference to normalize relations and solve outstanding problems. Chicherin replied, on 18 September, that the Soviet government desired friendly relations with Poland. On 18 October, in a speech to the Central Executive Committee of the Supreme Soviet, he declared that an improvement in Polish-Soviet relations was desirable and that it depended only on Poland.[23] Ten days later, Skrzyński told the Sejm that Poland would not cross her eastern frontier, undertake any crusades against Russia, or be the tool of any power against Russia. Poland, he said, wanted peace based on the Treaty of Riga and considered "moral disarmament" possible.[24] A new Soviet envoy, Pyotr Voykov, arrived in Warsaw in October and presented his credentials on 8 November. He was to work for the improvement of Polish-Soviet relations and to prepare for Chicherin's visit to Warsaw.

It seemed at this time that a Polish-Soviet rapprochement was possible. Both Poland and Russia feared an exclusively Western settlement with Germany, which would threaten their security. The "Zinoviev Letter" affair of late October in England—which will be discussed later—and the subsequent electoral defeat of the Labour government, increased Soviet fears. Skrzyński was not deterred by the Zinoviev affair or by the abortive Soviet coup in Estonia, which took place on 1 December. A departmental director in the Polish Ministry of Industry and Trade, Dr. Henryk Tennenbaum, stopped in Berlin on his way back from Paris and talked with Stefan Rayevsky, who was on the staff of the Soviet legation. According to Rayevsky, Tennenbaum said that the tendency to form an anti-Soviet bloc was clearly visible in Western Europe. Poland had the choice either of joining it or of concluding an agreement with Russia. He said that Premier Władysław Grabski and Foreign Minister Skrzyński favored the latter, since it would lead to the development of normal economic relations between Poland and the Soviet Union.[25]

Tennenbaum's statements were meant to worry the Soviet government and make it seek an understanding with Poland. His proposals included mutual recognition of the territorial status quo, nonintervention in each other's internal affairs, and nonparticipation in blocs aimed at either state.[26] Poland was not, however, prepared to conclude a bilateral pact with Russia. After his return from the Baltic Conference in Helsinki, Skrzyński told Voykov that he envisaged a multilateral nonaggression pact between Soviet

Russia, on the one hand, and Poland, the Baltic States, and Rumania on the other.[27] This was not a new aim, because Poland had been trying to organize such a Baltic bloc under her leadership since 1921 and because she was allied to Rumania. The Soviet government, however, insisted on a bilateral pact; so this rapprochement proved abortive.[28]

Alleged Soviet fears of a capitalist bloc led by Poland against the USSR were not the reason for Moscow's rejection of Skrzyński's proposal. It is most likely that the Soviet proposal for a bilateral pact with Poland was designed to put pressure on Germany. In the first place the Soviet leadership feared that Germany's entry into the league might force her to participate in some anti-Soviet action under article 16 of the League Covenant. (This article stipulated, among other things, that members of the league were to afford passage to armed forces of other members coming to the aid of a victim of aggression.)[29] A Soviet attack on Poland might confront Germany with such demands. Secondly, Soviet leaders professed to fear that a Western security pact would create a Western bloc directed against the Soviet Union. The German ambassador in Moscow, Count Ulrich von Brockdorff-Rantzau—who was in any case a staunch supporter of the "eastern orientation" in German policy—tried to reassure the Russians by playing the "Polish card." He did so with the permission of the head of the German Foreign Ministry, Baron Ago von Maltzan, known as the "Red Baron." The ambassador played this card in a conversation with Chicherin on 20 December 1924. He then said that the solution of the Polish Question would probably lie in "forcing Poland back to her ethnographic frontiers"—a euphemism for a new partition of Poland. Although Maltzan was soon thereafter appointed ambassador to Washington, the instruction was confirmed to Brockdorff-Rantzau by Maltzan's successor, Dr. Carl Theodor von Schubert. On receiving an account of the conversation, Schubert telegraphed the ambassador that his suggestion on Poland was consistent with the Foreign Ministry's line.[30] Chicherin, however, did not swallow the bait. What he wanted was a general discussion of policy; he hoped that this would lead not only to a trade treaty but also to a declaration of German neutrality in the event of conflict between the Western Powers and the Soviet Union. He was not averse to blackmail. As he told Brockdorff-Rantzau a few days later: "We shall do nothing with Herbette, if you don't do anything with Chamberlain."[31]

In the meanwhile, the British elections of October 1924 had led to the defeat of MacDonald's Labour government. A Conservative government was formed under Stanley Baldwin as prime minister, with Austen Chamberlain as foreign secretary. Here we should consider the curious Zinoviev Letter affair and the role of Polish Military Intelligence in it. The letter, allegedly signed by Grigory Zinoviev, then head of the Comintern; Arthur McManus, member of the presidium and head of the British Communist Party; and Otto

Kuusinen, head of the Finnish Communist Party and secretary of the presidium, appeared in the London press on 24 October 1924. It caused a furor. The letter urged the British Communists to work for the ratification of the Anglo-Soviet commercial treaties signed in August; it also instructed them to infiltrate the armed forces in preparation for a revolution. The letter, as published, was accompanied by a protest from John D. Gregory, head of the Foreign Office's Northern Department, to Christian Rakovsky, the Soviet chargé d'affaires in London, who was the chief negotiator of the commercial treaties.[32] The Zinoviev Letter, though it was immediately labeled a forgery by the Soviet government, gave an enormous boost to the Conservatives during the last stages of the election campaign, even though it did not determine the outcome, as was presumed at the time. In fact, Conservatives, Liberals, and powerful business interests already opposed the ratification of the treaties; and without Liberal support, the Labourites could not remain in power.

Polish involvement in this affair is curious. General Sikorski boasted to Rataj on 9 November that *he* was the author of the letter. He said that the instructions contained in it had been issued by the Third International (the Comintern). The Polish General Staff had acquired them, had "adapted them to British conditions," and then had added Zinoviev's signature. Sikorski claimed, moreover, that Gregory—whom he described as a candidate for the post of British minister in Warsaw—had "helped" with the "mystification."[33] Sikorski's claim to authorship is not borne out by available evidence, but Polish Military Intelligence was, indeed, involved. A certain Captain Paciorkowski, press attaché at the Polish legation in Berlin, had commissioned some Russian émigrés to forge the letter. The goal apparently was to prevent the ratification of the Anglo-Soviet commercial agreements. Gregory does not seem to have been involved, for he informed Sir Eyre Crowe that the letter looked like a forgery. Crowe felt obliged to allow it to be published when he learned that it was in the hands of Thomas Marlowe, the editor of the *Daily Mail*.[34]

As the year 1924 drew to a close, Polish worries about the conclusion of a purely Western security pact with Germany increased. Furthermore, Stresemann did not conceal his view that a revision of the Polish-German frontier was inevitable. In September he told the British ambassador in Berlin, Lord D'Abernon, that there could be no permanent peace without the Rhineland and Danzig again becoming part of Germany.[35] In a speech at Koenigsberg on 27 November, Stresemann said that East Prussia had been violently separated from Germany and that the day would come when it would be reunited with the Reich.[36] Such statements were not new, but they presented a more immediate danger in Polish eyes, when set in the context of a purely Western security pact. Therefore, the Polish minister in London,

Konstanty Skirmunt, warned Foreign Secretary Austen Chamberlain on 2 December 1924, that a pact that would guarantee only the western frontiers of Germany would encourage her to prepare for war in Eastern Europe. In the end, he warned, both France and Britain would be dragged into such a war.[37] Sikorski gave vent to the same fears at the end of the year. In a letter to Skrzyński he considered the possible forms that a Western pact might take and the consequences for Poland. He thought it likely that the British government would add such modifications to the Geneva Protocol as to make it worthless. In such a case, he foresaw the conclusion of an Anglo-French-Belgian security pact. This, he wrote, was being seriously considered in London; it also had the support of French public opinion. Another possibility was a pact guaranteeing Germany's frontiers with France and Belgium; France would simultaneously maintain her military agreements with Poland and Czechoslovakia. Sikorski thought that the first alternative would be murderous for Poland, while the second would be extremely dangerous. It would, he thought, lead Germany to concentrate her main attack, in case of war, on Poland; while in peacetime it would encourage hostile German activities against her.[38] With these dangers in mind, Polish diplomacy set its sights on a pact that would guarantee security equally in Western and in Eastern Europe. However, the prospects for success were dim from the outset.

The negative British reactions to the Geneva Protocol confirmed Polish fears. The prestigious Liberal *Manchester Guardian* expressed general British opinion that the protocol would encourage the existing system of military alliances and thus guarantee French "military hegemony" in Europe.[39] Furthermore, the paper claimed that the protocol would "petrify" the frontiers of 1919.[40] It claimed that real security would mean the elimination of those "injustices" which threatened peace and were the "cause" of armament production and large armies.[41] An uncritical rejection of the protocol would be disastrous, but a blind acceptance of it would be even worse.[42] However, the *Guardian* opposed a Franco-British-Belgian military treaty, since France needed no protection. Indeed, the phrase "French Security" was interpreted to mean the defense of France's "military system" in both Western and Eastern Europe. What was needed, said the *Guardian,* was a security system for all of Europe,[43] which meant a system that would include Germany. The *Guardian*'s distrust of France and her allies, and its critical attitude toward the Versailles Treaty, represented majority opinion in Britain as expressed in the press. E. L. Woodward summed it up as follows:

> Thus by 1925, the legend of the infamous treaty of Versailles had not only taken shape, but was accepted without question by large sections of conservative as well as progressive opinion in Great Britain. This legend was believed more easily because, in the average British view, the greatest

obstacles to European peace and recovery came not from Germany, but from France, and from the so-called client states of France in central and eastern Europe.[44]

It is against this background that we should consider the views of Austen Chamberlain. The new foreign secretary differed from the majority of the cabinet and from the bulk of the British press in believing that France must have security in order to improve her relations with Germany and that this security should take the form of an Anglo-French or an Anglo-French-Belgian alliance. His sympathy for France stemmed from a happy sojourn there as a young man, while his skepticism toward Germany was equally the result of a stay in that country.[45] In any event, by early January 1925 he believed that without the security of an alliance with Britain, France could drag the British into another Armageddon. He also believed that French security was a vital British interest, but he realized that an alliance with France would be much more difficult to conclude than in 1919, for public opinion in both Britain and the dominions opposed it. However, he thought that one would be possible if it excluded guarantees for Eastern Europe. This exclusion was in harmony with his own views, for "It is one thing to defend the channel or the eastern frontiers of the Low Countries and France. It is quite another thing to guarantee the very unstable situation in Eastern Europe which the Peace Treaties have 'balkanized' with a vengeance." With these considerations in mind, he asked the Central Department of the Foreign Office to prepare a statement on "Europe Today." He also asked James W. Headlam-Morley, the historical adviser to the Foreign Office, to write a paper on the historical position of Great Britain and how it applied to the present situation.[46] In the meanwhile, the Committee of Imperial Defense (CID) set up a subcommittee to study the Geneva Protocol. Rejection of the protocol by the CID was a foregone conclusion; the question was what to substitute for it.

Chamberlain found a strange ally for his project of a French alliance in Sir Maurice P. A. Hankey, the long-time secretary of the CID and secretary of the cabinet. Hankey's conversion was due mainly to fear either of a French attack on Britain or of a German attack on and domination of France and Belgium and hence a threat to Britain. He also thought that if Britain rejected the Geneva Protocol and did not offer France any compensation in security, the latter might react violently. Still he accepted an alliance only as a last resort; he preferred a collective-security system. He therefore thought that Sir Eyre Crowe's suggestion, as accepted by the subcommittee of the CID, indicated a way out of the dilemma.[47] Sir Eyre Crowe's proposal, which was incorporated into the subcommittee's report of 27 January 1925 on the Geneva Protocol, was for Britain, France, and Belgium to declare that they recognized the independence and integrity of their territories bordering on the

North Sea and the English Channel as being a "vital interest" to their respective countries. They would resist any unprovoked aggression in this area and, if such were to take place, would notify the League of Nations of their action under the provisions of article 16 of the League Covenant. At the same time, the CID report implied that no British aid would be forthcoming if Germany were to attack Poland or Czechoslovakia. Finally, Germany was to be a party to a comprehensive Western security system.[48] The CID paper confirmed Chamberlain's opinion that Britain could not ratify the Geneva Protocol as it stood. As far as Eastern Europe was concerned, he thought that French security in the west would in itself lessen the danger for that region. Here he cited Edouard Beneš, who had told him at the League Council session in Rome in December 1924 that "if Germany does not go to war with France, Czechoslovakia will be safe." Chamberlain thought much the same would apply to Poland.[49]

Although Chamberlain did not realize it at first, the German proposals for a Western security pact—which were transmitted by Lord D'Abernon to London on 20 January 1925—indicated a way out of the British dilemma. Before discussing them, however, we should consider the two memoranda that Chamberlain had requested from the Foreign Office in early January, for they reflect strikingly different views. The first, dated 23 January 1925 and circulated in a revised version dated 20 February, was written by Harold Nicolson of the Central Department. It was entitled "British Policy Considered in Relation to the European Situation."[50] It merits serious attention because, as Chamberlain wrote in the preface, it represented not only his own views but those of the Foreign Office as a whole. It is particularly important for us because of the light that it sheds on the views of the foreign secretary and of the Foreign Office regarding the Polish-German frontier.

Nicolson hoped that "the more intelligent Germans" would not desire a war of revenge with France, but

> it may be confidently asserted that so soon as Germany recovers, there will be a steady movement towards the righting of what are, for a German, the two most objectionable provisions of the Peace Settlement, namely, the Polish Corridor and the partition of Upper Silesia. . . . There is obviously a danger that a nation of over 60 millions will not permanently acquiesce in being sundered from the province which was the cradle of the Prussian State, or in being deprived of those mineral resources on which the national prosperity was largely based.

In considering the relation of British interests to European security, Nicolson thought that a British guarantee to France and Belgium would be an important contribution. Statesmen would know, as they did not in 1914, just where Britain stood. Germany would then not be likely to risk war with the

British Empire by attacking France, while France, for her part, would feel more secure. France's hitherto ''provocative'' policy would diminish and ''she will contemplate with less alarm the impending evacuation of the Rhineland; she will be less inclined to constitute the Little Entente as an armed camp to the east of Germany; she will be able to settle down to financial stabilization and to a policy of debt repayment.'' Nothing should stand in the way of including Germany in such a security system.

What then should be done about the ''injustices'' that Germany so bitterly resented? Like Chamberlain, Nicolson took a long view:

> Although in the present mood of Europe, it would be useless to mention the revision of the peace treaties, yet if the concert of Europe can thus be gradually recreated, saner councils will prevail. It is conceivable, especially if Germany, with French goodwill, becomes a member of the League of Nations, and obtains a permanent seat in the Council, that it may be possible eventually to revise by European agreement the dangerous conditions involved in the Silesian settlement and the Polish Corridor.

However, he concluded that ''until we can quieten France, no concert of Europe is possible, and we can only quieten France if we are in the position to speak to her with the authority of an Ally.''[51]

Chamberlain approved the memorandum. It represented his views and, as he claimed, those of the Foreign Office. They diverged significantly from the bulk of British opinion both in advocating an alliance with France and Belgium and in relegating the revision of the Polish-German frontier to some future date. Such a revision was, nonetheless, considered as the natural if delayed consequence of a Western security agreement that would include Germany. Only one voice was raised in the Foreign Office against this conclusion. Although it fell on deaf ears at the time, it is worth mentioning, since the author's views not only elicited some interesting comments from Austen Chamberlain but also proved remarkably prophetic.

As mentioned above, James Headlam-Morley had also been asked to write a memorandum. He had been closely involved in drawing up the Danzig articles of the Versailles Treaty, as well as those pertaining to the plebiscite in Upper Silesia. In his memorandum entitled ''The History of British Foreign Policy and the Geneva Protocol,''[52] he agreed with his colleagues on only one matter: ''As everyone knows, the danger point in Europe is not the Rhine, but the Vistula, not Alsace-Lorraine, but the Polish Corridor and Upper Silesia.'' His conclusions, however, were very different. Although he found no guide in history to justify British interests and responsibility in Eastern Europe—for Britain had neither opposed the partitions of Poland nor taken up arms on the latter's behalf during the nineteenth century—he observed that there had been good reasons for this passivity. Poland was then very remote from British shores, and nothing could be done for her anyway as long as the three Eastern Powers stood united. Now, however, the situation had changed. The three eastern monarchies had collapsed, and Britain could no longer remain indifferent to Poland's fate. This was primarily due to Britain's interest in preventing a Russo-German alliance, which would allow these two powers to dominate the Continent. Such an alliance would undoubtedly be cemented by an attack on and a partition of Poland. As far as Germany herself was concerned, he noted: "We cannot be indifferent if Germany breaks through upon the .east and there begins to acquire a new accession of territory and strength which would inevitably in the future be brought to bear upon the Rhine." France was right, he wrote, in assuming that the future of Europe was bound up with the new states, and he saw no reason for castigating her as a militarist power. He thought that Poland, in particular, was important. If Warsaw had fallen to the Bolsheviks, Europe would have been in turmoil, and no one could say where it would have ended. If Poland had depended on British aid, she would have been destroyed; it was French support that had saved Poland and Europe(!).

He then tackled the question of whether any British government could ask the dominions to go to war in order to protect the Polish Corridor and Upper Silesia. While admitting that East European frontiers left room for improvement, he stressed that the problem should be seen in a broader perspective, and asked:

> Has anyone attempted to realize what would happen if there were to be a new partition of Poland, or if the Czechoslovak State were to be so curtailed and dismembered that in fact it disappeared from the map of Europe? The whole of Europe would at once be in chaos. There would no longer be any principle, meaning or sense in the territorial arrangements of the continent. Imagine, for instance, that under some improbable condition Austria rejoined Germany, that Germany, using the discontented minority in Bohemia, demanded a new frontier far over the mountains, including Carlsbad and Pilsen, and at the same time, in alliance with Germany, the Hungarians recovered the southern slopes of the Carpathians. This would be catastrophic, and even if we neglected to intervene to prevent it happening, we should be driven to interfere, probably too late.

After stressing that, in general, the 1919 settlement was based on reason and justice and that the new East European states were now able to take their place with other secondary European states, he asked what they really wanted. He thought they needed to have confidence in British support at a time of crisis. It was no use telling them to seek support in the League of Nations; ultimately the latter's strength would depend on the Great Powers. Headlam-Morley agreed that British support for the East European states could not be the same as that afforded to France and Belgium, but he contended that passivity was neither wise nor practicable. He therefore suggested that the secretary of state make a statement, either in Parliament or to the dominions, that in certain cases the league could depend on British support. The statement should say that "we are interested in the maintenance of the new system in Europe, that we could not regard with equanimity the forcible overthrow of any of the new States, and that if a grave crisis arose, we should really carry out the obligations into which we have entered." Contending that "we cannot dissociate ourselves from responsibility in regard to what happened in Eastern and Central Europe," he saw the Council of the League as the forum in which Britain could exert her influence for conciliation. He believed that some European protocol was needed in order to create a security system that would be consistent with the League Covenant. Finally, he believed that Britain should help the new states commercially.[53]

We may well wonder how Headlam-Morley came to espouse conclusions so different from those of Austen Chamberlain and the majority of his colleagues in the Foreign Office. Presumably, they stemmed from his own extensive knowledge of Europe. We also know that he was susceptible to the opinions of his friend Lewis B. Namier, who had become a firm supporter of Poland's case against Germany—though not against Russia.[54] But Headlam-Morley's views were unacceptable to Austen Chamberlain. The foreign secretary noted that he had expected Headlam-Morley to deal with the security of the channel ports and of the Low Countries. While Chamberlain found much of interest in the memorandum, he differed from its author regarding British interests in Eastern Europe:

> But I must admit frankly that I am not at one with W. Headlam-Morley. I draw a far sharper distinction than he between the nature of our interests in the West and East of Europe, and between the character of the influence or intervention which we should seek to exercise in these two spheres. I would say broadly that in Western Europe we are a partner; that, comparatively speaking, in Eastern Europe our role should be rather that of a disinterested *amicus curiae*. Our safety in certain circumstances is bound up with that of France, or Belgium, or Holland. If this be secured, I do not believe that it is bound up with that of Rumania, for example; and if I rightly comprehend him, I would not contemplate linking our fortunes so closely with the Eastern States as he would do. Nor again until Russia is herself again under whatever form of Government, do I believe that a serious war will break out east of Germany if peace is firmly secured on Germany's western boundaries. But Russia is an imponderable factor, curiously enough as frightened of other people as other people are of her, or so, at least, it seems to me.[55]

Thus, Chamberlain based his hopes for European peace on an alliance between Britain, France, and Belgium, to be complemented by a broader security arrangement of which Germany, too, would be a member. By 21

February, when he penned his comments on Headlam-Morley's memorandum, the German proposals were, of course, known to him. They had been delivered in London, under seal of secrecy, on 20 January. Chamberlain had at first been suspicious. He thought that Stresemann's aim was to obtain the evacuation of the Rhineland and, at the same time, to drive a wedge between France and Britain so as to prevent their alliance. The secrecy also annoyed him. Two weeks later he wrote that the German proposal was "an endeavor to entrap me into conversations unknown to our Allies."[56] However, the Germans forwarded their proposal to Paris on 9 February,[57] and in early March, Chamberlain told the cabinet that "these overtures seem to offer the best chance of giving security to France and peace to the world. To turn it down would be to thrust Germany into the hands of Russia."[58]

While the timing of the German proposal of January 1925 had resulted from Allied refusal to evacuate the Cologne zone at that date—on the grounds that Germany had not fulfilled her treaty obligations on disarmament—and from Stresemann's fear of an Anglo-French alliance, the idea of a Western security pact was not new. Proposals to this effect had been put forward by Chancellor Wilhelm Cuno in December 1922, and again by Stresemann in September 1923.[59] The British ambassador in Berlin, Lord D'Abernon, urged Stresemann to make such an offer at the end of 1924. Only in this sense can D'Abernon be seen as the father of the German proposals of January/February 1925, which would eventually lead to the Locarno Treaties.[60] Still, Chamberlain was not far off the mark in his initial suspicions. In April 1925, Stresemann wrote to the German ambassador in Washington, Baron Ago von Maltzan, that such an agreement would secure the Rhineland against a renewed French assault, split the Allies, and open new possibilities in the east.[61]

The German offer first came under public discussion on 5 March 1925, during the House of Commons debate on the Geneva Protocol. While Chamberlain's remarks on Poland were friendly, the debate clearly demonstrated that in most minds any British guarantees of France were bound to include the security of her East European allies. This was unacceptable to many people who believed that revision of the Versailles Treaty was a necessary precondition for European security. Thus, Herbert Fisher spoke for the Liberals in opposing any Anglo-French-Belgian alliance. He noted that Lloyd George had refused to guarantee the frontiers of France's East European allies in 1922. He thought that the new German proposals sounded promising and that Germany should be free to seek territorial revision under article 19 of the League Covenant. He also mentioned Danzig and claimed that Poland was "constantly undermining its independence." Chamberlain answered that while he shared Fisher's desire for good German-Polish relations, Poland was "now coming of age," though he noted that she was still being menaced on her frontiers. In contrast to the early days of her independence, she could now, he thought, be expected to show "surety of judgement."

Despite Chamberlain's attitude, the opinion of the House of Commons was clearly that territorial revision must come first and security second. This was the line taken by Lt. Col. Sir Edward Grigg (Lloyd George's private secretary), Maj. Gen. Sir R. Hutchinson, Captain Garro-Jones, and Captain Ashmead-Bartlett. They all thought that the best way to avert war in Eastern Europe was to revise the territorial settlement. Ashmead-Bartlett also regretted the demise of the Habsburg Empire, which, he said, should have been preserved because it was "like a miniature League of Nations"(!).[62] Thus, Chamberlain had his work cut out for him. He had to fight a general consensus that opposed not only an alliance with France but even guarantees for the Franco-German frontier and demanded the revision of the Versailles Treaty.

It was not surprising that the cabinet rejected an alliance with France, though it did, rather gingerly, welcome the German proposals. Even so, it was highly ambivalent with regard to British participation in a multilateral guarantee pact to secure the frontiers of France and Belgium with Germany. On 2 March the cabinet approved instructions for Chamberlain's forthcoming conversation with Herriot. He was to say that while Britain could not contemplate a dual alliance with France, a quadruple pact between France, Germany, Britain, and Belgium, with Italian assent if possible, would be a different matter. Such a pact could assure European peace and therefore lead to disarmament. If the French agreed, the British government would begin discussions with the dominions. However, on the afternoon of 4 March, objections were raised to the rough draft of such a pact as presented by Chamberlain, especially against the provision that the parties should guarantee each other's frontiers. This, it was said, could mean a British guarantee, by force of arms, of the present frontiers of France and Belgium against German aggression. Such a commitment, it was claimed, was much more than public opinion in Britain or the dominions would accept, at least at this stage in the negotiations.[63]

Chamberlain went to Paris on 6 March and broke the news to Herriot, who was visibly shaken on being told that he could not count on a British guarantee pact with France that would be parallel to the multilateral security pact envisaged in the German proposals. Herriot said that France could not purchase her own security at the expense of her Polish ally. Chamberlain argued that an agreement in the west would lead to general appeasement and security everywhere.[64] However, privately he felt that it was imperative to promise France more security than the cabinet had authorized him to offer. He cabled Baldwin to this effect, and Sir Eyre Crowe suggested to the prime minister that Chamberlain be authorized to say that Britain might participate in a series of separate but connected pacts. Baldwin called the cabinet together, and a stormy discussion ensued. Churchill said that France should "stew in her own juice."[65] Leopold Amery, secretary for colonial affairs, thought that the dominions would not back any security pact, and he withdrew his support for it. Crowe sent a report of this discussion to Geneva, where Chamberlain had already informed the League Council of the reasons for Britain's rejection of the Geneva Protocol.[66] He suspected Baldwin of deserting him, and he thought about resigning. However, Crowe induced Baldwin to come out in full support of the foreign secretary. By 15 March the crisis was over.[67]

The attitude of the British cabinet and public opinion toward France and her allies augured ill both for Polish plans and for Poland's sympathizers in France, who at first clearly manifested their support for Warsaw and an all-European security arrangement. Poincaré thought that the German proposals were "detestable" and that they prophesied future German aggression.[68] Marshal Foch thought the German offer was "but the thin end of the wedge," designed to dismantle the Versailles Treaty piecemeal. He believed that the Germans would go first for the Polish Corridor, then for Austria and Czechoslovakia. After that, he said, Germany would have a population of 100 million, and it would be too late to stop her.[69] The powerful daily *Le Matin* declared on 8 and 9 March that if Poland and Czechoslovakia failed to receive guarantees of security, Germany would proceed to make violent changes on her eastern frontiers. The editor, Lausanne, wrote that if France were to agree to the loss of one piece of Polish territory in return for a scrap of paper, he would blush for shame. Former President Millerand also came out in favor of security for Poland's frontiers.[70]

The Poles were, of course, very worried. It was true, as Premier W. Grabski told the Sejm on 6 March, that France would—as her initial reply to Germany had stated on 20 February—first submit the proposals to her allies and then work with them to establish a security system within the framework of the Versailles Treaty.[71] At the same time, however, the Polish minister in Berlin, Kazimierz Olszowski, reported that the French ambassador, Pierre de Margerie, had said he was not convinced that the Polish Corridor had to stay in Polish hands.[72] It is not surprising that Foreign Minister Skrzyński and General Sikorski both appeared in Paris; the first in early March, the second in April. Indeed, Skrzyński said that France was "abandoning" Poland,[73] and he complained to a Havas journalist in Geneva that Poland had apparently been chosen as the nation to satisfy German demands. Why, he asked, was there no thought of giving Germany some colonies?[74] Nonetheless, despite his misgivings, Skrzyński saw no alternative to supporting Anglo-French cooperation, and he strove for a Polish rapprochement with Britain.[75]

He favored a security pact, but he hoped it would provide equal security for both Eastern and Western Europe.

In pursuit of this policy, he had a conversation with Austen Chamberlain in Geneva, but it was not encouraging. The foreign secretary did not tell Skrzyński in so many words what he had written in February to Lord Crewe, the British ambassador in Paris—namely, that no British government would ever risk the bones of a single British grenadier for the Polish Corridor.[76] But Chamberlain indicated that in the long run a revision of the Polish-German frontier was inevitable. As he wrote to Eyre Crowe, he had told Skrzyński on 13 March that

> Poland stood between two great nations in a position of danger which her tragic history must make only too plain. Surely it was in the interest of Poland to come to terms if possible with at least one of these Great Powers. Did he not think that it would be easier to cultivate good, and even friendly relations with the German Reich than with the Soviet Union?[77]

Still, he did not go quite as far as the *Times,* which advised Poland to consider "a generous effort and a reasonable compromise in the matter of frontiers."[78]

Skrzyński told Chamberlain he feared that a Western pact with Germany would appear to "legitimize" German aspirations in the east. Chamberlain disagreed, arguing that Germany's refusal to make exactly the same declaration on her eastern as on her western frontiers meant that she intended to keep her engagements (!). He also made it quite clear that Britain could not undertake any commitments in Eastern Europe: "I told him I had no idea of signing any pact which included a reference to the eastern frontiers of Germany. . . . Any pact into which we might enter . . . would necessarily be confined to those frontiers in which we had an immediate interest."[79]

The one positive result of this conversation was the favorable impression that Skrzyński made on Chamberlain. The foreign secretary wrote that Skrzyński's demeanor, as he had previously observed it in the League Council, was "all smiles and irony, but seemed to me to wear that air of uneasy assumption which those who are uncertain of their own position are apt to assume." Now, he wrote: "Having formed this unfavorable impression of M. Skrzyński, I was very favorably surprised when, opening our conversation in good English, he spoke simply and directly, with none of the swagger or conceit which had seemed to me a constant part of his public form."[80]

Despite Chamberlain's advice for Poland to seek good relations with Germany and his caveat against British commitments in Eastern Europe, Skrzyński found some reassurance in the foreign secretary's statements. He concluded that British policy was not aiming at a rapprochement with Germany and that she was not Britain's protégé. Finally, he was pleased with Chamberlain's assurance that the guarantee pact would not affect any provisions of the Versailles Treaty.[81] He would have been less pleased had he known the opinion of Aristide Briand, then the head of the French delegation in Geneva and soon again to be premier and foreign minister of France. As Chamberlain noted:

> Mr. Briand himself is under no illusions as to the impossibility of maintaining the present arrangements in Eastern Europe. He observed . . . that if Germany would only join the League and trust to time and article 19 of the Covenant, the council itself, after a series of such sittings as we had yesterday, would become convinced that some change must be made.[82]

This was a reference to the council's discussion of Polish-Danzig disputes, a fixed item on the agenda at almost every meeting.

Chamberlain's thoughts on the Polish-German frontier meshed perfectly with Briand's: revision was inevitable, but the issue should be left to the healing hand of time. Chamberlain therefore agreed with Headlam-Morley that immediate revision should not be encouraged. Commenting on the latter's memorandum to this effect, the foreign secretary wrote: "We deprecate premature discussion of a problem which time and good will alone can solve, at a moment when such discussion can only make more difficult and might easily entirely destroy such chances as exist of stabilizing peace."[83] He elaborated these views in a letter to Lord D'Abernon:

> I myself believe that within a reasonable number of years she [Germany] will find herself in a position where her economic and commercial support is so necessary and her political friendship so desirable to Poland that, without having recourse to the League machinery, she will be able to make a friendly arrangement on her own account directly with the Poles. This is what Briand said to me and what other members of the Council repeated. For the success of such a policy good will, patience, and tact are necessary. If the German public and press could be restrained from talking so much about the eastern frontiers, they might get more quickly to a solution.[84]

The foreign secretary took much the same stance publicly on 24 March, in the House of Commons debate on the Geneva Protocol. Speaking of German-Polish relations, he said that Poland had every interest in seeking good relations with Germany, while Germany could gain no advantage from attacking Poland. "Friendly adjustment," economic forces, and the free play of commercial interests would, with time, bring about a close friendship between the two states.[85] In discussing the German proposals, Chamberlain stated that Germany was willing to guarantee the status quo in the west and to renounce war as a means of changing European frontiers in both the east and the west.[86] Finally, he rebutted Lloyd George's violent attacks on Poland, particularly the latter's charge that Poland had refused to accept the League Council's decision on the mailbox dispute with Danzig, a decision that, as

Chamberlain pointed out, had not yet been made.[87] However, many speakers again advocated the revision of the Versailles Treaty as the precondition for a European security agreement.

Chamberlain's statement on Germany's readiness to renounce war as a means of changing her eastern frontiers provoked objections from the German ambassador in London. Dr. Friedrich Sthamer told Chamberlain that Germany did not wish to exclude war entirely in the east, since arbitration might not be accepted by both parties involved. Chamberlain was furious and threatened to tell the House of Commons that Germany had gone back on her proposals. Sthamer said that Germany had no such intentions, but the arbitration treaties that she had in mind would be modeled on those she already had with Sweden and Switzerland. In his report to Berlin, Sthamer expressed doubt that Chamberlain was familiar with these treaties, for they excluded frontier disputes from arbitration.[88] But Chamberlain knew this; however, his interpretation was different. As he told the House of Commons, by excluding frontiers from arbitration, Germany intended to settle disputes by conciliation and by mutual agreement; he believed that this meant she would renounce war. This was not the German view. As Schubert wrote to Brockdorff-Rantzau, the German government was adamantly opposed to any renunciation of war in the east, because this would put it on "the slippery slope" to the recognition of the Polish-German frontier.[89] Still, Chamberlain's strong reaction to Sthamer's statement did elicit an unofficial declaration that the German government explicitly rejected the use of force with regard to changing the Polish-German frontier.[90]

At this time, German aims were outlined by Herbert von Dirksen, the head of the Eastern Department in the Foreign Ministry, in a memorandum on German policy regarding Danzig and the Corridor. While noting that the moment was inopportune for raising the problem, he wrote that Germany should, at the right time, demand the return of Danzig and the Corridor. In the latter case, Germany should demand territory as far south as a line running from Schneidemühl (Piła) in the west and continuing through and including Bromberg (Bydgoszcz) and Thorn (Toruń) in the east. In exchange, Poland would be offered a free port in Danzig and the right to tariff-free road and rail communications with the city. She might also be offered another access to the sea at Memel through a special "corridor"—presumably through Lithuanian territory. Considering various alternatives, Dirksen rejected the amalgamation of Danzig and the Corridor into an enlarged free city-state, because the Corridor's preponderantly Polish population might lead to the Polonization of Danzig. He also rejected an exchange of populations as impracticable. In conclusion, he noted that these German demands could only be put to Poland if the latter should fall into complete decay. However, German representatives abroad were to prepare the ground for this solution by mentioning it in private conversations.[91] It is interesting that at this time Philip Kerr, formerly Lloyd George's private secretary, suggested to President Sahm of Danzig that a plebiscite might be held in the region between the sea and Bromberg. Sahm replied that such a procedure would be dangerous unless a distinction were to be made between voters living in the Corridor before and after 1918.[92] He thus implied that the population living in the Corridor before 1918 had been preponderantly German, an assumption contradicted by the results of the 1910 census in this area.[93]

Dirksen's views were shared by Gustav Stresemann. On 30 June 1925 the Foreign Ministry sent a directive to the principal German missions abroad, which even increased the amount of territory claimed by Germany in the Corridor. Upper Silesia was also to be returned to Germany.[94] But like Dirksen, Stresemann believed that the time was not ripe for raising the issue. He assumed that Germany's payment of reparations and her readiness to grant France security on the Rhine would ultimately produce Anglo-French support for the revision of the Polish-German frontier. He did not wish to rock the boat. As he told German journalists in March, they should leave the discussion of the "untenable" German-Polish frontier to the *Times* (London). He told them that even General von Seeckt thought that Germany could not possibly take any military action; Germany could not even hold her own frontiers in a defensive war, while an offensive one was unthinkable, given the resources at her disposal.[95] In the meanwhile, Stresemann contented himself with statements to the press and to the Reichstag that Germany would not officially recognize her frontier with Poland. He tried to mollify the leaders of his own German People's Party by claiming that Chamberlain, in his speech in the House of Commons, had at least indirectly recognized Germany's stand on revision.[96] In any case, Stresemann claimed that once Germany had taken her seat on the League Council, she would participate in all the important decisions on Danzig and the eastern boundaries—a clear reference to the implementation of article 19 of the League Covenant.[97] At the same time, he exerted pressure on the French and British ambassadors in Berlin. In March he told them that German public opinion was opposed to any cooperation with the West, unless Poland would give up Danzig and the Corridor. He also said that while the German government did not wish for a Polish-Soviet war, Soviet victory in such a war would mean the return of these territories to Germany.[98]

In the meanwhile, Herriot's government had fallen in April 1925. It was succeeded by a new one under Paul Painlevé, in which Aristide Briand again held the two posts of premier and foreign minister. At the end of that month, Briand stated his position to the Poles. He told Ambassador Alfred Chłapowski that while France wished to go as far as possible to obtain security for Poland's western frontier, she had to reckon with Britain, who was adamantly opposed to any security pact that included Poland. However, Briand declared, France would always observe the principle that the resulting western treaties should be in harmony with the Franco-Polish alliance and that they could not modify the Treaty of Versailles.[99] Thus, he implied that Poland would not be an equal partner in the forthcoming security negotiations. What is more, Briand told Sikorski that he would not register with the league the protocol signed by Herriot in November 1924. Briand explained this on the grounds that it did not have the character of an agreement, since it had not been ratified by the parliaments of both countries.[100] Though he did not say as much, the same applied to the Franco-Polish Military Convention of 1921. Indeed, as Jules Laroche told Aleksander Szembek, the Polish military chargé d'affaires in Paris, the convention would have to be revised so as to harmonize with the French Constitution and the League Covenant.[101]

Briand's policy toward Poland stemmed from his desire for closer relations with Britain on the one hand and with Germany on the other. He might have been obliged to take a line more favorable to Poland if the Poles and Czechs had stood together, but this was not the case. It is true that Beneš warned Chamberlain in early March against reopening the discussion on frontier questions; he said that if the question of East Prussia came up (i.e., the Corridor), all the other questions would follow—namely, the Vilna question, the Treaty of Trianon, Rumania, Czechoslovakia, Hungary, Bulgaria, the Balkans, and so forth. He specifically warned that the projected western treaty should not be interpreted as an abandonment of security on Germany's eastern frontiers. Nevertheless, he chose to accept a western security treaty, and this was known in Berlin.[102] By the same token, he opposed the Polish goal of obtaining equal security for both Eastern and Western Europe. As Beneš told Chamberlain, he was convinced that "it was Poland which was menaced and not Czechoslovakia."[103] While he stated repeatedly that security in the west equaled security in the east, he did so with this assumption in mind. Indeed, Czechoslovak ministers were fond of drawing a distinction between their country's good relations with Germany and the bad relations that existed between the latter and Poland. Despite Beneš's declarations to Niedziałkowski, the Czechoslovak ministers did not hide their support of German revisionist claims nor their critical attitude toward Poland. Thus, the secretary general of the Czechoslovak Foreign Ministry, Václav Girsa, told Dodd of the British legation that Czechoslovakia had no fear whatever that her present frontier would be changed. The Polish case was different: "Poland did not feel the corridor really belonged to her," while "Czechoslovakia has no borrowed coat and consequently is not nervous."[104] Speaking to the British minister, Sir George Clerk, Beneš himself said that if he were the Polish foreign minister, he would give up the Corridor while seeking to retain the Polish share of Upper Silesia; Poland could gain access to the sea through Memel.[105] At this time, Beneš also told the United States chargé d'affaires, Frederick I. Pearson, that he did not believe in the permanence of Polish frontiers and that, if severely pressed, Poland would accede to some demands for revision.[106] Beneš told the Czechoslovak parliament that Polish control over the Corridor and Upper Silesia could not last and that he recognized the need for some revision of Poland's western boundary.[107]

In the meanwhile, Beneš was warmly received in Warsaw, where he signed a series of treaties on 23 April. These included a treaty of arbitration and conciliation, which did not, however, cover territorial questions; a liquidation convention on matters arising from border delimitations; a treaty regularizing the treatment of respective minorities; a commercial treaty; and some technical conventions. Among the latter was an agreement for the transit of war material to Poland.[108] However, Beneš did not change this views. As he told Lewis Einstein, the American minister in Prague, in May, the Polish Corridor was an "absurdity" that Poland would abandon in twenty years' time.[109] In June, President Masaryk told the British minister that "the real problem of European peace lay in the Polish frontiers and in finding means to bring these frontiers into harmony with facts without another war." He denied that Czechoslovakia had any military agreement with Poland and said that this was absolutely out of the question. He also said that a smaller and more homogenous Poland would be more stable and added that "the Czech people would not stand for military commitments towards the Poles, of whose fondness for hazardous adventure they were profoundly suspicious."[110] On this occasion, Masaryk mentioned that an emissary sent by Stresemann had assured Beneš that Germany had no wish to seek any changes in the German-Czechoslovak frontier.[111] Masaryk may have been referring to the message that Stresemann sent to Prague at the end of March, in which he said that German strategy was identical for Poland and Czechoslovakia only because to proclaim otherwise would result in the open isolation of Poland.[112] While Beneš's attempts in May and June to establish direct contact with Berlin failed,[113] the cumulative effect of his statements could not but weaken Polish diplomacy while strengthening Briand's inclination not to risk any disruption of Franco-British relations or to endanger a French rapprochement with Germany by insisting on equal security for Germany's neighbors in the east and in the west.

It is not surprising, therefore, that, in May, Briand informed Chamberlain that he did not desire the same guarantees for both the eastern and the western frontiers of Germany.[114] Skrzyński, for his part, hoped for the best. Having seen the draft French reply to the German note, he instructed

Skirmunt to tell Chamberlain that he, Skrzyński, did not intend to ask for an explicit German acceptance of the Polish-German frontier and that he was satisfied with the references to it in the French draft.[115] A few days later the British minister in Warsaw reported Skrzyński as having said that while the assurances regarding the Polish-German frontier in the French draft were not as definite as Polish opinion might wish, yet "he counted on what was implied in the draft rather than on what was explicitly stated." Here Skrzyński mentioned French insistence on Germany's entry into the league and the statement that no eventual agreement should imply or lead to the revision of the peace treaties or to the Allies' renunciation of their rights and obligations under the treaties and the League Covenant.[116]

At this time, Briand apparently hoped to obtain Britain's participation in the projected Polish-German arbitration pact, either as a party to it or as a guarantor. Jules Laroche tried to persuade Ralph Wigram, of the British embassy in Paris, that such participation would not commit Britain to helping Poland but that a British "protest" against a German violation would give France the "moral right" to aid Poland. In this connection, Laroche hoped that the projected Rhine pact would not prevent France from helping Poland in case of German aggression.[117] While the first part of Laroche's proposal was unacceptable to London,[118] the second part was controversial, as we shall see later. As far as Warsaw was concerned, Briand instructed the French ambassador to say that France was only returning to the policy of 1921, when he (Briand) had tried to get an Anglo-French pact signed at Geneva. Briand claimed that France was not neglecting Polish interests and that in all Anglo-French conversations he was trying to secure indispensable guarantees for the Poles and Czechs.[119] In fact, like his protégé Philippe Berthelot, who once again became secretary general of the Quai d'Orsay, Briand envisaged a solution that had been considered for some time by the German Foreign Ministry. As Chamberlain noted on a conversation that he had with Briand in June at Geneva:

> Briand, who has a great sense of the real and practical, regrets that in the peace treaties the Poles bit off more than they can easily chew, and he appears to have some idea that eventually an arrangement may be made with Russia on the basis of some adjustment of territory, and with Germany at the expense of Lithuania, or so at least I suppose, for he said that it was in view of these considerations that they had postponed the coming into force of the Memel Convention at the Ambassadors' Conference.[120]

The implication of this statement was that Poland might be compensated for losing Danzig by receiving special rights in the port of Memel, or perhaps by getting possession of Memel itself. Berthelot made a similar suggestion to Ernest Remnant, the editor and owner of the *English Review*. As noted earlier, the French government had supported the idea of establishing Memel as a free city in 1922, but in March 1923 the Conference of Ambassadors had recognized Lithuania's sovereignty over the city, conditional on her granting it a certain autonomy.[121]

At Geneva, Chamberlain gave Briand an assurance that the French right to cross the Rhine under certain circumstances would not constitute a derogation from the mutual character of the proposed pact.[122] A Havas communique to this effect caused some excitement in Germany and Britain, and the Foreign Office denied that France could attack Germany in order to defend Poland.[123] The French reply to the German proposals was finally delivered in Berlin on 16 June. The French note specifically stipulated that Germany should conclude arbitration treaties with Poland and Czechoslovakia and that France would be their guarantor. Also, France reserved the right to go to the aid of her allies if they were attacked: the note stated that the Rhine Pact should not prevent her from doing so.[124] Chamberlain lent support to the French note—which had been drafted in common—in an instruction that was sent simultaneously to Joseph Addison, the British chargé d'affaires in Berlin, and to Sir William Max Muller in Warsaw. At the same time, Chamberlain took care to point out that some widely discussed solutions of the problem of the Polish-German frontier were unrealistic. He wrote that the German security proposals had "paradoxically" focused attention on the east and had aroused one of the periodic outbursts of criticism of the Versailles Treaty in Britain. In countering this criticism, he noted that the decisions of the Peace Conference had been at least "ethnographically correct and had provided the best solution possible at the time. With regard to the German-Polish frontier, he dismissed as unrealistic the suggestions of an exchange of Danzig for Memel, or of neutralizing East Prussia. He said that the first solution was futile because of the Polish-Lithuanian quarrel and the status of Memel. The second, seen as an alternative compensation for the loss of Polish rights in Danzig, Chamberlain thought would be unacceptable to Germany. He warned that it was dangerous to assume that a revision of the Polish-German frontier was inevitable and that, therefore, Britain should promote it. In his opinion, as little as possible should be changed until change proved necessary. Moreover, the idea that the British government favored change would only increase the feeling of insecurity. He had told the Polish minister in London that the latter's country should not irritate the Germans, and he told the German ambassador that Germany must not expect a change in the settlement. He concluded that "if the Germans are wise they will let the question sleep for a generation. If the Poles are wise they will make it possible for them to do so."[125]

A few days later, on 24 June, Chamberlain publicly took a stand against the immediate revision of the Versailles Treaty. In the House of Commons debate on the projected Security Pact, he stated that Britain's major concern was the guarantee of the Franco-German frontier but that "in seeking to make that frontier secure and to prevent war from breaking out there, nothing could be further from our thoughts than to cast any doubt upon the stability of the position elsewhere, or on the sanctity and obligations imposed by other provisions of the Treaties." If frontiers were to be changed, he said, this could only be done through article 19 of the League Covenant or through article 80 of the Treaties of Versailles and Saint-Germain (which stipulated that Germany recognized Austrian independence as inalienable, except with the consent of the League Council). He then argued against an immediate revision of the peace settlement:

> The idea that we should set to work within six years of the signature of the Treaty, and after all the labour they involved, rewrite the boundaries of Europe and tear up the settlements then arrived at—to try to create a fresh one—seems to me to be an idea that cannot be conceivable to anyone outside Bedlam.

However, he also declared that if Germany were to attack Poland, and if France were then to attack Germany, Britain's only obligation would be the one that she already had as a signatory of the League Covenant.[126]

This assurance did not appease the critics, nor were they convinced by Chamberlain's arguments against revision of the treaty. Lloyd George advocated British participation in the eastern arbitration treaties, but on the express condition of first changing the Danzig and Upper Silesian settlements. Captain Ashmead-Bartlett also urged that East European frontiers be revised first, after which Britain could guarantee the new settlement. In sum, there was more criticism than approval of the foreign secretary's statements.[127] The press, too, adamantly opposed any guarantee of the East European status quo. The manifesto of the National Reform Union stated that Britain should enter into no pacts with France that would solidify the eastern frontiers or which would close the doors to possible future revision.[128] The *Daily Herald* thought that the proposed pact would bind Britain to go to war whenever French politicans chose to drag her into one.[129] Thus, the German government had plenty of encouragement to oppose the demands set out in the French note of 16 June.

Right-wing German opinion reacted violently to this note, and the cabinet soon made its reservations known. As expected, the German government strongly objected to a French guarantee of the eastern arbitration treaties. Schubert told D'Abernon on 27 June, that according to the French note, France would be the sole judge of what constituted a hostile act and that she could act immediately as the guarantor of the German-Polish arbitration pact.[130] On the following day, Stresemann told D'Abernon that he could not accept the French demand to guarantee a German-Polish arbitration pact nor the French right to intervene by force under certain circumstances.[131] Chamberlain was angry and wondered whether the Germans were not using him as a dupe in order to get a better price from the Russians.[132]

Stresemann was, in fact, under great pressure from Moscow not to enter the League of Nations. The Soviet government's chief fear was Germany's participation in applying article 16 of the covenant against the USSR. However, Stresemann was able to use his objections to French demands as arguments to calm the Russians. This can be seen from the rough notes that Dirksen made prior to his departure with Brockdorff-Rantzau for Moscow, where they were to explain Stresemann's policy. According to these notes, the advantages that Germany would gain from the proposed security pact were to force Britain away from France and to weaken the latter's alliances with Poland and Czechoslovakia. Here Dirksen noted: "Germany was aware that to some extent she was meeting British wishes. [But] it was the only way of harnessing the British draught animals to the German cart."[133]

More important than Soviet pressure was the opposition that Stresemann faced at home. Thus, Gen. Hans von Seeckt, chief of the Heeresleitung (Army Command), objected to Germany's renunciation of the threat of force not only in Polish-German but also in Franco-German relations. The German National People's Party (DNVP) denounced Stresemann's alleged willingness to give up German lands and people in both the east and the west, and it tried to force him to resign. To parry these pressures, Stresemann secretly pledged that he would not sign the pact until the Ruhr had been evacuated and until the evacuation of the Cologne zone had been assured. Furthermore, he said, an early evacuation of the Rhineland would follow the signing of the security treaty.[134] Chancellor Hans Luther came to Stresemann's aid over the eastern territories—that is, Poland. Luther said that concern over these lands was understandable, "But after all, we could not start off by saying publicly that one of the inner motives for the German memorandum is the reestablishment of our former eastern boundaries."[135] The French helped Stresemann by announcing on 23 June that they would begin taking measures for the evacuation of the Ruhr.[136]

D'Abernon tried to pour oil on troubled waters by telling Schubert that the French guarantee of the eastern arbitration treaties would apply to Germany as well as to Poland. He also told Schubert that Britain would support the German point of view and that, in any case, France's relationship with Poland was like that of a man "who wanted to part from his mistress elegantly."[137] In the meanwhile, Chamberlain applied some economic pressure on Berlin. Credits for Germany were suspended in early July.[138] In mid July, Montagu Norman, the governor of the Bank of England, and Benjamin Strong, chairman of the Federal Reserve Bank of New York, visited

Germany. As they told Hjalmar Schacht, president of the Reichsbank, unless there were an improvement in the political atmosphere, Germany could not expect financial help from either the United States or England.[139] This pressure was, in fact, welcome to Stresemann. In the face of persistent opposition in the cabinet, he stated on 15 July that Britain and the United States had made it clear that if the security question were not resolved, Germany could not expect more money from them. He was then empowered to continue the negotiations.[140] Nonetheless, the German reply of 20 July reflected both Stresemann's aims and the views of German right-wing opposition leaders—particularly the DNVP—in rejecting the proposed French guarantee of the eastern arbitration treaties and the claim that the peace treaties could not be modified. Objections were also voiced to Germany's entry into the league, to article 16 of the League Covenant, and to the continued Allied occupation of the Rhineland.[141]

Chamberlain was angered by the German reply, which he saw as an "election manifesto."[142] However, he could understand Stresemann's domestic difficulties, since he also had his own. Aside from facing opposition in the press and Parliament to the projected British guarantee to France, Chamberlain had to prod the reluctant cabinet and the military. The Committee of Imperial Defense, for example, wanted a clause in the security pact to the effect that the pact could be terminated if the League Council should decide that the league itself provided sufficient protection. This was accepted in draft form by the cabinet and was sent to the dominions on 3 July.[143] The latter looked askance at any Continental commitment, and Chamberlain had to take time to tell Stanley M. Bruce, the Australian prime minister, that the security pact was not just a Continental problem.[144] As if these problems were not enough, Chamberlain felt that he had to moderate the French. Thus, on the one hand, he told the French ambassador on 11 July that it would be difficult to make a western settlement depend on a settlement between Germany and her eastern neighbors;[145] on the other hand, he told the French legal expert Henri Fromageot that Britain would act immediately if Germany were to attack France and that this assurance covered the Demilitarized Zone if German troops ever marched into it. To Undersecretary of State Locker Lampson's objections, the foreign secretary replied that he wanted to ensure that if war were to break out, it should be on a frontier removed as far as possible from Britain.[146] Clearly, he did not even think of the Vistula. The cabinet, in any case, took pains to ensure on 13 August that no British aid would be given automatically to France if she were to attack Germany after the latter had attacked Poland. In such a case, no British aid was to be forthcoming, even if German troops were standing on French soil.[147]

While striving to overcome cabinet and dominion opposition and while trying to influence France, Chamberlain also devoted some energy to cajoling the Germans into a more conciliatory frame of mind. Sir William Tyrrell, the permanent undersecretary of state, told Albert Dufour-Feronce, the German chargé d'affaires in London, that if Germany were to join the league, British opinion would shift in her favor. He also claimed that Briand was anxious to liquidate French obligations to Poland but could only secure Polish consent if France would guarantee the German-Polish arbitration treaty.[148] Chamberlain followed this line when he wrote to D'Abernon that a French guarantee of the Polish-German arbitration treaty was the only way of rewriting the Franco-Polish alliance.[149] There is no doubt that this was Briand's long-term goal. Briand told the German ambassador in Paris, Leopold von Hoesch, on 6 August, that there were no immediate prospects for frontier rectification, but that "once Germany had her seat on the Council and could speak as an equal of the representatives [of the Great Powers], then, under the influence of German economic superiority and other advantages, possibilities for a settlement by other methods would arise."[150]

Meanwhile, in Warsaw there were different views on what the Polish goals should be. On 21 June, in a letter to Premier W. Grabski, Sikorski outlined what he considered to be essential Polish desiderata. Here he enumerated four points: (1) Warsaw must insist on the maintenance of the Demilitarized Zone in the Rhineland; (2) the Franco-Polish Military Convention must be adapted to the new conditions, but without weakening the *casus foederis;* (3) there was to be a simultaneous signing of the Polish-German arbitration treaty, guaranteed by France, and of the Western security pact; and (4) Poland must obtain a permanent seat on the League Council.[151] Skrzyński took a stronger line. On 27 June he told Ambassador Panafieu that he considered it necessary to have a pact on Germany's eastern frontiers analogous to the projected Rhine pact. Skrzyński emphasized Poland's value to France by stating that in case of war, Poland could launch two hundred thousand men on a march to Berlin.[152] In a letter to W. Grabski, Skrzyński said that he wanted to keep Franco-Polish relations on the basis of partnership, and not of patron and client. He would offer Briand a Polish guarantee for the Franco-German frontier in return for a French guarantee of the Polish-German frontier. He also wanted to "modernize" the Franco-Polish alliance and to put it on the same foundations as the projected Rhine pact. This would, he thought, assure such an alliance the support of world opinion, especially British opinion.[153] On his way to the United States, Skrzyński stopped in Paris on 3 July. He wrote to Grabski three days later that Briand and Berthelot had agreed that the Polish requests were justified and that, in their view, military talks about the effects of the projected demilitarization of the Rhineland on the alliance should be held.[154] Since nothing was further from

French thoughts than acceding to Polish requests regarding the security pact and the demilitarization of the Rhineland, it is clear that Briand and Berthelot were seeking to avoid a public protest from Warsaw. Thus reassured, Skrzyński sailed for the United States, where he hoped to obtain not only American financial aid but also "moral" support for Polish demands regarding the security pact.[155] Meanwhile, Briand continued to soothe the Poles. After the German reply of 20 July, he assured Ambassador Alfred Chłapowski that the French government would inform its Polish ally in good time of its intentions and that it would not send a reply to Germany without prior consultation with Poland. Panafieu made an oral statement to this effect to the Polish Foreign Ministry in Warsaw.[156]

Apparently, these assurances were accepted. Whatever the case may be, a lengthy statement of Polish aims was drawn up at the end of July, reflecting Warsaw's view of the international situation. The author of the memorandum was most probably the undersecretary of state for foreign affairs, Kajetan Dzierżykraj-Morawski. In it we read that the aim of British policy was to ensure peace in Europe in order to safeguard the integrity of the British Empire. Britain was allegedly advancing toward this goal along two paths: by maintaining the balance of power between France and Germany—a balance seen as favoring Germany—and by aiming at a pact of guarantee. France was said to be afraid of this balancing policy. Soviet attention, it was noted, was focused on Asia, and this threatened British interests. Stresemann was trying to disturb Anglo-French relations, while at the same time posing as a man of peace in order to obtain U.S. financial aid. He was also aiming at a compromise with the Soviet Union. Stresemann, however, thought the author of the memorandum, would have to choose between the pact of guarantee and entry into the league, on the one hand, and revisionism and maintenance of the Rapallo Treaty with Russia on the other. Clearly, the author of the memorandum had in mind a pact of guarantee that would include both Eastern and Western Europe, for he went on to say that if such a pact were confined to Western Europe, it would leave Germany freedom of action in Eastern Europe, and thus would favor German-Soviet rapprochement.

In view of these considerations, Polish demands were formulated as follows: first, to ensure such a solution of the security problem as would (a) maintain the existing treaties unchanged, since change would entail the risk of armed conflict; (b) ensure the simultaneous and equal establishment of security on both the western and eastern frontiers of Germany; (c) ensure the immediacy and efficacy of sanctions in case of aggression; and (d) unmask the "insincere and artificial compromise" between the guarantee pact and the Rapallo Treaty, which was the aim of German policy. Second, Poland should aim (a) at maintaining the Franco-Polish alliance, while updating it to conform with the new international situation and the security problem; (b) at counteracting the German-Soviet rapprochement; (c) at exploiting the anti-Soviet orientation of British policy; and (d) at admitting Germany to the league only on condition that there be complete equality with other league members in regard to her rights and obligations and that there be an adequate assurance of Polish interests as a counterweight to German influence in the league.[157] It is not clear whether these objectives were approved by Skrzyński before he left for the United States, for they did not go as far as the views that he had expressed in his letters to Grabski. Whatever the case might be, when Skrzyński stopped in Paris on his way back from the United States in mid August, he crystallized his suggestions of early July. According to a French note, he then said that he viewed a Polish-French-German pact as a necessary complement to the Western security pact.[158]

Meanwhile, the French had been working on their reply to the German note of 20 July, and the French note was delivered in Berlin on 24 August. It stated that France and her allies agreed that neither the peace treaties nor the rights of the Allies and Germany should be impaired; nor could the guarantees for the execution of the peace treaties and the provisions governing them be modified by the proposed agreements. Further, Germany must enter the League of Nations. Finally, German objections to a French guarantee of the eastern arbitration treaties were rejected, especially the charge that France would thereby be empowered to decide unilaterally as to who was the aggressor. The aggressor, stated the French note, would define himself by committing an act of aggression. However, these statements were undermined by the assertion that it did not seem to be impossible to find dispositions that would be appropriate to the case envisaged and that means of ensuring an impartial decision on whether aggression had been committed or not could be sought.[159] At the same time, a verbal invitation to a Conference of Jurists was delivered by the French ambassador in Berlin. The German government accepted on 27 August.[160] It was clear that Briand would not insist too much on the French guarantee of the eastern arbitration pacts, or at least no more than was necessary in order to appease French public opinion.

At the end of August the Political Committee of the Polish Council of Ministers met to finalize Polish policy aims in the forthcoming security negotiations. The two key desiderata were that the Rhine pact not be allowed to weaken the existing treaties on which the Polish-German frontier was founded and that it must not weaken the Franco-Polish alliance. First, the French government must assure Poland that the Rhine pact would not in any way limit France's right to take armed action on the basis of her own decision in the event of any German armed threat against the frontiers of Poland—whether by regular troops or by volunteers. France must not submit the decision on whether Germany had threatened Polish frontiers to the League of Nations or to any third party but must reserve it for herself; nor could the pact prevent French armed aid to Poland because of the demilitarization of both banks of the Rhine. Second, Poland must strive to obtain recognition from the French and British governments of the principle that European security demanded the simultaneous conclusion of the Rhine pact—namely, the Anglo-French-Belgian-German security pact—and of a parallel and equal Polish-German-French security pact. If Germany should refuse to join the Franco-Polish pact—which was to guarantee mutual French and Polish aid in maintaining the integrity of their frontiers and to exclude military action against Germany, unless in self-defense against the latter—it would be left open for German accession at a later time. If this proposal were rejected by Britain, the Polish government would take the initiative in constructing a European security pact that would include Italy, Czechoslovakia, and possibly some smaller states.[161]

The Polish program seems unrealistic, but we must bear in mind that it was based at least in part on assurances that had repeatedly been given to Skrzyński by Briand and Berthelot. Thus, Britain, not France, was seen as the main obstacle, and the alternative goal of constructing another security pact with Italy, Czechoslovakia, and some other states seems to have been purely theoretical. The authors must have known that it had little chance of realization; perhaps they thought of it as a threat to use at the appropriate moment. Their trust in France stemmed, not from naïveté, but from misperception. They were right in believing that France and Poland had common security interests vis-à-vis Germany. What they failed to realize was that Briand and the Quai d'Orsay perceived Poland, not as vital to French security, but as a hindrance to the ''real'' security that they hoped to obtain from Great Britain and Germany. The price for this was, of course, French noninsistence on Germany's acceptance of equal obligations in Eastern and in Western Europe and, therefore, tacit French consent to the revision of the Polish-German frontier at some future time.

10

Poland at Locarno

The Polish objectives, as outlined by Skrzyński and the Polish Council of Ministers in July and August, were far removed from reality. The conference of jurists in London and the conference of foreign ministers, which followed at Locarno, confirmed the fact that Briand had no intention of insisting on equal security for both Western and Eastern Europe. His objective was to find formulas that would be acceptable to the Germans, the British, and, of course, to French public opinion.

British, French, Belgian, Italian, and German jurists met in London from 1 to 4 September in an attempt to iron out difficulties before the conference of foreign ministers. The German jurist Dr. Friedrich Gaus took heart from the fact that the draft treaty made more allowances for Germany than had been expected. He noticed, in particular, that the linkage between the eastern and western arbitration treaties was very tenuous and that this indicated a weak French position on this issue.[1] Dr. Ulrich Rauscher, the German minister in Warsaw, was also optimistic. He saw that the draft treaty distinguished between frontiers that were to be taken seriously and those that were not, relegating the Polish-German frontier to the second category. The Security Pact would, he wrote, result in weakening Franco-Polish cooperation against Germany and would devalue Poland as France's watchdog in the East.[2]

Gaus took a very determined stand on three major points: Germany's demands for special treatment under article 16 of the Covenant, the evacuation of the Rhineland, and the French guarantee of the eastern arbitration treaties. On the last point he stated that no German government could or would accept such a guarantee. Sir Cecil Hurst, the British legal expert, then asked if Germany would sign a declaration assuring Poland that Germany expressly renounced the use of force. Gaus would have none of this. He said that the German stand was well known: Germany had no intention of waging an aggressive war against Poland, but she saw no reason to accept an express obligation that went beyond the arbitration treaty and the provisions of the covenant that Germany would sign as a member of the league. Also, the Rhine Pact itself was so formulated that it meant nothing else but a renunciation of war. But if Germany were to undertake the same obligation to Poland as to France and Belgium, there would be no significant difference between the western and the eastern pacts. In that case, the foreign ministers might as well conclude a uniform treaty for both east and west. Therefore, as far as Germany was concerned, the only measures involving Poland should be the arbitration treaty and Germany's entry into the league. Even so, he claimed, both would be a heavy burden on German-Soviet relations.[3] It is strange that Gaus failed to mention a suggestion made by Hurst that France might give Poland a guarantee of the arbitration treaty in a *separate* instrument which would be communicated to the league.[4] As it turned out, this contained the seeds of the compromise later reached at Locarno, but at the London conference Gaus rejected it out of hand. President Hindenburg was pleased. He remarked that he was ''glad that Herr Gaus had so energetically shown his teeth to his Allied colleagues,'' and he agreed with Schubert that the forthcoming conference of foreign ministers would give Germany a chance ''of at last seizing the enemy by the throat.''[5] While these offstage snarls did not reach Allied ears, Gaus's stand was clearly understood. As Chamberlain noted on 9 September in Geneva, he agreed with Briand, Émile Vandervelde, and Vittorio Scialoja that the problem of Germany's eastern frontiers would be the key difficulty at the conference. Briand thereupon suggested a possible solution: to place the eastern arbitration treaties under the guarantee of the league, with France as the agent to implement it. He also agreed to Chamberlain's suggestion that negotiations should start with the western security pact, while the Polish and Czechoslovak representatives would be invited to join the conference later.[6]

It is clear that Briand completely ignored Skrzyński's memorandum, which he had received on 7 September. The Polish foreign minister demanded Polish participation in negotiations for the western security pact on the grounds that Italy, whose frontiers were not to be guaranteed either, was to be a participant. He then suggested that the Franco-Polish alliance be linked with the Rhine pact—a term frequently used to denote the western security pact— and that the Franco-Polish alliance be given the same legal force as that which, in Anglo-Saxon eyes, would be attributed to the Rhine pact.[7] Skrzyński seems not to have put the same demands to Chamberlain at the September council meeting. According to Chamberlain, the Polish foreign minister merely said that he would be satisfied if Polish-German negotiations began at the same time as those on the western pact.[8] However, Skrzyński made a speech in the League Council on 11 September, stating that Poland would remain faithful to the principles of the Geneva Protocol—thus underlining his view that security should be equal for both east and west—and that she was ready to conclude arbitration treaties.[9] Also, Poland and the three Baltic States agreed to support the principles of the Geneva Protocol.[10]

On 15 September, Germany was formally invited to attend a conference of foreign ministers. She accepted eleven days later, suggesting 5 October as the date and Locarno, Switzerland, as the place of the meeting.[11] However, the German ambassadors to France, Britain, Italy, and Belgium simultaneously delivered verbal notes demanding that the Allies officially deny Germany's war guilt and make a commitment to evacuate Cologne. Stresemann made a public declaration to the same effect. This was the result of pressures within the German cabinet, specially by the DNVP; and Stresemann had discussed the wording beforehand with the French and British ambassadors in Berlin. Briand had asked for some modifications so as to imply that the issue of war guilt had been raised only orally. Although the Germans refused this request, it was agreed that the Allied answer would be moderate.[12] Still, for the sake of French opinion, the Allied governments had to reject the German note.[13] Chamberlain was furious. He had already written to D'Abernon on 15 September: "Your Germans are very nearly intolerable." Now, after the German verbal note, Chamberlain exploded: "God forgive me if I have allowed myself to be duped by the Germans, but either Stresemann is crooked and a coward, or the value of any pact which may be made is, for the present, singularly discounted by the opposition which he meets."[14] This incident did not, however, cause a postponement of the conference.

At this time, Poland seemed to have a chance of emerging out of her isolation by concluding a nonaggression pact with Soviet Russia. Soviet soundings in this direction had been made through Karl Radek to Tennenbaum in July,[15] and Chicherin himself visited Warsaw from 27 to 29 September. However, as in 1924, the Soviets wanted a bilateral pact, while Poland insisted on a multilateral one that would include all of the Soviet Union's western neighbors.[16] The real Soviet objective was to bring pressure on Germany and thus prevent her from negotiating a security pact with the Western Powers. Berlin remained calm, since no one took the possibility of a Soviet-Polish rapprochement seriously.[17] Nor could Chicherin shake Stresemann when he arrived in Berlin on 30 September. Some feathers were ruffled when Chicherin recalled Brockdorff-Rantzau's proposal, of December 1924, that Germany and Soviet Russia cooperate to force Poland back to her "ethnographic frontiers." Stresemann denied having any knowledge of this, as did Schubert—who certainly knew better. Though admitting later that

Maltzan had authorized Brockdorff-Rantzau to make the statement, Stresemann refused to discuss the matter. However, he told Chicherin that he would work for such an interpretation of article 16 of the covenant as would ensure Russian security and that a German-Soviet trade treaty would be signed as soon as possible.[18] Thus, Chicherin's gesture toward Warsaw turned out to be a red herring and did not strengthen the Polish position.

Poland was further weakened by Beneš's demonstrative emphasis on an independent Czechoslovak approach to the projected western security pact. Beneš had tried vainly for months to arrange a meeting with Stresemann to discuss the German proposal.[19] When the Allied invitation to the conference reached Berlin on 15 September, D'Abernon told Schubert that "in questions concerning the arbitration treaties Beneš certainly attached no great importance to proceeding arm in arm with the Poles."[20] Stresemann took steps to confirm this; he was successful. At a press conference three days later, he stated that since neither Poland nor Czechoslovakia had answered the German note of 9 February, they were not interested in concluding arbitration treaties with Germany. Beneš immediately instructed the Czechoslovak minister in Berlin, Kamil Krofta, to tell Stresemann that Czechoslovakia did desire such a treaty. In the ensuing conversation, Stresemann told Krofta that the initial negotiations at Lorcarno would concern the Rhine pact, while the eastern arbitration treaties would come later. He therefore thought it would be better if Beneš did not participate in the opening stages of the conference. Krofta answered that this was also Beneš's view.[21]

Beneš gave a rather lame explanation of his policy to Dzierżykraj-Morawski in Geneva. Beneš said that his objective had been to deprive Stresemann of the argument that neither Poland nor Czechoslovakia had approached Berlin about the arbitration treaties and therefore had no right to attend the Locarno Conference. But he also stressed the fact that Germany had no territorial claims against Czechoslovakia and said that if Germany were to offer a more advantageous treaty to Prague than to Warsaw, he would accept it. Finally, he saw two alternatives: either a German-Czechoslovak arbitration treaty, or German access to the existing Franco-Czechoslovak alliance of 1924.[22] It is difficult to say whether he really aimed at the latter or merely said so because he knew that the Poles had a similar goal. In any case, he refused to make a common stand with Poland. Thus, Skrzyński was isolated.

Far from condemning Beneš's *démarche* in Berlin, the French government hinted that Poland might well make a similar move. Skrzyński rejected this in a dignified note of 29 September. He wrote that Poland had hitherto maintained an absolute reserve in the negotiations between Berlin, Paris, and London, in order to avoid unnecessary difficulties and also because she had been kept out of the negotiations on the arbitration treaties. Furthermore, a

Polish *démarche* in Berlin was bound to elicit a German reply, and the whole matter would provoke negative comments in the German press. He realized that Germany wished to avoid simultaneous negotiations (on the Rhine pact and the eastern arbitration treaties) at all costs, and he also realized that Poland's presence at Locarno would be due not to German good will but to the decision of the Allies. He thought it best if Briand would tell Stresemann that Poland desired negotiations with the German government in a spirit different from that of the past and that this was not due to the formal wish of the French government. He expressed full confidence in the latter.[23] Indeed, Briand assured Skrzyński that he would always treat Polish and Czechoslovak interests together with those of France and that the Locarno negotiations would not succeed unless France obtained both the guarantees that she wanted for her frontier with Germany and the necessary security and guarantees that she asked for her two allies.[24]

Let us now look at the attitudes of the major powers on the eve of the Locarno Conference. The Germans were determined to reject any linkage between the western security or Rhine pact and the eastern arbitration pacts; in particular, they opposed any French guarantees for the latter. Also, if Germany concluded an arbitration treaty with Poland, this could only be modeled on the arbitration treaties previously signed by Germany, which excluded territorial disputes.[25] Therefore, the guidelines for the German delegation stated that Germany could not resign from claims to any German territories and populations and that the eastern arbitration treaties would exclude frontier problems from any arbitration procedure.[26]

On the French side, Briand was ready to seek an accommodation with Germany provided French rights were *legally* preserved. As Chamberlain noted about Briand on 2 October:

> He is bound to respect the obligations of France to Poland and Czechoslo-
> vakia; but ever since the jurists' conversations he has been directing his
> efforts to finding a solution which shall put what is essential from the French
> point of view into a form acceptable to Germany. As he said to me at
> Geneva, he would not ''quarrel over words''; if a guarantee by France was
> unacceptable, he would be prepared to propose a guarantee by the League of
> Nations, placing, as it were, the army of France at the disposal of the League
> in support of that guarantee.

Chamberlain added that this was similar to a suggestion which had been made by the Committee on Imperial Defense on the form that a British guarantee to France might take in the Geneva Protocol.[27]

In this same memorandum, which Chamberlain wrote for the cabinet, he outlined his own attitude on the East European problem. He thought it would be a ''grave mistake'' to obtain a western pact without making corresponding security arrangements on the eastern frontiers of Germany. He reminded his colleagues that "the spark which kindled the Great War fell in Serbia." While Britain could not accept any obligations in the region, she could not be indifferent to a conflict there, "for it might easily raise issues and assume dimensions which would compel the Government of the day, free though it were from any treaty obligation, to take part." Therefore he would use his influence to secure success in the eastern negotiations, and "I should, as at present advised, not wish to go too far or too fast with the western negotiations until the eastern situation has developed." To strike a firm bargain with Germany in the west before there was a settlement in the east would, he thought, "militate strongly against the chances of such a settlement."[28] Chamberlain did not, of course, envisage equal security for Eastern and for Western Europe, but he seemed to give priority to the French guarantee of the projected arbitration treaties between Germany and her eastern neighbors.

The foreign ministers of France, Britain, Italy, and Germany gathered in Locarno on 4 October. The total number of delegates was reported as 121. The German delegation was the largest, numbering 40, headed by the German chancellor, Dr. Hans Luther. Some two hundred journalists descended on the little resort town on the shores of Lake Maggiore. The conference was held in the hall of the courthouse, which was described in one report as "a plain severe room, almost without decoration of any kind, save for a single painting and some woven heraldic curtains." On one side there was a view of the lake and the mountains; in the middle of the room stood a large oval table seating about forty persons. The German delegation checked into the Hotel Esplanade, about one mile from the center of town; all the others stayed in the Grand Palace Hotel, overlooking the lake.[29] On the first day of the conference, Chamberlain arrived at the courthouse with Miles W. Locker Lampson, head of the Central Department of the Foreign Office, and his private secretary, Walford Selby. They came "in an imposing white car," rented by the British delegation. It was reported to have "a wreath of white roses in *repoussé* work running round the body" and was a joy to behold. The foreign secretary told news correspondents that the Allies desired "to let the dead past bury its dead and to think only how the future could be made better than the past." He emphasized that the conference would be based on complete equality.[30]

But the past was very much alive. The chief problems were set out clearly from the beginning by the Germans. They would not enter the league unless article 16 of the League Covenant was modified; they would oppose a French guarantee of the eastern arbitration treaties, as well as any linkage between the latter and the Rhine or western security pact. Furthermore, they demanded the evacuation of the Rhineland. It was equally clear, however, that both the Germans and the French had assumed from the outset that some way would be found to circumvent the projected French guarantee. Briand made it clear that he would be ready to settle for some formula that was agreeable to Germany, and Schubert said as much to Lampson on 4 October.[31] Beneš said the same on the eve of his departure from Prague, when he stated that only the formulation of the guarantees for the eastern arbitration treaties would cause serious discussion.[32] The real problem, then, was to find a formula for safeguarding the principle of France's right to aid her eastern allies that would be acceptable to Germany.

To begin with, however, Briand's stated objective was to obtain German assent to the guarantee. This was a tactical move designed both as a bargaining point and as a demonstration for public opinion in France and Poland that Germany would never give her consent and that, therefore, some other arrangement would have to be found. At the first meeting of the conference, on 5 October, Stresemann stated that the second part of the article 6 of the draft Rhine pact, which tied it to the eastern arbitration treaties, could not be accepted by the German government. The matter was tabled, at Briand's suggestion. So was the German objection to article 11 of the Rhine Pact, which stated that the latter could not be ratified before Germany's entry into the league; this involved German objections to article 16 of the League Covenant.[33]

Article 6 of the draft Rhine Pact and article 16 of the League Covenant were discussed on the following day. Article 6 stated that the provisions of the present draft treaty left intact the rights and obligations of the High Contracting Parties stemming from the Versailles Treaty and complementary agreements, including the London Agreement of August 1924. Further, the same applied to the right of one of the High Contracting Parties (France) to implement the guarantee of the arbitration treaties to be signed the same day (as the western pact) between Germany, on the one hand, and Poland and Czechoslovakia on the other. The guarantee was to be operative if it was not contrary to the League Covenant and if one of the signatories (Germany) had recourse to force. Briand stated that France could not abandon her allies by accepting security for herself at their expense; French public opinion would not stand for it. However, if the difficulty was one of finding a formula that would be pleasing to German public opinion, then it could be found. He said that, in fact, the spirit of the League Covenant was dominant in article 6 of the draft treaty to such a degree that even if the French guarantee of the arbitration treaties were not written into it, he might almost have the right to say it was there. When Luther said that the German delegation would like for the French to find a formula, Briand countered that the Germans might find one.[34] As for article 16 of the League Covenant, Briand contended that it must be more closely defined. Chamberlain supported this view.[35]

But the Germans were not ready to smooth Briand's path, not immediately at any rate. They, too, had to put on a show for their public opinion.
Luther told Chamberlain on the evening of 6 October that "this question of
the eastern frontiers presented an almost insuperable difficulty." Chamberlain tried to persuade Luther that the real effect of the guarantee would be
to limit French obligations to Poland, as laid down in the existing alliance, by
defining and limiting the occasions on which assistance could be either
demanded or given. In support of this contention, Chamberlain even cited
Beneš's opinion that this was one of the reasons that he was satisfied with the
pact negotiations, for he did not wish to see Czechoslovakia involved in a
quarrel between France and Germany "arising out of a trifling matter"(!).[36]
However, Luther would not be moved.

The British delegation then met in Chamberlain's room to consider
possible solutions. As recorded by Lampson, the foreign secretary suggested a
note from Poland to France asking how the Security Pact would affect the
Franco-Polish alliance. The French would reply that if Poland were, in breach
of her arbitration treaty with Germany, subjected to unprovoked aggression,
the casus foederis would arise, and France would give the support promised in
the treaty of alliance. Another suggestion was for France to put on record that
if a Polish-German dispute should go before the council, she would place her
forces at the council's disposal. If the council should fail to reach a decision,
France would be free to act under article 15, paragraph 7, of the League
Covenant, under which the parties would recover their freedom of action.
Bennett made what was considered to be the most satisfactory proposal:
Germany should, in her arbitration treaties with Poland and Czechoslovakia,
give a specific undertaking not to resort to war. But in this case, the parties
would have to agree to give up the right to independent action as per article
15, paragraph 7, of the covenant (that is, if the League of Nations Council
should fail to reach a unanimous decision on how to resolve the dispute).[37]
This would eliminate unilateral French aid to Poland.

The jurists worked on these suggestions. At the third meeting of the
conference, on the afternoon of 7 October, Sir Cecil Hurst announced that
they had agreed to ask that article 2 of the draft treaty be reserved, since it was
connected with article 6 and the latter was still under discussion.[38] As it turned
out, what Hurst had in mind was the formulation of safeguards so that France
could not make use of article 15, paragraph 7, of the covenant unless
Germany had first committed an act of aggression. He submitted his revised
version to Chamberlain on the evening of 7 October and told him that the
jurists were satisfied that if the new text of article 2 were adopted, the disputed
part of article 6 could be eliminated. The key phrase in the revised version of
article 2, part 2, was that action according to article 15, paragraph 7, would be
possible only if "in this latter case the action is directed against a state which

has had recourse to war against another'' or if there was violation of the Demilitarized Zone in the Rhineland.[39] Although this eliminated French action in case of a *threat* of war, the Germans still dragged their feet. On the following day, Hurst reported that the Germans still wanted more security against possible French action under article 15, paragraph 7. Gaus stated that they were afraid that Poland might say that she had been attacked by Germany when this was not, in fact, the case. To guard against this, he thought that Germany would have to secure some kind of impartial examination of whether she had actually attacked Poland. Hurst concluded his note by saying that Luther was going to put the question to Briand.[40]

Briand and Luther did, indeed, have a private conversation on the same day. They went off by themselves to the small village of Ascona and conversed for some time without an interpreter (Luther spoke French). The meeting produced startling newspaper reports that Briand had dropped his demand for a French guarantee of the eastern arbitration treaties. The source for these reports, the *Berliner Tageblatt,* issued a denial, claiming that its reporter had been quoted out of context. Briand and Luther also issued denials.[41] There might, however, have been some truth in the reports, since Stresemann told Chamberlain on 8 October that he thought ''the question of the eastern frontiers and the French guarantee was in a fair way of settlement owing to the excellent work done by the lawyers.''[42]

In the meanwhile, Beneš arrived at Locarno on 7 October; Skrzyński followed on the next day. Skrzyński immediately asked to see Chamberlain and was received by him on the morning of 9 October. The British foreign secretary outlined the negotiations as they had developed, and Skrzyński said that Briand had informed him about them. Skrzyński then stated that he would be willing to substitute for the Franco-Polish alliance a tripartite treaty of mutual guarantee between France, Germany, and Poland. Chamberlain evaded this suggestion by asking Skrzyński to discuss it with Briand. Chamberlain indicated that the Polish minister should meet with Briand and follow Beneš's initiative in declaring his readiness to negotiate an arbitration treaty with Germany.[43]

Skrzyński stated the Polish position that same day at a press conference. He said that Poland would cooperate in the great work of peace, but the security problem could not be sliced up, since it formed one whole. The Polish government would abide by the principles of the Geneva Protocol, which it considered to be binding, because the protocol condemned war and proposed arbitration. He also did his best to counter press reports that only Polish intransigence was blocking the way to a security pact. When asked whether Poland would insist on French guarantees of the arbitration treaties, Skrzyński said: ''We are not here to insist on anything, but rather to find a loyal compromise between the just claims of Germany and the strict execution of the existing treaties.''[44] On the same day, the press noted a series of private conversations between the foreign ministers and also the fact that Beneš had worked many hours with the French legal expert Henri Fromageot to finalize a formula on Germany's entry into the league that would be acceptable to Berlin.[45]

On the morning of 10 October, Chamberlain stated that articles 6 and 7 still had to be agreed upon but that Briand preferred to continue to seek solutions in private conversations. Briand said that it was really a question of finding a formula and that private discussions were more appropriate than conference sessions for reaching agreement on the problems of the guarantee and of Germany's entry into the league. The Belgian foreign minister, Vandervelde, then proposed that the unresolved questions be submitted to a small group of five or six persons. Briand seized on this and asked whether Vandervelde thought that by sitting around a small table, the parties could get nearer to each other. However, both Briand and Chamberlain opposed holding conversations without the jurists, since, otherwise, incorrect interpretations might ensue.[46]

Vandervelde's suggestion may have inspired Briand to propose a boat excursion on Lake Maggiore that same afternoon. In any case, the Havas correspondent attributed the idea to Briand. The pretext for the excursion was Mrs. Chamberlain's birthday. The correspondent reported that the boat, the *Fiore d'Arancio* (Orange Blossom), left at 2:45 on a sunny afternoon and immediately took off for the Italian side of the lake, where the motorboats full of journalists were turned back. The journalists had, however, seen enough to guess the purpose of the excursion. In the drawing room of the boat they had observed a semicircular gaming table, covered with green cloth, and, seated round it, Chamberlain, Luther, Stresemann, Briand, Fromageot, Gaus, O. Hesnard (a professor of German and an expert on German affairs, who served as Briand's interpreter), and Hurst. The Havas correspondent thought that this conference dealt exclusively with the problem of Germany's entry into the league.[47]

As a matter of fact, the assembly dealt both with the conditions of Germany's entry into the league—that is, with her demands for the modification of article 16 of the covenant—and with the problem of the French guarantee of the eastern arbitration treaties. No detailed records of the discussions have survived,[48] but Stresemann described them briefly in a political speech of 14 December 1925. He then denied reports that the German delegates had enjoyed the cruise and said: "In fact, during this wonderful excursion, we sat for over five hours in the cabin, spending the first two and a half hours debating article 16, and the next two and half hours, the French guarantee for the eastern treaties. . . . I believe much of the criticism would be silenced if the protocols were available for reading."[49]

Agreement was reached, in principle, on German demands regarding article 16 of the covenant. It was embodied in the so-called *Texte de bateau* (Boat text), which was later included as Annex F of the security pact, entitled "Projet de lettre à la délégation allemande" (Draft letter to the German delegation). The essential point was that all member states were obligated to cooperate loyally and efficiently to make the covenant respected, but each one was to do so in proportion to its military situation and geographical position. This formula was not new. In 1923 the League Assembly had passed a resolution that the council should take into account the special circumstances and geographical position of each member in recommending military measures. Also, it was to leave to the government of each member state the decision on the degree to which it would use its military forces. However, the resolution failed because of one negative vote. The problem was tackled again in the Geneva Protocol, in 1924. Here it was suggested that all member states cooperate loyally in implementing sanctions against the aggressor, as prescribed in article 16 of the covenant. However, they were to do so as far as their geographical and military situation allowed. As we know, the Geneva Protocol failed because of British opposition to it. Thus, what Stresemann gained in the boat text was, in fact, final western acceptance of a proposal that had been debated in the league since 1923 and was now applied to German needs. Ironically, Beneš was the author of the formula. Briand wired Laroche on the afternoon of 12 October that the project accepted by the conference session that morning reproduced Beneš's report to the Sixth General Assembly of the League, in which Beneš had commented on the Geneva Protocol.[50] Poland was the loser, since Germany would now be entitled to refuse to allow the passage of troops and munitions to help Poland in case of Soviet aggression.

There now remained the problem of the French guarantee of the eastern arbitration treaties. A note by Hurst, dated 11 October, suggests that the Germans were still looking for a way to prevent French aid to Poland according to article 15, paragraph 7, of the covenant, while opposing any restriction on their own freedom of action against Poland. Chamberlain made a handwritten comment on the Hurst note: "Very important. You may tell M. Gaus that I do not see how any of us could refuse to support M. Briand if he made such a request, and ask him to inform the Chancellor and Foreign Minister."[51] Chamberlain's stand may have induced Stresemann to accept a compromise, or at least to choose the moment for doing so. In any event, on 11 October, Stresemann accepted a textual provision safeguarding the French right to aid Poland. The jurists were then instructed to search for a formula taking account of the different positions without damaging the basis of the French argument.[52]

Despite Stresemann's agreement of 11 October, however, the problem was not resolved. On the following day, Hurst noted that Gaus was still maintaining that Germany could not enter into any engagements with Poland and Czechoslovakia which excluded the right of going to war; but Gaus realized that Germany could not then ask France to "fetter herself with a restriction which Germany is not prepared to undertake." Gaus therefore proposed to try to induce his ministers to give up the stipulation that they had struggled so hard to obtain on the boat trip of 10 October.[53] There is no explanation of what this stipulation was, but it might have concerned the German demand for some "impartial inquiry" into the facts of the case if Germany were ever accused of commiting aggression against Poland. At any rate, this is what Gaus had told Hurst on 11 October.

The knotty problem was finally resolved by agreement on the revised text of part 2 of article 2 of the Rhine Pact. As Chamberlain cabled on the afternoon of 12 October, the "Eastern guarantee" was being discussed in informal conversations by the parties concerned. Chamberlain added that he had told Stresemann that the latter could not ask of France what he refused to give Poland. Apparently, agreement was reached on the evening of 12 October or the following morning, for Hurst presented the result and explained it to the conference at the afternoon session of 13 October. The first part of article 2 concerned exceptions to the renunciation of war. They were: cases of self-defense, or a flagrant violation of articles 42 and 43 of the Versailles Treaty (no German fortifications on the left or right bank of the Rhine); or if a troop concentration in the demilitarized zone necessitated immediate action; or in case of action on the basis of article 16 of the covenant. (These stipulations were in the Versailles Treaty.) It was stated that another exception would be action taken on the basis of a decision by the League Council, or on the basis of article 15, paragraph 7, of the covenant, provided however, that this action be directed against the state that had been the first to attack. Hurst stated that this last part of article 2, in fact, excluded all possibility of war, unless the other party had had recourse to arms, and that this therefore made it possible to strike out the last part of article 6 of the draft treaty to which the German government had objected—namely, France's right to aid her allies. Hurst's proposal met with unanimous approval. Briand agreed "in principle" and only asked for a short delay so that he could "out of loyalty" consult the interested parties before giving his official assent.[54] In the British version of the report, Hurst stated: "The Jurists believe that, in view of the existence of this project of article 2, France's right to give aid to Poland and Czechoslovakia, if absolutely necessary, is secure."[55] This was legally correct; however, the new formula not only dropped all reference to France's right of implementing her guarantee of the eastern arbitration treaties but also eliminated the guarantee altogether. Furthermore, this formula subordinated

France's alliances to the League Covenant and league machinery. This, of course, had been the French aim since the autumn of 1924.

And what were Beneš and Skrzyński doing? We can gather from press reports that on 9 October, Beneš helped Fromageot to work out the formula for the German acceptance of article 16 and that Briand talked with Vandervelde, Stresemann, and Skrzyński. Also on that day, Briand had lunch with Skrzyński and again saw Beneš. Skrzyński's telegram of 10 October to the Polish Foreign Ministry was optimistic. He reported that the link between eastern and western security was not questioned by anyone and it resulted from the very draft of the Rhine Pact itself (article 6). The French and British foreign ministers told him that the Germans had almost accepted the controversial principles, and the discussion now concerned formulas that would allow the German parliament to accept them. These principles were: first, that the Rhine Pact could neither limit France's rights and obligations under the covenant nor weaken the effectiveness of the Franco-Polish alliance; and second, that war would be completely excluded by arbitration. Skrzyński wrote that Poland could not conduct a "strong arm" policy or "intimidate" Europe; rather, she had to convince all parties of her moderation. He said that Briand's attitude was "clear, straight-forward, and loyal" and that Poland had the full support of Britain. Here he mentioned Chamberlain's declaration that the lack of Britain's guarantee for all frontiers did not mean a lack of interest in the eastern frontiers of Germany and that Britain recognized fully her obligations under article 16 of the covenant. (This was a statement to the press on 9 October.) Skrzyński ended his optimistic report thus: "At Locarno, the Anglo-French-British-Polish front is united: there are no differences of opinion, no suspicions. Let us leave to the Germans the task of creating different appearances; that is not our concern."[56]

It is difficult to determine whether Skrzyński really believed what he wrote or whether his optimistic tone was meant to prevent any moves in Warsaw which might make his position at Locarno more difficult. In any case, he does seem to have been informed by Briand of developments as they took place. On 12 October, Briand also arranged for the Polish minister to meet Stresemann for the first time and introduced them to each other.[57] Dzierżykraj-Morawski reported that the meeting had taken place in a "spirit of compromise."[58] (According to a press report, Briand "sat by and smoked cigarettes.")[59] The result of the meeting was that the Poles and the Czechs began to negotiate their arbitration treaties with the Germans.

Both the Poles and the Germans had their reservations, and Chamberlain tried to help in overcoming them. As he cabled on the afternoon of 12 October: "Monsieur Briand and Monsieur Benes are using all their influence to bring Poland into line."[60] It is most likely that on 12/13 October, Briand and Beneš were working on Skrzyński to make him accept the project of the revised articles 2 and 6 of the Rhine Pact. He might well have resisted these revisions, particularly article 6, since the new version dropped all reference to France's right to fulfill her guarantees of the eastern arbitration treaties. At the afternoon session on 13 October, when Briand asked for time to consult his allies, this meant only Skrzyński. He apparently gave in on that day in return for a separate French treaty with Poland (as with Czechoslovakia). In any case, at 7:55 P.M., Briand wired Paris that the afternoon session had resulted in fixing the terms of the Rhine security pact. He added that to complete ''the system,'' the French were preparing two conventions to be concluded with Poland and Czechoslovakia. These would ''consecrate'' the French right of intervention. He concluded: ''Our freedom of action is fully safeguarded and this is in agreement with our allies.''[61]

Meanwhile, after a last attempt by the German delegation to extract concessions on German disarmament as well as the speedy evacuation of Cologne, Dr. Kempner, Luther's secretary, was sent to Berlin to obtain the German cabinet's assent to the Rhine security pact. On the evening of 14 October, Luther announced the assent of his government. On the same day, the press reported that the issue of French guarantee had been resolved by means of special additional, direct treaties between France, on the one hand, and Poland and Czechoslovakia on the other.[62] No Polish sources seem to have survived to document this phase of Franco-Polish-Czechoslovak negotiations. It is, however, striking that the idea of replacing the French guarantee of the eastern arbitration treaties by separate French treaties with Poland and Czechoslovakia had been suggested by Beneš in a letter to Briand dated 20 September 1925. Since Briand approved this proposal two days later,[63] he may well have been aiming at this solution all along. His demand for German assent to a French guarantee of the eastern arbitration treaties was probably an elaborate maneuver to convince French public opinion that such assent was impossible. Skrzyński had no alternative but to accept the formula—which had been proposed by Beneš and had already been approved by the Germans, the British, and the French.

Thus it was that on 14 October the press gave a festive luncheon for the delegates. The menu, while amusing at the time, now has a ring or irony: ''Boiled eggs of Complete Security, Sauce Communique, Arbitration Salad, and Disarmament Meringue.'' The German delegation's digestion was, however, upset by Chamberlain's speech, in which he declared that the conference was at an end—while the Germans had not yet obtained the benefits that they had counted on, especially the promise of an early evacuation of the Rhineland.[64]

Beneš and Skrzyński entered the conference room on 15 October. This timing was probably due to Skrzyński. Kajetan Dzierżykraj-Morawski came to see Berthelot that morning. Morawski said Skrzyński considered it imperative that the Polish and Czechoslovak representatives join the conference that day. He also reminded Berthelot of Briand's assurance to Skrzyński, immediately after the latter's arrival at Locarno, that Poland was clearly entitled to be a member of the conference and could take her seat immediately. Skrzyński had not taken advantage of this invitation, said Morawski, since he did not wish to create the impression of conducting a policy of prestige; but now, for practical reasons, he could not agree to a further absence. When Fromageot objected, Morawski said that Poland had come to Locarno not merely to regulate her relations with Germany but also to participate in establishing peace in Europe. Furthermore, the Germans were aiming to exclude their treaty with Poland from the treaties to be signed at Locarno, while the Poles saw it as an integral part of these treaties. It was to demonstrate this point that Skrzyński demanded to be present at meetings at which eastern problems would *not* be discussed. Berthelot, who at first expressed reservations, then agreed and went to consult Briand. A few minutes later, Berthelot returned with the news that Briand would ask Chamberlain to invite Skrzyński and Beneš to attend the afternoon session.[65] This produced Chamberlain's invitation to the two ministers. Stresemann agreed, but on condition that a communiqué be issued stating that the participation of the Polish and Czechoslovak ministers was needed in conjunction with the arbitration treaties and that they had been invited by the major participants in the conference.[66] Skrzyński may have hastened this participation by a few hours, but he failed to achieve his goal of creating the impression that Poland and Czechoslovakia were at last being treated as equals.

On the same day, 15 October, there was a conference in Skrzyński's suite at the Grand Palace Hotel. It included the Polish foreign minister, the Polish legal expert Leon Babiński, Gaus, Fromageot, Hurst, Morawski, and Titus Komarnicki (director of the League of Nations Section of the Polish Foreign Ministry). The conference was to resolve three controversial points in the Polish-German negotiations: the preamble, article 1, and paragraph 2 of article 22 of the Polish draft of the treaty. Gaus objected to article 1, which stated that the contracting parties agreed not to resort to war except in the case of disputed facts concerning acts of aggression or in case of action that was in accordance with the League Covenant. He proposed the replacing of this article by a preamble, because German opinion could not accept such a total prohibition of war. He also opposed paragraph 2 of article 22 of the Polish draft, which stated that existing treaties could not be changed except by mutual consent. Gaus declared that he did not see the need for this kind of clause, since it obviously constituted one of the key principles of international law.[67] The Poles had to give in, and the final treaty omitted their desiderata. It is true that the preambles to both the German-Polish and German-

Czechoslovak treaties mentioned mutual agreement on the point that "the rights of a state cannot be modified without its consent," but as we shall see later, Stresemann was to describe the preambles as "collections of platitudes."

We should note that the German arbitration treaties with Poland and Czechoslovakia excluded territorial questions and were mainly concerned with conciliation procedures for other types of disputes. Each treaty specified that a permanent conciliation commission was to be set up; only when the parties failed to reach agreement were they to refer the disputes to arbitration, either by the Permanent Court of International Justice at The Hague or by an arbitration tribunal according to the conditions laid down by The Hague Convention of 1907. The treaties were initialed by Stresemann and Skrzyński and by Stresemann and Beneš, respectively, on the same day as the other Locarno Treaties—that is, on 16 October 1925.[68] It was arranged that this event coincide with Chamberlain's sixty-second birthday.

As agreed, France concluded identical treaties of mutual guarantee with her allies, Poland and Czechoslovakia. Each treaty contained a preamble and four articles. Article 1 stated that if either of the two contracting parties should suffer a failure of the undertakings arrived at between it and Germany, the other party, acting in application of article 16 of the League Covenant, would undertake to lend the first party immediate aid and assistance, provided that such failure was accompanied by an unprovoked recourse to arms. If the League Council failed to have its report accepted by all its members—exclusive of the representatives of the parties in dispute—and if either France or Poland were attacked without provocation, then France, or reciprocally Poland or Czechoslovakia, would immediately lend the other party aid and assistance by the application of article 15, paragraph 7, of the covenant. Article 2 stated that nothing in the present treaty diminished the rights and obligations of the contracting parties as members of the League of Nations, nor could it be interpreted as restricting the duty of the league to take action appropriate to the efficient safeguarding of world peace. Article 3 stated that the treaty would be registered with the League of Nations in conformity with the covenant. Article 4 stipulated that the treaty would be ratified; the ratifications would be deposited at Geneva with the League of Nations at the same time as the ratifications of the treaties concluded the same day between Germany, Belgium, France, Great Britain, and Italy and the treaty concluded by Germany and Poland (and Czechoslovakia). The Franco-Polish and Franco-Czechoslovak treaties would enter into and stay in force under the same conditions as the other treaties. The treaties were initialed by Briand and Skrzyński and by Briand and Beneš, respectively, on 16 October 1925.[69]

The fact that the Locarno Treaties made a distinction between the security of Germany's western neighbors, on the one hand, and those in the south and the east, on the other, was clear from the outset. It was, in fact, the Italian legal expert Massimo Pilotti who coined the term "first and second class frontiers."[70] However, while Italy's frontiers had not been guaranteed, the country that was most immediately affected by the discrimination was Poland, for she was the prime target of German revisionism and its accompanying propaganda. It was too much to claim, as Stresemann did in his report to the German cabinet on 19 October, that the Franco-Polish treaty of guarantee had invalidated the alliance between the two states,[71] but it was clear that the alliance had been weakened. Chamberlain told the British cabinet that France had "revised" her alliances with Poland and Czechoslovakia and had reduced her existing obligations.[72] Jules Laroche—who would soon be appointed ambassador to Poland (1926–35)—thought that the new treaty was "more imperative" than the alliance of 1921; the latter had only spoken of "concerting action," while the 1925 treaty spoke of "immediate aid." However, he admitted that the Locarno Treaty was more restrictive, since it was dependent on the League Covenant and covered only the case of direct German aggression. Léon Noël, who was to succeed Laroche as ambassador to Poland (1935–39), wrote in his reminiscences that the treaty of mutual guarantee was designed to make it easier for Poland to accept the political and juridical discrimination that Locarno had created between the eastern and western frontiers of Germany.[73]

Polish reactions to the Locarno Treaties were mixed but generally negative. Skrzyński, of course, tried to be optimistic. He claimed that the idea of peace had achieved a great victory, while the Franco-Polish alliance had been strengthened. He also claimed that Anglo-Polish relations had grown closer. Finally, he argued that the preamble of the German-Polish arbitration treaty clearly recognized the integrity of existing treaties. He said that he had left Locarno convinced that there was no danger of territorial revision.[74]

While the Polish cabinet accepted this evaluation, the same could not be said of public opinion. Although the National Democratic and Socialist press generally shared Skrzyński's point of view, others warned that a new partition of Poland was in the offing. There were attacks from both the Left and the Right in the Sejm. Stanisław Stroński, of the Christian National Club, said that while he and his colleagues appreciated Skrzyński's work, they differed from him in their evaluation of the treaties. They believed that the Franco-Polish alliance had been weakened, and they viewed as ominous the differentiation between the security of the eastern and the western frontiers of Germany. Marshal Piłsudski—who was then out of office, having resigned all of his posts in 1923—was also very critical of the Locarno Treaties. He believed that the balance between Eastern and Western Europe had been upset and should be restored. August Zaleski—who was then Polish minister in Rome and was to be foreign minister from 1926 to 1932—was particularly critical of Skrzyński. Zaleski wrote in his memoirs that Skrzyński always wanted everyone to like him, so he did not want to anger Chamberlain and Briand. Therefore he signed the Locarno Treaties and presented them as a victory for Polish diplomacy.[75]

While the legal adviser to the Polish Foreign Ministry, Leon Babiński, gave an optimistic analysis of French obligations to Poland under the Mutual Assistance Treaty, the evaluation of the Polish General Staff was much closer to the truth. Their observations were communicated to the Polish ambassador in Paris in February 1926.[76] Noting the accepted interpretation of the key articles of the League Covenant on which the Franco-Polish guarantee treaty was based—namely, article 16 and article 15, paragraph 7—the authors stripped them down to naked reality. According to article 16, the League Council had to pass a unanimous resolution naming the aggressor; at this point, economic-financial sanctions could be applied. Next, the council would issue directives on military sanctions; only then could the so-called immediate French intervention take place. (Here the memorandum cited Beneš's interpretation, given at the League session of 24 September 1924.) If the League Council's report were not accepted unanimously, then France could go to Poland's aid as per article 15, paragraph 7, of the League Covenant. But it was also noted that, according to article 12 of the League Covenant, if a dispute entailing the risk of war were submitted by both parties to arbitration or inquiry by the League Council, the parties would agree not to resort to war until three months after the award by arbitration or a report by the council. Thus, there could be a three month delay after which, according to article 15, Germany was entitled to wage a ''legal'' war against Poland in order to obtain her demands. Since French intervention depended on the occurrence of ''unprovoked'' German aggression against Poland, Germany was free to decide the time and form of exercising her right of ''legal'' war. Therefore, the first clash might not occur immediately after the expiry of three months, and when it did, it could take the form of diversionary incidents. In such a case, the incidents would once again come under article 16—that is, the League Council would report on the aggressor, and only after that could French aid be implemented as per the guarantee treaty. Furthermore, the authors of the memorandum foresaw the possibility that German demands for the return of the Corridor might find support from some members of the council, including Britain, who would try to find a compromise solution. French opinion would then be under great pressure to agree to such a solution—or else face the danger of Germany's ''legal'' war on Poland and its consequences.

The memorandum concluded that in comparison with the Franco-Polish treaty of 1921, the Locarno Treaty forced both parties to make their actions dependent on a third factor: the League of Nations, or the guarantee of the

Rhine Pact. This was so because, except for a quite obvious case of German aggression (and this was thought to be an absurdity), the only immediate French action possible—that of sending troops into the Demilitarized Zone of the Rhineland and thus threatening the Ruhr—could only take place with international sanction. This could cause a delay in effective French action or, at least, would not facilitate it, as per the Franco-Polish Military Convention of 1921. Therefore, Polish efforts had to be directed at eliminating the harmful consequences of this limitation by obtaining the confirmation and elaboration of the Military Convention. The Locarno Treaty merely provided the framework; the content had to be the Military Convention, appropriately adjusted to the new conditions.[77]

It is clear that Stresemann had achieved his major objectives. He had separated the security problems of Eastern and Western Europe and had weakened the Franco-Polish alliance. He obtained an interpretation of article 16 that satisfied both German and Russian wishes. He had also prevented the establishment of permanent league supervision over German disarmament. It is true that he failed to obtain the evacuation of Mainz and Coblenz, but he secured the promise that Cologne would soon be evacuated; this was done in January 1926. The evacuation of Cologne was, in fact, an Anglo-French bribe for the German signing of the Rhine Pact.[78] He also obtained a modification of the Allied occupation regime in the remaining towns.

As far as Germany's eastern borders were concerned, Stresemann constantly emphasized the fact that Locarno gave Germany the opportunity of recovering the territories she had lost to Poland. In his letter to the DNVP leader Walther von Keudell, Stresemann called Locarno an "armistice" which offered the possibility of recovering German territory in the east.[79] In his famous letter to the Prussian crown prince, he outlined the tasks that he foresaw for German foreign policy after Germany's entry into the league: namely, the revision of reparations; the protection of Germans who were living outside the Reich; the "correction" of the eastern frontier—that is, the return of Danzig and the Corridor to Germany; a border "correction" in Upper Silesia; and, finally, the union of Germany and Austria.[80] However, the most interesting exposition of Stresemann's views on the Locarno Treaties is to be found in his speech of 14 December 1925 to the Arbeitsgemeinschaft der deutscher Landsmannschaften in Gross-Berlin.

On this occasion, Stresemann told his audience that he had not made any moral renunciations at Locarno, such as the right to make war, since it would be lunacy for Germany to toy with the idea of a war with France. So, in return for giving up what he did not possess—the possibility of making war on France—he had obtained many concessions for Germany.[81] The most significant passage concerning Poland is that in which he explained his understanding of the phrase in the preambles to the German-Polish and German-Czechoslovak treaties, which stated that both sides agreed that "the rights of a state cannot be modified save with its consent." He took care to explain this matter, since some German newspapers had claimed that it implied Germany's recognition of her frontier with Poland. As Stresemann put it:

> When I read this phrase, since I am a layman in matters of international law, I asked Mr. Gaus what it meant. He then gave me an explanation which I have since heard from all sides, and which was declared to be correct by the conference of teachers of international law now in progress here. That is, that never in world history, not for thousands of years, has a change of frontiers taken place without the assent of the state in question, and this no matter how bad the treaties were, whether you take the treaties with Carthage after the Second Punic War or the Treaty of Versailles. It has always been the case that the defeated party must recognize the treaty as law, and since we rejected the preambles of Messrs. Beneš and Skrzyński, and since, unfortunately, a treaty has to have a preamble, we put in a collection of platitudes. For when you read this phrase, you will see that in all decisions on legal questions the law that prevails has jurisdiction. And what is the prevailing law? Briand said, as he read the preamble: "One could also put in here that the majority is as a rule greater than the minority." And this is the meaning of the phrase "the rights of either contracting party can only be changed with its consent."[82]

It is ironic that in the House of Commons debate of 18 November 1925 on the Locarno Treaties, Chamberlain claimed that they had produced a détente on the eastern frontier of Germany.[83] He spoke in good faith, but the perspectives for Poland were dismal. In fact, Stresemann was right when he said that Poland was the "Moor who had done his duty" and whose usefulness was over. France did not need Poland any more, and the latter was in a very difficult position. He wondered if the time had not come to "pull off her top clothes." However, he thought that Germany would first have to find friends or alliances or economic associations.[84]

The Locarno Treaties were the result of cooperation between Austen Chamberlain, Aristide Briand, and Gustav Stresemann, aided by Edouard Beneš. Poland and Czechoslovakia might have been able to obtain better guarantees for their security against Germany if they had stood together. But Beneš believed that his country was not threatened. It was he who suggested to Briand the solution of replacing the French guarantee of the eastern arbitration treaties by separate mutual-assistance treaties between France and her eastern allies. But, as the analysis by the Polish General Staff showed, these mutual-assistance treaties were based on articles 15 and 16 of the League Covenant. These articles, in turn, left plenty of room for delaying immediate French aid, which could only take the form of military entry into the Demilitarized Zone of the Rhineland, thus threatening the Ruhr. But such French action was doubtful under any circumstances other than those of flagrant German aggression, since it would depend on international sanction. This really meant British consent, and the British government was not ready to come to the aid of France if she attacked Germany to support Poland and was, in turn, attacked by Germany.

Chamberlain, Briand, and Stresemann each received the Nobel Peace Prize, but the peace they achieved was illusory. It depended on Germany's acceptance of the slow, peaceful, and "legal" revision of her eastern frontiers, which French and British statesmen believed to be inevitable in the course of time. This belief was originally a British one but was accepted by Briand, who thus gave up the original French concept of a strong Poland as the guarantor of France's security.

With Locarno, French policy came back full circle to 1919. As President Gaston Doumergue told Austen Chamberlain in March 1925, there probably would have been no Franco-Polish alliance if the Anglo-American pact had materialized in 1919.[85] Although the Rhine Pact fell far short of a Franco-British alliance, from the French point of view it was much more valuable than the alliances with Poland and Czechoslovakia, which were now seen as more of a burden than a guarantee of security. When Piłsudski returned to power in May 1926, he set himself the goal of "reestablishing the balance between Eastern and Western Europe."[86] However, all that he was able to achieve was a temporary Polish balance between Germany and Soviet Russia, based on the Polish-Soviet Nonaggression Pact of 1932 and the Polish-German Declaration of Nonaggression of 1934.

Locarno disguised the weakening of France's commitment to her eastern allies under the verbiage of articles 15 and 16 of the League Covenant. The reality behind the treaties was that Briand and Berthelot believed in the necessity of a French political and economic rapprochement with Germany. They also believed that Great Britain would never undertake any commitments to support Poland, Czechoslovakia, or any other East European state against aggression. In view of the above, it was easy for France to follow Britain's lead and assume that, with time, Germany would peacefully achieve some of her revisionist aims at Poland's expense and that such revisions would not threaten western security. It was also assumed that Poland would agree to give up the northern part of the Polish Corridor and her part of Upper Silesia and acquiesce in the return of Danzig to the Reich. Both assumptions were questioned by some astute observers at the time, but unfortunately, they were to persist into another era when the balance of power shifted in favor of Hitler's Germany. They then provided the justification for a western policy that was to bear bitter fruit in 1938/39.

11

Concluding Thoughts

Polish foreign policy in the period 1919 through 1925 has often been described as imperialistic, or at least romantic. No country can claim an unblemished record in either foreign or domestic policy, and Poland had her share of sins in both. But by the same token, simplistic stereotypes cannot explain complex problems. Reborn Poland emerged from a long period of foreign domination and oppression, particularly by the Germans and the Russians. It is not surprising, therefore, that Polish governments and public opinion rejected the idea—that was so frequently advanced in the west—of establishing good relations with at least one great neighbor, Germany, at the price of some territorial concessions. In the first place, however, such concessions would have made Poland a satellite of Germany. In the second place, Poland's very existence, whatever her boundaries, was resented by both of her powerful neighbors. She was thus compelled to seek support in the west, that is, in France.

However, in 1924/25, French statesmen came to believe that their East European allies did not offer adequate security against Germany. For this they looked to Britain. But Britain was opposed to any Continental commitments and, in particular, to commitments in Eastern Europe. Therefore, French statesmen soon came to look on their East European allies as more of a burden than a guarantee of security. They had, in any case, concluded their alliances with Poland and Czechoslovakia because the Anglo-American guarantee of 1919 had fallen through, and a non-Bolshevik Russia had failed to emerge from the civil war. In this sense, it was natural for France to agree with British policy goals and to sign the Rhine Pact at Locarno, which gave at least a partial guarantee to her frontier with Germany. At the same time, France's treaties of mutual assistance with Poland and Czechoslovakia gave them only a theoretical security, while undermining the earlier alliance treaties signed in 1921 and 1924 respectively.

The most logical instrument for strengthening these two countries would have been an alliance, which was also the aim of French policy. However, this was most unlikely, if not impossible, at the time. The Poles deeply resented the Czechoslovak seizure of western Teschen in 1919 and Beneš's sleight of hand in securing its award by the Conference of Ambassadors in 1920. Still, though Piłsudski had no faith in Czechoslovakia's survival, Skirmunt and Skrzyński did work for close cooperation with that country. But Masaryk and Beneš were not interested. They opposed western recognition of the Polish-Soviet frontier, supported West Ukrainian exiles, and looked on Russia as a future ally. At the same time, Masaryk and Beneš did not feel threatened by Germany, and they favored a revision of the Polish-German frontier. But when all is said and done, a Polish-Czechoslovak alliance would not, by itself, have sufficed to secure the two countries against German aggression. It could only have formed the eastern wing of a viable balance of power—provided that France and Britain were willing to form the western wing. This was also the key to overcoming mutual Polish-Czechoslovak distrust and resentment. Unfortunately, this key to security for the whole of Europe was missing—until it was too late to use it.

Poland's national minorities were a destabilizing factor, but they did not play a significant role in her foreign policy. Poland was not a multinational state like Czechoslovakia and Yugoslavia; the dominant Polish nationality constituted 60 percent of the population in the early 1920s, and the minorities, 40 percent. In the former Russian-Empire, now the Soviet Union, the dominant Russian nation constituted then and constitutes now only 50 percent of the population. Somehow, this was not perceived to be a Soviet weakness by western observers who perceived Poland's national makeup to be the source of her weakness.

Of Poland's national minorities, only the Ukrainians of East Galicia were a serious problem in the period 1919 to 1923. This was due less to their national aspirations than to Britain's refusal to recognize Polish sovereignty over the region until March 1923. While it is easy to understand and sympathize with the Ukrainians, it is difficult to see how they could have attained their goals in the interwar period, for majority Polish opinion opposed even territorial autonomy, let alone independence. There is no doubt that many western observers sincerely supported the Ukrainian cause on the grounds of self-determination, but its chief spokesman, Lloyd George, used it for his own political ends. In any case, it ill behooved him to accuse Poland of imperialism and of violating self-determination, when he imposed a vintage imperialist peace on the Ottoman Empire at the Treaty of Sèvres and supported outrageous Greek territorial claims against Turkey.

Given the problems and circumstances of the time, Polish statesmen achieved what was possible. They obtained an alliance with France, but they failed to establish close relations with Czechoslovakia or Lithuania. Their failure to secure lasting western commitments stemmed less from their errors of judgment than from irreconcilable differences of perception. It is always true that "all groups in society, including the government, work within a climate of opinion based on the dominant assumptions of a particular historical period." These assumptions, of course, circumscribe the range of policy options that are seriously considered by officials and the public.[1]

It so happened that the dominant western assumptions about Germany and Russia differed radically from those of the Poles. The Poles believed that German expansion at their expense would ultimately lead to German domination over Eastern and then Western Europe, and they held the same view regarding Russian expansion. However, western statesmen measured Germany and Russia with a yardstick that reflected their own experience, perceived interests, hopes, and beliefs. They wished to restore the old "Concert of Europe," that is, cooperation between the Great Powers based on mutual agreement as to their particular spheres of influence. Germany was expected, sooner or later, to return to the status of a Great Power, and the British, in particular, sav· Eastern Europe as Germany's sphere of influence. Since Germany refused to recognize her losses to Poland, the Polish-German frontier was seen as a danger to peace and therefore in need of revision. This view was bolstered by the belief that self-determination justified Germany's claims, although, in fact, this only applied to Danzig, which was a free city, outside of Poland's borders. The Polish-Soviet frontier was generally viewed as being unfair to the Russians and as being subject to revision, because Soviet Russia was a Great Power that would not rest until the frontier was changed. Many western observers believed that the Russian claims were based on self-determination, although, in fact, ethnic Russians in Poland's eastern territories numbered barely one hundred thousand. These attitudes and beliefs contributed to western sympathy for German claims up to 1939 and to sympathy with Russian claims after 1941. It is not surprising that World War II began with the German attack on Poland, while the Cold War has its roots in the brutal imposition of Soviet domination on that country in 1944/45.

Let us hope that this book will lead to a better understanding of Poland's foreign-policy problems and goals in the years 1919 through 1925 and, by extension, of Eastern Europe as a whole. Finally, let us hope that western statesmen and public opinion will cease to view the region as a natural sphere of influence for either Germany or Russia. This view has led to disastrous consequences, not only for the peoples of Eastern Europe, but also for Europe as a whole.

Notes

PREFACE

1. Titus Komarnicki, *Rebirth of the Polish Republic: A Study in the Diplomatic History of Europe, 1914–1920* (London, Melbourne, Toronto, 1957).

2. Jan Szembek, *Diariusz i teki Jana Szembeka, 1935–1945,* vols. 1–4 (London, 1964–69); vols. 1–3 edited by Tytus Komarnicki; vol. 4 edited by Jan Zarański.

3. Piotr S. Wandycz, *Soviet-Polish Relations, 1917–1921* (Cambridge, Mass., 1969), and *France and Her Eastern Allies, 1919–1925: French-Czechoslovak-Polish Relations from the Paris Peace Conference to Locarno* (Minneapolis, Minn., 1962).

4. Piotr Łossowski, *Stosunki polsko-litewskie w latach 1918–1920* (Warsaw, 1966).

5. Zofia Zaks, ''Aspekty międzynarodowe sprawy Galicji Wschodniej w latach 1918–1923'' (Ph.D. diss., University of Warsaw, 1963), and see Bibliography.

6. Maria Nowak-Kiełbikowa, *Polska-Wielka Brytania w latach 1918–1923* (Warsaw, 1975).

7. Wiesław Balcerak, *Polityka zagraniczna Polski w dobie Locarna* (Wrocław, etc., 1967).

8. Georges[-Henri] Soutou, ''Les Mines de Silésie et la rivalité franco-allemande, 1920–1923: Arme économique ou bonne affaire?'' *Relations internationales,* no. 1 (see Bibliography).

9. Denise Artaud, *La Question des dettes interalliées et la reconstruction de l'Europe (1917–1929)* (see Bibliography).

10. Eleanor Breuning, ''German Foreign Policy between East and West, 1921–1926'' (D.Phil. diss., Oxford, 1965).

11. Ann Orde, *Great Britain and International Security, 1920–1926* (London, 1978).

12. Sir James W. Headlam-Morley, *A Memoir of the Paris Peace Conference, 1919,* ed. Agnes Headlam-Morley, Russell Bryant, and Anna M. Cienciala (London, 1972).

INTRODUCTION

1. By 1916, 1.9 million Poles were serving in the armies of the Partitioning Powers. This included 4.0 percent of the population of Russian Poland; 14.8 percent of

Prussian Poland; and 16.3 percent of Austrian Poland, or Galicia. Military casualties accounted for about 460,000 of the losses; see Norman Davies, *God's Playground: A History of Poland in Two Volumes,* vol. 2: *1795 to the Present* (New York, 1982), p. 382.

2. See Piotr S. Wandycz, *The United States and Poland* (Cambridge, Mass., and London, 1980), pp. 171–72.

3. Stephen A. Schuker, *The End of French Predominance in Europe: The Financial Crisis of 1924 and the Adoption of the Dawes Plan* (Chapel Hill, N.C., 1976), p. 177.

4. Wandycz, *United States and Poland,* pp. 173–74; Norman Davies gives a somewhat different breakdown in *God's Playground,* 2:406.

5. Estimates for 1921 arrived at by the Polish economic historians Z. Landau and J. Tomaszewski by correcting official census figures; see Wandycz, *United States and Poland,* p. 173. Davies gives the 1931 census figures in *God's Playground,* 2:406.

6. See Victor S. Mamatey and Radomir Luza, eds., *A History of the Czechoslovak Republic, 1918–1948* (Princeton, N.J., 1973).

7. For a comparison of the two leaders see Hans J. Roos, ''Józef Piłsudski und Charles de Gaulle,'' *Vierteljahrshefte für Zeitsgeschichte* 8 (1960): 257–67.

8. Henry Kissinger, *White House Years* (Boston and Toronto, 1979), p. 1063.

9. For a short survey of the history of the Jews in Poland until 1939 see Norman Davies, *God's Playground,* vol. 2, chap. 9; for a detailed history up to 1800 see Bernard D. Weinryb, *The Jews of Poland: A Social and Economic History of the Jewish Community in Poland from 1100 to 1800* (Philadelphia, 1973). For the results of Sir Stuart Samuel's mission to Poland see his report of 1 July 1920, Command Papers (hereafter cited as Cmd.), no. 674, vol. 51, p. 1121. Norman Davies analyzes the reasons for British charges of anti-Semitism in Poland in ''Great Britain and the Polish Jews, 1918–1921,'' *Journal of Contemporary History* 8, no. 2 (1973): 119–42.

10. Cited by Wandycz, *United States and Poland,* p. 177; for more virulent views see Davies, *God's Playground,* 2:393.

11. See *Documents on British Foreign Policy, 1919–1939* (herefter cited as *DBFP*), 1st ser., vol. 23: *Poland and the Baltic States, 1921–23,* ed. W. N. Medlicott and Douglas Dakin, assisted by Gillian Bennett (London, 1981), p. xii.

12. Norman Davies, *God's Playground,* 2:492.

13. John D. Gregory, *On the Edge of Diplomacy: Rambles and Reflections, 1902–1928* (London, 1928), p. 184.

14. James W. Headlam-Morley, ''The History of British Policy and the Geneva Protocol,'' 12 February 1925, Public Record Office, London, Foreign Office Papers (hereafter cited as FO), 371/11064/9/W1252/98, cited extensively in chap. 9 below.

15. On the Prussian Colonisation Commission see Witold Jakóbczyk, *Pruska Komisja Osadnicza, 1886–1919* (Poznań, 1976) and ''The First Decade of the Prussian Settlement Commission's Activities (1886–1897),'' *Polish Review* 17, no. 1 (1972): 3–13; see also William W. Hagen, *Germans, Poles, and Jews: The Nationality Conflict in the Prussian East, 1772–1914* (Chicago and London, 1980), passim. According to article 91 of the Versailles Treaty, Poles in Germany and Germans in Poland could opt for the citizenship and residence of their choice. However, many Germans who opted for German citizenship and residence failed to understand that this disbarred them from permanent residence in Poland. Furthermore, the same article stipulated that German nationals who habitually resided in Poland could become Polish citizens provided they were domiciled there before 1 January 1908. However, the Minority Treaty stated that all Germans and other nationals who habitually resided in Poland, and were resident there *when the Treaty came into force,* could become Polish citizens (article 3). Also, Polish citizenship could be assumed by all persons born on Polish territory of parents who

habitually resided there, even if at the time the treaty came into force they were not habitually resident there (article 4). The Polish authorities chose to regard article 91 of the Versailles Treaty as binding, in order to reduce the number of Germans in Poland, while the German government insisted on the Minority Treaty in order to keep as many Germans in Poland as possible; hence many Polish-German disputes ensued. See Harald von Riekhoff, *German-Polish Relations, 1918–1933* (Baltimore, Md., and London, 1971), chap. 3 passim.

    16. See Wandycz, *Soviet-Polish Relations,* p. 45.

    17. See Anna M. Cienciala, "The Significance of the Declaration of Non-Aggression of January 26, 1934, in Polish-German and International Relations: A Reappraisal," *East European Quarterly* 1, no. 1 (1967): 1–30.

    18. Wandycz, *Soviet-Polish Relations,* p. 213.

CHAPTER 1
THE FRANCO-POLISH ALLIANCE AND POLAND IN FRANCO-BRITISH RELATIONS, 1920–22

    1. For Pierre Jacquin de Margerie's memoranda and views see Kalervo Hovi, *Cordon Sanitaire or Barriere de l'Est? The Emergence of the New French Eastern European Alliance Policy, 1917–1919* (Turku, 1975), pp. 72–73; for French policy regarding Poland from 1914 to 1917 see ibid., relevant sections; for de Margerie's life, career, and the diplomatic scene see Bernard Auffray, *Pierre de Margerie (1861–1942) et la vie diplomatique de son temps* (Paris, 1976), where some correspondence on Poland is cited on pp. 344–46, but not the memoranda. Piotr S. Wandycz has written a pioneering study of French relations with Poland and Czechoslovakia in *France and Her Eastern Allies, 1919–1924,* while Józef Kukułka wrote a detailed study for the years 1919–22 in *Francja a Polska po traktacie wersalskim (1919–1922)* (Warsaw, 1970). Jan Ciałowicz wrote an important study of the Franco-Polish alliance, edited by Marian Zgórniak: *Polsko-francuski sojusz wojskowy, 1921–1939* (Warsaw, 1970). However, French diplomatic documents for the period 1919–29 were closed until 1970. Two excellent studies of Franco-German relations and French policy up to 1924/25 are Jacques Bariéty, *Les Relations franco-allemandes après la Première Guerre mondiale, 10 novembre 1918–10 janvier 1925* (Paris, 1977), and Walter A. McDougall, *France's Rhineland Diplomacy, 1914–1924: The Last Bid for a Balance of Power in Europe* (Princeton, N.J., 1978). Both reflect primary French absorption with the issues of German reparations and the Rhineland.

    2. J. B. Barbier wrote about Poland at this time: "It would certainly be no exaggeration to say that in 1924, 95 per cent of the Poles were instinctively and almost blindly turned toward us, and that France inspired them with a sort of religious faith." J. B. Barbier, *Un frac de Nessus* (Rome, 1951), pp. 238–39 (trans. A. C.).

    3. Jacques Bainville, *La Russie et la barrière de l'Est* (Paris, 1937).

    4. See Hovi, *Cordon Sanitaire,* passim, and Janusz Pajewski, *Wokół sprawy polskiej, Paryż-Lozanna-Londyn, 1914–1918* (Poznań, 1970), passim; also Komarnicki, *Rebirth,* pp. 51–56 and passim.

    5. Bainville, *Russie,* p. 50. An example of current French views on Russia is to be found in Émile Haumant, *Le Problème de l'unité russe* (Paris, 1922). He hoped that the future great Russia would be neither autocratic nor centralized and that it would

conclude an honest agreement with Poland. For this, he put his trust in the "great Russian heart," ibid., pp. 6, 86, 127–28.

6. This was noted by Francesco Tommasini, the Italian minister to Poland from 1919 to 1923, in his book *La Risurrezione della Polonia* (Milan, 1925), pp. 275–76.

7. For the Teschen dispute see chap. 6 below.

8. For the Danzig question see chap. 4 below; for eastern questions see chaps. 5–8 below.

9. See George Bernard Noble, *Policies and Opinions at Paris, 1919: Wilsonian Diplomacy, the Versailles Peace, and French Public Opinion* (New York, 1935), pp. 389–93, 410.

10. Cited in Noble, *Policies and Opinions,* p. 357.

11. See Tommasini, *Risurrezione,* p. 282; Wandycz, *France,* p. 220, and "French Diplomats in Poland 1919–1926," *Journal of Central European Affairs* 23, no. 4 (January 1964): 443–45.

12. See Komarnicki, *Rebirth,* p. 409.

13. Cited in L. Litwiński, "Nafta małopolska i jej kulisy," *Kultura,* no. 11 (Paris, 1960); on East Galician oil in the diplomacy of 1918–23 see Zofia Zaks, "Walka dyplomatyczna o naftę wschodniogalicyjską, 1918–1923," *Z dziejów stosunków polsko-radzieckich: Studia i materiały* 4 (Warsaw, 1969): 37–60.

14. See discussion of Franco-Polish economic agreements later in this chapter and chap. 3 below.

15. For the economic and political background of French credits to Poland see Zbigniew Landau, "Gospodarcze i polityczne tło kredytów francuskich dla Polski w okresie 1921–1923," *Sprawy międzynarodowe,* nos. 7–8 (Warsaw, 1959), also Kukułka, *Francja,* p. 335.

16. See Maurice Pernot, *L'Épreuve de la Pologne* (Paris, 1921), p. 121.

17. Ferdynand Zweig, *Poland between Two Wars: A Critical Study of Social and Economic Changes* (London, 1944), p. 25.

18. Józef Piłsudski, *Pisma Zbiorowe,* vol. 5 (Warsaw, 1937), pp. 104–6 (trans. A. C.).

19. See Zbigniew Landau, "O kilku spornych zagadnieniach stosunków polsko-amerykańskich w latach 1918–1920," *Kwartalnik historyczny* 65, no. 4 (1958): 1093–1109, at 1097. For a detailed Polish estimate of February 1921 see Kukułka, *Francja,* p. 373. For French estimates, 2 February 1921, see Archives diplomatiques, Ministère des affaires étrangères, série Europe, 1918–1929, Pologne, vol. 131, p. 66 (hereafter cited as AD/MAE).

20. Vladimir I. Lenin, *Sochineniia,* vol. 25 (Moscow, 1935), p. 398.

21. See Komarnicki, *Rebirth,* pt. 2, chap. 5; also, Nowak-Kiełbikowa, *Polska-Wielka Brytania,* chap. 2 passim.

22. *DBFP,* 1st ser., vol. 6, no. 189.

23. Ibid., no. 243.

24. General Carton de Wiart, then head of the British Military Mission in Poland, wrote to Sir Walford Selby in July 1919: "Our one chance against the Germans in Russia was to use the Poles and Poland as our instrument for countering German commercial penetration" (see *DBFP,* 1st ser., vol. 6, no. 86). This suggestion was made again by Foreign Minister Aleksander Skrzyński in his conversation of 20 October 1919 with Sir Horace Rumbold, draft, Rumbold to Curzon, 20 October 1919, no. 371, FO, 668/1, f. 73. We should note that many Polish engineers and businessmen had worked in Russia before 1914.

25. Weygand wrote that while Foch believed that French aid to Poland was a clear obligation in view of the latter's loyalty to France and honorable Polish service under the French flag, he feared lest French leaders go too fast (*Mémoires*, vol. 2: *Mirages et réalité*, [Paris, 1957], p. 73).

26. Gen. Kazimierz Sosnkowski to Sapieha, 1 August 1921, cited in Landau, "Gospodarcze tło," p. 47 (see n. 15 above).

27. See Wandycz, *France*, p. 213.

28. For Sapieha's account of his talks with Panafieu see Ciałowicz, *Polsko-francuski sojusz*, p. 33; for the outline of the Polish draft military convention, based on the accounts of Gen. Władysław Sikorski and Capt. L. H. Morstin see ibid., p. 37. Niessel reported to Foch, on 1 January 1921, that according to secret and personal instructions (probably from Foch, A. C.), he was very reserved in a conversation with Gen. Kazimierz Sosnkowski, the minister of war, on 31 December 1920. Niessel told him that a military agreement was not feasible unless France simultaneously obtained "economic satisfactions" to which she had a right. Also, she should have an unquestioned influence in the Polish army as a guarantee of its "solidity." General Niessel to Marshal Foch, 1 January 1921, AD/MAE, Pologne, Z 695-9(39), p. 123.

29. Rumbold to Curzon, 14 September 1920, *DBFP*, 1st ser., vol. 11, no. 530.

30. *Le Journal de Pologne*, a French newspaper published in Warsaw, expressly rejected this accusation on 29 November 1920.

31. However, the National Democratic press expressed support for the alliance, which was also their goal. See Kukułka, *Francja*, p. 361.

32. Piłsudski, *Pisma*, 5:183 (trans. A. C.); see also Wandycz, *France*, pp. 213–14.

33. The Foreign Ministry's instruction of 2 January 1921 is in the archives of the former Polish embassy in London, now in the Polish Institute and Sikorski Museum (hereafter cited as APEL/PISM), cyphers; see also Kukułka, *Francja*, p. 358.

34. Cited in Jules Laroche, *La Pologne de Pilsudski: Souvenirs d'une ambassade, 1926–1935* (Paris, 1953), p. 13.

35. See Wandycz, *France*, p. 214.

36. Cited by Georges Suarez, *Briand: Sa vie—son oeuvre, avec son journal et des nombreux documents inédits*, vol. 5 (Paris, 1952), p. 107.

37. *Times* (London), 8 January 1921.

38. Władysław Baranowski, *Rozmowy z Piłsudskim, 1916–1931* (Warsaw, 1938), pp. 141–47, summarized in Wacław Jędrzejewicz, ed., *Kronika życia Józefa Piłsudskiego, 1867–1935*, vol. 2 (London, 1977), p. 13 (trans. A. C.).

39. Tommasini, *Risurrezione*, p. 288.

40. *DBFP*, 1st ser., vol. 11, no. 679, pp. 703–4.

41. *Times* (London), 18 February 1921.

42. Piłsudski, *Pisma*, 5:183–84.

43. Jędrzejewicz, *Kronika*, 2:17, 19 (trans. A. C.).

44. Marshal Foch to Premier, Foreign Minister, 3 February 1921, AD/MAE, Pologne, Z 698-1 (Jan. 1921–March 1921), IX, 211 Fa; also unsigned background paper on Polish affairs dated 4 February 1921, Fonds Millerand, 56:3–16.

45. Weygand, *Mémoires*, 2:179–80; Kukułka, *Francja*, pp. 368–69; text of the proposed communique is in AD/MAE, Pologne, 131:40.

46. Baranowski, *Rozmowy*, pp. 157–61; Jędrzejewicz, *Kronika*, 2:18–19 (trans. A. C.).

47. Colonel Joseph Beck, *Dernier rapport: Politique polonaise, 1926–1939* (Neufchâtel, 1951), p. 58 (trans. A. C.).

48. Charles Hardinge, Lord of Penshurst, *Old Diplomacy: The Reminiscences of Lord Hardinge of Penshurst* (London, 1947), p. 256.

49. See Wandycz, *France,* app. 1 (French text), p. 393.

50. Weygand, *Mémoires,* 2:181; for text of Foch memorandum of 11 February 1921 see AD/MAE, Pologne, 131:145.

51. The original is in "Conversation entre le Prince Sapieha et Monsieur Berthelot," 10 February 1921, ibid., pp. 122–40, also Fonds Millerand, 56:34–52; partly cited in Kukułka, *Francja,* pp. 373–74, from copy given by Berthelot to the Czechoslovak minister in Paris, Štefan Osuský; for Sapieha's objections see 18 February, Fonds Millerand, 56:58–61, and Pologne, 131:173–77.

52. Kukułka, *Francja,* p. 450.

53. Kukułka, ibid., p. 372, cites a draft by Sapieha; but Tadeusz Romer noted that this contained only general "postulates." In a retrospective article, Romer wrote that the Polish delegation had not brought any prepared drafts. On 7 February, Laroche asked Sapieha for drafts to be presented the next day, and the Polish minister agreed. Zamoyski informed Romer on the evening of 7 February, and both worked through the night to produce a draft of the political alliance. In this article, Romer published the memorandum of the Polish legation, Paris, that was sent to Warsaw on 15 January 1921, outlining issues and suggesting positions to be taken during the Paris talks. See Tadeusz Romer, "U kolebki pewnego sojuszu," *Zeszyty historyczne,* no. 13 (Paris, 1968): 119–39; the original is in the Modern Polish Archives, Warsaw— Archiwum Akt Nowych (hereafter cited as AAN), Amb. Paryż, 110:46–63. For the Polish alliance project, see Ciałowicz, *Polsko-francuski sojusz,* app. 1, p. 401; the French original is in AD/MAE, Pologne, 131:108–10; see also ibid., p. 148.

54. See n. 51 above.

55. A detailed summary of Sosnkowski's project is given by Ciałowicz on the basis of the general's letter to him; see *Polsko-francuski sojusz,* pp. 58–62. Kukułka mentions it briefly as the final Polish project (*Francja,* pp. 372–73), but according to Sosnkowski's account, as given in Ciałowicz, on 10 February the general presented a different project modeled on the Franco-Russian military convention of 1892 (see Ciałowicz, *Polsko-francuski sojusz,* p. 63). Sosnkowski's projects are enclosed in a letter from Foch to Briand of 9 February 1921. The first consists of nine articles and is likely the revised project of 10 February. The second, labeled "strictly secret," is much longer, consisting of eighteen articles, including the sending of the French fleet into the Baltic. This is probably Sosnkowski's original proposal. Some points are crossed out, probably by Foch and/or Weygand, see AD/MAE, Pologne, 131:111–17.

56. Sapieha's report of 14 February 1921, cited in Kukułka, *Francja,* pp. 374–75.

57. For the French text see Wandycz, *France,* app. 2, p. 393.

58. For the French text of the Military Convention see Kazimiera Mazurowa, "Przymierze polsko-francuskie z roku 1921," *Najnowsze dzieje Polski: Materiały i studia z okresu 1914–1939* 11 (1967): 212–14. The annex stipulated that the French government committed itself to grant Poland a military loan totaling 400 million francs, of which 80 million would be in surplus French demobilization stock. In principle, 200 million would be advanced in 1921/22, excluding the 80 million mentioned above.

59. See Ciałowicz, *Polsko-francuski sojusz,* p. 43.

60. Cited in Kukułka, *Francja,* p. 351 n. 47.

61. Peretti de la Rocca to Berthelot, 7 March 1921, telegram no. 731; Berthelot to Peretti de la Rocca, London, 8 March 1921, telegram no. 23 (trans. A. C.). In telegram no. 23b of the same day, Berthelot corrected himself, stating that Briand had

written the revision with the consent of Sapieha and Sosnkowski, not Zamoyski, see AD/MAE, Pologne, 132:7–9.

62. See n. 58 above; also Wandycz, *France,* p. 219.

63. Ciałowicz, *Polsko-francuski sojusz,* p. 73.

64. See AD/MAE, Pologne, 131:195.

65. See n. 51 above.

66. See n. 63 above.

67. Cit. Kukułka, *Francja,* p. 484.

68. For these conventions see Kukułka, ibid., pts. 3 and 4, chap. 1, passim.

69. See Zaks, cited in n. 13 above.

70. Note on Poland: Financial and Commercial questions, 18 July 1922, AD/MAE, Pologne, 132:106.

71. Robert Lansing, *The Peace Negotiations* (Boston, 1921), pp. 159–60.

72. Edgar Vincent D'Abernon, *An Ambassador of Peace,* 3 vols. (London, 1929–30), 1:184–85 (1:193–94 of U.S. ed.).

73. Sir Maurice P. A. Hankey to Prime Minister, 25 June 1921, Lloyd George Papers, Beaverbrook Library, London, F/25/1/48 (hereafter cited as LLGP).

74. Philip Kerr to Prime Minister, 2 September 1920, LLGP, F/90/1/18.

75. See *Papers Respecting Negotiations for an Anglo-French Pact,* Cmd. 2169, no. 9, pp. 108 ff.; for the French collection see *Documents relatifs aux négociations concernant les garanties de sécurité contre une aggression de l'Allemagne* (Paris, 1924); see also McDougall, *France's Rhineland Diplomacy,* p. 176, and Orde, *Great Britain,* pp. 12–13; chapter 1 of Orde's work deals with the negotiations for an Anglo-French pact during the period 1921 to 1923.

76. Notes of a conversation between Mr. Lloyd George and M. Briand . . . December 21, 1921, *DBFP,* 1st ser., vol. 15, no. 110, pp. 785–87; also Thomas Jones, *Whitehall Diary,* vol. 1: *1916–1925* (London, 1969), p. 187. For the French version see Suarez, *Briand,* 5:350–51, English translation in J. Néré, *The Foreign Policy of France from 1914 to 1945* (London and Boston, 1975), pp. 275–76; see also McDougall, *France's Rhineland Diplomacy,* pp. 176–77, and Orde, *Great Britain,* p. 13.

77. Curzon, Memorandum on the Question of the Anglo-French Alliance, 28 December 1921, *DBFP,* 1st ser., vol. 16, no. 768, pp. 864, 865–70; also Orde, *Great Britain,* p. 14.

78. January 4, 1922, *DBFP,* 1st ser., vol. 19, no. 1, pp. 1–7; see also Suarez, *Briand,* 5:358 ff., and Orde, *Great Britain,* p. 15.

79. January 5, 1922, *DBFP,* vol. 19, no. 3, pp. 11–15; also Orde, *Great Britain,* pp. 15–16.

80. Suarez, *Briand,* 5:373–75, partially translated into English in Néré, *Foreign Policy,* pp. 276–78; original: "Exposé des vues du gouvernement français," 8 Jan. 1922, AD/MAE, Grande Bretagne, 69:134–40, cited in McDougall, *France's Rhineland Diplomacy,* p. 179 n. 2; see also Orde, *Great Britain,* p. 14.

81. January 8, 1922, *DBFP,* vol. 19, no. 10, pp. 56–58; see also Orde, *Great Britain,* p. 17.

82. See 9 January 1922, *DBFP,* vol. 19, no. 11, pp. 58–59, and 10 January 1922, no. 18, pp. 87–89.

83. CAB 1 (22), 10 January 1922, CAB 23/29, pp. 1–6, cited in McDougall, *France's Rhineland Diplomacy,* p. 179 n. 4.

84. See McDougall, *France's Rhineland Diplomacy,* p. 180; also Édouard Bonnefous, *Histoire politique de la Troisième République,* vol. 3: *L' Après-guerre (1919–1924),* 2d ed. (Paris, 1968), p. 281; Jacques Chastenet, *Histoire de la Troisième République,* vol. 5:

Les Années d'illusions, 1918–1931 (Paris, 1960), pp. 92–93; also Orde, *Great Britain,* p. 19.

85. See McDougall, *France's Rhineland Diplomacy,* pp. 183–84, and Orde, *Great Britain,* p. 24.

86. Chargé d'affaires, Polish legation, Paris, no. 49/22/P, "On the general situation," 14 January 1922, AAN, Amb. Paryż, 70:133–38. For Briand's delay in ratifying the alliance see Georges-Henri Soutou, "L'Alliance franco-polonaise (1925–1933): ou Comment s'en débarrasser?" *Revue d'historie diplomatique,* April–December 1981, nos. 2, 3, and 4, pp. 295–348.

87. Cited in McDougall, *France's Rhineland Diplomacy,* p. 184; also Orde, *Great Britain,* p. 25.

88. McDougall, *France's Rhineland Diplomacy,* pp. 185, 187, and Orde, *Great Britain,* p. 26.

89. McDougall, *France's Rhineland Diplomacy,* pp. 189–90; Orde, *Great Britain,* pp. 27–36.

90. James W. Headlam-Morley, "Memorandum respecting the Guarantee Treaties, 1814-15-1919," 17 January 1922, FO, 371/11064/9/W1252/98, pp. 162–64 (1–6).

91. Hardinge, *Old Diplomacy,* p. 268.

92. Arnold J. Toynbee, *Survey of International Affairs, 1924* (London, 1928), p. 28.

93. On the ideas of Tyrrell and Crowe see Orde, *Great Britain,* pp. 7–8, 31.

94. See Auguste Bréal, *Philippe Berthelot* (Paris, 1937), pp. 198–99.

95. For these projects see Bariéty, *Relations franco-allemandes,* pt. 1, chaps. 3 and 4, and McDougall, *France's Rhineland Diplomacy,* chap. 5, pp. 206–13. French attempts to reach agreement with German industrialists in Upper Silesia are discussed in chap. 3 below.

96. Cited in *Kurjer Warszawski,* 8 January 1922.

97. See Jules Laroche, *Au Quai D'Orsay avec Briand et Poincaré, 1913–1926* (Paris, 1957), p. 137.

CHAPTER 2
THE STRUGGLE FOR UPPER SILESIA: THE BACKGROUND AND DEVELOPMENT FROM 1919 TO THE PLEBISCITE OF 20 MARCH 1921

1. For an excellent short study of the diplomatic aspects of the dispute see F. Gregory Campbell, "The Struggle for Upper Silesia, 1919–1922," *Journal of Modern History* 42, no. 3 (September 1970): 361–85; for the problem at the Peace Conference see Kay Lundgreen-Nielsen, *The Polish Problem at the Paris Peace Conference: A Study of the Policies of the Great Powers and the Poles, 1918–1919* (Odense, 1979), chap. 8, pp. 357–80; see also Joseph F. Harrington, Jr., "Upper Silesia and the Paris Peace Conference," *Polish Review* 19, no. 2 (1974): 25–45, and "The League of Nations and the Upper Silesian Boundary Dispute, 1921–1922," *Polish Review* 23, no. 3 (1978): 86–101. For the context of the problem in Franco-Polish relations see Wandycz, *France and Her Eastern Allies,* pp. 225–37, and Kukułka, *Francja a Polska po traktacie wersalskim,* chaps. 4 and 5 passim. For British policy see Patricia A. Gajda, *Postscript to Victory: British Policy and the German-Polish Borderlands, 1919–1925* (Washington, D.C., 1982). For Polish policy see Tadeusz Jędruszczak, *Polityka Polski w sprawie Górnego Śląska, 1918–1922*

(Warsaw, 1958). Sarah Wambaugh's useful account of the plebiscite dispute is based on published official documents; see her *Plebiscites since the World War,* 2 vols. (Washington, D.C., 1933), vol. 1, chap. 6, pp. 206-70, key documents in vol. 2, nos. 64-89, pp. 163-260. For two older studies see William J. Rose, *The Drama of Upper Silesia: A Regional Study* (London, 1936), and Robert Machray, *The Problem of Upper Silesia* (London, 1945). For an economic study see Norman J. G. Pounds, *The Upper Silesian Industrial Region* (Bloomington, Ind., 1958). For legal aspects of the problem after the plebiscite and for an account of the working of the Upper Silesian Convention see Georges Kaeckenbeeck, *The International Experiment of Upper Silesia* (Oxford, 1942); for a study of the Interallied Governing and Plebiscite Commission see Jan Przewłocki, *Międzysojusznicza Komisja Rządząca i Plebiscytowa na Górnym Śląsku w latach 1920-1922* (Wrocław, etc., 1970).

2. See G. W. Prothero, gen. ed., *Handbooks Prepared under the Direction of the Historical Section of the Foreign Office,* no. 40: *Upper Silesia* (London, 1920), pp. 4-7.

3. Supreme Council, 15 July 1919, "Report on the Composition and Size of the Army of Occupation in the Plebiscite Areas," *DBFP,* 1st ser., vol. 1, no. 11, app. E, p. 101.

4. See Machray, *Problem,* p. 66.

5. Ibid.: for the census of 1896 see map facing p. 65; for the census of 1910 see map facing p. 72; and see maps 1 and 2 supra.

6. H. J. Paton, "Upper Silesia," *Journal of the British Institute of International Affairs* 1 and 2 (1922/23): 15.

7. *Upper Silesia,* (see n. 2 above).

8. Machray, *Problem,* p. 41.

9. Memorandum of the Mines and Foundry Works Association of Upper Silesia to the Secretary of State for Foreign Affairs, Dr. Richard von Kuhlmann, 6 December 1917, cited in Kazimierz Popiołek, *Zaborcze plany kapitalistów śląskich* (Katowice-Wrocław, 1947), pp. 61-62.

10. Memorandum by Gerhard Williger, spokesman for Upper Silesian industrialists, to Reich Chancellor Theobald von Bethmann-Hollweg, November 1915, cited in Rose, *Drama,* p. 163; see also *Nécessité de l'union de la Haute Silésie à la Pologne (D'apres des documents secrets allemands de 1917)* (Warsaw, April 1921; in French, English, Italian).

11. Rose, *Drama,* p. 164.

12. See *Economist* (London), 26 March 1921.

13. J. M. Keynes, *The Economic Consequences of the Peace* (London, 1919), p. 246.

14. Étienne Mantoux, *The Carthaginian Peace: or The Economic Consequences of Mr. Keynes* (Oxford, 1946; reprint New York, 1952), pp. 79-80.

15. For a discussion of the Polish-German tariff war see Riekhoff, *German-Polish Relations,* chap. 7; a more detailed treatment is in Jerzy Krasuski, *Stosunki polsko-niemieckie, 1919-1925* (Poznań, 1962), chap. 5.

16. *New York Times,* 22 June 1925.

17. A. J. Toynbee, *Survey of International Affairs, 1925* (London, 1928), 2:239.

18. See Komarnicki, *Rebirth,* pp. 338-49, and see works listed in n. 1 above.

19. As James W. Headlam-Morley wrote in April 1921: "The adoption of the plebiscite was really a political device to overcome an immediate practical difficulty. The cardinal point was, would the Germans sign and what would happen if they refused to sign?" *DBFP,* 1st ser., vol. 16, no. 13, annex, p. 27 (11 D).

20. For the text of the Fontainebleau Memorandum see Martin Gilbert, *The Roots of Appeasement* (London, 1966), app. 1.

21. D'Abernon, *Ambassador of Peace,* 1:139 (entry for 22 March 1921): "The concession, therefore, was really of the nature of a bargain with Germany. The Germans, by signing, accepted our offer; it follows from this that there is an absolute obligation honestly to carry out our side of the bargain—that is, to abide by the result of the plebiscite (see n. 19 above).

22. Cited in Luigi Aldrovandi Marescotti, *Nuovi ricordi e frammenti di diario per far seguito a guerra diplomatica (1914–1919)* (Milan, 1938), p. 63.

23. The first proposal to this end is in "Anlage zum Protokoll der Kabinettssitzung" of 21 March 1919: see Weltkrieg nr. 30, bd. 32, 4080/D924260, Archiv des Auswärtigen Amtes, Bonn (henceforth cited as WK, AAN). Then see Reichskabinett, 21 April, 15 May, 1919, Akten der Alten Reichskanzlei, Kabinett Protokolle (hereafter cited as AARK/KP), German Foreign Ministry microfilms (hereafter cited as GFM), 2.3438/2, Foreign Office and Commonwealth Library, London.

24. Manfred Laubert, *Die oberschlesische Volksbewegung* (Breslau, 1938), p. 37.

25. Ibid., p. 43.

26. Report by Reich Commissioner, Otto Hörsing, to the German Cabinet, 28 August 1919, Reichskabinett, 28 August 1919, AARK/KP, GFM, 2.3438/3.

27. See below.

28. See Ernst Sontag, *Adalbert Korfanty: Ein Beitrag zur Geschichte der polnischen Ansprüche auf Oberschlesien* (Kitzingen/Main, 1954), p. 77.

29. On Bishop Bogedein see Rose, *Drama,* pp. 69 ff., also Tadeusz Gospodarek, *Walka o kulturę narodową ludu na Śląsku (1815–1863)* (Wrocław, 1968).

30. In the Stresemann Papers we read (6 November 1921) that land reform would be of dubious value to Upper Silesian industry because of its close links with the great landowners, Stresemann Nachlass, GFM, 2.6996H.

31. See Gen. Karl Hoefer, *Oberschlesien in der Aufstandszeit, 1918–1921* (Berlin, 1938).

32. See F. W. von Oertzen, *Die deutschen Freikorps, 1918–1923,* 5th ed. (Berlin, 1939), p. 118.

33. Robert G. L. Waite, *Vanguard of Nazism: The Free Corps Movement in Postwar Germany, 1918–1923* (Cambridge, Mass., 1952), p. 107.

34. Hoefer, *Oberschlesien,* p. 21.

35. Waite, *Vanguard,* p. 226.

36. *Times* (London), 21 February 1921. The title of the book under review was *Mit Erhard durch Deutschland.*

37. This was the Oberschlesisches Freiwilligenkorps; see Hoefer, *Oberschlesien,* p. 24.

38. For the proclamation see ibid., pp. 58–59.

39. Ibid., p. 22.

40. Jędruszczak, *Polityka Polski,* p. 104.

41. Ibid., p. 116.

42. POW, Silesian Command, report of 5 August 1919, to the Intelligence Section (Section 2) of the Polish High Command, Warsaw, cited in Jędruszczak, *Polityka Polski,* pp. 118–19; see also Tadeusz Jędruszczak and Halina Janowska, eds., *Powstanie II Rzeczypospolitej: Wybór dokumentów 1866–1925* (Warsaw, 1981), no. 262, pp. 516–17.

43. See n. 26.

44. Hoefer denied that the uprising was Spartacist and blamed it on the Poles of Poland (*Oberschlesien,* p. 38).

45. Ibid., p. 46.

46. For Henrys's report of 19 August and Dupont's of 21 August 1919 see *DBFP*, 1st ser., vol. 1, no. 37, app. D; no. 39, app. B, pp. 440, 470–71.

47. Ibid., no. 41, app. B, pp. 500–501.

48. Ibid., no. 37, p. 441, statement by Philippe Berthelot.

49. Ibid., no. 38, p. 451.

50. Foch to Henrys, and Pichon to Zamoyski, see Kukułka, *Francja,* pp. 89–90.

51. See Polish note of 18 August 1919, *DBFP*, 1st ser., vol. 6, no. 130.

52. Sir Percy Wyndham's report of 21 August 1919, ibid., no. 131.

53. See *Papers Relating to the Foreign Relations of the United States: Paris Peace Conference* (hereafter cited as *FRUS/PPC*), 7:735.

54. See Hoefer, *Oberschlesien,* p. 47.

55. Reichskabinett, 28 August 1919, AARK/KP, GFM, 2.3438/3.

56. *DBFP*, vol. 6, no. 172.

57. Ibid.

58. Pichon and Clemenceau told Zamoyski that the Allies could not occupy Upper Silesia; see Kukułka, *Francja,* pp. 90–91. Von Haniel reported that Foch had given up the demand that the industrial region be removed from German control; see Nachlass Waffenstillstandskommission, GFM, 2.9105/7.

59. Hoefer, *Oberschlesien,* p. 48; Laubert, *Oberschlesische Volksbewegung,* p. 93.

60. Oertzen, *Deutschen Freikorps,* p. 128.

61. See Colonel Percival to Lord Curzon, 18 August 1920, *DBFP*, 1st ser., vol. 11, no. 26.

62. Oertzen, *Deutschen Freikorps,* p. 132; Hoefer, *Oberschlesien,* p. 77.

63. Count Carlo Sforza, *Diplomatic Europe since the Treaty of Versailles* (New Haven, Conn., 1928), p. 22.

64. Rose, *Drama,* p. 173.

65. Wambaugh, *Plebiscites,* 1:238.

66. Reichskabinett, *Akten der Reichskanzlei der Weimarer Republik, Kabinett Protokole* (hereafter cited as *ARKWR/KP*), in *Das Kabinett Fehrenbach, 25 Juni 1920 bis 4 Mai 1921* (hereafter cited as *Kabinett Fehrenbach*), ed. Peter Wolf (Boppard am Rhein, 1972), nos. 63, 64, pp. 153–60.

67. See Laubert, *Obserschlesische Volksbewegung,* p. 176. For a brief discussion of the problem of national consciousness in Upper Silesia at this time see Harry K. Rosenthal, "National Self-Determination: The Example of Upper Silesia," *Journal of Contemporary History* 7, nos. 3 and 4 (July–October 1972): 231–41.

68. Laubert, *Oberschlesische Volksbewegung,* pp. 4–6; for a study of Polish and German propaganda in Upper Silesia see Władysław Zieliński, *Polska i niemiecka propaganda plebiscytowa na Górnym Śląsku* (Ossolineum, Wrocław, etc., 1972).

69. Laubert, *Oberschlesische Volksbewegung,* pp. 75, 84.

70. *ARKWR/KP, Kabinett Fehrenbach,* 20 November 1920, no. 116, p. 293.

71. T. Jędruszczak believes that Korfanty and his political activists only decided to call for another Polish uprising in May 1921 because they feared that all other means to prevent Poland's loss of Upper Silesia had failed; see *Polityka Polski,* pp. 318–19.

72. See Hoefer, *Oberschlesien,* p. 84.

73. Ibid.; Laubert, *Oberschlesische Volksbewegung,* p. 84.

74. Oertzen writes that people who were suspected of conniving with the Poles or the French could not be openly knifed or sentenced to the Feme, so they would disappear and never be seen again, *Deutschen Freikorps,* pp. 138–39; see also E. J. Gumbel, *"Verräter verfallen der Feme"* (Berlin, 1929).

75. See Oertzen, *Deutschen Freikorps,* p. 140.

76. Ibid., p. 143.

77. Ibid., p. 144.

78. For an explanation of the decision on outvoter rights in Upper Silesia see the memorandum by James W. Headlam-Morley of 6 April 1921, *DBFP*, vol. 16, no. 13, annex, point no. 14, p. 29. According to this, the chairman of the Plebiscite Commission, Gen. Henri Le Rond, suggested that the regulations set up for plebiscites in Allenstein (Olsztyn) and Slesvig be adopted for Upper Silesia. See also *A Memoir of the Paris Peace Conference, 1919,* pp. 135, 143–44, 150–54, 156–57, 163.

79. See Gajda, *Postscript to Victory,* pp. 75–76.

80. See Wambaugh, *Plebiscites,* 1:242. Polish miners in the Ruhr constituted up to 35 percent of the population in some towns. See also Gajda, *Postscript to Victory,* p. 77.

81. Wambaugh, *Plebiscites,* 1:248–49; Jędruszczak estimates that 182,288 German outvoters came to Upper Silesia for the plebiscite; see *Polityka Polski,* p. 287.

82. Jędruszczak, *Polityka Polski,* p. 289; see also Wambaugh, *Plebiscites,* 1:250.

83. Rose, *Drama,* p. 181; in Neustadt and Leobschutz, which the Poles never claimed, they obtained only 5,000 votes; see Frank P. Walters, *A History of the League of Nations* (Oxford, 1952), p. 152.

84. See memorandum of the Prussian Minister for Trade and Industry to the Foreign Ministry, 30 March 1921, *ARKWR/KP, Kabinett Fehrenbach,* no. 223, pp. 618–20.

CHAPTER 3
THE STRUGGLE FOR UPPER SILESIA: INTERPRETING THE PLEBISCITE, 20 MARCH TO 10 OCTOBER 1921

1. *Times* (London), 7 April 1921; *DBFP,* 1st ser., vol. 16, nos. 13 and 14.

2. *ARKWR/KP, Kabinett Fehrenbach,* nos. 1, 129, 201.

3. Lloyd George's statement of 21 July 1921, *Parliamentary Debates, House of Commons* (hereafter cited as *Parl.Deb.H.C.*), 5th ser., vol. 132, cols. 502–3; at the London Conference on Reparations in March 1921, he had said: "The reservation concerning Upper Silesia is a most important one"; see *DBFP,* 1st ser., vol. 15, no. 42, pp. 313–14; this was a reference to the German government's statement that it could not undertake to sign a reparations agreement before a decision on the fate of Upper Silesia was made.

4. See Harold Nicolson, *Curzon: The Last Phase, 1919–1925: A Study in Post-War Diplomacy* (London, 1934), p. 55.

5. See Gajda, *Postscript to Victory,* p. 212.

6. See Wambaugh, *Plebiscites,* 1:251; see map 3 supra.

7. *Times* (London), 28 March 1921.

8. Wambaugh, *Plebiscites,* 1:253 and vol. 2, no. 88, pp. 240–42.

9. See Kazimierz Smogorzewski, *La Silésie polonaise* (Paris, 1932), pp. 319–27.

10. Polish Foreign Minister to Polish Legation, London (undated, probably around 6 or 7 April 1921), APEL/PISM.

11. See D'Abernon, *Ambassador of Peace,* 1:139.

12. Curzon to Percival, 22 March 1921, *DBFP,* vol. 16, no. 1; Cabinet Conclusions, 22 March 1921, 14 (21), Cab. 23/24, p. 175.

13. *Parl.Deb.H.C.,* 5th ser., 5 May 1921, vol. 141, col. 1351.

14. 13 May 1921, ibid., cols. 2360–61.

15. See Tommasini, *Risurrezione,* p. 173; Marinis's reports accorded with the pro-German and anti-French attitudes then prevalent in Rome; see Stanisław Sierpowski, *Stosunki polsko-włoskie w latach 1918–1940* (Warsaw, 1975), p. 83.

16. See Wambaugh, *Plebiscites,* vol. 2, no. 88; summary in *DBFP,* vol. 16, no. 26, report dated 26 April 1921; see map in Gajda, *Postscript to Victory,* p. 89.

17. See Sierpowski, *Stosunki,* p. 89; Sforza, *Diplomatic Europe,* pp. 24–25.

18. See Jędruszczak, *Polityka Polski,* pp. 314–15.

19. See Rose, *Drama,* p. 172.

20. See Campbell, "Struggle for Upper Silesia," p. 378 (see above, n. 1 of chap. 2).

21. Jędruszczak, *Polityka Polski,* pp. 311–18. Korfanty tried to control the movement by claiming to lead it: see his Manifesto of 3 May 1921 in Jędruszczak and Janowska, *Powstanie,* no. 315, pp. 641–42.

22. Erasm Piltz to Polish legation, London, 2 May 1921, APEL/PISM.

23. Jędruszczak, *Polityka Polski,* p. 305.

24. Piltz to Polish Legation, London, 4 May 1921, APEL/PISM.

25. See *Times* (London), 5 and 8 May 1921; also *DBFP,* vol. 16, nos. 29, 35, 44, 47.

26. *Times* (London), 6 May 1921.

27. Sapieha to Foreign Minister, 4 May 1921, APEL/PISM.

28. Jędruszczak, *Polityka Polski,* p. 341; see also Wacław Ryżewski, *Trzecie powstanie śląskie, 1921* (Warsaw, 1977), pp. 275–76; *DBFP,* vol. 16, nos. 43, 52.

29. For the text of the resolutions and the Polish government's reply of 14 May 1921 see Smogorzewski, *Silésie polonaise,* pp. 340–41; also *DBFP,* vol. 16, nos. 38, 45.

30. Cabinet Meeting, 7 May 1921, *ARKWR/KP, Kabinett Fehrenbach,* no. 250, p. 668.

31. See Hoefer, *Oberschlesien,* p. 33.

32. Stresemann Memorandum of May 1921, Stresemann Nachlass, GFM, 2.7600H.

33. D'Abernon, *Ambassador of Peace,* 1:165.

34. Ibid., p. 166.

35. Hardinge to Curzon, 9 May 1921, *DBFP,* vol. 16, no. 45, p. 66.

36. D'Abernon, *Ambassador of Peace,* 1:168–69; Curzon to D'Abernon, 10 May 1921, *DBFP,* vol. 16, no. 612, pp. 664–65; see also Gajda, *Postscript to Victory,* p. 98.

37. *Times* (London), 30 July 1921. Stresemann was worried by the disclosure; he would have preferred, as he wrote on 16 August, that his negotiations with D'Abernon not be publicized until the Upper Silesian question had been settled, Stresemann Nachlass, GFM, 2.6998H.

38. For Frassati's attitude see Ministerio degli affari esteri, *I Documenti diplomatici italiani* (Rome, 1953; hereafter cited as *DDI*), 7th ser., 1:58, 60; also D'Abernon, *Ambassador of Peace,* 1:187, 202; for Kenworthy's speech, 13 May, see n. 14 above.

39. Curzon to Hardinge, *DBFP,* vol. 16, no. 50, p. 71.

40. Percival to Curzon, 11 May 1921, ibid., no. 52, and see n. 28 above.

41. Gajda, *Postscript,* pp. 104–5.

42. *Parl. Deb. H. C.,* 5th ser., vol. 141, 13 May 1921, cols. 2380–88.

43. Hardinge to Curzon, 14 May 1921, *DBFP,* vol. 16, no. 63; for the French press see n. 64.

44. For the press interview see *Times* (London), 16 May 1921. In his *aide-mémoire,* Briand denied French intentions to grant the whole industrial district to

Poland and said that the award should be based on the will of the population. However, he also said that Poland recognized the need for the Allies to have economic and industrial control over the mining regions awarded to her; see *DBFP*, vol. 16, no. 66, especially p. 87.

45. Jędruszczak, *Polityka Polski*, pp. 352–53.

46. Curzon to Cheetham, 16 May 1921, *DBFP*, vol. 16, no. 70, pp. 90–91.

47. Ibid., nos. 71, 73, pp. 91–93.

48. Percival to Lloyd George, 15 May 1921, LLGP, F/57/6/23.

49. Statement by Prime Minister, *Times* (London), 19 May 1921.

50. Maj.-Gen. Sir C. E. Callwell, ed., *Field-Marshal Sir Henry Wilson, Bart., G.C.B., D.S.O.: His Life and Letters,* vol. 2 (London, 1927), p. 290.

51. See Jędruszczak, *Polityka Polski*, p. 351; the note is summarized in a report by Sir William Max Muller, British minister in Warsaw, 15 May 1921, *DBFP*, vol. 16, no. 67, p. 89.

52. Copy of telegram from Korfanty to Lloyd George, LLGP, F/57/5/18.

53. Percival to Curzon, 18 May 1921, *DBFP*, vol. 16, no. 76, p. 96 n. 1.

54. Muller to Curzon, 17 May 1921, ibid., no. 74, p. 95.

55. Jędruszczak, *Polityka Polski*, p. 354.

56. Oertzen, *Deutschen Freikorps,* pp. 151–52; Sierpowski, *Stosunki,* p. 97, gives the number of Italians killed as 23.

57. Oertzen, *Deutschen Freikorps,* p. 156.

58. Waite, *Vanguard,* p. 228.

59. Hoefer, *Oberschlesien,* p. 116.

60. W. N. Medlicott, *British Foreign Policy since Versailles* (London, 1940), p. 21; rev. ed., p. 10 (the author misspelled the general's name).

61. *ARKWR/KP, Die Kabinette Wirth, I und II, v. I, Marz 1921–Marz 1922,* ed. Ingrid Schulze (Boppard am Rhein, 1973; hereafter cited as *ARKWR/KP, Kabinette Wirth*), *I,* no. 13, pp. 25–26 and n. 2.

62. Hoefer, *Oberschlesien,* pp. 146, 148.

63. Otto Gessler, *Reichswehrpolitik in der Weimarer Zeit* (Stuttgart, 1958), p. 221.

64. Stresemann wrote on 16 August that he had learned from the Reichswehr that a central fund for the Selbstschutz existed in Breslau, but that the soldiers' pay was insufficient, Stresemann Nachlass, GFM, 2.6996H.

65. Bruno E. Buchrucker, *Im Schatten Seeckt's: Die Geschichte der "Schwarzen Reichswehr"* (Berlin, 1928); Friedrich von Rabenau, *Seeckt: Aus seinem Leben, 1918–1936* (Leipzig, 1940), p. 300.

66. Hoefer, *Oberschlesien,* pp. 204–5.

67. *Times* (London), 21 May 1921.

68. Hoefer, *Oberschlesien,* p. 114.

69. Ibid., p. 178; Colonel Percival denied that Keatinge or any other British officers were in command of the German "Self-Protection" forces; but he claimed that to withdraw the British officers attached to the German forces would leave him completely dependent on French intelligence, *DBFP*, vol. 16, nos. 112, 117, pp. 139–40, 144.

70. Hoefer, *Oberschlesien,* p. 189.

71. Chancellor's decree forbidding military associations, 24 May 1921, *Reichsgesetzblatt, Erstes Halbjahr 1921,* pp. 711–12.

72. See Muller to Curzon, 29 June 1921, *DBFP*, vol. 16, no. 205, p. 228. Jean Monnet erred when he wrote that the "Polish army" had occupied the region and so

the German forces had had to come in; see Jean Monnet, *Mémoires* (Paris, 1976), p. 102.

73. Jędruszczak, *Polityka Polski,* pp. 355–56.

74. Ibid., p. 359.

75. *Economist,* 4 June 1921.

76. See *Times* (London), 25 May 1920; *Temps* (Paris), 26 May 1920.

77. On the same day, the German ambassador in London, Friedrich Sthamer, told Sir Eyre Crowe that the German government believed the whole of Upper Silesia should remain with Germany, *DBFP,* vol. 16, no. 147, pp. 169–70.

78. See *Times* (London), 19 May 1921; for French reactions see *DBFP,* vol. 16, no. 92, p. 113; they insisted that the decision must be unanimous.

79. Sforza's proposals—which were communicated to the British ambassador in Rome, Sir George Buchanan, and were transmitted to London on 24 May—envisaged two possible formulas, both entailing the division of the Upper Silesian industrial region. As Major Ottley noted, under the first formula, Germany would obtain about 8.5 million tons of coal of the output according to 1913 figures; under the second, she would have obtained 18.05 out of the total 1913 production of 43 million tons, *DBFP,* vol. 16, no. 109, n. 6, pp. 136–37. For the article in *Corriere della sera* see Sierpowski, *Stosunki,* p. 101.

80. See *Times* (London), 30 May 1921, report from Oppeln. The same paper reported on 7 June that German planes had dropped leaflets over Kattowitz, announcing that British troops had already gone into action against Polish insurgents; see also *DBFP,* vol. 16, no. 158, n. 1, p. 180; and Gajda, *Postscript,* p. 122.

81. Laubert cites such a conversation with a "prominent Englishman," unnamed, see *Oberschlesische Volksbewegung,* p. 132. E. H. Carr, then a member of the Foreign Office, wrote in his report of a tour of Danzig, Warsaw, and the Eastern Plebiscite Areas in June 1920: "It seems to me so nearly a certainty that, within a generation, Upper Silesia (barring some unforeseen developments) must in some guise or other again form part of Germany, that any expedient which might lead peacefully and without bloodshed to that consummation should be very seriously considered" (*DBFP,* vol. 11, no. 18, p. 26).

82. *Times* (London), 7 and 8 June 1921; *DBFP,* vol. 16, no. 162, n. 4, p. 183.

83. AARK/KP, GFM, 2.3428/10.

84. *ARKWR/KP, Kabinette Wirth,* no. 30, pp. 69–70.

85. Ibid., no. 34a, pp. 81–82.

86. Oertzen, *Deutschen Freikorps,* pp. 194–95.

87. Stresemann letter to Senator Bierman, 16 August 1921, Stresemann Nachlass, GFM, 2.6998H; see also Hans W. Gatzke, *Stresemann and the Rearmament of Germany* (New York, 1969), p. 8.

88. Spiecker at cabinet meeting, 19 September 1921, *ARKWR/KP, Kabinette Wirth,* no. 95, p. 273.

89. *Parl.Deb.H.C.,* 5th ser., vol. 144, col. 877.

90. Sforza, *Diplomatic Europe,* pp. 99–100; *DBFP,* 1st ser., vol. 15, no. 90, pp. 606–7.

91. Sierpowski, *Stosunki,* p. 102.

92. D'Abernon's diary for 1 July 1921, sent to Sir Maurice P. A. Hankey, 2 July, for Lloyd George, LLGP, F/54/1/30; on Sforza's proposals see notes 79 and 91 above. On reference to "W" and his view of the Greek issue see D'Abernon's diary for 6 July 1921, LLGP, F/54/1/32.

93. See *DBFP,* vol. 16, no. 219, p. 241.

94. It should be noted that Briand had earlier declared his readiness to send thirty thousand French troops to Upper Silesia if General Hoefer continued to resist Allied demands (19 June 1921, *DBFP,* vol. 15, no. 89); on French demands see memorandum of French ambassador to Curzon, 16 July 1921, *DBFP,* vol. 16, no. 225, also nos. 226, 227, 250, 251; see also Suarez, *Briand,* 5:201ff., and *Times* (London), 21–30 July 1921.

95. See Curzon to Cheetham on his "most serious conversation" with the French ambassador, 27 July 1921, *DBFP,* vol. 16, no. 247, also nos. 257, 262, 264, 266, 272, 282; and Gajda, *Postscript,* pp. 130–133.

96. *Deutsche Zeitung,* 30 July 1921.

97. Hardinge to Curzon, 29 July 1921, *DBFP,* vol. 16, no. 273. Briand accepted Hardinge's "informal proposals" and presented them to the French Council of Ministers as his own, ibid., p. 298 n. 7.

98. As early as 1 June, Crowe had warned Sthamer that the German claim to all of Upper Silesia was not practical politics, *DBFP,* vol. 16, no. 147, pp. 169–70.

99. Ibid., nos. 286, 288.

100. *DBFP,* vol. 15, no. 91, app. 1.

101. Ibid., chap. 5, especially nos. 91, 92, 93, and ff.

102. Jules Laroche, *Au Quai d'Orsay,* p. 142.

103. *Times* (London), 10 August 1921.

104. *DBFP,* vol. 15, no. 97, pp. 689, 691, also no. 99, p. 693; for the second report of the Committee of Experts see nos. 92 and 96, app., pp. 681–88; see also Gajda, *Postscript,* pp. 134–36.

105. For the French refusal of British proposals and for the decision to submit the problem to the League of Nations see *DBFP,* vol. 15, nos. 101, 102.

106. Jones, *Whitehall Diary,* 1:167.

107. Ibid., p. 202.

108. See Conversation between British and Italian Prime Ministers and Foreign Ministers at dinner (Hotel) Crillon, 11 August 1921, 8:15 P.M., *DBFP,* vol. 15, no. 100, pp. 695–96. D'Abernon reported Frassati's claim that he had "brought Torretta round to a sound view on Upper Silesia." He had worked hard with Marinis and had succeeded in convincing Torretta to support English policy; D'Abernon's diary, 15 August 1921, LLGP, F/54/1/37.

109. See Poincaré's article in *Le Matin* and G. Scelles's in *L'Information,* both of 15 August 1921.

110. *Parl.Deb.H.C.,* 5th ser., vol. 146, col. 1230.

111. D'Abernon, *Ambassador of Peace,* 1:202.

112. *Economist,* 20 August 1921.

113. Prof. Bernardo Attolico telephoned the secretary general, Sir Eric Drummond, on 13 August, informing him that the league's decision would be accepted by the Powers. He thought that the league should make an independent investigation and that it should make sure that Germany was heard, League of Nations Archives, Geneva (hereafter cited as LNA), Upper Silesia, IIA/11/14688/529. For the official directive of the Supreme Council to the League Council see *DBFP,* vol. 15, no. 710; see also cover letter, Briand to Ishii, 24 August 1921, LNA, IIA/15118/14724. Jean Monnet, who was closely involved, noted in his memoirs that this was the first time the secretariat had had powers of investigation with its decision accepted in advance (Monnet, *Mémoires,* p. 103).

114. Draft Articles on the Preparation of the Council's Recommendations regarding Upper Silesia, LNA, IIA/15257/14724. Interestingly enough, the composi-

tion of the committee closely resembled one of the alternatives suggested by Sir Cecil Hurst, chief legal adviser of the Foreign Office, on 15 August 1921. Curzon disagreed. He noted: "This has merits but would hand over a great European case to China, Brazil *(sic)* and Spain—surely almost a joke" *(DBFP,* vol. 16, no. 303, p. 328 n. 8). Apart from some records kept by the secretariat, there is an informative collection of documents in *The Minutes of the Extraordinary Session of the Council of the League of Nations held at Geneva from August 29th to October 12th 1921 to Consider the Question of Upper Silesia* (Geneva 1921); a good summary is in Smogorzewski, *Silésie polonaise,* pp. 398–438. The basic decision to give priority to the wishes of the population while finding ways to permit the continuation of the economic life of the region was apparently made at the fourth meeting (no date, but probably 9 September 1921), LNA, IIA/15257/14724.

115. F. Hodač was the secretary general of the Czechoslovak Manufacturers' Federation and a member of the governing body of the International Labour Office; Herald was director of the railways of Toggenburg, a professor at the University of Zurich, and a member of the Technical and Advisory Committee on Transit and Communications of the league's secretariat.

116. Sir Eyre Crowe noted that Beneš had only said that he thought the chances of a lasting peace would be greater if Poland, and not Germany, were to receive the industrial area; see Campbell, "Struggle for Upper Silesia," p. 384 n. 65. Beneš was, however, more explicit in his conversation with Balfour. Beneš then said that he thought the area should be divided on ethnic lines as far as possible. He said that the frontier problem in Teschen was rather similar, and claimed that he had pressed for an ethnic, rather than an industrial, frontier there (this was not true, A. C.). However, he also thought that the property of German industrialists on the Polish side of the frontier should be immune from expropriation for about twenty-five years; see Balfour to Léon Bourgeois, head of the French Delegation, Geneva, 10 September 1921, LNA, IIA/15257/14724.

117. See n. 114 above.

118. See James Barros, *The Åland Islands Question: Its Settlement by the League of Nations* (New Haven, Conn., and London, 1968).

119. See *DBFP,* vol. 15, no. 102, p. 702.

120. See n. 127 below.

121. Copy of Simons's speech to the German League of Nations Association, sent to Sir Eric Drummond on 10 September 1921, LNA, IIA/15753/14724.

122. On 8 September 1921, Stresemann wrote to a certain Herr Loeser in London: "I cannot possibly leave the Gentlemen in London without a clear answer. As you said this noon, Oberbedarf must deliver the shares. This can, immediately, if opportune, only take place when the basis of the commitment: 'the Reich guarantees to pay the equivalent value,' is unconditionally fulfilled. The Reich bears full responsibility for this. In our country's interest, I would always regret it if our English friends were proved correct in their repeated observations that the matter was purposely drawn out on our side" (Stresemann Nachlass, GFM, 2.6997H, trans. A. C.).

123. Balfour to Secretary of the Cabinet (Hankey), 29 September, LLGP, F/25/2/25, cited in *DBFP,* vol. 16, no. 324, p. 343, no. 3.

124. D'Abernon, *Ambassador of Peace,* 1:216, and LLGP, F/54/2/5.

125. See Smogorzewski, *Silésie polonaise,* p. 410 and n. 10.

126. See n. 124 above.

127. Hankey to Sir Eric Drummond, Private and Personal, 21 October 1921, LLGP, F/25/2/35.

128. Sir Eric Drummond to Hankey, 24 October 1921, ibid., F/25/2/36; Hankey noted that he did not find it convincing.

129. Drummond to Hankey, Private and Personal, 29 October 1921, and Hankey's note that he found the letter interesting, throwing a good deal of light on the matter, LLGP, F/25/2/39. Hankey's biographer simply repeats his hero's conviction that "French influence proved dominant" and claims that Hankey's judgment was "much more realistic than Drummond's"; see Stephen Roskill, *Hankey: Man of Secrets,* vol. 2: *1919–1931* (London, 1972), p. 234.

130. Blanche Dugdale, *Balfour,* 2:228–30.

131. Sir E. Drummond to Sir J. Simon, Rome, 1 December 1933, FO 411/17, no. 259, pp. 398–99.

132. See article by Lord Robert Cecil, "The Question of Upper Silesia," in *Nineteenth Century and After,* December 1921, pp. 967–68.

133. See Wandycz, *France,* p. 229 and Georges-[Henri] Soutou, "La Politique économique de la France en Pologne (1920–1924)," *Revue historique,* no. 509 (1974): 85–116; also Zbigniew Landau, "Gospodarcze"; and Franciszek Ryszka, "Kulisy decyzji w sprawie Śląska w r.1921," *Kwartalnik Historyczny* 60, no. 1 (Warsaw, 1953): 127–67.

134. Soutou, "Mines de Silésie," pp. 135–54.

135. See Ryszka, n. 133 above, also Z. Landau and J. Tomaszewski, "Misja Profesora A. Benisa," *Teki Archiwalne,* no. 4: *Materiały do historii klasy robotniczej w Polsce, 1916–1938,* ed. M. Motas and I. Motasowa (Warsaw, 1955), pp. 34–225.

136. Soutou, "Mines de Silésie," p. 138.

137. Ibid., pp. 140–41.

138. Ibid., p. 145.

139. Soutou, "Politique économique," see n. 133 above.

140. Ibid.

141. Wandycz, *France,* p. 229; Soutou, "Mines de Silésie," pp. 147–48.

142. In 1922 a British group proposed to work the principal part of the Polish-owned industrial triangle. Money was promised by Lazards and Lloyds, while the British Shareholders' Trust would underwrite the business and then become debenture holders when the shares were offered to the public. However, the Foreign Office opposed the scheme, which it saw not only as a purely commercial venture but also as a political one, because, as Owen O'Malley correctly said, "the industrial triangle is to Central and Eastern Europe what Wesphalia and Essen are to Western Europe, or what South Wales, Leeds, and Sheffield are to England (interview of Lieutenant Commander Kenworthy, M.P., with Owen O'Malley, 7 March 1922, cited in Gajda, *Postscript,* p. 163). For British control of certain mines see ibid., p. 161.

143. 12 October 1921, *Kabinette Wirth,* no. 111, p. 315; see also Foreign Minister Rosen's letter to Curzon, 6 October 1921, *DBFP,* vol. 16, no. 316, pp. 336–37.

144. Stresemann to D'Abernon, 11 October 1921, in Stresemann Nachlass, GFM 2.6996H. Curzon warned D'Abernon against having discussions with Stresemann, since the latter was not a member of the German government, *DBFP,* vol. 16, no. 353, p. 371.

145. Telegram from Polish Legation, London, to Foreign Minister, 12 October 1921, APEL/PISM; two days later, Curzon told the German ambassador: "If I were a German I would make the best of it," *DBFP,* vol. 16, no. 336, p. 353. Monnet mentions the objections of the Quai d'Orsay but claims that Briand refused to allow

the breakdown of the Bourgeois-Balfour agreement and had the project adopted on 12 October 1921 (*Mémoires,* p. 105).

146. For the decision of the Conference of Ambassadors of 19 October 1921 see *DBFP,* vol. 16, no. 352, pp. 369–70; also Kaeckenbeeck, *International Experiment,* pp. 558–65. For the discussions preceding the decision see *DBFP,* vol. 16, nos. 341, 344, 345, 346.

147. Stresemann note of 23 October 1921, Stresemann Nachlass, GFM, 2.6992H.

148. *DBFP,* vol. 16, no. 358, pp. 375–76.

149. See A. Szczepański, *Górny Śląsk w świetle wykonania Konwencji Genewskiej* (Warsaw, 1929); M. S. Korowicz, *Górnośląska ochrona mniejszości* (Katowice, 1938; unauthorized translation published by the Preussisches Staatsarchiv, Berlin-Dahlem, 1938, as *Der Oberschlesische Minderheitensschutz*); see also *Oberschlesien und der Genfer schiedsspruch,* Osteuropa Institut Breslau (Berlin, 1925). The text of the convention is in *Convention germano-polonaise relative à la Haute Silésie, faite à Genève le 15 mai 1922* (Geneva, 1922; French and Polish texts).

150. Kaeckenbeeck, *International Experiment* (see n. 1 above).

151. Foreign Minister, telegram to Polish Legation, London, 13 October 1921, APEL/PISM.

152. *Concise Statistical Yearbook of Poland, 1938* (Warsaw, 1938), p. 22, table 14.

153. *Verhandlungen des Reichstag: Stenographische Berichte,* vol. 351, 26 October 1921 (Berlin).

154. *Sitzungsberichte des preussischen Landtags,* 60 Sitzung, 21 October 1921 (Berlin).

155. D'Abernon, *Ambassador of Peace,* 1:83.

156. Brockdorff-Rantzau Nachlass, GFM, 2.6812H; Stresemann criticized Wirth's statement as imprudent, ibid.

157. For Severing see *Schulthess' europäischer Geschichtskalender, 1926* (Munich, 1927), p. 81; for Hindenburg see *Times* (London), 19 September 1928.

158. See Margarete Gärtner, *Bostschafterin des guten Willens* (Bonn, 1955).

159. See Restytut W. Staniewicz, *Mniejszość niemiecka w województwie śląskim w latach 1922–1933* (Katowice, 1965); for a table of Polish, German, and Jewish complaints submitted to the president of the Mixed Commission in the years 1922–27 see Stanisław Potocki, *Położenie mniejszości niemieckiej w Polsce 1918–1938* (Gdańsk, 1969), p. 310.

160. For an excellent study of Weimar Germany's propaganda against Poland see Janusz Sobczak, *Propaganda zagraniczna Niemiec weimarskich wobec Polski* (Poznań, 1973); for the effects of German propaganda in Britain see Anna M. Cienciala, "German Propaganda for the Revision of the Polish-German Frontier in Danzig and the Corridor: Its Effects on British Opinion and the British Policy-making Elite in the Years 1919–1933," *Antemurale* 20 (Rome, 1976): 77–129.

CHAPTER 4
THE FREE CITY OF DANZIG: AN UNWORKABLE COMPROMISE, 1919–25

1. *Danziger Statistisches Taschenbuch,* 1933, table 9, p. 16 (Danzig, 1933).

2. Wacław Borowski, "Ludność i struktura zatrudnienia w Wolnym Mieście Gdańsku," in *Studia z dziejów Gdańska, 1918–1939,* ed. Stanisław Potocki, Komunikaty

Instytutu Bałtyckiego, Zeszyt specjalny no. 2 (Gdańsk, 1975), p. 14. Borowski cites the estimates of T. Kijeński, an official in the Polish Commissariat General in Danzig, 1928/29.

3. Roman Wodzicki, *Wspomnienia: Gdańsk—Warszawa—Berlin, 1928–1939* (Warsaw, 1972), p. 128. Wodzicki was an official in the Polish Commissariat General in Danzig from 1928 to 1935.

4. Prof. Bernard Pares, "The Polish Question," 8 October 1914, FO, 800/74 (Grey Papers).

5. See Malbone W. Graham, ed., *New Governments of Eastern Europe* (New York, 1927), pp. 751–52.

6. Arthur J. Balfour, "The Peace Settlement in Europe," 4 October 1916; see David Lloyd George, *War Memoirs of David Lloyd George*, vol. 1 (London, 1938), pp. 523–29, and Blanche Elizabeth Campbell Dugdale, *Arthur James Balfour* (London, 1936), vol. 2, app. 2, pp. 323–28.

7. For example, Louis Barthou's statement at the Sorbonne, 28 January 1916, cited in Pajewski, *Wokół sprawy polskiej*, p. 33.

8. Address to the United States Senate, 22 January 1917, Senate Document 685, 64th Cong., 2d sess., cited in Ray Stannard Baker and William E. Dodd, eds., *The Public Papers of Woodrow Wilson: The New Democracy* (New York, 1926), 2:411.

9. James W. Gerard, *My Four Years in Germany* (New York, 1917), p. 268.

10. Dmowski wrote that he had presented his memorandum to Balfour at the end of March 1917; see Roman Dmowski, *Polityka polska i odbudowanie państwa*, 2d ed. (Warsaw, 1926), p. 445; for the date, 25 March, see Marian Leczyk, *Komitet Narodowy Polski a Ententa i Stany Zjednoczone, 1917–1919* (Warsaw, 1966), p. 71.

11. Cited in Harold I. Nelson, *Land and Power: British and Allied Policy on Germany's Frontiers, 1916–19* (London and Toronto, 1963), pp. 17–18; for text of Balfour's statement see *FRUS, The Lansing Papers, 1914–1920,* vol. 1 (Washington, D.C., 1939), pp. 19–20.

12. Memorandum by Prof. Charles Oman on the Western Boundaries of Poland, November/December 1918, cited in James W. Headlam-Morley, "The Eastern Frontiers of Germany," 4 April 1925, FO, 417/18, pt. 12, no. 27, pp. 79–80. See also Nelson, *Land and Power*, p. 99, for Foreign Office's line see map 2 supra.

13. "Note on the most practicable Western boundary of Poland," 23 November 1918, FO, 371/4354, PID file, pc. (piece) 46, pp. 107 ff.

14. "Memorandum on Poland," Confidential, 9 December 1918, ibid.

15. See Col. Edward House and Walter Lippmann, "Commentary on the Fourteen Points," October 1918, in *The Intimate Papers of Colonel House*, ed. Charles Seymour (Boston, 1928), 4:200. For Allied and Polish views on the eve of the peace conference see Lundgreen-Nielsen, *The Polish Problem*, pt. 1, chap. 1 passim: for his treatment of the Danzig question see sections on the Frontier Problem and the German-Polish Frontier Problem, under chronological subdivisions.

16. "La Question de Pologne," 26 November 1917, signed by (Pierre) de Margerie, AD/MAE, série Paix, Pologne, A.391–2, p. 4; see also chap. 1, n. 1, above.

17. Cited in Nelson, *Land and Power*, pp. 117–18; full text in Pajewski, *Wokół sprawy polskiej*, pp. 229–39 (the date is misprinted as 1968 instead of 1918, A. C.).

18. Alma Luckau, *The German Delegation at the Paris Peace Conference* (New York, 1941), p. 36; see also Komarnicki, *Rebirth*, p. 246.

19. See Christoph M. Kimmich, *The Free City: Danzig and German Foreign Policy, 1919–1934* (New Haven, Conn., and London, 1968), p. 16.

20. Records of the United States delegation, cited in Nelson, *Land and Power*, p. 121.

21. James W. Headlam-Morley wrote: "When the Paris Peace Conference began, no authoritative decision or instructions as to British policy on this matter had been given, but there appears to have been a general consensus of opinion against the tranference of Danzig to Poland," in "The Eastern Frontiers of Germany," p. 3, point 10; see n. 12 above.

22. See Headlam-Morley, *Memoir*, p. 39 n. 2, and "The Eastern Frontiers of Germany," points 9, 11.

23. Namier's criticism of the Polish National Committee, and especially of Dmowski, had aroused so much French and Polish resentment that Paton was sent instead of Namier to replace Esme Howard, when the latter went to Poland in early February. Namier wrote to Headlam-Morley: "The fact that Paton has been summoned and I have been passed over will be exploited by my enemies"; see Headlam-Morley, *Memoir*, p. 29 n. 1.

24. Headlam-Morley, *Memoir*, p. 41.

25. 12 February 1919, *Parl.Deb.H.C.*, 5th ser., vol. 112, col. 191.

26. *Intimate Papers of Col. House*, 4:334–35.

27. *Verhandlungen der verfassungsgebenden deutschen Nationalversammlung*, vol. 1 (Berlin, 1919), p. 254.

28. *FRUS/PPC*, 4:414; the report was dated 19 March 1919. For the commission's deliberations see Nelson, *Land and Power*, pp. 151–66.

29. Paul C. Helmreich, *From Paris to Sèvres: The Partition of the Ottoman Empire at the Peace Conference of 1919–1920* (Columbus, Ohio, 1974), p. 65.

30. Nelson, *Land and Power*, pp. 221–22.

31. Ibid., pp. 171–73; *FRUS/PPC*, 4:413–19.

32. Nelson, *Land and Power*, pp. 173–74; Headlam-Morley, *Memoir*, p. 53.

33. Headlam-Morley, *Memoir*, p. 57 n. 1.

34. David Lloyd George, *The Truth about the Peace Treaties* (London, 1938), 1:413 ff.; text in Gilbert, *Roots of Appeasement*, pp. 189–96.

35. Paul Mantoux, ed., *Les Délibérations du Conseil des Quatre: 24 mars–28 juin 1919*, 2 vols. (Paris, 1955), 1:41–58.

36. Sir Eyre Crowe noted on the evening of 27 March that Lloyd George "wants me to have the decision of the Conference [*sic*, A. C.] reversed. He therefore requests me to prepare an alternative scheme of frontiers which will lock off Poland from the sea" (note dated 28 March 1919, courtesy of Dr. Sybil Crowe).

37. Dr. Sidney E. Mezes to the President, 1 April 1919, cited in Headlam-Morley, "Papers and Correspondence dealing with the Establishment of Danzig as a Free City," dated 31 August 1919, FO, 608/66, pc. 20216, pp. 4–6; also "The Eastern Frontiers of Germany," p. 82 (5).

38. Mantoux, *Délibérations*, 1:110–14.

39. Lloyd George to President Wilson, 2 April 1919, cited in Nelson, *Land and Power*, p. 228.

40. Lloyd George to Bonar Law, 31 March 1919, LLGP, F/30/3/40; Nelson, *Land and Power*, p. 236; Helmreich, *Paris to Sèvres*, pp. 68–69.

41. Headlam-Morley, *Memoir*, p. 84.

42. Article 104 stated:

The Principal and Associated Powers undertake to negotiate a Treaty between the Polish Government and the Free City of Danzig, which shall come into force at the same time as the establishment of the said Free City, with the following objects:

1. To effect the inclusion of the Free City of Danzig within the Polish Customs Frontiers, and to establish a free area in the port;

2. To ensure to Poland without any restriction the free use and service of all waterways, docks, basins, wharves and other works within the territory of the Free City necessary for Polish imports and exports;

3. To ensure to Poland the control and administration of the Vistula and of the whole railway system within the Free City, except such street and other railways as serve primarily the needs of the Free City, and of postal, telegraphic and telephonic communications between Poland and the port of Danzig;

4. To ensure to Poland the right to develop and improve the waterways, docks, basins, wharves, railways and other means of communication mentioned in this Article, as well as to lease or purchase through appropriate purchases such land and other property as may be necessary for these purposes;

5. To provide against any discrimination within the Free City of Danzig to the detriment of the citizens of Poland and other persons of Polish origin or speech;

6. To provide that the Polish Government shall undertake the conduct of the foreign relations of the Free City of Danzig as well as the diplomatic protection of citizens of that city when abroad.

Article 107 stated:

All property situated within the territory of the Free City of Danzig belonging to the German Empire or any other German State shall pass to the Principal Allied and Associated Powers for transfer to the Free City of Danzig or the Polish State as they may consider equitable.

Article 108 stated:

The proportion and nature of the financial liabilities of Germany and Prussia to be borne by the Free City of Danzig shall be fixed in accordance with Article 254 of Part IX of the present Treaty.

All other questions which may arise from the cession of the Territory referred to in Article 100, shall be settled by further agreements.

Article 103 stated:

A constitution for the Free City of Danzig shall be drawn up by the duly appointed representatives of the Free City in agreement with a High Commissioner to be appointed by the League of Nations. This constitution shall be placed under the protection of the League of Nations.

The High Commissioner will also be entrusted with the duty of dealing in the first instance with all differences arising between Poland and the Free City in regard to this treaty or any arrangements or agreements made thereunder.

The High Commissioner shall reside at Danzig.

For the Treaty of Versailles, section 11, The Free City of Danzig, see Fred L. Israel, ed., *Major Peace Treaties of Modern History, 1648–1967,* vol. 3 (New York, 1967); also John Brown Mason, *The Danzig Dilemma: A Study in Peacemaking by Compromise* (Stanford, Calif., and Oxford, England, 1946), app. A, pp. 323–25.

43. On 4 March 1919, Count Eberhard zu Solms-Sonnenwald of the German legation at The Hague reported British advice, transmitted through the Dutch

minister for colonies, that Germany should refuse permission for Haller's army (the Polish army formed in France, A. C.) to land in Danzig, Political Archives, Foreign Ministry, Bonn (hereafter cited as PA), Weltkrieg, nr. 30, bd. 28,4080/D923514; Baron Ago von Maltzan reported the same advice on 1 April, from "American friends," ibid., bd. 34,4091/D924836. On 28 March, Gen. Sir Richard Haking, head of the British Armistice Commission at Spa, told Gen. Kurt von Hammerstein-Equord, head of the German Armistice Commission, that as soon as the peace treaty was signed, England would again stand with Germany; Hammerstein-Equord to Matthias Erzberger, 28 March 1919, ibid., D924678–79. Two days later, the American diplomat Hugh Gibson and Lloyd George's adviser F. E. Wise told Brockdorff-Rantzau that Britain had no desire to destroy Germany; she wished for German recovery and prosperity; see also Arno J. Mayer, *Politics and Diplomacy of Peacemaking: Containment and Counterrevolution at Versailles, 1918–1919* (London, 1968), pp. 754–55. On 4 April, Breithaupt reported the American minister in The Hague, [John] Wiley, as having said that the United States expected that there would be a breakup of the Peace Conference, especially if the German cabinet had the courage to resign rather than accept "impossible" conditions. Wiley thought that the resignation would lead to the fall of Clemenceau and his being replaced by the "more moderate" Briand. Finally, Wiley believed that Germany's refusal to sign the peace treaty would give her great Socialist support abroad; see report of 4 April 1919, Hague, Weltkrieg, nr. 30, bd. 35,D925318/9. Ten days later, Breithaupt reported another conversation with Wiley, in which the latter asked what he thought of a separate U.S.–German peace and gave him a list of peace conditions to which he was to write yes or no. These conditions listed Germany's return of Alsace-Lorraine to France; N. Schleswig to Denmark; predominantly Polish provinces (on the basis of the German wartime census) to Poland. Furthermore, the U.S. was said to have no interest in the Danzig solution (?), and in case of a union of Germany and Austria, Germany was to guarantee the Czechoslovak state, ibid., bd. 37,D925650-52.

44. For the establishment of the International Shipbuilding and Engineering Company Ltd. see below.

45. *Parl.Deb.H.C.*, 5th ser., 27 July 1936, vol. 315, cols. 1202–3.

46. On 26 June 1919, Winthrop Bell, who had been sent on a fact-finding mission to East Prussia by Sir Maurice P. A. Hankey, reported to the latter on the views of Dr. Heinrich Sahm, then mayor of Danzig. Sahm thought that the genuineness of Danzig's proposed autonomy depended on the interpretation of articles 104, 107, and 108. He expressed particular concern regarding article 104, since Polish control of the harbor and communications would mean the Polonization of the city; Winthrop Bell to Sir Maurice P. A. Hankey, 26 June 1919, FO, 371/3898, f. (file) 73, pc. 99063. In July, Sahm expressed the same concern to Gen. Sir Ian Malcolm, head of the British Military Mission, Berlin. Malcolm forwarded the report to the Foreign Office, where it was date-stamped 31 July 1919, FO, 608/65, pc. 7298.

47. See Kimmich, *Free City*, p. 40.

48. Ibid., p. 18.

49. *DBFP*, 1st ser., vol. 1, no. 31, pp. 375–77; vol. 2, no. 2, pp. 12–15.

50. 18 August 1919, FO, 608/65, 130/61, pc. 18040.

51. The agreement was summarized in a note of 10 February 1920, sent by telegram by Philippe Berthelot, head of the French Foreign Ministry, to the French embassy, London, AD/MAE, Pologne (Dantzig), Z931-3 (20), p. 24; see Anna M. Cienciala, "An Aspect of the German Problem in the Interwar Period: The Secret

Anglo-French Agreement on Danzig and the Saar, and Its Consequences, 1919–1926,'' *Zeitschrift für Ostforschung* 27, no. 3 (Marburg, 1978): 434–55.

52. Comments of Sir Cecil Hurst, James W. Headlam-Morley, Sir Eric Drummond, and Eric Colban on the Polish project (text in French), FO, 608/65, 130/61, pc. 18477.

53. ''Sir Reginald Tower's Journey to Danzig'' and Extract of Conversation between Sir R. Tower and Polish Representatives in Paris, 27 and 28 November 1919, *DBFP*, 1st ser., vol. 6, nos. 342, 352, 403.

54. Note by E. H. Carr, 21 November 1919, FO, 608/61, pc. 10572.

55. See n. 53 above.

56. Haking to Tower, 4 February 1920, FO, 371/3925/117922/178169/55.

57. There appears to be only a Polish account of the conversation between Tower and Polish delegates in Paris, 4 February 1920. It is in a collection of copied documents compiled by Dr. Henryk M. Serejski, a Polish historian, and entitled ''Kolekcja opracowań i odpisów dokumentów dotyczących stosunków Polski z Łotwą, Litwą, Rosją Radziecką, Gdańskiem i Ukrainą w latach 1914–1928'' (hereafter cited as Kolekcja), AAN, MSZ, sygn. 45/11, vol. 23, pp. 52–56.

58. On Prussian-German policy toward the Poles of Prussian Poland during the Partition period see Martin Broszat, *200 Jahre deutsche Polenpolitik* (Munich, 1963). The older work of R. W. Tims, *Germanizing Prussian Poland: The H-K-T Society and the Struggle for the Eastern Marches in the German Empire, 1894–1919* (New York, 1941), while still useful, has been superseded by William W. Hagen, *Germans, Poles, and Jews: The Nationality Conflict in the Prussian East, 1772–1914* (Chicago and London, 1980). Polish studies include Adam Galos, F. H. Gentzen, and W. Jakóbczyk, *Dzieje Hakaty,* ed. Janusz Pajewski (Poznań, 1966); Lech Trzeciakowski, *Kulturkampf w zaborze pruskim* (Poznań, 1970) and *Pod pruskim zaborem, 1850–1918* (Warsaw, 1973). The most important older German work is Manfred Laubert, *Die preussische Polenpoltik von 1772–1914* (Berlin, 1920). The most important older Polish work is Józef Buzek, *Historya polityki narodowościowej rządu pruskiego wobec Polaków* (Lwów, 1909).

59. Tower to Carr, 25 February 1920, FO, 371/3934/188296/190163/55.

60. Gen. Paul Henrys to Marshal Foch, 7 March 1920, 2-ème Bureau no. 346-360, AD/MAE, Pologne (Dantzig), Z931-1 (1.I-31.III 1920), pp. 160–61.

61. Tower report no. 47 to the Conference of Ambassadors, 17 March 1920, *DBFP*, 1st ser., vol. 11, no. 226, pp. 253–55.

62. Haking to Chief, Imperial General Staff, and memorandum by H. N. Crookshank, 23 April 1920, FO, 371/3931/182599/195583, also FO, 371/3934/188296/192558/55.

63. 29 April 1920, Conference of Ambassadors (hereafter cited as CA), FO, 893.3, pp. 4–16.

64. 7 May 1920, CA, FO, 893.4, pp. 7–22; also Lord Derby to Curzon, 7 May 1920, *DBFP*, vol. 11, no. 265.

65. Haking to Chief, Imperial General Staff, 14 May 1920, FO, 371/3901/73/199261/55.

66. Heinrich Sahm, *Erinnerungen aus meinen Danziger Jahren, 1919–1930* (Marburg/Lahn, 1958), p. 52.

67. See Wandycz, *Soviet-Polish Relations,* pp. 211–12.

68. *DBFP*, vol. 8, no. 62, p. 551.

69. Ibid., app. 8, 9, pp. 557–58.

70. See Norman Davies, ''Sir Maurice Hankey and the Inter-Allied Mission to Poland, July–August 1920,'' *Historical Journal* 15, no. 3 (1972): 553–61.

71. See Norman Davies, *White Eagle, Red Star: The Polish-Soviet War, 1919–20* (London, 1972).

72. Conference at 10 Downing Street, 6 August 1920, 3:30 P.M., *DBFP*, vol. 8, no. 82; see also Richard H. Ullman, *Anglo-Soviet Relations, 1917–1921*, vol. 3: *The Anglo-Soviet Accord* (Princeton, N.J., 1972), pp. 204–5 and, on events in Danzig, 249–52.

73. Tower report to Curzon, 18 August 1920, *DBFP*, 1st ser., vol. 11, no. 359. Tower cabled that the Danzig Constituent Assembly had asked him to declare the city's neutrality. Two days later the assembly made the declaration in its own name.

74. Foch's instructions to the Commander of the Gueydon, dated 20 August 1920, AD/MAE, Pologne (Dantzig), Z931-1 (1.VI-31.VIII 1920), B2888.

75. *DBFP*, 1st ser., vol. 8, no. 89, p. 780; here he named it the "Danzig Council."

76. Col. Tadeusz Wenda wrote a memorandum on 20 June 1920 on the possibility of developing the Polish coast and the port of Danzig. He pointed out Gdynia as the site for a Polish naval, fishing, and eventually trade port; see Andrzej Rzepniewski, "Memoriał Tadeusza Wendy z 20 czerwca 1920r. w sprawie możliwości rozwojowych wybrzeża polskiego i portu gdańskiego," *Zapiski historyczne poświęcone historii Pomorza* 29, no. 4 (1964): 45–63. It is worth noting that in 1919 a representative of the British shipbuilding firm Vickers also thought a port in Gdynia was quite feasible. This finding was confirmed by Lieutenant Buchanan, R.N., in spring 1921; see Gajda, *Postscript to Victory*, pp. 112–13.

77. *DBFP*, vol. 11, no. 52, and FO, 371/5407, p. 20.

78. Sahm, *Erinnerungen*, p. 20.

79. For the commission's draft see Derby to Curzon, 15 October 1920, *DBFP*, vol. 11, no. 584, and Conference of Ambassadors, FO, 893/8, no. 80.

80. Count Ishii's report on the Polish Defense Mandate for Danzig, 22 June 1921, League of Nations, Council Series, Danzig Documents, League of Nations Library, Geneva, C151, M113, 1921.I (hereafter cited as Danzig Documents).

81. See Col. A. B. Barber's memorandum "Polish-Danzig Convention: Order of Work under articles 102, 104 and 107 of the Treaty of Versailles," 12 September 1920, in files of the Polish Commissariat General, Gdańsk (hereafter cited as PCG/G), Wojewódzkie Archiwum Panstwowe, Gdańsk (hereafter cited as WAP/G), I.259/9. There is a note that a copy was sent to Mieczysław Jałowiecki, who had been the Polish delegate in Danzig in 1919 and was a member of the Polish delegation in Paris in the fall of 1920; see Anna M. Cienciala, "USA a sprawa W.M. Gdańska w latach 1919–1920" (Przyczynek do historii stosunków polsko-amerykańskich), *Ameryka Północna, Studia*, vol. 2, ed. Marian Marek Drozdowski (Warsaw, 1978), pp. 146–69.

82. Lt. Comdr. Eric Wharton, R.N., "Some Observations on my time as Adviser to the Polish Delegation attending in Paris on the subject of the Polish-Danzig Convention," 2 November 1920, FO, 688/4, f.28-65, cited in Cienciala, "USA a sprawa" (see n. 81 above).

83. Sahm to Tower, 22 November 1922, files of the Danzig Senate (hereafter cited as Dzg.Sen), WAP/G, I.260/585, pp. 31–34; also, Sahm, *Erinnerungen*, p. 39.

84. Kimmich, *Free City*, pp. 49–51. For Stinnes see Derby's statement to the Conference of Ambassadors, 15 October 1920, FO, CA, 893/8, no. 81, p. 10.

85. Report of Professor (Bernardo) Attolico, ex-High Commissioner, Danzig, Paris, 23 February 1921, Danzig Documents, 1921, vol. 1, no. 41, original in Administrative Commissions, LNA, 21/41/39, 21/68/59.

86. Memorandum by Joseph Avenol, deputy secretary general, League of Nations, 15 March 1922, C.220.1922, Danzig Documents, 1922, vol. 1, no. 173.

87. Haking report of 3 February 1921, FO, 371/6820/N2533, p. 348, also, C151. 4/1085/8528, Danzig Documents, 1921.

88. Herbert von Dirksen, the German consul general in Danzig, report dated 31 August 1922, cited in Kimmich, *Free City,* pp. 51–52.

89. For the law establishing the company see *Gesetzblatt für die Freie Stadt Danzig,* 10 January 1923; also, Sahm, *Erinnerungen,* app. 8. For a detailed account of the establishment of the International Shipbuilding and Engineering Company Ltd. see Anna M. Cienciala, "Powstanie Międzynarodowego Towarzystwa Budowy Okrętów i Maszyn w Gdańsku: Przyczynek do historii Wolnego Miasta Gdańska w latach 1919–1923," in *Z dziejów Słowiańszczyzny i Europy Środkowej w XIX i XX wieku,* Zbiór studiów pod redakcją Tadeusza Cieślaka (Wrocław, etc., 1980), pp. 135 ff. In June 1937, Charles F. Spencer, for many years chairman of the board of directors, told Ernst Woermann, counsellor at the German embassy in London, that the aim of dividing the shares—30% each for France and Britain, and 20% each for Poland and Danzig—was to balance French and Polish capital with British and Danzig capital; see note by Woermann, GFM, PA, 1728H/40710-13. The British shares were ultimately sold to Danzig through a German firm, ibid., 407124-18; see also *Documents on German Foreign Policy,* ser. D, vol. 5, nos. 15, 17, 24.

90. Warsaw Convention, 24 October 1921, Polish text in *Dziennik Ustaw,* 21 March 1922; English and French texts in *League of Nations Treaty Series,* vol. 116, no. 2699, pp. 5–311, corrections in vol. 117, pp. 459–60.

91. Franciszek Marszałek, *Prawa polskie w Wolnym Mieście Gdańsku (Ich źródła, zakres i obrona)* (Gdansk, 1959; reprint from Rocznik Gdański, vol. 15/16 [1956/57]), p. 9. See also list of the high commissioners' decisions, 1921–1933, in Mason, *Danzig Dilemma,* app. I, pp. 355–63.

92. Max Muller to Curzon, 7 June 1923, *DBFP,* 1st ser., vol. 23, no. 706, pp. 884–86; for a Foreign Office view of Polish-Danzig relations and Polish aims see Selby's memorandum of 5 June 1923, ibid., no. 705, pp. 866–84; for Consul Fry's notes on Memel on 9 December 1923 see ibid., no. 509, pp. 633–38.

93. For the Danzig-Saar agreement see n. 51 above; for a summary of discussions at the League Council in July 1923 see Headlam-Morley to Selby, 11 July 1923, *DBFP,* vol. 23, no. 720, pp. 908–13; for his longer memorandum of 10 August 1923 see ibid., app., pp. 1046–64.

94. See *Zusammenstellung der zwischen der Freien Stadt Danzig und der Republik Polen abgeschlossennen Verträge, Abkommen und Vereinbarungen 1920–1938,* vol. 3 (Danzig, 1923–39), also, Sahm, *Erinnerungen,* p. 86.

95. Sahm, *Erinnerungen,* p. 86.

96. The *Times* (London), 21 December 1923, reported that the Bank of England had supplied ₤200,000; cited in Gajda, *Postscript,* p. 176. The vice-president of the Danzig Senate, Dr. Ernst Ziehm, noted that the Bank of England held a security fund, put up by a British financial group, for the Bank of Danzig (*Aus meiner politischen Arbeit in Danzig, 1914–1939,* 2d ed. [Marburg/Lahn, 1960], p. 54).

97. Sahm, *Erinnerungen,* p. 89.

98. See Protocol of Agreement, 23 January 1924, *League of Nations Official Journal* (hereafter cited as *LNOJ*), August 1924, p. 1062.

99. Note on a conversation between Ziehm and MacDonnell, 2–4 April 1924, Dzg.Sen., WAP/G, I.260/661, pp. 9–11.

100. Note on a conversation between Sahm and MacDonnell, 7 July 1924, ibid., pp. 33–34.

101. Consul Aschmann, Geneva, 15 November 1924, cited in Kimmich, *Free City*, p. 54 n. 17.

102. Harold Nicolson, "British Policy Considered in Relation to the European Situation," 20 February 1925, FO, 371/10727/C2201/459/18, pp. 138 ff.; Austen Chamberlain's preface, p. 137 (see chap. 9 below).

103. These suggestions were made by James W. Headlam-Morley in his memorandum "The History of British Foreign Policy and the Geneva Protocol," 12 February 1925, FO, 371/11064/9/W1522/9/98 (see chap. 9 below).

104. See Austen Chamberlain's note on Danzig and the Polish-German frontier, 7 October 1926, *DBFP*, ser. IA, vol. 2, no. 245, n. 3, p. 428.

105. Commenting on a Foreign Office memorandum of 4 May 1929, dealing with German demands for colonies and revision of the Polish-German frontier, Austen Chamberlain wrote: "I dream my own dreams; whether they will ever come true is another matter and if they do, it will be after my time. But I can imagine that after long years the relations between Germany and Poland might conceivably be so improved and their common interests so great that both would be willing to put an end to the ancient feuds and that for this purpose *Poland* might make *some* territorial concession for reciprocal advantages. And it is conceivable that the League might be the decisive factor in bringing about such an arrangement—on condition that it does not move till the right moment comes." The FO memorandum is in *DBFP*, ser. IA, vol. 6, no. 134, pp. 272–73; Chamberlain's handwritten comment is on the original copy of the memorandum by J. V. Perowne, FO, 371/13617/45/18, pp. 57 ff. See also Anna M. Cienciala, "Nastawienie Austena Chamberlaina do Polski w latach 1924–1933," in *Polska-Niemcy-Europa: Studia z dziejów myśli politycznej i stosunków międzynarodowych,* ed. Antoni Czubiński (Poznań, 1977), pp. 481–94.

106. 38th session of the League Council, Secret Session, Wed. 11 March 1925, A.M., LNA, 14/9887/2385/XV.

107. *LNOJ*, April 1925, no. 1460, pp. 469–71; no. 1461, pp. 472–73.

108. Ibid., nos. 1464, 1466.

109. *LNOJ*, July 1925, no. 1516, pp. 882–96.

110. *LNOJ*, October 1925, no. 1566, pp. 1371–77.

111. Ibid., no. 1565, pp. 1367–77.

112. *LNOJ*, February 1926, no. 1630, pp. 162–63 (session of 12 December 1925, A.M.).

113. For German objections to Hamel and the harassment he suffered see Kimmich, *Free City*, pp. 96–97. Hamel's report, which was very critical of German revisionist policy and of Danzig's cooperation with Berlin, was circulated to members of the League Council in a limited edition; see report of 10 May 1929, C.221, Danzig Documents, 1929, vol. 1, no. 4: correspondence in LNA, 2/10458/2339, 22 February–4 May 1929. Hamel reproduced the gist of the report in his paper "Observations et suggestions au sujet de Dantzig et le 'Corridor Polonais,'" in *Dantzig et quelques aspects du problème germano-polonais,* ed. H. Strasburger et al. (Paris, 1932), pp. 287 ff.

114. See Kimmich, *Free City,* pp. 73–75.

115. Sahm, *Erinnerungen,* pp. 112, 114.

116. D'Abernon, *Ambassador of Peace,* 3:221.

117. A. W. G. Randall, "The Problem of Danzig," 21 August 1926, FO, 371/10998/115/N4780/55, p. 104.

118. See Joseph Beck's instruction to Ambassador Józef Lipski, 25 March 1939. Beck asked Lipski to stress Piłsudski's view of Danzig as the touchstone of Polish-German relations in his forthcoming conversation with Ribbentrop; see Wacław

Jędrzejewicz, ed., *Diplomat in Berlin, 1933-1939: Papers and Memoirs of Józef Lipski, Ambassador of Poland* (New York, 1968), pp. 506-7.

CHAPTER 5
THE POLISH-LITHUANIAN DISPUTE OVER VILNA, 1918-22

1. The key works dealing with the Vilna dispute, Polish-Lithuanian relations, and Polish federalism are: Alfred Erich Senn, *The Emergence of Modern Lithuania* (New York, 1959) and *The Great Powers, Lithuania and the Vilna Question, 1920-1928* (Leiden, 1966); M. K. Dziewanowski, *Joseph Piłsudski: A European Federalist, 1918-1922* (Stanford, Calif., 1969); Piotr S. Wandycz, "Polish Federalism 1919-20 and Its Historical Antecedents," *East European Quarterly* 4, no. 1 (1970): 25-39; Józef Lewandowski, *Federalizm: Litwa i Białoruś w polityce obozu belwederskiego (XI 1918-IV 1920)* (Warsaw, 1962); Łossowski, *Stosunki polsko-litewskie;* Aleksy Deruga, *Polityka wschodnia Polski wobec ziem Litwy, Białorusi i Ukrainy, (1918-1919)* (Warsaw, 1969); Sergiusz Mikulicz, *Prometeizm w polityce II Rzeczypospolitej* (Warsaw, 1971). For older works giving the Polish point of view see Stanisław Kutrzeba, *La Question de Wilno,* Extrait de *La Revue générale de droit international public* (Paris, 1928); Władysław Wielhorski, *Polska a Litwa: Stosunki wzajemne w biegu dziejów* (London, 1947); Adam Żółtowski, *Border of Europe: A Study of the Polish Eastern Provinces* (London, 1950). For the Lithuanian point of view see Ladas Natkevičius, *Aspect politique et juridique du différend polono-lithuanien,* 3d ed. (Paris and Kaunas, 1930).

2. For a short history of Lithuania see C. R. Jurgela, *History of the Lithuanian Nation* (New York, 1948); see also Jerzy Ochmański, *Historia Litwy* (Ossolineum, Wrocław, etc., 1967). For a short account of the development of modern Lithuanian nationalism see Senn, *Emergence,* chap. 1 passim; for a more detailed study in Polish see Jerzy Ochmański, *Litewski ruch narodowo-kulturalny w XIX wieku (do 1890r.)* (Białystok, 1965). For an excellent socio-economic-cultural study of the roots of the Lithuanian elite that emerged in the second half of the nineteenth century see Saulius A. Suziedelis, "The Lithuanian Peasantry of Trans-Niemen Lithuania, 1807-1864: A Study of Social, Economic and Cultural Change" (Ph.D. diss., University of Kansas, 1977).

3. See, for example, the views of a leading Lithuanian political writer, Mykolas Biržiška, cited in Łossowski, *Stosunki,* pp. 37-38.

4. Dmowski's statement at a meeting of the Polish National Council, Paris, 27 February 1918, cited ibid., p. 65.

5. For a detailed study of Polish federal concepts in the period 1864-1918 see Karol Grünberg, *Polskie Koncepcje federalistyczne, 1864-1918* (Warsaw, 1971). We should note that the founding of the First International in April 1864 was intimately connected with the Polish uprising of 1863/64. The International appealed for help to the Poles; see Lidia Ciołkoszowie and Adam Ciołkoszowie, *Zarys dziejów socjalizmu polskiego,* vol. 2 (London, 1972), pp. 215-45. For the First International and the Polish question see Henryk Katz, ed., *Pierwsza Międzynarodówka a sprawa polska* (Warsaw, 1964), and Marian Żychowski, *Pierwsza Międzynarodówka a sprawa polska: Dokumenty i materiały* (Warsaw, 1965); for St. Mendelson see Jerzy W. Borejsza, *W kręgu wielkich wygnańców, 1848-1895* (Warsaw, 1963), passim, and Feliks Perl (Res), *Dzieje ruchu socjalistycznego w zaborze rosyjskim (do powstania PPS)* (Warsaw, 1958), p. 454.

6. For the Congress of July 1892 see Perl, *Dzieje,* pp. 472–73, and K. Grünberg and Cz. Kozłowski, *Historia polskiego ruchu robotniczego, 1864–1918* (Warsaw, 1962), p. 96; for the split with SDKP, see Grünberg and Kozłowski, *Historia,* pp. 97 ff., also Kazimiera Janina Cottam, *Boleslaw Limanowski (1835–1935): A Study in Socialism and Nationalism* (Boulder, Colo., and New York, 1978), chaps. 6 and 7 passim.

7. For Piłsudski's 1894 article on Russia see Józef Piłsudski, *Pisma,* vol. 1 (Warsaw, 1937), pp. 90–91 (trans. A. C.).

8. For Piłsudski's Tokyo memorandum of July 1904 see ibid., 2:249–58, also Dziewanowski, *Joseph Pilsudski,* pp. 36–37, and Jerzy J. Lerski, "A Polish Chapter in the Russo-Japanese War," *Transactions of the Asiatic Society of Japan,* 3d. ser., 7 (November 1959).

9. For Piłsudski's prophetic view of the course of the World War and its results, as expressed in Paris, February 1914, see the memoirs of one of the leaders of the Russian Social Revolutionary Party, Victor Chernov, *Pered Buriei* (New York, 1953), and Jędrzejewicz, *Kronika,* 1:265–66.

10. For a summary of Leon Wasilewski's article on the eastern frontiers of the Polish state see Lewandowski, *Federalizm,* pp. 64–66.

11. See Senn, *Emergence,* p. 23.

12. On Biržiška see Łossowski, *Stosunki,* pp. 37–38; for Gabrys's map see ibid., p. 37.

13. See table 23 (I) in Władysław Czapliński and Tadeusz Ladogórski, *Atlas historyczny polski,* 2d ed. (Warsaw, 1970).

14. For the census figures see Łossowski, *Stosunki,* pp. 18–20; see also maps 1 and 5 supra.

15. See Senn, *Emergence,* pp. 13–14; Łossowski, *Stosunki,* p. 42; also Wiktor Sukiennicki, ed., "Memoriał w sprawie litewskiej złożony przez Prof. W. Zawadzkiego, 7.11.1917," *Zeszyty historyczne,* no. 30 (Paris, 1974), pp. 69–76. Zawadzki, the vice-president of the Polish Committee in Vilna, submitted the memorial to the German-controlled Polish Regency Council in Warsaw.

16. See Piłsudski, *Pisma,* 5:42; Łossowski, *Stosunki,* pp. 47–48.

17. Senn, *Great Powers,* p. 16.

18. Cited in Senn, *Emergence,* p. 45.

19. See Harry R. Rudin, *Armistice 1918* (New Haven, Conn., 1944), pp. 310–12.

20. A copy of Dmowski's memorandum "The Territory of Poland" was sent to the British foreign secretary, Lord Balfour, by Colville Barclay of the British embassy, Washington, on 23 October 1918; see FO, 371/3279/3361/188822/55. The date stamp for reception in the Foreign Office was 11 November 1918—Armistice Day.

21. Full text in *Sprawy polskie na konferencji pokojowej w Paryżu w 1919r.,* ed. Remigiusz Bierzanek and Jósef Kukułka, vols. 1–3 (Warsaw, 1965–68; hereafter cited as *SPKPP*), vol. 1, no. 10, pp. 45–56; summary in *FRUS/PPC,* 3:772–82.

22. 2 March 1919, in *SPKPP,* vol. 1, no. 22, pp. 77–104; see also Dziewanowski, *Joseph Pilsudski,* pp. 95–97, and Lundgreen-Nielsen, *Polish Problem,* pp. 207–13.

23. *Documents diplomatiques: Conflit polono-lithuanien: Question de Vilna* (Kaunas, 1924), no. 6, p. 7 (hereafter cited as *DDCPLQV*); Lundgreen-Nielsen, *Polish Problem,* pp. 253–54.

24. "Pologne, Conférence du 29 janvier 1919," AD/MAE, Pologne, Z-698-1 (1.1–3.3.1919), pp. 228–32; partly cited in Hovi, *Cordon Sanitaire,* p. 175.

25. "Memorandum by the British Delegation on the former Russian Empire," 20 January 1919, *Printed Papers, British Delegation, Paris,* FO, 374/20, pp. 71–73.

26. See David Hunter Miller, *My Diary at the Conference of Paris,* vol. 4 (New York, 1928), pp. 224–26.

27. "Supply of Arms to the Poles," 7 January 1919, note signed LBN (Lewis B. Namier), RAL (Reginald Allen Leeper), Sir R. Graham, FO, 371/3896/73/8921/55.

28. For the Russian Conference in Paris see Dziewanowski, *Joseph Pilsudski,* pp. 85–88; Wandycz, *Soviet-Polish Relations,* p. 101. For an excellent study of Polish–White Russian relations from 1918 to 1920 see Adolf Juzwenko, *Polska a "Biała" Rosja (od listopada 1918 do kwietnia 1920r)* (Wrocław, etc., 1973).

29. For Namier's comments, dated 27 December 1918, on Dmowski's memorandum "The Territory of Poland" (see n. 20 above); Namier cited H. J. Paton of the Admiralty Intelligence Department as a doubter.

30. Namier to William Tyrrell, 19 December 1918, comments on report of 9 December 1918 by Sir Horace Rumbold, British minister in Switzerland, on his conversation with a Polish delegation from the province of Grodno, FO, 371/3279/3361/205808/55.

31. Namier's comments on Sir Esme Howard's report from Poland of 26 March 1919, FO, 371/3898/73/55014/55 (section: Lithuania and White Russia); for Pichon see Lundgreen-Nielsen, *Polish Problem,* p. 253.

32. See Piłsudski, *Pisma,* 5:75–76, also Dziewanowski, *Joseph Pilsudski,* chap. 4 passim. For Piłsudski's admission that he decided to take Vilna while the Sejm was recessed for Easter see his interview with Ignacy Rosner in *Kurier Polski,* 6 January 1923, reprinted in *Pisma,* 6:11; also Jędrzejewicz, *Kronika,* 2:90. Piłsudski said that deputy Aleksander Skarbek, one of the National Democratic leaders, had threatened revolution if Piłsudski carried out his plans with respect to Vilna.

33. Łossowski, *Stosunki,* p. 66.

34. Dziewanowski, *Joseph Pilsudski,* pp. 98–99.

35. Piłsudski to Sir Percy Wyndham, British minister in Warsaw, 16 July 1919, cited in Nowak-Kiełbikowa, *Polska-Wielka Brytania,* pp. 129–30. Wyndham's full report is in FO, 371/3898/73/105824/55.

36. Leon Wasilewski, *Józef Pilsudski, jakim go znałem* (Warsaw, 1935), p. 175.

37. As per Lundgreen-Nielsen, *Polish Problem,* p. 258; but see Wandycz, *Soviet-Polish Relations,* pp. 99–100.

38. J. Karszo-Siedlecki's telegram to Ignacy Paderewski, about 23–26 April 1919, *Archiwum polityczne Ignacego Paderewskiego,* ed. Halina Janowska et al., vol. 2: *1919–1921,* ed. Andrzej Piber and Witold Stankiewicz, Polska Akademia Nauk, Instytut Historii (Ossolineum, Wrocław, etc., 1974), no. 83, p. 105 (hereafter cited as *APIP*); see also Lewandowski, *Federalizm,* pp. 170–71.

39. See Nowak-Kiełbikowa, *Polska-Wielka Brytania,* p. 107.

40. See *FRUS/PPC,* 4:628–29.

41. Paderewski to Foreign Minister, Paris, 26 April 1919, *APIP,* vol. 2, no. 90, p. 117.

42. *SPKPP,* vol. 2, no. 47, pp. 436–37; also Lewandowski, *Federalizm,* p. 171.

43. *DDCPLQV,* no. 5, pp. 15–17.

44. Note of 26 May 1919 to Admiral Kolchak, *FRUS, 1919, Russia,* pp. 369–70, and *DBFP,* 1st ser., vol. 3, no. 233, pp. 331–32.

45. Senn, *Emergence,* p. 122.

46. *Conférence de la paix, 1919–1920: Recueil des actes de la conférence,* Partie IV, Commissions de la Conférence, C. Questions Territoriales, 7 (Paris, 1924), pp. 48–49 (hereafter cited as *CPRAC*).

47. Conference of Foreign Ministers, 24 May 1919, *FRUS/PPC,* 4:766–73.

48. For British views see James W. Headlam-Morley's letter to Rex Leeper, 30 May 1919, Headlam-Morley, *Memoir,* p. 132; for the statement in July 1919 see Esme Howard in Commission for Baltic Affairs, 7 July 1919, *CPRAC,* C(7), Proces Verbal no. 14, p. 148, partly cited in Łossowski, *Stosunki,* p. 174, no. 69. In April 1920, Gregory wrote retrospectively on British policy toward the Baltic States: "It was held to be undersirable to afford full recognition to these new states so long as there was a chance in the near future of a reconstruction of Russia under anti-Bolshevik leaders which might result in their re-absorption into a 'Great Russia.' . . . Eventually, therefore, the component parts of the old Russian Empire are bound to come together again, but this time in a strictly limited economic federalism, and decentralized politically to the fullest extent" (*DBFP,* 1st ser., vol. 11, no. 292). For French views opposing Polish-Lithuanian federation see Pichon to French Minister in Warsaw, 12 May 1919, AD/MAE, Pologne, Z698-1 (12.XI.18–20.VII.19); for Voldemaras's appeal to V. A. Maklakov and the latter's letter to Kammerer, 9 May 1919, see ibid.

49. For the Polish-Lithuanian conversations and exchanges of notes in June 1919 see Łossowski, *Stosunki,* pp. 96–99, and *SPKPP,* vol. 2, nos. 30, 51, 56.

50. *Glos Litwy,* 29 May 1919, no. 13, cited in Łossowski, *Stosunki,* p. 94.

51. Paris, 7 July 1919, *APIP,* vol. 2, no. 196 (2d), p. 256.

52. Władysław Skrzyński to Paderewski, Warsaw, 10 July 1919, ibid., no. 205, p. 266; see also Juzwenko, *Polska,* pp. 168–69.

53. For Namier's comments on Sir Esme Howard's report of 26 March 1919 see n. 31 above.

54. *CPRAC,* pt. IV, C(2), pp. 426 ff.

55. W. Skrzyński, telegram to Foreign Ministry, Paris, May 1919 (no day), *APIP,* vol. 2, no. 143, p. 175.

56. See n. 47 above.

57. See Entente Line of 18 June 1919 on map 4 supra.

58. Gen. Tadeusz Rozwadowski, head of Polish Military Mission in France, to Marshal Foch, Paris, 15 July 1919, *SPKPP,* vol. 2, no. 59, pp. 454–55.

59. See map cited in n. 57 above, shown on map 6 in this book.

60. By southern Suwałki Province we mean Augustów County; here 66.8% of the population was Polish-speaking and 8.5% Lithuanian; the rest were Russians, Germans, and Jews; see Łossowski, *Stosunki,* p. 21.

61. Cited in Nowak-Kiełbikowa, *Polska-Wielka Brytania,* p. 131, and Łossowski, *Stosunki,* p. 173; Nowak-Kiełbikowa cites Serejski, *Kolekcja;* Łossowski cites A. Bezverchnis, "Imperialistu sekimai itraukti Lietuva i kara pries tarybu Rusija antro antantes zygio metu," in *Uz socialistine Lietuva,* p. 144; he notes that the author used Lithuanian government documents now in the Central State Archives, Vilna.

62. See n. 35 above.

63. Namier's comments of 23 July 1919, in file entitled "Limitation of Polish Advance on the Bolshevik Front," FO, 371/3899/73/103944/55.

64. See G. W. Prothero, gen. ed., *Handbooks Prepared under the Direction of the Historical Section of the Foreign Office,* no. 44: *Russian Poland, Lithuania and White Russia* (London, 1920), p. 20. The source cites the Russian census of 1897 as follows: White Russians (Belorussians, A. C.)—5,447,000; Jews—1,414,000; Lithuanians—1,408,000; Poles—565,000; Great Russians—500,000; Little Russians (Ruthenians)—380,000; Letts (Latvians, A. C.)—308,000. However, the author also states: "The Great Russian population at the date of the census was chiefly composed of officials and soldiers who did not settle permanently in the district. There is no doubt that the Polish populataion is much larger than these figures allow."

65. See Senn, *Emergence,* p. 147; Łossowski, *Stosunki,* p. 118.

66. Senn, *Emergence;* for L. Wasilewski's report of 15 August 1919, see *SPKPP,* vol. 2, no. 62, pp. 457–59.

67. See Nowak-Kiełbikowa, *Polska-Wielka Brytania,* p. 132.

68. According to L. Wasilewski, Brodie was an anglicized Jew from Kiev (Brodsky); he claimed to be tremendously impressed by Piłsudski and played the role of an unofficial mediator between the Poles and Lithuanians (Wasilewski, *Piłsudski,* p. 204).

69. For the view that Polish expectations of an uprising were unfounded, see Łossowski, *Stosunki,* pp. 133–34, also Lewandowski, *Federalizm,* pp. 188–89. For internal unrest in Lithuania, also on S. Narutavičius and S. Žukauskas, see Wiktor Sukiennicki, "Wojna?—Nie, Dialog," *Zeszyty historyczne,* no. 48 (Paris, 1978), especially pp. 27–33; see also Tadeusz Katelbach, "Moja misja kowieńska," ibid., no. 36 (Paris, 1976): 60–96. Katelbach writes that in a conversation of 1 June 1919, Piłsudski definitely forbade a POW rising in Suwałki Province but later changed his mind.

70. According to Lithuanian documents captured by the Poles, the twenty-one British officers served in the Lituanian army from September 1919 to February 1920; eleven American officers also served (see Łossowski, *Stosunki,* p. 174). According to A. M. Andreev, *Bor'ba litovskogo naroda za sovetskuiu vlast' (1918–1919)* (Moscow, 1954), p. 128, who cites Lithuanian archival documents, the British also gave the Lithuanians 15,000 rifles, 500 machine guns, 12 tanks, and 10 airplanes (cited in Łossowski, *Stosunki,* p. 174 n. 71); see also Brig. Gen. F. P. Crozier, *Impressions and Recollections* (London, 1930), chap. 11, "Lithuania." Paderewski asked Sir Horace Rumbold, British minister in Warsaw, on 29 October 1919, about rumors that there were British instructors in the Lithuanian army. Paderewski then expounded his view that Poland could not maintain its position in Danzig without being able to exercise pressure on East Prussia from Lithuania; he also stated his disbelief that an independent Lithuania was possible, for, in his view, it would always serve as a corridor between Germany and Russia (draft, H. Rumbold to Curzon, no. 409, 29 October 1919, FO, 688/1, f. 6/156).

71. See Wasilewski's report to Skrzyński on the Special Mission to Kaunas and Vilna, 24 September 1919, cited in Łossowski, *Stosunki,* pp. 154–55.

72. Senn, *Great Powers,* p. 22; Sukiennicki sees British financial aid to Lithuania as the decisive factor in the failure of the uprising (see n. 69 above).

73. Senn, *Emergence,* pp. 165–66. In 1917, Sablin was listed as counsellor and chargé d'affaires in the Russian embassy, London; see *The Statesman's Year-book* (London, 1917).

74. Memorandum by R. H. Hoare, 22 December 1919, *DBFP,* 1st ser., vol. 3, no. 619, pp. 735–38.

75. Memorandum by H. P. B. Maxse, *DBFP,* 1st ser., vol. 12, no. 787.

76. *Le Temps,* 4 October 1919, cited in Senn, *Emergence,* p. 162.

77. For the view that France's primary object in establishing the "Cordon sanitaire" was the separation of Germany and Russia in order to prevent German domination of Russia see K. Hovi, *Cordon Sanitaire,* passim, and chap. 1 above.

78. On 22 September 1919, W. Skrzyński wrote Paderewski that the latter's telegram from Paris (not printed) was unclear. According to (Eugene) Pralon, the French minister in Warsaw, Paderewski had promised that in return for Foch's order to German troops in the northeast to withdraw, Poland would not intervene independently in the "Baltic states." Kukułka believes that the French feared that another Polish *fait accompli* would make their Russian policy more difficult and that

they therefore desired the annulment of the planned Polish military action (see Kukułka, *Francja,* p. 126).

79. The Supreme Council's line of 8 December 1919 was the same as the Curzon Line (1920) down to the border of East Galicia; see map 1 supra. For the Supreme Council's statement of 8 December 1919, see *FRUS/PPC,* vol. 9, p. 447, also Wandycz, *Soviet-Polish Relations,* p. 148.

80. Wandycz, *Soviet-Polish Relations,* pp. 148–49; see also Lewandowski, *Federalizm,* pp. 146–55, who cites Denikin's memoirs. For the Polish Military Mission to Denikin see Juzwenko, *Polska,* pp. 235–46.

81. Łossowski, *Stosunki,* p. 149.

82. Wasilewski, *Piłsudski,* pp. 209–13.

83. Łossowski, *Stosunki,* p. 186.

84. Senn, *Emergence,* p. 194; see also Andrzej Skrzypek, *Związek bałtycki, 1919–1924: Litwa, Łotwa, Estonia i Finlandia w polityce Polski i ZSRR w latach 1919–1925* (Warsaw, 1972), pp. 48–49.

85. Skrzypek, *Związek,* p. 50.

86. Nowak-Kiełbikowa, *Polska-Wielka Brytania,* p. 171.

87. Ibid.; the author cites Polish archives; also Łossowski, *Stosunki,* p. 192, citing a report by the Latvian minister in London, Biesenieks, 12 February 1920, from Vilnis Sipols, *Die ausländische Intervention in Lettland, 1918–1920* (Berlin, 1961), p. 211.

88. See "Conclusions of a Conference of Ministers, 27 January 1920," where the conversation with Patek was discussed, Cab. 23/20, pp. 109–10; and see Curzon to Rumbold, 27 January 1920, *DBFP,* 1st ser., vol. 3, no. 664, pp. 803–5.

89. Carton de Wiart, head of the British Military Mission in Poland, came to see Piłsudski with Colonel Robinson, head of the British Mission in Kaunas. Carton de Wiart's message was reported in the Socialist paper *Robotnik,* 17 April 1920, which, however, misinterpreted his statement that Britain would see any Polish "defensive action" as being justified to mean a British warning to Lithuania (cited in Nowak-Kiełbikowa, *Polska-Wielka Brytania,* p. 173).

90. *DBFP,* vol. 11, nos. 241 and 243, pp. 27–72; see also vol. 7, no. 75, pp. 677–78.

91. Senn, *Emergence,* pp. 204–5.

92. Łossowski, *Stosunki,* pp. 189–90; Skrzypek, *Związek,* pp. 53–64.

93. *Pravda,* no. 73, 3 April 1920, cited in Senn, *Emergence,* p. 212.

94. Senn, *Emergence,* p. 213.

95. See Ward to Curzon, 28 May 1920, and (Alfred) Tyszkiewicz (Lithuanian minister in London) to Curzon, 31 May 1920, *DBFP,* vol. 11, nos. 283 and 285, pp. 338–40. Tyszkiewicz was formerly a secretary in the tsarist Russian embassy in London (see Senn, *Emergence,* p. 178). The Lithuanian foreign minister told Colonel Ward that he expected the Russians to defeat the Poles if the Entente did not intervene. He also stated that the Soviet government's first condition for accepting Lithuania's (territorial) demands was that she would make no treaty with Poland, see ibid., no. 283, cited above.

96. *Documents diplomatiques concernant les relations Polono-Lithuaniennes* (Warsaw, 1921), no. 28, p. 40 (hereafter cited as *DDRPL*).

97. *DBFP,* 1st ser., vol. 8, no. 57. app. 2c, p. 518.

98. See *Dokumenty vneshnei politiki SSSR,* vol. 3 (Moscow, 1959), pp. 38–42 (hereafter cited as *DVPSSSR*). The English text of the Soviet-Lithuanian treaty is in *British and Foreign State Papers,* vol. 113 (London, 1923), pp. 1121–22; see also Wandycz, *Soviet-Polish Relations,* p. 209; Dziewanowski, *Joseph Pilsudski,* p. 314; and

Senn, *Great Powers,* p. 32, where Senn notes: "Since the Bolsheviks were acting as the legal heirs of the Tsarist Government, the treaty marked the legal birth of the Lithuanian state."

99. Lithuanian-Soviet agreement of 6 August 1920, cited according to captured Lithuanian documents in Łossowski, *Stosunki,* p. 221.

100. *DDCPLQV,* no. 32 and annex, pp. 43–44; Łossowski, *Stosunki,* p. 219.

101. Opinion paper of Polish Military Intelligence, signed by Gen. Tadeusz Rozwadowski, cited in Łossowski, *Stosunki,* p. 220. The Polish emissaries left for Kaunas on 21 August 1920 (ibid.).

102. See ibid., p. 227; the Polish proposals were published in *DDRPL,* no. 35 and annex, pp. 51–53.

103. Adam Romer's report, cited in Łossowski, *Stosunki,* pp. 228–29.

104. *DDCPLQV,* no. 22, p. 42; *DDRPL,* no. 33, p. 45. Łossowski notes that the Polish document erroneously cites Grajewo instead of Grabowo (*Stosunki,* pp. 230–31). See map 4 supra.

105. *DDCPLQV,* no. 23, p. 46; *DDRPL,* no. 34, p. 45.

106. Curzon to Rumbold, 31 August 1920, *DBFP,* vol. 11, no. 499, p. 537.

107. The Lithuanian Military Intelligence report of 10 September 1920 assumed that a Soviet offensive would begin along the whole Polish front on 20 or 21 September (see captured Lithuanian documents cited in Łossowski, *Stosunki,* p. 233).

108. Records of the Polish State Council of 4 September 1920, cited ibid., pp. 235–36 (trans. A. C.).

109. *DDRPL,* no. 39, pp. 61–62; *DDCPLQV,* no. 39, pp. 69–70.

110. See n. 106 above.

111. Curzon to Rumbold, 2 September 1920, *DBFP,* vol. 11, no. 509, p. 542.

112. Rumbold to Curzon, 4 September 1920, ibid., no. 513, pp. 544–45.

113. Gustaw Szura, Paderewski's representative in Paris, reported on 6 September 1920 that the Quai d'Orsay feared that the latest Polish-Lithuanian incident might be the first step in a Polish advance on Vilna. However, Mikołaj Jurystowski, first counsellor at the Polish legation, Paris, was informed at the same time that Poland's attitude was completely satisfactory, *APIP,* vol. 2, no. 360, p. 469. Kukułka notes that in September the French military, influenced by the reports of the French Military Mission in Poland, began to understand and support Polish strategic arguments (*Francja,* p. 291).

114. See Wandycz, *Soviet-Polish Relations,* map facing p. 254; the line was slightly east of the Polish-Soviet frontier as later fixed by the Treaty of Riga, March 1921.

115. Note from Jan Ciechanowski, Polish chargé in London, to Curzon, 6 September 1920, *DBFP,* vol. 11, no 518, pp. 548–49. See also Łossowski, *Stosunki,* p. 240.

116. Ciechanowski report on a conversation with Lord Hardinge, 12 September 1920, cited in Łossowski, *Stosunki,* p. 240; see also Curzon to Derby, *DBFP,* vol. 11, no. 523, pp. 555–56.

117. Curzon to Rumbold, 10 September 1920, *DBFP,* vol. 11, no. 521, p. 533; see also memorandum by Gregory on the attitude of the British government toward de jure recognition of Estonia, Latvia, and Lithuania, 2 November 1920, ibid., no. 630, p. 653, and Curzon to Dewhurst (Riga), 6 January 1921, ibid., no. 681, p. 707.

118. On 11 May 1920 the French government gave de facto recognition to Latvia and Lithuania. It sent a special commissioner to the Baltic States, and the director general of the so-called Noulens bank group arrived in Riga (see *DBFP,* vol. 11, no. 274, p. 320, and Kukułka, *Francja,* p. 287).

119. See Łossowski, *Stosunki,* pp. 243–45.
120. See Rumbold to Curzon, 13 September 1920, FO, 800/156. At this time, Ciechanowski complained to Lord Hardinge about Ward, but considered the suggested candidacy of Stephen Tallents, British commissioner in the Baltic States, to be even worse (see Nowak-Kiełbikowa, *Polska-Wielka Brytania,* p. 267).
121. See Senn, *Great Powers,* p. 40; for Paderewski's speech of 16 September 1920 to the League of Nations Council see *APIP,* vol. 2, no. 366, pp. 490–92; for Voldemaras's statement of 16 September and Hymans's report of 20 September see *DDCPLQV,* nos. 39, 40, also *DDRPL,* no. 39, and *LNOJ,* 1920, nos. 19–23; summary in Łossowski, *Stosunki,* pp. 247–48.
122. See *APIP,* vol. 2, nos. 370 and 371, pp. 497–98.
123. *DVPSSSR,* vol. 3, p. 212; Senn, *Great Powers,* p. 40.
124. Rumbold to Curzon, 23 September 1920, *DBFP,* vol. 11, no. 541, pp. 571–72.
125. See Łossowski, *Stosunki,* p. 260 n. 154.
126. *DDRPL,* no. 45, p. 76; *DDCPLQV,* no. 45, pp. 78–79; *APIP,* vol. 2, no. 374, pp. 503–4.
127. Curzon to Derby, 5 October 1920, *DBFP,* vol. 11, no. 554, pp. 583–84.
128. Derby to Curzon, 7 October 1920, ibid., no. 556, pp. 584–85.
129. Loraine to Curzon, 7 October 1920, ibid., no. 558, p. 586.
130. Curzon to Derby, 7 October 1920, ibid., no. 561, pp. 587–88.
131. Askenazy report of 10 October 1920, cited in Łossowski, *Stosunki,* p. 266. However, on 2 October, the premier and foreign minister, Georges Leygues, told the Polish minister, Maurycy Zamoyski, that a Polish occupation of Vilna was inadvisable, and Gen. Maxime Weygand told Capt. Ludwig Morstin, Polish liaison officer with Marshal Foch's staff, that the Poles must bear in mind the reaction of world opinion, particularly the British (cited in Kukułka, *Francja,* p. 293). Leygues advised: "Show more moderation and you will get what you deserve later" (Paderewski to Sapieha, 29 September 1920, *APIP,* vol. 2, no. 375, p. 305; trans. A. C.).
132. Paderewski to Sapieha, 3 October 1920, *APIP,* vol. 2, no. 377, p. 508.
133. See chaps. 2 and 4 above.
134. Cited in Dziewanowski, *Joseph Pilsudski,* p. 316, and Łossowski, *Stosunki,* p. 269.
135. Account by Zeligowski, cited in Łossowski, *Stosunki,* p. 271; and see Lucjan Żeligowski, "Notatki z roku 1920," *Niepodległość,* n.s. 3 (London, 1951); also, Adam Koc, "Józef Piłsudski we wspomnieniach tych którzy go znali," *Na Antenie,* no. 58 (London, 1958), cited in Jędrzejewicz, *Kronika,* 1:523, 525.
136. For the Suwałki Conference see Senn, *Great Powers,* pp. 44–46 and n. 63, and Dziewanowski, *Joseph Pilsudski,* pp. 316–18. For a detailed account see Łossowski, *Stosunki,* pp. 227–85; for the demarcation line proposed at Suwałki by the Polish and Lithuanian delegations see map 4 supra.
137. See Wacław Chocianowicz, "Historia dywizji litewsko-białoruskiej w świetle listów Józefa Piłsudskiego," *Niepodległość,* n.s. 3 (London, 1962): 212; Katelbach, "Moja misja kowieńska," cited in Jędrzejewicz, *Kronika,* 1:525; see also Dziewanowski, *Joseph Pilsudski,* chap. 16 passim and p. 316. For a detailed account see Łossowski, *Stosunki,* pp. 272–74, 280, 290–93.
138. Łossowski, *Stosunki,* pp. 293–94.
139. Ibid., pp. 294–97.
140. Colonel Ward to Curzon, Vilna, 8 October 1920 (marked "received 20 October"), FO, 417/9, no. 6, pp. 105–6.

141. Senn, *Great Powers,* pp. 48–49; Łossowski, *Stosunki,* pp. 300–302.

142. Łossowski, *Stosunki,* p. 305.

143. Ibid., p. 307; Colonel Ward to Curzon, Vilna, 10 October 1920 (received 20 October), FO, 419/9, no. 82, pp. 137–47.

144. Łossowski, *Stosunki,* p. 308.

145. Ibid.

146. Record by Mr. (J. D.) Gregory of a conversation with Mr. (J.) Ciechanowski, 11 October 1920, *DBFP,* vol. 11, no. 566, pp. 593–94; see also Ciechanowski to Paderewski, 11 October, *APIP,* vol. 2, no. 382, pp. 517–18.

147. Curzon to Derby, 11 October 1920, *DBFP,* vol. 11, no. 564, p. 592.

148. For Gregory to Ciechanowski see n. 146 above. The Polish-Soviet agreement was mentioned in a letter from S. Dąbrowski to Paderewski, Warsaw, 5 October 1920, *APIP,* vol. 2, no. 380, pp. 512–13. Dąbrowski warned Paderewski of Piłsudski's plans to march on Vilna.

149. See Kukułka, *Francja,* pp. 296–97.

150. See ibid., pp. 298–99.

151. Curzon's note on Gregory's report of 11 October on conversation with Ciechanowski (see n. 146 above).

152. Curzon to Derby, 12 October 1920, *DBFP,* vol. 11, no. 574, pp. 600–601.

153. See *DBFP,* vol. 11, no. 556, p. 584–85.

154. Ibid., no. 576, pp. 602–4.

155. Loraine to Curzon, 14 October, ibid., no. 578, pp. 605–7. Paderewski was so upset that he offered his resignation to Foreign Minister Sapieha on 15 October, *APIP,* vol. 2, no. 387, pp. 520–21. Sapieha, in a letter to Paderewski of 17 October, admitted that the government had expected the action and that athough it condemned Żeligowski, it also believed his action was "the only way to save Vilna" (ibid., no. 389, pp. 521–22). In early December 1922, when Piłsudski was about to give up his post as chief of state to the president-elect, Gabriel Narutowicz, he told the ministers of France, Britain, Italy, and the United States the truth about the Vilna affair (see Jędrzejewicz, *Kronika,* 2:77).

156. Curzon to Derby, Loraine to Curzon, *DBFP,* vol. 11, nos. 582 and 583, pp. 610–12.

157. Ibid., no. 590, pp. 617–18.

158. Łossowski, *Stosunki,* pp. 312–13.

159. Ibid., p. 314.

160. Ibid., p. 311–12.

161. Ibid., p. 317.

162. Gregory memorandum, 17 October 1920, FO, 371/5400/N695/272/55, cited in Nowak-Kiełbikowa, *Polska-Wielka Brytania,* p. 274.

163. Sapieha mentioned "information from our Legation in London," *APIP,* vol. 2, no. 389, p. 522. For Sir Eyre Crowe's favorable attitude toward a Polish-Lithuanian federation see FO, 371/5401/N541/55, cited in Tadeusz Piszczkowski, *Anglia a Polska, 1914–1939: W świetle dokumentów brytyjskich* (London, 1975), pp. 177–78.

164. Draft telegram, Loraine to Gregory, 21 October 1920, FO, 688/14/3438, p. 3.

165. Curzon to G. Graham, 27 October 1920, *DBFP,* vol. 11, no. 617, pp. 641–42.

166. See Kukułka, *Francja,* pp. 428–29. Léon Bourgeois had denounced Żeligowski's action as a violation of Poland's obligation to the league and warned that if he

did not withdraw, the league would act (see Senn, *Great Powers*, p. 51; for the league session, ibid., pp. 53–54, and Łossowski, *Stosunki*, pp. 342–45; also *DDCPLQV*, chap. 2 passim).

167. Sapieha to Paderewski, 17 October 1920, *APIP*, vol. 2, no. 389, pp. 522–23.

168. Paderewski and Askenazy to Léon Bourgeois, 7 November 1920, ibid., no. 419, pp. 556–57; *LNOJ*, Special Supplement no. 4, 1920, no. 86; *DDCPLQV*, no. 64, pp. 111–12.

169. Senn, *Great Powers*, p. 54; *DDCPLQV*, no. 63, pp. 108–10.

170. Senn, *Great Powers*, p. 55 n. 39; full text in Voldemaras to L. Bourgeois, 23 November 1920, *DDCPLQV*, no. 65, p. 113 (trans. A. C.).

171. Curzon to Balfour, 27 October 1920, FO, 371/6794/N463/55, cited in Piszczkowski, *Anglia*, p. 180.

172. Łossowski, *Stosunki*, pp. 350–52.

173. Ibid., pp. 364–65; for the armistice protocol of 29 November 1920 see *DDCPLQV*, no. 69 and annex, pp. 123–24.

174. See Loraine to Curzon, 12 December 1920, *DBFP*, vol. 11, no. 671, p. 696; for the French view as reported by the Polish legation in Paris, 15 January 1921, see AAN, Amb.Pol.Paryż, vol. 110, pp. 46–63. However, the French opposed Polish annexation of Grodno and proposed that Memel be available for use by both Lithuania and Poland.

175. Senn, *Great Powers*, p. 60.

176. Ibid., p. 62; *DDCPLQV*, no. 87, pp. 164–65.

177. See Muller's report, 23 March 1921, *DBFP*, 1st ser., vol. 23, no. 3, pp. 4–6.

178. Ibid., p. 6 n. 7.

179. *DBFP*, vol. 23, no. 11, pp. 14–15.

180. See Muller's report, 19 April 1921, ibid., no. 22, pp. 29–34.

181. Memorandum by Col. Stanisław Laudański, "Les frontières actuelles de la Pologne par rapport à son role en Europe," sent to Gen. Henri Niessel, head of French Military Mission in Poland, April 1921, cited in Kukułka, *Francja*, p. 551. Laudański was attached to the Polish General Staff.

182. Hardinge to Curzon, 26 April, 1921, *DBFP*, vol. 23, no. 28, encl. 1, pp. 38–41; this was a reply to the British note of 16 April.

183. Foreign Office memorandum of 7 May 1921, FO, 371/7698/N5084/55, cited in Piszczkowski, *Anglia*, pp. 183–84; see also *DBFP*, vol. 23, nos. 42, 43.

184. Kukułka, *Francja*, p. 552.

185. Senn, *Great Powers*, pp. 68 ff.; for the Brussels negotiations see *LNOJ*, September 1921, no. 7, and *DDCPLQV*, nos. 95 and 96 and annexes, pp. 176–236; see also *DBFP*, vol. 23, no. 52.

186. Senn, *Great Powers*, p. 69.

187. Ibid., pp. 69–70; *DDCPLQV*, annex 7 to no. 95, pp. 228-29.

188. Senn, *Great Powers*, pp. 71–72; *DDCPLQV*, annexes 10 and 11 to nos. 95 and 96, pp. 234–36; *LNOJ*, Special Supplement no. 4, 1921; and *DBFP*, vol. 23, no. 63.

189. See Skrzypek, *Związek*, pp. 112–13.

190. Senn, *Great Powers*, p. 73; *DDCPLQV*, nos. 97–100, pp. 237–43; *LNOJ*, Special Supplement no. 4, 1921.

191. Senn, *Great Powers*, pp. ·74–75; *DDCPLQV*, no. 100, pp. 243–46.

192. *DDCPLQV*, no. 102, pp. 247–52.

193. Senn, *Great Powers*, pp. 75–76; *DDCPLQV*, nos. 103-6, pp. 253–58.

194. Senn, *Great Powers*, pp. 76–77; *DDCPLQV*, no. 108, pp. 264–65.

195. Kukułka, *Francja*, p. 553.

196. Zamoyski's report of 4 October 1921, cited ibid., p. 554.
197. Ibid.
198. Senn, *Great Powers*, p. 78; for Piłsudski's policy statement see *Pisma*, 5:226–28.
199. Zamoyski's statement to the Political Committee of the Council of Ministers, 10 January 1922, cited in Kukułka, *Francja*, p. 556.
200. Ibid.
201. See *DVPSSSR*, 4:331, 338–39, cited in Senn, *Great Powers*, p. 80. On 28 April 1921, Chicherin instructed S. Aralov, Soviet plenipotentiary representative in Kaunas, that Lithuania's fate, her foreign policy, and her international position would play an extremely important role in Soviet policy. He claimed that there was no word (in the Treaty of Riga) about Soviet lack of interest in relations with Lithuania, nor any violation of the Moscow (Soviet-Lithuanian) Treaty of 12 July 1920. The Treaty of Riga's stipulation that the Vilna question should be decided by Poland and Lithuania did not mean that until such time as the latter decided to give Vilna to Poland, she was not sovereign there. Chicherin wrote that there was every reason to think the Żeligowski "adventure" was to prepare the way for the use of hostile forces against the Soviet Union. Lithuania was one of Soviet Russia's vital international interests; hence the aim of Soviet policy would be to prevent Lithuania from becoming an economic vassal of the Western Powers (*DVPSSSR*, 4:86–88, also *Dokumenty i materiały do historii stosunkow polsko-radzieckich*, ed. Natalia Gąsiorowska-Grabowska, I. A. Khrienov, et al., vol. 4: April 1921–May 1926, ed. Aleksy Deruga et al. [Warsaw, 1965], no. 5, pp. 7–8 [hereafter cited as *DIM*]).
202. Senn, *Great Powers*, p. 82; *DDCPLQV*, no. 109, pp. 266–67; also *DBFP*, vol. 23, no. 244.
203. Cited in Nowak-Kiełbikowa, *Polska-Wielka Brytania*, p. 347.
204. Ibid., pp. 347–48. French pressure was also strong; Briand sent a letter deprecating annexation as "an act of folly" (see *DBFP*, vol. 23, no. 263, p. 333).
205. Senn, *Great Powers*, p. 85.
206. Ibid., pp. 85–86.
207. Ibid., pp. 84–85; *LNOJ*, vol. 3 (1921), pp. 138–39; *DDCPLQV*, no. 109 and annex, pp. 267–70.
208. Cited in Nowak-Kiełbikowa, *Polska-Wielka Brytania*, p. 348.
209. Ibid., p. 349.
210. See chap. 8 below.
211. See Anna M. Cienciala, *Poland and the Western Powers, 1938–39: A Study in the Interdependence of Eastern and Western Europe* (London and Toronto, 1968), pp. 49–52.

CHAPTER 6
EAST GALICIA AND THE QUESTION OF POLAND'S EASTERN FRONTIER, NOVEMBER 1918 TO DECEMBER 1921

1. On the negotiations for the Polish-Rumanian alliance see Henryk Bułhak, "Początki sojuszu polsko-rumuńskiego i przebieg rokowań o konwencję woiskową w latach 1919–1921," *Dzieje Najnowsze*, 1973, no. 3:21–52. For a brief survey of Polish-Rumanian relations see Henryk Bułhak and Antoni Zieliński, "Pologne et Roumanie 1918-1939," *Acta Poloniae Historica* 41 (Warsaw, 1980): 171–77.

2. See G. W. Prothero, gen. ed., *Handbooks Prepared under the Direction of the Historical Section of the Foreign Office,* no. 46: *Austrian Poland* (London, 1920). According to the Austrian census of 1910, the Ukrainian population of East Galicia amounted to 59 percent and the Poles to 39 percent (ibid., p. 10). Since the Ukrainians protested that the Polish percentage was too high, the figure of 35 percent is accepted here (see maps 1 and 5 supra).

3. See Ivan L. Rudnytsky, "Polish-Ukrainian Relations: The Burden of History," and Frank E. Sysyn, "Ukrainian-Polish Relations in the Seventeenth Century: The Role of National Consciousness and National Conflict in the Khmelnytsky Movement," in *Poland and Ukraine: Past and Present,* ed. Peter J. Potichnyj (Edmonton and Toronto, 1980), pp. 11, 58–82.

4. Mykhailo Hrushevs'kyi, *Istoriia Ukraiiny-Rusy,* 10 vols. (Kiev and Lwow, 1898–1936; reprint, New York, 1954). There is a one-volume summary in English: *Outline of the History of the Ukraine* (London, 1904), and *A History of the Ukraine* (New Haven, Conn., 1941); see also Ivan L. Rudnytsky, "The Ukrainians in Galicia under Austrian Rule," and Piotr Wandycz, "The Poles in the Habsburg Monarchy," chaps. 2 and 3 in *Nationbuilding and the Politics of Nationalism: Essays on Austrian Galicia,* ed. Andrei S. Markovits and Frank E. Sysyn (Cambridge, Mass., 1982), pp. 23–67, 68–93.

5. On East Ukraine see Steven L. Guthier, "The Popular Base of Ukrainian Nationalism in 1917," *Slavic Review* 38, no. 1 (1979): 30–47; John S. Reshetar, Jr., *The Ukrainian Revolution, 1917–1920: A Study in Nationalism* (Princeton, N.J., 1952); also covers East Galicia. For a Ukrainian view of the Polish-Ukrainian struggle see *Ukraine: A Concise Encyclopaedia,* vol. 1 (Toronto, 1963), pp. 770–86, and vol. 2 (Toronto, 1971), pp. 63–66. For an older Ukrainian view see W. Kutschabsky, *Die Westukraine im Kampfe mit Polen und dem Bolschewismus in den Jahren 1918–1923* (Berlin, 1934). For list of Ukrainian-language works see the bibliography in Michael Yaremko, *Galicia-Halychyna: From Separation to Unity* (Toronto, New York, and Paris, 1967). For a recent Polish interpretation see Dziewanowski, *Joseph Pilsudski,* pp. 217–32; Władysław A. Serczyk, *Historia Ukrainy* (Wrocław, etc., 1979), is good up to 1917; two older Polish works worth citing are Józef Skrzypek, *Ukraińcy w Austrii podczas wielkiej wojny i geneza zamachu na Lwów* (Warsaw, 1939), and Leon Wasilewski, *Ukraińska sprawa narodowa w jej rozwoju historycznym* (Warsaw, 1925).

6. See John W. Wheeler-Bennett, *Brest-Litovsk: The Forgotten Peace, March 1918,* 1st ed. (London, 1938; reprint, London and New York, 1963), app. 4; also *Texts of the Ukrainian "Peace"* (Department of State, Washington, D.C., 1918); Reshetar, *Ukrainian Revolution,* p. 181.

7. See Helga Grebing, "Österreich-Ungarn und die 'Ukrainische Aktion' 1914–18," *Jahrbücher für Geschichte Osteuropas* 7, no. 3 (Munich, 1959): 270–96; see also Fritz Fischer, *Germany's Aims in the First World War* (New York, 1967), pt. 3, pp. 534–62.

8. See Arnold Margolin, *Ukraine and Policy of the Entente* (n.p., 1977), translation of *Ukraina i politika Antanty* (Berlin, 1921), by V. P. Sokoloff, chap. 10 passim; also Arnold D. Margolin, *From a Political Diary: Russia, the Ukraine, and America, 1905–1945* (New York, 1946), chap. 4 passim.

9. J. Skrzypek, *Ukraińcy w Austrii,* pp. 107 ff.

10. Balfour memorandum, 4 October 1916, cited in Nelson, *Land and Power,* p. 9; also Lloyd George, *War Memoirs,* 2:523–29, and Dugdale, *Arthur James Balfour,* vol. 2, app. 2, pp. 323–27.

11. Balfour memorandum on Poland, 18 October 1918, cited in Nelson, *Land and Power*, pp. 63–65.

12. "Memorandum on Poland," 3 May 1917, FO, 371/30001, f. 6784, pc. 9238, cited (in Polish) in Anna M. Cienciala, "Polityka brytyjska wobec odrodzenia Polski, 1914–1918," *Zeszyty historyczne* 16 (Paris, 1969): 77.

13. Namier note, 3 May 1918, FO, 371/3278, f. 3361, pc. 7431.

14. Namier, comment on letter by G. Sackville-West, 26 August 1918, FO, 371/3276, f. 3361, pc. 148264.

15. "The Problem of East Galicia," received 13 November 1918, submitted by Mr. Namier for delegation, FO, 371/4352, f. 6, pc. 6, pp. 123–30.

16. "Poland: Report On," 3 December 1918, FO, 371/4354, Peace Conference Series Files, PID file 46, pc. 73, pp. 122–23.

17. German Foreign Ministry memoranda, November 1918–June 1919, cited in Mayer, *Politics and Diplomacy of Peacemaking*, p. 231.

18. This is my view of Namier's role, as expressed in the article cited in note 12 above; Kay Lundgreen-Nielsen thinks this is still an open question (see *Polish Problem*, p. 59).

19. Note by Namier, 8 November 1918, FO, 371/3279/3361/189358/55.

20. See S. Filasiewicz, *La Question polonaise pendant la première guerre mondiale: Recueil des actes diplomatiques, traités et documents concernant la Pologne* (Paris, 1920), vol. 2, no. 280, p. 579, also *SPKPP*, vol. 2, no. 2, p. 217; original in documents cited in n. 19 above.

21. Memorandum by R. A. Leeper, "Russia and the Peace Conference," November 1918, FO, 371/4352/13/24, pp. 171–75.

22. See Lundgreen-Nielsen, *Polish Problem*, p. 88.

23. "Une méthode d'action en Pologne: Nécessité d'une Pologne forte," 20 December 1918, cited in Pajewski, *Wokół sprawy polskiej*, app. 4; also cited by Lundgreen-Nielsen, *Polish Problem*, p. 75.

24. "Une méthode," in Pajewski, *Wokół sprawy polskiej*, pp. 234–35.

25. See Lundgreen-Nielsen, *Polish Problem*, pp. 571–73.

26. Memorandum by the British Delegation on the Former Russian Empire, 20 January 1919, FO, 374/20, no. 16; Esme Howard wrote the section on Poland.

27. Namier note to M. Tilley, with comments on interview between Lieutenant Colonel Kisch and General Haller, 20 January 1919, FO, 371/3896/73/5255.

28. On the question of Haller's army see Lundgreen-Nielsen, *Polish Problem*, chaps. 3, 4, and 5 passim.

29. See ibid., p. 183.

30. Zofia Zaks, "Walka dyplomatyczna," pp. 37–38.

31. Ibid., pp. 42–43.

32. S. Szczepanowski to Paderewski, 2 February 1919, *APIP*, vol. 2, no. 28, p. 37.

33. Zaks, "Walka dyplomatyczna," pp. 44–45.

34. Perkins to Balfour, 28 March 1919, cited ibid., p. 45, after Barbara Ratyńska, *Rola nafty w kształtowaniu stosunku państw zachodnich do sprawy Galicji Wschodniej (1918–1919): Zbiór Dokumentów* (Warsaw, 1957), pp. 48–49; see also Litwinski's letters to Perkins, March 1919, FO, 371/39006/28011/48975/55.

35. Helmreich, *Paris to Sèvres*, p. 208 and p. 225 n. 34.

36. Ibid., pp. 209–10.

37. Ibid., p. 212.

38. See n. 33 above.

39. General Staff, Desiderata regarding Territorial Adjustments . . . C. 1, Former Russian Empire . . . iii, Poland, 19 February 1919, FO, 374/20, no. 40, pp. 179–80.

40. Zaks, *Aspekty międzynarodowe,* chap. 1, p. 35.

41. Saint Aulaire's report, Bucharest, 29 April 1919, AD/MAE, ser. Europe, Russie, vol. 31, Z-722-1, no. 355. We should note that more-ambitious Ukrainian proposals had been made earlier. A French report from Berne on 29 March 1919 reported Sevriuk's claim that in early February the Directorate had offered the French representative in Odessa, General Anselme, its cooperation with Denikin if the Allies would end the Polish-Ukrainian war in East Galicia and would force the Poles to retreat beyond the San River. Anselme allegedly refused all Ukrainian proposals on 10 February (see ibid.). However, the French Foreign Ministry seemed to favor the Ukrainian proposals (see n. 45 below).

42. See Lundgreen-Nielsen, *Polish Problem,* p. 217.

43. Commission report, 14 March 1919, AD/MAE, ser. Europe, Pologne, vol. 83, pp. 112–13; for discussion in the Council of Ten, 15 March 1919, see *FRUS/PPC,* 4:379–83.

44. In 1898, Ukrainians constituted 16.95 percent of all secondary-school students in East Galicia, as compared with 80.48 percent Poles, 2.35 percent Germans, and 0.22 percent others. In 1899, Ukrainians constituted 28.8 percent of students at Lwów University; 1.2 percent at the Jagiellonian University, Kraków; 4.9 percent at the Lwów Polytechnic; and 8.1 percent at the University of Chernovets (see T. Piłat, ed., *Podręcznik statystyki Galicji* [Lwów, 1900], pp. 95, 111, 114; courtesy of Prof. Juliusz Bardach, Historical Institute, University of Warsaw).

45. Foreign Minister to President of the Council, Minister of War, 16 March 1919, AD/MAE, Pologne, vol. 83, pp. 115–16.

46. *FRUS/PPC,* 4:410.

47. Memorandum by Mr. Selby, 6 June 1919, in Curzon to Balfour, 11 June 1919, *DBFP,* 1st ser., vol. 3, no. 256, p. 366.

48. Russian Political Conference to the President of the Peace Conference, Paris, 9 April 1919, AD/MAE, Russie, vol. 594–95, pp. 118–20.

49. Eastern Frontiers of Poland, report no. 2 of the Commission on Polish Affairs, 21 April 1919, FO, 371/3893/73/64310/55; for discussion on 26 April see *FRUS/PPC,* 4:624–26.

50. Laroche, Note on the Eastern Frontiers of Poland, 24 April 1919, AD/MAE, Pologne, vol. 137, pp. 1–4.

51. Namier note on the Polish Socialist Party, 25 April 1919, FO, 371/3922/ 60635/55.

52. Commission on Polish Affairs, report no. 2 on Eastern Frontiers of Poland, see n. 49 above.

53. *Gazeta Polska,* 27 April 1919, p. 1.

54. Lundgreen-Nielsen, *Polish Problem,* p. 223.

55. W. Jodko-Narkiewicz to Paderewski, Warsaw, 30 April 1919, *APIP,* vol. 2, no. 95, pp. 121–22.

56. Lord Acton, Berne, 28 April 1919, FO, 371/3907/28011/67131, pp. 2–3.

57. Zaks, *Aspekty Międzynarodowe,* chap. 1, pp. 46–47.

58. Lundgreen-Nielsen, *Polish Problem,* p. 289.

59. Wandycz, *Soviet-Polish Relations,* p. 126.

60. They compared Poland's offensive in East Galicia with the German invasion of Belgium in 1914 (!) (Lundgreen-Nielsen, *Polish Problem,* p. 322).

61. Russian Political Conference, memorandum to Clemenceau, 10 May 1919, *DBFP,* 1st ser., vol. 3, no. 721, n. 1.

62. Namier's comments on Lord Acton's report of interview with Vassylko (28 April), 10 May 1919 (see n. 56 above).

63. Dmowski to Paderewski, Paris, 15 May 1919, *APIP,* vol. 2, no. 121, p. 155; see also Lundgreen-Nielsen, *Polish Problem,* pp. 318, 322.

64. *FRUS/PPC,* 4:711.

65. Lundgreen-Nielsen, *Polish Problem,* pp. 324–26.

66. Ibid., p. 319.

67. French text in *APIP,* vol. 2, no. 136; English text in *DIM,* 2:259–60.

68. *DBFP,* vol. 3, no. 231.

69. Ibid., no. 233.

70. Pralon report, 31 May 1919, ibid., no. 240, app. 1.

71. Piłsudski to Paderewski, 21 May 1919, *SPKPP,* vol. 2, no. 90, and *DIM,* 2:262–67.

72. *DBFP,* vol. 3, no. 247.

73. Telegram from de Martel, Omsk, 4 June 1919, ibid., no. 255, app. 2.

74. Report, 2-ème Bureau, 12 June 1919, AD/MAE, Pologne, vol. 84, pp. 111–12.

75. Lundgreen-Nielsen, *Polish Problem,* pp. 385–86.

76. Zaks, "Walka dyplomatyczna," p. 47.

77. Report no. 3, Commission on Polish Affairs, 17 June 1919, *DBFP,* 1st ser., vol. 3, no. 699, map facing p. 840, showing lines A and B; see map 5 supra.

78. *DBFP,* vol. 3, no. 700.

79. Ibid., no. 701; note to Polish government, ibid., no. 702.

80. Zaks, "Walka dyplomatyczna," p. 49.

81. *DBFP,* vol. 3, no. 713; Balfour's answer to Perkins was sent to Warsaw on 27 August, 1919, FO, 371/39007/28011/122777.

82. Wandycz, *Soviet-Polish Relations,* p. 127.

83. Ibid., p. 133.

84. Report by General Henrys, 22 November 1919, AD/MAE, Pologne, vol. 137, 2-ème Bureau, no. 1254/2B; cf. Polish Foreign Ministry to Zamoyski on Maklakov report, to the same effect, *DIM,* vol. 2, no. 242.

85. Wandycz, *Soviet-Polish Relations,* pp. 133–34.

86. Polish Delegation to the President of the Peace Conference, 25 August 1919, *DBFP,* vol. 3, no. 712.

87. E. Smal-Stocky to Clemenceau, Prague, tel. no. 45, 20 August 1919, AD/MAE, Pologne, vol. 85, p. 15.

88. 19 September 1919, *DBFP,* 1st ser., vol. 1, no. 61, p. 735.

89. Ibid., no. 63, pp. 770–72.

90. Paderewski to Piłsudski, 23 September 1919, *APIP,* vol. 2, no. 261.

91. Rozwadowski to Piłsudski, 24 September 1919, *DIM,* 2:374.

92. Report no. 6, Commission on Polish Affairs, of 1 September, discussed on 25 September 1919, *DBFP,* vol. 1, no. 64, app. L, pp. 788–92.

93. J. Cambon to Paderewski, 25 September 1919, *APIP,* vol. 2, no. 262.

94. Memorandum of Russian embassy, Paris, to Clemenceau, 27 September 1919, *DBFP,* vol. 3, no. 721, encl., pp. 893–94.

95. Extract from Canadian Parliamentary Debates, 8 October 1919, FO, 371/3908/28011/157544.

96. M. P. A. Hankey to Foreign Secretary, 10 October 1919, FO, 371/3907/ 28011/140861/55; see also Curzon to Crowe, 13 October 1919, *DBFP,* vol. 3, no. 723.

97. Ibid., nos. 729–31.

98. Ibid., vol. 2, no. 34, p. 470.

99. Ibid., no. 27, pp. 363–65.

100. Ibid., no. 44, p. 582, and vol. 3, nos. 738–40.

101. See n. 21 above.

102. Rumbold, Warsaw, 16 December 1919, draft, FO, 688/1/73/72.

103. Pralon, Warsaw, 12 January 1920, no. 19, AD/MAE, Pologne, vol. 137, pp. 25 ff.

104. Pralon, Warsaw, 29 January 1920, no. 56, ibid., vol. 86, p. 30.

105. Rumbold, 23 January 1920, *DBFP,* vol. 3, no. 660.

106. Polish proposals, *DIM,* vol. 2, no. 318.

107. Millerand to Panafieu, 4 March 1920, AD/MAE, Pologne, vol. 137, pp. 48–55.

108. Derby to Curzon, 24 February 1920, encl. Memorandum by British Delegation to Ambassadors Conference, *DBFP* 1st ser., vol. 11, no. 206.

109. Rumbold, 14 March 1920, ibid., no. 220.

110. Palairet wrote that the Allies should not support the Poles east of the "Paris line." He thought that the armistice should be signed but that there should be no peace negotiations until the "return" *(sic)* of Russia to the League of Nations, Polish Peace Conditions, 20 March 1920, FO, 371/3913/40430/55.

111. Namier's comments on Polish peace terms, ibid.

112. Rumbold, 26 March 1920, *DBFP,* vol. 11, no. 237.

113. Eric Drummond, note on conversation with Gregory, 27 April 1920, LNA, 11/4074/2361.

114. Panafieu, Warsaw, 15 April 1920, no. 110, AD/MAE, Pologne, vol. 137, pp. 73–74.

115. See Wandycz, *Soviet-Polish Relations,* pp. 192–93; Polish text of alliance in *DIM,* 2:745–47; English text in Reshetar, *Ukrainian Revolution,* pp. 301–2; Polish text of Military Convention in *DIM,* 2:749–53.

116. Zofia Zaks, "Radziecka Rosja i Ukraina wobec sprawy państwowej przynależności Galicji Wschodniej 1920–1923," *Z dziejów stosunków polsko-radzieckich: Studia i materiały* 6 (Warsaw, 1970): 71 (hereafter cited as "Radziecka Rosja i Ukraina").

117. Wandycz, *Soviet-Polish Relations,* pp. 194–95.

118. Note by Paul Mantoux, 1 May 1920, LNA, 11/4074/2361.

119. Rozwadowski report, cited in Zaks, *Aspekty międzynarodowe,* chap. 2, p. 79 (trans. A. C.).

120. "La Paix dans l'est Européen, ses conditions et ses adversitées: A propos de la guerre entre la Pologne et la Russie," May 1920, cited in Zaks, *Aspekty międzynarodowe,* chap. 2, p. 83.

121. Chamber of Deputies, 26 May 1920, sess. 73, p. 1639, cited ibid., p. 80.

122. Foreign Office note, 1 June 1919, FO, 371/3908/20811/197430/55.

123. Polish Foreign Ministry, instruction to Missions, 5 June 1920, cited in Zaks, *Aspekty międzynarodowe,* chap. 2, p. 80.

124. Kidston, Helsingfors, 13 June 1920, *DBFP,* vol. 11, no. 293.

125. See Rumbold, 19 June 1920, ibid., no. 300, and Rumbold, 22 June 1920, FO, 417/9, no. 3, pp. 3–5.

126. *DBFP*, vol. 11, no. 310.

127. Report from Spa, 7 July 1920, cited in Zaks, *Aspekty międzynarodowe*, chap. 2, p. 103.

128. *DBFP*, vol. 8, no. 51A.

129. Zaks, "Radziecka Rosja i Ukraina," p. 77.

130. See *DBFP*, vol. 8, no. 59, app. 2; see chap. 1 above.

131. See Norman Davies, "Lloyd George and Poland, 1919–20," *Journal of Contemporary History* 6, no. 3 (1971): 132–54; see map 5 supra.

132. White Russian representatives at Spa, N. Basil and P. Struve, told Erazm Piltz that Russia would never give up her claims to East Galicia: see Korespondencja K. Smogorzewskiego ze Spa, 6 July 1920, cited in Zofia Zaks, "Problem Galicji Wschodniej w czasie wojny polsko-radzieckiej," *Studia z Dziejów ZSRR i Europy Środkowej* 8:100–101 (hereafter cited as: "Problem Galicji Wschodniej"). Basil and Struve only repeated the standard White Russian line propagated by the Russian Conference in Paris.

133. Foreign Minister to Warsaw, Bucharest, London, Rome, Berlin, Prague, 22 July 1920, AD/MAE, Pologne, vol. 86, p. 176.

134. Wandycz, *France*, chap. 3 passim.

135. Beneš to Laroche, Holograph Letter, Spa, 11 July 1920, AD/MAE, Allemagne-Pologne, Z698-6, vol. 102, pp. 128–29.

136. Erazm Piltz, note for President Grabski (Władysław Grabski was president of the Polish Delegation), Spa, 11 July 1920, *APIP*, vol. 2, no. 332, encl., pp. 425–26.

137. See n. 135 above, also Wandycz, *France*, p. 158; Laroche, *Au Quai d'Orsay*, pp. 24–26.

138. Curzon to Rumbold, 10 August 1920, *DBFP*, vol. 11, no. 411.

139. Helmreich, *Paris to Sèvres*, p. 324.

140. See n. 77 above; for the text of the treaty of 10 August 1920 see *British and Foreign State Papers, 1920*, vol. 113 (London, 1923), pp. 866–73.

141. Erazm Piltz to Paderewski, 22 July 1920, *APIP*, vol. 2, no. 338, pp. 431–33.

142. Zdenek Sládek and Jaroslav Valenta, "Sprawy ukraińskie w czechosłowackiej polityce wschodniej w latach 1918–1922," *Z dziejów stosunków polsko-radzieckich: Studia i materiały* 3 (Warsaw, 1968): 139.

143. Beneš's note of 25 February 1919, cited ibid., p. 141.

144. Ibid., pp. 144–46.

145. See Krzysztof Lewandowski, "W kręgu problematyki stosunków czechosłowacko-ukraińsko-polskich 1918–1922," *Z dziejów stosunków polsko-radzieckich: Studia i materiały* 6 (Warsaw, 1970): 183, and *Sprawa ukraińska w polityce zagranicznej Czechosłowacji w latach 1918–1932* (Wrocław, etc., 1974), chap. 2.

146. Szarota report, Vienna, 10 July 1919, AMSZ, kol. 71, cited in Lewandowski, *Sprawa ukraińska*, p. 135.

147. Cited in Zaks, *Aspekty międzynarodowe*, chap. 2, p. 92.

148. Cited ibid., p. 93.

149. Cited ibid., p. 94.

150. S. R., "Halychyna i novi derzhavy Ievropy," *Ukrainskyi Prapor* (Vienna, 1921), pp. 10–11, cited in Alexander J. Motyl, *The Turn to the Right: The Ideological Origins and Development of Ukrainian Nationalism, 1919–1929* (Boulder, Colo., and New York, 1980), p. 34.

151. Cited in Zaks, "Problem Galicji Wschodniej," p. 106.

152. See n. 78 above.

153. See Wandycz, *Soviet-Polish Relations*, chap. 11 passim.

154. *DIM,* vol. 3, no. 222.

155. Ibid., no. 221.

156. Ibid., no. 224.

157. Cited in Zaks, *Aspekty międzynarodowe,* chap. 3, pp. 18–21.

158. Gregory to Eyre Crowe, 14 October 1920, FO, 371/5412/N911/911/55.

159. Askenazy report, Paris, 10 October 1920, cited in Zofia Zaks, "Sprawa Galicji Wschodniej w Lidze Narodów (1920–1922)," *Najnowsze dzieje polski, 1914–1939* 12 (Warsaw, 1967): 129–30 (hereafter cited as "Sprawa Galicji Wschodniej").

160. Note on Polish Petroleum, 3 February 1921, AD/MAE, Pologne, vol. 131, p. 71; also note on East Galicia, 11 June 1921, ibid., vol. 87, pp. 11–13.

161. Zaks, "Sprawa Galicji Wschodniej," pp. 132–33.

162. Ibid., p. 139.

163. Ibid., pp. 136–37.

164. Sir George Clerk, Prague, 29 December 1920, and Gregory's comments, 10 January 1921, FO, 371/6807/N100/77/55.

165. Foch to president of the Council, 3 February 1921, AD/MAE, Pologne, Z 698-1 (January–March 1921), and see chap. 1 above.

166. See chap. 1 above.

167. Sapieha's report, 13 February 1921, cited in Zaks, "Sprawa Galicji Wschodniej," pp. 144–45.

168. Memorandum by Gregory . . . (iii) Eastern Galicia, *DBFP,* vol. 11, no. 693.

169. Zaks, "Radziecka Rosja i Ukraina," p. 84.

170. Jerzy Kumaniecki, *Po traktacie ryskim: Stosunki polsko-radzieckie, 1921–1923* (Warsaw, 1971), pp. 47–48.

171. Ibid., p. 59.

172. Zaks, "Radziecka Rosja i Ukraina," p. 87, cites A. D. Yaroshenko, *Komunistichna partiia Zakhidnoi Ukraiiny* (Kiev, 1957), pp. 23–24, where the date on which "Zakordot" was established is given as December 1921. However, the Polish-Soviet exchange of notes, cited below, indicates an earlier date.

173. Cited in Zaks, "Radziecka Rosja i Ukraina," p. 86.

174. Ibid., p. 87; also Kumaniecki, *Po traktacie ryskim,* pp. 60–61.

175. Kumaniecki, *Po traktacie ryskim,* pp. 62–73; text in *DVPSSSR,* 4:394–96, also *DIM,* vol. 4, no. 60.

176. Kumaniecki, *Po traktacie ryskim* (see n. 174 above).

177. See Sergiusz Mikulicz, *Prometeizm w polityce II Rzeczypospolitej,* passim.

178. See Andrzej Garlicki, "Myśl polityczna Sanacji wobec problemów bezpieczeństwa II Rzeczypospolitej," in *Na warsztatach historyków polskiej myśli politycznej,* ed. Jan St. Miś, *Polska myśl polityczna XIX i XX wieku,* ed. Henryk Zieliński, no. 4 (Wrocław, etc., 1980), p. 193.

179. See M. K. Dziewanowski, *The Communist Party of Poland: An Outline of History* (Cambridge, Mass., 1959), chap. 6 passim.

180. See Wandycz, *France,* pp. 248–49; also Alina Szklarska-Lohmannowa, *Polsko-czechosłowackie stosunki dyplomatyczne w latach 1918–1925* (Wrocław, etc., 1967), chap. 3 passim.

181. See Motyl, *Turn to the Right,* pp. 52–53.

182. Report of the British Military Attaché, T. Cunningham, Vienna, 24 August 1921, in John Cecil to Curzon, Prague, 23 September 1921, FO, 371/6811/N10950/77/55.

183. Motyl, *Turn to the Right,* pp. 86–87.

184. Mirosława Papierzyńska-Turek, *Sprawa ukraińska w drugiej Rzeczypospolitej, 1922–1926* (Kraków, 1979), p. 37.

185. See chap. 8 below.

186. See Papierzyńska-Turek, *Sprawa ukraińska*, pp. 303–4 n. 64.

187. See chap. 3 above.

188. Memorandum by J. W. Headlam-Morley respecting Upper Silesia and Eastern Galicia, 31 March 1921, *DBFP*, vol. 16, no. 8, pp. 8–10.

189. J. W. Headlam-Morley, no. 1, East Galicia, 19 April 1921, FO, 371/6808/77/N4819/55, and N5097, ibid.

190. Philip Kerr to Vansittart, 18 April 1921, encl. Tomaschivsky letter, FO, note 28, April 1921, FO, 371/6808/77/N4832/55.

191. Crookshank memorandum, 8 June 1921, comment by Crowe, 17 June 1921, *DBFP*, vol. 23, no. 74, pp. 92–97.

192. Panafieu, Warsaw, 3 June 1921, no. 159, AD/MAE, Pologne, vol. 89, pp. 37–38.

193. Panafieu, Warsaw, 16 August 1921, no. 222, ibid., pp. 276–78.

194. President of the Council and Foreign Minister to Panafieu, Paris, 3 August 1921, no. 564, ibid., pp. 205–6.

195. Max Muller memorandum to Polish Foreign Ministry, cited in Zaks, "Walka dyplomatyczna," p. 56.

196. Max Muller to Curzon, Warsaw, 15 July 1921, *DBFP*, vol. 23, no. 100, pp. 127–29.

197. *Parl.Deb.H.C.*, 6 July 1921, 5th ser., vol. 144, cols. 394–95.

198. Balfour telegram, 16 September 1921, and comments, FO, 371/6810/77/N10575/55; see also *DBFP*, vol. 23, no. 159, pp. 193–94.

199. See *League of Nations: Minutes of the Fourteenth Session of the Council of the League of Nations held at Geneva August 30–October 19, 1921* (Geneva, 1921), pp. 119, 174.

200. Max Muller to Curzon, 22 September 1921, no. 552, FO, 371/6828/362/N11018/55.

201. Zamoyski report, Paris, 29 September 1921, cited in Zofia Zaks, "Galicja Wschodnia w polskiej polityce zagranicznej (1921–1923)," *Z dziejów stosunków polsko-radzieckich: Studia i materiały* 8 (Warsaw, 1971; hereafter cited as "Galicja Wschodnia"): 7.

202. Max Muller to Curzon, Warsaw, 6 November 1921, *DBFP*, vol. 23, no. 211, p. 269.

203. Zaks, "Galicja Wschodnia," pp. 7–8.

204. See n. 202 above (p. 270).

205. Max Muller to Gregory, letter, Warsaw, 15 November 1921, FO, 371/6811/77/N13044/55.

206. Notes by Tyrrell, Crowe, Curzon, 6 December 1921, ibid., N13488.

207. Nowak-Kiełbikowa, *Polska-Wielka Brytania*, p. 354.

208. Foreign Office correspondence, cited ibid. This matter is not mentioned in the official British records of the Briand–Lloyd George talks in London in late December 1921 (see chap. 1 of this book and see n. 30 of chap. 7 below).

CHAPTER 7
EAST GALICIA AND POLAND'S EASTERN FRONTIER: THE GENOA CONFERENCE, JANUARY–JUNE 1922

1. Chicherin note, 28 October 1921, *DVPSSSR*, vol. 4, no. 278, pp. 445–48.

2. See Artaud, *Question des dettes interalliées,* pp. 381 ff.

3. Jones, *Whitehall Diary,* 1:187; see also *Times* (London), 7 January 1922.

4. Seydoux to Peretti de la Rocca, 29 December 1921, cited in Jay L. Kaplan, "France's Road to Genoa: Strategic, Economic, and Ideological Factors in French Foreign Policy, 1921–1922" (Ph.D. diss., Columbia University, 1974), p. 114.

5. On the question of Russian debts and French investments in Russia see René Girault, *Emprunts russes et investissements français en Russie, 1887–1914,* Publications de la Sorbonne, recherches 3 (Paris, 1973).

6. French Foreign Office memorandum, 5 August 1921, cited in Kaplan, "France's Road to Genoa," p. 81.

7. *DBFP,* vol. 19, no. 6, app. 6, pp. 35–36.

8. See chap. 1 above.

9. Polish reports from London, cited in Nowak-Kiełbikowa, *Polska-Wielka Brytania,* p. 375.

10. See chap. 1 above.

11. Instructions to the Polish Minister, Moscow, 7 March 1922, cited in Nowak-Kiełbikowa, *Polska-Wielka Brytania,* p. 373.

12. See Gerald Freund, *Unholy Alliance: Russian-German Relations from the Treaty of Brest-Litovsk to the Treaty of Berlin* (London, 1957), chap. 5, "The Rapallo Alliance."

13. D'Abernon, *Ambassador of Peace,* 1:250–53 (1:262–63 of U.S. ed.).

14. Bonnefous, *Histoire politique,* 3:288–89; on German-Soviet ties see Freund, *Unholy Alliance,* chap. 4.

15. Skirmunt to Polish legation, London, 3 March 1922, APEL/PISM, cyphers; see also Kukułka, *Francja,* pt. 4, chap. 7.

16. See A. Young, report, Belgrade, 16 March 1922, *DBFP,* 1st ser., vol. 19, no. 45, and Dering report, Bucharest, 17 March 1922, ibid., no. 47.

17. Ibid., no. 34, p. 192.

18. See Skrzypek, *Związek,* pp. 87–90.

19. Władysław Pobóg-Malinowski, *Najnowsza historia polityczna Polski, 1864–1945,* vol. 2, pt. 1 (London, 1956), p. 404.

20. Kumaniecki, *Po traktacie ryskim,* pp. 91–92.

21. Ibid.; see also *DIM,* vol. 2, no. 103.

22. See *DBFP,* vol. 23, nos. 338, 340, 345, 352, 358; for protocol, ibid., pp. 447–50; also *DBFP,* vol. 20, no. 488.

23. Kumaniecki, *Po traktacie ryskim,* p. 95.

24. See *DBFP,* vol. 23, no. 343.

25. For the English text of the protocol see *DBFP,* vol. 19, no. 47, n. 2; French text in *DIM,* vol. 4, no. 104; see also *DBFP,* vol. 23, no. 363.

26. *Journal de Pologne,* 5 April 1922; see also Kumaniecki, *Po traktacie ryskim,* p. 110.

27. Skirmunt interview in *Petit Parisien,* cited ibid., p. 111; on the attitudes of Polish political parties see ibid., pp. 104 ff.

28. Konstanty Skirmunt, "Moje wspomnienia"—Photocopy of typescript (courtesy of the Catholic University of Lublin Library), pp. 97–99 (hereafter cited as Skirmunt, *Memoirs*).

29. Frontiers of Poland, Note for the President of the Council, 3 April 1922, with handwritten addition by J. Laroche, AD/MAE, Pologne, vol. 137, p. 132.

30. Note on the Frontiers of Poland, 4 April 1922, ibid., p. 135.

31. Polish Legation, report no. 7, cited in Nowak-Kiełbikowa, *Polska-Wielka Brytania,* p. 376.

32. *DBFP,* vol. 19, no. 62, pp. 298–99 n. 3.

33. Note by Peretti de la Rocca, 10 April 1922, AD/MAE, Pologne, vol. 137, p. 137.

34. Skirmunt, *Memoirs,* p. 101.

35. "Treaties with Russia," received 6 April 1922, *DBFP,* vol. 19, no. 61, pp. 293–95.

36. Draft Polish note to President of the Council, 6 April 1922, AD/MAE, Pologne, vol. 137, pp. 138–40; Note signed by Zamoyski, 11 April 1922, ibid., pp. 140–42.

37. See Gregory's telegram, 15 April 1922, *DBFP,* vol. 19, no. 95, p. 566 n. 2.

38. Ibid., no. 74, p. 419.

39. See Freund, *Unholy Alliance,* pp. 116–17.

40. *DBFP,* vol. 19, no. 76, p. 437.

41. Ibid., no. 77, pp. 447, 449.

42. Poincaré to Zamoyski, Paris, 19 April 1922, AD/MAE, Pologne, vol. 137, pp. 144–45.

43. The Polish Socialist Party had proposed that (a) the autonomous territory include all the counties of the Lwów, Stanisławów, and Tarnopol voivodships lying east of the Cieszanów-Stary Sambor line; (b) the Polish Sejm should retain competence in military, industrial, mining, and trade-customs affairs, as well as labor legislation, agricultural reform, the parceling out of land, railways, post, and telegraph services; (c) the Polish Constitution of March 1921, was to apply fully in East Galicia; (d) the autonomous authorities were to consist of the Provincial Sejm, the Provincial Council, and a minister for East Galician Affairs; (e) the Provincial Sejm was to be competent in matters of language, education, and religion; (f) the two official languages would be Polish and Ukrainian; (g) educational matters would be dealt with by Polish and Ukrainian school councils. See "Communique on the Polish Socialist Party's Autonomy Project," sent to all regional organizations by the secretariat general of the party, Warsaw, 15 February 1922, photocopy, Central Archives of the Central Committee of the Polish Workers' Party, Warsaw. See also Hoare report, Warsaw, 19 May 1922, *DBFP,* vol. 23, no. 388, pp. 486–87.

44. *DBFP,* vol. 19, no. 93, p. 558.

45. Skirmunt, *Memoirs,* p. 102.

46. *DBFP,* vol. 19, no. 95, pp. 565–70.

47. See F. Gregory Campbell, *Confrontation in Central Europe: Weimar Germany and Czechoslovakia* (Chicago and London, 1975), p. 112. The Czechoslovak trade treaties with Soviet Russia and Soviet Ukraine were signed on 5 and 6 June 1922.

48. See *DBFP,* vol. 19, no. 95, p. 570 n. 14.

49. Cited in John Saxon Mills, *The Genoa Conference* (London, 1922), pp. 117–19.

50. See memorandum by Mr. Gregory on the "Pact of Non-Aggression," 1 December 1922, *DBFP,* vol. 20, no. 569, pp. 954–55.

51. *DBFP,* vol. 19, no. 98, p. 588.

52. 29 April 1922, 11 A.M., ibid., no. 102, pp. 630–36, especially p. 635.

53. 2 May 1922, ibid., no. 106, p. 677.

54. Ibid., p. 678.

55. Ibid., p. 679.

56. Barthou telegrams nos. 330–33, Genoa, 2 May 1922, AD/MAE, Pologne, vol. 137, pp. 147–50. For the draft statute on Ruthenian autonomy in Czechoslovakia see Walter K. Hanak, *The Subcarpathian-Ruthene Church, 1918–1945* (The Bishop Takach Carpatho-Ruthene Historical Society, Greek-Catholic Union Messenger,

Munhall, Pa., 1962), pp. 16–17; for the revised statute of April 1920 see ibid., pp. 10–20. On Memel see French Foreign Office Note on the Question of Polish Frontiers, 2 May 1922, and Poincaré's telegram to Barthou, 3 May 1922, AD/MAE, Pologne, vol. 137, pp. 151 ff.

57. Chicherin's letter to Skirmunt, Genoa, 24 April 1922, *DVPSSSR*, 5:266–68; *DIM*, vol. 4, no. 108.

58. Skirmunt note to Chicherin, 25 April 1922, *DIM*, vol. 4, no. 109.

59. Cited in Zaks, *Aspekty międzynarodowe*, chap. 5, p. 43.

60. Notes of a Conversation . . . 5 May 1922, between Lloyd George and Skirmunt, *DBFP*, vol. 19, no. 112, p. 741.

61. Ibid.; see also Skirmunt, *Memoirs*, p. 105.

62. *DBFP*, vol. 19, no. 112, pp. 742–43.

63. Ibid., pp. 744–46.

64. Ibid., no. 212, pp. 799–803.

65. Kumaniecki, *Po traktacie ryskim*, p. 218, citing Polish press of 11 and 12 May 1922; see also Hoare's report, Warsaw, 13 May 1922, *DBFP*, vol. 23, no. 385, pp. 483–84, and Hankey's note to Eyre Crowe, 30 May 1922, and comments, ibid., no. 390, pp. 489–91.

66. *DBFP*, vol. 19, no. 128, p. 875.

67. Ibid., no. 130, p. 892.

68. Ibid., no. 133, pp. 920–21.

69. *Times* (London), 16 May 1922.

70. Meeting, 15 May 1922, *DBFP*, vol. 19, no. 135, p. 938.

71. Meeting, 17 May 1922, ibid., no. 137, p. 974.

72. 18 May, ibid., no. 138, p. 985.

73. Crowe's note, 20 May 1922, on answer to a parliamentary question on East Galicia by Lord R. Cecil, FO, 371/8122/64/N5030/55.

74. Gregory's comment, 12 June 1922, on report of Hoare, Warsaw, 1 June 1922, ibid., N5447.

75. See n. 43 above.

76. Skirmunt, *Memoirs*, pp. 108–9; Jędrzejewicz, *Kronika*, 2:55.

77. Panafieu to President of the Council, 10 June 1922, no. 169, AD/MAE, Pologne, Z698-1, vol. 73, pp. 135–36.

78. Note on Peretti de la Rocca–Zamoyski conversation, 16 May 1922, ibid., pp. 116–17.

CHAPTER 8

EAST GALICIA, VILNA, MEMEL, AND THE RECOGNITION OF POLAND'S EASTERN FRONTIER, JUNE 1922 TO MARCH 1923

1. Cited in Zaks, "Galicja Wschodnia," p. 20.

2. R. H. Hoare to Ovey, Warsaw, 12 July 1922, *DBFP*, 1st ser., vol. 23, no. 416, pp. 512–14, especially p. 513.

3. Polish Legation, London, report of 8 July 1922, cited in Zaks, *Aspekty międzynarodowe*, chap. 5, p. 12, and n. 1 above.

4. Memorandum by Mr. Emrys Evans, "The Status of Eastern Galicia," 28 July 1919, *DBFP*, vol. 23, no. 430, pp. 526–28.

5. Zaks, "Galicja Wschodnia," p. 20.

6. Papierzyńska-Turek, *Sprawa ukraińska,* p. 118.

7. Zaks, "Galicja Wschodnia," pp. 20–21.

8. Ibid., p. 21.

9. See *DBFP,* 1st ser., vol. 2, no. 27, app. F, pp. 372–76, and no. 28, app. A, pp. 383–84 (cited in chap. 6 above).

10. See Lewandowski, *Sprawa ukraińska,* pp. 128, 201 ff.

11. See Zaks, "Galicja Wschodnia," p. 21.

12. See Elizabeth Wiskemann, *Czechs and Germans: A Study of the Struggle in the Historic Provinces of Bohemia and Moravia* (London, New York, and Toronto, 1938), pp. 51–52, 110, 112, 259.

13. William Max Muller, 16 August 1922, telegram no. 97, FO, 371/8122/64/N7759/55.

14. Max Muller, 16 August 1922, telegram no. 98, ibid., N7790; also 17 August 1922, *DBFP,* vol. 23, no. 441, pp. 539–42.

15. Max Muller, 21 August 1922, and comments by Emrys Evans, Esmond Ovey, R. C. Lindsay, and Curzon, FO, 371/8122/64/N7855/55.

16. Cited in Zaks, "Galicja Wschodnia," p. 13.

17. Wielowieyski's letter to Peretti de la Rocca, 22 August 1922, AD/MAE, Pologne, vol. 137, pp. 159–61.

18. Wielowieyski's reports, 25 August and 2 September 1922, cited in Zaks, "Galicja Wschodnia," p. 14.

19. French Foreign Office note, 6 September 1922, and comments by British Foreign Office officials, FO, 371/8122/64/N8349/55.

20. Internal Foreign Office minutes, 17 and 19 September, FO, 371/8122/N8420/64/55.

21. Polish Legation, London, report no. 42, and Polish Foreign Ministry to Polish Legation, Paris, 3 October 1922, cited in Nowak-Kiełbikowa, *Polska-Wielka Brytania,* pp. 387–88; and Zaks, "Galicja Wschodnia," p. 14.

22. See Zaks, "Galicja Wschodnia," p. 15.

23. Polish Foreign Ministry telegram to Polish Missions, cited in Zaks, ibid.

24. Polish Legation, Rome, 15 September 1922, cited ibid.

25. British Delegation, Geneva, 12 September 1922, *DBFP,* vol. 23, no. 463, pp. 568–69 n. 2.

26. British Delegation, Geneva, 18 September 1922, FO, 371/8122/N8803/64/55.

27. Curzon's telegram for "Mr. London" (Balfour), *DBFP,* vol. 23, no. 463, pp. 538–39.

28. Cited in Zaks, "Sprawa Galicji Wschodniej," p. 151.

29. See Zaks, "Galicja Wschodnia," pp. 22–23.

30. Panafieu, no. 290, 2 October 1922, AD/MAE, Pologne, vol. 137, pp. 162–63; see also Muller to Curzon, 5 October 1922, *DBFP,* vol. 23, no. 476, pp. 580–82.

31. Curzon to Max Muller, 26 September 1922, *DBFP,* vol. 23, no. 471, pp. 576–77.

32. Aide-mémoire, Max Muller to Polish Government, 4 October 1922, copy, FO, 371/8123/64/N9202/55.

33. Max Muller to Curzon, 11 October 1922, *DBFP,* vol. 23, no. 480, p. 594.

34. Curzon to Max Muller, 26 October 1922, ibid., no. 5; for Italian attitude see Sir R. Graham, Rome, 13 October 1922, ibid., no. 482.

35. See Motyl, *Turn to the Right,* chap. 8 passim.

36. Papierzyńska-Turek, *Sprawa ukraińska,* pp. 129–31.

37. See table 2, ibid., p. 130.

38. Ibid., p. 131.

39. Ibid., p. 132.

40. Ibid., pp. 134–35.

41. For the Ukrainian population according to the 1921 census see ibid., p. 136; on the elections see Max Muller's reports, 9 and 30 November 1922, *DBFP,* vol. 23, nos. 499 and 504, pp. 614–17, 625–26.

42. *Manchester Guardian,* 22 October and 25 November 1922; *Daily Herald,* 28 October 1922, cited in Nowak-Kiełbikowa, *Polska-Wielka Brytania,* pp. 395–96.

43 For election results, the presidential election, and the assassination of Gabriel Narutowicz see Andrzej Ajnenkiel, *Od rządów ludowych do przewrotu majowego: Zarys dziejów politycznych Polski 1918–1926* (Warsaw, 1964), pp. 208 ff., or 2d ed. (Warsaw, 1978), pp. 286 ff. For an excellent survey of Polish political life at this time see Antony Polonsky, *Politics in Independent Poland, 1921–1939* (Oxford, 1972), chap. 2 passim.

44. *Izvestia,* 13 January 1923.

45. Maltzan to Madeyski, 11 January 1923, GFM, 170/K024175; see also Riekhoff, *German-Polish Relations,* p. 73.

46. *Kurjer Warszawski,* 17 January 1923.

47. *Izvestia,* 21 January, 1923.

48. Maltzan to Madeyski, 23 January 1923; see Riekhoff, *German-Polish Relations,* p. 74.

49. Prussian Census 1910, figures for Memel region, Stefan Kanerol, "Kłajpeda," offprint from *Sprawy Obce* 5 (Warsaw, 1930): 6.

50. *FRUS/PPC,* 6:191–201; Polish text in *SPKPP,* 1:212–21.

51. See Sergiusz Mikulicz, *Kłajpeda w polityce europejskiej, 1918–1939* (Warsaw, 1976), p. 41.

52. Ibid.

53. Ibid., pp. 44–45.

54. Ibid., p. 55.

55. For the Hymans Plans see chap. 6 above.

56. See Mikulicz, *Kłajpeda,* pp. 58–60.

57. Ibid., pp. 60–61.

58. See Hardinge to Curzon, 8 December 1922, and Curzon to Dilley, 20 December 1922, *DBFP,* vol. 23, nos. 508 and 515, pp. 631 and 645; for the Conference Committee's draft report of 9 January 1923, proposing autonomy for Memel, see ibid., no. 523, pp. 652–61.

59. German Foreign Ministry's statement, November 1922, cited in Senn, *Great Powers,* p. 109 n. 14.

60. See Julius P. Slavenas, "General Hans von Seeckt and the Baltic Question," in *The Baltic States in Peace and War, 1917–1945,* ed. V. Stanley Vardys and Romuald J. Misiunas (University Park, Pa., and London, 1978), pp. 123–25.

61. J. Łukasiewicz, "Polityka litewska w sprawie Kłajpedy," *Przegląd polityczny,* 1 April 1924, pp. 12–13, cited in Mikulicz, *Kłajpeda,* p. 82.

62. Galvanauskassin, *Draugas,* 25 January 1961, cited in Senn, *Great Powers,* p. 108 n. 13. See also R. Ziugzda, "Kaip buju prarasta Klajpeda," in *Gimtasis Krasztas* (Vilnius, 1969), cited in Mikulicz, *Kłajpeda,* p. 38, and R. Ziugzda, *Po diplomatijos skraiste: Klaipedas krastas imperialisiiniu valstybiu planuose 1919–1924 metais* (Vilnius, 1973), pp. 130–39, Russian-language summary, ibid., pp. 203–5 (courtesy Dr. Zofia Zaks).

63. *DVPSSSR*, vol. 6, no. 50, pp. 110–11.

64. Cited in Mikulicz, *Kłajpeda*, p. 66; see also Dilley to Curzon, 8 January 1923, *DBFP*, vol. 23, no. 519, p. 649; for the French Council of Ministers' decision of 3 January 1923 see McDougall, *France's Rhineland Diplomacy*, p. 243.

65. Cited in Mikulicz, *Kłajpeda*, pp. 66–67.

66. See Crewe to Curzon, 9 January 1923, *DBFP*, vol. 23, nos. 521 and 522, pp. 650–52; also Dilley to Curzon, 17 January 1923, ibid., no. 546, pp. 678–79.

67. Conference of Ambassadors, Note to Lithuanian Government, 11 January 1923, ibid., no. 527, pp. 662–63.

68. See Crewe to Curzon, 13 January 1923, ibid., no. 532, p. 667.

69. Crewe to Curzon, 13 January 1923, ibid., no. 533, pp. 667–68.

70. Crewe to Curzon, 15 January 1923, ibid., no. 540, p. 675 (here the name is misspelled as Troussau, A. C.).

71. Le May to Curzon and Dilley to Curzon, 16 January 1923, ibid., nos. 542 and 543, pp. 676–77.

72. Crewe to Curzon, 17 January 1923, ibid., no. 548, pp. 680–81.

73. Captain North (H.M.S. *Caledon*) to Admiralty, 20 January 1923, ibid., no. 554, p. 687.

74. Crewe to Curzon, 20 January 1923, ibid., no. 556, pp. 688–89.

75. Ibid.

76. Sargent's letter to Gregory, 24 January 1923, ibid., no. 564, pp. 694–96; also Curzon to Crewe, 25 January, ibid., no. 566, p. 697.

77. Curzon's note, ibid., no. 569, p. 699 n. 3.

78. Crewe to Curzon, 31 January and 4 February 1923, ibid., nos. 578 and 586, pp. 707–9, 714–17.

79. Draft decision, in Crewe to Curzon, 12 February 1923, ibid., no. 602, pp. 736–39.

80. See Nowak-Kiełbikowa, *Polska-Wielka Brytania*, pp. 396–97; Zaks, "Galicja Wschodnia," p. 27.

81. Sikorski to Rataj, 31 January 1923, Sikorski also said that the British "confidentially" reported that the Lithuanians were preparing an attack on Vilna on 10 February (see Rataj, *Pamiętniki*, p. 156). This was no doubt a scare tactic to prevent the Poles from taking military action against Memel or Danzig. However, Skirmunt had already assured Curzon of peaceful Polish intentions (see Skirmunt, *Memoirs*, p. 188), and there is no evidence of any Polish plans to act in either direction; see also *DBFP*, vol. 23, no. 582.

82. Zaks, "Galicja Wschodnia," p. 28.

83. Peretti de la Rocca's note on Zamoyski's visit; Zamoyski's letter to Poincaré, 8 February 1923, AD/MAE, Pologne, vol. 137, pp. 183–84.

84. Handelsman Papers, cited in Zaks, *Aspekty międzynarodowe*, chap. 5, p. 70; also Tommasini to Mussolini, 24 February 1923, *DDI*, 7th ser., vol. 1, no. 546; also see Sierpowski, *Stosunki*, pp. 219–20.

85. Note, 10 February 1923, AD/MAE, Pologne, vol. 137, p. 193.

86. Poincaré to Zamoyski, summary telegraphed to Warsaw and Rome, by courier to London, 10 February 1923, ibid., pp. 186–87; text of letter of 12 February 1923, ibid., pp. 198–99; see also Wandycz, *France*, p. 273.

87. Poincaré to Zamoyski, summary, see n. 86 above; see also Crewe to Curzon, 13 February 1923, *DBFP*, vol. 23, no. 605, p. 742.

88. Max Muller to Curzon, 12 February 1923, ibid., no. 601, pp. 735–36.

89. Sikorski letter to Poincaré, 12 February 1923, delivered to French Foreign Office 16 February, AD/MAE, Pologne, vol. 137, pp. 200–202, and Peretti de la Rocca's note on Zamoyski's visit, 16 February 1923, ibid., p. 205; see also Wandycz, *France,* p. 273; also Muller to Curzon, 15 February 1923, *DBFP,* vol. 23, no. 612, pp. 748–49, and Crewe to Curzon, 21 February 1923, ibid., no. 627, pp. 762–63.

90. Polish Delegation to the Peace Conference to President Poincaré, President of the Peace Conference and of the Conference of Ambassadors, 15 February 1923, AD/MAE, Pologne, vol. 137, pp. 209–10.

91. *Lithuanian White Book,* pp. 62–63, cited in Senn, *Great Powers,* p. 111; also *The Lithuanian-Polish Dispute,* vol. 3 (London, 1923), no. 36, pp. 96–97, and Crewe and Curzon, 16 February 1923, *DBFP,* vol. 23, no. 617, pp. 752–53; text of decision in *Documents diplomatiques: Relations Polono-Lithuaniennes: Conférences de Copenhague et de Lugano* (Warsaw, 1929), no. 1, pp. 11–13.

92. Cited in Sierpowski, *Stosunki,* pp. 220–21.

93. Le May to Curzon, 20 February 1923, *DBFP,* vol. 23, no. 624, p. 759; and Max Muller to Curzon, 21 February 1923, ibid., no. 626, pp. 760–61.

94. Poincaré's telegram to Warsaw, 21 February 1923, no. 316, AD/MAE, Pologne, vol. 137, pp. 206, 211.

95. CA, Resolution 207 (1), 21 February 1923, ibid., p. 207; see also Crewe to Curzon, 21 February 1923, and Vaughan to Curzon, 25 February 1923, *DBFP,* vol. 23, nos. 617 and 632, pp. 762–63, 771; on Polish reply to Soviet note see Max Muller to Curzon, 26 February 1923, ibid., no. 634, pp. 773–74.

96. Telegrams nos. 323–31, Paris, 22 February 1923, to Warsaw, Geneva, and Memel, copies to Conference, Marshal Foch, AD/MAE, Pologne, vol. 137, pp. 213–14.

97. See Sierpowski, *Stosunki,* pp. 221–22.

98. See *DBFP,* vol. 23, no. 629, p. 767 n. 4.

99. Paris, 24 February 1923, telegrams to London, Rome, and Warsaw, AD/ MAE, Pologne, vol. 137, pp. 228–29.

100. Laroche note on visit by Łukasiewicz, 25 February 1923, ibid., p. 232.

101. Note for the President of the Council, 23 February 1923 (stamped over—26 February, A. C.), ibid., pp. 230–31.

102. Saint Aulaire, 27 February 1923, no. 204; reply to telegrams 683–84, received by courier at 14 hrs., ibid., pp. 236–37; see also Curzon to Crewe, 26 February 1923, *DBFP,* vol. 23, no. 637, pp. 775–76.

103. Memorandum from British Embassy to Conference of Ambassadors, 28 February 1923, AD/MAE, Pologne, vol. 137, pp. 243–45.

104. Crewe to Curzon, 2 and 3 March 1923, *DBFP,* vol. 23, no. 639 and 641, pp. 777–79, 781.

105. Curzon to Crewe, 6 March 1923, ibid., no. 644, pp. 783–84.

106. Curzon to Cecil, 9 March 1923, ibid., no. 654, pp. 794–95.

107. Committee of Jewish Delegations, Paris, to Conference of Ambassadors, 28 February 1923, AD/MAE, Pologne, vol. 138, pp. 45–48.

108. Crewe to Curzon, 7 March 1923, *DBFP,* vol. 23, no. 649, pp. 787–88.

109. Note for the President of the Council, 2 March 1923, stating Sargent's letter was received at 18.45 hrs., AD/MAE, Pologne, vol. 138, pp. 7–10.

110. Note of 3 March 1923, ibid., pp. 11–13.

111. Gregory-Ciechanowski conversation, 6 and 8 March 1923, cited in Nowak-Kiełbikowa, *Polska-Wielka Brytania,* pp. 403–4; for Sargent-Gregory correspondence see ibid., pp. 406–7; see also *DBFP,* vol. 23, no. 648.

112. See Sargent letter to Gregory, 12 March 1923, *DBFP,* vol. 23, no. 658, pp. 797–98.
113. Handelsman Papers, cited in Zaks, "Galicja Wschodnia," p. 31 and n. 231.
114. Ibid.
115. *DIM,* vol. 4, no. 156.
116. Zaks, "Galicja Wschodnia," p. 32.
117. Note by J. Laroche on forthcoming Skrzyński visit to Paris, 13 March 1923, AD/MAE, Pologne, vol. 138, p. 60; report from French Minister, Prague, 16 March 1923, ibid., p. 93; see also Wandycz, *France,* p. 267.
118. Laroche note, 13 March 1923, see note 117 above.
119. Ibid., p. 61.
120. Zaks, "Walka dyplomatyczna," p. 58.
121. *DVPSSSR,* vol. 6, no. 126, pp. 224–26; *DIM,* vol. 4, no. 158.
122. See Vaughan to Curzon, 11 and 13 March 1923, *DBFP,* vol. 23, nos. 655, 656, and 659, pp. 795–96, 798.
123. See Phipps to Curzon, 14 March 1923, ibid., no. 661, pp. 799–801.
124. Poincaré to French Minister, Warsaw, 14 March 1923, 14.15 hrs., AD/MAE, Pologne, vol. 138, p. 76.
125. For French text of decision as published 15 March 1923, see *Documents on Polish-Soviet Relations, 1939–1945,* vol. 1 (General Sikorski Historical Institute, London, 1961), no. 4; see also *League of Nations Treaty Series,* vol. 15, no. 398 (Geneva, 1923), pp. 260–65.
126. See n. 125 above.
127. Sikorski to Poincaré, 17 March 1923, AD/MAE, Pologne, vol. 138, p. 98.
128. Note for the President of the Council, 17 March 1923, ibid., pp. 100–102.
129. For draft, internal correspondence, and final note see ibid., pp. 102, 114, 136–37.
130. Papierzyńska-Turek, *Sprawa ukraińska,* p. 185; Zaks, "Galicja Wschodnia," pp. 33–34.
131. Zaks, "Galicja Wschodnia," pp. 33–34.
132. Polish Legation, Prague, 23 March 1923, cited in Zaks, *Aspekty międzynarodowe,* chap. 5, p. 80.
133. Ibid., pp. 86–87.
134. Papierzyńska-Turek, *Sprawa ukraińska,* p. 186.
135. Ibid., pp. 188–89.
136. See Motyl, *Turn to the Right,* pp. 119 ff.
137. Cited in Zaks, "Radziecka Rosja i Ukraina," p. 94.
138. *Izvestia,* 17 March 1923; *Kurjer Warszawski,* 25 March 1923.
139. See Zaks, n. 137 above.

CHAPTER 9

TOWARD LOCARNO: POLAND, THE WESTERN POWERS, AND GERMANY, JANUARY 1924 TO SEPTEMBER 1925

1. For the Ruhr occupation, Poincaré's policy, and the fall of the franc see J. Bariéty, *Les relations franco-allemandes,* chaps. 6–9; McDougall, *France's Rhineland Diplomacy,* chaps. 6–8; Stephen A. Schuker, *The End of French Predominance in Europe,* pt. 1. For an excellent summary of the war-debts problem see Artaud, "Question des

dettes interalliées et la reconstruction de l'Europe," *Revue historique* 261, no. 2 (Paris, 1979): 363–82. On the Ruhr occupation, see Artaud's "Die Hintergründe der Ruhrbesetzung 1923: Das Problem der interallierten Schulden," *Vierteljahrshefte für Zeitgeschichte* 1979, pt. 2:241–59. For the German side see David Felix, *Walther Rathenau and the Weimar Republic: The Politics of Reparations* (Baltimore, Md., and London, 1971). For a detailed analysis of the evolution of the Dawes Plan see Artaud, *Question des dettes interalliées et la reconstruction de l'Europe,* vol. 2, chap. 5. On Franco-British relations see Ann Orde, *Great Britain,* chap. 2. For a critical review of recent literature on French foreign policy see Jon Jacobson, "Strategies of French Foreign Policy after World War I," *Journal of Modern History* 55, no. 1 (March 1983): 78–95.

 2. Toynbee, *Survey of International Affairs, 1924,* p. 378.

 3. See Walters, *History of the League of Nations,* 1:264.

 4. Stresemann's speech, 14 December 1924, *Akten zur deutschen auswärtigen Politik, 1918–1945,* ser. B, vol. 1, pt. 1 (Göttingen, 1966; hereafter cited as *ADAP*), p. 733.

 5. *Daily Herald* (London), 4 February 1924.

 6. Konstanty Skirmunt, Political Report no. 8/24, 27 February 1924, AAN, Amb. Londyn, vol. 102, pp. 71–73, and *Memoirs,* pp. 125–26. For MacDonald's speech, 23 February 1924, see *Parl.Deb.H.C.,* 5th ser., vol. 170, cols. 45–46.

 7. *Daily Herald* (London), 27 February 1924.

 8. *Manchester Guardian,* 26 February 1924.

 9. Ibid., 10 March 1924.

 10. Jan Ciechanowski, Political Report, 1/24, 2 January 1924, AAN, Amb. Londyn, vol. 102, p. 4.

 11. Foch memorandum, 16 February 1924, cited in Karol Bader, *Stosunki polsko-czeskie* (Warsaw, 1928), p. 31. Foch stressed the need for Polish-Czechoslovak military cooperation on 28 April in a conversation with the Polish minister in Paris, Alfred Chłapowski (cited in Szklarska-Lohmannowa, *Polsko-czechosłowackie stosunki,* p. 117 n. 155). Foch stressed this need again in Franco-Polish staff conversations in May and October 1924 (see Henryk Bułhak, "Polsko-francuskie koncepcje wojny obronnej z Niemcami z lat 1921–1926," *Studia z dziejów ZSRR i Europy środkowej,* vol. 15 (Wrocław, etc., 1979), pp. 85–89, and Henryk Bułhak and Piotr Stawecki, "Rozmowy sztabowe polsko-francuskie w Paryżu (maj 1924)," *Przegląd historyczny* 66, no. 1 (1975): 56–70. The Franco-Czechoslovak alliance was concluded on 25 January 1924 (see Wandycz, *France,* chap. 11 passim; also Laroche, *Au .Quai d'Orsay,* pp. 185–86).

 12. See Soutou, "L'Alliance franco-polonaise (1925–1933)," p. 299.

 13. Maciej Rataj, *Pamiętniki,* entry for 13 September 1924, pp. 228–29.

 14. Ibid., entry for 17 September 1924, pp. 232–33.

 15. See Walters, *History of the League of Nations,* vol. 1, chap. 22 passim; Toynbee, *Survey of International Affairs, 1924,* pp. 36–63; text of Protocol in *World Peace Foundation Pamphlets,* vol. 7, no. 7 (Boston, 1924), pp. 401–19 (hereafter cited as *WPFP*); see also Orde, *Great Britain,* chap. 3 passim.

 16. For the Chicherin-Herbette conversation, 11 August 1924, see *DVPSSSR,* 8:487–89.

 17. On 21 October 1924 Rataj noted Skrzyński's statement that Sikorski's trip to Paris was not only unncessary but also harmful (*Pamiętniki,* p. 240).

 18. See Henryk Bułhak, "Rozmowy polsko-francuskie w Paryżu (październik-listopad 1924)," *Przegląd historyczny* 61, no. 1 (1970): 680–83 (trans. A. C.); see also Ciałowicz, *Polsko-francuski sojusz,* p. 113. For Sikorski's letter to the chief of the Polish

General Staff and his report to the Council of Ministers see Balcerak, *Polityka zagraniczna,* p. 43.

19. Entries for 4 and 9 November 1924, in Rataj, *Pamiętniki,* pp. 245, 247.

20. See Soutou, "L'Alliance franco-polonaise," p. 301; Piotr S. Wandycz, "La Pologne face à la politique locarnienne de Briand," *Revue d'histoire diplomatique,* April–December 1981, nos. 2, 3, 4, p. 244.

21. Rataj, *Pamiętniki,* p. 247; for a detailed account of Sikorski's talks in Paris see Bułhak and Ciałowicz, n. 18 above.

22. Rataj, *Pamiętniki,* p. 237.

23. See Balcerak, *Polityka zagraniczna,* p. 63; for Chicherin's speech of 18 October 1924 see *DIM,* vol. 4, no. 236, pp. 358–59.

24. Skrzyński's speech, 28 October 1924, cited in Balcerak, *Polityka zagraniczna,* pp. 63–64 n. 70.

25. Balcerak, ibid., p. 64 n. 76; see also Marian Leczyk, *Polityka II Rzeczypospolitej wobec ZSRR w latach 1925-1934* (Warsaw, 1976), p. 22; and *DVPSSSR,* 7:573–74.

26. *DVPSSSR,* 7:573–74.

27. See Leczyk, *Polityka II Rzeczypospolitej,* p. 21; also Balcerak, *Polityka zagraniczna,* p. 68; Chicherin's reply, *DVPSSSR,* 7:438–41.

28. Balcerak, *Polityka zagraniczna,* p. 68; Leczyk, *Polityka II Rzeczypospolitej,* pp. 52–53.

29. Article 16 of the League Covenant stated that if a member of the league were to resort to war in disregard of articles 12, 13, or 15 (arbitration and conciliation), the others would sever trade or financial relations, contribute armed forces as the league recommended, and afford passage through their territory to those members who were coming to the aid of the victim of aggression (see League Covenant, Preamble to the Versailles Treaty).

30. Maltzan to Brockdorff-Rantzau, 13 December 1924, GFM, 4562/ 194574–75; Brockdorff-Rantzau report on conversation with Chicherin, 20 December 1924, 2860/554569-71; Schubert to Brockdorff-Rantzau, 29 December, ibid., cited in Breuning, "German Foreign Policy," pp. 294–99 (courtesy of Dr. Breuning).

31. Brockdorff-Rantzau report of 29 December 1924, GFM, 4562H/154921-30, cited in Breuning, "German Foreign Policy," p. 302. See also Zygmunt J. Gąsiorowski, "Stresemann and Poland before Locarno," *Journal of Central European Affairs* 18, no. 1 (1958): 32–33.

32. The texts of both letters are in *Survey of International Affairs, 1924,* pp. 492–93.

33. Rataj, *Pamiętniki,* 9 November 1924, p. 247.

34. See Lewis Chester, Stephen Fay, and Hugo Young, *The Zinoviev Letter* (London, 1967); also Sybil Crowe, "The Zinoviev Letter: A Reappraisal," *Journal of Contemporary History* 10, no. 3 (July 1975): 407–32. Sybil Crowe stresses that several Foreign Office departments were consulted on the letter and that Sir Eyre Crowe was convinced that it was genuine because his source of information on Russia had never been mistaken.

35. D'Abernon, *Ambassador of Peace,* 3:101, September 14, 1924.

36. *Vossische Zeitung,* 28 November 1924, cited in Balcerak, *Polityka zagraniczna,* p. 81.

37. Skirmunt, Political Report no. 27/24, 2 December 1924, AAN, MSZ, vol. 2657, pp. 227–32.

38. Sikorski to Skrzyński, 15 December 1924, cited in Balcerak, *Polityka zagraniczna,* pp. 41–42 n. 70.

39. *Manchester Guardian,* 27 August 1924.

40. Ibid., 20 September 1924.

41. Ibid., 22 September 1924.

42. Ibid., 10 November 1924.

43. Ibid.

44. Sir (Ernest) Llewellyn Woodward, *Great Britain and the War of 1914–1918* (London, 1967), p. 583.

45. See Austen Chamberlain, *Down the Years* (London, 1935), chap. 1; also Charles Petrie, *The Chamberlain Tradition* (London, 1938), p. 143.

46. Minute by Secretary of State, 4 January 1925, FO, 371/11064/9/W362/98, pp. 38–40; see also Orde, *Great Britain,* p. 75.

47. Memorandum by Hankey, 23 January 1925, FO, 371/10727/459/C1218/18.

48. CID paper 559-13, Cab. 4/12, cited in Orde, *Great Britain,* p. 74.

49. Austen Chamberlain to Esme Howard (Washington), 28 January 1925, FO, 800/257, and see Orde, *Great Britain,* p. 73.

50. "British Policy Considered in Relation to the European Situation," Memorandum by Mr. Harold Nicolson of the Foreign Office Prepared in Pursuance of Directions from the Secretary of State, February 20, 1925, FO, 371/10727/459/C2201/18, pp. 137–41, and see Orde, ibid., pp. 75–76.

51. Nicolson memorandum (see n. 50 above).

52. James W. Headlam-Morley, "The History of British Policy and the Geneva Protocol," 12 February 1925, FO, 371/11064/9/W1252/98, pp. 150 ff., partially cited in Orde, *Great Britain,* p. 77.

53. Headlam-Morley memorandum (see n. 52 above).

54. For his correspondence with Namier during the Peace Conference see Headlam-Morley, *Memoir,* passim; see also references to Headlam-Morley in Julia Namier, *Lewis Namier: A Biography* (London, 1971).

55. Chamberlain's handwritten comments on Headlam-Morley memorandum, pp. 152–54 (see n. 52 above).

56. Chamberlain to D'Abernon, 3 February 1925, AC 52/256, original in D'Abernon Papers (British Museum), 48928, cited in Jon Jacobson, *Locarno Diplomacy: Germany and the West, 1925–1929* (Princeton, N.J., 1972), p. 13; see also Orde, *Great Britain,* p. 88.

57. French text in *Pacte de sécurité: Neuf pieces relatives à la proposition faite le 9 février 1925 par le Gouvernement allemand et à la réponse du Gouvernement français (9 février 1925–16 juin 1925)* (République française, Ministère des affaires étrangères, Paris, 1925), no. 1, p. 3 (hereafter cited as *Pacte de sécurité,* 1); English text in *WPFP,* vol. 9 (Boston, 1926), pp. 33–34.

58. Cabinet 4, March 1925, Cabinet Minutes, CAB, 23/49, p. 322 (hereafter cited as CAB).

59. For Cuno's proposal of an agreement with France and other Great Powers interested in the Rhineland see D'Abernon to Curzon, 31 December 1922, *DBFP,* vol. 20, no. 163, p. 369; also McDougall, *France's Rhineland Diplomacy,* p. 241. For Stresemann's proposal on security pact see Sir G. Grahame to Curzon, 5 September 1923, *DBFP* vol. 21, no. 348, pp. 505–6.

60. See F. G. Stambrook, " '*Das Kind*'—Lord D'Abernon and the Origins of the Locarno Pact," *Central European History* 1, no. 3 (1968): 233–63; also Orde, *Great Britain,* p. 84.

61. Stresemann, *Vermächtnis*, 2:281; see also Gąsiorowski, "Stresemann and Poland before Locarno," pp. 37–38.

62. 5 March 1925, *Parl.Deb.H.C.*, 5th ser., vol. 181, cols. 649–99, 703–4, 723, 759–60, 764, 788–89.

63. For 2 March 1925 see Orde, *Great Britain*, p. 90; for 4 March, afternoon, see Cab. 14 (25), CAB, 23/49, pp. 320–21; Orde, *Great Britain*, p. 91; see also Roskill, *Hankey*, 2:396, and Douglas Johnson, "Austen Chamberlain and the Locarno Agreements," *University of Birmingham Historical Journal* 8, no. 1 (1961): 73–74, where the author erroneously stated that Chamberlain gained approval for British participation in a multilateral guarantee pact. He corrected himself in a revised version, "The Locarno Treaties," published in *Troubled Neighbours: Franco-British Relations in the Twentieth Century*, ed. Neville Waites (London, 1971), pp. 113–14; see also Orde, *Great Britain*, pp. 90–91.

64. Johnson, "Locarno Treaties," p. 114; Orde, *Great Britain*, pp. 91–93.

65. Johnson, "Locarno Treaties," p. 115; Orde, *Great Britain*, pp. 94–95.

66. For Chamberlain's statement on the Protocol at Geneva, 12 March 1925, see *LNOJ*, April 1925, pp. 446–50; also Cmd. 2368, 1925.

67. Johnson, "Locarno Treaties," pp. 115–16; Orde, *Great Britain*, pp. 95–96; also Sybil Eyre Crowe, "Sir Eyre Crowe and the Locarno Pact," *English Historical Review* 87, no. 342 (1972): 49–74.

68. Crowe to Chamberlain, 5 March 1925, FO, 371/10728/459/C3202/18, p. 38.

69. Memorandum by Eric Phipps on a conversation with Marshal Foch, 11 March 1925, ibid., C3531, p. 122; see also Foch's letter to Sikorski, 6 March 1925, in Henryk Bułhak, "Lettre du Maréchal Foch au Général Sikorski en date du 6 mars 1925," *Revue internationale d'histoire militaire*, 1969, no. 28:675–78.

70. See Wandycz, *France*, p. 331.

71. Ibid.; for French reply of 20 February see *Pacte de sécurité*, 1, no. 2, p. 4; English text in *WPFP*, 9:34.

72. K. Olszowski's report of 12 March 1925, on conversation with Margerie, cited in Balcerak, *Polityka zagraniczna*, p. 48 n. 2.

73. See Wandycz, "Pologne," pp. 241–42.

74. Cited in Balcerak, *Polityka zagraniczna*, p. 55.

75. Ibid., p. 60.

76. Cited in Charles A. Petrie, *The Life and Letters of the Right Hon. Sir Austen Chamberlain*, vol. 2 (London, 1940), p. 259; full text in FO, 371/10727/459/C2450/18, and FO, 800/257, p. 322.

77. Chamberlain to Crowe, 14 March 1925, FO, 371/10728/459/C3753/18, p. 192 (1), circulated to the cabinet.

78. *Times* (London), 4 March 1925.

79. See n. 77 above.

80. Ibid.

81. Cited in Balcerak, *Polityka zagraniczna*, p. 51.

82. Chamberlain to Crowe, see n. 77 above; Briand repeated this view almost verbatim to the German ambassador in Paris, Leopold von Hoesch, on 6 August 1925, adding that it was shared by Chamberlain and Beneš; see Hoesch's report of 6 August 1925, cited in Gąsiorowski, "Stresemann and Poland before Locarno," p. 43.

83. Chamberlain's handwritten comment, dated 26 March 1925, on Headlam-Morley's memorandum of 17 March, "European Security and Proposed Revision of Eastern Frontiers of Germany," FO, 371/10729/459/C3975/18, p. 33.

84. Chamberlain's private and personal letter to D'Abernon, 18 March 1923, ibid., C4171, p. 126, partially cited in Robert Grathwol, "Gustav Stresemann: Reflections on His Foreign Policy," *Journal of Modern History* 45, no. 1 (1973): 54.

85. 24 March 1925, *Parl.Deb.H.C.*, 5th ser., vol. 182, cols. 320-21.

86. Ibid., cols. 317-18.

87. Ibid., col. 332.

88. Sthamer to Schubert, 25 March 1925, GFM, 3241/D606241-2, cited in Gaines Post, Jr., *The Civil-Military Fabric of Weimar Foreign Policy* (Princeton, N.J., 1973), p. 29.

89. Schubert to Brockdorff-Rantzau, 12 February 1925, GFM, 4562/E154966-69, cited in Breuning, "German Foreign Policy," pp. 311-14.

90. Schubert to Sthamer, 29 March 1925, GFM, 2945/D571620-1, cited in Post, *Civil Fabric*, p. 30.

91. Dirksen memorandum, 21 March 1925, "Aufzeichnung über die Aufrollung der Korridorfrage," GFM, 4569H/E168384-85, cited in Kimmich, *Free City*, p. 73; also Post, *Civil Fabric*, pp. 22-23, 33-34.

92. As Kerr told D'Abernon: "The only plan would be ultimately to have a plebiscite in the northern portion of the Corridor, i.e. in the country between Bromberg and the sea—the strip of West Prussian territory lying West of Danzig and inhabited by a population neither very German nor very Polish"(!) (D'Abernon, *Ambassador of Peace*, vol. 3, entry for 18 March 1925, p. 150); see also memorandum by Dirksen, 18 March 1925, GFM, 4569H/E168896-98, cited in Kimmich, *Free City*, p. 72.

93. See Cienciala, "An Aspect of the German Problem in the Inter-War Period," pp. 440-41 n. 24, and map of Poznań and West Prussia from Otto Hoetsch et al., *Die deutsche Ostmark* (Lissa, 1913); see maps 1 and 2 supra.

94. Stresemann to Missions, 30 June 1925, GFM, 4556H/E149414-34, cited in Kimmich, *Free City*, pp. 73-74, and more extensively in Gąsiorowski, "Stresemann and Poland before Locarno," p. 42.

95. Cited in Robert Grathwol, *Stresemann and the DNVP: Reconciliation or Revenge in German Foreign Policy, 1924-1928* (Lawrence, Kans., 1980), pp. 68-69.

96. *Kölnische Zeitung*, 13 March 1925; *Neue freie Presse*, 11 April 1925.

97. Stresemann, *Vermächtnis*, 2:88, cited in Gąsiorowski, "Stresemann and Poland before Locarno," p. 37.

98. K. Olszowski, report of 28 March 1925 for Skrzyński's eyes only, cited in Krasuski, *Stosunki*, p. 402. The conversation between Stresemann and the French ambassador is summarized in Stresemann, *Vermächtnis*, 2:84, cited in Gąsiorowski, "Stresemann and Poland before Locarno," p. 35.

99. Chłapowski report of 25 April 1925, cited in Balcerak, *Polityka zagraniczna*, p. 97 n. 256.

100. See *Polskie siły zbrojne w drugiej wojnie światowej*, vol. 1, pt. 1 (London, 1951), p. 90: see also Balcerak, *Polityka zagraniczna*, p. 98 n. 259, citing a report by Lt. Col. Franciszek Kleeberg, dated Paris, 7 July 1925.

101. Aleksander Szembek, report of 8 September 1925, cited in Krasuski, *Stosunki*, p. 410.

102. Beneš to Chamberlain, 16 March 1925, encl., FO, 371/10729/C3878/459/18.

103. Chamberlain to Crowe, 12 March 1925, FO, 371/10728/459/C3726/18.

104. Dodd to Chamberlain, 13 March 1925, FO, 371/10729/459/C3851/18.

105. Cited in Campbell, *Confrontation*, p. 145.

106. Cited in Wandycz, *France,* pp. 336–37.

107. Ibid., p. 337.

108. Ibid., pp. 343–44. Skrzyński visited Prague in the spring of 1926, not 1925 as stated by Wandycz.

109. Ibid., p. 344.

110. Prague dispatch no. 209, 12 June 1925, FO, 371/10674/256/C8043/12.

111. Ibid.

112. See Campbell, *Confrontation,* pp. 145–46.

113. See ibid., pp. 144–45.

114. See "Memorandum communicated informally by French Embassy on May 18 in reply to certain enquiries which Mr. Austen Chamberlain made of the French Ambassador on May 14 when the latter handed to him the French Draft Note to Germany on the Subject of Security"; Briand spoke of a British "moral guarantee" of Germany's eastern frontiers, FO, 371/10731, no. 8, archives, also FO, 371/ C6708/459/18.

115. See "Allied-German Negotiations regarding proposed European security pact," chap. 2, point 21, Conversation with Polish Minister, May 19, FO, 371/ 10737/459/C10079/18 (p. 7).

116. Ibid., point 33 (conversation between British minister, Warsaw, and Polish foreign minister, p. 10).

117. Eric Phipps to Miles Lampson, 21 May 1925, Phipps Papers, courtesy of Lady Frances Phipps (1969).

118. Lampson wrote to Phipps on 29 May 1925: "The answer to Laroche is briefly that there is no need to fly to specially guaranteed arbitration treaties to meet the situation which he contemplates. The remedy is already provided by the terms of the League Covenant." Lampson then quoted an opinion to this effect by Sir Cecil Hurst and wrote that Chamberlain had approved the suggestion that Phipps privately let this be known at the Quai D'Orsay, Phipps Papers.

119. Briand to French Ambassador, Warsaw, nos. 138–43, 5 June 1925, AD/ MAE, Pologne (France-Pologne), Z 698, 12 and 13, pp. 104–7.

120. Chamberlain to Tyrrell, 8 June 1925, FO, 371/10997/459/C37862/18. The Memel Convention was signed on 17 May 1924 but was not ratified until 25 August 1925.

121. For Remnant's report see FO, 371/10997/43/N3028/55, p. 136. For French and Polish interests in Memel and the decision of 14 March 1923 see chap. 8 above.

122. See "Allied-German Negotiations," chap. 2, point 51, pp. 17–18; also Orde, *Great Britain,* p. 108.

123. See "Allied-German Negotiations," chap. 2, points 54–60, pp. 18–20.

124. For the text of the French note of 16 June 1925 see *Pacte de sécurité,* 1, no. 9, pp. 27–29; also *WPFP,* 9:35–41.

125. Chamberlain to Joseph Addison, Berlin, and Sir William Max Muller, Warsaw, 16 June 1925, FO, 417/8, no. 39, pp. 111–14; also FO, 371/10737/98/ 24-99/25.

126. 24 June 1925, *Parl.Deb.H.C.,* 5th ser., vol. 185, cols. 1562–63. The last statement was based on a memorandum by Sir Cecil Hurst of 17 June 1925; see "The Proposed Rhineland Pact in Relation to France's Commitments to Poland, Memorandum by Sir C. Hurst," in "Memorandum on the proposed Security Settlement on Germany's Western Frontier, in its relation to Germany's Eastern Frontiers," CP, 317 (25), CAB, 24/174. Here the only case in which France could help Poland was if Germany attacked the latter, thus violating article 16 of the League Covenant. Hurst

wrote: "Such action will not violate the Rhineland Pact, nor bring the British guarantee to protect the Rhineland into play."

127. 24 June 1925, *Parl.Deb.H.C.,* vol. 185, cols. 1588–93, 1609–44.

128. *Manchester Guardian,* 7 July 1925.

129. *Daily Herald* (London), 10 June 1925.

130. "Allied-German Negotiations," chap. 2, point 89, p. 33; see also Orde, *Great Britain,* p. 110.

131. "Allied-German Negotiations," chap. 2, point 89, p. 33.

132. Chamberlain to Berlin, telegram no. 135, 30 June 1925, FO, 371/10735/C8770/459/18, cited in Orde, *Great Britain,* p. 110.

133. Dirksen notes of 23 June 1925, GFM, 6698/H107159-53, cited in Breuning, "German Foreign Policy," pp. 396–99.

134. For Seeckt's objections see Gąsiorowski, "Stresemann and Poland before Locarno," p. 40; for Stresemann's pledge and for Seeckt see Jacobson, *Locarno Diplomacy,* pp. 52–53, and Grathwol, *Stresemann and the DNVP,* p. 86.

135. Cited in Grathwol, *Stresemann and the DNVP,* pp. 88–89.

136. "Allied-German Negotiations," chap. 2, point 81, p. 27.

137. Memorandum by Schubert, 8 July 1925, GFM, 4509/E127066-70.

138. Chamberlain to Churchill, 29 June 1925, and Churchill to Chamberlain, 3 July 1925, FO, 800/258, pp. 246–47, 263.

139. D'Abernon to Chamberlain, 14 July 1925, ibid., p. 325.

140. Stresemann in Cabinet, 15 July 1925, GFM, 3343/765345-55, cited in Breuning, "German Foreign Policy," p. 426; Grathwol ascribes cabinet support for Stresemann to internal political considerations (see *Stresemann and the DNVP,* pp. 94–99).

141. French text in *Pacte de sécurité,* 2, no. 1, pp. 1–8; English in Cmd. 2468, 1923; also *WPFP,* 9:41–45.

142. See Orde, *Great Britain,* p. 113.

143. Ibid., p. 112; such a provision had been included in the Anglo-American guarantee to France of 28 June 1919.

144. Ibid., p. 113.

145. Chamberlain to Fleuriau, 11 July 1925, FO, 371/10736/459/C9185/18, and AD/MAE, Grande Bretagne, vol. 79, and see Orde, *Great Britain,* pp. 115–16.

146. 22 July 1925, ibid., C9784.

147. See Orde, *Great Britain,* p. 118.

148. Dufour-Feronce, report of 7 August 1925, GFM, 4509/E127504-06, 127551-6, 127633-47.

149. Chamberlain to D'Abernon, 11 August 1925, FO, 800/258, and D'Abernon Papers, British Museum, Add. Manuscript 48929, cited in Orde, *Great Britain,* p. 119.

150. Hoesch's telegram to Stresemann, 6 August 1925, cited in n. 82 above.

151. Wandycz, *France,* pp. 349–50.

152. Panafieu to Secretary General (Berthelot), 27 June 1925, AD/MAE, Pologne-France, Z 689, 12 and 13 (135), pp. 118–20.

153. Skrzyński's letter to W. Grabski, 27 June 1925, cited in Balcerak, *Polityka zagraniczna,* pp. 103–4.

154. Cited ibid, pp. 104–5.

155. Ibid., pp. 105 ff.

156. K. Dzierżykraj-Morawski to Olszowski (Berlin), 24 July 1925, and Panafieu, verbal note, cited ibid., p. 117.

157. Memorandum, 27 July 1925, Polish Foreign Ministry to Diplomatic Missions, cited ibid., pp. 118–20.

158. Note by Blanchet, 13 August 1925, AD/MAE, Pologne, Z 698-1, vol. 74, pp. 222–24.

159. See *Pacte de sécurité*, 2, no. 2, pp. 6–8; also *WPFP*, 9:44–49.

160. *Pacte de sécurité*, 2, no. 3, p. 9; *WPFP*, 9:49-50.

161. Cited in Balcerak, *Polityka zagraniczna*, pp. 144–45.

CHAPTER 10
POLAND AT LOCARNO

1. See Gaus's report on Jurists' Conference, London, 18 September 1925, *Locarno-Konferenz, 1925: Eine Dokumentensammlung,* Deutsche Demokratische Republick, Ministerium für auswärtigen Angelegenheiten (Berlin, 1962; hereafter cited as *LK 1925*), no. 20, pp. 120–38; this is a collection of the notes and reports of the German jurists at the London Conference and of the German delegation at Locarno. The Locarno Conference notes of the British, French, German, and Italian delegations are given in Russian translation in *Lokarnskaia Konferentsiia 1925g.*, Ministerstvo Inostrannykh Del (Moscow, 1959). Detailed reports of the conference are also to be found in *Documents diplomatiques belges, 1920–1940: La Politique de sécurité extériure* (Brussels, 1964–65), vol. 2, pp. 316–25. For the British draft discussed at the Jurists' Conference see CP, 311(25), 312(25), 27 June 1925, CAB, 24/174, cited in Orde, *Great Britain*, p. 114. For German acquisition of the British draft through a confidant in Dublin see ibid., p. 116 n. 2.

2. Rauscher's report, 31 August 1925, cited in Breuning, "German Foreign Policy," p. 462.

3. Gaus's report, 18 September, see *LK 1925*, no. 20.

4. Hurst's reports, 4 and 5 September 1925, cited in Orde, *Great Britain*, pp. 121–22.

5. Memorandum by Schubert, 9 September 1925, GFM, 4509/E127927-31, cited in Breuning, "German Foreign Policy," p. 470.

6. Memorandum by A. Chamberlain, 9 September 1925, FO, 371/10739/C11670/18, cited in Orde, *Great Britain*, p. 122.

7. Polish memorandum, received by Briand 7 September 1925, cited in Balcerak, *Polityka zagraniczna*, pp. 150–51; French orginal, with Skrzyński's cover letter to Briand, Geneva, 7 September 1925, in AD/MAE, Grande Bretagne, vol. 82, pp. 230–36, cited in Orde, *Great Britain*, p. 122 n. 3.

8. Memorandum by Chamberlain, 11 September 1925, FO, 371/10740/C11813-14/459/18, cited in Orde, *Great Britain*, p. 122 n. 3.

9. *LNOJ*, sixth assembly, p. 43, cited in Balcerak, *Polityka zagraniczna*, p. 153.

10. Agreement reached by Skrzyński on 5 September 1925, with the foreign ministers of Estonia, Finland, and Latvia (see Balcerak, *Polityka zagraniczna*, p. 153).

11. For the texts of the notes of 15 and 26 September 1925 see *Pacte de sécurité*, 2, nos. 4, 5; also, *WPFP*, 9:50.

12. See Grathwol, *Stresemann and the DNVP*, pp. 111–16.

13. *WPFP*, 9:50.

14. Chamberlain to D'Abernon, 15 and 30 September 1925, Austen Chamberlain Papers, 52/295,297, cited in Jacobson, *Locarno Diplomacy*, p. 59; also Orde, *Great Britain*, p. 123.

15. Tennenbaum to W. Grabski, 15 July 1925, cited in Balcerak, *Polityka zagraniczna*, p. 114 n. 1.

16. See *DVPSSSR*, 8:552–55; for Polish press comments see Balcerak, *Polityka zagraniczna*, pp. 164–67.

17. See Freund, *Unholy Alliance*, p. 231; also Orde, *Great Britain*, pp. 124–30.

18. Stresemann's conversations with Chicherin, 30 September and 2 October 1925, see Freund, *Unholy Alliance*, pp. 232–34.

19. See Campbell, *Confrontation*, p. 151.

20. Schubert's memorandum, 21 September 1925, GFM, 4509/E128100-07, cited in Breuning, "German Foreign Policy," p. 471.

21. See Campbell, *Confrontation*, pp. 151–52; Wandycz, *France*, p. 356.

22. Wandycz, *France*, p. 357; see also De Vaux, Warsaw, 29 September 1925, AD/MAE, Grande Bretagne, vol. 84, pp. 26–27.

23. Skrzyński to Briand, typewritten copy, 29 September 1925, ibid., pp. 33–34.

24. Briand to French Ambassadors, Warsaw, Prague, communicated to London, Brussels, Rome, Berlin, 30 September 1925, ibid., pp. 60–64; also, according to text in Czechoslovak archives, Balcerak, *Polityka zagraniczna*, p. 174 n. 13 (with some typographical errors).

25. German Cabinet meeting, 24 September 1925, cited in Breuning, "German Foreign Policy," pp. 500–501.

26. See Instructions for German Delegation, Locarno, *LK 1925*, no. 24, p. 143; also Grathwol, *Stresemann and the DNVP*, pp. 121–22.

27. Memorandum by Chamberlain, 2 October 1925, FO, 371/10741/459/C12491/18, p. 1.

28. Ibid., p. 2.

29. *Times* (London), 5 October 1925.

30. Ibid., 6 October 1925.

31. Lampson report of 4 October 1925, Locarno Security Conference, FO, 371/10741/459/C12660/18; the notes and reports of the British delegation are in volumes 10742–44 (hereafter cited as Locarno).

32. *Manchester Guardian*, 5 October 1925, p. 10, col. 3; for Beneš's suggestions on how the guarantee could be formulated see below.

33. For German notes see *LK 1925*, pp. 147, 149; for British notes see Locarno, 1st session; see also Briand, 5 October 1925, AD/MAE, Grande Bretagne, 84:118–20.

34. See British secretary's notes on second meeting between British, Belgian, French, and German delegations, 6 October 1925, Locarno, 10741/459/C12747/18; French summary in Berthelot's telegram, 6 October 1925, AD/MAE, Grande Bretagne, 84:133–38, and Laroche to Margerie, ibid., pp. 149–50.

35. See British and French notes, cited in n. 34 above.

36. Chamberlain memorandum, 7 October 1925, Locarno, 10741/459/C12747/18, cited in Orde, *Great Britain*, p. 133.

37. Memorandum by M. W. Lampson, 7 October 1925, in Chamberlain to Tyrrell, 7 October, Locarno, C12749.

38. See British secretary's notes of third meeting, 7 October 1925, 4 P.M., Locarno, C12750, cited in Orde, *Great Britain*, p. 134.

39. Locarno, C12750, annex A, pp. 185–86, and notes of a meeting between members of the British delegation, 7 October, 10 P.M., C12791, "Guarantee of Eastern Arbitration Treaties," pp. 262–63.

40. Note by Hurst, 8 October 1925, FO, 840/1/6, p. 276 (5).

41. *Manchester Guardian; Le Temps*, 9 October 1925.

42. Chamberlain memorandum, 8 October 1925, Locarno, C12881, p. 72 (1).
43. Chamberlain memorandum, 9 October 1925, Locarno, C12818.
44. *Le Temps,* 11 October 1925 (trans. A. C.).
45. Ibid.
46. See British secretary's notes, 10 October 1925, fifth meeting, Locarno.
47. *Le Temps,* 12 October 1925.
48. See Chamberlain's account, cited in Orde, *Great Britain,* pp. 139–40 and 140 n. 1. There is a summary account in Berthelot's telegram of 11 October 1925, AD/ MAE, Grande Bretagne, 84:214–16.
49. Rede Dr. Stresemanns vor der "Arbeitsgemeinschaft deutscher Landmannschaften in Gross-Berlin," 14 December 1925, *ADAP,* vol. 1, pt. 1, app. 2, p. 737 (trans. A. C.); abbreviated and edited version in Stresemann, *Vermächtnis,* 1:231–44.
50. For the proposals of 1923/24 see Orde, *Great Britain,* pp. 40 n. 2 and 68; for Briand's telegram see AD/MAE, Grand Bretagne, 84:221; for the Boat Text as amended on 12 October, see *Pacte de sécurité,* 2, annex F, p. 36; German text in *LK 1925,* pp. 182–83; see also Orde, *Great Britain,* pp. 139–40.
51. Note by Hurst and handwritten comment by A. Chamberlain, 11 October 1925, Locarno, 10744/459/C13634/18, pp. 58–59.
52. Berthelot, telegram 11 October 1925, AD/MAE, Grande Bretagne, 84:214–16.
53. Note by Hurst, 12 October 1925, FO, 840/1/7, p. 291.
54. For Chamberlain's telegram, 12 October, see Locarno, 459/C12899/18, p. 73; for discussions and agreement on revised text see *LK 1925,* pp. 183–90; French text, AD/MAE, Grande Bretagne, 84:233; British text, Locarno, seventh meeting, 13 October, 5 P.M., *Lokarnskaia Konferentsiia,* pp. 271 ff.
55. Locarno, seventh meeting, 13 October, 5 P.M., *Lokaenskaia Konferentsiia,* pp. 273–74.
56. Cited in Balcerak, *Polityka zagraniczna,* p. 180 n. 9 (trans. A. C.).
57. *Le Temps,* 13 October 1925.
58. Cited in Balcerak, *Polityka zagraniczna,* p. 183 n. 2.
59. *Le Temps,* 13 October 1925.
60. Chamberlain's telegram, 12 October (see n. 54 above).
61. Briand's telegrams, nos. 42 and 43, 13 October 1925, AD/MAE, Grande Bretagne, 84:236–38 (trans. A. C.).
62. *Le Temps,* 14 October 1925; for Kempner's trip to Berlin and his report to the cabinet see Grathwol, *Stresemann and the DNVP,* pp. 125–27.
63. Beneš to Berthelot, Geneva, 20 September 1925, and Quai d'Orsay telegram to French Consul General, Geneva, 22 September 1925, AD/MAE, Grande Bretagne, 83:77–83, 106, partially cited in Orde, *Great Britain,* p. 134 n. 5. In his letter of 20 September, Beneš wrote that if Germany absolutely refused the French guarantee of the eastern arbitration treaties, "then we should give this guarantee to ourselves. Thus, we shall change our arbitration treaty into a treaty of guarantee which would be more precise and more definite than the old treaty." He added that the French guarantee would apply strictly within the framework of the League Covenant and that France should be able to enter the Demilitarized Zone in the Rhineland if Germany threatened or attacked Czechoslovakia and the League Council was not unanimous. The Quai d'Orsay telegram of 22 September, probably sent by Berthelot, stated: "Please tell Beneš that Briand agrees on the essential principles of his letter to Berthelot and approves the latter's letter sent via you today to Czechoslovak Foreign Ministry" (trans. A. C.).
64. Stresemann, *Vermächtnis,* 2:199.

65. Dzierżykraj-Morawski's report of 19 October 1925, cited in Balcerak, *Polityka zagraniczna,* p. 185 n. 89.

66. Stresemann, *Vermächtnis,* 2:197.

67. Titus Komarnicki's report on the jurists' meeting, cited in Balcerak, *Polityka zagraniczna,* p. 187.

68. For the texts of the Polish-German and Czechoslovak-German Arbitration Treaties, see *Pacte de sécurité,* 2, annexes D and E, pp. 28-35; also, *WPFP,* 9:73-75.

69. See *Pacte de sécurité,* 2, pp. 37-38; Wandycz, *France,* app. 8, pp. 401-2; *WPFP,* 9:73-75.

70. Kempner's diary at the Locarno Conference, cited in Breuning, "German Foreign Policy," p. 505.

71. Stresemann to German Cabinet, 19 October 1925, GFM, 3242/713903, cited in Breuning, "German Foreign Policy," p. 506; for an account of Stresemann's report—without this point—and the ensuing discussion see Grathwol, *Stresemann and the DNVP,* pp. 131-35.

72. 21 October 1925, Cab. 49 (25), CAB, 23/51, p. 30.

73. Laroche, *Pologne,* p. 17; Léon Noël, *L'Agression allemande contre la Pologne: Une Ambassade à Varsovie, 1935-1939* (Paris, 1946), p. 102.

74. Balcerak, *Polityka zagraniczna,* p. 201.

75. Ibid., p. 205; for Piłsudski's view see n. 86 below; for Zaleski, see Piotr S. Wandycz, *August Zaleski: Minister spraw zagranicznych RP 1926-1932 w świetle wspomnień i dokumentów,* Instytut literacki (Paris, 1980), Biblioteka "Kultury," vol. 317, pp. 22-23.

76. Attaché Wojskowy i Morski w Paryżu, Pro Memoria dla Pana Ambasadora, Paryz, 3/II/1926r, see Piotr Wandycz, "Ocena traktatów sojuszniczych polsko-francuskich: Dokument," *Niepodległość* 16 (New York, 1983): 61-74.

77. Ibid.; for an unduly optimistic Polish legal analysis, by legal adviser of Foreign Ministry, Leon Babiński, see Krasuski, *Stosunki,* pp. 440-50.

78. Jacobson, *Locarno Diplomacy,* p. 65.

79. Stresemann to Keudell, 27 November 1925, Stresemann, *Vermächtnis,* 2:246.

80. Stresemann to Crown Prince, 7 September 1925, ibid., p. 533; full text in Stresemann Nachlass, GFM, 3168/7318/15971 ff.

81. *ADAP,* vol. 1, pt. 1, app. 2, p. 738.

82. Ibid., p. 741 (trans. A. C.).

83. 18 November 1925, *Parl.Deb.H.C.,* 5th ser., vol. 188, col. 429.

84. *ADAP,* vol. 1, pt. 1, p. 745.

85. Chamberlain to Eyre Crowe, Paris, 7 March 1925, FO, 371/10996/459/C3368/18.

86. Beck, *Dernier Rapport,* p. 6.

CHAPTER 11
CONCLUDING THOUGHTS

1. Ralph B. Levering, *The Public and American Foreign Policy, 1918-1978* (New York, 1978), p. 30.

Bibliography

ARCHIVAL SOURCES

British
    Public Record Office, London
        Cabinet Conclusions, Memoranda, Papers
        Foreign Office, General Correspondence: Poland; British Embassy, Warsaw; Conference of Ambassadors; Locarno Conference; Private Papers; Printed Papers
    Private Papers outside of Public Record Office
        Note by Sir Eyre Crowe, 28 March 1919, courtesy Dr. Sybil Crowe
        Lloyd George Papers, Beaverbrook Library, London
        Papers of Sir Eric Phipps, courtesy of Lady Phipps

French
    Archives Diplomatiques, Ministère des Affaires Étrangères, Paris
        Fonds Millerand
        Série Europe, 1918–1929: Allemagne, Grande Bretagne, Pologne, Russie
        Série Paix: Pologne, Russie

German
    Foreign Office and Commonwealth Library, London
        Akten der Alten Reichskanzlei
        Brockdorff-Rantzau Nachlass
        German Foreign Ministry Microfilms
        Stresemann Nachlass
    Archiv des Aswärtigen Amtes, Bonn
        Abteilung IV: Politik, Polen, Wirtschaft, Geheim
        General Konsulat Danzig; Abteilung IA: Weltkrieg

League of Nations Archives, Palace of Nations, Geneva
    Administrative Commissions, 1919–25
    Danzig Documents: Council Series, 1919–25

League of Nations Council: Secret Sessions, 1919–25.

Polish
Archiwum Akt Nowych, Warsaw
Ambasada London; Paryż; Ministerstwo Spraw Zagranicznych; Dr. Henryk
M. Serejski, "Kolekcja opracowań i odpisów dokumentów dotyczących
stosunków Polski z Łotwa, Litwą, Rosją Radziecką, Gdańskiem i Ukrainą
w latach 1914–1928"
Władysław Grabski, Wspomnienia z konferencji w Spa
Wojewódzkie Archiwum Państwowe, Gdańsk
Akta Komisariatu Generalnego Rzeczypospolitej Polski
Akta Senatu Wolnego Miasta Gdańska (in German)
Polish Institute and Sikorski Museum, London
Ambasada Polska, Londyn
Szyfry
Józef Piłsudski Institute of America, New York
Akta Adiutatury Generalnej Naczelnego Dowództwa, 1918–1922
Kaltolicki Uniwersytet, Lublin. Konstanty Skirmunt, "Moje wspomnienia"
(typescript; photocopy, courtesy of Catholic University of Lublin Library)

PUBLISHED SOURCES

General
Graham, Malbone W., Jr. *New Governments of Eastern Europe.* New York. 1927.
Israel, Fred L., ed. *Major Peace Treaties of Modern History, 1648–1967.* 4 vols. New
York, 1967.
World Peace Foundation Pamphlets. Boston, 1924–26.

Belgian
Documents diplomatiques belges, 1920–1940: La Politque de sécurité extérieure. Edited by
Ch. de Visscher and F. Van Langenhove. 5 vols. Brussels, 1964–65.

British
British and Foreign State Papers. London, 1841–.
Documents on British Foreign Policy, 1918–1945. Edited by E. L. Woodward, R.
Butler, W. N. Medlicott, Douglas Dakin, M. E. Lambert. 1st ser., vols. 1–23.
London, 1947–81. Ser. IA, vol. 1. London, 1966.
Papers Respecting Negotiations for an Anglo-French Pact. Cmd. 2169, no. 9. London,
1924.
Parliamentary Debates: House of Commons. 5th series.
Samuel, Sir Stuart. "Report on Mission to Poland," 1 July 1920. In *Papers by
Command,* vol. 51, 1121, cmd. 674, pp. 1–17.

French
Bułhak, Henryk, ed. "Lettre du Maréchal Foch au Général Sikorski en date du 6
mars 1925." *Revue internationale d'histoire militaire,* 1969, no. 28:675–78.
_____. "Rozmowy polsko-francuskie w Paryżu (październik-listopad 1924)"
(protocol of military conferences). *Przegląd historyczny* 61, no. 1 (1970): 681–83.
Conférence de la paix, 1919–1920: Recueil des actes de la conférence, Partie IV:
Commissions de la Conférence. C. Questions Territoriales. 2. Commission des
Affaires Polonaises. Paris, 1924.

Décisions de la Conférence des ambassadeurs. Paris, 1932.

Les Délibérations du Conseil des Quatre: 24 mars–28 juin 1919. Edited by Paul Mantoux. 2 vols. Paris, 1955.

Documents relatifs aux négociations concernant les garanties de sécurité contre une agression de l'Allemagne (10 janvier 1919–7 décembre 1923). Ministère des affaires étrangères. Paris, 1924.

Pacte de sécurité: Neuf pièces relatives à la proposition faite le 9 février 1925 par le Gouvernement allemand et à la réponse du Gouvernement français (9 février–16 juin 1925). Ministère des affaires étrangères. Paris, 1925.

Pacte de sécurité, II: Documents signés ou paraphés à Locarno le 16 octobre 1925, précédes de six pièces relatives aux négociations préliminaires (20 juillet–16 octobre 1925). Ministère des affaires étrangères. Paris, 1925.

German

Auswärtiges Amt. *Akten zur deutschen auswärtigen Politik 1918–1945.* Ser. B, 1925–1933, vol. 1, pt. 1. Edited by Hans Rothfels et al. Göttingen, 1966.

Bundesarchiv. *Akten des Reichskanzlei Weimarer Republik: Das Kabinett Fehrenbach, 25 Juni 1920 bis 4 Mai 1921.* Edited by Peter Wolf. Boppard am Rhein, 1972.

Documents on German Foreign Policy. Ser. D, vol. 5. Edited by the Honorable Margaret Lambert et al. London and Washington, D.C., 1953.

Gesetzblatt für die Freie Stadt Danzig.

Die Kabinette Wirth I und II, Marz 1921–Marz 1922. Edited by Ingrid Schulze. Boppard am Rhein, 1973.

Locarno-Konferenz, 1925: Eine Dokumentensammlung. Deutsche Demokratische Republik, Ministerium für auswärtigen Angelegenheiten. Berlin, 1962.

Reichsgesetzblatt.

Sitzungsberichte des preussischen Landtags. 60 Sitzung, 21 Oktober 1921. Berlin, 1921.

Verhandlungen der verfassungsgebenden deutschen Nationalversammlung. Berlin, 1919.

Verhandlungen des Reichstags: Stenographische Berichte. Vol. 351. Berlin, 1921.

Zusammenstellung der zwischen der Freien Stadt Danzig und der Republik Polen abgeschlossenen Verträge, Abkommen und Vereinbarungen 1920–1938. Danzig, 1923–39.

Italian

Ministerio degli affari esteri. *I Documenti diplomatici italiani.* 7th ser. Rome, 1953–.

League of Nations

League of Nations Official Journal. Geneva, 1920–26.

League of Nations Treaty Series. Geneva, 1920–23.

The Minutes of the Extraordinary Session of the Council of the League of Nations Held at Geneva from August 29th to October 12th 1921 to Consider the Question of Upper Silesia. Geneva, 1921.

The Minutes of the Fourteenth Session of the Council of the League of Nations Held at Geneva August 30–October 19, 1921. Geneva, 1921.

Lithuanian

Lithuanian Information Agency. *The Lithuanian-Polish Dispute.* Vol. 3. London, 1923.

Ministère des affaires étrangères de la République lithuanienne. *Documents diplomatiques: Conflit polono-lithuanien: Question de Vilna.* Kaunas, 1924.

Polish

Archiwum polityczne Ignacego Paderewskiego. Edited by Halina Janowska et al. Vol. 2: *1919–1921.* Edited by Witold Stankiewcz and Andrzej Piber. Wrocław, etc., 1974.

Documents on Polish-Soviet Relations, 1939–1945. General Sikorski Historical Institute. Vol. 1. London, 1961.

Dokumenty i materiały do historii stosunków polsko-radzieckich. Polska Akademia Nauk i Akademia Nauk ZSRR. Edited by Natalia Gąsiorowska-Grabowska, I. A. Khrienov, et al. Vols. 1–4. Warsaw, 1962–65.

Dziennik Ustaw Rzeczypospolitej Polskiej. Warsaw, 1919–.

Filasiewicz, S., ed. *La Question polonaise pendant la première guerre mondiale: Recueil des actes diplomatiques, traités et documents concernant la Pologne.* Paris, 1920.

Jędruszczak, Tadeusz, and Janowska, Halina, eds. *Powstanie II Rzeczypospolitej: Wybór dokumentów 1866–1925.* Warsaw, 1981.

Ministère des affaires étrangères de la République polonaise. *Actes et documents de la conférence polono-allemande tenue à Vienne du 30 avril au 20 aôut 1924.* Vienna, 1924.

———. *Convention germano-polonaise relative à la Haute Silésie, faite à Genève le 15 mai 1922.* Geneva, 1922.

———. *Documents diplomatiques concernant les relations polono-lithuaniennes.* Vols. 1–3. Warsaw, 1920–21.

———. *Documents diplomatiques: Relations polono-lithuaniennes: Conférences de Copenhague et de Lugano.* Warsaw, 1929.

———. *Nécessité de l'union de la Haute Silésie à la Pologne (d'après des documents secrets allemands de 1917).* Warsaw, April 1921 (in French, English, Italian).

Rzepniewski, Andrzej. "Memoriał Tadeusza Wendy z 20 czerwca 1920r. w sprawie możliwości rozwojowych wybrzeża polskiego i portu gdańskiego." *Zapiski historyczne poświęcone historii Pomorza,* Toruń, 29, no. 4 (1964).

Sprawy polskie na konferencji pokojowej w Paryżu w 1919r. Edited by Remigiusz Bierzanek and Józef Kukułka. Vols. 1–3. Warsaw, 1965–68.

Sukiennicki, Wiktor. "Memoriał w sprawie litewskiej złożony przez Prof. W. Zawadzkiego, 7.11.1917." *Zeszyty historyczne,* no. 30 (Paris, 1974): 69–76.

Zbiór dokumentów urzędowych dotyczących stosunku Wolnego Miasta Gdańska do Rzeczypospolitej Polskiej. Vols. 1–11, 1918–36. Zebrane i wydane przez Komisariat Generalny Rzeczypospolitej Polskiej w Gdańsku (Polish Commissariat General, Danzig). Gdańsk, 1923–37.

Russian

Degras, Jane, ed. *Soviet Documents on Foreign Policy.* Vol. 1: 1917–24. London and New York, 1951.

Ministerstvo Inostrannykh Del SSSR. *Dokumenty vneshnei politiki SSSR,* vols. 1–8. Moscow, 1959–.

———. *Lokarnskaia Konferentsiia 1925 g.* Moscow, 1959.

United States of America

Barber, A. B. *Report on American Technical Advisers' Mission to Poland, 1919–1922.* New York, 1923.

Department of State. *Papers Relating to the Foreign Relations of the United States, 1920.* Vol. 3. Washington, D.C., 1936.

———. *The Lansing Papers, 1914–1920.* 3 vols. Washington, D.C., 1939–40.

———. *The Paris Peace Conference.* 13 vols. Washington, D.C., 1942–47.

———. *Texts of the Ukrainian "Peace."* Washington, D.C., 1918.

BIOGRAPHIES, CHRONICLES, DIARIES, MEMOIRS, AND PAPERS

Aldrovandi Marescotti, Luigi. *Nuovi ricordi e frammenti di diario per far séguito a guerra diplomatica (1914–1919)*. Milan, 1938.
Auffray, Bernard. *Pierre de Margerie (1861–1942) et la vie diplomatique de son temps*. Paris, 1976.
Baker, Ray Stannard, and Dodd, William E., eds. *The Public Papers of Woodrow Wilson*. Vol. 2: *The New Democracy*. New York, 1926.
Barbier, J. B. *Un frac de Nessus*. Rome, 1951.
Beck, Colonel Joseph. *Dernier rapport: Politique polonaise, 1926–1939*. Neufchâtel, Switzerland, 1951.
Bismarck, Otto von. *Die gesammelten Werke*. Vol. 1: *Politische Schriften*. Edited by Herman von Petersdorff. Berlin, 1924.
Bréal, Auguste. *Philippe Berthelot*. Paris, 1937.
Brockdorff-Rantzau, Ulrich von. *Dokumente und Gedanken um Versailles*. 2d ed. Berlin, 1925.
Callwell, Major-General Sir C. E., ed. *Field-Marshal Sir Henry Wilson, Bart., G.C.B., D.S.O.: His Life and Letters*. 2 vols. London, 1927.
Chamberlain, Austen. *Down the Years*. London, 1935.
Chernov, Viktor. *Pered Buriei*. New York, 1953.
———. "Polsko-russkoe Otnosheniia." *Novy zhurnal* 28 (New York, 1952): 228–37.
Chocianowicz, Wacław. "Historia dywizji litewsko-białoruskiej w świetle listów Józefa Piłsudskiego." *Niepodległość*, n.s. 3 (London, 1962).
Clemenceau, Georges. *Grandeur and Misery of Victory*. London, 1930.
Crozier, Brig. Gen. F. P. *Impressions and Recollections*. London, 1930.
D'Abernon, Edgar Vincent, Viscount. *An Ambassador of Peace*. 3 vols. London, 1929–30.
———. *Versailles to Rapallo, 1920–1922: The Diary of an Ambassador*. With historical notes by Maurice Alfred Gerothwohl (U.S. edition of vol. 1). New York, 1929.
Dmowski, Roman. *Polityka polska i odbudowanie państwa*. 2d ed. Warsaw, 1926.
Dugdale, Blanche Elizabeth Campbell. *Arthur James Balfour*. 2 vols. London, 1936.
Gärtner, Margarete. *Botschafterin des guten Willens*. Bonn, 1955.
Gerard, James W. *My Four Years in Germany*. New York, 1917.
Gregory, John D. *On the Edge of Diplomacy: Rambles and Reflections, 1902–1928*. London, 1928.
Hancock, W. K. *Smuts: The Sanguine Years, 1870–1919*. Cambridge, 1962.
Hankey, Sir Maurice P. A. *The Supreme Control at the Paris Peace Conference, 1919*. London, 1963.
Hardinge, Charles, Lord of Penshurst. *Old Diplomacy: The Reminiscences of Lord Hardinge of Penshurst*. London, 1947.
Headlam-Morley, Sir James W. *A Memoir of the Paris Peace Conference, 1919*. Edited by Agnes Headlam-Morley, Russell Bryant, and Anna M. Cienciala. London, 1972.
———. *Studies in Diplomatic History*. London, 1930.
Hoefer, Gen. Karl. *Oberschlesien in der Aufstandszeit, 1918–1921*. Berlin, 1938.
House, Edward Mandell. *The Intimate Papers of Colonel House*. Edited by Charles Seymour. Vol. 4. Boston, 1928.
———, and Charles Seymour. *What Really Happened at Paris*. London, 1921.
Jędrzejewicz, Wacław, ed. *Kronika życia Józefa Piłsudskiego, 1867–1935*. 2 vols. London, 1977.
Jones, Thomas. *Whitehall Diary*. Vol. 1: *1916–1925*. Edited by Keith Middlemas. London, 1969.

Jouvenel, Bertrand de. *D'une guerre à l'autre*. Vol. 1. Paris, 1940.

Katelbach, Tadeusz. "Moja misja kowieńska." *Zeszyty historyczne*, no. 36 (Paris, 1976): 60–97.

Kessler, Harry. *Walther Rathenau: His Life and Work*. London, 1929.

Kissinger, Henry. *White House Years*. Boston and Toronto, 1979.

Koc, Adam. "Józef Piłsudski we wspomnieniach tych którzy go znali." *Na Antenie*, no. 58 (London, 1958).

Lansing, Robert. *The Peace Negotiations*. Boston, 1921.

Laroche, Jules. *Au Quai d'Orsay avec Briand et Poincaré, 1913–1926*. Paris, 1957.

———. *La Pologne de Pilsudski: Souvenirs d'une ambassade, 1926–1935*. Paris, 1953.

Lenin, Vladimir I. *Sochineniia*. Vol. 25. Moscow, 1935.

Lerski, George J., comp. *Herbert Hoover and Poland: A Documentary History of a Friendship*. Stanford, Calif., 1977.

Lipski, Józef. *Diplomat in Berlin, 1933–1939: Papers and Memoirs of Józef Lipski, Ambassador of Poland*. Edited by Wacław Jędrzejewicz. New York, 1968.

Litwiński, L. "Nafta małopolska i jej kulisy." *Kultura*, no. 11 (Paris, 1960).

Lloyd George, David. *The Truth about the Peace Treaties*. Vol. 1. London, 1938.

———. *War Memoirs of David Lloyd George*. Vol. 1. London, 1938

Margolin, Arnold D. *From a Political Diary: Russia, the Ukraine, and America, 1905–1945*. New York, 1946.

———. *Ukraine and Policy of the Entente*. Translation of *Ukraina i politika Antanty* (Berlin, 1921), by V. P. Sokoloff. N.p., 1977.

Miller, David Hunter. *My Diary at the Conference of Paris*. Vol. 4. New York, 1928.

Monnet, Jean. *Mémoires*. Paris, 1976.

Namier, Julia. *Lewis Namier: A Biography*. London, 1971.

Noël, Léon. *L'Agression allemande contre la Pologne: Une ambassade à Varsovie, 1935–1939*. Paris, 1946.

Petrie, Charles A. *The Life and Letters of the Right Hon. Sir Austen Chamberlain*. Vol. 2. London, 1940.

Piłsudski, Józef. *Pisma zbiorowe*. 10 vols. Warsaw, 1937–38.

———. *Year 1920 and Its Climax*. London, 1972.

Rabenau, Friedrich von. *Seeckt: Aus seinem Leben, 1918–1936*. Leipzig, 1940.

Rataj, Maciej. *Pamiętniki*. Edited by Jan Dębski. Warsaw, 1965.

Riddell, George Allardice, ed. *Lord Riddell's Intimate Diary of the Peace Conference and After, 1918–1923*. London, 1933.

Romer, Tadeusz. "U kolebki pewnego sojuszu." *Zeszyty historyczne*, no. 13 (Paris, 1968): 119–39.

Roskill, Stephen. *Hankey: Man of Secrets*. Vol. 2: *1919–1931*. London, 1972.

Sahm, Heinrich. *Erinnerungen aus meinen Danziger Jahren, 1919–1930*. Marburg/Lahn, 1958.

Seeckt, Gen. Hans von. *Aus meinem Leben*. Vol. 2. Leipzig, 1941.

Seydoux, Jacques. *De Versailles au plan Young*. Paris, 1932.

Sforza, Count Carlo. *Diplomatic Europe since the Treaty of Versailles*. New Haven, Conn., 1928.

Sokolnicki, Michał. *Rok czternasty*. London, 1961.

Sontag, Ernst. *Adalbert Korfanty: Ein Beitrag zur Geschichte der polnischen Ansprüche auf Oberschlesien*. Kitzingen/Main, 1954.

Stresemann, Gustav. *Gustav Stresemann: His Diaries, Letters, and Papers*. Edited and translated by Eric Sutton. 3 vols. New York, 1935–40.

————. *Vermächtnis: Der Nachlass in drei Bänden.* Edited by Henry Bernhard. Vol. 3. Berlin, 1933.

Suarez, Georges. *Briand: Sa vie, son oeuvre, avec son journal et des nombreux documents inédits.* 6 vols. Paris, 1938-52.

Szembek, Jan. *Diariusz i teki Jana Szembeka, 1935-1945.* Vols. 1-4. London, 1964-69. Vols. 1-3 edited by Tytus Komarnicki; vol. 4 edited by Jan Zarański.

Tommasini, Francesco. *La Risurrezione della Polonia.* Milan, 1925. Polish translation: *Odrodzenie Polski.* Warsaw, 1928.

Trotsky, Leon. *Stalin.* Edited and translated by Charles Malamuth. London, 1947.

Wasilewski, Leon. *Józef Piłsudski, jakim go znałem.* Warsaw, 1935.

Wędziagolski, Karol. *Pamiętniki.* London, 1972.

Weygand, Maxime. *Mémoires.* Vol. 2: *Mirages et réalité.* Paris, 1957.

Wilson, Trevor, ed. *The Political Diaries of C. P. Scott, 1911-1928.* Ithaca, N.Y., 1970.

Wodzicki, Roman. *Wspomnienia: Gdańsk—Warszawa—Berlin, 1928-1939.* Warsaw, 1972.

Żeligowski, Lucjan. "Notatki z roku 1920." *Niepodległość,* n.s. 3 (London, 1951).

Ziehm, Ernst. *Aus meiner politischen Arbeit in Danzig, 1914-1939.* 2d ed. Marburg/Lahn, 1960.

ARTICLES, MONOGRAPHS, HISTORIES, AND SURVEYS

Ajnenkiel, Andrzej. *Od rządow ludowych do przewrotu majowego: Zarys dziejów politycznych Polski, 1918-1926.* Warsaw, 1964; 4th ed., 1978.

Artaud, Denise. "Die Hintergründe der Ruhrbesetzung 1923: Das Problem der interallierten Schulden." *Vierteljahrshefte für Zeitgeschichte,* 1979, no. 2:241-59.

————. *La Question des dettes interaliées et la reconstruction de l'Europe (1917-1929).* Thèse presentée devant l'Université de Paris 1, le 22 mai 1976; Atelier de reproduction des thèses, Université de Lille III, Lille (Diffusion, Librairie Honoré Champion, Paris). 2 vols. 1978.

————. "La Question des dettes interalliées et la reconstruction de l'Europe." *Revue historique* 261, no. 2 (1979): 363-82.

Bader, Karol. *Stosunki polsko-czeskie.* Warsaw, 1928.

Bainville, Jacques. *La Russie et la barrière de l'Est.* Paris, 1937.

Balcerak, Wiesław. *Polityka zagraniczna Polski w dobie Locarna.* Wrocław, etc., 1967.

Bariéty, Jacques. *Les Relations franco-allemandes après la Premiere Guerre mondiale, 10 novembre 1918-10 janvier 1925.* Paris, 1977.

Barros, James. *The Åland Islands Question: Its Settlement by the League of Nations.* New Haven, Conn., and London, 1968.

Bernhard, Ludwig. *Das polnische Gemeinwesen im preussischen Staat.* Munich and Leipzig, 1907; 3d ed., rev., *Die Polenfrage: Der Nationalitätenkampf der Polen in Preussen,* 1920.

Blücher, Wipert von. *Deutschlands Weg nach Rapallo.* Wiesbaden, 1951.

Bonnefous, Édouard. *Histoire politique de la Troisième République.* Vol. 3: *L'Après-guerre (1919-1924).* 2d ed. Paris, 1968.

Bonsal, Stephen. *Unfinished Business.* Garden City, N.Y., 1944.

Borejsza, Jerzy W. *W kręgu wielkich wygnańców, 1848-1895.* Warsaw, 1963.

Borkenau, Franz. *The Communist International.* London, 1938.

Borowski, Wacław. "Ludność i struktura zatrudnienia w Wolnym Mieście Gdańsku." In *Studia z dziejów Gdańska 1918-1939,* edited by Stanisław Potocki, pp. 9-30. Komunikaty Instytutu Bałtyckiego, Zeszyt specjalny nr. 2. Gdańsk, 1975.

Breuning, Eleanor. "German Foreign Policy between East and West, 1921–1926." D.Phil. diss., Oxford, 1965.

Broszat, Martin. *200 Jahre deutsche Polenpolitik.* Munich, 1963.

Brozek, Andrzej. "The Concept of 'Ostflucht' in Germany." *Poland and Germany* (a quarterly review, London), April–June 1966, pp. 20–34.

Buchrucker, Bruno E. *Im Schatten Seeckt's: Die Geschichte der "Schwarzen Reichswehr."* Berlin, 1928.

Bułhak, Henryk. "Początki sojuszu polsko-rumuńskiego i przebieg rokowań o konwencję wojskową w latach 1919–1921." *Dzieje najnowsze,* 1973, no. 3:21–52.

————. "Polsko-francuskie koncepcje wojny obronnej z Niemcami z lat 1921–1926." *Studia z dziejów ZSRR i Europy środkowej* 15 (Wrocław, etc., 1979): 69–91.

————, and Stawecki, Piotr. "Rozmowy sztabowe polsko-francuskie w Paryżu (maj 1924). *Przegląd historyczny* 66, no. 1 (1975): 56–70.

————, and Zieliński, Antoni. "Pologne et Roumanie 1918–1939." *Acta Poloniae Historica* 41 (Warsaw, 1980): 171–77.

Buzek, Józef. *Historya polityki narodowościowej rządu pruskiego wobec Polaków.* Lwów, 1909.

Campbell, F. Gregory. *Confrontation in Central Europe: Weimar Germany and Czechoslovakia.* Chicago and London, 1975.

————. "The Struggle for Upper Silesia, 1919–1922." *Journal of Modern History* 42, no. 3 (September 1970): 361–85.

Chastenet, Jacques. *Histoire de la Troisième République.* Vol. 5: *Les Années d'illusions, 1918–1931.* Paris, 1960.

Chester, Lewis; Fay, Stephen; and Young, Hugo. *The Zinoviev Letter.* London, 1967.

Ciałowicz, Jan. *Polsko-francuski sojusz wojskowy, 1921–1939.* Edited by Marian Zgórniak. Warsaw, 1970.

Cienciala, Anna M. "An Aspect of the German Problem in the Interwar Period: The Secret Anglo-French Agreement on Danzig and the Saar, and Its Consequences, 1919–1926." *Zeitschrift für Ostforschung* 27, no. 3 (Marburg, 1978): 434–55.

————. "German Propaganda for the Revision of the Polish-German Frontier in Danzig and the Corridor: Its Effects on British Opinion and the British Policy-making Elite in the Years 1919–1933." *Antemurale* 20 (Rome, 1976): 77–129.

————. "Nastawienie Austena Chamberlaina do Polski w latach 1924–1933." In *Polska-Niemcy-Europa: Studia z dziejów myśli politycznej i stosunków międzynarodowych,* edited by Antoni Czubiński, pp. 482–94. Poznań, 1977.

————. *Poland and the Western Powers, 1938–1939: A Study in the Interdependence of Eastern and Western Europe.* London and Toronto, 1968.

————. "Polityka brytyjska wobec odrodzenia Polski, 1914–1918." *Zeszyty historyczne* 16 (Paris, 1969): 67–94.

————. "Powstanie Międzynarodowego Towarzystwa Budowy Okrętów i Maszyn w Gdańsku: Przyczynek do historii Wolnego Miasta Gdańska w latach 1919–1923." In *Z dziejów Słowiańszczyzny i Europy Środkowej w XIX i XX wieku,* Zbiór studiów pod redakcją Tadeusza Cieślaka, pp. 59–74. Wrocław, etc., 1980.

————. "The Significance of the Declaration of Non-Aggression of January 26, 1934, in Polish-German and International Relations: A Reappraisal." *East European Quarterly* 1, no. 1 (1967): 1–30.

————. "USA a sprawa W.M. Gdańska w latach 1919–1920" (Przyczynek do historii stosunków polsko-amerykańskich). *Ameryka Północna, Studia.* Vol. 2, edited by Marian Marek Drozdowski, pp. 146–69. Warsaw, 1978.

Ciołkoszowie, Lidia, and Ciołkoszowie, Adam. *Zarys dziejów socjalizmu polskiego.* Vol. 2. London, 1972.

Conze, Werner. *Polnische Nation und deutsche Politik im Ersten Weltkrieg.* Cologne, 1958.
Cottam, Kazimiera Janina. *Boleslaw Limanowski (1835-1935): A Study in Socialism and Nationalism.* Boulder, Colo., and New York, 1978.
Crowe, Sybil Eyre. "Sir Eyre Crowe and the Locarno Pact." *English Historical Review* 87, no. 342 (1972): 49-74.
————. "The Zinoviev Letter: A Reappraisal." *Journal of Contemporary History* 10, no. 3 (July 1975): 407-32.
D'Abernon, Edgar Vincent, Viscount. *The Eighteenth Decisive Battle of the World: Warsaw, 1920.* London, 1931.
Davies, Norman. *God's Playground: A History of Poland in Two Volumes.* Vol. 2: *1795 to the Present.* New York, 1982.
————. "Lloyd George and Poland, 1919-20." *Journal of Contemporary History* 6, no. 3 (1971): 132-54.
————. "Sir Maurice Hankey and the Inter-Allied Mission to Poland, July–August 1920." *Historical Journal* 15, no. 3 (1972): 553-61.
————. *White Eagle, Red Star: The Polish-Soviet War, 1919-20.* London, 1972.
Deruga, Aleksy. *Polityka wschodnia Polski wobec ziem Litwy, Białorusi i Ukrainy (1918-1919).* Warsaw, 1969.
Dziewanowski, M. K. *The Communist Party of Poland: An Outline of History.* Cambridge, Mass., 1959.
————. *Joseph Piłsudski: A European Federalist, 1918-1922.* Stanford, Calif., 1969.
Eyck, Erich. *A History of the Weimar Republic.* 2 vols. New York, 1967.
Felix, David. *Walther Rathenau and the Weimar Republic: The Politics of Reparations.* Baltimore, Md., and London, 1971.
Fischer, Fritz. *Germany's Aims in the First World War.* New York, 1967.
Freund, Gerald. *Unholy Alliance: Russian-German Relations from the Treaty of Brest-Litovsk to the Treaty of Berlin.* London, 1957.
Gajda, Patricia A. *Postscript to Victory: British Policy and the German-Polish Borderlands, 1919-1925.* Washington, D.C., 1982.
Galos, Adam; Gentzen, F. H.; and Jakobczyk, W. *Dzieje hakaty.* Edited by Janusz Pajewski. Poznań, 1966.
Garlicki, Andrzej. "Myśl polityczna Sanacji wobec problemów bezpieczeństwa II Rzeczypospolitej." In *Polska myśl polityczna XIX i XX wieku,* edited by Henryk Zieliński, no. 4:191-99, of *Na warsztatach historyków polskiej myśli politycznej,* edited by Jan St. Miś. Wrocław, etc., 1980.
Gąsiorowski, Zygmunt J. "Stresemann and Poland before Locarno." *Journal of Central European Affairs* 18, no. 1 (1958): 25-47.
Gatzke, Hans W. *Stresemann and the Rearmament of Germany.* Baltimore, Md., 1954; New York, 1969.
Gayre, Robert R. *Teuton and Slav on the Polish Frontier.* London, 1944.
Geiss, Imanuel. *Der polnische Gernzstreifen, 1914-1918.* Ein Beitrag zur deutschen Kriegszielpolitik im Ersten Weltkrieg, *Historische Studien,* edited by Wilhelm Berges et al., no. 378. Lübeck and Hamburg, 1960.
Gessler, Otto. *Reichswehrpolitik in der Weimarer Zeit.* Stuttgart, 1958.
Gilbert, Martin. *The Roots of Appeasement.* London, 1966.
Girault, René. *Emprunts russes et investissements français en Russie, 1887-1914* Publications de la Sorbonne, n.s. recherches 3. Paris, 1973.
Gospodarek, Tadeusz. *Walka o kulturę narodową ludu na Śląsku (1815-1863).* Wrocław, 1968.
Grathwol, Robert. "Gustav Stresemann: Reflections on His Foreign Policy." *Journal of Modern History* 45, no. 1 (1973): 52-70.

_____. *Stresemann and the DNVP: Reconciliation or Revenge in German Foreign Policy, 1924–1928*. Lawrence, Kans., 1980.

Grebing, Helga. "Österreich-Ungarn und die 'Ukrainische Aktion' 1914–18." *Jahrbücher für Geschichte Osteuropas* 7, no. 3 (Munich, 1959): 270–96.

Grosfeld, Leon. "Piłsudski et Savinkov." *Acta Poloniae Historica* 14 (Warsaw, 1966): 49–73.

Grünberg, Karol. *Polskie koncepcje federalistyczne, 1864–1918*. Warsaw, 1971.

_____, and Kozłowski, Cz. *Historia polskiego ruchu robotniczego, 1864–1918*. Warsaw, 1962.

Gumbel, E. J. *"Verräter verfallen der Feme."* Berlin, 1929.

Guthier, Steven L. "The Popular Base of Ukrainian Nationalism in 1917." *Slavic Review* 38, no. 1 (1979): 30–47.

Hagen, William W. *Germans, Poles, and Jews: The Nationality Conflict in the Prussian East, 1772–1914*. Chicago and London, 1980.

Hallgarten, George W. F. "General Hans von Seeckt and Russia, 1920–1922." *Journal of Modern History* 21, no. 1 (1949): 28–34.

Hanak, Walter K. *The Subcarpathian-Ruthene Church, 1918–1945*. Munhall, Pa.: The Bishop Takach Carpatho-Ruthene Historical Society, Greek-Catholic Union Messenger, 1962.

Harrington, Joseph F., Jr. "The League of Nations and the Upper Silesian Boundary Dispute, 1921–1922." *Polish Review* 23, no. 3 (1978): 86–101.

_____. "Upper Silesia and the Paris Peace Conference." *Polish Review* 19, no. 2 (1974): 25–45.

Haumant, Émile. *Le Problème de l'unité russe*. Paris, 1922.

Helmreich, Paul C. *From Paris to Sèvres: The Partition of the Ottoman Empire at the Peace Conference of 1919–1920*. Columbus, Ohio, 1974.

Hilger, Gustav, and Meyer, Alfred G. *The Incompatible Allies: A Memoir-History of German-Soviet Relations, 1918–1941*. New York, 1953.

Höltje, Christian. *Die Weimarer Republik und das Ostlocarno-Problem, 1919–1934: Revision oder Garantie der deutschen Ostgrenze von 1919*. Würzburg, 1958.

Hötzsch (Hoetsch), Otto, et al. *Die deutsche Ostmark*. Lissa, 1913.

Hovi, Kalervo. *Cordon Sanitaire or Barriere de l'Est? The Emergence of the New French Eastern European Alliance Policy, 1917–1919*. Annales Universitatis Turkuensis, ser. B OSA— tom. 135. Turku, 1975.

Hughes, Judith M. *To the Maginot Line: The Politics of French Military Preparation in the 1920's*. Cambridge, Mass., 1971.

Hunczak, Taras, ed. *The Ukraine, 1917–1921: A Study in Revolution*. Cambridge, Mass., 1977.

Jacobson, Jon. *Locarno Diplomacy: Germany and the West, 1925–1929*. Princeton, N.J., 1972.

_____. "Strategies of French Foreign Policy after World War I." *Journal of Modern History* 55, no. 1 (March 1983): 78–95.

Jakóbczyk, Witold. "The First Decade of the Prussian Settlement Commission's Activities (1886–1897)." *Polish Review* 17, no. 1 (1972): 3–13.

_____. *Pruska komisja osadnicza, 1886–1919*. Poznań, 1976.

Jędruszczak, Tadeusz. *Polityka Polski w sprawie Górnego Śląska, 1918–1922*. Warsaw, 1958.

Jeżowa, Kazimiera. *Die Bevölkerungs- und Wirtschaftsverhältnisse im westlichen Polen . . . Zu Rauschnings Buch: "Die Entdeutschung Westpreussens und Posens."* Danzig, 1933.

Johnson, Douglas. "Austen Chamberlain and the Locarno Agreements." *University of Birmingham Historical Journal* 8, no. 1 (1961): 62–81.

———. "The Locarno Treaties." In *Troubled Neighbours: Franco-British Relations in the Twentieth Century*, edited by Neville Waites. London, 1971.

Jordan, William M. *Great Britain, France, and the German Problem, 1918–1939*. London, 1943.

Jurgela, C. R. *History of the Lithuanian Nation*. New York, 1948.

Juzwenko, Adolf. *Polska a "Biała" Rosja od listopada 1918 do kwietnia 1920 r.* Wrocław, etc., 1973.

Kaeckenbeeck, Georges. *The International Experiment of Upper Silesia*. Oxford, 1942.

Kaplan, Jay L. "France's Road to Genoa: Strategic, Economic, and Ideological Factors in French Foreign Policy, 1921–1922." Ph.D. diss., Columbia University, 1974.

Katz, Henryk, ed. *Pierwsza międzynarodówka a sprawa polska*. Warsaw, 1964.

Kennan, George F. *American Diplomacy, 1900–1950*. Chicago, 1951.

Keynes, John M. *The Economic Consequences of the Peace*. London, 1919.

Kimmich, Christoph M. *The Free City: Danzig and German Foreign Policy, 1919–1934*. New Haven, Conn., and London, 1968.

Kochan, Lionel. *Russia and the Weimar Republic*. Cambridge, 1954.

Komarnicki, Titus. *Rebirth of the Polish Republic: A Study in the Diplomatic History of Europe, 1914–1920*. London, Melbourne, and Toronto, 1957.

Korbel, Josef. *Poland between East and West: Soviet and German Diplomacy toward Poland, 1919–1933*. Princeton, N.J., 1963.

Korowicz, M. S. *Górnośląska ochrona mniejszości*. Katowice, 1938.

Krasuski, Jerzy. *Stosunki polsko-niemieckie, 1919–1925*. Poznań, 1962.

———. *Stosunki polsko-niemieckie, 1926–1932*. Poznań, 1964.

———. *Stosunki polsko-niemieckie, 1919–1932*. 2d ed., rev. Poznań, 1975.

Krüger, Peter. "La Politique extérieure allemande et les relations franco-polonaises (1918–1921)." *Revue d'histoire diplomatique*, nos. 2, 3, and 4 (April–December 1981): 264–94.

Kukułka, Józef. *Francja a Polska po traktacie wersalskim (1919–1922)*. Warsaw, 1970.

Kumaniecki, Jerzy. *Po traktacie ryskim: Stosunki polsko-radzieckie, 1921–1923*. Warsaw, 1971.

Kutrzeba, Stanisław. *La Question de Wilno*. Extract from *La Revue générale de droit international public*. Paris, 1928.

Kutschabsky, W. *Die Westukraine im Kampfe mit Polen und dem Bolschewismus in den Jahren 1918–1923*. Berlin, 1934.

Landau, Zbigniew. "Gospodarcze i polityczne tło kredytów francuskich dla Polski w okresie 1921–1923." *Sprawy międzynarodowe*, nos. 7 and 8 (Warsaw, 1959).

———. "O kilku spornych zagadnieniach stosunków polsko-amerykańskich w latach 1918–1920." *Kwartalnik historyczny* 65, no. 4 (1958): 1093–1109.

———. "Quelques problèmes économiques des relations polono-americaines en 1918–1920." *Studia Historia Oeconomicae* 3 (1968; Poznań, 1969): 201–20 (translation of article above).

———, and Tomaszewski, J. "Misja Profesora A. Benisa." *Teki archiwalne*, no. 4:34–225. *Materiały do historii klasy robotniczej w Polsce, 1916–1938*, edited by M. Motas and I. Motasowa. Warsaw, 1955.

Laubert, Manfred. *Die oberschlesische Volksbewegung*. Breslau, 1938.

———. *Die preussische Polenpolitik von 1772–1914*. Berlin, 1920.

Leczyk, Marian. *Komitet Narodowy Polski a Ententa i Stany Zjednoczone, 1917–1919.* Warsaw, 1966.

———. *Polityka II Rzeczypospolitej wobec ZSRR w latach 1925–1934.* Warsaw, 1976.

Lemke, Heinz. *Allianz und Rivalität: Die Mittelmächte und Polen im ersten Weltkreig (Bis zur Februarrevolution).* Vienna, Cologne, and Graz, 1977.

Lerski, Jerzy J. "A Polish Chapter of the Russo-Japanese War." *Transactions of the Asiatic Society of Japan,* 3d ser., 7 (November 1959): 69–97.

Levering, Ralph B. *The Public and American Foreign Policy, 1918–1978.* New York, 1978.

Lewandowski, Józef. *Federalizm: Litwa i Białoruś w polityce obozu belwederskiego (XI 1918–IV 1920).* Warsaw, 1962.

———. *Imperializm słabości: Kształtowanie się koncepcji polityki wschodniej piłsudezyków, 1921–1926.* Warsaw, 1967.

Lewandowski, Krzysztof. *Sprawa ukraińska w polityce zagranicznej Czechosłowacji w latach 1918–1932.* Wrocław, etc., 1974.

———. "W kręgu problematyki stosunków czechosłowacko-ukraińsko-polskich 1918–1922." *Z dziejów stosunków polsko-radzieckich: Studia i materiały* 6 (Warsaw, 1970): 183–95.

Łossowski, Piotr. *Stosunki polsko-litewskie w latach 1918–1920.* Warsaw, 1966.

Luckau, Alma. *The German Delegation at the Paris Peace Conference.* New York, 1941.

Lundgreen-Nielsen, Kay. *The Polish Problem at the Paris Peace Conference: A Study of the Policies of the Great Powers and the Poles, 1918–1919.* Odense University Studies in History and Social Sciences, vol. 59. Odense, 1979.

McDougall, Walter A. *France's Rhineland Diplomacy, 1914–1924: The Last Bid for a Balance of Power in Europe.* Princeton, N.J., 1978.

Machray, Robert. *The Polish-German Problem.* London, 1941.

———. *The Problem of Upper Silesia.* London, 1945.

Mamatey, Victor S., and Luza, Radomir, eds. *A History of the Czechoslovak Republic, 1918/1948.* Princeton, N.J., 1973.

Mantoux, Étienne. *The Carthaginian Peace: Or The Economic Consequences of Mr. Keynes.* Oxford, 1946; reprint, New York, 1952.

Markovits, Andrei S., and Sysyn, Frank E., eds. *Nationbuilding and the Politics of Nationalism: Essays on Austrian Galicia.* Cambridge, Mass., 1982.

Marszałek, Franciszek. *Prawa polskie w Wolnym Mieście Gdańsku (Ich zródła, zakres i obrona).* Gdańsk, 1959; reprint from *Rocznik Gdański* 15/16 (1956/57).

Mason, John Brown. *The Danzig Dilemma: A Study in Peacemaking by Compromise.* Stanford, Calif., and Oxford, 1946.

Mayer, Arno J. *Politics and Diplomacy of Peacemaking: Containment and Counterrevolution at Versailles, 1918–1919.* London, 1968.

Mazurowa, Kazimiera. "Przymierze polsko-francuskie z roku 1921." *Najnowsze dzieje Polski: Materiały i studia z okresu 1914–1939* 11 (1967): 212–14.

Medlicott, W. N. *British Foreign Policy since Versailles.* London, 1940. 2d ed., rev. and enl.: *British Foreign Policy since Versailles, 1919–1963.* London, 1968.

Mickiewicz, Adam. *Pan Tadeusz: Or The Last Foray in Lithuania.* Translated by Kenneth Mackenzie. London, 1964.

Mikos, Stanisław. *Działalność Komisariatu Generalnego Rzeczypospolitej Polskiej w Wolnym Mieście Gdańsku, 1920–1939.* Warsaw, 1971.

———. *Wolne Miasto Gdańsk a Liga Narodów 1920–1939.* Gdańsk, 1979.

Mikulicz, Sergiusz. *Kłajpeda w polityce europejskiej, 1918–1939.* Warsaw, 1976.

———. *Prometeizm w polityce II Rzeczypospolitej.* Warsaw, 1971.

Mills, John Saxon. *The Genoa Conference.* London, 1922.

Morrow, Ian F. D. *The Peace Settlement in the German-Polish Borderlands.* London and Oxford, 1936.

Motyl, Alexander J. *The Turn to the Right: The Ideological Origins and Development of Ukrainian Nationalism, 1919–1929.* Boulder, Colo., and New York, 1980.

Natkevičius, Ladas. *Aspect politique et juridique du différend polono-lithuanien.* 3d ed. Paris and Kaunas, 1930.

Nelson, Harold I. *Land and Power: British and Allied Policy on Germany's Frontiers, 1916–19.* London and Toronto, 1963.

Néré, J. *The Foreign Policy of France from 1914 to 1945.* London and Boston, 1975.

Nichtweiss, Johannes. *Die ausländischen Saisonarbeiter in der Landwirtschaft der östlichen und mittleren Gebiete des Deutschen Reiches: Ein Beitrag zur Geschichte der preussisch-deutschen Politik von 1890 bis 1914.* Berlin, 1959.

Nicolson, Harold. *Curzon: The Last Phase, 1919–1925: A Study in Post-War Diplomacy.* London, 1934.

————. *Diplomacy.* London, 1939.

————. *King George the Fifth: His Life and Reign.* London, 1952; Garden City, N.Y., 1953.

Noble, George Bernard. *Policies and Opinions at Paris, 1919: Wilsonian Diplomacy, the Versailles Peace, and French Public Opinion.* New York, 1935.

Nowak-Kiełbikowa, Maria. *Polska-Wielka Brytania w latach 1918–1923.* Warsaw, 1975.

Oberschlesien und der Genfer Schiedsspruch. Osteuropa Institut, Breslau. Berlin, 1925.

Ochmański, Jerzy. *Historia Litwy.* Wrocław, etc., 1967.

————. *Litewski ruch narodowo-kulturalny w XIX wieku do 1890 r.* Białystok, 1965.

Oertzen, F. W. von. *Die deutschen Freikorps, 1918–1923.* 5th ed. Berlin, 1939.

Orde, Ann. *Great Britain and International Security, 1920–1926.* London, 1978.

Pajewski, Janusz. *Wokół sprawy polskiej: Paryż-Lozanna-Londyn, 1914–1918.* Poznań, 1970.

Papierzyńska-Turek, Mirosława. *Sprawa ukraińska w drugiej Rzeczypospolitej, 1922–1926.* Kraków, 1979.

Paton, H. J. "Upper Silesia." *Journal of the British Institute of International Affairs* 1 and 2 (1922/23): 14–28.

Perl, Feliks (Res). *Dzieje ruchu socjalistycznego w zaborze rosyjskim (do powstania PPS).* Warsaw, 1958.

Pernot, M. *L'Epreuve de la Pologne.* Paris, 1921.

Petrie, Charles. *The Chamberlain Tradition.* London, 1938.

Piłat, T., ed. *Podręcznik statystyki Galicyi.* Lwów, 1900.

Piszczkowski, Tadeusz. *Anglia a Polska, 1914–1939: W świetle dokumentów brytyjskich.* London, 1975.

Pobóg-Malinowski, Władysław. *Najnowsza historia polityczna Polski, 1864–1945.* Vol. 2. London, 1956.

Polonsky, Antony. *Politics in Independent Poland, 1921–1939.* Oxford, 1972.

Polskie siły zbrojne w drugiej wojnie światowej. General Sikorski Historical Institute. Vol. 1, pt. 1. London, 1951.

Popiołek, Kazimierz. *Zaborcze plany kapitalistów śląskich.* Katowice-Wrocław, 1947.

Post, Gaines, Jr. *The Civil-Military Fabric of Weimar Foreign Policy.* Princeton, N.J., 1973.

Potocki, Stanisław. *Położenie mniejszości niemieckiej w Polsce 1918–1938.* Gdańsk, 1969.

————, ed. *Studia z dziejów Gdańska, 1918–1939.* Komunikaty Instytutu Bałtyckiego. Zeszyt specjalny, nr. 2. Gdańsk, 1975.

Pounds, Norman J. G. *The Upper Silesian Industrial Region.* Bloomington, Ind., 1958.

Przewłocki, Jan. *Międzysojusznicza Komisja Rządząca i Plebiscytowa na Górnym Śląsku w latach 1920-1922.* Wrocław, etc., 1970.

Rauschning, Hermann. *Die Entdeutschung Westpreussens und Posens: Zehn Jahre polnischer Politik.* Berlin, 1930.

Reshetar, John S., Jr. *The Ukrainian Revolution, 1917-1920: A Study in Nationalism.* Princeton, N.J., 1952.

Riekhoff, Harald von. *German-Polish Relations, 1918-1933.* Baltimore, Md., and London, 1971.

Roos, Hans J. "Józef Piłsudski und Charles de Gaulle." *Vierteljahrshefte für Zeitsgeschichte* 8 (1960): 257-67.

Rose, William J. *The Drama of Upper Silesia: A Regional Study.* London, 1936.

_____. *The Rise of Polish Democracy.* London, 1944.

Rosenthal, Harry Kenneth. *German and Pole: National Conflict and Modern Myth.* Gainesville, Fla., 1976.

_____. "National Self-Determination: The Example of Upper Silesia." *Journal of Contemporary History* 7, nos. 3 and 4 (1972): 231-41.

Rotschild, Joseph. *Piłsudski's Coup d'Etat.* New York, 1966.

Rubinstein, N. L. *Vneshnaia politika sovetskogo gosudarstva v 1921-1925 godakh.* Moscow, 1953.

Rudin, Harry R. *Armistice 1918.* New Haven, Conn., 1944.

Rudnytsky, Ivan L. "Polish-Ukrainian Relations: The Burden of History." In *Poland and Ukraine: Past and Present,* edited by Peter J. Potichnyj, pp. 3-31. Edmonton and Toronto, 1980.

_____. "The Ukrainians in Galicia under Austrian Rule," in *Nationbuilding and the Politics of Nationalism: Essays on Austrian Galicia,* edited by Andrei S. Markovits and Frank S. Sysyn, pp. 23-67. Cambridge, Mass., 1982.

Ryszka, Franciszek. "Kulisy decyzji w sprawie Śląska w r. 1921." *Kwartalnik historyczny* 60, no. 1 (Warsaw, 1953): 127-67.

Ryżewski, Wacław. *Trzecie powstanie śląskie, 1921.* Warsaw, 1977.

Schmitt, Bernadotte E., ed. *Poland.* Berkeley and Los Angeles, 1945.

Schuker, Stephen A. *The End of French Predominance in Europe: The Financial Crisis of 1924 and the Adoption of the Dawes Plan.* Chapel Hill, N.C., 1976.

Senn, Alfred Erich. *The Emergence of Modern Lithuania.* New York, 1959.

_____. *The Great Powers, Lithuania and the Vilna Question, 1920-1928.* Leiden, 1966.

Serczyk, Władysław A. *Historia Ukrainy.* Ossolineum, Wrocław, etc., 1979.

Sforza, Carlo. *Diplomatic Europe since the Treaty of Versailles.* New Haven, Conn., 1928.

Sierpowski, Stanisław. *Stosunki polsko-włoskie w latach 1918-1940.* Warsaw, 1975.

Sipols, Vilnis. *Die ausländische Intervention in Lettland, 1918-1920.* Berlin, 1961.

Skrzypek, Andrzej. *Związek bałtycki, 1919-1924: Litwa, Łotwa, Estonia i Finlandia w polityce Polski i ZSRR w latach 1919-1925.* Warsaw, 1972.

Skrzypek, Józef. *Ukraińcy w Austrii podczas wielkiej wojny i geneza zamachu na Lwów.* Warsaw, 1939.

Skrzypek, Stanisław. *The Problem of Eastern Galicia.* London, 1948.

Sládek, Zdenek, and Valenta, Jaroslav. "Sprawy ukraińskie w czechosłowackiej polityce wschodniej w latach 1918-1922." *Z dziejów stosunków polsko-radzieckich: Studia i materiały* 3 (Warsaw, 1968): 137-69.

Slavenas, Julius P. "General Hans von Seeckt and the Baltic Question." In *The Baltic States in Peace and War, 1917-1945,* edited by Vytas Stanley Vardys and Romuald J. Misiunas. University Park, Pa., and London, 1978.

Smogorzewski, Kazimierz M. *Francja a Polska: Studium polityczne.* Warsaw, 1930.

————. *Poland's Access to the Sea.* London, 1934.

————. *La Silésie polonaise.* Paris, 1932.

Sobczak, Janusz. *Propaganda zagraniczna Niemiec weimarskich wobec Polski.* Poznań, 1973.

Soutou, Georges-Henri. "L'Alliance franco-polonaise (1925–1933): ou Comment s'en débarrasser?" *Revue d'histoire diplomatique,* nos. 2, 3, and 4 (April–December 1981): 295–348.

————. "Les Mines de Silésie et la rivalité franco-allemande, 1920–1923: Arme économique ou bonne affaire?" *Relations internationales,* no. 1 (n.d.), L'Institut universitaire des hautes études internationales (Genève) et l'Institut d'histoire des relations internationales contemporaines (I.H.R.I.C. Paris I—Panthéon-Sorbonne), pp. 135–54.

————. "La Politique économique de la France en Pologne (1920–1924)." *Revue historique,* no. 509 (1974): 85–116.

Srokowski, Stanisław. *East Prussia.* Toruń, 1934.

Stambrook, F. G. " 'Das Kind'—Lord D'Abernon and the Origins of the Locarno Pact." *Central European History* 1, no. 3 (1968): 233–63.

Staniewicz, Restytut W. "Mniejszość niemiecka w Polsce—V kolumna Hitlera?" *Przegląd Zachodni* 15 (Poznań, 1959): 395–438; translated as "A Polish Comment on a Book [by L. de Jong] Dealing with the German Fifth Column." *Polish Western Affairs* 1, no. 1 (Poznań, 1960): 110–30.

————. *Mniejszość niemiecka w województwie śląskim w latach 1922–1933.* Katowice, 1965.

Stolper, Gustav. *The German Economy, 1870–1940: Issues and Trends.* New York, 1940.

Strasburger, H., et al., eds. *Dantzig et quelques aspects du problème germano-polonais.* Paris, 1932.

Sukiennicki, Wiktor. "Wojna?—Nie, dialog." *Zeszyty historyczne,* no. 48 (Paris, 1978): 16–44.

Suziedelis, Saulius A. "The Lithuanian Peasantry of Trans-Niemen Lithuania, 1807–1864: A Study of Social, Economic and Cultural Change." Ph.D. diss., University of Kansas, 1977.

Sysyn, Frank E. "Ukrainian-Polish Relations in the Seventeenth Century: The Role of National Consciousness and National Conflict in the Khmelnytsky Movement." In *Poland and Ukraine: Past and Present,* edited by Peter J. Potichnyj, pp. 58–82. Edmonton and Toronto, 1980.

Szczepański, Aleksander. *Górny Śląsk w świetle wykonania Konwencji Genewskiej.* Warsaw, 1929.

Szklarska-Lohmannowa, Alina. *Polsko-czechosłowackie stosunki dyplomatyczne w latach 1918–1925.* Ossolineum, Wrocław, etc., 1967.

Tims, Richard Wonser. *Germanizing Prussian Poland: The H-K-T Society and the Struggle for the Eastern Marches in the German Empire, 1894–1919.* New York, 1941.

Toynbee, Arnold J. *Survey of International Affairs, 1920–1923.* London, 1925.

————. *Survey of International Affairs, 1924.* London, 1928.

————. *Survey of International Affairs, 1925.* Vol. 2. London, 1928.

Trzeciakowski, Lech. *Kulturkampf w zaborze pruskim.* Poznań, 1970.

————. *Pod pruskim zaborem, 1850–1918.* Warsaw, 1973.

Ullman, Richard H. *Anglo-Soviet Relations, 1917–1921.* Vol. 3: *The Anglo-Soviet Accord.* Princeton, N.J., 1972.

Vardys, V. Stanley, and Misiunas, Romuald J., eds. *The Baltic States in Peace and War, 1917–1945.* University Park, Pa., and London, 1978.

Wagner, Gerhard von. *Deutschland und der polnisch-sowjetische Krieg, 1920.* Wiesbaden, 1979.

Waite, Robert G. L. *Vanguard of Nazism: The Free Corps Movement in Postwar Germany, 1918-1923.* Cambridge, Mass., 1952.

Walters, Francis P. *A History of the League of Nations.* Vol. 1. Oxford, 1952.

Wambaugh, Sarah. *Plebiscites since the World War.* 2 vols. Washington, D.C., 1933.

Wandycz, Piotr S. *August Zaleski: Minister spraw zagranicznych RP 1926-1932 w świetle wspomnień i dokumentów.* Instytut Literacki, Biblioteka "Kultury," vol. 317. Paris, 1980.

————. *France and Her Eastern Allies, 1919-1925: French-Czechoslovak-Polish Relations from the Paris Peace Conference to Locarno.* Minneapolis, Minn., 1962.

————. "French Diplomats in Poland 1919-1926." *Journal of Central European Affairs* 23, no. 4 (January 1964): 440-50.

————. "General Weygand and the Battle of Warsaw of 1920." *Journal of Central European Affairs* 19, no. 4 (1960): 357-65.

————. "Ocena traktatów sojuszniczych polsko-francuskich: Dokument." *Niepodległość* 16 (New York, 1983): 61-74.

————. "The Poles in the Habsburg Monarchy," in *Nationbuilding and the Politics of Nationalism: Essays on Austrian Galicia,* edited by Andrei S. Markovits and Frank S. Sysyn, pp. 68-93. Cambridge, Mass., 1982.

————. "Polish Federalism 1919-20 and Its Historical Antecedents." *East European Quarterly* 4, no. 1 (1970): 25-39.

————. "La Pologne face à la politique locarnienne de Briand." *Revue d'histoire diplomatique,* nos. 2, 3, and 4 (April–December 1981): 237-63.

————. *Soviet-Polish Relations, 1917-1921.* Cambridge, Mass., 1969.

————. *The United States and Poland.* Cambridge, Mass., and London, 1980.

Wasilewski, Leon. *Ukraińska sprawa narodowa w jej rozwoju historycznym.* Warsaw, 1925.

Weinryb, Bernard D. *The Jews of Poland: A Social and Economic History of the Jewish Community in Poland from 1100 to 1800.* Philadelphia, 1973.

Wellisz, Leopold. *Foreign Capital in Poland.* London, 1944.

Wheeler-Bennett, John W. *Brest-Litovsk: The Forgotten Peace, March 1918.* London, 1938; reprint, London and New York, 1963.

————. *The Nemesis of Power: The German Army in Politics, 1918-1945.* New York, 1967.

Wielhorski, Władysław. *Polska a Litwa: Stosunki wzajemne w biegu dziejów.* London, 1947.

Wiskemann, Elizabeth. *Czechs and Germans: A Study of the Struggle in the Historic Provinces of Bohemia and Moravia.* London, New York, and Toronto, 1938.

Woodward, Sir Ernest Llewellyn. *Great Britain and the War of 1914-1918.* London, 1967.

Yaremko, Michael. *Galicia-Halychyna: From Separation to Unity.* Toronto, New York, and Paris, 1967.

Zaks, Zofia. "Aspekty międzynarodowe sprawy Galicji Wschodniej w latach 1918-1923." Ph.D. diss., University of Warsaw, 1963.

————. "Galicja Wschodnia w polskiej polityce zagranicznej (1921-1923)." *Z dziejów stosunków polsko-radzieckich: Studia i materiały* 8 (Warsaw, 1971): 3-36.

————. "Problem Galicji Wschodniej w czasie wojny polsko-radzieckiej." *Studia z dziejów ZSRR i Europy środkowej* 8 (Wrocław, etc., 1972): 79-109.

————. "Radziecka Rosja i Ukraina wobec sprawy państwowej przynależności Galicji Wschodniej 1920-1923." *Z dziejów stosunków polsko-radzieckich: Studia i materiały* 6 (Warsaw, 1970): 69-95.

————. "Sprawa Galicji Wschodniej w lidze narodów (1920-1922)." *Najnowsze dzieje Polski, 1914-1939* 12 (Warsaw, 1967): 127-53.

_____. "Walka dyplomatyczna o naftę wschodniogalicyjską, 1918–1923." *Z dziejów stosunków polsko-radzieckich: Studia i materiały* 4 (Warsaw, 1969): 37–60.

Zieliński, Władysław. *Polska i niemiecka propaganda plebiscytowa na Górnym Śląsku.* Wrocław, etc., 1972.

Ziugzda, R. *Po diplomatijos skraiste: Klaipedas Krastas imperialistiniu valstybiu planuose 1919–1924 metais.* Vilnius, 1973.

Żółtowski, Adam. *Border of Europe: A Study of the Polish Eastern Provinces.* London, 1950.

Zweig, Ferynand. *Poland between Two Wars: A Critical Study of Social and Economic Changes.* London, 1944.

Żychowski, Marian. *Pierwsza Międzynarodówka a sprawa polska: Dokumenty i materiały.* Warsaw, 1965.

CONTEMPORARY NEWSPAPERS AND PERIODICALS

British
Daily Herald, London
Economist, London
Manchester Guardian
Times, London
French
Le Temps, Paris
German
Kölnische Zeitung
Vossische Zeitung, Berlin
Polish
Gazeta Polska, Warsaw
Kurjer Warszawski
Rzeczpospolita, Warsaw
Russian
Izvestia, Moscow
Pravda, Moscow
United States
New York Times

ATLASES, CALENDARS, ENCYCLOPEDIAS, HANDBOOKS, AND YEARBOOKS

Bourgeois, Émile. *Manuel historique de politique étrangère.* 11th ed. Paris, 1948.

Concise Statistical Yearbook of Poland, 1938. Warsaw, 1938.

Creutzburg, Nikolaus, et al. *Atlas der Freien Stadt Danzig.* Danzig, 1936.

Czapliński, Władysław, and Ładogórski, Tadeusz, eds. *Atlas historyczny Polski.* 2d ed. Warsaw, 1970.

Danziger Statistisches Taschenbuch. Danzig, 1933.

Handbuch für die internationale Petroleum-Industrie 1921. Berlin, 1921.

Prothero, G. W., ed. *Handbooks Prepared under the Direction of the Historical Section of the Foreign Office.* No. 40: *Upper Silesia;* no. 44: *Russian Poland, Lithuania and White Russia;* no. 46: *Austrian Poland;* no. 52: *Prussian Poland.* London, 1919–20.

Rocznik służby zagranicznej Rzeczypospolitej Polskiej według stanu na l kwietnia 1936. Warsaw, 1936.

Schulthess' europäischer Geschichtskalender, 1926. Munich, 1927.

The Statesman's Year-book. London, 1917.

Ukraine: A Concise Encyclopaedia. Vol. 1. Toronto, 1963. Vol. 2. Toronto, 1971.

Index